THE PAPERS OF

WOODROW WILSON

VOLUME 62

JULY 26–SEPTEMBER 3, 1919

SPONSORED BY THE WOODROW WILSON
FOUNDATION
AND PRINCETON UNIVERSITY

THE PAPERS OF

WOODROW WILSON

ARTHUR S. LINK, *EDITOR*

JOHN E. LITTLE, *ASSOCIATE EDITOR*

MANFRED F. BOEMEKE, *ASSOCIATE EDITOR*

L. KATHLEEN AMON, *ASSISTANT EDITOR*

PHYLLIS MARCHAND, *INDEXER*

Volume 62
July 26–September 3, 1919

PRINCETON, NEW JERSEY

PRINCETON UNIVERSITY PRESS

1990

INTRODUCTION

THE opening of this volume on July 26, 1919, finds Wilson facing domestic and international problems nearly as complex and urgent as those he had faced in Paris a month before.

His main task is to assure the Senate's approval of the Treaty of Versailles so he can speedily join in the process of exchange of ratifications that is already under way. By various tactics, Senator Lodge is pursuing a policy of delay in the Foreign Relations Committee in order to give opponents of the Treaty time to mount a nationwide campaign against it. The Massachusetts Senator's stratagem is to this point not succeeding, mainly because of the vigorous pro-League propaganda of the bipartisan League to Enforce Peace led by former President Taft and President Lowell of Harvard University. Most Democrats in the Senate will follow Wilson's lead in the controversy, hence Wilson's most important potential allies are Republican leaders like Taft and a group of about twenty Republican senators, called "mild reservationists," who favor consent to ratification with reservations to be attached to the articles of ratification. Seven leaders of this group on July 31 publish what they say are four necessary compromise interpretive reservations. They relate to the right of withdrawal from the League, the military obligations of the United States under Article X, the jurisdiction of the League over the domestic affairs of member states, and the Monroe Doctrine.

Wilson's response to this and other such compromise overtures, from Democrats and Republicans alike, is severely compromised by what was almost certainly a "small" stroke on July 19, which adversely affects his temperament, judgment, leadership, and memory. In circumstances which are full of promise for the success of the Treaty, Wilson makes not a single move to get in touch with and rally his supporters, either in the country at large or in the Senate. He does meet for over three hours with the members of the Foreign Relations Committee on August 19 and says that he is willing to accept interpretive reservations. He privately approves when one of his spokesmen, Pittman, introduces a resolution in the Senate on August 20 that embodies the reservations of seven Republican supporters of the Treaty. And, on September 3, Wilson sends a secret memorandum to Senator Hitchcock, the Democratic minority leader on the Foreign Relations Committee, which puts into his own words the "interpretations" of the Republican seven. All along, however, Wilson insists that these reservations must not be incorporated in the articles of ratification by the United States Government. A pro-League coalition of two thirds of the members of the Senate and victory on nearly all of Wilson's terms is now in sight. Yet, in a fit of anger, he decides on August 25 to embark upon a month-long speaking tour in the Middle West and West on behalf of the League. As this volume ends, Wilson and his party leave for what, in light of Wilson's very precarious health, will be a journey with disastrous consequences.

Another reason for Wilson's unwillingness to stay in Washington to press for the Senate's consent to ratification of a mildly reserved treaty is his petulant, angry, and profoundly discouraged reactions to signs of what seems to be a continuance if not resurgence of the traditional imperialism of the Entente Powers: the refusal of Japan to say outright that she will restore full sovereignty over Shantung Province to China forthwith; Rumania's grab for all of Transylvania and Bessarabia; an Anglo-Persian agreement that gives a monopoly of Persian oil to Great Britain; Greece's demands for all of Thrace; France's refusal to agree to the establishment of Class A mandates in the Levant; and Italy's continued refusal to abandon her claim to Fiume. "When I see such conduct . . . and when I think of the great and utter selfishness of it all," he tells Lansing on August 21, "I am almost inclined to refuse to permit this country to be a member of the League of Nations when it is composed of such intriguers and robbers. I am disposed to throw up the whole business and get out." It is the third time he has threatened to withdraw the Versailles Treaty from the Senate. The conviction, present in his mind for a long time, that only the United States (and he, himself, personally) could create a redemptive, reformist, and democraticizing League becomes intensified in his thinking and is undoubtedly a prime factor in his refusal to agree to any reservations to the Treaty that might seem to cast any doubt upon the eagerness of his country to lead the world out of darkness into the light.

Meanwhile, Wilson gives further evidence of ebbing mental and physical power during the weeks covered by this volume. He wants to grant amnesty to Debs and other so-called political prisoners but cannot muster enough physical energy to force his Attorney General to take such action. He is no longer able to cope personally with important domestic crises and relies upon subordinates in drafting an anti-inflation program and dealing with a threatened railroad strike. He reacts weakly, if at all, to problems that once would have evoked daring and innovative responses. Most noticeably, his once photographic memory becomes like a sieve. It is all a portentous background to what lies immediately ahead—the greatest mental and physical stresses that he has yet endured.

Translating and editing Paul Mantoux's *Les Délibérations du Conseil des Quatre* has caused us to make an intensive review of the Peace Conference Volumes, and that review suggests a few clarifications that we think might be helpful.

We gave a great deal of space to the documents relating to the dialogue between the German delegation and the Council of Four about the preliminary treaty presented to the German delegation on May 7, 1919. This interchange has been largely overlooked by historians, who usually go from the presentation of the preliminary treaty to the Germans on May 7 to the signing of the Versailles Treaty on June 28 without taking notice of the results, favorable to Germany, of this voluminous exchange.

The Four did not regard the preliminary treaty as an ultimatum, but as a document to be negotiated between themselves and the Germans. This point comes out clearly in the documents in the Peace Conference Volumes. What needs to be emphasized are the following facts:

1. The Four themselves, on April 26, 1919, sent to the German delegation a list of questions to be discussed between themselves and the German delegation and indicated the time limit for the return of observations by the Germans. This list of subjects included all important issues raised by the preliminary treaty. *PPC*, V, 297-98, noted in Vol. 58, p. 150.

2. The German delegation replied on these subjects and others in what were called counterproposals, and we print or summarize them seriatim in the Peace Conference Volumes. Then began the long process of reply by the Four. We print the most important of these replies and note and summarize the rest. All these replies were combined into a single document, which was sent to the German delegation on June 16 and is printed in *PPC*, VI, 926-96.

3. Toward the end of these negotiations, the Germans asked whether certain concessions made by the Four in their replies, which had not been incorporated in the final text of the Versailles Treaty, were to be regarded as amendments of that treaty. The Council replied on June 21 that the concessions stipulated in its note of June 16 and not incorporated in the treaty should be considered as binding engagements, and they embodied these changes in a protocol. The Council's note of June 21, which included the protocol, is printed in *PPC*, VI, 601-604. We took note of this protocol in n. 1 to the extract from the Desk Diary of Robert Lansing printed at July 30, 1919, in this (Vol. 62) volume.

A SECOND NOTE TO OUR READERS

We have decided to omit in this and following volumes the section *"Verbatim et Literatim,"* which explains our editorial methods. It has been printed many times in previous volumes, and the reader unacquainted with it can find it by looking, say, at the Introduction to Volume 61.

We are indebted, first of all, to Dr. Bert E. Park for his essay on Wilson's health problems during the summer of 1919, which we print as an Appendix to this volume. Dr. Park's conclusions are our own. We refer readers who might be interested in the problem of "small strokes" and their effect on personality and behavior to the pioneer work, Walter C. Alvarez, *Little Strokes* (Philadelphia, 1966).

We continue to be grateful to John Milton Cooper, Jr., William H. Harbaugh, Richard W. Leopold, and Betty Miller Unterberger for reading the manuscript of this volume and being helpful critics. Alice Calaprice was its editor for Princeton University Press. Dr. Timothy Connelly of the staff of the National Historical Publications and Records Commission supplied numerous copies of documents and the pictures in the illustration section.

THE EDITORS

Princeton, New Jersey
October 9, 1989

CONTENTS

The Papers, July 26-September 3, 1919
Domestic Affairs

Diplomatic, Military, and Naval Affairs

Personal Affairs

ILLUSTRATIONS

Following page 328

SOME PRINCIPALS IN THE EARLY CONTROVERSY
OVER THE VERSAILLES TREATY

ABBREVIATIONS

AJB	Arthur James Balfour
ALS	autograph letter signed
AMP	Alexander Mitchell Palmer
CC	carbon copy
CCL	carbon copy of letter
CCLI	carbon copy of letter initialed
DFH	David Franklin Houston
EBW	Edith Bolling Galt Wilson
EMH	Edward Mandell House
ENH	Edward Nash Hurley
FDR	Franklin Delano Roosevelt
FKL	Franklin Knight Lane
FLP	Frank Lyon Polk
FR	*Papers Relating to the Foreign Relations of the United States*
FR 1918, Russia	*Papers Relating to the Foreign Relations of the United States, 1918, Russia*
FR 1919, Russia	*Papers Relating to the Foreign Relations of the United States, 1919, Russia*
GFC	Gilbert Fairchild Close
HCH	Herbert Clark Hoover
HCL	Henry Cabot Lodge
Hw, hw	handwritten, handwriting
JD	Josephus Daniels
JFD	John Foster Dulles
JPT	Joseph Patrick Tumulty
MS, MSS	manuscript, manuscripts
NDB	Newton Diehl Baker
PPC	*Papers Relating to the Foreign Relations of the United States, The Paris Peace Conference, 1919*
PWW	*The Papers of Woodrow Wilson*
RG	record group
RL	Robert Lansing
T	typed
TC	typed copy
TCL	typed copy of letter
THB	Tasker Howard Bliss
TI	typed initialed
TL	typed letter
TLI	typed letter initialed
TLS	typed letter signed
TNP	Thomas Nelson Page
TS	typed signed
WBW	William Bauchop Wilson
WCR	William Cox Redfield
WDH	Walker Downer Hines
WGM	William Gibbs McAdoo
WHP	Walter Hines Page
WW	Woodrow Wilson

WWhw	Woodrow Wilson handwriting, handwritten
WWsh	Woodrow Wilson shorthand
WWT	Woodrow Wilson typed
WWTLI	Woodrow Wilson typed letter initialed
WWTLS	Woodrow Wilson typed letter signed

ABBREVIATIONS FOR COLLECTIONS AND REPOSITORIES

Following the National Union Catalog of the Library of Congress

CSmH	Henry E. Huntington Library
CSt-H	Hoover Institution on War, Revolution and Peace
CtY	Yale University
DLC	Library of Congress
DNA	National Archives
ICHi	Chicago Historical Society
InND	University of Notre Dame
JDR	Justice Department Records
MH-BA	Harvard University Graduate School of Business Administration
NcD	Duke University
NHpR	Franklin D. Roosevelt Library
NjP	Princeton University
NjP-Ar	Princeton University Archives
SDR	State Department Records
ViU	University of Virginia
VtU	University of Vermont
WC, NjP	Woodrow Wilson Collection, Princeton University
WP, DLC	Woodrow Wilson Papers, Library of Congress

SYMBOLS

[July 26, 1919]	publication date of published writing; also date of document when date is not part of text
[*July 28, 1919*]	composition date when publication date differs
[[July 31, 1919]]	delivery date of speech when publication date differs
* * * * * * *	text deleted by author of document

THE PAPERS OF

WOODROW WILSON

VOLUME 62

JULY 26–SEPTEMBER 3, 1919

THE PAPERS OF
WOODROW WILSON

A News Report

[July 26, 1919]

SHANTUNG PROBLEM NEARING A SOLUTION
Wilson Hopes Developments Will Come in Few Days.

CONFERS AGAIN ON LEAGUE

Diplomatic discussions with Japan over the Shantung provision in the peace treaty have reached a stage where President Wilson is represented as very hopeful of developments within a few days that will clear the air and remove much of the opposition to the provision in the Senate.

This interpretation of the President's expectations was expressed by Senator Spencer,[1] Republican, Missouri, after a long talk with Mr. Wilson yesterday about the treaty. The senator declined to go into details as to the exact steps being taken, and both the White House and the State Department were silent on the subject. There were indications, however, that the conversations with Japan, though quite informal in character, had as their object such a declaration from Tokyo as would satisfy China and result in her acceptance of the treaty.

Senator Spencer also discussed at length with the President the subject of reservations in the Senate ratification of the treaty, taking with him to the White House a draft of five reservations drawn up and submitted to the President, it is understood, at the suggestion of Chairman Lodge, of the foreign relations committee.[2]

The draft also is said to have been shown to other Republicans of varying shades of opinion, but Mr. Spencer made it clear in presenting them that he alone stood sponsor for their phraseology.

The reservations covered the Monroe doctrine, withdrawal, Shantung, national determination of domestic issues and independence of action under Article X.

Mr. Spencer told the President that without some such qualifications the treaty never could be ratified, while if they were included ratification would come quickly.

Senator Spencer said Mr. Wilson promised to give the proposed reservations his earnest consideration and conveyed the impression that he personally was not opposed to such a course, except for the complications that might result should the treaty be returned for renegotiation.

Senator Spencer would not say on what assurances the President based his hope of important developments in the near future. It is understood, however, that a full account of the feeling aroused here against the Shantung provision has gone forward to Tokyo as a result of a conference Thursday between Katsuji Debuchi, the Japanese charge d'affaires, and Secretary Lansing.[3]

There were indications that no reply to these representations had been received last night, though what preliminary information the President might have was uncertain.

The President has been told by Republican senators that most of the Senate opposition to this provision would disappear if he were able to induce Japan to give such assurances for the future return of Shantung to China as would result in the latter signing the treaty.

It is believed that view has been reflected in the conversations with Tokyo, and that the suggestion has been made that this end could be accomplished by a formal declaration to China, or to all of the allied and associated powers.

The reservations submitted by Senator Spencer are in some respects similar to the interpretations proposed as a middle ground by former President Taft,[4] and are understood to follow in general the plan discussed among the group of Republicans favoring a league.

They would provide:

That the Monroe doctrine is "an essential national policy" whose application and enforcement must be determined "by the United States alone."

That "internal questions entirely domestic in character, such as immigration and the tariff" are to be "determined solely by the country in which they arise."

That the United States "cannot bind itself in advance" to make war "without the express authorization of Congress at the time."

That the right of a nation to withdraw "includes the right to determine for itself" whether it has fulfilled its obligations as provided in the covenant.

That the Shantung settlement is viewed with "deep regret" as "disregardful" of the rights and desires of inhabitants of the peninsula, "unjust" to China, and "threatening" to future peace.

Mr. Spencer said the President showed no antagonism to a reservation program that would follow these lines.

Mr. Wilson even indicated, the senator declared, that he had no disposition individually to stand for unreserved ratification if the Senate really thought reservations necessary, but said he hoped senators would fully realize the possibilities of renegotiation.

Senator Warren,[5] Republican, Wyoming, also saw the President, but he declined to discuss their talk. Last night no other Republicans had been invited to the White House, though it was thought likely others would be given invitations next week.

Notice also was taken at the White House during the day of Senate discussion of the defensive treaty with France, which Senator Lodge, and others have charged the President is withholding from the Senate in direct violation of the treaty's own terms.

Without making any explanation, White House officials made it clear that Mr. Wilson has no intention of submitting the Franco-American agreement for Senate ratification until consideration of the treaty with Germany is well under way.

The President plans, it was stated, to present the French treaty after his tour of the country, which will not begin until about August 10 and may continue for several weeks.

In debate senators have pointed out that published texts of the document require that it must be laid before the Senate "at the same time" as the Versailles treaty, which was presented more than two weeks ago.

The foreign relations committee made such progress yesterday in its reading of the treaty that members thought it might be completed at one more meeting.

Adjournment was taken until Monday, however, and it was decided that after the reading was completed the document would be laid aside for a short while to permit action on the Colombian treaty.[6] The Senate also adjourned until Monday.

Today Chairman Lodge will see Secretary Lansing, and while the conference primarily concerns the Colombian treaty it is expected that various matters concerning the Versailles negotiations also will be discussed.

Mr. Lodge may take the opportunity to secure certain documents to aid the committee in its work and to get a digest of some of the opinions on various subjects given the American delegation by its expert advisers.

Senator Lodge did not call up yesterday his resolution asking the President to transmit the French treaty, and it was indicated that action on the measure might not be sought for the present. The subject is expected to be revived, however, as Senate debate continues.

A proposal for a new national organization with headquarters here to hasten ratification of the treaty was discussed with Democratic senators during the day by Vance McCormick, former chairman of the war trade board, who recently returned from the Versailles conference.

It was said that although the suggestion found considerable favor, Mr. McCormick's plans had not yet taken definite shape.

Printed in the *Washington Post*, July 26, 1919.
[1] That is, Selden Palmer Spencer.
[2] For the text of the Spencer resolution, see the first news report printed at July 25, 1919, Vol. 61.
[3] Actually, on Friday, July 25. See n. 2 to *ibid.*
[4] See the Enclosure printed with JPT to WW, July 23, 1919 (second letter of that date), and the memorandum by W. H. Taft printed at July 23, 1919, both in Vol. 61.
[5] That is, Francis Emroy Warren.
[6] On the Treaty of Bogotá, signed on April 6, 1914, between the United States and Colombia, and the repeated attempts by the Wilson administration to secure its approval by the Senate, see the index references under "Colombia and the United States" in Vols. 39, 41, and 52 of this series and Arthur S. Link, *Wilson: The New Freedom* (Princeton, N. J., 1956), pp. 320-24.
    Frank L. Polk in January 1919 had drafted a new version of the treaty and secured its acceptance by Senators Lodge and Knox late that month. The clause expressing mutual regret by the United States and Colombia for any previous unfriendly actions was deleted; the United States was to pay $5,000,000 to Colombia within six months of ratification, with an additional $5,000,000 annually over the next four years; and Colombia was to agree not to use any of the $25,000,000 for legal fees incurred during the ratification process. The Colombian government agreed to these modifications in late February 1919.
    The Senate Foreign Relations Committee, by a unanimous vote, reported the revised treaty favorably to the Senate on July 29, 1919. However, on August 7, Lodge requested the Senate to recommit the treaty to the Foreign Relations Committee. The committee, he said, had just learned of a decree promulgated by the Colombian government on June 20, 1919, which regulated petroleum exploration and affirmed national ownership of subsoil oil and mineral rights. In fact, Lansing had informed Lodge of the Colombian decree. The Senate took no further action on the treaty until after the inauguration of President Harding in 1921. See Richard L. Lael, *Arrogant Diplomacy: U. S. Policy toward Colombia, 1903-1922* (Wilmington, Del., 1987), pp. 118-19, 144, 149-50, 155, and *FR 1919*, I, 726-38.

To Albert, King of the Belgians

Washington, July 26, 1919.

463 Your 294, July 23, noon.[1] Please convey to the King the following message:

QUOTE Having heard from Mr. Whitlock that it might be possible for Your Majesty to come to this country for a short time in the autumn I hasten to tender on behalf of the American Government a most cordial invitation to Your Majesty and to Her Majesty the Queen of the Belgians to visit the United States at such time as may best suit your convenience.

May I add a personal expression of the great pleasure that it will give me to receive you and the Queen as the honored guests of the Nation.   Woodrow Wilson. UNQUOTE.   Lansing

TS telegram (SDR, RG 59, 033.5511/12, DNA).
[1] B. Whitlock to WW, July 23, 1919, Vol. 61.

From Norman Hezekiah Davis

My dear Mr. President: Stockbridge, Mass., July 26, 1919.

I find that quite a number of substantial people (principally Republicans who favor the ratification of the Treaty) think it most important that you make public explanations of it at an early date. One gentleman,[1] in whose judgment I have considerable confidence, is strongly of the opinion that further delay is dangerous, and that, instead of delivering addresses of explanation throughout the country, it would be more effective if you would deliver a series of messages or addresses of explanation to the full Senate. This suggestion has impressed me very favorably, and I am therefore taking the liberty of giving it to you for what it may be worth.

I also find that some people (favorably inclined toward the ratification of the Treaty) have gathered the impression, from your private interviews with Senators, that there are many things about the Treaty which the public cannot be told. It is, of course, advisable to avoid any such erroneous impression, and such people are anxiously awaiting public explanations from you.

Apparently the Republican opposition in the Senate is determined, obstinate, prejudiced, and vicious, and I am reluctantly convinced that they do not wish to be persuaded, that they will not accept your offer to enlighten them on doubtful points, and that the only thing that will change them will be pressure from the outside. It therefore seems to me most important that you make an early public explanation, and it occurs to me that it might be advisable for you to deliver one or more messages of explanation to the Senate before making a tour of the country. This would minimize the importance of the Senate opposition and would appear as a patient endeavor to explain points which are evident from a study of the Treaty which the Republican Senators have failed to make. To tour the country before delivering at least one message of explanation to the Senate might create the impression that the fight was so serious that you felt the necessity of going over the heads of the Senate by appealing direct to the people.

I do not consider, however, that addresses to the Senate would serve as a substitute for a tour of the country, for, while these addresses would reach the public through the press, they would lack the personal touch with the people themselves, which I think it most important that you should get at the earliest possible moment, partly on account of having been absent from the country.

I hope you will not consider me presumptuous in writing this letter, and beg to remain, my dear Mr. President, with high esteem and cordial regards.   Faithfully yours,   Norman H. Davis

P.S. I have just presented the above views to Baruch, who quite agrees with the advisability of the procedure indicated, provided it be in accord with usage for you so to address the Senate. I realize there may be several reasons which would make it inadvisable to follow my suggestions.

TLS (WP, DLC).
[1] Thomas W. Lamont. See T. W. Lamont to WW, July 25, 1919, Vol. 61.

From Michael A. O'Leary[1]

Mr. President: Boston, Mass. July 26, 1919.

The Democratic State Committee in meeting, July 26, adopted this resolution.

Resolved:

That the Democratic State Committee of Massachusetts is unalterably opposed to the attempt of England and her Allies to force upon the American people, a so-called Covenant of a League of Nations which attempts to commit this Republic to recognize, and hold forever, the title of England, to own and to rule Ireland against the expressed will of an overwhelming majority of the Irish people.[2]

Respectfully submitted: Michael A. O Leary

TLS (WP, DLC).
[1] Chairman of the Massachusetts Democratic State Committee.
[2] In a letter to Tumulty of the same day, O'Leary pointed out that the resolution had been "the result of bitter conflict" and had been adopted over his protest. M. A. O'Leary to JPT, July 26, 1919, TLS (WP, DLC).

From Newton Diehl Baker

My dear Mr. President: Washington. July 26, 1919.

When the Government of the United States purchased the Panama Canal rights it acquired, among other things, the Panama Railroad. This railroad is an incorporated company of which the Secretary of War, on behalf of the Government, owns all the stock. Its operation, however, is that of a private corporation.

The Panama Railroad owns, and has operated continuously, a lime [line] of steamers from New York to the Panama Canal. The continuance of this service was deemed essential during the period of canal construction, and I think it is conceded by everybody that the Panama Railroad steamers have done an excellent service in a thoroughly business-like way, saved the Government great costs in transportation charges, for material and personnel connected with

the Panama Canal, and maintained fair rates of transportation between New York and the Canal Zone.

It is my belief that this service ought to be extended by adding
to it other steamers, and changing its route so as practically to
cover the Caribbean Sea, thus making a Government-owned and
operated line, with the advantages of private corporation management, between the United States and Cuba, Hayti, Porto Rico, San
Domingo, the Virgin Islands, the Panama Canal Zone, and such
other ports and points in the Caribbean as develop traffic to justify
the service.

Until now our line has operated only between the Canal Zone
and New York, except that during the war our steamers stopped at
Hayti at the request of the Shipping Board. The rest of the Caribbean traffic has been monopolized by the Royal Dutch Line and
the British Lines.

The Shipping Board disapproves of my suggestion, and proposes
the discontinuance of the Government operated line to the Panama
Canal Zone, believing that the ships should be disposed of and the
route operated by private individuals and corporations in accordance with the general policy of the Shipping Board which favors
private rather than Government operation.

Secretary Redfield, at my request, considered the matter, and
sought the advice of the Commissioner of Navigation, Mr. E. T.
Chamberlain,[1] who agrees with the Shipping Board. Mr. Redfield's
personal view is that the Panama Canal line should be maintained
as it now is, but should not be largely extended, even in the Caribbean.

I do not know whether this question will be presented to you by
the Shipping Board, but I have given considerable study to the
question, and feel strongly the wisdom of my own preference in
the matter.

The Caribbean Sea has been called the American Mediterranean. It lies at our door. We have a certain responsibility in the
matter of its police, notably in Porto Rico which belongs to the
United States, and in Cuba where our interests and obligations are
obvious. Generally throughout the islands and the Central and
South American coast which surround the Caribbean Sea, the natural lines of trade, interest and association are with the United
States as against any European country. The Panama Canal is a
great possession which it is our duty to maintain and protect. Its
protection requires not merely adequate military foresight but
commercial facilities which will be created and nursed in the interest of solidarity of commercial interests between the countries
and islands surrounding the Caribbean, and the United States.

The maintenance of an adequate commercial fleet for the Caribbean trade, not only under the American flag but in the hands of the Government, would afford us in any emergency at least that many ships to be devoted to the transportation of troops and materials. The ownership and management of such a fleet would have a general effect in controlling transportation charges between the United States and South American ports, on both the East and West Coasts.

I do not believe that the maintenance of Government owned and controlled ships in the Caribbean is an inconsistent exception, even if the policy of the Shipping Board be generally accepted as sound. I myself would not accept it as sound, however, but for the practical considerations which make Government operation of steamship lines generally inadvisable at this time because public opinion is not properly prepared for such extensive and general Governmental activities in this country.

I do not want to press the question on you for consideration at this time, but, in the event it is brought to your attention from any other source, I should be glad to be heard and place in your hands some studies I have on this subject which ought to be considered before a determination is made adverse to the extension of the Panama Railroad steamship line, much less a conclusion reached which would in any way interfere with the pre-war service rendered by it. I think I may say that neither the Shipping Board nor the Bureau of Navigation of the Department of Commerce questions in the slightest degree the fairness and excellence of the service hitherto rendered by the line, nor the value of the unusual service it was able to render during the war.

Respectfully yours,   Newton D. Baker

TLS (WP, DLC).
  [1] Eugene Tyler Chamberlain.

Thomas Riley Marshall to Joseph Patrick Tumulty

My dear Tumulty,   Washington. 26" July 1919.

I enclose you resolutions which may or may not have been forwarded to you.[1] Two of the signers are Republicans.

Without too much trouble could you find out whether the President wants me to stay here while he is on his tour. As I see it nothing will be done and no question arise upon which I am needed to vote.

Thanking you for an answer

I am   Yours sincerely   Thos. R. Marshall[2]

ALS (WP, DLC).

¹ The enclosures are missing in WP, DLC.
² "The President does not think it is necessary for the Vice President to stay in Washington. He appreciates his consulting him." GFC, "Memo," c. Aug. 2, 1919, T MS (WP, DLC).

From Henry White

Paris, July 26, 1919.

3323. For the President. Referring to your number 2594 July 18, noon.¹ I communicated yesterday afternoon to the Council of Five the President's decision which caused considerable disappointment. An informal conversation entirely friendly in tone thereupon ensued in the course of which Balfour created a distinction between belligerency and warfare, which latter he said is now going on to a considerable extent in those parts and British soldiers are being killed. He and Clemenceau finally decided that the latter should make an appeal to the President by telegraph for reconsideration his decision on grounds to be set forth in the telegram which I understand is to be drafted by Balfour and despatched by Clemenceau this evening.   American Mission.

T telegram (SDR, RG 59, 661.119/444, DNA).
¹ FLP to H. White, July 18, 1919, Vol. 61.

From the Desk Diary of Robert Lansing

Sunday July 27 [1919]

6:20 pm President called at house and discussed "reservations & interpretations." Also asked me to tell Japanese Chargé negotiations with China on basis of agreements of 1915 & 1918¹ would not be tolerate[d].

Hw bound diary (R. Lansing Papers, DLC).
¹ About which, see, e.g., ns. 4 and 5 to Mantoux's notes of a meeting of the Council of Four printed at April 18, 1919, 11 a.m., Vol. 57, and the index references under "Japan: and China on treaties and claims regarding Shantung Province and Kiaochow," *ibid.*, and "China," "China and the United States," and "Japan and the United States," Vol. 39.

A News Report

[July 27, 1919]

PRESIDENT MAY YIELD
Statement From White House Expected on Interpretations

The most important move in the Senate disagreement over reservations to the peace treaty is expected to come from President Wilson.

Having canvassed the Senate situation in his conferences with fifteen Republican senators, all of whom are said to have told him they would support certain reservations, it is expected the President soon will make known definitely his attitude toward such a course. It was indicated at the White House yesterday that expression of his views on the subject might not await his speaking tour, to begin two weeks hence, but might be embodied in a public statement within the next few days.

This aroused great interest among Republican senators, though they said it was not wholly unexpected. Several Republicans have told Mr. Wilson the treaty never could be ratified without interpretative qualifications, and Friday at the suggestion, it is understood, of Republican Leader Lodge, a tentative draft of reservations indicating in a general way the trend of opinion among many Republican senators was laid before the President by Senator Spencer, Republican, Missouri.[1] The leaders for reservations say it is now the President's move.

The group of Republicans who, under the lead of Senators McCumber and McNary, are working on a reservation program designed to clarify the league of nations covenant without vitally weakening it, believes the President will announce his acceptance of such a course and that quick ratification of the treaty will ensue.

In their talks with Mr. Wilson, they say, he has indicated no radical antagonism to Senate qualifications, his only fear being that the whole subject might be thrown back into renegotiation.

The President's Democratic supporters in the Senate, however, are not in accord with this view and predict that he will assert himself for unreserved ratification and then go to the country in an effort to fortify public sentiment behind that stand.

Yesterday Chairman Lodge discussed some features of the treaty with Secretary Lansing. Mr. Lodge is understood to have suggested that the committee have the benefit of expert advice on some sections, particularly those dealing with alien enemy property.

It is expected that Bradley Palmer[2] and others who advised the American delegation at Versailles on these matters will appear before the committee this week.

President Wilson had intended, it was said at the White House, to go to the Capitol yesterday afternoon and talk over the treaty situation with administration senators. He abandoned the plan, however, when he learned that the Senate was not in session and that Senator Hitchcock, administration leader in the treaty fight, was out of town. The foreign relations committee had also recessed over yesterday, and will meet again tomorrow when it expects to complete preliminary reading of the treaty text.

In the opinion of many Republican senators the lines to be drawn in the reservation controversy rest entirely with the President. They say if he gives his assent to a reservation program designed to further safeguard national interests they quickly can come to such an agreement as to insure ratification of the treaty.

But if he takes an uncompromising stand for unreserved ratification and then by public speeches attempts to discredit the senators who are holding out against it the opposition leaders look for a long and bitter fight.

Printed in the *Washington Post*, July 27, 1919.
  [1] See the first news report printed at July 25, 1919, Vol. 61.
  [2] That is, Bradley Webster Palmer, former assistant counsel to the Alien Property Custodian, who had been an adviser on economic and commercial questions in the American delegation at the peace conference.

To George V

[The White House, c. July 27, 1919]

It is with gratification that I learn of Your Majesty's acceptance of the invitation[1] extended to His Royal Highness the Prince of Wales to visit the United States upon the occasion of his journey to Canada. I anticipate much pleasure in having the Prince with us even for so short a time and will do all in my power to make his visit a pleasant one in the hope that he may return to Great Britain with as warm a feeling for this country and with as pleasant memories as those which we cherish of our recent visit to London. Mrs. Wilson joins in extending warmest regards to Your Majesty and the Queen.   Woodrow Wilson.

TC telegram (Royal Archives, Windsor Castle).
  [1] Ambassador John W. Davis had suggested to Lansing on May 26, 1919, that, in view of the forthcoming visit of the Prince of Wales to Canada in August, he be invited to visit the United States. After Wilson and Lansing had agreed, Davis had extended a formal invitation to the Prince on July 3, and George had accepted the invitation for him on July 24. As it turned out, he visited the United States from November 10 to November 22, 1919. About this matter, see the documents printed in *FR 1919*, II, 247-50.

From Thomas Staples Martin

Dear Mr. President: Charlottesville, Va., July 27, 1919.

As pleasing as it was to me to have a letter from you, I confess I was surprised that you could find time to write even a few lines of sympathy,[1] confronted with the difficulties that have surrounded you.

Of course, the treaty could not in all respects be entirely satisfactory to you or to any other one person, but I trust you will pardon me for saying that I think you worked out a wonderful result. It will be a real pleasure to me to vote for it just as you have sent it to the Senate. Of course, there are things which I would prefer to have seen shaped differently, but I am really surprised that you should get so good a result in the midst of the difficulties that surrounded you. You had to meet difficulties with foreign governments and you were continually nagged, as you are now being nagged, by political enemies at home. I trust, however, you will be able to prevail in carrying out your purposes.

I have had a very severe spell. Indeed, I have been on the sick list since last January, doing only such work from time to time as my strength permitted. I was finally compelled to surrender. However, I expect to be in Washington to vote on the treaty when it is ready for a vote. I am confident I can manage it by getting in a drawing room on the train and returning to Charlottesville after voting. I do not expect to be paired, but to vote on the treaty just as you have sent it to the Senate, unless in some particulars you should see fit to approve some modifications or reservations.

With kindest regards to Mrs. Wilson and yourself, I am,

Very sincerely yours,   Thomas S. Martin

TLS (WP, DLC).
[1] WW to T. S. Martin, July 16, 1919, Vol. 61.

From Henry White

Paris July 27, 1919.

Urgent 3354. For the President. Mr. Clemenceau requests me to transmit to you the following message from my British, French, Italian, and Japanese colleagues relative to the proposed blockade of Soviet Russia:[1]

"British, French, Italian, Japanese members of the Council of Five, respectfully offer the following on the President's message relating to neutral trade in the gulf of Finland.[2] They do not desire to express any opinion upon the statement of International law laid down in the telegram. It may well be true that where there is no state of belligerency there can be no legal blockade; but they would point out that the situation in Russia and in the Gulf of Finland is at the present moment such as hardly to permit rigid application of rules which in ordinary cases are quite uncontested. Language in which international law is expressed is fitted to describe the relations between organized states but it is not so well fitted to describe the relations between the organized states on the one hand and unorganized chaos on the other hand. Russia during this period of transition is not a state but a collection of 'de facto' Governments at war with each other and though it is quite true to say that the

Allied and Associated Powers are not in a state of belligerency with Russia it is also true they are involved in military operations with one of these 'de facto' governments and that they are supplying arms and ammunition to the others.

It may not be proper to describe this condition of things as war but it cannot be right to treat it as peace, nor can the international rules applicable to a state of peace be applied to it without qualification. The case is a special one, and must be specially treated.

We would venture to point out some of the ill consequences which in the present case would follow from neglecting this consideration.

Allied and Associated troops are defending themselves in circumstances of very great difficulty against Bolshevist attacks in Archangel. Yet we permit the Bolshevist troops, who are making these attacks, to receive supplies which we could easily cut off.

We are furnishing the Siberian army of Koltchak with military equipment, and at the same time we are permitting military equipment to go to his enemy. We have gone far in the direction of recognizing the Esthonians, and other non Russian people, who are struggling to resist Bolshevist attacks; yet we leave neutral traders free to strengthen the Bolshevist armies, and to convey unhindered information to a hostile navy as to the number and disposition of our own ships of war.

It may be urged, indeed, that to interfere with neutral commerce will not so much have the effect of hampering the military operations of those who are engaged in attacking us and our friends, as in aggravating the misery under which the innocent civil population is already suffering. So far as our information goes, however, this will not be the result. Every cargo successfully brought through the Gulf of Finland to Petrograd supplies a new instrument to the Bolshevists for adding recruits to their army. None of it will reach anyone but soldiers and officials. Its distribution will be determined by considerations which are military and not philanthropic. It will not diminish the sufferings of humanity; it will add to them.

It has been suggested that it might be possible for the four other great powers to maintain the control of imports into the Gulf of Finland without the participation of the United States. We feel however the stronger objection to adopting any policy not accepted by our principal allied and associated power and even apart from this overwhelming consideration we cannot ignore the fact that if in such circumstances an American ship were to enter the gulf an incident might easily occur where consequences would be well nigh intolerable.

It is for these reasons that we would most earnestly request the

United States Government to consider their decision and to concur in a policy which as it seems to us is of so special and exceptional a character as to be quite outside the ordinary rules laid down by international law for the conduct of maritime blockade.["] White.

American Mission

T telegram (SDR, RG 59, 763.72112/12393, DNA).
¹ There is a copy of the following memorandum, initialed by A. J. Balfour and dated July 25, 1919, in the A. J. Balfour Papers, Add. MSS, 49751, British Library.
² FLP to H. White, July 18, 1919, Vol. 61.

A News Report

[July 28, 1919]

TALKS WITH 11 DEMOCRATS
President Tells Senators European Stability Requires
Early Ratification.
FIRM AGAINST AMENDMENTS
Fears Reservations Would Recommit Convention to Paris
and Cause Indefinite Delay.

Washington, July 28.—In a conference with eleven Democratic Senators at the Capitol late today, President Wilson urged speed in consideration by the Senate of the treaty with Germany. The President pictured to the Senators the economic crisis in Europe and argued that quick ratification of the treaty, with the League of Nations covenant included, was imperative, to bring about order and effect an adjustment of international affairs.

The President deplored any tendency toward delay in reaching the stage of ratification. He expressed disapproval, several Senators said, of the threat of the Republican opposition to press reservations. The President felt, he told the Senators, that the treaty ought to be ratified exactly as submitted to the Senate.

Mr. Wilson, it was said, told the Senators that he would submit to the Senate within a day or so, the Anglo-American-French treaty; he was criticised by Senate Republicans last week for having failed to send this treaty in along with the treaty of Versailles. He did not know that the Senate was anxious to get that treaty at once, he said, and had held it with the intention of submitting it with a special message.

The President took up the Shantung award to Japan in the Peace Treaty, giving the impression that an announcement would be forthcoming within a few days that would throw a different light on the matter. Mr. Wilson did not indicate whether this announcement would come from him or through Japanese sources. The impression at the Capitol after the President's conference was that, if the Japanese Government failed to make a public announcement on the subject, the President would do so. No inkling was conveyed by Mr. Wilson as to the nature of the forthcoming development regarding Shantung, but it is understood that it will embrace a statement explicitly defining Japan's intention to return within a reasonable period the rights given to her in the Chinese peninsula.

Secretary Lansing conferred with the Counselor of the Japanese Embassy, Mr. Debuchi, on Shantung, and Mr. Debuchi subsequently indicated in an interview that Japan was only awaiting the signature of China to the Peace Treaty to give satisfactory assurances as to the return of the peninsula to Chinese sovereignty.

Mr. Wilson gave the emphatic impression to the Democratic Senators that he was still unalterably opposed to any reservations in the Peace Treaty. He was as much against "interpretive" reservations, such as Mr. Taft had suggested, as any others. The President's idea was expressed later as being that he felt that any reservations would have the effect of recommitting the treaty to the Peace Conference, entailing indefinite delay in final ratification.

The President's visit to the Capitol was unheralded. He had conferred earlier in the day with Senator Thomas, Democrat, of Colorado, who had told him that he had not made up his mind how he stood as to the necessity for reservations. Before his conference at the White House he had been generally put down as intending to vote for the treaty without change. After his talk with the President, Mr. Thomas said, he had not come to any definite judgment as to reservations and would have to read the treaty over again before making up his mind.

The President also conferred at the White House with Senators Johnson of South Dakota and Smith of Arizona. To both he insisted that reservations would have the effect of sending the treaty back to the Paris conference and urged that the treaty be ratified without change.

After his conference with the eleven Democrats at the Capitol, which lasted exactly an hour, Mr. Wilson, facing a group of newspaper men, smiled broadly. Before any one could put a question to him the President remarked:

"There is no crisis in the country today, gentlemen."

The President declined to discuss the nature of his talk with the Democrats.

"We were just visiting," he said. The President appeared at the Capitol at 4:30 o'clock, just after the Senate had adjourned for the day. He met the Democratic Senators in his own room, on the Senate floor. At the conference were Swanson of Virginia, King of

Utah, Pittman of Nevada, Overman of North Carolina, Pomerene of Ohio, Harrison of Mississippi, Nugent of Idaho, Jones of New Mexico, Henderson of Nevada,[1] Shields of Tennessee, and Wolcott of Delaware. Senator Hitchcock, ranking Democratic member of the Foreign Relations Committee, who has been leading the Senate fight for ratification of the treaty, along with Senator Swanson, did not attend the conference, not having reached Washington from his week-end trip to Swampscott, Mass.

Exactly how the President happened to have the particular eleven Democats at the conference did not develop, but it was assumed that the meeting was arranged at his suggestion. Many other Democrats were at the Capitol during the day—nearly all of the forty-seven, in fact—but all, excepting the eleven, left the Senate just as the President arrived.

The President stood at the marble table in the President's room during his hour's talk with the Senators. Mr. Wilson spoke earnestly to the Senators, especially when he urged speedy ratification of the treaty. He laid stress upon the necessity of getting affairs in Europe readjusted. This, he said, could not be done until the Peace Treaty had become operative, with the League of Nations covenant as a part of it.

After the conference the Senators, while not going into detail as to what the President had said, indicated that he was particularly emphatic as to the urgency of expeditious handling of the treaty. All spoke of the President as apparently unwavering in his attitude against reservations.

The President, Senators said, referred only briefly to the Anglo-American-French treaty. From what he said, the Senators expect the treaty will be submitted to the Senate by Wednesday. His reference to the opposition's fight in the Senate on the Shantung award was more extended. Mr. Wilson seemed to be confident, the Senators said, that when the contemplated announcement was made respecting the award there would be a change of sentiment. Mr. Wilson, the Senators inferred, expects that the Shantung provision will remain in the treaty. At least, they gathered the impression that he would fight for it to the end, as an essential part of the treaty.

The President is understood to have gone into the reasons for putting the Shantung award into the treaty, as he has in his conferences at the White House. His explanation, it was said, as expressed to the Senators, was that it was done to keep Japan from declining to sign the treaty. Mr. Wilson is reported to have stated that, in the face of the treaty entered into by Great Britain, France, and Japan during the early days of the war, no other course appeared open than to decide in favor of bestowing the Shantung rights upon Japan. He is also said to have emphatically stated his confidence that Japan would restore the privileges granted within a reasonable time.

As an outcome of the conference with the President, the Administration forces, it was understood, would redouble their efforts to get speedy action in the Foreign Relations Committee, and to expedite consideration of the Treaty when it reaches the Senate. Also, the fight against reservations will go on, without compromise.

In his conference with the President at the White House, Senator Thomas frankly told Mr. Wilson that he had been unable to reach a conclusion as to reservations. Speaking of the conference, Mr. Thomas said he told the President that he had read the treaty three times and would have to read it again before he could decide what to do.

Senator Thomas objects, he said, to the Shantung provision and also to that for delivering the Sarre Basin to France. As to the Sarre Basin award, the Senator said, the treaty appeared to leave it for the League of Nations to determine when France should give it back, rather than to a plebiscite. He thought it should be determined by a vote of the people themselves and favored an explicit plebiscite clause.

Senator Johnson, after his talk with the President, said the President had urged that the treaty must be accepted without change if it was to be an effective instrument for world peace. Senator Johnson expressed it as his own opinion that the treaty either must be accepted in toto or rejected. He would not believe, he said, that the Senate would throw it out.

The expectation that the Japanese Government, if China agrees to sign the Peace Treaty, would make a formal statement concerning the Shantung question which would clear up that feature of the fight against the League of Nations was increased today following a conference between Secretary of State Lansing and Katsuji Debuchi, Counselor and Chargé d'Affaires for Japan. Mr. Debuchi, while emphasizing the fact that he was not speaking on behalf of his Government, but solely as an individual, expressed an optimistic view of the situation, predicting that Japan would restore to China, within a reasonable time, sovereignty over the leased territory of Kiau-Chau.

Mr. Debuchi was in conference at the State Department with Secretary Lansing this morning. Neither the Japanese Embassy nor the State Department would give any intimation of the progress of the conversations going forward between the Japanese and American Governments in regard to the recommendation, made originally at Paris by the United States, that Japan make a public declaration in respect of her intentions concerning Shantung.[2]

It was learned at the State Department that the United States never had withdrawn the request the American delegation made of the Japanese delegation at Paris that an official Japanese declaration be made, and there is excellent reason to believe, not only that President Wilson has directed, since his return to Washington, the attention of the Japanese Government to the American advice given at Paris, but also that the Japanese Government itself is interested in the popular opinion of the United States, which has manifested concern for a public declaration by the Japanese Government. . . .

Printed in the *New York Times*, July 29, 1919.
    [1] Charles Belknap Henderson, Democrat.
    [2] See the memorandum by Robert Lansing printed at June 28, 1919, and n. 5 thereto, Vol. 61.

From Walker Downer Hines, with Enclosure

Dear Mr. President: Washington July 28, 1919.

By way of reply to the question you asked me today, I enclose memorandum which I have prepared after carefully considering the matter.

Since my return to the office I have received a letter from the President of the National Coal Association[1] (representing the bituminous operators) in which he refers to the propaganda urging people to buy coal at once, as follows:

"The National Coal Association has felt that it has a duty to perform in placing the situation squarely before the public, so that when the rush comes, and the coal is difficult to obtain, and clamor for coal will undoubtedly bring on increased prices, there will be an attack on the coal industry through the press, and the coal operators would have been blamed for not advising the public of the true situation."

I think the real meaning is that the coal operators have refrained from inducing purchases during the summer by reducing prices and they propose to make up for this by heavily increasing the prices somewhat later on, unless effective action can be taken to protect the public. The operators seem to suspend the law of supply and demand while the supply exceeds the demand, but they propose to give the law full swing when the demand exceeds the supply.   Cordially yours,   Walker D Hines

TLS (WP, DLC).

[1] Henry Noble Taylor of Kansas City, president of the General Wilmington Co. and the Monon Coal Co. and vice-president and general manager of the Central Coal & Coke Co. During the war, he had been a deputy director of the United States Fuel Administration and a member of the War Industries Board.

E N C L O S U R E

MEMORANDUM:

Further increases in prices through the continued development of the profiteering spirit will hamper the furnishing by the United States of its part of the capital needed for the rehabilitation of Europe.

This is true because further increases in prices will bring about further increases in wages; the increases both in prices and in wages will increase the cost of production and hence will increase the domestic demands upon capital. A 25% increase in the cost of production would not only tie up large additional amounts of capital in current operations, but would correspondingly tie up additional capital in all new construction.

On the other hand, to the extent that the present exorbitant prices are diminished there will be a diminution of the strain on credit and correspondingly additional capital will be made available for use in Europe.

Of course if a policy were adopted which were so drastic as to destroy hope of reasonable profit, such a course would be prejudicial to the financial situation, but without going to such extremes it is believed a great deal can be accomplished to put a curb on profiteering and to give hope to the working classes.

Walker D Hines

TS MS (WP, DLC).

From Robert Heberton Terrell[1]

Sir: Washington, July 28, 1919.

Permit me to call your attention to the splendid services rendered by the Hon. John F. Costello, the Recorder of Deeds for the District of Columbia, last week when our city was disturbed by a race riot.[2] From the beginning to the end of that trouble Mr. Costello was unceasing in his efforts to bring peace to our community and to restore harmony between the races here. His impartial attitude, his spirit of fairness and his willingness to listen to the men who represented the colored people as they told him of their grievances and laid before him their side of the situation that had developed, won for him their complete confidence and made it possible for him to do effective work among both races. On all sides the colored people have appreciated and commended Mr. Costello's work, and I think it is not improper for me, as a colored man, to bring to your attention that so worthy a citizen, and one who represents your administration in this District, has rendered all the citizens of the Nation's Capital, regardless of race or politics, such effective services at a time when they were so sorely needed.

Respectfully yours,   Robert H Terrell

TLS (WP, DLC).
[1] A Negro judge on the Municipal Court of the District of Columbia. Appointed to this position by Theodore Roosevelt in 1902, he had been reappointed by Wilson in 1914 and confirmed over the strong protest of some southern Democrats. See the index references to Terrell in Vol. 29 of this series.
[2] See J. R. Shillady to WW, July 21, 1919, n. 2, Vol. 61.

From Robert Lansing, with Enclosure

Balfour on Italy and the pending questions[1]

My dear Mr. President: Washington July 28, 1919.

I am transmitting to you herewith a copy of a personal telegram I have just received from Mr. White containing a draft of a communication which has been prepared by Mr. Balfour at M. Clemenceau's request regarding the Italian situation and which is intended to answer a note presented to the Council of Five by the Italian delegate.   Faithfully yours,   Robert Lansing

TLS (WP, DLC).
[1] WWhw and WWsh.

E N C L O S U R E

Paris, July 25, 1919.

3313. Personal for Lansing. The following is a draft reply written by Balfour at Clemenceau's request to the note presented to the Council of Five by Tittoni[1] in reply to the note addressed to his predecessor on the twenty-eighth of June.[2]

"We beg to acknowledge receipt of Your Excellency's reply to joint note signed by the Prime Ministers of France and Great Britain and sent on the 28th. of June to Your Excellency's predecessor in office, Baron Sonnino. The greater part of this reply is concerned with certain matters of historical controversy raised in the joint note, with these [which?] we proposed briefly to deal in another communication but for the moment it seems essential to isolate the most important of the immediate issues and to lay before Your Excellency the exact nature of the difficulties which render the problem of the Adriatic so hard of solution.

We must preface what we have to say by correcting a serious error into which your Excellency has fallen. You say explicitly in one passage, and you constantly imply that we consider the Treaty of London as no longer binding. We have never said this. What we have said is that Italy has treated it and is and [at] this very moment treating it as no longer binding which is a very different thing. The declarations of her statesmen; the articles in her newspapers; the demonstrations in her Parliament; and the incidents, often most lamentable, which have happened in her streets all combine to show that in the opinion of her people the question of Fiume is an open one and that if Italy wants it there is no valid reason why Italy should not have it. But according to the Treaty of London the question is not an open one, and those who are ready to repudiate the Treaty in the matter of Fiume have evidently no right whatever to claim it as binding in cases where its provisions are more to their liking.

We must trust Your Excellency will believe that we do not again raise this point, important as it certainly is, merely for controversial purposes. Our object is very different. We desire to impress upon Your Excellency that a satisfactory settlement of the Adriatic question must take account of other things besides the Treaty of London and to remind you that in this opinion though from another point of view Your Excellency and all Italy thinks as we do.

The full difficulty of the problem becomes manifest as soon as we enumerate all the conditions which its complete solution must satisfy. One condition there is which must be treated as irreducible. The settlement, whatever be its character, must be accepted by all the Associated Powers. Otherwise it is no settlement at all— but a public and ignominious confession of diplomatic failure. Other conditions are perhaps less absolute in their character though each taken separately has claim to be included in any ideal arrangement. Such an arrangement would enable every power to fulfill all the obligations into which it has entered; all the principles which it has proclaimed; all the hopes which it has expressed; all the ambition which it has cherished. How nearly can this ideal be reached? That is the question.

That it is a question very difficult to answer is evident if we consider it from the point of the power most immediately concerned. Italy desires to maintain the Treaty of London; and also to obtain Fiume. She cannot evidently do both. Italy desires to regulate European frontiers according to the principle of self determination;

and also to obtain large portions of the Dalmatian Coast and the adjacent islands. After all she cannot do both. Italy recognizes the need for including America in any settlement that may be arrived at but she also desires to acquire territories which cannot be hers with the good will of America if the latter adheres to President Wilson's declared *interruption* (interpretation?) of the fourteen points. Again we must observe that no one has yet suggested a scheme by which these two apparent incompatibles may be reconciled.

The difficulties we have enumerated are familiar to Your Excellency and doubtless all the other Associated Powers are in their several (?) confronted like Italy with problems arising out of the unforseen historical developments of the last four years. But so far as the Adriatic question is concerned it is Italy which should provide us with a solution. Firstly, Italy alone among the Associated Powers of the west has material ambition to satisfy. All four are pledged to the principle of self determination; three have signed the Treaty of London. But only to Italy can it matter from a territorial, military, naval or economic point of view what arrangement be finally adopted. Let Italy then suggest a policy which, without being forgetful of her interest, is consistent with her principles and with ours.

There is one subsidiary contention contained in Your Excellency's memorandum on which it is necessary to say a word before bringing this portion our reply to a close.

Your Excellency writes as if Italy were receiving less considerate treatment from her associates than other Allied states and in particular, as in the principle of self determination and nationality, were applied in her case with a rigidity of interpretation quite absent in the cases for example of Poland or Bohemia.

We are unable to agree with this view. It is of course true that in this world of complex relations no abstract rule can be sighted [cited] and (as it were) had never mechanically applied. Considerations based on history and ethnology; on religion, culture and language, on administrative conveniences; on economic interdependence and military security, may unite districts which would otherwise be separated and separate districts which would otherwise be united. The determination of the new frontier of Italy in the north presents an example of this procedure which to many lovers of Italy has been a cause of painful surprise. They say, and say truly, that if language, race, and the wishes of the neutral powers had in this case governed the decision of the Conference southern Tyrol would never have been Italian. Self determination, however, and nationality were outweighed by strategic considerations and Italy obtained what she desired, the frontier of the Alps.

The case of Bohemia also presented difficulties. Here also there is a German area included in a non-German state and here also geographic and strategical reasons may be fairly urged in favor of the *anomaly*. But historical and economic considerations have ever a greater weight. Since the middle ages Bohemia has been a political unity, sometimes a separate and independent Kingdom, sometimes an independent Kingdon united to its neighbors through the person of its monarch, sometimes within and sometimes without the Holy Roman Empire, latterly a unit in the Austrian half of the Dual Monarchy. But through every change she has possessed a continuous unity, and a national territory immemorially divided from Germany proper by its range of encircling mountains. To cut this territory in two by a strictly linguistic frontier in defiance of historic sentiment and economic expansion would surely have been to misuse the principles of self determination. With this view we know that Your Excellency agrees, we are also confident that you hold with us that no parallel case can be found [in] the Italian populations sparsely scattered along the Dalmatia coast.

With these two exceptions, southern Tyrol and German speaking Bohemia, we are unaware of any case in which frontiers have been so drawn as to leave important areas on what they would deem to be the wrong side of the line. No doubt there are many cases of isolated settlements which have necessarily been left in the midst of an alien population. This is inevitable. No doubt there are also cases where for sufficient geographical, economic or greater reason, slight deflections of the ethnographical frontier have been deliberately sanctioned by the Conference. But broadly speaking we see no ground for Your Excellency's suggestion that our principles are inflexible only where Italy is concerned. On the contrary we think that if Italy would apply to the Istrian and Dalmatia coast line south of Pola the methods which, in conjunction with her Allies, she has applied elsewhere, the Adriatic question would not exist. Signed A. J. Balfour."

In sending it Balfour writes me as follows:

"It may possibly be found necessary to supplement my draft with more detailed replies to the specific points raised by Tittoni, such as the question of when and why Italy went to war and more especially [with] respect to Asia Minor, but my object has been to isolate and set out what seems to me to be [at] the moment the essential question. I think it is really important to get rid of this (?) dragging in of the treaty of London and my endeavor has been to make clear once and for all the exact position as regards that instrument. The view I have expressed is taken from the British standpoint, and I do not know how far Clemenceau will accept it or wish to modify or amplify it unqualifiedly, but I am anxious that

you should have full possession of what I conceive to be a fair statement of the British position." White.[3]   American Mission.

T telegram (WP, DLC).
    [1] For which, see W. Phillips to WW, July 22, 1919 (second letter of that date), Vol. 61.
    [2] That is, the note printed as the Appendix to the minutes of the Council of Four
printed at June 28, 1919, 6 p.m., Vol. 61.
    [3] A few hours later, White added: "Referring to my No. 3313, Balfour has just told me
that Clemenceau has accepted his draft note which will be signed by them both and
presented to Tittoni tomorrow. 3317." T telegram (SDR, RG 256, 186.3411/725B,
DNA).

From the Most Reverend Aluigi Cossio,[1]
with Enclosure

Your Excellency: Washington, D. C. July 28, 1919.

    I have the honor of forwarding, herewith enclosed, an autograph
letter of Pope Benedict XV,[2] which I have received for Your Excellency from the Papal Secretary of State, His Eminence Cardinal
Gasparri.
    With sentiments of profound respect and high esteem, I have
the honor to be,

                    Your humble servant,   Mons. Aluigi Cossio
                                           Chargé d'affaires.

TLS (WP, DLC).
    [1] Chargé d'Affaires of the Apostolic Delegation in the United States.
    [2] It accompanies this document in WP, DLC.

                    E   N   C   L   O   S   U   R   E

                        DRAFT TRANSLATION
                        TO HIS EXCELLENCY
                    DOCTOR WOODROW WILSON
                PRESIDENT OF THE UNITED STATES.

    Excellency,
    Monsignor Cerretti,[1] upon his return from Paris, hastened to in-
form Us with what spirit of moderation Your Excellency examined
the demands regarding the Catholic Missions which We presented
to the Peace Conference, and with what zeal Your Excellency subsequently supported these demands. We desire to express to you
Our sincere gratitude and at the same time We urge Your Excellency to be good enough to employ your great influence, also, in
order to prevent the action, which according to the Peace Treaty
with Germany, it is desired to bring against the Kaiser and the
highly placed German commanders. This action could only render
more bitter national hatred and postpone for a long time that paci-

fication of souls for which all nations long. Furthermore, this trial, if the rules of justice are to be observed, would meet insurmountable difficulties as may be seen from the attached article from the Osservatore Romano,[2] which deals exclusively with the trial of the Kaiser, the newspaper reserving right to treat in another article the question of the trial of the generals.

It pleases Us to take advantage of this new occasion to renew to Your Excellency the wishes which We entertain for your prosperity and that of your family, as well as for the happiness of the inhabitants of the Confederation of the United States.

Rome, The Vatican, 1st July, 1919.
(Signed) Benedictus PP. XV.

T MS (WP, DLC).
  [1] That is, the Most Rev. Bonaventura Cerretti, Papal Undersecretary of State and Secretary of Extraordinary Ecclesiastical Affairs.
  [2] "The Trial of the Kaiser," English translation from *Osservatore Romano*, June 25, 1919, T MS (WP, DLC). A French translation of the article is also attached to these documents.

From the Desk Diary of Robert Lansing

Tuesday July 29 [1919]

Cabinet meeting 2:30-4:15. Conferred with Prest. He will not go west when he intended. Also on Shantung and sending Harbord to Armenia.[1]

  [1] About this proposed mission, see NDB to WW, July 15, 1919 (second letter of that date), and particularly its Enclosure, Vol. 61. Wilson appointed Harbord to head this mission on August 1, 1919. For further details, see James B. Gidney, *A Mandate for Armenia* (Kent, Ohio, 1967), pp. 168-91, and Richard G. Hovannisian, *The Republic of Armenia* (2 vols. to date, Berkeley, Calif., etc., 1971-82), II, *passim*.

To the Senate

GENTLEMEN OF THE SENATE: The White House 29 July, 1919.

I take pleasure in laying before you a treaty with the Republic of France the object of which is to secure that Republic of the immediate aid of the United States of America in case of any unprovoked movement of aggression against her on the part of Germany. I earnestly hope that this treaty will meet with your cordial approval and will receive an early ratification at your hands, along with the treaty of peace with Germany. Now that you have had an opportunity to examine the great document I presented to you two weeks ago, it seems opportune to lay before you this treaty which is meant to be in effect a part of it.

It was signed on the same day with the treaty of peace and is intended as a temporary supplement to it. It is believed that the treaty of peace with Germany itself provides adequate protection to France against aggression from her recent enemy on the east; but the years immediately ahead of us contain many incalculable possibilities. The Covenant of the League of Nations provides for military action for the protection of its members only upon advice of the Council of the League—advice given, it is to be presumed, only upon deliberation and acted upon by each of the governments of the member States only if its own judgment justifies such action. The object of the special treaty with France which I now submit to you is to provide for immediate military assistance to France by the United States in case of any unprovoked movement of aggression against her by Germany without waiting for the advice of the Council of the League of Nations that such action be taken. It is to be an arrangement, not independent of the League of Nations, but under it.

It is, therefore, expressly provided that this treaty shall be made the subject of consideration at the same time with the treaty of peace with Germany; that this special arrangement shall receive the approval of the Council of the League; and that this special provision for the safety of France shall remain in force only until, upon the application of one of the parties to it, the Council of the League, acting, if necessary, by a majority vote, shall agree that the provisions of the Covenant of the League afford her sufficient protection.

I was moved to sign this treaty by considerations which will, I hope, seem as persuasive and as irresistible to you as they seemed to me. We are bound to France by ties of Friendship which we have always regarded, and shall always regard, as peculiarly sacred. She assisted us to win our freedom as a nation. It is seriously to be doubted whether we could have won it without her gallant and timely aid. We have recently had the privilege of assisting in driving enemies, who were also enemies of the world, from her soil; but that does not pay our debt to her. Nothing can pay such a debt. She now desires that we should promise to lend our great force to keep her safe against the power she has had most reason to fear. Another great nation volunteers the same promise. It is one of the fine reversals of history that that other nation should be the very power from whom France fought to set us free. A new day has dawned. Old antagonisms are forgotten. The common cause of freedom and enlightenment has created new comradeships and a new perception of what it is wise and necessary for great nations to do to free the world of intolerable fear. Two governments who wish to be members of the League of Nations ask leave of the

Council of the League to be permitted to go to the assistance of a friend whose situation has been found to be one of peculiar peril, without awaiting the advice of the League to act.

It is by taking such pledges as this that we prove ourselves faithful to the utmost to the high obligations of gratitude and tested friendship. Such an act as this seems to me one of the proofs that we are a people that sees the true heart of duty and prefers honour to its own separate course of peace.   Woodrow Wilson[1]

T MS (WP, DLC).
 [1] There is a WWT draft of this document, with WWhw (left-handed) emendations, in WP, DLC. Wilson's message, along with the English and French texts of the treaty, is printed in *Assistance to France in the Event of Unprovoked Aggression by Germany. Message from the President of the United States,* 66th Cong., 1st sess., Sen. Doc. No. 63 (Washington, 1919). The English version of the text of this treaty is printed as the Appendix to Mantoux's notes of a meeting of the Council of Four printed at June 28, 1919, 10:30 a.m., Vol. 61.

To Warren Gamaliel Harding

My dear Senator: [The White House] 29 July, 1919.

Matters of so grave a consequence are now under consideration that I would very much appreciate an opportunity to have a talk with you about the Treaty and all that it involves. I wonder if it would be possible for you to see me at the White House at 11 o'clock tomorrow, Wednesday morning.
        Cordially and sincerely yours,   Woodrow Wilson[1]

TLS (Letterpress Books, WP, DLC).
 [1] Wilson sent the same letter on the same date, *mutatis mutandis,* to Senators William Paul Dillingham, Republican of Vermont; James Eli Watson and Harry Stewart New, Republicans of Indiana; Henry Wilder Keyes, Republican of New Hampshire; Irvine Luther Lenroot, Republican of Wisconsin; and Bert Manfred Fernald, Republican of Maine. These letters are all TLS, Letterpress Books, WP, DLC.

From Albert, King of the Belgians

Bruxelles [July 29, 1919]

The gracious message that Your Excellency has just sent me[1] coincides perfectly with the desire of the Queen and myself to express our gratitude and that of all Belgium to the noble American nation. I hasten to accept your kind invitation to visit the United States with the Queen this autumn, and I shall be happy thus to be able to return the visit that Your Excellency paid us at Brussels.

I send to Your Excellency the assurance of my sincere friendship.   Albert.

T telegram (WP, DLC).
 [1] WW to Albert, July 26, 1919.

From Robert Lansing

My dear Mr. President: Washington July 29, 1919.

I am sending you an authenticated edition of the Treaties signed at Versailles which I was requested to bring to you from Paris as a presentation copy.

A special edition of these Treaties is being retained at the Department of State.   Faithfully yours,   Robert Lansing

TLS (WP, DLC).

From George P. Hampton[1]

Dear Mr. President: Washington, D. C. July 29, 1919

The people I have the honor to represent are deeply stirred over the question as to whether the Covenant of the League of Nations and the Peace Treaty with Germany should be adopted without change, with amendments, with clearly defined reservations, or rejected entirely. They feel that the real significance of these two documents and their bearing upon the welfare for many years to come, not only of the American people, but of the entire world, can be understood only after the most careful study and discussion.

To this end we recommend that following the series of addresses we understand you will make on a trip to the Pacific Coast and return, and the counter addresses of Senators and others opposed to the Covenant and Treaty, as they stand, that the people be given opportunity through a referendum vote to register their will on these documents. We hold it to be of the very essence of that free government which it was one of the prime purposes of our entering the war to establish, that there should be widely diffused responsibility. You, Mr. President, and the Senate, and the people and representatives of other nations, are entitled, on a matter so vitally affecting our country and the world at large, to have the conscientious and thoughtful expression of the opinion of the American people.

In this spirit and belief, we are now petitioning Congress to immediately enact the necessary legislation for an advisory referendum of every voter in the United States on the ratification by our country of both the Covenant of the League of Nations and the Peace Treaty with Germany. Such a referendum without a constitutional amendment cannot be made binding upon the Senate, but such an expression of public opinion will unquestionably have enormous weight and will reveal to all the world the desire of the people of this great nation.

We trust, Mr. President, that this action will meet with your hearty approval.   Yours sincerely,   Geo. P. Hampton

TLS (WP, DLC).
  [1] Managing Director of the Farmers' National Council, previously known as the Farmers' National Headquarters. Organized with the support of the American Society of Equity, the National Gleaner Federation, the North Carolina Farmers' Union, and various state granges, the Farmers' National Council was the most radical of the four agricultural lobbying groups based in Washington at this time.

From Warren Sanford Stone

Cleveland, Ohio, July 29, 1919.

Myself and associate grand officers, consisting of twelve members composing the advisory board of the Brotherhood of Locomotive Engineers, urgently request an interview with you and Cabinet, or the members thereof that may be quickly available for the purpose of placing before you a grave situation[1] that concerns all the people and obtaining advice that we think is necessary to guide our future movements. We will arrive in Washington Wednesday morning. Communication will reach me at National Hotel.
                W. S. Stone, Grand Chief Engineer
                Brotherhood of Locomotive Engineers.

T telegram (WP, DLC).
  [1] Stone and his associates saw Wilson at the White House on July 30 at 5 p.m. On that occasion, they presented to Wilson a statement which deplored the high cost of living and pointed out that the large increase in the price of basic commodities had created a "widespread spirit of unrest" among all workers. Due to this inflation, the statement continued, current real wages were actually lower than before the war and no longer provided the workers with "adequate food, shelter and raiment for themselves and families." As a solution to this problem, Stone and his associates then urged the following:
  "We believe the true remedy for the situation and one that will result in lifting the burden under which the whole people are struggling is for the Government to take some adequate measures to reduce the cost of the necessaries of life to a figure that the present wages and income of the people will meet. Should this not be considered feasible, we will be forced to urge that those whom we represent by [be] granted an increase in wages to meet the deterioration of the purchasing price of the dollar, be that what it may, which can be easily determined by competent authorities." *New York Times*, July 31, 1919.

From William Cox Redfield

Dear Mr. President: Washington July 29, 1919.

The report of the Bureau of Foreign and Domestic Commerce on the foreign trade of the country for the last fiscal year is startling, even to those who thought they were keeping track of it:

The exports for the single month of June were $918,000,000, which exceeds the record by over $200,000,000.

The total exports for the year were $7,225,000,000, an excess of $1,300,000,000 over the previous year and three times the normal record before the war.

The excess of exports was $4,129,000,000, an increased excess of over $1,100,000,000.

These are not only national records but world records. Nothing like them has ever been known.

I write them, however, not with elation but with concern, for they show the world problem we face. The enormous volume of export business at current prices is a measure of the world's need, which we alone can adequately supply. The excessive balance due us is a measure of the world's call on us for credits, which we alone can sufficiently furnish.

Clearly this condition cannot continue, for were it to proceed as now it does and on its present scale, it would exhaust the world's supply of credits and of cash to pay us. Nor can the balance be made good either by services or merchandise, for we require neither in sufficient quantity. A net excess in our favor of over $11,000,000 every day in the year cannot be adequately met by any normal means hitherto or now existing. Were this process to continue to an extreme it would impoverish the nations and place their fiscal futures in our hands.

One sees in the above figures why the problem of exchange is difficult and why, in addition to current high prices, the difference of exchange imposes a heavy additional burden upon the world at the time when it is least able to bear it. If America desires, as we know she does, to help the world effectively, it cannot be done long in the present way, for the continuance of the process, whose results I have noted, means financial starvation (and because of it other starvation in goods as well as in foods) for the nations.

Here lies the reason for this letter. Recently a friend, who is a Republican but a moderate and wise man, said to me, respecting these very figures, that the Republicans in Congress had before them a great political opportunity which they were neglecting, devoting themselves instead to muckraking and to partisan squabbling. Some individuals see the need, and Senators Edge and Owen have made an attempt at a remedy (S.2472 and S.2590).[1] The constructive opportunity, however, is going almost untouched and I think that, if you seize it, the ground can be cut from under the opposition in Congress, who will be forced to follow your lead, however reluctantly, because of the essential truth and necessity of what you suggest.

This is it. We have the ability to supply credits and goods (both raw and manufactured) in the necessary quantities and no other

nation is now able to do so. We have not, however, the organization. The task is too vast for private enterprise to do it on an adequate scale. It is a nation's job, akin in its size to the placing of a
Liberty Loan and must be based upon the same foundation of national faith.

I think the present emergency is as severe a test of America as
was the military part of the war; that the crisis, though of a different nature, is as great, and that its effect upon our national future
may be even greater. We have won the military fight. The economic test has come and we are not now ready for it, though we
have sufficient resources. I think a conference of such officers as
will at once occur to you would develop the outline of a plan which
stated to Congress and to the country would compel assent. Essential to it is, of course, the League of Nations as the first step toward
the establishing of credit for the small nations, who for a time must
in the general judgment of the world depend upon the League for
their security against external aggression. You could show that today without the League there can be no adequate credits for these
small peoples and that in order for America to use her opportunity
for service and for commerce the League is essential. Those who
oppose it are opposing not merely a political matter but a human,
industrial and commercial one, upon which depends the credit and
perhaps the existence of other nations and employment and prosperity in our own.

To illustrate, there lies before me the matter of supplying Poland
with locomotives and cars. She has railroads and no equipment.
Our men in England report through our Ambassador that the English banks cannot now handle the matter. We can and would,
were there an organization through which it could be done, but
Poland has no credit until secured by the League against external
aggression and here the matter rests while Poland waits.

Again the State of South Dakota has officially asked my assistance in marketing a large number of horses in and near Poland
where they are known to be greatly needed. I have been obliged to
tell the State authorities that although I should be glad to help
them by sending a man, if need be, to Poland to aid in selling the
horses yet the matter must rest till the Treaty is ratified and until
there shall be provided thereafter a credit organization, which does
not now exist, adequate to the purpose.

No present organization covers the matter adequately. There is
needed, after and in addition to the League, an organization in
which the Government either has a direct part or which is under
Government supervision to take over the securities not only of Poland itself and of other nations like her but of corporations, utilities,

cities, etc., and to issue its own obligations against these and with Government cooperation as suggested to place these in the hands of American investors. There will be required certainly two billions and probably three billions of these credits, and time presses. The need is now.

Because there had been started under the lead of Mr. Henry P. Davison, of J. P. Morgan & Company, a movement to meet the situation, if possible, by private capital, I wrote Mr. Davison as per attached copy.[2] Having had no reply, I think there should be no further delay in bringing the matter before you. Attached are the following pertinent papers:

Senate bill S.2472 (Mr. Edge) and report thereon embodying letter from the Governor of the Federal Reserve Board.

Senate bill S.2590 (Mr. Owen).

Copy of letter to Mr. H. P. Davison referred to above.

Copy of letter to Hon. Peter Norbeck, Governor of South Dakota.[3]

Clipping giving brief statement of James S. Alexander,[4] President of the National Bank of Commerce in New York.[5]

I trust I have not trespassed too long upon your courtesy.

Yours very truly,   William C. Redfield

TLS (WP, DLC).
    [1] About these bills, see R. L. Owen to WW, July 16, 1919, and ns. 3 and 4 thereto, Vol. 61.
    [2] W. C. Redfield to H. P. Davison, July 25, 1919, CCL (WP, DLC).
    [3] W. C. Redfield to P. Norbeck, July 28, 1919, CCL (WP, DLC).
    [4] James Strange Alexander.
    [5] It is attached to this letter in WP, DLC.

From Norman Hapgood

Dear Mr. President: Copenhagen July 29, 1919.

As I cannot tell when the Russian question may be precipitated I am taking the liberty of enclosing the two last reports sent in by correspondents of the *Manchester Guardian*,[1] which steadily keeps better track of Russian affairs than any other publication that I know.   Yours sincerely,   Norman Hapgood

TLS (WP, DLC).
    [1] The first clipping was from the *Manchester Guardian* of July 21, 1919. It was written by William T. Goode, the *Guardian*'s special correspondent on the Estonian front, and was dispatched via Reval (Tallinn) on June 16. Goode wrote that he had been a "prisoner" of the Bolsheviks in the Pskov area and had been treated kindly and generously and that, on the whole, conditions in the region were excellent. "Petrograd," he concluded, "will never be taken by the North Russian Corps nor Moscow by Koltchak or Deniken."
    The second clipping, presumably from the same issue of the *Guardian*, was a report by its correspondent "lately in the Far East," entitled "Russia's Civil War. Great Britain's

Support of Koltchak." This correspondent praised Kolchak for his high character and dedication to Russia. Kolchak, he said, had accepted the dictatorship of the Omsk government only because he had been pressed into doing so by General Alfred W. F. Knox, commander of the British contingent in Siberia. Knox had assured Kolchak that two British divisions would be sent to support him. This British decision to participate in the Russian Civil War had no doubt been based on purely military considerations, but it had involved the British government in the responsibility for subsequent political events. The most serious consequence of the decision to support Kolchak, the correspondent went on, had been the alienation of the United States. He continued:

"The Koltchak party in Siberia has a great affection for the British, because the British have given them military help. But they criticise the Americans, who have refused to fight. . . . The American Government has steadily refused to take sides in the civil war, and one or two officers who urged a change of policy have been sharply rebuked. The result is that the Americans are accused of sympathising with Bolshevism, and an official Japanese report has declared that among the Bolsheviks killed by them in one of their skirmishes were some American deserters. The same accusation has been made by English people in Siberia."

The article concluded by saying that the Japanese, except for keeping order in the Maritime Province, had been of "no value" to Kolchak. The Japanese were interested only in exploiting the country they occupied, and it was difficult to exaggerate the Russians' contempt for and hatred of the Japanese.

The correspondent also had high praise for the relief efforts in Siberia of the American Red Cross and for John F. Stevens for his efforts to restore railway communications.

File[1]

Jacob Allen Metzger[2] to Robert Lansing

Dear Mr. Secretary: [Washington] July 29, 1919.

In his speech published in the CONGRESSIONAL RECORD of July 25, Senator Pittman takes the position "that any annex or reservation or addition or qualification" by the United States Government of the Peace Treaty, as now before the Senate for its advice and consent to ratification, must be submitted to the parliaments or officers, of the other governments parties to the Treaty authorized to consent to and approve treaties. It is understood that you desire a brief on the question whether this Government can ratify a treaty with reservations or interpretations; whether such action would, as Senator Pittman contends, necessitate the resubmission of the treaty by the other governments parties thereto to the parliaments or officers of the signatory states having power of ratification or whether the ratification of the treaty as signed by those states could stand notwithstanding the reservations or interpretations made by this Government.

Senator Pittman bases his contention mainly on the decision of the Supreme Court in the case of Doe against Braden (16 Howard 635) 1853. This was an action in ejec[t]ment, the plaintiff claiming title under the grant of the King of Spain to the Duke of Alagon. The Treaty concluded February 22, 1819, between the United

---

[1] WWhw.
[2] Assistant Solicitor for the Department of State.

States and Spain, by which the United States acquired the Floridas contained an Article providing as follows:

"All grants made since the twenty-fourth of January, 1818, when the first proposal on the part of His Catholic Majesty for the cession of the Floridas was made are hereby declared and agreed to be null and void."

The United States Senate gave its advice and consent to the ratification of this Treaty on February 24, 1819; the King of Spain ratified the Treaty on October 24, 1820, and made a declaration in his ratification that the grant of land in favor of the Duke of Alagon was invalid and null. This ratification was submitted to the Senate and on February 19, 1821, it again gave its advice and consent to ratification, observing in its resolution that the Senate had seen the ratification of the King of Spain.

Senator Pittman contends that because this Treaty was submitted to the Senate for action after the King of Spain had included in his ratification a declaration explaining one of the Articles of the Treaty, it follows that "any annex or reservation or addition or qualification to the written Treaty must be submitted to the other parliaments or officers authorized to consent and approve treaties." The Senator regards the case of Doe against Braden, referred to above, as authority for his contention.

Although the Treaty, which the court was considering, had been resubmitted to the Senate after ratification by the King of Spain, it is not believed that the decision referred to decides the question of the necessity of having submitted it again to the Senate. The case did decide that the declaration of the King of Spain having been ratified by the United States was a part of the Treaty, but did not decide that if the King's declaration had been included in the instrument or ratification without resubmission to the Senate it would not have been effective or that the second action by the Senate was necessary.

The other decision upon which Senator Pittman relies, the Diamond Rings case, (183 United States 182) 1901, had to do with the effect of a resolution of the Senate passed after the Treaty was in effect, purporting to explain or interpret the Treaty. The court used some general language as to limitation of the powers of the Senate in advising and consenting to the ratifications of the treaties, but the case could not be regarded as authority on the proposition for which it is cited, the resolution of the Senate having been adopted after the Treaty was in force and not in giving the advice and consent to ratification.

Whatever may be the force of the case of Doe against Braden as showing that it is necessary to resubmit to the Senate of the United

States a treaty with a foreign country when the ratifications of that country contain an interpretation or reservation, the practice in the United States in such matters is governed by the Constitutional system prevailing in this country, and neither our practice nor our court decisions can be determinative of what it would be necessary to do in other countries, if this Government ratifies a treaty with reservations or interpretations. The practice of other states is as much dependent upon the peculiarities of their Constitutional systems as our own practice is dependent upon our Constitutional system.

There are, however, instances in which reservations and interpretations were made upon the exchange of ratifications without subsequent reference to the Senate. In the exchange of ratifications of the Clayton-Bulwer Treaty between the United States and Great Britain, Sir Henry Butler [Bulwer], by direction of the British Government, made a declaration to the effect that the British settlement at Honduras and its dependencies were not subject to the provisions of the Treaty against the occupation of [or?] colonization of Central America. Mr. Clayton, representing the United States, made a counter declaration accepting this view. This declaration was not submitted to the Senate (MOORE'S INTERNATIONAL LAW DIGEST, Vol. V, page 206).

Before exchanging ratifications of the Treaty of Guadelupe Hidalgo, between the United States and Mexico, representatives of the two Governments signed a protocol interpreting amendments which had been made by the United States Senate and ratified by the Mexican Congress. This protocol was not submitted to the United States Senate.

A distinction exists between the cases of the Spanish Treaty which was the subject of the court decision in the case of Doe against Braden and the cases of the Clayton-Bulwer Treaty and the Treaty of Guadelupe Hidalgo. In the former case the declaration made by the King of Spain in his ratification of the Treaty was mentioned in the resolution of the Senate, giving its advice and consent to the ratification on the part of the United States, the court holding that in these circumstances the declaration of the King of Spain was annexed to the Treaty and was as obligatory as if the declaration had been inserted in the body of the Treaty itself. In the latter cases, however, the declarations were not in the instrument of ratification and could be regarded only as an expression of the views of the Governments concerned as to the meaning of the provisions of the Treaty, to which the declarations related.

Perhaps the precedents most nearly in point with the pending Peace Treaty are found in the action of this Government and other governments with respect to the various Hague Conventions. The United States Senate gave its advice and consent to the ratification of the Convention for the Pacific Settlement of International Disputes, concluded at the First International Peace Conference at The Hague, 1899, with the reservation[3] quoted below:

"Nothing contained in this convention shall be so construed as to require the United States of America to depart from its traditional policy of not intruding upon, interfering with, or entangling itself in the political questions of policy or internal administration of any foreign state; nor shall anything contained in the said convention be construed to imply a relinquishment by the United States of America of its traditional attitude toward purely American questions;"

The Resolution of the Senate advising and consenting to the ratification of the Convention for the Pacific Settlement of International Disputes signed at the 1907 Hague Peace Conference contained a reservation identical with that made with respect to the corresponding Convention of the 1899 Conference and the following additional reservation:

"*Resolved further, as a part of this act of ratification*, That the United States approves this convention with the understanding that recourse to the permanent court for the settlement of differences can be had only by agreement thereto through general or special treaties of arbitration heretofore or hereafter concluded between the parties in dispute; and the United States now exercises the option contained in article fifty-three of said convention, to exclude the formulation of the 'compromis' by the permanent court, and hereby excludes from the competence of the permanent court the power to frame the 'compromis' required by general or special treaties of arbitration concluded or hereafter to be concluded by the United States, and further expressly declares that the 'compromis' required by any treaty of arbitration to which the United States may be a party shall be settled only by agreement between the contracting parties, unless such treaty shall expressly provide otherwise."

The Resolution of the Senate advising and consenting to the ratification of the Convention respecting the Limitation of the Employment of Force for the Recovery of Contract Debts, signed at The Hague in 1907, reads as follows:

"*Resolved* (two thirds of the Senators present concurring therein), that the Senate advise and consent to the ratification of

---

[3] Actually, this reservation was a declaration read by the American delegation at the final Plenary Session of the Hague Conference of 1899. See D. H. Miller to G. Auchincloss, June 26, 1919, Vol. 61.

a convention signed by the delegates of the United States to the Second International Peace Conference held at The Hague from June 15 to October 18, 1907, respecting the limitation of the employment of force for the recovery of contract debts.

"*Resolved further*, as a part of this act of ratification, that the United States approves this convention with the understanding that recourse to the permanent court for the settlement of the differences referred to in said convention can be had only by agreement thereto through general or special treaties of arbitration heretofore or hereafter concluded between the parties in dispute."

The Hague Conventions referred to were signed by the delegates of the United States with reservations. The reservations included in the Senate Resolution, giving advice and consent to ratifications, were incorporated in the instruments of ratification deposited at The Hague. The delegates of various powers attending the several Hague Conferences made ratifications upon signing the Conventions and in most cases these reservations were continued effective upon ratification.

The general Act of the International Conference at Algeciras and an additional Protocol signed April 7, 1906, were signed under reservations by representatives of the United States Government. The Senate gave its advice and consent to the ratification of this Agreement with reservations. The declaration of the representatives of the United States made at signature, and the reservations made in ratification were brought to the attention of the representatives of the other powers at Madrid at the time the ratifications were deposited. The question arose as to whether the declarations and reservations should be set out at length in the Protocol signed by all the parties at the time of ratification. Owing to objections on the part of representatives of some of the other nations to the phraseology of the Senate reservation, the full text thereof appears not to have been set forth in the Protocol, but reference was made to the reservation, and the representative of the United States was assured that the United States need have no fear as to the effectiveness of the reservation, although the reservation was not set forth in full.

In a despatch dated December 29, 1906, the American Minister at Madrid, reporting regarding the depositing of ratifications of the Algeciras Convention stated:

"His Excellency (the Spanish Minister of State) after examining the document of ratification averred that the fact that both the declaration and Senate resolutions appeared therein was all that was necessary to exempt the United States from all obligations to secure the execution of the provisions of the Act of Algeciras. He suggested that I read at the time of signing a statement containing both the declaration and resolutions, both of which would be referred to in the Procès Verbal, which would thus be brought to the cognizance of the powers before signing."

In conclusion, it is submitted that the result of the ratification of the Peace Treaty by this Government with interpretations or reservations included in the instrument of ratification deposited at Paris, so far as action by other states is concerned, would depend upon the law existing and the practice established in those countries, but that the practice followed by various powers including the United States in making reservations in signing and ratifying The Hague Conventions and other Conventions, notably the general Act of Algeciras, would indicate that reservations or interpretations could be incorporated in the instrument of ratification to be deposited at Paris without necessitating further action by the Governments of other states on that account. I find no authoritative statements as to the effect which such action would have on the obligations of this Government to the other signatory powers or of those powers to this Government. It would seem, however, that unless any interpretation or reservations which this Government might make were ratified and adopted by the other states, they would not be binding on them, and that the only effect of such interpretations or reservations would be to give notice of the position of this Government with respect to the provisions of the Treaty in relation to which the interpretation or reservations were made.

JAM

TI MS (WP, DLC).

A Memorandum by Breckinridge Long

MEMORANDUM OF CONVERSATION WITH THE
JAPANESE CHARGÉ D'AFFAIRES.
July 29, 1919.

(NOTE: After my conversation with Mr. Debuchi on last Thursday, July 24, in which he said that his Government did not feel that they could make an announcement of their intentions in Shantung at that time, I had a conversation with Mr. Lansing in which I reported the substance of Debuchi's statement. Mr. Lansing then said that the President had authorized him to say to Debuchi the following day that unless Japan made some definite and satisfactory statement that he, the President, would do so.)[1]

Mr. Debuchi came in this afternoon shortly after my return to town and reviewed the happenings in the Shantung matter since our last interview. He related the fact that the Secretary had talked to him on Friday and deplored that news in regard to the subject matter of their conversation had been printed in the papers, and stated that it was particularly regret[t]able that the statement had been made that unless Japan answered in less than forty-eight hours that the President himself would make an announcement. He said that he feared very much the effect that that statement would have in Japan; that he had immediately cabled Japan the substance of his conversation with the Secretary; that he had received a wire on Sunday which he had communicated to Mr. Lansing on Monday at the same time that he communicated a despatch also received from Baron Makino at Paris which stated that he was cabling the Japanese Government advising that they make a statement.

Debuchi very apparently considered the situation as very tense and several time[s] characterized it as a "crisis," and as being "the most important moment in Japanese-American relations."

He asked whether in view of the fact that time had elapsed the statement would be immediately forthcoming. I told him that I did not know, but that I would say to the Secretary that in view of the distance which separates Paris and Tokyo, and the fact that cable communication had been necessary between Paris and Tokyo after receipt in Tokyo of advices from Mr. Debuchi, and the added fact that both he and Baron Makino had cabled urging his Government to make a statement, that I would suggest to the Secretary that the statement threatened by the President be withheld for several days.

Mr. Debuchi was apparently considerably alarmed at the situation. He expressed the hope that some decision would be arrived at as to the withholding of the statement by the President, and hoped that he might be informally advised so as to relieve what he termed his nervous tension.

He said that he had talked to Mr. Lansing about the Treaties of 1915 and 1918, and their application to the Treaty of Versailles; that Mr. Lansing had not confirmed the impression Debuchi had had from Mr. Polk that the Treaties of 1915 and 1918 were annulled, but had given him the impression that they did not enter into the calculations upon which the Treaty of Versailles was made, and that they were separate and distinct matters. I told him that my impression was that, whereas, we had never recognized the 1915 and 1918 Treaties, and did not now intend to, that we looked upon the Treaty of Versailles as superseding any former treaties on the subject, and as confirming to Japan the rights held by Germany as of August, 1914, without amendment of any kind, and without enlargement of any kind, and subject only to the statements made by the Japanese delegates in Paris as to their intentions in regard to the rights which they were to acquire.

Breckinridge Long

TS MS (SDR, RG 59, 793.94/953, DNA).
   [1] See n. 2 to the first news report printed at July 25, 1919, Vol. 61.

From Harry Augustus Garfield

Dear Mr. President: Williamstown, Mass. July 29, 1919.

Jessie and Frank[1] are in town for a day or two and I am happy to say that we see a good deal of them. I know that you will be pleased to have a line testifying to their good health and their happiness in the arrangement Frank has made for the next five years at Harvard. I am sorry to lose him, but appreciate the importance to him of the change.[2]

Cordially and faithfully yours,   H. A. Garfield.

TLS (WP, DLC).
   [1] That is, Jessie Woodrow Wilson Sayre and Francis Bowes Sayre.
   [2] Sayre, who had been an assistant to Garfield, President of Williams College, from 1914 to 1917, had just been appointed Assistant Professor at the Harvard Law School.

From John Knox Coit[1]

My dear Mr. Wilson: Sautee, Georgia July 29, '19

On account of the tremendous pressure under which you have been laboring, we have allowed our usual annual reminder of your $50.00 Scholarship to lapse for a few months.

I am sure you will be interested to know that we have just received a letter from Alvin C. York, the famous soldier of Pall Mall, Tenn.,[2] making application for his own brother[3] to enter our School. Mr. York lives in our larger mountain neighborhood and we want to help many of his brothers.

Sincerely yours,   J. K. Coit Supt.

TLS (WP, DLC).
   [1] According to the letterhead, he was superintendent of the Nacoochee Institute, a "Christian Industrial Home School" in Nacoochee, Georgia.
   [2] Alvin Cullum York, also known as "Sergeant York," the most popular American war hero of the First World War. On October 8, 1917, during the Meuse-Argonne offensive, York, then a corporal in Company G, 328th Infantry, had, singlehanded, destroyed an entire German battalion. After shooting at least twenty-five enemy soldiers, he had taken 132 prisoners and captured thirty-five machine guns. Promoted to sergeant on November 1, 1918, he received the Congressional Medal of Honor in addition to some fifty other decorations, and his fame reached such proportions that he was the subject

of a Hollywood motion picture in 1941. See Tom Skeyhill, ed., *Sergeant York: His Own Life Story and War Diary* (Garden City, N. Y., 1928); Sam K. Cowan, *Sergeant York and His People* (New York, 1922); and the extensive obituary in the *New York Times*, Sept. 3, 1964, pp. 1, 26.

[3] He cannot be identified. Alvin C. York had ten brothers and sisters.

A News Report

[*July 30, 1919*]

FEARS REOPENING TREATY
President Says Germany Would Probably Make
Further Demands

Washington, July 30.—Four Republican Senators told President Wilson at the White House today that reservations must be adopted in the ratification of the Versailles treaty, if it is to be accepted by the majority of the upper body. His callers, each of whom talked about an hour with the President, were Dillingham of Vermont, Fernald of Maine, Harding of Ohio, and Lenroot of Wisconsin.

President Wilson, the Senators said, expressed himself as insistent that reservations should not be made, saying they would endanger the treaty. For the Senate to amend the document, the President told the Senators, would be embarrassing to the United States after it had assumed a leading part in the treaty negotiations. Through the reopening of negotiations, which, the President said, would be forced, if reservations were made, complications were likely to develop. Germany, encouraged by whatever changes had been effected by the Senate, would seize upon it as an opening for further demands.

The President, touching upon the Franco-American Treaty, said it had been urged by Premier Clemenceau as necessary for the protection of France. The French people wanted some assurance of support in the event of an attack by Germany outside of that provided in the League of Nations.

The four Senators, after the conference, said that, while the President had not changed in his opposition to reservations, he had not succeeded in influencing them to abandon their fight.

The Senators touched every phase of the treaty pertaining to reservations. Senator Dillingham said he asked "a great many questions" and Mr. Wilson freely answered them.

"In fact," said Mr. Dillingham, "the President was so frank as to make it rather embarrassing for me to keep on with my questions."

The President, Mr. Dillingham said, spoke particularly of the effect reservations would have in reopening the treaty negotiations.

Drastic terms had been laid down to Germany, the President said, and the peace conferees felt that the provisions of the treaty as finally submitted to Germany ought to stand.

Mr. Dillingham outlined reservations touching upon Article X, respecting territorial guarantees; the Monroe Doctrine; purely domestic questions, such as immigration and the tariff; and withdrawal from the League after two years' notice, the United States to decide if its obligations to the league had been fulfilled. These, the Lermont [Vermont] Senator said, if written into the resolution of ratification, undoubtedly would mean prompt acceptance of the treaty. Unless they were embraced in it, Mr. Dillingham said, the treaty stood in danger of being rejected.

To this Mr. Wilson replied that he hoped the Senate would carefully weigh the consequences of adopting reservations that would recommit the treaty to Paris. It would take many months, the President said, to have the treaty renegotiated.

Mr. Dillingham gathered from his talk with the President that Mr. Wilson was not so much opposed to the reservations suggested as to sending the treaty back to the conference. He felt that any reservations would have that effect.

Mr. Wilson adverted to the Shantung award, saying he expected hourly that Japan would make an official announcement regarding it. Mr. Wilson did not indicate the nature of the expected announcement, but it is understood to embrace a statement by Japan as to the relinquishment of rights on the Chinese peninsula within a short time.

As to the Franco-American Treaty, Mr. Dillingham gathered the impression that the President regarded it as advisable from the viewpoint of promoting friendship between the two countries, while affording France an assurance of protection if a crisis with Germany should develop.

Senator Harding discussed with the President reservations along the line followed by Mr. Dillingham. The President told the Ohio Senator that for the United States to write reservations into the ratifying resolution would encourage other nations to do the same and that endless delay would ensue. Senator Harding said he regarded the interests of the United States as paramount and regarded them as threatened unless the reservations were adopted.

Senator Fernald informed the President that there were enough votes in the Senate to reject the treaty unless amended through reservations. The Senator remarked afterward that the President apparently was not persuaded to change his attitude against reservations, while the Senator came away as determined as ever that they must be adopted.

Senator Lenroot told the President he favored an explicit reservation on Article X. and on purely domestic questions. He suggested an interpretative reservation as to the Monroe Doctrine and the withdrawal provision. Mr. Lenroot told the President that changes must be made if he expected to have the treaty ratified.

Printed in the *New York Times*, July 31, 1919.

From the Desk Diary of Robert Lansing

Wednesday July 30 [1919]

9:15 pm. Prest came to my house much perturbed over fact that protocol with Germany[1] had not been sent to Senate. Will take matter up in the morning.

[1] Six supplementary provisions to the Versailles Treaty, printed in *PPC, VI*, 604. Wilson sent this document to the Senate on July 31, 1919.

From Josephus Daniels

My Dear Mr. President: Washington. July 30, 1919.

At present the opponents of the League are guessing and do not seem able to get together. Is it not wise for them so to continue? I had a long talk with Swanson this morning. He strongly believes:

1. That at present you ought to make no statement. Lodge fears Borah will join with the Democrats and prevent any reservations, and they are at sea. For the present our course should be to let them flounder.

2. If you feel called upon to make any expression such as was discussed in the Cabinet yesterday, Swanson thinks by all means it should be made to the Senate in their Chamber and not in a letter. The first has impressiveness which the latter lacks.

Sincerely yours,   Josephus Daniels

I am sure your conferences with the Senators has done good, and that if possible you ought to see every Senator Democrat and Republican except the handful who are impossible.

ALS (WP, DLC).

From Josephus Daniels, with Enclosures

My dear Mr. President: Washington. July 30, 1919.

Speaking yesterday about the oil legislation,[1] you said you did not clearly recall what you had agreed to. I am enclosing herewith a copy of a letter which you wrote from Paris on January 17, 1919, to the Secretary of the Interior.[2] Because you may not have it in your files in Washington, and for the purpose of refreshing your recollection you may wish it, I am also enclosing you a statement which I obtained from Attorney General Gregory, giving a succinct statement of the old question, particularly with reference to the Honolulu claim, which I think he gave to you, but which you might like to have together with the letter I am enclosing you, which you wrote on January 17th. As you said you were going to study the whole matter, I thought these statements would be of value to you.   Sincerely yours,   Josephus Daniels

I am also enclosing you a copy of the Swanson amendment which we all agreed to as the best compromise.   J.D

TLS (WP, DLC).
   [1] That is, the pending general leasing bill, once again before Congress, about which see A. M. Palmer to WW, July 18, 1919, Vol. 61.
   [2] WW to F. K. Lane, Jan. 7 (not 17), 1919, printed at that date in Vol. 53.

E N C L O S U R E   I

On September 27, 1909, the President by executive order withdrew from disposal under the mining laws large areas of oil lands in California and Wyoming. The validity of this order was sustained by the Supreme Court on February 23, 1915, in United States v. Midwest Oil Company, 236 U.S. 459.

On December 13, 1912, the President by executive order established Naval Reserve No. 2 in California "for the exclusive use or benefit of the United States Navy." The lands in this reserve are within the area withdrawn September 27, 1909.

The executive order of September 27, 1909, excepted "all locations or claims existing and valid" on that date, and the "Pickett Act" of June 25, 1910, 36 Stat. 847, saved the rights of any person who, at the date of the executive order, was "a bona fide occupant or claimant of oil or gas bearing lands," and "in diligent prosecution of work leading to discovery of oil or gas."

In April, 1915, the Honolulu Consolidated Oil Company, claiming under the saving clause of the Pickett Act, applied for patents to 17 quarter sections of 160 acres each under the placer mining law, located in the heart of Naval Reserve No. 2 and constituting the most valuable part of the reserve.

Thereupon Special Agents of the General Land Office investigated the claims and reported their invalidity for want of discovery work in good faith on September 27, 1909, and also as to four of the claims because the original locators were dummies.

On December 15, 1915, the Commissioner[1] rendered his decision on the Special Agents' reports and the *ex parte* showing made by the Company, clear-listing all of the 17 claims for patent, except the 4 charged with dummy location, and as to those he directed a hearing on that charge before the Register and Receiver of the local Land Office. On the question of the diligent prosecution of discovery work at the date of the withdrawal, the Commissioner ruled that, although no drilling was begun on any one of the claims until February, 1910, four and one-half months after the withdrawal, and although drilling was only begun thereafter on others at various dates as late as March 3, 1911, a year and five months after the withdrawal, yet the Company had shown general preparations for drilling before the withdrawal sufficient to constitute diligent work in good faith at the date of the withdrawal as to each claim.

On December 24, 1915, the Secretary of the Interior stated in a letter to the Attorney General that the Commissioner's decision "seems to me to be correct."

The Secretary of the Navy having protested against the Commissioner's decision, at the suggestion of the President the Secretary of the Interior agreed to withhold the patents until the Attorney General could examine into the basis of the Commissioner's decision.

On April 12, 1916, the Attorney General wrote to the Secretary of the Interior expressing his disagreement with the theory of "group development" which appeared to be the basis of the Commissioner's decision, but stated that he could not pass a definite opinion on the case without more certain findings of fact than the Commissioner had made with respect to the time and extent of the work claimed to have been done by the Company.

June 28, 1916, the Commissioner wrote to the Secretary of the Interior criticizing various disconnected statements of the Attorney General's letter and adhering to his former decision. He closed his letter with the following recommendation:

I am strongly persuaded, therefore, particularly in view of the course the chief law officer of the Government has seen fit to take in this matter, that one of two things should be done forthwith with this case, viz., either (a) the Attorney General should withdraw his objections to the granting of patents in these cases, or (b) suits should be started at once and diligently prosecuted to secure a judicial determination of the controverted questions; and I have to recommend that the Attorney General be requested to follow one of these two courses without delay.

June 29, 1916, the Secretary of the Interior transmitted the Commissioner's letter to the Attorney General with the following statement:

I concur in Mr. Tallman's conclusion, as you know, and would respectfully urge that the suggestion made that patents be longer withheld be withdrawn, or that the matter be taken into court at once if you are convinced that our view is erroneous.

August 5, 1916, the Attorney General wrote to the Secretary of the Interior giving more extended reasons for his disagreement with the apparent basis of the Commissioner's decision, and pointing out that the matter could not be taken into court unless the Commissioner's clear-listing decision were revoked and a hearing ordered before the Register and Receiver.

On August 9, 1916, the Secretary of the Interior answered the Attorney General, declining to order a hearing, saying that "as to the controlling facts, there is little, if any dispute."

On August 17, 1916, the Attorney General responded, adhering to his previous view that it would be useless to attempt to secure any court action unless it could be shown that the validity of the claims was at least questionable in the Interior Department, and that unless a hearing were ordered the case would show that the claims were not questioned.

Further correspondence ensued without result until January 29, 1917, when the Secretary of the Interior, at the President's behest, set aside the Commissioner's decision and "directed that the entire matter be reopened for further consideration of any new testimony that may be presented." Yet he still refused to order a hearing.

In the summer of 1917, Assistant Attorney General Kearful[2] went to California and discovered unquestioned documentary evidence which had not been before the Commissioner and which, in the Attorney General's opinion, clearly established the fraudulent character of all the Honolulu claims, and also showed that the supposed preparatory work prior to the withdrawal on which the Commissioner relied was merely a cheap pretense and intended for the purpose of excluding bona fide prospectors until the completion of a well on adjoining land in private ownership might demonstrate the oil-bearing character of the claims in question.

October 19, 1917, the Attorney General filed in the General Land Office a protest on behalf of the Secretary of the Navy against the applications of the Honolulu Company, founded upon the newly discovered evidence and asked for a hearing, and on December 10, 1917, the Commissioner ordered a hearing before the Register and Receiver.

November 20, 1917, the Attorney General caused a bill to be filed in the District Court of the United States for the Southern District of California, setting out the same facts alleged in the Navy protest and praying for an injunction against the drilling of new wells, for a receiver to take charge of the operations pending a final determination in the Interior Department and for permanent relief after final action by that Department. On March 2, 1918, the court granted the injunction and appointed the receiver and suspended further proceedings pending a final determination of the matter in the Interior Department.

July 13, 1918, the Register and Receiver, after a hearing, rendered their decision in favor of the Government, finding that the claimant "was not in good faith diligently prosecuting work for the development of oil" on any of the 17 claims on September 27, 1909. The Honolulu Company appealed to the Commissioner, before whom oral arguments were made and printed briefs were filed.

On February 11, 1919, the Commissioner rendered his decision reversing the decision of the Register and Receiver and dismissing the Navy protest. The reasons given were substantially the same as those stated in his first decision. The newly discovered evidence was not regarded by him as of any special significance.

Under the rules of practice of the General Land Office the protestant has a right of appeal from the Commissioner to the Secretary of the Interior, and such appeal has been directed.

It should be noted that, although the Navy protest was dismissed, the Commissioner found that four of the claims were fraudulent because initiated by dummy locators in accordance with the charge made by the Special Agents. It is believed that the evidence shows no substantial difference between those four claims and the others in that respect.

T MS (WP, DLC).
[1] Clay Tallman, Commissioner of the General Land Office in the Department of the Interior.
[2] Francis Joseph Kearful, Assistant Attorney General in charge of the Public Lands Division from March 19, 1917, to July 15, 1919.

ENCLOSURE II

The amendment proposed by Senator Swanson is as follows: "That any claimant, who either in person or through his predecessor in interest, entered upon any of the lands embraced within the executive order of withdrawal dated September 27, 1909, prior to July 3, 1910, honestly and in good faith for the purpose of prospecting for oil or gas, and thereupon commenced discovery work thereon, and thereafter prosecuted such work to a discovery of oil or gas, shall be entitled to lease from the United States any producing oil or gas well resulting from such work, at a royalty of not

less than one-eighth of all the oil and gas produced therefrom, together with an area of land sufficient for the operation thereof, but
without the right to drill any other or additional wells; provided,
that such claimant shall first pay to the United States an amount
equal to not less than the value of one-eighth of all the oil and gas
already produced from such well; and provided further, that this
act shall not apply to any well involved in any suit brought by the
United States, or in any application for patent, unless within ninety
days after the approval of this act the claimant shall relinquish to
the United States all rights claimed by him in such suit or application; and provided further, that all such leases shall be made,
and the amount to be paid for oil and gas already produced shall
be fixed, by the Secretary of the Interior under appropriate rules
and regulations."

CC MS (WP, DLC).

From Walker Downer Hines

Dear Mr. President: Washington July 30, 1919

Referring to our conference this morning I inclose a better draft[1]
of the provisional recommendation which I handed you at that
time. The first three pages are substantially the same as the draft
I handed you[2] except further investigation indicates that an increase of 12¢ per hour to the shop men would probably mean a
total increase to all railroad employes of $800,000,000 instead of
$600,000,000.

Page 4 has been rewritten so as to bring out more clearly the
insufficient character of the present machinery for dealing with
general wage problems under peace time conditions.

I call your especial attention to the last paragraph in the letter.
This is intended to allay a well founded anxiety that reference to
Congress would mean indefinite delay and irremediable loss. I
think the paragraph is fair and reasonable and in itself will do
much to compose the situation. Of course if the cost of living begins to diminish the paragraph will not have substantial effect. If
the cost of living continues to increase the employes ought to have
the protection.

Further thought confirms me in the opinion that it would help
the general legislative situation to call upon Congress for prompt
legislation dealing with the wage problems. This would bring out
clearly the branch of the subject which so far has received the least
attention. Prompt study by Congress of the wage question would
contribute to its realizing more promptly the difficulties which

must be faced and the necessity for getting away from the old methods.

My thought is that the specific recommendation which I submit could be made without any commitment as to your position on the other phases of railroad legislation, because this method of dealing with the wage matter would be equally desirable and fitting no matter what might be the plan adopted as to the other features.

I have told the executive of the shop men today that the Railroad Administration is willing to make a National Agreement with them. This of course is a matter which it is not necessary to hold in abeyance pending action by Congress.

Cordially yours,   Walker D Hines.

TLS (WP, DLC).
    [1] W. D. Hines to WW, July 30, 1919, TLS (WP, DLC). Wilson, with Close's assistance, slightly emended this draft and sent it back to Hines, who then had the emended version retyped and sent as W. D. Hines to WW, July 31, 1919. It is printed at that date.
    [2] This first draft is missing in WP, DLC.

Julius Howland Barnes to Joseph Patrick Tumulty, with Enclosure

My dear Mr. Secretary: New York July 30, 1919.

At my conference today with the President, it was suggested that I submit a statement of the wheat situation to him in such form and covering such details that it could be released to the press. The President was also kind enough to suggest that I make a suggested reply suitable to the statement which I was to submit. I am enclosing you the statement which incorporates some of the suggestions of the President in conference, and also a suggested form of response.[1]

May I ask you please to submit this exchange to the President for his immediate approval and the immediate release to the press[2] as wheat marketing is under way and the producer should be advised of this change of market opportunity before any further portion of his crop should have left his hands so that further marketing will be with full knowledge on his part.

If for any reason the President desires to make modification or alteration, it is, of course, perfectly agreeable that should be done without conference with me, or I can be reached readily by phone through the wheat director's office here to my office in New York.

Thanking you for your aid,

Very truly yours,   By Julius H. Barnes

TLS (WP, DLC).

¹ Printed below as WW to J. H. Barnes, July 30, 1919, which Barnes had drafted and Wilson simply signed.
² However, see JPT to WW, Aug. 1, 1919.

E N C L O S U R E

From Julius Howland Barnes

My dear Mr. President: New York July 29, 1919

Unfavorable crop developments have occasioned a startling change in the wheat situation of the world. In sections of our spring-sown acreage and that of Canada, deterioration has been severe. Since June first, North American wheat promise has fallen possibly 400,000,000 bushels.

In Argentina, where the world looked for cheap wheat, recent advances stimulated by foreign buying have exceeded sixty cents per bushel. The present Buenos Aires wheat price, $2.29 per bushel, will net an average farmer price in Argentina as high as our own under our fair price guarantee. With longer voyage and higher ocean freights, Argentine wheat delivered in European markets to-day will cost fully fifty cents per bushel more than wheat bought in America at the guarantee price level.

Australia, popularly supposed possessed of large reserves accumulated by restricted shipping outlet of the past few years, has, since the armistice, reduced its unsold surplus until to-day it does not exceed one-tenth the overseas world wheat requirements of this year.

Russia, Roumania, and India, formerly contributing annually 300,000,000 bushels of wheat and rye, are apparently definitely out for the coming year.

Canada, which until recently had hoped to supply overseas 200,000,000 bushels, will be unable to equal even the 90,000,000 bushels contribution of this last crop. Recent prices for new-crop wheat in Winnipeg reached twenty-five cents over our own guarantee equivalent.

America, by these developments, becomes the reservoir of the world's wheat supply and the Government guarantee price the low price of the world. This will be startling to our people, accustomed to statements that the wheat price in America was inflated and sustained only by the Government guarantee, and that if America's wheat market were thrown open to world influences, our wheat price must decline.

It is well that these basic facts be clearly understood:

First: The stabilized fair price maintained in America for almost two years resulted in an average farm price for wheat of $2.05 per bushel.

Second: During the last calendar year, the average farm price in the United Kingdom was $2.28 per bushel.

Third: The four big producing countries—United States, Canada, Argentina and Australia—producing 1,500,000,000 bushels, work out an average grower price of $1.94.

Fourth: The fifteen consuming countries of the world, largely under guaranteed prices, producing 800,000,000 bushels of home-grown wheat, work out an average grower price of $3.75 per bushel.

Fifth: An average of all these wheat growers, weighted according to the size of their contribution to the total crop of the world, works out an average world grower price of $2.46.

Viewing these facts in the light of the altered crop outlook of the world, we are faced with the necessity for immediate decision on some basic policies. For two years, associated with the Allied Nations at war with Germany, we have provided their necessities to the utmost and at fair prices. With the Export Embargo administered by the War Trade Board we have done this with full protection of necessary food supplies at home. We have also preserved industrial peace by thus preventing price disturbances which unrestrained war buying of food would have occasioned. This security to trade at home reflected into fair trade margins, and thus cumulatively protected our own people.

The price measure used in that allied food cooperation was the price pronounced in August, 1917 as "fair" between producer and consumer by your Fair Price Commission, after careful examination.

This was justified in the protection of all our people and because transport and finance, broken by war, obstructed the usual protection of supply and demand influences.

That war has been fought to a successful conclusion and, broadly speaking, our obligations to these Allied Countries have been dissolved. The Food Administration, though nominally still in existence, lacks any appropriation for effective administration, even should it be wise to exercise its former authority in what are probably the last days of its authorized existence. During its existence, and by its authority, producers and dealers of the country have learned to think of the wheat fair price basis as practically a fixed price basis. That wheat price level is the one now perpetuated in the National Guarantee effective for this coming crop. That minimum guarantee and its administration under the Act of March 4th, last, differs as to powers and obligations. If there are to be, therefore, changes of policy and a different market opportunity, decisions should be reached so that the wheat movement which is now starting should be with full knowledge by the producer of any altered conditions.

Possibly, in this period of reconstruction, as in time of war, wheat should still be controlled as to price and distribution. The Wheat Director, however, in administering the powers delegated to him under the Act, must adhere to the purposes stated, namely: "To carry out the guaranties made to producers of wheat" and "to protect the United States against undue enhancement of its liabilities under said guaranties." This leads to the following conclusions:

Imports of wheat could be prohibited in order to prevent foreign producers taking advantage of a price guarantee established for the benefit of our own producers. When that possibility no longer "enhances the liabilities of the United States," have we a right to maintain the Import Embargo?

Exports of wheat could be prohibited in order to prevent private competition needlessly undermining foreign sales of national accumulations.

Authority to sell at home or abroad, for cash or credit, at the guarantee price, or other price, was clearly intended for the protection of our consuming public to the world price level. A large appropriation was made in case necessity forced sales abroad and at home at lower than the cost of the guarantee purchases.

We should not sell our surplus wheat abroad at a possibly lower world's price without reflecting to our consumers, in the form of flour, the equivalent reduction.

Many thousands of Trade Contracts with Grain Dealers, Millers, Flour Jobbers, and Bakers, assure that any such reduction made by payments from the National Treasury should be immediately reflected through the different trade processes to our consumers.

Certain sections of our people have urged an arbitrarily lowered price on flour on the assumption that our pledged guarantee price was above a world supply and demand price. They should not object, therefore, should the reinstatement of supply and demand create a higher price level than the guarantee.

Another section of our people advocate a lower resale price of flour, artificially subsidized by the National Treasury. Wherever in countries abroad this has been done, it has tended to stifle production and certainly has delayed a return to normal processes of trade. Producers, constantly fearing the arbitrarily reduced price of flour as the measure of their returns, reduced wheat production until reassured by a guarantee price, unduly high in many instances, to offset the distrust already engendered. Such guarantee thus placed too high again disturbs the proper balance of other crops, and the vicious circle widens. The economic effect of this national policy, where tried, has been bad. It has been used oftentimes as the excuse to deny better living and social conditions. Such policy of National subsidy would force National charity to the table of every American, needy or affluent. I have a conception that our Americanism is the sturdy, self-respecting kind that wants no such unsought charity. In all events, embarkation on a deliberate policy of food subsidy should be undertaken only when authorized by the National Congress in terms so explicit that there can be no possible misunderstanding. This has not been done in the Wheat Guarantee Act.

Similarly, if the Export Embargo control authorized in the Act were intended to maintain supplies at home, it should be clearly so stated. This has not been done in the Wheat Guarantee Act.

Private trade and private facilities will probably, for a time, prove inadequate in carrying overseas commerce because of difficulties in transport and in international finance. It is probable that the Grain Corporation must conduct part of the wheat and flour marketing of the country.

Nevertheless, there exists the obligation to help reknit the broken processes of trade. It is undesirable that the injection of Government War Agencies shall be extended a single day beyond the actual necessity of liquidating war commitments. Even in that respect, encouragement should be given trade agencies to reassume their normal function. Both in America, fortunate and intact, and in Europe, prostrate and devastated, there exists the great duty to help to their feet these normal processes of trade that insure economic stability and general employment. Whether higher or lower prices here will result is beside the question, as long as supply and demand influences are reinstated and fairly controlled against abuse.

The Grain Corporation may still buy a portion of the crop at the guarantee prices. Should there result therefrom the accumulation of nationally-owned stocks, some portion may be fairly retained for resale in our domestic markets as some surety against excessive prices before the new crop. Beyond that, foreign sales should be fairly apportioned among the various claimants, if there are such still unable to deal through private agencies.

The Grain Corporation proposes also to maintain, in various cities, stocks of such standard flour as properly reflect the guarantee price, and to resell in the customary trade manner such flour as need develops, as an assurance that consumers may, at all times, be sure of a standard and nutritious flour at a proper reflection of the wheat price.

It is well to remember also, in the consumer's protection, that while our crop shrinkage from earlier prospects has been unfortunately large, we are still apparently assured of a crop above the average and that the difficulties of transport and of international finance will control the foreign draft upon that crop to the limit of their bare necessities.

Should certain consumers desire special classes and special qualities of flour, and pay therefor the premium necessary because of a perhaps restricted supply of those particular varieties of wheat from which such special qualities are produced, then that may well be their privilege. The flour thus handled by the Grain Corporation will be the standard flours with which it has supplied our Allies for two years and of a quality equal to, or better than, that produced to-day under Government control milling in practically all of the consuming countries abroad.

For the same reasons, the result of thus restoring world trade in wheat may disappoint the producer expecting that to result in higher prices, but at least the influence of arbitrary price influences and the substitution of natural influences will have been largely accomplished and the producer now marketing twenty million bushels weekly is entitled to know at once the enlarged trade opportunity thus restored and to reach his own decision as to the effect of such trade restoration.

Summarizing the wheat situation to-day: a crop practically secured, large but below expectations; crop deterioriation and price advances in our wheat competitors; the urgent need to encourage the restoration of private trade enterprise and to eliminate the suspicion that governmental influence prevents wheat prices made by world supply and demand influences; a belief that consumers will not unduly suffer and that all classes have a right to the protection of natural trade influences as far as they can be reinstated.

I feel justified in making the following recommendation: that, subject to cancellation should necessity develop and subject to such regulations as will help to protect railroad and port facilities against congestion, we announce now that until December 31st next, at least, exports and imports of wheat will be permitted.

I believe a practical reinstatement of world-wide trade influences can be made without enlarging the liabilities of the Government under the Guarantee; that the producer will be convinced no effort is made to limit his opportunity, if such exists beyond the guaranteed price; that the consumer will be content to pay his own self-respecting way as long as he feels that the price he pays is fixed by proper trade influences, free and unhampered; and that a long step will have been taken to encourage, both here and abroad, that private enterprise which means trade activity and orderly employment.   Respectfully,   Julius H Barnes

TLS (WP, DLC).

To Julius Howland Barnes

My dear Mr. Barnes: The White House, July 30, 1919

I have your statement of the twenty-ninth, outlining the wheat situation of the world as it has recently developed, and asking my expression on certain proposed National policies of wheat administration.

I am convinced of the desirability of eliminating Government War Agencies at the earliest possible moment, and, meantime, step by step, recreating the private agencies which must take up the burden of trade.

I agree with you that the rigorous control and the interference with normal trade which export and import embargoes create should not be used except in furtherance of the purposes distinctly named by Congress in the Wheat Guarantee Act. I heartily approve the policy expressed by you that our own consumers shall have in our domestic markets the reflection of a world supply and demand price as far as it can be ascertained, and to this protection they are entitled.

The fact that our wheat crop, though disappointing, is still a very large one, that transport and finance will limit the foreign call upon us to the barest necessities together with the steps suggested by you in protection of both producer and consumer, warrants me in believing that certain steps can be taken along the lines of your suggestion, probably without large price disturbances and distinctly in the line of proper progress.

As tending to reconstruct private enterprise, to afford both producers and consumers the fairer test of world influences, and, at the same time, not apparently enhancing the liabilities of the Government, while also protecting the National pledge of the Guaranteed Price, I express my approval of the relaxation of export and import embargoes recommended by you.

                    Sincerely,   Woodrow Wilson

TLS (WP, DLC).

From Alexander Mitchell Palmer, with Enclosure

Washington, D. C. July 30, 1919.

MEMORANDUM FOR THE PRESIDENT.

I promised Clarence Darrow to hand you the attached letter.

Debs' sentence of ten years is too long and ought to be commuted, but I am firmly of the opinion that the time is not yet ripe for such action. He has been in prison only a couple of months, is absolutely unrepentant, will not personally make any application for clemency, and a pardon now would be bitterly resented by a very large portion of the population who consider him a dangerous leader in the ultra-radical class war movement.

When we release Debs, we shall have to release also two or three other leaders of the same class. Their release now would be used by many opponents of the peace treaty as evidence of too great leniency toward law violators of the radical element in the labor classes, in a way that would prejudice many people against the liberal labor provisions of the treaty.

My own judgment is that we should wait until the peace treaty is ratified and out of the way and conditions in the country have settled down somewhat before we seriously consider executive clemency for these leaders. We have already commuted the sentences of more than a hundred persons convicted under the Espionage Act and my plan is to make recommendations to you with respect to the remainder of the cases (including Debs) at or about the time of the actual going into force of the treaty of peace.

A Mitchell Palmer

TS MS (WP, DLC).

E N C L O S U R E

From Clarence Seward Darrow

Dear Mr. President: Washington, D. C., July 29, 1919.

I earnestly petition the Government for the release of Eugene V. Debs from the Federal prison at Atlanta, Georgia, where he is now held for violation of the Espionage Act. This I do as a friend of Mr. Debs for more than twenty-five years and after full consultation with him in prison.

I am aware that Mr. Debs did violate the Act and in his argument to the jury and address to the court, he fully and freely stated that he did. I know that Mr. Debs, like many other sincere men and women, did not believe in war and that he could not bring himself to think that the United States was justified in entering the conflict.

From the time the German army invaded Belgium, I believed that the civilized world should unite to drive it out and that this country must ultimately do its part. When the United States entered the war, I gave my time and energy without reserve to support the Allies' cause. I was sorry for many men and women who were sent to jail for speaking what they believed to be the truth in opposition to the act of Congress in declaring war. I believe that many of these were guilty of no moral wrong, but I likewise know that self-preservation is the first law of nations as well as of men and that while the war was on we could not weigh individual motives, but were bound to take all necessary measures to protect ourselves, even from those who committed no moral wrong. This course the Government followed—not with malice or hatred, but as a stern duty in meeting a grave emergency. Any Government, however liberal, would have done the same.

But the war is over and it is right to examine the motives of men; and to keep in prison one who felt it his duty to disagree, after the need has passed, would not be self-defense but a punishment undeserved.

I confess to the deepest affection for Mr. Debs, an affection which has made me glad to travel hundreds of miles in trying weather and to sacrifice a much needed rest and vacation, that I might aid in obtaining his release from prison. He is courageous, honest, emotional and loving. He has freely given his life to help his fellow men and proclaimed the truth as he saw the truth. More than this no man can do, for it is not given to any of us to be sure that the opinions we hold are right. He is sixty-four years old and in prison for speaking what he believed to be the truth and now, when the war is over and the danger is passed, he should be released.

I am very sure that I do not ask this alone for my friend. The work of the world today is to heal the deep wounds of war, and I am most anxious that this Government, which has always tolerated differences and upheld the freedom of thought and speech, should show that stern measures were only used for self-protection and that it has acted without malice or hatred and is willing and anxious not only to be just, but forgiving. I know of nothing that could make this so plain to intelligent men as the pardon of Eugene V. Debs.   Very respectfully,   Clarence Darrow

TLS (WP, DLC).

From Edward Mandell House

Dear Governor: London, July 30, 1919.

Almost as soon as I arrived in England I sensed an antagonism to the United States. The English are quite as cordial and hospitable to the individual American as ever, but they dislike us collectively.

The war has left but two great powers in the world, where before there were seven. While Russia has collapsed internally, and Germany and Austria have fallen through defeat, France and Japan have gone from first to second rate powers because the United States and Great Britain have become so powerful. While the British Empire vastly exceeds the United States in area and population and while their aggregate wealth is perhaps greater than ours, yet our position is much more favorable. It is because of this that the relations between the two countries are beginning to assume the same character as that of England and Germany before the war.

By her industry and organization Germany was forging ahead as the first power in the world, but she lost everything by her arrogance and lack of statesmanship. Will it be Great Britain or the United States who will next commit this colossal blunder. If we are farsighted we will conduct ourselves so as to merit the friendship of all nations, for it is to me conceivable that there may come a time when we will need it.

Our war expenditures gave a spectacular exhibition of our wealth which has excited the envy of the world, and which if we are unwise, may lead to a great coalition against us. It looks now as if it would be necessary for us to supply coal to those who formerly looked to England for this commodity, and if we continue our merchant marine building on the present scale, we will be hitting at two of her most lucrative industries.

Labor in Europe is showing a strange disinclination for work, and English labor is lagging behind more and more. This accentuates the widening economic position between us. The advanced liberals are questioning the Government as to the reason for their big navy estimates for next year. The Government's answer is that when the war was ended Great Britain was going at top speed in naval construction, and that it would be a great waste not to finish the ships now on the ways. It was brought out that there would be eighty-four ships of the larger class and some thirty-five destroyers. It was the Government's intention, so it was said, to use the newer types to replace the older ones now in use. The truth is this new construction is because of us, and for no other reason.

Haldane, Grey[1] and I dined together on Sunday. The purpose of the conference was to discuss the Government's request to Grey to become Ambassador at Washington. Curzon, acting Minister of Foreign Affairs, at Lloyd George's instance, asked Haldane to use his good offices with Grey, and Haldane, in turn, asked me to help. Haldane told Grey and me that the three matters that the Government had in mind to settle with the United States were, first, the naval building program, second, the Irish question, and third, the League of Nations.

Grey said that in no circumstances would he become Ambassador, but he would consider going out on a special mission for the purpose of discussing these questions, provided the Government agreed with him about them. He thought there would be no difficulty in regard to the League of Nations or the naval program, but he was insistent that they should outline their Irish policy and that it should be one with which he could agree. I suggested that Lloyd George and Curzon be told that it was impossible to discusss [discuss] an abstract question, and that he Grey wanted to know what was their Irish program before even considering the question of accepting their offer. This would place the burden on the Government rather than upon Grey.

As to the naval building program, Grey told Haldane that he would write him a memorandum which he could hand to the Government. This memorandum would outline his, Grey's, views which are as follows:

That in no circumstances would Great Britain build against the United States no matter how many keels we laid. However, England would hold herself free to build against any European power in any quantity that seemed to her best. On the other hand, the United States could exercise her own judgment about building, without regard to Great Britain, as against Japan, and they would consider it a matter of no concern to them.

Grey told me in this conversation, and in another I had with him some two weeks ago, that the British Government's policy during the time he was in office was to disregard the naval program of the United States. In the first place they thought war between the two nations was inconceivable, and in the second, that in a rivalry it was admitted the United States could outbuild Great Britain. In discussing this matter further with Grey he admitted that this was the liberal point of view and not the conservative, or the one held in naval circles. I predict that when they receive Grey's memorandum concerning these questions, they will soften in their insistence that he go to Washington.

You may be surprised that I am not taking into account the League of Nations as a preventive, not only for trouble with Great Britain but also as a deterrent in naval armaments. I consider the League as the great hope of a peaceful solution of all these vexatious international jealousies, but we must admit that it is a long cry from today to the time when the League shall have proved itself such an instrument as we all hope it may be. The fact that this Government wishes an Ambassador of Grey's standing to go to America to discuss the question of naval armaments, indicates that they do not expect it to be reached through the League of Nations.

You will have noticed that the British have been very insistent upon reduction of standing armies, but they never protest against naval armaments. One of the necessary things to be done, in my opinion, is the creation of an international code of laws covering both land and sea. It is your belief that in the next war there will be no neutrals, therefore, there is no necessity for a revision of the laws of the sea. I do not agree with this position. It is quite conceivable that war might come between, say, France and England, in which no other nations would be Involved. However, the lack of sea laws would almost inevitably bring us into the conflict. If, on the other hand, we had a chart which all nations had accepted, then any two belligerents would of necessity have to conform to it or bring the world in arms upon themselves. This question of the freedom of the seas is the one thing above all others that brought us into the war, and yet it is no nearer solution today than it was before Germany collapsed. If If [sic] there were a Liberal Government here I am sure they would recognize the seriousness of this menace.

I do not know that I would advise doing anything more at present than to call attention to the fact that it was your purpose to ask consideration of the question sometime within the near future. In the meantime, there might be a Government here sympathetic to the view that a general international understanding upon this subject should be reached.

It is my judgment that we should go ahead as rapidly as possible with the organization of the League of Nations, and at the first meeting of the Assembly bring up the question of a reduction of armaments and seek an agreement. Do you not think also that our people should be warned not to expect complete payment of loans to the Entente? Should they not be asked to consider a large share of these loans as a part of our necessary war expenditures, and should not an adjustment be suggested by us and not by our debtors? If this is done then it would be well to do it with a *beau geste*. For instance, I notice we have sold our one billion of war material in France to the French Government for three hundred millions. Would it not have been better to have made this a gift in name as, indeed, it is in fact?

The one coalition which might conceivably prove dangerous to us is that of Great Britain and Japan, and yet a large section of our people, notably those of Irish and German descent, would welcome trouble in this direction. On the other hand, we have those that are trying to make difficulties with Japan.

If I were you I should take some early occasion to invoke the sober attention of our people to these dangers. The world is in a belligerent mood, and the next ten years will be the most dangerous to its peace. If we can get over this period safely and get the League in satisfactory operation, war may conceivably become almost obsolete. Could you serve mankind better at the moment than to caution all to sit steady in the boat, and do what is possible to bring things back to the normal. At present, the world is a long way from being safe, and another upheaval now may completely wreck civilization.   Affectionately yours,   E. M. House

P.S. Hoover, who has just left, is in one of his most pessimistic moods. He is simply reveling in gloom. He gives Europe but thirty days longer of orderly life—after that it is to be revolution, starvation and chaos. In his opinion the coal situation is the most menacing.

TLS (WP, DLC).
    [1] That is, Richard Burdon Haldane, 1st Viscount Haldane of Cloan, Secretary of State for War (1905-1912) and Lord High Chancellor of Great Britain, 1912-1915; and Edward Grey, 1st Viscount Grey of Fallodon, Secretary of State for Foreign Affairs from 1905 to 1916.

From Robert Lansing, with Enclosure

My dear Mr. President: Washington July 30, 1919.

A recent mail despatch from our Embassy at Tokyo, containing voluminous newspaper clippings from Japanese papers relating to the developments in China resulting from the recognition by the Peace Conference of Japan's claims in Shantung, throws some interesting light on the point of view of the Japanese public. I am enclosing a memorandum containing the principal points brought out in the Ambassador's despatch.

                    Faithfully yours,   Robert Lansing

TLS (WP, DLC).

E N C L O S U R E

MEMORANDUM.

An outstanding feature of the Japanese attitude is the inability to understand why the award of the Peace Conference should have aroused such opposition among the Chinese. The comments in this connection are illuminating evidence of the genuine conviction that prevails in Japan as to the justice of its position and the uprightness of its aims. Japanese believe that they are striving to promote cordiality between the two nations and to secure the safety and well being of China, and they are accordingly pained at China's "ingratitude." Very few can see any other side to this question. They justify their desire for territorial footholds on the plea that from such points of vantage they can the better guard China from Occidental aggression, and they base their eagerness to secure mining and other concessions on the necessity of providing for the sinews of war to "preserve the peace of the Far East."

The inability of the Japanese to appreciate the Chinese point of view makes them all the more ready to attribute the Chinese agitation to British and American instigation. Various exaggerated and entirely unfounded reports of the sinister activity of British and American agents in inflaming students and others to organize boycotts and commit acts of violence against Japanese are given credence and widely circulated in the Japanese press. Unfortunately, the anti-Japanese feeling prevailing among the majority of foreign residents in China, which frequently finds expression in the foreign language press of that country, lends color to these reports. The resolution passed by the Anglo-American Association at a meeting when both the British and American Ministers were said to be present and the resolution of the American Chamber of Commerce at Shanghai denouncing the Shantung settlement, have added to the resentment in Japan against the attitude of the British and American residents in China.

The ASAHI's views as to the origin of the disturbances are saner than those of the majority of the press. It ascribes them to the prevailing belief among Chinese that Japan is behind the reactionary military clique, thus standing as an effectual bar to political progress, and to a desire among a section of the merchant class to check Japan's economic encroachment. The journal, however, also admits that it is quite conceivable that the direct and indirect assistance given by foreigners has had the effect of swelling the anti-Japanese agitation to its present dimensions, and alludes to the opinion prevailing among certain Japanese business men that Americans are taking advantage of this movement to extend their markets.

The JIJI, which is better informed on China than most vernacular papers, not only believes that there are no immediate prospects of the disturbances being quelled, but anticipates a further aggravation of the situation, which may spread to all sections of the country, in view of the conflicting political ambitions which lie at the roots of the movement. It also hints that there are Bolshevik influences at work fomenting the spirit of revolution and anarchy.

The HOCHI demands, if the Chinese Government is powerless to deal with the situation, that Japan should land troops herself. Also that it should take appropriate measures against British and American officials in China, should they prove to have participated in the resolution of the Anglo-American Association. A correspondent of the YAMATO, who suffers from chronic anti-Americanism, has been so impressed with America's responsibility for the demonstrations, that he has become convinced that the solution of the troubles lies in an appeal to arms against the United States.

In view of the general tendency to attribute the causes for the troubles to conflicting ambitions of Chinese politicians, Anglo-American instigation, Bolshevik propaganda and in fact everything except Japanese aggressiveness, and to seek remedies accordingly, the views of the CHUO KORON (Central Review) are like a voice crying in the wilderness:

"The short cut to quieting the anti-Japanese agitation in China would be for the Japanese to restrain the Chinese policy of the bureaucrats and capitalists, so that the genuine peaceful requirements of the Japanese nation may be laid frankly before our neighbors. It should not be attempted to suppress the dissatisfaction of the Chinese people by rendering assistance to Tsao, Chang[1] and other so-called pro-Japanese.

"For many years we have been striving for the emancipation of Japan from the grip of the bureaucrats and militarists. In this respect the object for which the Chinese students are struggling must be described as the same as our own object. In this sense it must be said that the success of the Chinese agitation would mean the success of our own efforts for the emancipation of Japan from the baneful influence of the bureaucrats and militarists. If this be done, it will be possible to found the real national friendship between Japan and China on a sound and secure basis. It will be observed that all attempts at the promotion of Sino-Japanese friendship tried in the past have proved more harmful than beneficial."

T MS (WP, DLC).
    [1] That is, Ts'ao Ju-lin and Chang Tsung-hsiang.

From Robert Lansing

My dear Mr. President: Washington July 30, 1919.

When the Armistice was signed American bankers and investors were constrained to look abroad for new fields in which to employ the surplus wealth recently acquired through the growth of American production and accumulation of capital. Although the Departments of State and Commerce have looked with approval upon the extension of foreign trade, opportunities for such investment are being neglected because of the alleged lack of cooperation between our Government and Americans willing to invest abroad. A clarification of the relation between the Government and the American foreign investor is necessary to improve the situation.

There are still many Americans who consider that the Government regards them as commercial adventurers merely because they invest in foreign fields, and they resent this attitude, as evidenced by the complaints of many honest investors who have suffered the loss of their relatives, agents and property in Mexico.

In view of these conditions, and regarding this present time as particularly auspicious, when you have just concluded a covenant of amity and better understanding between the nations of the world, it is respectfully suggested that a Commission, composed of Americans of wide experience in matters of world trade, should be formed to study and advise upon the question of a definite policy of Governmental protection. Its findings would be of great service in guiding the Department to formulate a constructive policy toward foreign trade, and at the same time would dispel misunderstanding, stimulate our business abroad and disseminate those American principles which should govern our commercial and trade activities. Moreover it is thought that a most beneficial effect would be produced by the calling together at this time of those who are now, or are soon to become the most important American investors in foreign fields, in order to ask their advice and counsel regarding foreign trade and protection.

The enclosed list of representative Americans,[1] who are interested in foreign fields, has been prepared with the thought that the Commission idea might appeal to you and the task of selecting its personnel be simplified by placing before you these names.

I will be pleased to outline several ways in which the details of such a plan might be handled effectively should you so desire.

                              Faithfully yours,   Robert Lansing.

TLS (WP, DLC).
   [1] The list (T MS, WP, DLC) reads like a *Who's Who* of Americans active in international business, communications, mining, petroleum, and finance.

A News Report

SEVEN REPUBLICAN SENATORS PREPARE
FOUR 'MILD RESERVATIONS' TO COVENANT;
WILL URGE THEM AS BASIS OF SETTLEMENT

                                                    [*July 31, 1919*]

Washington, July 31.—In an effort to reach an agreement on changes in the League of Nations covenant seven Republican Senators, who favor mild reservations, conferred late today at the Capitol. In the conference were McCumber of North Dakota, Cummins of Iowa, Kellogg of Minnesota, Lenroot of Wisconsin, Spencer of Missouri, McNary of Oregon, and Colt of Rhode Island.

As explained by the conferees, their idea is to find a basis of compromise between the forces that demand drastic reservations and those who feel that less drastic ones would suffice. All the conferees except Mr. Colt and Mr. McNary have announced themselves as favoring reservations of some sort. Some of the five advocating reservations are inclined to go further than others.

The seven Senators discussed the reservations question for three hours. Afterward it was stated that they discussed reservations on Article X., on the Monroe Doctrine, on purely domestic matters, such as the tariff and immigration, and on a two-year withdrawal clause. The question of a reservation on the Shantung award was also referred to, but the conferees devoted themselves today to proposed covenant reservations.

All the Senators except Colt and McNary, it was stated, seemed to agree that the four reservations suggested were desirable. As to the Monroe Doctrine, the matter of domestic questions and the two-year withdrawal, with the United States determining whether its obligations to the League had been fulfilled, all seven expressed themselves, it is understood, as willing to vote for reservations. The only question was as to phraseology. Some Senators urged merely interpretive reservations on these three provisions; others thought the reservations should go further, but not so far as to constitute amendments.

As to Article X. there are wider differences of opinion. Senators McCumber, Cummins, and others advocated an explicit statement of the right of Congress alone to determine whether American soldiers were to be sent into foreign lands. This would take authority out of the hands of the League to put the United States into war. Senators Colt and McNary are said to have favored leaving Article X intact. They argued, it is stated, that Congress in any event had the right to vote war, and that the League could not interfere.

The seven conferees, it was stated, felt that further explanations were necessary from the White House or State Department before any decision could be reached respecting a reservation on Shantung.

The conference was called because of the apparent inability of Republican leaders in the Senate to concentrate on a reservation policy.

Among the opponents of the League there is a group, including Borah, Johnson, Brandegee and Moses,[1] who insist upon amendments rather than reservations. Some of this group, if not all, would vote for reservations if not able, as seems unlikely, to put through a program of amendments.

There is another group of opponents of the covenant who talk of "explicit reservations," not "interpretative" ones. This includes Lodge, Knox and others of the conservative Republicans. They regard the reservations they advocate, which follow the lines of those suggested by Elihu Root,[2] as having the same effect as direct amendments.

The seven Senators who met today hope in later conferences to reach a basis of agreement. Then the result will be laid before the Republican leaders and discussed with other Senators.

The leaders among the "mild reservationists" expected to win sixteen to twenty-one Senators to their program. With this as a basis they believe it will be not difficult to decide on the policy to be pursued when the Senate acts on the treaty. With the Republicans united on a reservation policy, with perhaps an exception or two, the majority party, with the aid of at least two Democratic Senators, Reed and Gore,[3] would be in position, they believe, to force through its program.

Senator Colt expressed the opinion tonight that a workable program would be evolved. He believed the advocates of changes which would "clarify" the covenant would bring about a situation that would put the onus on the Democrats of rejecting the treaty if they saw fit to do so, rather than on the Republicans.

Senator Hitchcock, ranking Democratic member of the Foreign Relations Committee, told President Wilson on Monday at the White House that the League's opponents were "hopelessly floundering." When he heard today of the conference of "mild reservationists," he remarked that it gave fresh indication of the muddle in the opposition camp.

Senator Hitchcock gave this analysis of the fight made by opponents of the League:

"First, they advocated separating the League of Nations covenant from the treaty.

"Next they abandoned that idea and talked of rejecting the treaty.

"Next they declared for direct amendments.

"Next there came talk of reservations.

"Now comes the effort for 'mild' reservations.

"And later on," Senator Hitchcock predicted, "the fight of the League opponents will come to nothing at all, with the treaty being ratified exactly as submitted to the Senate."

Opposition Senators, however, asserted tonight that they were not "floundering," but that the movement for changes in the treaty was making progress day by day. Conservative leaders spoke of the conference of the "mild" reservationists as nothing but an individual effort of these Senators to see how far they wanted to go in reservations. As to the outcome of the fight for reservations, the leaders said, there was no doubt. They predicted that changes would be made before the treaty was ratified.

Although a reservation to the Peace Treaty to express the sense of the Senate in favor of international prohibition is being urged by prohibition advocates, Senator Sheppard[4] of Texas, who was reported as intending to offer it, stated today that he had no such intention.

In a letter to the Rev. A. I. Cameron of Altus, Okla., Senator Gore has written that he thought it opportune to insert an amendment to the treaty for prohibition against international shipment of intoxicants. He also advocates one appealing to the Supreme Being to "justify the treaty by its fruits."

Printed in the *New York Times*, August 1, 1919.
  [1] That is, Frank Bosworth Brandegee of Connecticut and George Higgins Moses of New Hampshire.
  [2] See JPT to WW, June 21, 1919, n. 3, Vol. 61.
  [3] That is, Thomas Pryor Gore of Oklahoma.
  [4] That is, Morris Sheppard.

To Francis Joseph Heney

My dear Mr. Heney: [The White House] 31 July, 1919.

Your letter of July 18th[1] has given me a great deal of pleasure, and I must turn aside from the duties of even these hectic days to express in at least a line my very great appreciation. It is fine of you to remember to cheer me in these anxious days.

Cordially and sincerely yours,   Woodrow Wilson

TLS (Letterpress Books, WP, DLC).
  [1] F. J. Heney to WW, July 18, 1919, Vol. 61.

To Newton Diehl Baker

My dear Mr. Secretary: [The White House] 31 July, 1919.

It is hard to find a satisfactory "official" name for the war, but the best, I think, that has been suggested is "The World War," and I hope that your judgment will concur.[1]

I know you will understand the brevity of this note.

Cordially and faithfully yours,   Woodrow Wilson

TLS (Letterpress Books, WP, DLC).
  [1] Wilson was replying to NDB to WW, July 23, 1919 (third letter of that date), Vol. 61.

From Carter Glass

Dear Mr. President: Washington July 31, 1919.

I understand that you have given Mr. Norman H. Davis an appointment to see you at 2:30 this afternoon. With your approval, I have asked Mr. Davis to accept appointment as Assistant Secretary of the Treasury in charge of foreign loans in place of Mr. Rathbone, who for personal reasons, is very anxious to be permitted to resign.

In the Treasury, we think that Mr. Davis is exceptionally equipped both by rare judgment and ability and by the unique experience which he has had during the past two years in the Treasury in Washington and with you in Europe, to deal with the problem of European reconstruction, which is now perhaps the most important problem confronting American finance, both private and public.

It will not be easy for Mr. Davis to make the further sacrifice involved in accepting the office. If, however, you should feel disposed to add to the invitation which I have already extended to Mr. Davis, your personal request that he accept the office and so round out his fine record of public service, I feel sure that he would accept it as a clear duty.

I should be very grateful for any help you can give me in securing the service of Mr. Davis, which seems to me to be well nigh indispensable at this critical juncture.

Sincerely yours,   Carter Glass.

TLS (WP, DLC).

Two Letters from William Gibbs McAdoo

PERSONAL

Dear Governor: New York July 31, 1919.

Some time ago I accepted an invitation to become a member of the Executive Committee of the League to Enforce Peace. Vance McCormick is also a member.

An important meeting of the Committee was held this morning which McCormick told me he could not attend. For that reason, I thought yesterday that it might be necessary for me to go to Washington to confer with you after the meeting today, but I subsequently changed my mind about this.

At today's meeting the Executive Committee adopted a resolution[1]—which I had the opportunity to prepare—declaring for an unconditional ratification of the League of Nations Covenant and opposing any amendments or reservations. There was a long discussion but the vote was unanimous. Mr. Taft's letters to Mr. Hays[2] have caused a good deal of embarrassment to the League but this emphatic declaration of the League's position, which is going to be put out as in harmony with Mr. Taft's own views, will, I hope, correct the unfortunate effects of his suggestions to Mr. Hays.

We have also arranged for an effective publicity campaign which I think will help you enormously in your fight. I am strongly convinced that we should make no concessions whatever in the way of reservations—certainly not at this time. I believe the Treaty can be ratified without such concessions if we all stand firm.

I understand that a committee of the League is to confer with you about this matter at your convenience.

Love for all.   Affectionately,   W G McAdoo

[1] "RESOLUTION ADOPTED BY EXECUTIVE COMMITTEE LEAGUE TO ENFORCE PEACE," July 31, 1919, T MS (WP, DLC).
[2] About which, see JPT to WW, July 23, 1919, n. 1, and the Enclosure with this letter, Vol. 61. See also the memorandum by Taft printed at July 23, 1919, and n. 1 thereto, *ibid.*

PERSONAL.

Dear Governor: New York July 31, 1919.

Now that I am in the audience and no longer on the stage, I am learning more about what the public is thinking than I could possibly learn at Washington.

The two things which are concerning the average man and woman more than anything else are, first, the high cost of living and, second, taxation. The Republicans have assiduously created the impression that the Administration,—by that they mean you, the President,—can do something to reduce the cost of living and to change existing conditions, and that you are not doing it; also, that you are responsible for the high taxation and that the responsibility of changing it rests with you. This notwithstanding your recent message recommending a revision of the tax laws.

The Republican House is about to adjourn for five weeks and the country has not been made to understand that such an adjournment is indefensible in the circumstances. Before you called the special session, the Republicans made the country believe that these very problems of the high cost of living and taxation would be dealt with by them and relief granted if you would call an extra session. No sooner had you done so, than the insincerity and hypocrisy of the Republican majority became manifest.

It seems to me that you could make a tremendous point by immediately sending a special message, requesting the House of Representatives not to adjourn, in view of the fact that the high cost of living and the burden of taxation present problems to which the House should immediately devote its best energies and intelligence; that if relief can be found through legislation, it rests with the Congress to enact the necessary laws; that so far as the revision of the burdensome tax laws are concerned, the House should devote itself to the preparation of the necessary measures while the Senate is debating the Peace Treaty because taxation measures must originate in the House and time will be saved if the House prepares and passes the necessary measures, so that they may be acted upon promptly by the Senate as soon as it has disposed of the Peace Treaty.

I think, also, that, if you would send such a message, calling attention to the fact that the power of the Government to deal with the high cost of living problems is quite limited, since its jurisdiction is restricted to interstate commerce, and that the States, themselves, have a larger power to deal with these problems, since most of them concern intrastate commerce, you would do a serviceable thing to the country by fixing and lodging in the public mind, the proper measure of responsibility as between the Federal and State Governments.

I am writing very hastily and I do not believe I am giving you the idea as I should like to, but I hope there is at least a germ of intelligence in it.

I am thoroughly convinced that the country would applaud your appeal to make the House of Representatives stay in session and to do the job which it has assured the country all along that it would do if you gave it an opportunity by calling a special session.

Hastily, and affectionately,   W G McAdoo

TLS (WP, DLC).

From Walker Downer Hines

Dear Mr. President: Washington July 31, 1919.

Several months ago the railroad shop employes asked for an increase in wages.[1] The matter was considered by the Railroad Administration's Board of Wages and Working Conditions, which is composed of three representatives of labor and three representatives of the railroad managements. This Board was unable to agree and therefore took no action as a Board, but on July 16th I received two reports from members of the Board, one from the three labor

[1] For the background of this matter, see W. D. Hines to WW, July 18, 1919, Vol. 61.

members recommending a general increase in wages (for example increasing the wages of machinists from 68¢ per hour to 80¢ per hour and proportionately increasing the wages of other classes of shop employes), and another report from the three management members recommending against any general increase in wages, although recommending certain readjustments of the wages of some classes of the employes.

The position of the labor members of the Board is that the wages of railroad shopmen are substantially below the wages paid similar classes of employes in the Navy Yards, Arsenals and Shipyards, and in many industrial enterprises in the principal cities of the country, and that substantial increases in the wages in the ship yards and outside industrial enterprises have taken place since the wages of the shop employes were established in the summer of 1918, and that the cost of living has been, and is steadily rising. The position of the management members on the Board is that the wages of shop employes are not properly comparable with the wages of non-railroad employes cited by the employes and their representatives and that these latter industries have differentiating conditions which account for the high wages paid by them, and that a further wage increase at this time would simply begin a new cycle in the increased cost of living which would not benefit the employes. They urge instead, the adoption of effective methods of reducing the cost of living; but they add that unless some action can be taken within a reasonable time to accomplish this result they see no alternative but to continue the wage cycle increases with corresponding increased cycles of living costs.

On July 28th a conference was begun in accordance with an arrangement made on July 8th between the representatives of the Railroad Administration and representatives of the shop employes. At this conference the representatives of the employes made it plain to my associates that their members expected, and believed that they were entitled to, a substantial increase in wages retroactive to January 1st, 1919, and that the state of unrest was so great that it was of the highest importance that a definite answer be given on the wage matter without delay. These representatives expressed the same views to me yesterday.

On July 17th the Shop Crafts Convention, meeting at Atlanta, Ga., and representing employes from 16 railroads in the Southeast, strongly urged the necessity for substantial increases in wages by August 1st, retroactive to January 1st, 1919.

The earnest insistence that immediate action be taken to equalize wages with the rapid increase in the cost of living is not confined to the shop employes.

The Triennial Convention of the Brotherhood of Railroad Trainmen representing about 160,000 railroad employes meeting at Columbus, Ohio, adopted on May 31st a resolution strongly urging substantial additional increases in wages to meet the cost of living.

The Triennial Convention of the Brotherhood of Locomotive Firemen, meeting at Denver from June 9th to July 15th and representing about 116,000 employes, likewise adopted resolutions insisting upon the necessity for substantial increases in wages to meet the increased cost of living.

The Thirteenth Annual Convention of Railway Signalmen of America in session at Kansas City on July 15th strongly urged a further increase in wages and similar action was taken at Boston on July 27th by 150 delegates to the Convention of the United Brotherhood of Maintenance of Way Employes and Railroad Shop Employes of the railroad systems of New England and New York. The International Convention of the Brotherhood of Railway Clerks, which was held in Cincinnati from May 12th to 24th, endorsed proposals to the Railroad Administration which also urged an increase and readjustment of the wages of the employes represented by that organization.

The representatives of the Railroad Administration have had assurances from representatives of practically all classes of employes that the continuance in the increase in the cost of living would necessarily involve very substantial increases in wages and that increases in wages given to any one class of railroad employes would necessitate corresponding increases to all other classes of railroad employes.

The situation thus presented involves the following considerations:

We have received the most positive assurances that any general increases to shop employes will result in demands for corresponding increases to every other class of railroad employes. The situation, therefore, cannot be viewed except as a whole for the entire two million railroad employes. Viewing it as a whole, every increase of one cent per hour means an increase of $50,000,000 per year in operating expenses for straight time with a substantial addition for necessary overtime. An increase of 12¢ per hour as asked for by the shop employes would, if applied to all employes, mean (including necessary overtime) an increase of probably $800,000,000 per year in operating expenses.

The Government is already incurring a deficit at the rate of several hundred million dollars per year in operating the railroads, because the increase in transportation rates has been proportionately less than the increases in wages already granted and the increases in prices which have taken place. Therefore there is no fund whatever out of which additional wages can be paid, so that additional wages cannot be paid unless new revenues are produced through an increase in transportation rates and any immediate payment of additional wages would necessitate for several months an appropriation by Congress out of the Treasury because substantial increases in rates could not be made immediately effective.

While you may find it expedient to use the temporary rate-making power, which was conferred upon you as a war emergency during Federal control, to prevent the continuance of the deficit now being incurred which grows out of increases in wages and prices due to the war, you would not, in my opinion, be justified in regarding that rate-making power as a sufficient warrant for making still additional increases in rates for the purpose of paying still additional increases in wages to be established under existing peace conditions, and to be controlling as the wage basis in the future.

The question presented for an additional increase in wages, whether the total amount be $800,000,000 or any proportion of that sum, is a peace-time question between the entire American public on the one hand and the two million railroad employes and the members of their families on the other hand. It is a question which I do not believe the Executive ought to undertake to decide unless specific authority is conferred upon him for the express purpose of deciding it.

The fact that these demands are made and are so urgently pressed emphasizes the great necessity of having for their decision legislation which will provide adequate machinery representing both the public and the employes. Obviously any such machinery should include a method whereby revenues will be provided to the extent required to pay the increased wages awarded.

While the general powers implied in the Federal Control Act were sufficient to admit of taking as war measures the necessary steps to deal with the wage problems that arose during the war they are not sufficient to satisfy the requirements arising in connection with any present proposals for general wage increases. Under the existing machinery the ultimate public interest is exclusively represented by the Railroad Administration in the making of wages but by the Interstate Commerce Commission in the final decision upon rates. Moreover, the Railroad Administration while thus charged with the final decision as to what wages are proper as between the American public and railroad labor is also charged with the responsibilities incident to the day to day operation of the railroads. On the one hand a decision by the Railroad Administration against an increase in wages will be regarded by the employes as a decision dictated more by the immediate difficulties of railroad management than by the broad interests of the public as a whole.

On the other hand a decision by the Railroad Administration in favor of an increase in wages will not necessarily be binding on the Interstate Commerce Commission which is now the final representative of the public as to transportation rates. To deal with these problems under peace time conditions there ought to be a final and authoritative representation of the public whose decision when in favor of a wage increase would carry with it the obligation on the part of the final rate-making power to prescribe rates which would furnish the necessary funds with which to pay the increased wages. It is obvious that no wage increases could be put into effect at the moment except on the theory that for several months they would be paid by an appropriation of Congress because even under the existing machinery rate increases could not actually be put into effect for a substantial period. Undoubtedly any rate increases of a general character ought at the present time to be considered by the Interstate Commerce Commission before they shall be put into effect.

The conclusion to which I have come has been forced upon me by the recent developments above referred to.

When I announced last March the increases in wages for the employes in train and engine service I stated that they completed the war cycle of wage increases.

When it developed in May and June that the continued pressure of the increase in the cost of living was causing railroad employes generally to urge that they be given substantial protection through further important increases in wages if the cost of living was not reduced, I realized that the question was assuming such wide and deep significance to the American public as well as to railroad employes that the question ought not to be dealt with in the same way in which the railroad wages had been increased in connection with the war emergency. I therefore advised the Board of Railroad Wages & Working Conditions on July 3rd that they could not regard themselves as vested with jurisdiction to formulate and recommend further general wage increases to be made by me but that in all cases thereafter arising, they should report the facts to me that I might decide in the light of the facts upon a fair and just procedure.

The receipt of the observations of the members of the Board with reference to the shop employes, the hearings now in progress before the Board with reference to the Brotherhood of Railroad Trainmen, the conferences I have had in the last three days with the representatives of the shop employes and the conferences which my associates and I have been having recently with the representatives of practically all classes of railroad labor with reference to the menace in the continued increase in the cost of living, force me to the definite conclusion that the problem is too great and has too much permanent significance to the American Public as well as to railroad labor to admit of its being decided through the exercise of the war emergency powers of the Federal Control Act and which are subject to the limitations and embarrassments above pointed out. I feel that the developments have now reached the point where the situation has taken a sufficiently concrete form to serve as the basis for a positive recommendation.

I therefore respectfully recommend that Congress be asked promptly to adopt legislation providing a properly constituted body on which the public and labor will be adequately represented and which will be empowered to pass on these and all railroad wage problems, but not on rules and working conditions, (because the latter cannot be satisfactorily separated from the current handling of railroad operations and therefore should continue to be dealt with by the Railroad Administration). Such legislation should also provide that if wage increases shall be decided upon it shall be mandatory upon the rate-making body to provide where necessary increased rates to take care of the resulting increases in the cost of operating the railroads.

I do not think that we can properly deal with this great problem without a full recognition of the fact that the cost of living is rapidly rising and that every month that passes promises to impair still further the purchasing power of the existing wages of railroad employes unless the rise in the cost of living can be successful[l]y restrained (as I earnestly hope in the general public interest it can speedily be). I therefore further recommend that Congress be asked to provide in any such legislation that any increases in railroad wages which may be made by the tribunal constituted for that purpose shall be made effective as of August 1, 1919, to such extent as that tribunal may regard reasonable and proper in order to give railroad employes from that date the benefit which the tribunal may think they were then entitled to. In this way the delay necessarily incident to the creation of such tribunal and its action will not be prejudicial to the fair interests of the railroad employes.

Cordially yours,   Walker D Hines

TLS (WP, DLC).

Two Letters from Edward Nash Hurley

My dear Mr. President: Washington July 31, 1919.

On this, my last day as Chairman of the Shipping Board, as I visualize the future of a real American Merchant Marine, I am confident that we—by we I mean you, the Executive and Administrative Departments of the Government, Congress, American shipping men, and the public—will realize its attainment. The domestic elements in the program will adjust themselves from now on as developments indicate. What may be called the International problems, however, will need careful attention. Of the International problems, not forgetting the necessity of building up trade agencies and developing banking facilities in foreign countries, none is more essential than that of fuel oil supply in foreign parts. May I, therefore, suggest the vital necessity of the protection of the American Merchant Marine and the United States Navy in the matter of fuel oil supply.

As you know, the merchant fleet's use of fuel oil already exceeds very largely the use of coal. Furthermore, coal-burning ships are rapidly being converted into oil-burning ships. In the not distant future, Diesel Motorship vessels will be added to the oil-burning steamships. A positive assurance of a definite supply of fuel oil, therefore, becomes the prime essential to successful operation.

There have been many reports made by interested parties; there have been many reports made by Government officials. The last one I have had before me is that by Van H. Manning,[1] Director of the Bureau of Mines to the Secretary of the Interior, under date of May 15, 1919. This is a full report and, to my mind, shows clearly that the United States is not protected in the matter of bunker fuel oil in foreign waters. It will, of course, be quite obvious to you that many of our ships may not return for years to United States ports to be bunkered, and that while the steam radius on oil bunkering for ships is greater than in the case of coal, yet in possibly two-thirds of the world the United States will be at the mercy of foreign bunkering stations for fuel oil.

Great Britain has recognized this and has taken immediate steps to protect her merchant marine and navy in this respect, and, as the report of Mr. Manning shows, she has under Government control scattered holdings of oil producing fields, having at the present time tremendous capacity and with extraordinary future potentialities. Great Britain holdings primarily through the Royal Dutch Shell Company, control producing fields in all the important districts in the United States and in Mexico and various parts of Europe, including Roumania, Russia. She also owns control of the stock of the Anglo-Persian Oil Co. which controls exclusively the Persian Gulf Field.

On the other hand, outside of the United States the only American holdings of any moment are those in Mexico and those of the Standard Oil Company in Roumania. The Roumanian Government has undertaken to confiscate the latter.

As an assured, continuing supply of oil fuel for bunkering purposes lies close to the heart of the successful operation of our merchant marine, it would seem to me that steps should be taken to
plan a definite protection. I suggest that the matter is properly one
that should be in the hands of the Secretary of the Interior. I also
suggest for your consideration, that he be definitely instructed to
outline a plan for meeting this situation, so that active steps be
taken as promptly as possible to make the assurance of a bunkering supply definite and certain.

                   Faithfully yours,   Edward N. Hurley

[1] Vannoy Hartrog Manning. The Editors have not found a copy of his report.

My dear Mr. President: Washington July 31, 1919.

Pursuant to the permission you have so graciously accorded me,
I relinquish today the chairmanship of the United States Shipping
Board. In doing so I feel it my duty to place in your hands a summary of the work done and projected toward the establishment,
development and maintenance of an adequate merchant marine
under the American flag. This summary does not in any way anticipate the forthcoming annual report of the Shipping Board. Its
preparation has been inspired by an appreciation of your desire to
keep currently informed concerning the status, progress and prospects of every constructive national enterprise.

In the attached report[1] I am confident you will find assurance
that American ships can hold their own anywhere in competition
with the ships of other nations, notwithstanding that we have set
a high standard for the wages and living quarters of seamen; that
our requirements concerning seaworthiness and the safety of life
are more rigorous, and that our ships receive no subsidy of any
kind.

This is possible because our plan contemplates a merchant marine free from certain blighting influences which affect every other
merchant marine in the world and compel other governments to
grant subsidies. The merchant marine we have planned is to be
wholly American, not only in ownership and equipment, but also
in collateral branches such as ship classification and marine insurance. We have every reason to expect it will be a model American
enterprise of high efficiency and widely-distributed ownership;
closely linked with every industrial and commercial interest of the
American people; always responsive to enlightened public opinion,
and safeguarded against financial exploitation.

To witness the early crystalization of this hope into fact is one of my most fervent wishes. I say crystalization because the figure faithfully pictures the process by which I conceive the American merchant marine must come into existence in finished form. I believe a spontaneous popular appreciation of the opportunit[i]es the merchant marine has to offer will bring about the progressive rehabilitation of our traditions on the sea.

Faithfully yours,   Edward N. Hurley

TLS (WP, DLC).
¹ E. N. Hurley, "REPORT TO THE PRESIDENT OF THE UNITED STATES ON WORK DONE TOWARD THE ESTABLISHMENT AND MAINTENANCE UNDER THE AMERICAN FLAG OF A MERCHANT MARINE ADEQUATE TO THE NEEDS OF AMERICAN OVERSEAS TRADE," July 31, 1919, T MS (WP, DLC). This report was fifty-nine pages in length; Wilson apparently did not read it.

From William Cox Redfield

My dear President: Washington July 31, 1919.

Respectfully recalling to your thought my letter of July 29th on the general subject of foreign credits, permit me to add the following arising from conferences had by me yesterday in New York with a group of gentlemen representing a number of competing interests in the general line of railway equipment and comprising men of both parties.

These men approach the problem of supplying all kinds of railway equipment to Europe in a helpful spirit and are not afraid of the long credits which may be necessary if some organization can be arranged through which can be worked out a satisfactory arrangement of credits on some sound basis. They deprecate the somewhat selfish, or perhaps one would better say self-centered attitude of some of our international bankers, whose viewpoint is rather toward the profit possible under existing conditions than toward the maximum amount of help that may be rendered.

For some countries (Poland and Serbia are examples) transportation is the first and the most urgent necessity. Other commerce cannot follow, nor can even food be distributed sufficiently until adequate means of transportation are provided. First and foremost, therefore, among the steps to be taken and which we alone can effectively take is the providing of cars and engines to haul freight. Furthermore, thus much of commercial interests enters that if transportation equipment cannot be supplied by us to these countries until after through long debate laws are passed and a foreign credit corporation gotten into working order, it is almost certain that our competitors will have put their plants into some sort of working order and have had their credits arranged and will be taking and filling orders. The nature of the business is such that if equipment is provided from other countries it is not thereafter easy to add to it from our own, for the standards are in most respects unlike. The normal thing would be to continue purchasing equipment from the country which supplied the original lot.

The point is that this phase of the foreign credit problem is urgent and will not wait either from the point of view of the people we desire to help abroad or from our own. Is it not possible, therefore, to avoid the necessary delay that would seem otherwise sure by having the War Finance Corporation act in some special way in connection with this equipment matter and, perhaps, as regards others of whose urgency you may know. I do not know whether it can be done by executive order, but, if it can be so done, I suggest that it ought to be. If it cannot be treated this way or by any other prompt and executive method, would not an emergency amendment to the law governing the War Finance Corporation receive quicker action, if its nature were carefully explained, than would be possible with a bill intended broadly to deal with the whole great subject.

My present understanding is that, through no fault of its own, the great credit authorized to the War Finance Corporation[1] lies dormant and that bankers are not specially anxious to have it wake up. Nevertheless, now, rather than four or six months since, is the time when it is needed.

Yours very truly,   William C. Redfield

TLS (WP, DLC).
[1] By an Act of Congress, signed by Wilson on March 3, 1919, the War Finance Corporation was empowered to make advances to any person, firm, corporation, or association in the United States engaged in the business of exporting domestic products to foreign countries, if such person or organization was, in the opinion of the board of directors of the W.F.C. unable to obtain funds upon reasonable terms from banks. Any such advance was to be made only for the purpose of assisting in the exportation of domestic products and was to be limited in amount to "not more than the contract price therefor, including insurance and carrying or transportation charges to the foreign point of destination." The W.F.C. might also make advances to banks, which in turn could make advances to individuals or organizations engaged in such export trade. The W.F.C. was authorized to make advances for these purposes up to a total of $1,000,000,000. See Sec. 9 of 40 *Statutes at Large* 1309. See also the Enclosure printed with N. H. Davis to WW, May 9, 1919 (second letter of that date), Vol. 58.

To Francis Edward Clark

My dear Dr. Clark: [The White House] 31 July, 1919.

Your letter of July 23rd[1] gave me a great deal of pleasure and reassurance. I can assure you that your confidence and approval mean a vast deal to me.

I dare not hope to be present at the Biennial Meeting to which

you so generously invite me, but you may be sure that my heart will go out to them and that I know what I am missing in missing the opportunity to address so great and influential a body on a matter so near my heart.   Cordially and sincerely yours,
                                        Woodrow Wilson

TLS (Letterpress Books, WP, DLC).
 ¹ F. E. Clark to WW, July 23, 1919, Vol. 61.

From Newton Diehl Baker, with Enclosure

My dear Mr. President: Washington. July 31, 1919.

I enclose a copy of a letter just received from General Graves, which I feel sure will be interesting to you. I have attached copies of all exclosures [enclosures]¹ except one which is apparently a circular printed in Russian.

I have handed to the Secretary of State, for his files, a copy of a very voluminous inquiry² made by our Military Intelligence officers in Siberia into the Czecho-Slovak military situation which takes up the organization of the Czecho-Slovak forces which operated first in Russia and later in Siberia. The report traces their entire course, and attempts to appraise the influences which from time to time dominated their actions. The paper is much too long for your reading, but I have talked with Mr. Lansing about it, and indicated to him that, in my judgment, the report shows with fair conclusiveness that the Czecho-Slovak forces could have gotten out of Russia, but that influence was brought to bear (perhaps by the French who were interested in having them remain in Russia), and that at least a part of their difficulties with the Russians grew out of this changed desire on their part.
                              Respectfully yours,   Newton D. Baker

TLS (WP, DLC).
 ¹ The first of the two attachments was W. S. Graves, "PROCLAMATION, TO THE RUSSIAN PEOPLE," April 21, 1919, T MS (WP, DLC). Graves describes it, as attachment "A," at the beginning of the Enclosure printed as the next document. The second attachment, mentioned as "B" in the following Enclosure, was H. Kelch to W. S. Graves, June 19, 1919, TCL (WP, DLC). Kelch, the Vladivostok agent of the National City Bank of New York, related an incident in which a woman "claiming to be a Russian" had complained to him because the American bank would give her no gold in exchange for American paper currency.
 ² This report, dated April 15, 1919, which Wilson obviously never saw, was entitled "THE CZECHO-SLOVAKS IN RUSSIA. AUGUST, 1919 [sic] * * * TO * * * FEBRUARY, 1919," and was prepared by Laurence Bradford Packard, then a captain in the United States Army attached to General Graves' headquarters. Packard, whose graduate studies in history had been interrupted by the war, received the Ph.D. degree from Harvard University in 1921. He taught at the University of Rochester, 1913-1925, and at Amherst College from 1925 to 1955 and was also, from time to time, a lecturer or visiting professor of history at various universities, including Harvard and Yale. He died in 1955.
    The original of Packard's report is filed with Security Classified Reports, Studies, Monographs, and Other Records Relating to the Activities of the American Expeditionary Forces in Siberia ("Historical File"), Records of the American Expeditionary Forces, Siberia, 1918-1920, No. 21-23.7, Records of the United States Army Overseas Opera-

tions and Commands, RG 395, DNA. A copy of this report is filed with NDB to RL, July 28, 1919, RG 59, 861.00/6052, DNA. Another copy was at some time transferred from the records of the War Department, RG 165, DNA, to the Historical Section of the War Department and is now missing in that collection. The copy in the Records of the American Expeditionary Forces, Siberia, was declassified on March 12, 1947.

The Packard Report was based upon the reports of U. S. Army intelligence officers attached to the so-called Czech Legion, reports obtained from officers of that legion, and other sources. Packard carefully listed what he called his "authorities." Packard's report was 114 pages in length, and he, himself, provided the best short summary of it, as follows:

"This sketch is based on very limited and really inadequate material. So far as possible an effort has been made to present the main aspects of a complicated subject, with a proper sense of proportion and chronology. Some bias may be traced in the emphasis upon certain features, but so far as the actual evidence is available it is difficult to get away from the following conclusions,—which may perhaps, in the light of more evidence, fail of substantiation:

"1. The Czecho-Slovak claims that they were treacherously attacked by Bolsheviks, German Agents and war prisoners are unfounded in fact.

"2. The Czecho-Slovak Armies never needed 'rescue': their original purpose of withdrawal could have been safely accomplished.

"3. The Czecho-Slovaks did not fully abide by their promise to surrender their arms and keep out of Russian internal affairs.

"4. The Czecho-Slovak military achievements have been much overrated; during the period when they were so 'brilliantly successful,' they met with practically no serious military opposition. When they finally encountered real enemy organization and fighting spirit there was a distinct limitation of their glory and exploits."

Baker aptly characterizes the report in his letter to Wilson.

The Packard Report is one of the most important documents of this period, and, if it had been used by scholars, would have long ago conclusively answered some important questions, for example:

(1) Whether the Czech Legion in Siberia was in fact threatened by the Red Army and by former German and Austro-Hungarian prisoners of war and had to be "rescued" if it was to survive. Packard says emphatically "no."

(2) The responsibility for starting the fight between the Czechs and the Bolsheviks at Cheliabinsk on May 14, 1918, which set off general hostilities between the two contending forces and, in fact, precipitated the Russian Civil War. Packard ascribes full responsibility for this incident to the Czech forces.

(3) The general disposition of the leaders of the Czech Legion. Packard describes them as in no way feeling beleaguered or threatened but, on the contrary, as being confident and aggressive in the knowledge that they were the only effective organized military force in all of Siberia.

(4) Whether the Czech Legion was a pawn in the hands of British and French leaders, on the one side, who hoped to use the legion to reestablish the eastern front, and, on the other side, of Masaryk and Beneš, who cooperated with the British and French in return for their diplomatic recognition of the Czech National Council. Packard concludes that this was true.

The great mystery is why scholars have failed to find and use the Packard Report and, particularly, the important reports upon which it was based. This lapse has finally been ended by Betty Miller Unterberger, *The United States, Revolutionary Russia, and the Rise of Czechoslovakia* (Chapel Hill, N. C., 1989).

E N C L O S U R E

Vladivostok, June 21, 1919.

Confidential.

From: The Commanding General.
To: The Adjutant General of the Army, Washington, D. C.
Subject: Conditions in Siberia.

1. The situation with reference to guarding the railroad has not materially improved since my last report. During the last ten days we have had more or less trouble in the sector between Spasskoe

and Ussuri. I have issued a proclamation (copy hereto attached, marked "A") with reference to our object and duty connected with guarding the railway, and have sent sufficient copies to all Commanding Officers so that people in the neighboring villages and all anti-Kolchak people have complete information as to our intentions regarding the use of American troops. Where there is interference with the railroad, I contemplate inflicting punishment on the party or parties interfering with the railroad. This is not difficult where bodies of armed troops interfere with the road, because we go to their villages and inflict punishment there or anywhere we can find them. This seems to have the effect of making them respect our duties and obligations. We have had no trouble in the Souchan [Suchan] Sector for almost one month. The last week we have had no interference in the Spasskoe-Ussuri Sector, but it is too early to state definitely what their intentions are with reference to the railroad. The Japanese, south of Spasskoe, have recently been having a great deal more trouble than we have. The Bolsheviks have one of our men a prisoner. We are making every effort to get him and I hope for success. The question as to disposition of Bolshevik prisoners falling into our hands is a rather difficult one. The Japanese and Russians undoubtedly kill some of their prisoners. Private Floyd M. Pickel, Company "G," 31st Infantry, states that on the evening of June 14th, at Spasskoe, he saw two Japanese sentinels bringing a Russian prisoner past the station. As the prisoner passed three American soldiers, he, the prisoner, asked for help, whereupon the Japanese sentinel in the rear ran up and kicked him across the car track. Several people followed the prisoner and his guard until they went behind a fence surrounding a Japanese storehouse. A short time after this, Private Pickel's attention was attracted by a noise back of this fence. He went to the fence and looking over he recognized the prisoner being dragged off by one of the sentinels. The prisoner was apparently dead. He asked a Russian, who was at the fence, what had happened and was informed that the Japanese sentinel, walking in the rear of the prisoner, bayoneted the prisoner in the back and when the prisoner fell stuck his bayonet through the neck. The general belief is that a mere statement that a man is a Bolshevik, is, generally speaking, enough to cause him to disappear. The Russian soldiers are very bitter and the so-called Russian "Intelligentzia" are launching a campaign against Americans because we put two Bolshevik wounded in our hospital and have eleven prisoners. They claim we are feeding Bolsheviks and looking out for their sick. General Horvath[1] came to see me a few days ago and asked me to designate

[1] That is, Gen. Dmitrii Leonidovich Horvat, or Horvath.

a couple of American officers to go out with Russian columns sent after Bolsheviks. He said that he was as much opposed to the past action of Russian troops as I was and it was his desire to stop it. He thought the mere presence of Americans would cause Russian troops to desist from their former treatment of the people. I informed him that under certain conditions I would have no objection, i.e., if he were operating against men who had actually interfered with the operation of the railroad, or against Americans, I did not consider it wise for American officers to be attached to Russian troops. He has not asked for American officers to be attached to Russian troops. He has not asked for any American officers, so I assume he was not [?] satisfied with my reply. As to my proclamation above referred to, Mr. Smith,[2] American Representative, Inter-Allied Railway Committee, informed me yesterday that the Technical Board, now here from Harbin, had a meeting with the Inter-Allied Railway Committee yesterday morning and informed them my proclamation was exactly what they thought ought to be followed in all sections of the railway and they would like to see it put up in all railway stations as outlining the policy of Allied Troops. While apparently General Horvath, acting head of the Inter-Allied Railway Committee, concurred in this view, I feel certain in my own mind that he will try to block the proposed action of the Inter-Allied Railway Committee. This proclamation has been criticized by the Russians, not only here, but in Omsk, because I did not mention specifically the Bolsheviks could not interfere with the railroad.

2. The action of the Koltchak governmental class here is such that in my mind the Department should have a clear statement of the results of this action. While the railroad is operating under what is known as the Railroad Agreement,[3] the Russian military practically and absolutely controls the shipment of supplies and the transportation of persons. By this means this Army Officer class is depriving the peasants in various sections of the country of the absolute necessities of life. They have established what they call passport control stations and examine all passengers to determine whether they are authorized to travel on the train. In these peasant villages no one has authority to give them permission to travel on the trains, consequently they are deprived of this privilege. If caught on the train without passports they are put in jail. There are thousands and thousands of peasants who have no means to prevent so-called Bolsheviks from coming into their

[2] That is, Charles Hadden Smith.
[3] About which, see FLP to RL, Dec. 21, 1918, n. 1, and FLP to RL, Dec. 30, 1918, n. 4, both in Vol. 53.

country if they so desire, who have not been permitted to have one pound of food shipped to them since the Allies took over the guarding of the railway. Nearly two months ago the peasants in the Olga District selected two representatives to come to Vladivostok, with the object of acquainting the Consular Body of their situation. These two peasants were immediately arrested upon arrival in Vladivostok and are still in jail. Two other representatives were sent down about two weeks ago with the idea of appealing to General Horvath for assistance. They have been here twelve days and General Horvath nor any representative of his would talk to them. This governmental class tries to justify their actions by saying, "they are Bolsheviks." The Koltchak representatives recently requested the British Cruiser "Kent" to go to the Olga District for the purpose of evacuating certain Koltchak adherents. As I see this question, we become a party, by guarding the railroad, to the action of this governmental class in depriving the peasants of food. This naturally causes a resentment not only against Koltchak and his representatives but against all the Allies. Two days ago I was informed by the representatives of the peasants in the Olga District that they did not believe the President of the United States knew the result of the action of U. S. troops in this country. I am convinced in my own mind that there is no possibility of settling this trouble by such oppressive, unjust and inhumane actions as are being committed by the Koltchak representatives here in Eastern Siberia, as outlined above. I know of my own knowledge a case here in Vladivostok where a political prisoner escaped from prison. The Koltchak representatives immediately arrested his wife and have had her in prison for two months. Last week I sent an officer to Colonel Butenko[4] to ask if she was going to be tried, and if so, what the charges were against her. Yesterday this woman came to my office and had a paper where they had released her for one day, ordering her to report to the militia at Nikolsk. This was done so the militia there would arrest her and put her in jail, where they had informed her she would be kept until her husband returned. I know this woman had nothing to do with the escape of her husband, because she was convinced he had been taken out at night and killed and came to my Intelligence Officer after her husband had departed, weeping, and asking the Intelligence Officer to help her find her husband's body.

3. The Semenoff situation[5] in the Transbaikal is temporarily

---

[4] Commander of the fortress at Vladivostok.

[5] That is, Gen. Grigorii Mikhailovich Semenov. P. S. Reinsch to FLP [c. June 14, 1919], printed in FR 1919, Russia, pp. 506-07, explains the "Semenoff situation" as follows: "Trouble which threatened to be serious occurred at Verchneudinsk June 9th and 10th between Americans and Semenoff forces, Colonel Morrow demanded removal

cleared up. Colonel Morrow's[6] controversy with Semenoff has apparently been settled satisfactorily. In my judgment, Semenoff will have to be eliminated before the railroad can operate satisfactorily. If Semenoff were himself a good, honest, and patriotic citizen, which he is not, the removal of his troops would still be necessary because they are composed of Russians, Chinamen, Buriats, and Mongols, and live by graft, theft, and money received from the Japanese. The Japanese can probably control him. They say they will, but this must be determined by future developments. I very much fear Semenoff is doing exactly what they want him to do. Rumors constantly float around that the Japanese military in Transbaikal have been interested in sending supplies for civilian use to that section in military trains and passed as military supplies. I am unable to establish this fact, but believe it is true. Japanese headquarters here has recently shown an inclination to cooperate and work harmoniously with us. I know so well the object, desires, and intentions of the Japanese military in this section of the world, that I am convinced, if they really desire to work with the United States, it is because they have been forced to this action from Tokio.

4. The Omsk Government recently called in all the Kerensky money. The reason given was the flood of Karenskies which had been issued by the Bolsheviks in European Russia. The Central Imperial Bank has published the results of this action. The Roubles turned in from the various towns are as follows:

PLACE.	ROUBLES.	PLACE.	ROUBLES.
Barnaul	23,000,000	Ekaterinburg	42,975,000
Irkutsk	26,198,000	Krasnoyarsk	11,500,000
Novo-Nikolaevsk	16,435,000	Perm	40,668,000
Tobolsk	8,400,000	Tiumen	11,760,000
Tomsk	12,439,000	Ufa	9,913,000
Cheliabinsk	28,200,000	Chita	19,840,000
Yakutsk	11,940,000	Shadrinsk	16,782,000
Syzran	171,000	Vladivostok	147,000,000
Omsk	37,000,000	Semipalatinsk	5,543,000

It will be seen from this table that Vladivostok is far and above all the other towns. This is not unexpected to me. If there is anything dishonorable or discreditable going on in Siberia, Vladivostok

---

of Semenoff armoured train and called out troops to enforce demand. Train was finally removed. Semenoff claims trouble was misunderstanding, brought about purposely by Russian-Jewish interpreters with American forces. He adds that he has now been officially notified of Allied control of railroad, will see that nothing of the kind occurs again and will do all in his power to work in accord with Allied forces and railroad engineers. Mr. Stevens called upon Semenoff today and was given assurance."

[6] That is, Col. Charles H. Morrow.

will certainly have its share. If some of these speculators realized that Kerensky money could be printed and passed, there is no doubt in my mind they would soon establish a printing press. Russian army officers parade the streets of Vladivostok, apparently without any means of support, and without any occupation, but apparently are able to give banquets, go to cafes, and spend all kinds of money. If this money comes from the Omsk government, there is an immense leak somewhere.

5. The propaganda against the United States continues, but is not so bad as formerly, because, in my judgment, General Horvath and Colonel Butenko, the Fortress Commander, are trying to stop it. There is quite a little evidence that this propaganda is now being directed by the old German agents who were here representing Germany when the armistice was signed and who are still here. Mr. Kurtif,[7] a Russian, Secretary of the Chamber of Commerce, has stated that this is a fact but it is purely local, that these people have no connection whatever with the German Government. There is no question in my mind that these German representatives, the Japanese military, and the Russian army officer class, with a few exceptions, have an understanding as to their course of action. As to whether this extends beyond Lake Baikal, I am not able to say. I have just learned that the Russian (Professor Spalvin,)[8] who is in charge of censorship and with whom we have been working, has been writing, under an assumed name, many of the anti-American articles. The operations of this clique are sometimes very crude, but with the newspapers subsidized they can easily get the intelligent class to believe anything they say. There are many evidences of their deliberate and wilful intention to insult American soldiers, with the idea of spreading propaganda against the Americans by representing that the American soldiers attack them without any reason. My only fear is that the American soldiers will soon become so prejudiced that there will be cause for their complaints, but so far this has not been the case and they have acted in a way that has met with my absolute approval. I inclose copy of a letter written by the Agent of the National City Bank here (hereto attached, marked "B") which also tends to confirm the belief that there is strong propaganda against Americans directed by German agents. Mr. Kelch, the Agent of the National City Bank, had previously informed me that there were many evidences of this propaganda. False and incorrect reports are constantly being sent out from Japanese headquarters, but when their attention is called to this they

[7] He cannot be further identified.
[8] Evgenii Genrikovich Spal'vin, scholar of the Japanese language, culture, and history.

profusely apologize and claim a nonintentional error, when I, of course, must then say their explanation is satisfactory. By these reports they accomplish their object, even if they deny it later, because their papers all over Eastern Siberia and Japan publish these reports but never publish the denial. As a sample of the action of the Japanese, their Communique of June 20th stated:—"The American detachment which was sent to Uspenka was obliged to retire, sustaining a loss of 5 killed and 14 wounded." This statement is not only false, but the Japanese had our Communique giving the facts in their headquarters when this false communique was given out to all the Allied representatives here, and undoubtedly sent to Japan. I have directed the Intelligence Officer to try and get complete information as to the extent of this combination above referred to and the object.

6. The papers are commenting on a London dispatch of June 6th in which Mr. Winston Churchill, in the House of Commons, on that date said, with reference to Siberia, "that the British Government had furnished no men but had equipped the army with munitions, and went on to say that financial assistance had been given to the Omsk Government as an honorable obligation, seeing that the British Government had called it into being for our own aid at a time when necessity demanded it." This statement accords with the general belief in Eastern Siberia that General Knox,[9] British Mission, took a prominent part in putting Koltchak in power. So far as I know, this statement in the House of Commons is the first acknowledgment of that fact. General Knox is very anti-American and has no hesitancy in expressing openly his antagonism to President Wilson's views. He has never so expressed himself to me, but Americans have told me that they have heard him so express himself. General Knox evidently thinks that the Ambassador in Tokio and I are responsible for the policy of the United States in Siberia. I make this statement because of his request to Mr. Caldwell,[10] the American Consul, to send a cablegram requesting that both of us be removed, as we were not representing the views of the United States. As General Knox is so closely associated with Admiral Koltchak and the Omsk Government, it is possible that he had something to do with the anti-American feeling which exists in the Government class. He, however, apparently denies this, as I one day informed Colonel Summerville,[11] representing the British Mission, that I was getting tired of this pin-pricking from Britishers here in Vladivostok and if they desire to fight the United States' represen-

9 That is, Maj. Gen. Alfred William Fortescue Knox.
10 That is, John Kenneth Caldwell.
11 Col. John Arthur Coghill Somerville.

tatives to come out in the open, like I expected Anglo-Saxons to do, and we could have a show down, then I felt we would have a better understanding. He telegraphed my statement to General Knox, who requested that I specify what I meant. This I did in writing, but did not make official the fact that General Knox had asked Mr. Caldwell to ask for my recall. When I gave my reply to Colonel Summerville, I told him that I knew of this and could have made it official but thought it better to leave that disagreeable incident off paper. Colonel Summerville said he was very glad I had. I have heard nothing more of my statement. I received from Colonel Summerville most hearty cooperation, as well as from his successor, Colonel Grogan,[12] who is now in charge of the British Mission. They have shown a desire to cooperate and work harmoniously. I can not say so much for the British Mission while in charge of General Knox and General Blair.[13]

(signed) Wm. S. Graves.

TCL (WP, DLC).
[12] Col. Edward Ion Beresford Grogan.
[13] Brig. Gen. James Molesworth Blair, deputy chief of the British Military Mission in Siberia.

Three News Reports

[Aug. 1, 1919]

NEW FOR U. S. FIRST
On League Question "I Am an American,"
He Tells Wilson.
INSISTS ON RESERVATIONS

The fight for and against the league of nations covenant has now reached a point where both sides are awaiting developments and not attempting to force matters. Administration leaders, like Senator Hitchcock, for example, still claim to be confident that opposition will dwindle in the end and attach great importance to what they describe as lack of unity among their opponents as to what plans for reservations or amendments should be followed.

Leaders of the opposition, on the other hand, claim to have scored heavily during the past week or so because of the effect [fact] that President Wilson's personal appeals to individual senators have made no impression and because the country is believed to be veering away from its earlier vague but sincere approval of "a league of nations," irrespective of the exact form it takes.

Letters from all parts of the country show that the people are now becoming more concerned over the effect the league may have on the United States than on world conditions.

President Wilson yesterday continued his conferences with Republican senators regarding the treaty and the league covenant. He talked with Senator New, of Indiana, known to be strongly opposed to the covenant. After the conference Senator New said:

"I told the President I would not vote for the league without reservations. I also told him I did not want to give the impression I would vote for the league even with reservations, because they must be of a kind that will protect the things I think need to be protected."

Senator New emphasized that the league of nations is a contract about to be entered into by the nations, and that it is so indefinitely worded that many of the contracting parties are disagreeing about what it means. He told the President he was sure the league covenant could not be put through without reservations.

Senator New said he did not question the intention of the President to devise a means of preventing warfare in future."What I do question," said Senator New, "is your method of arriving at a way of preventing warfare." The President told Senator New that he really was not concerned so much about the proposed reservations of the Senate, but that he was concerned about the fact that if this country makes reservations others will do likewise and the whole league would be endangered.

To this Senator New replied that he could not see the justice of the argument that the United States forego its case and yield on vital questions of principle because of its fear that other nations might insist on stating their cases. Senator New also told the President he was a nationalist first. "I am an American" he said. "My first concern is for this country. The other nations come afterward with me. I am not an internationalist and I don't believe in any supergovernment or superstate. I believe in the U. S. A."

The President emphasized to Senator New the bankrupt conditions of the world and the appeal the other nations are making to the United States to save them. He asked Mr. New if he did not think it right for the United States to take the lead in saving these distressed nations.

"I think we should help them all we can," said Senator New, "but I don't think we should take on a greater load than we can carry. It is like going to the aid of a drowning man. If the rescuer is not careful he will drown himself."

Regarding the Shantung affair, the President told Senator New that he did not like the arrangement, but that certain concessions had been agreed to by the Japanese, which would make the arrangement look a little less harsh when they were made public. The President intimated that he had information that the Japanese would make a formal statement on Shantung in a few days. But the President did not intimate that he expected the Japanese to name a definite date for the return of Shantung to China.

Senator Watson was to have gone to the White House yesterday, but could not arrange his engagements to permit it, so he will confer with the President today instead.

Senator Keyes conferred with the President yesterday.

About this visit, Senator Keyes said he had passed a very pleasant hour and that the ratification of the treaty was very frankly discussed. He also said that he was of course not at liberty to quote anything the President said, but that he left the White House if anything more fully convinced than ever that several "reservations," or, to use a word which he understood the President prefers, "interpretations," should be adopted. The senator said:

"The Senate, notwithstanding the persistent misrepresentation on the part of some, is, in my opinion, most anxious to meet fairly and squarely the situation confronting the world, of which this country is a most important part, and that partisan politics will receive slight recognition."

Pressed for a further statement, the senator added: "I feel that we should not assume tremendous reponsibilities, new to our traditions and policies, without at least having it made clear, so far as possible, what those responsibilities are. We must not make a false start.

"Whatever we agree to do we must do. Certainly if the language in certain articles of the treaty is not clear or is subject to various interpretations, now is the time to record our interpretation and understanding. This interpretation could be made in Washington by Americans and not in Geneva by other nations no matter how apparently friendly."

Printed in the *Washington Post*, August 1, 1919.

[*Aug. 1, 1919*]

WILSON FEARS CRASH IN EUROPE IF TREATY WAITS
Tells Senator Watson That Some Nation Might Precipitate
a Grave Crisis.

Washington, Aug. 1.—Chaos might reign in Europe before the League of Nations could be put in working order if Senators demanding reservations to the Peace Treaty were allowed their way, President Wilson fears. He indicated his fear today to Senator Watson of Indiana, his only Republican caller during the day.

The President told Mr. Watson that he was afraid the whole of next Winter would be required to bring about final ratification of the treaty and get the League going as an effective bulwark against trouble if the Senate opened the doors to reservations. In the meantime, Mr. Wilson pointed out, there might come a breakdown in Europe of some nation which easily might precipitate a crisis. If the League were promptly set up, he said, wabbly nations would be taken care of and bolstered up through the precarious days of the near future.

The delay, the President told Mr. Watson, would come through the acceptance by foreign nations of the adoption of reservations here as an opportunity to put their own interpretations on certain treaty provisions. Long parleys would be required, in his opinion, to reconcile conflicts and get matters back to the point where they are today.

Senator Watson dissented, telling the President that he did not believe American interests should be sacrificed or endangered just to prevent other nations from expressing their understanding of the League. He called Mr. Wilson an internationalist, but this name the President declined to accept. He said that he was not an internationalist.

The Indiana Senator spoke out vigorously for reservations, both to the League covenant and the Shantung provision of the treaty, and told the President that he could not support the treaty unless such reservations were made.

"I believe that our effectiveness in the war and a great deal of what you were able to accomplish at the Peace Conference were due to the independent position the United States occupied," said Mr. Watson.

He found the President partly in agreement on this, he said, but it was urged upon him again that conditions in Europe make it imperative that the United States join in the work of stabilization without delay.

Russia, the President is said to have told Mr. Watson, would have to be left to work out her own salvation.

The President repeated to the Senator what he had told others on Shantung, that unless Japan speedily made clear the status in which the peace conferees left the matter, the President would feel compelled to take the American people into his confidence by disclosing facts in his possession.

Meanwhile, many Senators are drawing up their own reservations. When the question comes before the reservationsts for some union on a program that could be put through, it is expected that a wide variance will be shown in degree and wording.

Leaders of those insisting on reservations as the price of their

support for the treaty were encouraged, they said today, in the belief that before long a common ground would be found which
would prove so unassailable that President Wilson would be convinced beyond doubt that he must yield to the demands of the reservationists or lose the treaty entirely.

Week-end conferences are in prospect to canvass the whole situation and plan further moves for next week, when a revival of the
Senate debate is looked for.

Printed in the *New York Times*, Aug. 2, 1919.

FOOD PROBLEM AT THE FORE
President, Cabinet and Congress Tackling Cost of Living

[Aug. 1, 1919]

Washington, Aug. 1.—The question of the cost of living has now
become the absorbing problem in Government and Congressional
circles.

This was brought home with force today when President Wilson
called upon the House of Representatives to abandon its plans for
a recess until September and remain in Washington to take up the
matter.

It is generally believed that President Wilson will abandon temporarily his proposed trip to the Pacific coast and remain at his post
because of the crisis created by recent developments.

Both in the House, where it was voted to assent to the President's request, and in the Senate the cost of living was the subject
of discussion.

It became known during the day that at the Cabinet meeting
yesterday a special committee was named to consider means of reducing the high cost of living, and report to the Cabinet Tuesday
when further steps will be taken.

This committee is composed of Walter [Walker] D. Hines, Direc-
tor of Railroads; F. B. [William B.] Colver of the Federal Trade
Commission, and Assistant Secretary Leffingwell of the Treasury
Department.

Attorney General Palmer and Postmaster General Burleson were
among those who conferred today with President Wilson. Mr. Palmer, it is said, went over the main features of the conference which
took place at his office yesterday and promised the President that
there would be an early report.

It was reported that the Government might endeavor to bring
about decreased prices of breadstuffs by selling wheat for domestic
consumption at 75 cents to $1 below the guaranteed price of $2.26,

the Government meeting the difference out of the $1,000,000,000 guarantee fund provided by Congress.

This policy has been discussed at some length at the conference with Attorney General Palmer, and, while no definite decision had been reached, there was much sentiment for the adoption of such a course. The opinion was expressed by some that such a reduction in wheat prices to the consumer would do more to bring about a general reduction of living costs than almost any other policy that might be pursued.

Strength was given to the reports that action was to be taken to reduce wheat prices, by the announcement that Julius Barnes, head of the United States Grain Corporation, who is said to be opposed to such a policy, had been summoned to Washington to take part in the conference Tuesday with Attorney General Palmer and other officials. As the proposition stands, it is said, cheaper wheat will be realized soon unless the opponents of this policy are able to convince the President that it is unsound economically.

There has been considerable agitation in the House of Representatives in favor of selling wheat for domestic consumption at a loss to the Government from the guaranteed price and the indications are that the course, if adopted, will be favorably received in legislative circles.

The President and the officials who made up the conference in Attorney General Palmer's offices yesterday are determined also to get at hoarders, profiteers and speculators if the law can be made effective in that connection. Statements were made at yesterday's conference, it is understood, that hoarding for speculative purposes had become almost a mania and was in no small measure responsible for the tremendous increases in cost to the ultimate consumer. . . .

Printed in the *New York Times*, August 2, 1919.

To William Bauchop Wilson, with Enclosure

My dear Mr. Secretary: [The White House] 1 August, 1919.

The enclosed memorandum, as you will see, is not new. It has been lying on my desk for some time, and much of the subject matter of it was covered in our recent conversation. I am sending it to you now, in order to get your judgment with regard to paragraphs three and four, which I would very much appreciate.

Cordially and faithfully yours,   Woodrow Wilson

TLS (Letterpress Books, WP, DLC).

E N C L O S U R E

From James Thomson Shotwell

MEMORANDUM FOR THE PRESIDENT.

July 16th, 1919.

In accordance with your instructions concerning the preparation for the International Labor Conference, I have made a careful survey of the situation in Washington, and beg to report as follows:

1. The Department of Labor should prepare studies of the subject matter of the agenda (the eight hour day; unemployment, women and children in industry). This can be done with perfect propriety as a normal activity of the Department, even if no Conference were ever called. The Department, however, is not prepared to do this without word from the President.

2. I strongly advise that Senator Kenyon and Congressman Smith (Michigan) and Nolan,[1] heads of the Labor Committees of both Houses, be sent for for a short conference, as they have expressed a willingness to cooperate by helping to find a way to bring Congress to pass appropriate measures to secure the success of the Labor Conference. Senator Kenyon might make a statement from the floor, if encouraged.

3. I am convinced from what I have been told here, that the Labor clauses can be used to real advantage in gaining support for the Treaty. Radicals like Mrs. Raymond Robins,[2] President of the Woman's Trade Union League, a bitter opponent of the Treaty and even of the League of Nations, have already promised to reconsider their opposition if it endangers the Labor Clauses.

I have discussed this phase of the question with several in New York and Washington, but especially with Mr. Edward P. Costigan,[3] of the Tariff Board, who is both an ardent supporter of the Treaty, and has the confidence of those who oppose it.

4. I suggest that as a provisional measure, at least until the ratification of the treaty, a Committee of Citizens be either called by the President or given his endorsement. The membership of such a Committee might be discussed with Senator Kenyon, but I suggest, tentatively, some such leading citizens as the following, with power to add to their numbers:

> William Howard Taft, Chairman,
> Samuel Gompers, Vice Chairman,
> Thomas R. Chadbourne, Treasurer,[4]
> Samuel M. Lindsay, Secretary,[5]
> Miss Julia Lathrop,[6]
> Edward P. Costigan,

John Mitchell,[7]
Thomas Lamont,
Mrs. Raymond Robins,
Matthew Woll,[8]
Mary Anderson.[9]
Respectfully submitted,   James T. Shotwell

TS MS (WP, DLC).
  [1] William Squire Kenyon, chairman of the Senate Education and Labor Committee; John McMunn C. Smith, Republican, chairman of the House Committee on Labor; and John Ignatius Nolan, Republican of California, a member of that committee.
  [2] That is, Margaret Dreier (Mrs. Raymond) Robins.
  [3] That is, Edward Prentiss Costigan.
  [4] Actually, Thomas Lincoln Chadbourne, Jr.
  [5] That is, Samuel McCune Lindsay.
  [6] That is, Julia Clifford Lathrop.
  [7] At this time, chairman of the New York State Industrial Commission.
  [8] One of the vice-presidents of the American Federation of Labor.
  [9] Mary Anderson, Assistant Director of the Woman in Industry Service of the Department of Labor, which had been established in July 1918 to advise the Secretary of Labor and to coordinate the efforts of various agencies and departments with regard to the employment of women in industry. When the Service was transformed into the Women's Bureau of the Labor Department in July 1920, Miss Anderson was appointed as its director and served in that position until 1944.

Two Letters to Newton Diehl Baker

My dear Mr. Secretary: The White House 1 August, 1919.

At last I have read what I ought to have read long ago, your letter of the first of July about conscientious objectors.[1] I have already orally approved of the action proposed for the first group, and now that I have read the document, I am prepared to approve the whole programme suggested. Please pardon my long delay and temporary oversight.

Cordially and faithfully yours,   Woodrow Wilson

  [1] It is printed at that date in Vol. 61.

My dear Baker: The White House 1 August, 1919.

I have your letter of July 26th about the boats owned by the Panama Railroad, and want to say at once that I am inclined to agree with your judgment about them. If you will keep an eye on the matter, I shall wish to be in at the final determination. Thank you very much indeed for your careful memorandum about it.

Cordially and faithfully yours,   Woodrow Wilson

TLS (N. D. Baker Papers, DLC).

To Alexander Mitchell Palmer

My dear Palmer: The White House 1 August, 1919.

Thank you for your letter enclosing the letter of Mr. Clarence Darrow.[1] I entirely agree with your judgment about the suggestion with regard to Debs, and shall hope to consult with you later as to the policy we ought to adopt.

Cordially and faithfully yours,   Woodrow Wilson

TLS (A. M. Palmer Papers, DLC).
    [1] AMP to WW, July 30, 1919.

To Frederick Huntington Gillett

My dear Mr. Speaker: [The White House] 1 August 1919.

The Director General of Railroads informs me that the situation with reference to the railroads is growing so critical every hour that I hope it will be possible for the House to postpone its recess until some definite action is taken upon the recommendations contained in my letter to Mr. Esch. Officials of the Government have been in consultation with reference to the problems growing out of the high cost of living, upon which I expect recommendations to be made within a fortnight. I sincerely trust that the proposed recess of Congress may be postponed at least until such time as we may know definitely the problems which confront us, growing out of this intricate situation.

Cordially and sincerely yours,   Woodrow Wilson[1]

TLS (Letterpress Books, WP, DLC).
    [1] Wilson sent the same letter, *mutatis mutandis*: WW to F. W. Mondell, Aug. 1, 1919, TLS (Letterpress Books, WP, DLC). Frank Wheeler Mondell, Republican of Wyoming, was the Majority Leader in the House of Representatives.

To John Jacob Esch[1]

My dear Mr. Esch: [The White House] 1 August, 1919.

I take the liberty of enclosing a copy of a letter[2] which I have just received from Mr. Walker D. Hines, the Director General of Railroads, and which I am sure you will agree with me in thinking contains matter for very serious thought and for action also.

May I not say that I concur in the suggestions which Mr. Hines makes in the two concluding paragraphs of his letter? I hope that it will be possible for your Committee to consider and recommend legislation which will provide a body of the proper constitution, authorized to investigate and determine all questions concerning the wages of railway employees, and which will also make the decisions of that body mandatory upon the rate-making body and provide, when necessary, increased rates to cover any recommended increases in wages and, therefore, in the cost of operating the railroads. In view also of the indisputable facts with regard to the increased cost of living, I concur in Mr. Hines' suggestion that the legislation undertaken should authorize the body thus set up to make its findings with regard to wage increases retroactive to the first of August, 1919, at any rate to the extent that that tribunal may regard reasonable and proper, in order to give real relief to the employees concerned.

I need not, I am sure, urge upon you the importance of this matter, which seems vital from more than one point of view, and I hope that you will think this form of action the proper and necessary one.　　　Cordially and sincerely yours,　　Woodrow Wilson[3]

TLS (Letterpress Books, WP, DLC).
　[1] To repeat, Republican congressman from Wisconsin and chairman of the House Committee on Interstate and Foreign Commerce.
　[2] W. D. Hines to WW, July 31, 1919.
　[3] Wilson sent the same letter, *mutatis mutandis*: WW to A. B. Cummins, Aug. 1, 1919, TLS (Letterpress Books, WP, DLC). Albert Baird Cummins, Republican of Iowa, was chairman of the Senate Committee on Interstate Commerce.

To William Gibbs McAdoo

My dear Mac:　　　　　　　　　[The White House] 1 August, 1919.

I am very much cheered by your letter of yesterday about the action of the Executive Committee of the League to Enforce Peace. It will help immensely.

We were disappointed that we did not get a glimpse of you and Nell. I hope something will bring you both down soon. We miss you both immensely, as I need not tell you.

I also have your suggestion about urging the House not to adjourn, but unfortunately it had adjourned and the Senate had concurred, without my being consulted, and the thing is done. I think from one or two editorials that I have seen that the attention of the country is being called to the insincerity and farce of the whole Republican profession with regard to a programme of public service, and I think we can be certain that it won't escape notice anywhere. We are hoping to do something—the little that we can do by federal pressure—with regard to the cost of living, and we can at least emphasize the whole business by our investigations and pressure.

In haste, with affectionate messages from us all and dearest love to Nell,　　　　　Affectionately yours,　　Woodrow Wilson

TLS (Letterpress Books, WP, DLC).

To Vance Criswell McCormick

My dear McCormick: [The White House] 1 August, 1919.

I received your letter of July 24th[1] about the winding up and the transferrence of the duties of the War Trade Board, and cannot let the matter pass without saying how high a value I have put upon your services in this great matter, as well as upon the services of your colleagues, and how thoroughly I have admired the devotion, the intelligence, and the statesmanlike breadth of the way in which the whole matter has been conducted under your direction. Critics can make no hole in it, and those of us who are on the inside know how to value and admire what has been done.

With warmest regard and sincere congratulation,

Faithfully yours,   Woodrow Wilson

TLS (Letterpress Books, WP, DLC).
[1] V. C. McCormick to WW, July 24, 1919, TLS (WP, DLC).

To Thomas William Lamont

My dear Lamont: The White House 1 August, 1919.

I am sure I need never explain to you why I am delayed in replying to letters, but I am nevertheless sorry not to have acknowledged sooner your letter of the 25th of July.[1] I thank you sincerely for every ray of light you shed on the present perplexed and somewhat distressing situation, and you do shed many that help me to see the path.

In unavoidable haste,

Cordially and sincerely yours,   Woodrow Wilson

TLS (T. W. Lamont Papers, MH-BA).
[1] It is printed at that date in Vol. 61.

To Robert Heberton Terrell

My dear Judge Terrell: [The White House] 1 August, 1919.

Thank you for your letter about Mr. John F. Costello, the Recorder of Deeds.[1] I have great confidence in Mr. Costello and am very glad indeed to get such testimony as to his friendly and helpful services.   Sincerely yours,   Woodrow Wilson

TLS (Letterpress Books, WP, DLC).
[1] H. B. Terrell to WW, July 28, 1919.

To Frank William Taussig

My dear Taussig: [The White House] 1 August, 1919.

Just a line, the brevity of which you will understand, to thank you with all my heart for your personal letter of July 24th,[1] which touched and pleased me mightily. I think you cannot know how I value the approval of such a man as I know you to be.

    Cordially and faithfully yours, Woodrow Wilson

TLS (Letterpress Books, WP, DLC).
 [1] It is printed at that date in Vol. 61.

To Norman Hapgood

My dear Hapgood: [The White House] 1 August, 1919.

Your letters[1] are most informing and helpful, and I hope that you will know that they are appreciated, even when I do not have the time or opportunity to send you direct acknowledgements of them.

I am glad that you are keeping your eye and your thought on the Russian situation. It is the most difficult now in sight, and the direct lights and sidelights you throw on it in your dispatches are very valuable.

In haste, with warmest regard and best wishes,

    Faithfully yours, Woodrow Wilson

TLS (Letterpress Books, WP, DLC).
 [1] Attached to the carbon copy of this letter in WP, DLC, are N. Hapgood to RL, July 12 and 13, 1919, CCL (WP, DLC).

To Harry Augustus Garfield

Dear Garfield: The White House 1 August, 1919.

Thank you for your two letters of July 29th. It was thoughtful of you to send me the one about Jessie and Frank, and it is delightful to get news of them directly from you.

Thank you also for the letter about turning over the files of the Fuel Administration to the Department of the Interior.[1] You do these things so thoroughly that you leave me nothing to worry about.

With the warmest regards to you all,

    Cordially and faithfully yours, Woodrow Wilson

TLS (H. A. Garfield Papers, DLC).
 [1] H. A. Garfield to WW, July 29, 1919, TLS (WP, DLC).

To Edward Parker Davis

My dear E.P.:   [The White House] 1 August, 1919.

You always understand without explanations being volunteered, and you will know, therefore, that it is not my heart but only my voice that has been silent with regard to the delightful letter and the splendid verses you sent to greet me when I got back.[1] I have read them with real and deep comfort. These are strenuous times, in which I realize the full significance of the old expression about "testing men's souls," and reassurances such as you generously give me are a necessary food for the heart.

The verses about the classmates buried at Princeton were very touching and very stirring at the same time, and the verses read at the Reunion lifted one's thoughts to the real significance of such comings together of old comrades. I bless you for your confidence in me and shall treasure these lines and the little book[2] as among my most heartening possessions.

Mrs. Wilson joins me in affectionate messages to you both.
                    Your devoted friend,   Woodrow Wilson

TLS (Letterpress Books, WP, DLC).
  [1] E. P. Davis to WW, June 24, 1919, ALS (WP, DLC).
  [2] *The Man and the Hour* (Chicago, 1919), a copy of which is in the Wilson Library, DLC.

To William Blackshear Moore[1]

My dear Mr. Moore: The White House 1 August, 1919.

I learn with sincere interest of the booklet which you intend presently to publish in memory of the twenty men of the Class of 1917 who gave their lives to the service of their country during the great war,[2] and I crave the privilege of joining with you and your classmates in paying my tribute of admiration and affection to the men who made this great sacrifice, and of sympathy from the bottom of my heart for those whom they have left behind them, bereaved and lonely. The whole Nation is deeply proud of men like your classmates who did this great thing, and I join in your tribute not only personally as a Princeton man, but also officially as the head of the great military forces of the government, of which we are all so intensely proud.

                    Cordially and sincerely yours,   Woodrow Wilson

TLS (NjP-Ar).
  [1] President of the Class of 1917, Princeton University.
  [2] W. B. Moore to WW, July 26, 1919, TLS (WP, DLC), in which Moore told Wilson about the plans of the Class of 1917 to publish a booklet dedicated to the memory of the

twenty men of that class who had died in the service of their country during the war. Moore asked Wilson for a tribute to their memory to be included in the book.

From Frederick Huntington Gillett

Sir: Washington, D. C. August 1, 1919.

I have received your letter of this date expressing the wish that Congress should not recess at present. I presume it is in lieu of the ordinary method of communicating your views to Congress and will cause it to be read to the House.

I regret that you did not arrive at these conclusions sooner and advise us when the subject was under consideration by Congress some days ago, as of course it will now interfere with many perfected plans. But if as intimated in your letter you expect soon to recommend to us important legislation, I have no doubt that the House will be glad to await and consider the proposals you are preparing.

As to railroad legislation, I supposed by Act of Congress you had now full authority, and one of the reasons of our recess was that the Committee of the House might, uninterrupted by the business of the House, prepare the legislation which will be necessary when your authority ceases.

Respectfully yours,   Fredk H Gillett

TLS (WP, DLC).

From William Cox Redfield

Confidential

Dear Mr. President   Washington Aug. 1. 1919

I write to inform you of a decision not wholly easy to make but at which I have arrived after very careful thought. Long neglected personal affairs which have necessarily been subordinated for over eight years now naturally require care. It seems my clear duty to take up business work again and I trust to be able to do so in such a way as will still permit some general service.

Therefore, let me ask that you kindly release me from duty as Secretary of Commerce as soon as certain matters are worked out—say on October 15th next. Before then I hope to finish my annual report, to prepare the estimates for the coming year and to complete the organization for the census of 1920 in addition to several other departmental matters. May I suggest that publicity of this be deferred until September. During August I hope to get a short rest.

I must add my heartfelt thanks for your unvarying courtesy and kindness to me and my appreciation of your noble purposes. You will not forbid a word also of personal affection and of sincere regret that I may not longer continue to serve in your official family.
Sincerely Yours   William C. Redfield

ALS (WP, DLC).

From Joseph Patrick Tumulty, with Enclosure

Dear Governor: The White House, 1 August 1919.

Mr. Leffingwell has read the Barnes letters. He says, "If the programme outlined in these letters is adopted, it means the end of the campaign to reduce the high cost of living."

I have telegraphed Mr. Branes [Barnes] requesting him to attend the conference at the Attorney General's office on Tuesday. In the meantime, I have held up, as you suggested, the Barnes letters and have so notified Mr. Barnes.   Sincerely yours,   Tumulty

TLS (WP, DLC).

E N C L O S U R E

Russell Cornell Leffingwell to Joseph Patrick Tumulty

MEMORANDUM FOR THE SECRETARY: July 29, 1919.

Once more concerning wheat:

The Treasury cannot undertake to say what the price of wheat should be, nor how the United States Wheat Administrator should perform his duties. I submit merely that Mr. Barnes' letters and public utterances show that it is his definite policy to keep the price of wheat on the basis of $2.26 Chicago in any event, and to do it by buying our exportable surplus with cash taken from the United States Treasury and selling it on credit (very long and very doubtful credit at that) in Europe.

Mr. Barnes' address at the Chamber of Commerce in New York on June 10th at the conference of the trade representatives of the United States Wheat Director is an eloquent and ingenious argument in support of a preconceived determination to maintain wheat prices on the basis of $2.26 Chicago, no more, no less. In this address, page 12, he says:

"It is evident that, with the size of the crop now in sight, that the pressure for marketing will, shortly, force wheat prices in this country back to the Government guarantee basis and that *buying of wheat in large quantities at that basis by the Government will be the decisive factor* in wheat prices of this country, stabilizing them at that Government guarantee level."

In his letter of July 21st to you, Mr. Barnes says, referring to the needs of Europe:

"My point is that, particularly as to wheat and wheat flour, if these countries do not arrange a partial payment, we may, *both in the interests of marketing our crops and of broad humanity*, have to consider extension of complete credit to them."

In his letter of July 23rd to me, Mr. Barnes says:

"Our net exports of wheat and wheat flour for the crop-year just ended July 1st amounted to 301,000,000 bushels, from a crop estimated by the Government to be 918,000,000 bushels. It is quite probable that on a crop now of 1,000,000,000 bushels we would have difficulty in exporting, in view of the new influences, more than 300,000,000 bushels, or say a valuation of $750,000,000.

"There is, of course, always present the possibility of a readjusted lower resale price of wheat at a loss to the National Treasury, between the guarantee price and such lower resale price. This last condition, in view of the shrinkage in our own crop, and in Canada, and in European crops, is far more remote than the popular estimate of two months ago. *It should be avoided in the interest of administration alone until its need is imperatively demonstrated.*

"Summing it all up, and as a veritable guess subject to wide variation because of influences yet to develop, I would say that the probability is that no loss will fall upon the United States Treasury by the resale price of wheat, but that a large amount of the funds which we must take from the Treasury will be returned in the form of foreign obligations at the end of the guarantee period."

On the basis of Mr. Barnes' figures and plans, as indicated in the latter letter, the actual cash outgo from the Treasury from his operations will be $750,000,000, against which he proposes to hand to the Treasury obligations of foreign Governments which will not, it is safe to say, be paid, if at all, for long years to come.

If the whole wheat crop of 1,000,000,000 bushels could be sold for cash at a price reduced by $.75 a bushel, the current cash loss to the Treasury would be the same $750,000,000, and I submit it would be better business, better economics and better humanity.

It will be little comfort to this Administration and to the American people, suffering from the high cost of living at this time, to be obliged to provide in taxes and loans the cash to pay a war price for this staple food product, and to be told that future generations may receive payment from the Poles, Czecho-Slovaks, etc., etc., of the sum of $750,000,000.

Nor will the peoples of Europe be grateful for aid furnished them on such hard terms. European credit is strained to the utmost. The policy of the Wheat Director is to maintain a bread line in Europe. So long as the Governments of Europe can obtain bread without paying for it, they will maintain the bread line. Their people will not go back to work while they are fed without work. European credit should not be used to obtain stuffs consumable in their use. It should be devoted to obtaining raw materials and finished products necessary to restore business activity. To pursue an homely illustration: The Wheat Director's policy is to maintain the bread line; the Treasury's policy is to establish a wood yard where those willing to work may find the means of livelihood.

The question is, not whether the United States shall take a loss on its wheat guarantee, but whether the loss which is inevitable shall be camouflaged by placing in the Treasury obligations of doubtful value which will not be paid, if at all, before the expiration of many years, and at the cost of maintaining the present high cost of living.   (Signed) R. C. Leffingwell

CC MS (WP, DLC).

From James Edward McCulloch and Edwin Courtland Dinwiddie[1]

Washington, D. C.

To the President: August first, Nineteen-nineteen.

The Southern Sociological Congress,[2] in harmony with your deliverance on the subject of mob rule in America, at its meeting in Knoxville, Tenn., May 12, 1919, adopted the following resolution:

"The Southern Sociological Congress strongly condemns lynching and mob rule which are un-American and subversive of law and order. We pledge ourselves to do everything possible to prevent lynching and we call upon the editors of the public press, the ministers, the teachers and other leaders responsible for creating public sentiment to proclaim against this practice which constitutes both a disgrace and menace in our own land and also discredits American democracy abroad; and we urge the immediate exercise of all possible State and Federal power to put a speedy end to these outrages throughout the country."

For the purpose of furthering the movement against lynching our Governing Board, having the same subject under consideration, decided that this matter should be brought to the attention of the Executive Heads of the several States and finally concreted the expression of their judgment in the subjoined resolution which they unanimously approved and to which we respectfully invite your attention:

"In pursuance of the resolution on lynching by the Southern Sociological Congress at its last annual session, in accord with The President's address to the country on this subject, be it resolved that we, on behalf of the constituency of said Congress, earnestly petition The President to call a conference of the Governors of the several States to meet in conference at Washington at such date as he may consider most opportune for the purpose of adopting measures for the prevention of lynching and mob violence.

The Governing Board of the Southern Sociological
        Congress, by
                    Bishop Theodore D. Bratton,
                    Chairman, Miss.
                    James H. Dillard, Va.
                    W. D. Weatherford, N. C.
                    W. W. Alexander, Ga.
                    J. A. McCullough, Ga.
                    Edwin C. Dinwiddie, D. C.
                    J. A. C. Chandler, Va."

We hope you may concur in the wisdom of the conference which we recommend, and that you may see your way clear to lend the weight of your personal and official influence in behalf of a discussion of this very important question which so intimately affects our relations at home and, in this crucial time of World affairs, our standing as a Democracy abroad.

With assurances of our highest consideration and regards, we remain

Very sincerely yours, For the Southern Sociological Congress
                    J. E. McCulloch   Exec. Secy.
                    Edwin C. Dinwiddie   Treasurer.

TLS (WP, DLC).

[1] McCulloch, a Methodist minister and social worker, was the principal founder and educational secretary of the Southern Sociological Congress. Dinwiddie, a Lutheran minister and legislative superintendent of the Anti-Saloon League, was treasurer of the Congress.

[2] About this organization, see WW to S. Axson, April 12, 1918, n. 1, Vol. 47. The members of its Governing Board, listed below, in addition to Dinwiddie, were the Rt. Rev. Dr. Theodore DuBose Bratton, Protestant Episcopal Bishop of Mississippi; James Hardy Dillard, president of the Negro Rural School Fund (commonly known as the Jeanes Fund) and the John F. Slater Fund; Willis Duke Weatherford, president of the Southern College of the Y.M.C.A. in Nashville; Will Winton Alexander, a Methodist minister, founder and leader of the organization soon to be known as the Commission

on Interracial Cooperation; Joseph Allen McCullough, lawyer of Baltimore; and Julian Alvin Carroll Chandler, President of William and Mary College.
    There is a large literature on this, the first important southern movement for racial reform and alleviation. For the best bibliography of the subject, see John T. Kneebone, *Southern Liberal Journalists and the Issue of Race, 1920–1944* (Chapel Hill, N. C., 1985), pp. 280-98.

From Robert Lansing, with Enclosure

My dear Mr. President: [Washington] August 1, 1919.

    I prepared the enclosed instruction to the American Commission in accordance with our talk yesterday afternoon concerning the blockade of the Bolshevik ports in the Baltic which the representatives of the Allied Governments are so desirous of instituting. Will you be good enough to give me your comments or changes in the telegram if it meets generally with your approval?

                         Faithfully yours,   Robert Lansing

CCL (SDR, RG 59, 763.72112/12393, DNA).

E N C L O S U R E

                                              August 1, 1919

    Your 3354, July 27, 12 p.m.[1]
    The President desires me to send the following answer to the message of your British, French, Italian and Japanese colleagues relative to the blockade of Soviet Russia.
    PARAGRAPH (QUOTE) The President is not unmindful of the serious situation which exists in relation to neutral trade in the Baltic with the Russian ports controlled by the Bolsheviks. He has given careful consideration to the arguments advanced in the message transmitted at the request of M. Clemenceau and is not unmindful of their force in support of the proposed interruption of commerce with the ports mentioned. However, while he fully understands the reasons for employing war measures to prevent the importation of munitions and food supplies into the portion of Russia now in the hands of the Bolsheviks, he labors under the difficulty of being without constitutional right to prosecute an act of war such as a blockade affecting neutrals unless there has been a declaration of war by the Congress of the United States against the nation so blockaded.
    PARAGRAPH The landing of troops at Archangel and Murmansk was done to protect the property and supplies of the American and Allied Governments until they could be removed. The sending of troops to Siberia was to keep open the railway for the protection of

Americans engaged in its operation and to make safe from possible German and Austrian attack the retiring Czecho-Slovaks. The furnishing of supplies to the Russians in Siberia, while indicating a sympathy with the efforts to restore order and safety of life and property, cannot be construed as a belligerent act.

PARAGRAPH The President is convinced that, if proper representations are made to the countries neutral during the war, they can be induced to prohibit traffic in arms and munitions with the portions of Russia controlled by the Bolsheviks. The avowed hostility of the Bolsheviks to all governments and the announced program of international revolution make them as great a menace to the national safety of neutral countries as to Allied countries. For any government to permit them to increase their power through commercial intercourse with its nationals would be to encourage a movement which is frankly directed against all governments and would certainly invite the condemnation of all peoples desirous of restoring peace and social order.

PARAGRAPH The President cannot believe that any government, whose people might be in a position to carry on commerce with the Russian ports referred to, would be so indifferent to the opinion of the civilized world as to permit supplies to be exported to those ports directly or indirectly.

PARAGRAPH The President, therefore, suggests that the so-called neutral governments be approached by the Allied and Associated Governments in a joint note setting forth the facts of the case and the menace to such countries and to the world of any increase of the Bolshevik power, and requesting the neutral governments to take immediate steps to prevent trade and commerce with Bolshevik Russia and to give assurances that such policy will be rigorously enforced in conjunction with other governments which are equally menaced. (UNQUOTE)

PARAGRAPH Confidentially I believe that the action proposed by your colleagues, of which the approval of the President is urged, would arouse serious criticism by Congress if the President acted accordingly on the legal ground of having exceeded his constitutional powers and on the politic ground of interference in the domestic affairs of Russia. With the present partisan feeling in Congress, while the ratification of the Treaty of Peace is undecided, any action which would bring about a new controversy or a new excuse for criticism would be manifestly unwise.

PARAGRAPH In carrying out a general policy of non-intercourse with the Bolshevik territory this Government could deny clearance to all American vessels for the Baltic ports referred to as well as passports to persons seeking to visit those regions, and the same action by other governments would accomplish the same purpose as a hostile blockade.

PARAGRAPH You may discreetly use the foregoing arguments in explanation of the President's unwillingness to reverse the decision as to instituting a blockade of Russian ports in the Baltic.[2]

CC MS (SDR, RG 59, 763.72112/12393, DNA).
   [1] H. White to WW, July 27, 1919.
   [2] This was sent, verbatim, as RL to Ammission, No. 2714, Aug. 2, 1919, T telegram (SDR, RG 59, 763.72112/12393, DNA).

From Frank Lyon Polk

Paris August 1st, 1919

Urgent. 3441. Strictly confidential. For the President and Secretary of State. Question of West Thrace[1] was discussed at length by Council of Heads of Delegation yesterday afternoon and vigorous arguments were made by Tardieu and Balfour for giving West Thrace to Greece. A proposed compromise that proclaims Thrace should be made part of the international state of Constantinople was received with great surprise by the French and there is every indication that it will be bitterly fought. It is clear that a deal has been made by the British arbiters. Tittoni admits arrangements with Greece by which Italy is to get Meander Valley in Asia-Minor. In return he is willing to support Greek claims in Thrace but tells us privately he prefers our proposal and hopes that it will be accepted. Debate on that question has been adjourned until Saturday. We would like to know, as soon as possible, if we are authorized to make whatever settlement appears to us the only one possible even to the extent of ceding West Thrace to Greece. Personally, I have no desire or intention of backing such proposal but we merely wish to know the scope of our authority. Commission is unanimously of the opinion that it may be necessary to take a strong position now in regard to the Bulgarian treaty pointing out to other powers that unless absolute justice is done it will be necessary for us to refuse to sign the treaty. Personally, from a very limited examination of the subject, it would seem to me almost desirable to inform the great powers that we are seriously thinking of withdrawing from the negotiations in respect to the Bulgarian and Turkish treaties. It is very evident that these negotiations are being carried on in a spirit of barter and that it is to be in the end a land grabbing scheme. It will be difficult, if not impossible to secure a treaty in either case which will not be subject to gravest criticism by the American people. Do you not think it would be wise to point out to Clemenceau and Balfour our fears and are we

authorized to say that we may withdraw from all further negotiations. It may be that this suggestion would be welcomed by
French, Greeks and Italians as they might then make a division
without a hard fight. Great Britain would probably wish us to remain in the negotiations as she is not disposed to look with favor
on claims of other three. We thought we should point out that
there is a slight chance that this threat, on our part, might be
promptly accepted and for that reason you may prefer to remain a
party to the negotiations on account of the League of Nations
being guarantor of boundaries. Polk.   American Mission.

T telegram (SDR, RG 59, 763.72119/5920, DNA).
    [1] For earlier discussions on this subject, see H. White to WW, July 20 and 22, 1919,
and WW to H. White, July 25, 1919, all in Vol. 61.

Robert Lansing to Joseph Patrick Tumulty

Dear Mr. Tumulty: Washington August 1st, 1919.

The Charge d'Affaires of Belgium[1] has called at the Department
with Dr. P. J. de Strycker,[2] Vice-Rector of the American College
and Associate of the University of Louvain. The subject of their
conversation was the visit of His Eminence Cardinal Mercier, who
will arrive in this country about the 22nd or 23rd of September. He
will attend in Washington a meeting of the Catholic Hierarchy of
America on September 24th. He wants to pay his respects to the
President before doing anything else, even before meeting his colleague Cardinal Gibbons. I understand the President will be back
from his trip before the 22nd or 23rd of September. Will you advise
me whether the President will receive him about that time and
whether he will invite His Eminence to lunch during the time he
will be in Washington.

The Cardinal will not be on an official mission so he probably
will not be treated as a guest of the Government, but in view of his
international reputation and his very great service to the Allied
cause during the war the President might feel inclined to facilitate
the travels of His Eminence around the country to the extent of
providing him with a private car. He intends to travel to the Pacific
Coast and back making various stops en route.

If the President feels inclined to extend this semi-official courtesy I think the Department of State could arrange to pay for it.

If you will advise me of the President's pleasure I will be glad to
see that his wishes are complied with.

                    Faithfully yours,   Robert Lansing.[3]

TLS (WP, DLC).

[1] Charles Symon, Counselor of Legation and Chargé d'Affaires ad interim since March 7, 1919.

[2] The Rev. Peter Joseph De Strycker, Vice Rector of the American College of the Immaculate Conception of the Blessed Virgin Mary, affiliated with the University of Louvain.

[3] "I will be very glad to act upon the Secretary's suggestion with regard to a private car, which of necessity must be paid for by the State Department because I have no funds available for the purpose. I sincerely hope I shall be in Washington when Cardinal Mercier arrives." WW to JPT, Aug. 8, 1919, TL (WP, DLC).

A News Report

[Aug. 2, 1919]

MADE PART OF TREATY

Proposals of 7 Republicans Not Merely Reservations.

The reservation proposal agreed to by seven Republican senators as the basis of ratification of the league of nations covenant[1] is so worded, it became known last night, that the "reservations and understandings" enumerated shall become "a part of the treaty" and shall not stand simply as a detached interpretation by the Senate.

While some of the sponsors of the program regard it as merely interpretive in effect, clarifying the language of the covenant without changing the meaning of any provision, others of the seven believe it goes further and greatly softens certain features which, they say, violate national rights.

The reservations, as agreed to, in definite terms are embodied in a proposed ratification resolution reading as follows:

"That the Senate of the United States advise and consent to the ratification of said treaty with the following reservations and understandings, to be made a part of the treaty by the instrument of ratification:

"1. That whenever the two-year notice of withdrawal from the league of nations shall have been given by the United States as provided in Article 1, the United States shall be the sole judge whether all its international obligations and all its obligations under this covenant shall have been fulfilled at the time of withdrawal.

"2. That the suggestions of the council of the league of nations as to the means of carrying the obligations of article 10 into effect are only advisory, and that any undertaking under the provisions of article 10, the execution of which may require the use of American military or naval forces or economic measures can under the constitution be carried out only by the action of the Congress, and that the failure of the Congress to adopt the suggestions of the council of the league, or to provide such military or naval forces or economic measures, shall not constitute a violation of the treaty.

"3. The United States reserves to itself the right to decide what questions are within its domestic jurisdiction and declares that all domestic and political questions relating to its internal affairs, including immigration, coastwise traffic, the tariff, commerce and all other purely domestic questions, are solely within the jurisdiction of the United States and are not by this covenant submitted in any way either to arbitration or to the consideration of the council or the assembly of the league of nations or to the decision or recommendation of any other power.

"4. The United States does not bind itself to submit for arbitration or inquiry by the assembly or the council any question which in the judgment of the United States depends upon or involves its long-established policy commonly known as the Monroe doctrine, and it is preserved unaffected by any provision in the said treaty contained."

The seven Republicans who agreed to this proposal as a basis for the effort to bring on a middle ground senators of both parties who favor the league plan in general outline, were Senators McNary, Oregon; McCumber, North Dakota; Colt, Rhode Island; Spencer, Missouri; Cummins, Iowa; Kellog, Minnesota, and Lenroot, Wisconsin.

It became known last night that the proposed resolution had not been presented either to Republican Leader Lodge or to Senator Hitchcock, administration leader in the treaty fight, and that the efforts of the group sponsoring the plan probably would be directed for the present toward enlarging their number in order to hold indisputably the balance of power.

Negotiations with administration leaders along the general line laid down in the resolution have been in progress, however, for several days.

League opponents declared yesterday that all possibility of unreserved ratification of the league had been removed by the willingness of Senators McCumber and McNary, regarded as the warmest friends of the league among the Republican majority, to accept reservations. To this administration senators replied that a vote on ratification still was a long way off, adding that seven Republicans lined up for reservations of the character proposed, there was no longer a possibility that more radical qualifications could be included in the ratification.

Although the McCumber-McNary reservation program held the center of interest in discussion among senators during the day several other angles of the treaty controversy came to the surface.

President Wilson submitted a short protocol to the Versailles treaty containing a number of supplementary provisions[2] and Chairman Lodge put into the record an agreement hitherto unpublished in this country, in which Mr. Wilson and Premier Clemenceau and Lloyd George had embodied certain regulations for the government of the Rhine provinces.[3]

Mr. Lodge also presented a copy of the treaty between the "Big Five" powers and Poland,[4] not yet submitted to the Senate for ratification.

Senator Watson, Indiana, was the only Republican senator who saw President Wilson during the day and afterward he said there had been a very pleasant discussion of the treaty including the league of nations and the Shantung issue. His views on these subjects, he said, were not changed by the conference.

Printed in the *Washington Post*, August 2, 1919.
[1] For the background of this initiative, see the news report printed at July 31, 1919.
[2] See n. 1 to the extract from the Lansing Desk Diary printed at July 30, 1919.
[3] For which, see Appendix II to the minutes of the Council of Four printed at June 13, 1919, 12 noon, Vol. 60.
[4] It is printed in *PPC*, XIII, 791-808.

To Edward Nash Hurley

My dear Hurley: The White House 2 August, 1919.

Thank you for your thoughtful letter of July 31st about the oil supply situation and its bearings on the future of our merchant marine. I have several times had the matter called to my attention and have been very much disturbed that there seemed to be no method by which we could assure ourselves of the necessary supply alike at home and abroad. I shall take real pleasure in acting upon your suggestion that I consult the Secretary of the Interior, who, I am sure, can and will be most helpful.

With warmest regard,

Faithfully yours,   Woodrow Wilson

TLS (E. N. Hurley Papers, InNd).

To Franklin Knight Lane

My dear Lane: [The White House] 2 August, 1919.

I would be very much obliged if you would read the enclosed letter from Hurley and return it to me with such comments and suggestions as you may feel prepared to give me. I know you will regard the matter he speaks of as of as critical importance as it seems to me, and yet I am at present without constructive thought in the matter.

Cordially and faithfully yours,   Woodrow Wilson

TLS (Letterpress Books, WP, DLC).

To William Cox Redfield

PERSONAL AND CONFIDENTIAL

My dear Mr. Secretary: The White House 2 August, 1919.

It is with deep and genuine distress that I read your letter of August first. I had no idea that you were contemplating leaving the office in which you have done such distinguished service. I do not feel at liberty, in view of the reasons you give, to attempt to dissuade you, because I have no right to ask you to continue to sacrifice your personal interests, but I must say I shall be at a great loss to find a successor, and that I shall sadly miss your counsels and your efficient, active, and watchful services as the Head of your Department. I have throughout my administration been able to think of the Department without any concern because I had such perfect confidence in you and was so sure that everything would be looked after as it should be.

Of course I will observe your wishes about the method in which the suggestion is to be treated, and I shall hope to have some direct personal words with you before you make your final decision.

With genuine distress and equally genuine gratitude,

Cordially and faithfully yours,   Woodrow Wilson

TLS (W. C. Redfield Papers, DLC).

To Thomas Dixon, Jr.

My dear Dixon: [The White House] 2 August, 1919.

Not on your life![1] I am of course genuinely interested in any play you may put on the boards, but I would not go to see a serious play, no matter how fine, which dealt with the critical matters now daily pressing upon my judgment as matters of policy, for anything in the world. The weight of this weary, unintelligible world is great enough anyhow on those of us poor devils who have to take some part in straightening things out, and when I go to the theatre I must, for psychological reasons see something that does not extend the strain of the day. You will understand.

Faithfully yours,   Woodrow Wilson

TLS (Letterpress Books, WP, DLC).
   [1] Wilson was replying to T. Dixon, Jr., to WW, July 23, 1919, ALS (WP, DLC). Dixon had invited the Wilsons to attend the opening of his new play, *The Red Dawn: A Drama of Revolution*, at the Schubert Belasco Theatre in Washington on July 28. "I've done my best," he commented, "to defend American Ideals against Red Communism. Senator [Lee Slater] Overman will be there with the entire Judiciary Committee."

To John Sharp Williams

My dear Senator: The White House 2 August, 1919.

There is undoubtedly something in the suggestion made by Mr. Gerard,[1] and I am going to transmit it to the other side of the water. I thank you sincerely for letting me see it. I have so many things to think about and attend to these days that one feels all the time as if there were something left undone.

Cordially and faithfully yours,   Woodrow Wilson

TLS (J. S. Williams Papers, DLC).
[1] Wilson was replying to J. S. Williams to WW, Aug. 1, 1919, TLS, enclosing James Watson Gerard to J. S. Williams, July 31, 1919, T telegram, both in WP, DLC. Gerard warned that "Turco Tartars" were moving in on the Armenians from three sides and that, unless immediate preventive measures were taken, the "Armenian nation" would meet with an "appalling catastrophe." He urged that Williams and Lodge exert pressure on Lansing to take action on behalf of Armenia. The United States and the Allies should declare immediately that any further Turkish aggression against Armenia would force upon all "civilized nations" the "inevitable and fixed duty of terminating Turkish rule altogether." He also suggested that British troops should intervene "in Caucasus." Williams, in his covering note to Wilson, attempted to interpret Gerard's somewhat incoherent telegraphic prose, "How would it do," he said, "to make the declaration which Mr. Gerard suggests, to wit, that further aggression against Armenia would be the absolute dissolution of the Turkish Empire not only in Europe but in Asia? As to getting any military help to them, I don't see how we can do that. Maybe the British, being on the ground, can."

To Frank Lyon Polk

The White House, 2 August, 1919.

Might it not be a wise course for the Allied and Associated Powers to warn Turkey that aggressive action on the part of her forces or subjects against the Armenians might result in the absolute dissolution of the Turkish Empire and a complete alteration of the conditions of peace?   Woodrow Wilson

T telegram (WP, DLC).

To Newton Diehl Baker

My dear Baker: The White House 2 August, 1919.

Thank you very much for sending me Graves' report of June 21st.[1] You may be sure I shall give it a most careful reading.

Cordially and faithfully yours,   Woodrow Wilson

TLS (N. D. Baker Papers, DLC).
[1] Printed as an Enclosure with NDB to WW, July 31, 1919.

From John Jacob Esch

My dear Mr. President,   Washington, D. C. August 2, 1919.

Your letter of August 1st was presented to me yesterday accompanied by a copy of a letter addressed to you by the Director General, Mr. Hines, wherein he urged certain legislation providing for a body authorized to investigate and determine all questions concerning wages of railway employees and which will also make the decisions of that board mandatory upon the rate making body.

Senator Cummins was present at the conference and we went over the situation with the Director General and suggested that he place the above recommendations in bill form so that they could be introduced in the Senate and House and referred to the appropriate committees.

You doubtless have already been advised of the action of the House in rescinding its order providing for a recess to September 9th beginning today.

I wish to assure you that our Committee on Interstate and Foreign Commerce will give due consideration to any measure seeking to carry out the above purpose.

With greatest respect, I remain,

Yours very truly,   John J Esch

TLS (WP, DLC).

From Albert Baird Cummins

Dear Mr. President: [Washington] 2 August 1919

I have received your note of the first instant, together with a copy of the communication from Mr. Walker D. Hines, the Director General of Railroads.

It is obvious to every observing man and has been for some time that the railroad situation is not only exceedingly serious but really alarming. The railroad men have always been the most conservative of all the laborers of the country. There is upon every side abundant evidence that they are losing some measure of the confidence which they formerly had in the justice of the laws.

I will cooperate in every way to bring about a better state of affairs, but I am not sure that the plan you suggest is comprehensive enough even to meet present conditions. I will call a meeting of the Committee on Interstate Commerce for next Tuesday, and we will take up for discussion the very vital subject you have submitted to me.   Yours sincerely,   Albert B. Cummins

TLS (WP, DLC).

From William Hugh Johnston and Others

Dear Mr. President: Washington, D. C. August 2, 1919.

The undersigned Chief Executive Officers and Committee of one hundred, selected by approximately 500,000 members of the organizations hereinafter named, have before us a copy of a letter transmitted to you under date of July 30th, by the Director General of Railroads.[1] We note with particular interest that the Director General has made the following recommendation:

"I therefore respectfully recommend that Congress be asked promptly to adopt legislation providing a properly constituted body on which the public and labor will be adequately represented and which will be empowered to pass on these and all railroad wage problems, but not on rules and working conditions, (because the latter cannot be satisfactorily separated from the current handling of railroad operations and therefore should continue to be dealt with by the Railroad Administration). Such legislation should also provide that if wage increases shall be decided upon it shall be mandatory upon the rate-making body to provide where necessary increased rates to take care of the resulting increases in the cost of operating the railroads.

I do not think that we can properly deal with this great problem without a full recognition of the fact that the cost of living is rapidly rising and that every month that passes promises to impair still further the purchasing power of the existing wages of railroad employees unless the rise in the cost of living can be successfully restrained (as I earnestly hope in the general public interest it can speedily be). I therefore further recommend that Congress be asked to provide in any such legislation that any increases in railroad wages which may be made by the tribunal constituted for that purpose shall be made effective as of August 1, 1919, to such extent as that tribunal may regard reasonable and proper in order to give railroad employees from that date the benefit which the tribunal may think they were then entitled to. In this way the delay necessarily incident to the creation of such tribunal and its action will not be prejudicial to the fair interests of the railroad employees."

In a conference August 1, with the Director General, we were advised that you have unqualifiedly endorsed the above recommendation in a letter addressed to Senator Cummings, Chairman Interstate Commerce Commission and Congressman, Esch, Chairman Committee on Interstate and Foreign Commerce.[2]

On January 7, 1919, a request was submitted to the Railroad

[1] W. D. Hines to WW, July 30, 1919.
[2] WW to J. J. Esch, Aug. 1, 1919, and n. 1 thereto.

Administration, embodying increases of 17 cents per hour for mechanics, 15 cents per hour for helpers and 10 cents per hour for apprentices, effective January 1, 1919, which we at that time felt were absolutely necessary to meet the conditions that then existed. This question was referred to the Board of Wages and Working Conditions on February 8th, by the Director General, with instructions to hold hearings and submit their recommendations to him.

We quote the following excerpt from letter submitted by the Director General to you under date of July 30, 1919;

"I therefore advised the Board of Railroad Wages and Working Conditions on July 3rd, that they could not regard themselves as vested with jurisdiction to formulate and recommend further general wage increases to be made by me, but that in all cases thereafter arising they should report the facts to me that I might decide in the light of the facts upon a fair and just procedure."

Therefore, it will be seen that our request was placed in the hands of the Wage Board with instructions to make recommendation to the Director General prior to the time the above quoted instructions were given to the Wage Board.

Public hearings were held during the months of March and April. The recommendations of the Board of Railroad Wages and Working Conditions, were filed with the Director General on July 16th, 1919.

Correspondence starting July 8, 1919, resulted in a conference being arranged for with the Director General and the undersigned representatives on July 28th, 1919, at which time it was expected we would be advised as to the conclusions arrived at in connection with the above referred to request. After waiting approximately 7 months for this decision, it is with some surprise that we are now confronted with a proposition which is entirely unacceptable, both as to the method of procedure and the delay which must necessarily follow, should Congress favorably consider the suggested plan of disposing of this question.

We have not been consulted as to this entirely new departure and it is only fair to say to you that, the suggested plan does not at this time meet with our approval, nor are we willing to say that we are prepared to endorse any such procedure as the basis upon which wage rates shall be finally determined. From our point of view to do so would, in a great measure, deny to the men we represent the right of collective bargaining as we under-stand it.

The Railroad Wage Commission of which Mr. Franklin K. Lane, Secretary of the Interior, was Chairman, after an exhaustive study, recommended to the Director General, the creation of a Board which should be authorized to deal with the following questions:

"(1) Inequalities as to wages and working conditions whether as to individual employees or classes of employees.

(2) Conditions arising from competition with employees in other industries.

(3) Rules and working conditions for the several classes of employees, either for the country as a whole or for different parts of the country.

The board shall also hear and investigate other matters affecting wages and conditions of employment referred to it by the Director General.

This board shall be solely an advisory body and shall submit its recommendations to the Director General for his determination."

This Board was appointed June 1, 1918, and from that date to the present time has been exclusively engaged in handling questions coming within its jurisdiction, as above prescribed.

The personnel of the Board consists of three railroad officials and three representatives chosen from organizations representing railroad employees.

It is fair to assume that, in the selection only men with practical experience and knowledge of railroad wages and schedules were chosen.

The letters of transmittal accompanying the recommendations, submitted by the Board of Railroad Wages and Working Conditions to the Director General, copies of which have been furnished us by the Director General, do not materially differ as to the necessity of meeting to a reasonable degree the increase of wages to the men we represent. The difference being only to the extent that the three labor members of the Board recommend a specific increase, specified in the amount to be paid per hour. The three members representing the railroads, qualifying their recommendation to the extent of saying that unless costs of living could be reduced, thereby increasing the purchasing value of the dollar earned, it would be necessary to meet the situation by granting increases in wages.

We herewith submit the letter of transmittal accompanying the recommendation made by the labor members of the Board, which represents a concise statement of their reasons upon which the recommendation was made.

We particularly call your attention to the position now occupied by the railroad employees whom we represent. The only increase they have received since the railroads were placed under Federal control is that provided for under Supplement No. 4. effective January 1, 1918.

Practically all other employees of the railroads have received substantial increases under General Order No. 27, effective as of January 1, 1918, and other adjustments creating substantial increases were granted by the issuance of Supplements Nos. 7 and 8. effective September 1, 1918, and subsequent supplemental orders issued up to as late as April 14, 1919, effective to January 1, 1919.

Members of these same organizations, engaged in other industries, have received substantial increases, establishing a differential in rates of pay, ranging from 10 to 30 cents per hour in excess of that now paid to the men in the railroad service, reversing, in a large degree, the pre-war conditions, as the railroad employees at that time received, as a general proposition, equal compensation paid men in other industries.

As a result of this changed condition, and the disappointment resulting from the long delay in disposing of the question which was submitted last January, we are now confronted with a situation which is nearing a point that we can no longer control.

Information received within the last 48 hours is to the effect that, not less than 20,000 of our railroad members have suspended work as a protest against this long deferred decision.

In view of this condition, there is but one course open for us to pursue. That is, to submit to the entire membership the proposition as it has now been presented to us by the Director General, with a request that by their vote they shall decide what further action they may deem necessary to secure the much needed relief.

We are in accord with the thought that an increase in wages of itself, will not altogether solve the problem, but it is well to bear in mind that, the classes of employees herein referred to and for whom we speak, feel, and, we believe, justly so, are entitled to an increase in wages, which will restore them to the same relative position as compared to their fellow members employed in outside industries. We are not aware that this condition applies with equal force to other classes of railroad employees.

May we urge upon you the necessity of meeting the present situation, by putting into effect our original request, as submitted to the Director General on January 7, 1919?

Yours truly,   Wm. H. Johnston
Int'l Ass'n. of Machinists.
John J. Hynes
Sheet Metal Workers I. A.
Fred C. Bolam
Bro. of Blacksmiths & Helpers.
Jas. P. Noonan
Int. Bro. of Electrical Wkrs.

Wm Atkinson
   Bro. of Boilermakers I. S. B. & H.
Martin F. Ryan
   Bro. Railway Carmen of America.
B. M. Jewell
   Actg. Pres. Ry. Employees Dpt.
   A. F. of L.

TLS (WP, DLC).

From William Delahunty[1]

My dear Mr President: New York Aug. 2, 1919.

The stand you are taking to lessen the burdens of the common people is creating wide spread attention and favorable comment.

As the former secretary of the Silk Textile Workers of America— of which Mr Powderly[2] of the Department of Labor, Senator Calder, of New York and President Gompers of the American Federation of Labor, can tell you—the textile workers together with the great industrial masses of our country bid you God speed in your efforts to lower the high cost of living and to curb the profiteers.

You will recall the incident between yourself and President Cleveland on a great labor matter, when Mr Cleveland asked you what you would do had you been in his place, and you remember what your reply was.[3] Now Mr President I, as the one to whom you related the incident while at Sea Girt, N. J., believe, with all my heart, you will do what you told President Cleveland you would do, if you were in his place, and sure enough—thank God—you are now where Mr Cleveland was when he asked your advice, yes and we all believe you will make good.

It has been my pleasure to tell our people many times of the pleasant interview I had with you at Sea Girt in October 1912, and of your sincere sympathy with all the legitimate efforts of the wage earning masses to better their condition.

Believe me Mr President, as ever
                    Yours faithfully   Wm Delahunty

TLS (WP, DLC).
   [1] A printer of New York. He had been an enthusiastic supporter of Wilson in the campaign for the governorship of New Jersey in 1910 and in the presidential campaign of 1912. At that time, he had been the publisher of a weekly labor newspaper, *The Industrial News*. He still called himself a "Publisher" on his letterhead, but the Editors have been unable to determine whether *The Industrial News* was extant in 1919. See W. Delahunty to WW, Aug. 2 and 13, Oct. 7, Nov. 7 and 16, 1910, and Feb. 9, 27, and 28, 1913, all ALS (WP, DLC).
   [2] Terence Vincent Powderly, head of the Knights of Labor, 1879-1893; Commissioner

General of Immigration, 1897-1902; and chief of the Division of Information of the Bureau of Immigration, 1907-1921.
³ Nothing is known about this conversation between Wilson and Cleveland. However, one can only infer that Wilson had said to Cleveland that he would not have intervened in the Chicago railroad strike of 1893 if he had been President then.

Frank Lyon Polk to Robert Lansing

Paris August 3, 1919.

Urgent 3489 Following sent to AmLegation Bucharest. "August 3, 4 pm. The commission desires you to inform the Roumanian Government that it is entirely opposed to a Roumanian advance upon Budapest¹ and feels that any occupation however limited or temporary would seriously affect the attitude of the United States towards Roumania. Kindly make this clear to the Roumanian Government without delay. Acknowledge receipt." Polk.

American Mission

T telegram (SDR, RG 59, 864.00/100, DNA).
¹ Béla Kun resigned on August 1, and the Supreme Council were at this point attempting to negotiate a settlement with the new Hungarian government under Gyula (Julius) Peidl, Minister of Welfare in the Károlyi government and a moderate socialist. However, the Brătianu government in Bucharest had made it clear that it would not accept the Rumanian boundaries already laid down by the Big Four and was already beginning preparations for an advance on Budapest, news of which had reached Paris at least by August 2. See Francis Deák, *Hungary at the Paris Peace Conference: The Diplomatic History of the Treaty of Trianon* (New York, 1942), particularly pp. 102-110.
A copy of Polk's telegram was sent to Wilson August 5, 1919.

Two Telegrams from Herbert Clark Hoover

August 3rd [1919] London

Secretary of State, Washington Important 2690 Aug. 3, 2 PM Secret

Please deliver the following telegram American Relief Administration Washington

Quote for Barnes Rickard¹ from Hoover

Please present following to the President for me.

At Supreme Economic Council today France England Italy produced and adopted in principle a plan providing for restriction of cooperation in purchase of foodstuffs. We took the attitude that we have no authority to even discuss the matter, but advised them that it was not to the world's interest to use such powers to the detriment of the farmers of the world or they would decrease the world's production and starve themselves, but that they should seek to place it on a basis of cooperation with the United States or otherwise they would create in the mind of the American producer the impression of such combinations against him. Further, that if the impression of such combinations was to gain currency it would destroy the hope of Allied credits in the United States. We stated that the American people would sympathize with any plan for dealing with speculation and profiteering.

It was finally decided that the other Governments propose to you for acceptance a plan to be further amplified by a Committee on which we decided we would not be represented.   Davis.

---

[1] Edgar Rickard, assistant to Hoover in the Food Administration, Acting Food Administrator since November 1918, Director of the American Relief Administration since March 1919.

London Aug. 3, 1919.
Secretary of State Washington Important 2691 Aug. 3rd 2 PM Secret

For Barnes Rickard from Hoover
Second. Please forward the following to the President as a cable for me.

The degeneration of the world's food supplies situation during the last month, the outbreak of speculation and profiteering all over the world due partially to this but principally to a moral slackening in all the avenues of life, and the action as shown in my cable today of the Allies through which they propose in effect to restore collective buying which should reduce speculation, but unless controlled on our side may work great hardships on the American farmer, seem to me to necessitate laying of the position before Congress for it to decide whether protection is needed both for consumer and producer.

There has been a steady degeneration of cereal crops during the last 30 to 60 days, and the promise of marginal supplies, the weight of which would control speculation has greatly diminished, and while there is sufficient balance to meet the world's needs during the next year if properly distributed, the margins are sufficiently narrow to create great danger of speculation and profiteering.

In respect to even wheat, the indications now are that while the price might remain near the guarantee during the heavy marketing season and free world prices, it would probably rise very materially before the next harvest.

In the matter of pork products and fats generally the margin over the world's need is very narrow, but such surplus production of the United States comes with a rush during a short season. Combinations of European buying, unless they are controlled, may result in depreciation of prices below cost of production, and unless some control is exerted either through provision of Congress for accumulation of surplus for subsequent distribution, or through the control of the European credits by which righteous prices may be insisted upon as a condition of such credits there is some danger from this to the producer in the heavy marketing season and second to the consumer through subsequent rises in price and uncontrolled speculation.

In order to clear the decks it seems to me desireable to brush away the remains of the old Food Administration. In my view if it were decided to take interest in the matter nothing could do that without new legislation because although the present Food Act is technically in force, it will expire at any moment with the ratification of peace; it is based on war powers and even this extended its legal foundations could be intact in peace. It should be noted also that the act taken alone would have been entirely ineffective against profiteering for the success of the previous administration was based not on the Act but on the voluntary cooperation of the trades, the form of which would be illegal in peace without specific legislation.

In any event, acting under your original instructions we demobilized the Food Administration as rapidly as possible after the armistice. By the end of March the largest part of safeguarding activities were brought, in my view, very immaturely to an end under pressure of the Cabinet, and all those functions still outstanding have been finally completed within the last 30 days by the setting up of the Wheat Directorate, the only outstanding matter being the liquidation of the sugar contracts. Failure of Congress to make any appropriations for the continuation of the Food Administration but finally indicates the desire for its separation.

With regard to the sugar contracts I have telegraphed you separately[1] but in any event so far as the existing contract and the existing sugar corporation are concerned they can be completed without the continuation of the Food Administration, and if temporary use of the Food Act is necessary for this perhaps it can be delegated to the President of the Board by executive order.

In order that the last vestige of the old administration may be eliminated I would be glad if you would consider that my oral resignation as Food Dictator given to you personally before leaving Paris should be considered as effective from that date, namely July 1st. I will of course, if you desire, continue as Director General of Relief until the completion of its accounting.

In conclusion it seems to me that Congress should give careful consideration as to whether legislation is needed and the erection of such (?) administration as may be necessary. I do not feel that after eight months absence I am sufficiently in touch with the American conditions and sentiment to advise as to methods to be pursued but feel it my duty to point out the conditions which are likely to obtain during the next twelve months.   Davis.

T telegrams (WP, DLC).
¹ HCH to J. H. Barnes (for WW), July 23, 1919, T telegram (Hoover Archives, CSt-H).

To Alexander Mitchell Palmer, with Enclosure

                                                      The White House
My dear Mr. Attorney General: 4 August, 1919.

I hope that you will have the patience to examine the enclosed. The writer of the letter, John Nevin Sayre, I know very well and trust very completely, and I would be very much obliged if you would have the papers attached to his letter carefully gone over, and a brief memorandum made concerning them, for our guidance with regard to this perplexing matter in which, as you know, I am anxious to act at an early date.

                    Cordially and sincerely yours,   Woodrow Wilson

TLS (A. M. Palmer Papers, DLC).

E N C L O S U R E

From John Nevin Sayre

My dear Mr. President: Katonah, N. Y. August 1, 1919.

Of course I can understand how in the present rush of business it is not possible for you to see Mr. Wood, Mr. DeSilver¹ or myself.² But following up the very kind suggestion in your letter of July 15th, I am writing this letter to you, and I beg to submit herewith a Memorandum and Exhibits³ drawn up by my friend Walter Nelles, Counsel for the National Civil Liberties Bureau.

I have personally worked for more than a year with Mr. Nelles and the National Civil Liberties Bureau and I have every confidence that the statements made by Mr. Nelles are substantially accurate, and that the Memorandum and Exhibits give a not overdrawn picture of the circumstances attending many convictions under the Espionage Law. I sincerely hope that you may be able to afford the time to personally examine these documents.

On the whole question of general amnesty may I urge the following points?

First, the war is now over, and with it has passed the principal dangers which the Espionage Act sought to guard against. This

Act was admittedly a war measure, passed by Congress under war conditions and its aim was to prevent the propagation of words or actions which might conceivably hinder or delay us in winning the war. The war being now won and the power of German militarism broken, it is impossible any longer for Espionage Act offenders to give dangerous aid or comfort to the enemy, even though they all should be released from jail tomorrow. The further imprisonment of these men and women can therefore hardly serve any useful social end, unless it be held that they are deserving of further punishment. But because of your progressive views on penology, and because of the unscientific and unstandardized character of the sentences imposed, I do not believe this punishment theory will appeal to you.

Secondly, The circumstances of the convictions of offenders against the Espionage Act were such as to make it highly questionable whether equal justice was done. I am not alluding here to the possible miscarriage of justice in a few exceptional instances, but to the broad facts (1) that most of the convictions were for expressions of opinion, rather than overt acts, and (2) that there was no uniform standard throughout the country, by which juries and judges could determine the proportionate guilt and penalty of various offenders. The limits of what it was safe or unsafe to say without incurring imprisonment were often not so much determined by the law as by the temper of popular opinion in the locality where a person happened to be. Similarly the sentences of judges varied greatly in accordance with the preconceptions and personality of each judge. All this is well covered by Mr. Nelles' Memorandum and Exhibits. Furthermore, because of the difficulty of any attempt to reconstruct all the circumstances of any particular case, it seems next to impossible now to secure a fair review of all Espionage Act cases and by revision of sentences to meet out equal justice. Another difficulty is the fact that many persons said far worse things against the government than did others who were apprehended and imprisoned, and yet the former, by reason of their social, financial or political connections went scot free. It is not practicable to try them now. Would not a general amnesty then be, on the whole, the fairest course that the government could take?

Thirdly, The present need of reconciliation between all groups and classes in America grows more urgent every day. The continued imprisonment of those whom their comrades regard as sufferers for the cause of social justice, can only widen and not close up, dangerous breeches which divide modern society. Where there was a suspicion, as in the cases of many socialist[s] and I.W.W.s, that these persons were really imprisoned not so much for their opposition to the war as for their opposition to class privilege, that suspicion is bound to intensify for each day that these persons are kept in jail beyond that moment when the German danger was palpably over. In this connection it seems to be coming true that the blood of martyrs (even if they are only supposed ones) is the seed of radical organization.

Mr. President, I am sure that these arguments are not new to you, and that you can yourself give cogency to them in far more effective words than I. I state them simply as the expression of my deep belief, and of the conviction of my associates of the National Civil Liberties Bureau, and I feel sure also, of thousands of our countrymen. We appeal to you, the one person in the nation, who now has power to grant the general amnesty we desire.

Sincerely and respectfully yours,   John Nevin Sayre

Enclosures: One Memorandum as to persons imprisoned
    for violation of the War Laws
    One Exhibit, accompanying same.

TLS (General Records of the Department of Justice, D. J. Central Files—Straight Numerical Files, File No. 197009-1-2, RG 60, DNA).
    [1] That is, Levi Hollingsworth Wood and Albert De Silver.
    [2] See J. N. Sayre to WW, July 7, 1919, and WW to J. N. Sayre, July 15, 1919, both in Vol. 61.
    [3] W. Nelles, "MEMORANDUM TO THE PRESIDENT OF THE UNITED STATES AS TO PERSONS IMPRISONED FOR VIOLATIONS OF THE WAR LAWS," TS MS, and National Civil Liberties Bureau, "EXHIBITS SUBMITTED WITH MEMORANDUM TO THE PRESIDENT AS TO PERSONS IMPRISONED FOR VIOLATIONS OF WAR LAWS," T MS, both in General Records of the Department of Justice, D. J. Central Files—Straight Numerical Files, File No. 197009-1-2, RG 60, DNA. Nelles' memorandum summarized the general characteristics and similarities of the cases of persons convicted of violations of war statutes or for alleged conspiracies in wartime. He stressed that he was not concerned with the cases of men imprisoned for refusal of military service. Rather, he was concerned primarily with those convicted for expressions of opinion. "The question," he wrote, "which we hope to leave before you for consideration is simply this: Is it desirable that punishment of conduct such as these convictions involve should continue after the passing of the emergency in which it was made criminal?" The "Exhibits" gave summaries of the cases of nineteen individuals convicted under the Espionage Act and other so-called "war laws," the best known of whom were Debs, Charles T. Schenck, and Rose Harriet Pastor Stokes.

To James Edward McCulloch

My dear Mr. McCulloch: [The White House] 4 August, 1919.

I have received and examined with the greatest interest the proceedings of the Southern Sociological Congress, to which you call my attention in your interesting letter of the first of August, and note your suggestion that a conference of the Governors of the several States be called to consider the very serious question of lynching and race riots. I hasten to apprise you that the regular annual meeting of the Conference of Governors will occur August 19th to

21st, at Salt Lake City, Utah, and I suggest that the Southern Sociological Congress take steps to call this matter formally to the attention of that conference. I am sure they will regard it as of the utmost importance.

Cordially and sincerely yours,   Woodrow Wilson

TLS (Letterpress Books, WP, DLC).

From William Cox Redfield

My dear Mr. President: Washington August 4, 1919.

Apropos of our conference with the Attorney General, 31st ultimo,[1] and of your letter to Mr. Esch of the 1st instant, I venture a few suggestions.

I am, of course, in full sympathy with using the law against malefactors. Wherever profiteering exists the power of the law should be exerted against it. If the law is not strong enough for the task, it should be made so. We should not, however, have prejudices or fancies as to who the profiteers are. Ten days ago a purchaser at a public market here was asked forty five cents a pound for roasting beef. In a store near the market it was bought the same day for thirty seven cents. On Friday last it was advertised at thirty cents. There is some danger of our ranging rather far afield in this phase of the matter.

I suspect the profiteers are all about us. The feeling of high prices is in the air, no little stimulated by current taxes. At best, however, the use of the law is a negative attack on the problem; an affirmative one is possible. House Document No. 155[2] herewith speaks for itself. Had we available here one-half the average sum we have turned back into the Treasury each of the past six years untouched, we could put into every leading sea port and lake port demonstrators showing how to use great quantities of food now untouched and available at low cost. We have done this for two years but Congress has just stopped it. Let me, however, urge on your thought the fact that there are quantities of unused, wholesome and palatable foods which can for a moderate sum be made broadly available.

Proper complaint is made of the high cost of shoes, yet an almost unlimited supply of leather is available at low prices from aquatic sources. Tanners are regularly working on it. Again, this could be largely developed had we such a sum for the purpose as is above suggested. I am not sure how far you would go in direct aid of a new industry of this kind but there is no question whatever as to the leather that there is available, a huge untouched supply, practically to be had for the taking.

May I be pardoned for suggesting that it is curious, to say the least, that we discuss so vigorously the high cost of living, while we allow available supplies of food and of leather to go untouched and while Congress, with the facts before it, refuses to permit the development of unused and cheap foods.

We ought also to consider just how the high cost of living bears upon many of our people, for there seems no doubt that in some cases it takes a modified form of the cost of high living. It is, I think, true that many wage earners are by reason of larger incomes living upon a scale different from that before the war. This is of course desirable; any advance in the standard of living is welcome which adds to the comfort, happiness and efficiency of life. Is it not, however, of doubtful wisdom, having advanced the standards of living considerably, to make the cost of this advance an argument for further claims based upon the expenses thus incurred? There is at least enough truth in this to warrant reflection. A woman recently buying butter for her own household at sixty cents per pound was succeeded by a woman clearly poor who paid seventy five cents a pound for a fancy brand. My experience leads me to believe there is much possible in the way of teaching wise expenditure.

Little is said in current discussion of such practical things as cooperative stores and of definite efforts to reduce the excessive cost of distribution. This last, I think, bears more heavily than the cost of transportation of which we talk so much. Yet cooperative stores are successful and there have grown up establishments which, by cutting out distributing cost and other overhead charges, are selling at reduced prices, to learn of which we have only to look in current advertisements.

Believing, as an employer, in high wages as the basis of low productive cost, welcoming any advance in the economic scale for labor, believing firmly that the toiler must have a larger share of the economic product than heretofore, I yet seriously question the wisdom of advancing wages today as a solution of the so-called high cost of living. On the contrary this seems to me a step in a vicious circle, which when completed adds weight to the problem that presses hard upon the worker. Better far is the method of making present wages more effective.

This, in part, can be done by processes of law, in part by such affirmative processes as I have suggested, but chiefly I think by something not yet tried but which would be effective if well and promptly done. If I judge the public temper correctly, the people are eager to do something about this matter of high prices if they knew what to do. For lack of definite leadership one says "Lo! here," another "Lo! there" and we hear discordant voices. Can you not by a public statement call to the attention of the whole country the social effects of prevailing prices, pointing out sternly how seriously profiteering menaces the public weal, calling upon the great business bodies to second your demand that it be stopped, calling upon the people to conserve in food and other expenditures as they did in the war and because the emergency is as great as then it was, and calling upon labor unions, fraternal societies, religious bodies, and the organizations which did such wonderful work during the war, each to take up the demand in their own particular place? Point out that he who spends unnecessarily injures his country by promoting unrest and so adds to the forces of disorder and that abstention from unnecessary purchases now means not only a direct addition to personal and national wealth but strikes a direct blow at the high prevailing prices. Then, as a complement to this, call upon labor to produce as fully as possible, making it plain that these two things—production and thrift—and these two alone can be a full and final answer to the question that concerns us.

The people are in a mood to rise to leadership of this kind. They welcome the use of the law and of every other affirmative means but if to every household is sent a call to something it can do the people will, I think, welcome this still more.

Yours very truly,   William C. Redfield

TLS (WP, DLC).
[1] About which, see the third news report printed at Aug. 1, 1919.
[2] It is missing in WP, DLC. However, it was *Methods of Preparing and Cooking Fish. Letter from the Secretary of Commerce* . . . , 66th Cong., 1st sess., H. Doc. No. 155 (Washington, 1919). Redfield's letter of July 19, 1919, was written in support of an earlier request for a supplemental appropriation of $15,000 for the Bureau of Fisheries to continue to "conduct demonstrations and impart instructions in correct, cheap, wholesome methods of preparing and cooking fish for consumption" as a means of showing American housewives how to reduce the high cost of living.

Two Letters from William Bauchop Wilson

My dear Mr. President: Washington August 4, 1919.

I am sure you will be interested in knowing that in the latter part of last week I succeeded in getting the Senate and House, unanimously, to adopt the following joint resolution:

"RESOLVED, etc., That the President of the United States be, and he hereby is, authorized to convene and to make arrangements for the organization of a general international labor conference, to be held in Washington, D. C.: Provided, however, That nothing herein shall be held to authorize the President to appoint any delegates to represent the United States of America at such conference or to authorize the United States of America to participate therein unless and until the Senate shall have ratified the provisions of the proposed treaty of peace with Germany with reference to a general international labor conference."

This will permit of the calling of the Labor Conference, and the matter of appointing delegates thereto and securing the necessary appropriation can wait until the Treaty has been passed upon by the Senate.

I am having a proposed call of the Conference prepared for your consideration.   Faithfully yours,   W B Wilson

My dear Mr. President: Washington August 4, 1919.

I am in receipt of your note of the 1st instant, inclosing memorandum from Dr. Shotwell relative to the International Labor Conference, which I am returning herewith.

Radicals of the group that Mrs. Raymond Robins belongs to are opposed to the Treaty of Peace and the League of Nations in part because they do not believe the labor features are sufficiently radical. They fail to attach sufficient importance to the fact that the International Labor Conference has within itself the elements of its own development. If it could be shown to them that labor would be injured by the failure of the Treaty, I am sure it would go a long way to remove their opposition. However, I do not believe that can be done without arousing other antagonisms that are now passive. The members of the so-called invisible government, representatives of a certain group in the Manufacturers' Association, exposed during the Congressional investigations in the Mulhall episode,[1] are now extremely active in driving against everything and anything that has the label of labor attached to it. Thus far they have paid no attention to the labor features of the Treaty, but if any attempt is made to concentrate attention upon the labor features, in an effort to convert the element referred to, they will no doubt become active in their opposition.

I have lived long enough to know the value of the aphorism to "let sleeping dogs alone." I am, therefore, of the opinion that it would not be advisable to make any public effort to convert this group, although something may be done in a quiet and indirect way.

As to paragraph 4, referring to the appointment of a committee, I think it is too early yet to consider the advisability of appointing such committee. The Department is undertaking to work out the arrangements for the Conference, and if a committee of this character is appointed they will undoubtedly assume that their appointment carries with it some work for them to do, which might very readily get the Department and the proposed committee with their wires crossed.

When the details of the arrangements have been worked out and it becomes necessary to select some important personages as a reception committee, then I think that it might be well to consider the suggestion made by Dr. Shotwell. Until then no action should be taken.   Faithfully yours,   W. B. Wilson

TLS (WP, DLC).
    [1] About which, see WW to R. Pulitzer, Oct. 9, 1913, and the notes thereto, Vol. 28.

From Walker Downer Hines

Dear Mr. President: Washington August 4, 1919.

I understand you have an appointment to see Mr. Jewell[1] of the Railroad Shop Crafts at 2.50 this afternoon.

He and the other railroad labor representatives show pronounced opposition to the proposal for a statute providing for a board which will determine the wages to be made good by rates which the Commission will be compelled to fix.

They claim that the President, under the powers of the Federal Control Act, ought to fix the necessary wages and the rates necessary to support those wages, or rely on Congress to make appropriations to make good the resulting deficit.

I have explained to them that we have been forced to the conclusion that the President can not as a practical proposition at this date exercise his war power for the purpose of making an increase in wages approximating $800,000,000 per year and either increase rates to pay therefor (in addition to the rate increase necessary to make up the existing deficit of perhaps $350,000,000 per ye[a]r) or expect Congress to pass an appropriation; that such action would involve a commitment which could not be carried out and would be extremely prejudicial to a liberal solution of the railroad problem.

Most of the objections of the labor representatives are to features which need not necessarily be a part of the plan, such as compelling employes to work, appointing a tribunal which will take many months to reach a decision, etc.

I have said to these representatives that we will be glad to consider any plan they can suggest other than the plan of your under-

taking at this time, without congressional sanction or even acquiescence, to increase operating costs by such a large amount with
its consequences either of increased rates or increased deficit to be
made good by appropriations.

I thought you might be interested in this statement preparatory
to your seeing Mr. Jewell.

I have tried to impress on these representatives the fact that the
Senate has already passed a bill giving the Interstate Commerce
Commission the power to suspend rates and the bill is now pending in the House Committee and I understand the sentiment in
both houses is almost unanimous in favor of the adoption of the
measure; and hence that the President would not have at the necessary time the power which they assume of making general increases in rates to take care of future increases in wages; and that
any assumption by him of that power at the moment in the face of
the existing sentiment would be most prejudicial to the just solution of the railroad problem and to the interests of the employes
themselves.   Sincerely yours,   Walker D. Hines

TLS (WP, DLC).
  ¹ Bert Mark Jewell, president of the Railway Employees' Department of the A. F. of
L.

A News Report

[*Aug. 4, 1919*]

REJECT WILSON'S PROPOSAL
SHOPMEN THREATEN TO PARALYZE NATION
IF DEMANDS ARE NOT MET.

Washington, Aug. 4.—Organized labor, as represented by the
railroad shopmen, today flatly rejected the program recommended
by President Wilson for the establishment of a Federal Commission
to adjust wage disputes and to dictate rates, and served notice on
the President and Director General of Railroads Hines that unless
Congress provided the money for a cash settlement of their demands the railroad systems would be tied up by a strike not later
than Sept. 2. Mr. Hines told the men that he did not have the
money with which to pay the increase. The President, according to
the railroad representatives, did not definitely state his position.

The shopmen's representatives, after conferences with President
Wilson and Director General of Railroads Hines this afternoon,
were in a bellicose frame of mind and spoke plainly of their attitude. B. M. Jewell, acting President of the Railways Employees' Department of the American Federation of Labor, who acted as their

spokesman, said the temper of the men was such that he did not know whether they could be controlled until the strike vote now being taken was completed.

The men were in a mood, he said, to demand the democratization, not only of the railways, but of the basic industries, such as steel, coal, the packing industry, and possibly others, along lines suggested in the so-called Plumb plan,[1] which would require the Government to purchase the industries and to give the workers a share of the profits.

"As we see it," he said, "there is only one satisfactory settlement of the problem confronting the nation. That has two parts. First, cash payment to meet the demands of the employe as a temporary measure of relief; second, the application of the Plum plan to the railroads and to the basic industries. There is a growing demand upon the part of the working men for this movement. It is the only effective cure."

This position also was taken today by the Railroad Brotherhoods in a statement issued through the Plumb Plan League and signed by Warren S. Stone, Grand Chief of the Brotherhood of Locomotive Engineers, and other prominent officials. In this statement, while attempting to deprecate published reports that the Brotherhoods were taking advantage of the present economic situation to hold up Congress, the railroad chiefs said that "it marks the step by which organized labor passes from demands for wage increases to demands that the system of profits in industry be overhauled."

The statement also says "We demand that the owners of capital, who represent only financial interest as distinguished from operating brains and energy, be retired from management."

The attitude of the shopmen and the statement of the Brotherhood Chiefs were viewed with much concern, both in Administration circles and on Capitol Hill. To add to the tenseness of the situation, a strike threat was voiced by the Brotherhood of Railway and Steamship Clerks, Freight Handlers, and Station Employes, who assert that they control 450,000 men, if their demands for increased wages and readjusted working hours are not met forthwith.

The shopmen, who now appear as among the strongest advocates of the Plumb plan, had an interview with President Wilson today and laid before him a lengthy statement, firm in tone, in which they asserted that the President's program for a Federal Wage Board would not be accepted. They said they could not await

[1] About which, see n. 2 to the Enclosure printed with W. D. Hines to WW, Feb. 24, 1919, Vol. 55, and the digest printed as an Enclosure with W. D. Hines to WW, Aug. 8, 1919.

such a delay, and that the principles of the plan were unsatisfactory.

The shopmen claim to control 500,000 men in the United States and 10,000 in Canada, and their spokesman, B. M. Jewell, said tonight that the other unions connected with railway operation, including the four brotherhoods, were in sympathy with their attitude, and were definitely lined up against the legislation which President Wilson has recommended to Congress.

"Absolutely no," he replied, when asked if the legislation would prove satisfactory. "We will tie up the railroads so tight that they never will run again if that legislation is passed. We are all opposed to it. That much was agreed to among the fourteen branches of organized labor which called upon Mr. Hines today.

The shopmen are demanding increases which would approximate $165,000,000 annually, and these, added to the demands for wages made by the four brotherhoods and other branches of the railway employes, would bring the total asked to at least $800,000,000.

The leaders of the employes frankly state that they do not see how the Railroad Administration can meet the emergency unless there is an immediate appropriation made by Congress. Mr. Jewell said that in his opinion such an appropriation was the only way in which a strike could be averted, and that the employes were beyond the stage where promises would satisfy.

The visit paid by Mr. Jewell and the representatives of five other branches of the shopmen to the President was the first big development of the day. The delegation took with it a copy of a statement addressed to the President,[2] in which they review their case and rejected forthwith the President's program for Congressional action. They told Mr. Wilson that the shopmen had not been granted an increase since Jan. 1, 1918, and that the wages were not commensurate to those received by machinists and other shopmen employed by the navy and shipyards and in privately controlled industries.

They discussed the cost of living with the President, Mr. Jewell said, and told him that present conditions were intolerable. The Plumb plan for Government purchase of railroads was discussed briefly, but not in detail, Mr. Jewell said. He added that the President said he had all Government agencies at work in an effort to reduce living costs, but that any move in that direction would take some time. But Mr. Wilson, he added, did not give any definite reply concerning the opposition of the shopmen to the recommen-

---

[2] W. H. Johnston *et al.* to WW, Aug. 2, 1919.

dations which he had made to Congress concerning the proposed Federal Wage Board.

In their statement to the President the officials of the Railroad Shopmen Union quoted Director General Hines's recommendation that a body be constituted by Congress to pass upon all railroad wage problems. They add that they have been advised by the Director General that the President has indorsed the recommendation, and after reviewing the seven months' delay in acting on their demands the statement continues: . . .[3]

The long conference which the shopmen's representatives, along with the representatives of the four brotherhoods and representatives of the Maintenance of Way and Telegrapher's Union held with Director General of Railroads Hines today brought no more definite results as to when the Government might be willing to meet their wage demands. There were, in all, fourteen of the prominent organizations of railway employes represented at this conference.

Mr. Jewell said that Director General Hines admitted that the Railroad Administration did not have the necessary funds to meet their demands. Mr. Hines, he said, stated that Congress apparently was going to pass the Cummins bill returning to the Interstate Commerce Commission full power to fix rates as before the war and that Congress had restricted his appropriation to the $750,000,000 which would not permit him to meet the wage increases out of the Railroad Administration funds.

Under such conditions, Mr. Jewell said, the situation was an impossible one, unless Congress would grant the Railroad Administration the money to meet the demands of the men. There could be no holding off until Congress made lengthy surveys of the situation, before that time a strike would be on, he added, and the country's transportation systems effectively crippled.

The union officials doubted that large communities could not [sic] long stand the effects of a railroad strike. It is stated that retail dealers have not stocked up to any large extent because of the danger of a break in the market, and it was said that New York City could not very well stand a break in communication lines for more than six or seven days without finding itself short of foodstuffs.

The statement of the brotherhoods, which was put out by the Plumb Plan League stirred up much comment because of the radical assertions made concerning the movement for the democratization of industries. It increased rather than softened the emotions which had been created on Saturday when the brotherhoods

[3] Here follows a quotation from *idem* to the end of the letter.

sprung the Sims bill[4] for the purchase of the railroads by the Government. Here is the statement:

"The innuendoes in telegraphed dispatches from Washington, appearing also in the speech of Representative Blanton[5] of Texas, that the railroad unions are holding up Congress and the Government, may as well cease.

"This appeal is made to the American people direct. It invokes the judgment and common sense of public sentiment of all the public which earns a wage or a stipend. We recognize that the only way in which we can exist under the present system is to demand further increases in wages, but we agree with Representative Blanton that this affords but temporary relief. It does not offer a remedy.

"Labor's bill, on the other hand, provides a remedy and we ask merely that its terms be scrutinized. Our full argument in support of these terms will be scrutinized. Our argument in support of these terms will be presented on Wednesday before the House Committee on Interstate Commerce by Warren S. Stone, Grand Chief, Brotherhood Locomotive Engineers; Frank Morrison, Secretary of the American Federation of Labor, and Glenn E. Plumb, general counsel for the Organized Railway Employes of America. In this statement we are sounding the notes of our basic principles.

"That this rôle originates with labor is merely because labor happens to have firm organizations through which it may become articulate. It is not to benefit labor as labor alone; it is to benef[i]t the consuming public, of which labor at present is the audible part. In labor's bill providing that the public take over the railroads and establish a tripartite control between the public, the railway operating management, and the employes, the labor organizations of America have established this new policy which envisages their condition, not only as producers, but also as consumers.

"It marks the step by which organized labor passes from demands for wage increases to demands that the system of profits in industry be overhauled. Hitherto during successive wage negotiations and arbitration awards we have called for provisional attention only of questions arising out of differences as to wages, hours and conditions of labor. That principle of genuine co-operation and partnership based upon a real community of interest and participation in control, of which President Wilson has spoken to Congress, has been ignored both by labor and by the private owners of the railroads.

"What wage increases have been received during the past few years resulted only in immediately being followed by more than

[4] About which, see T. R. Marshall to WW, Aug. 7, 1919, n. 2.
[5] Thomas Lindsay Blanton, Democrat.

proportionate increases in the cost of living. Each rise in wages has turned out to mean only temporary relief for the affected workers. When the increases have gone around the circle, labor as producer loses the advantage of the new wages through the additional cost it pays as consumer. Moreover, through compounded profits taken on the wage increased each cycle becomes an upward spiral of costs, which the consuming public vainly reaches to control.

"As the major part of the consuming public, labor is entitled to representation on the directorate of the public railroads; as a producer of capital it is entitled to representation on the directorate of the railroads. To capital, which is the fruit of yesterday's labor, we now propose to discharge every just obligation. We demand that the owners of capital, who represent only financial interest as distinguished from operating brains and energy, be relieved from management, receiving Government bonds with a fixed interest return for every honest dollar that they have invested in the railway industry. We ask that the railroads of the United States be vested in the public—that those actually engaged in conducting that industry, not from Wall Street but from the railroad offices and yards and out on the railroad lines, shall take charge of this service for the public.

"These represent all the brains, skill, and energy that is in the business. They are entitled to that measure of control which is equal to their ability and their responsibility for operating the transportation properties. Then and only then, will the service be primarily for the public, not primarily for profits to speculators and inflaters of capital. As a means for accomplishing this end, we ask that a lease be granted to a corporation, created not for profit but for public service. We ask that this corporation be controlled in its management by an equal representation of the three fundamental interests upon which industry is based. The public, operating managers, and wage earners will then guarantee both the integrity of the investment required for the conduct of the industry, and that return which induces it, by investing, to enter the public service.

"The public as consumers and the operating managers and wage earners as producers having joined in that guarantee, will then share equally all earnings in excess of the amounts required to meet the guarantee.

"This is provided by granting to the wage earners and management one-half of the savings, which they, through their perfected organizations can make, and by securing to the public the other half to be enjoyed by the consumers, either by increasing the means for service without increasing fixed charges, or by reducing the cost of the service, which the machinery then in existence can render, thus the cost of transportation is automatically reduced exactly in proportion as benefits accrue to the producers of transportation. Increase in earning power of producers under this system cannot be reflected in increased costs, it must be balanced by decreased costs.

"The railroads are the key industry of the nation. The[y] affect at once the price of every necessity. As increased transportation costs are reflected in the increased price of all commodities, so a reduction in those costs must be reflected by the reduced prices.

"We say this because of labor's interest as consumer, as part of an overburdened public. This fundamental statement of principle we respectfully submit to the American people.

"Warren S. Stone, Grand Chief, Brotherhood of Locomotive Engineers.

"Timothy Shea, acting chief, Brotherhood of Firemen and Engineers.

"L[ucius]. E[lmer]. Sheppard, President, Association of Railway Conductors.

"B. M. Jewell, Acting President, Railway Employes Department, American Federation of Labor."

W[illiam]. G[ranville]. Lee, President, Brotherhood of Railway Trainmen, who was a signer of the first statement issued by the railway brotherhood officials, was absent from Washington at the time of issuance of this statement, but is understood to concur in it.

The possibility of action by the railroad clerks, freight handlers, and express and station employes similar to that taken by the shopmen is intimated in a statement issued today by J[ames]. J[oseph]. Forrester, Grand President of the Brotherhood of Railway and Steamship Clerks, Freight Handlers, Express and Station employes. A referendum, in effect a strike ballot, will be taken upon whatever reply the Railroad Administration makes to pending demands for a wage increase and improved working rules. The organization has a membership of 450,000.

Demands for a forty-four-hour week and a 20 cents an hour increase in wages have been made, and the brotherood expects a definite reply immediately. A letter has gone to the administration, Mr. Forrester said today, asking a hearing.

Printed in the *New York Times*, Aug. 5, 1919.

From Franklin Knight Lane

My dear Mr. President: Washington August 4, 1919.

Several months ago I sent you a copy of the report to which Mr. Hurley refers, regarding the situation as to the fuel oil for our shipping.[1] Mr. Hurley later learning of it, asked me for a copy, which I sent to him. I shall be very glad to help you with suggestions as to a constructive policy to meet the situation.

Cordially and faithfully yours,   Franklin K. Lane

TLS (WP, DLC).
  [1] See ENH to WW, July 31, 1919 (first letter of that date). Lane was replying to WW to FKL, Aug. 2, 1919.

Two Letters to Robert Lansing

My dear Mr. Secretary,   The White House, 4 August, 1919.

I am distressed by these developments.[1] That Ven[i]zelos and Tittoni should be suffered in any way or degree to prejudge the Asia Minor settlements by agreements entered into between Greece and Italy without the concurrence or approval of the other Powers is little less than intolerable; and the more the Greek hand is shown in this business the less I like the way it is used. I am clear in the judgment that Greece should *not* be given Bulgarian Thrace and I think our representatives ought to take a firm stand against it; and yet I see how serious a matter it is to assign it again to Bulgaria, who deserves no consideration whatever at our hands.

We have a clear right to a voice in these matters, for we are to be among the guarantors of their permanent settlement, and we ought to make it clear that we will not stand for assignments of territory which will mean, not peace, but disquiet, disturbance and an early rekindling of the Balkan wars. If they suspect us of wishing territorial aggrandizement (which in that quarter is ridiculous),[2] let them make some temporary arrangement for Bulgarian Thrace under the League of Nations, pending a thorough inquiry by an impartial commission and a subsequent determination based unpo [upon] the preferences and interests of the population, and on nothing else.

We ought to make it plain now that we will not stand for the grabbing of territory anywhere contrary to the principles we have all along insisted on, and, that if our cooperation is to be obtained, the suggested settlements much [must] clearly square with those principles. We are in danger of cutting the ground from under our feet in our dealings with Italy, if we permit other considerations to slip in in Asia Minor, or if we do not make it clear that we will not permit any dealings between Greece and Italy to complicate the situation so far as we are concerned.

I should assume that Mr. Venezelos is clear-headed enough to see that he can gain no advantage by alienating us and making us regret that we ever let him take possession of Smyrna.

If you concur in these views, will you not be kind enough to embody them in an immediate despatch to the Mission in Paris?[3]

Faithfully Yours,   W.W.

WWTLI (SDR, RG 59, 763.72119/5920, DNA).
  [1] See FLP to WW and RL, Aug. 1, 1919.
  [2] About this charge, see, in particular, H. White to WW, July 20, 1919, Vol. 61.
  [3] Wilson's letter, except for the first sentence and the last paragraph, was conveyed verbatim in RL to Ammission, No. 2714½, Aug. 4, 1919, T telegram (SDR, RG 59, 763.72119/5920, DNA).

My dear Mr. Secretary,   The White House, 4 August, 1919.

I am ashamed to say that I carried the enclosed[1] across the water with me and brought it back without reading it until yesterday, when I was down the river in the Mayflower, away from all interruptions, and took occasion to look over postponed papers of various kinds.

I wonder if Fletcher would still make the same analysis and the some [same] suggestions? And, if these are still his suggested courses of action, what, under the second course suggested, would he propose to do if Mexico did not respond to our "call" do [to] do her duty internationally? Are there any memoranda in your office which would answer these questions, or is Fletcher still here to answer them directly?   Faithfully Yours,   W.W.

WWTLI (SDR, RG 59, 711.12/187, DNA).
  [1] FLP to WW, March 1, 1919, enclosing H. P. Fletcher to WW, March 1, 1919, printed at that date in Vol. 55.

To Robert Lansing, with Enclosure

My dear Mr. Secretary,   The White House, 4 August, 1919.

Do you not think that it would be well for you to see Mr. Lodge personally and lay this message before him, with strong emphasis upon the perhaps irreparable damage we are doing to American business interests by not taking part in these preliminary determinations? I hope that you will, and that it will be possible for you to do it at once. We ought to be sending some of our very best men over to safeguard our interests.

I do not think that we ought in any ciscumstances [sic] to withdr.w [sic] altogether.   Faithfully, W.W.

WWTLI (SDR, RG 59, 763.72119/6778, DNA).

Paris July 31, 1919

Urgent. 3416. Personal for the Secretary of State from Polk and Dulles.

Many of the most important problems with which Mission is now dealing relate to existing treaty with Germany. As previously reported an interim reparation committee has been formed which through acute economic situation in Europe has been led already to take up economic problems of great importance to Europe and also, though less directly, to the United States. The coal negotiations of this commission have been forwarded Mission's 3298, July 24, 6 pm and 3320, July 26, 7 pm.[1] The Allied Maritime Transport Executive in London has now been authorized by reparation commission to study the allocation of ceded German ships. German dyestuff experts will be here next week. Broad reconstruction plans are under consideration.

The committee on execution of the treaty with Germany has made a number of reports which the Supreme Council has approved and which emphasize the necessity of immediate action in selecting, provisionally, the members of the Commissions so that they can enter promptly and intelligently upon their functions in such disturbed districts as Silesia, Schleswig, Danzig, etcetera.

The committee, dealing with the Rhineland Occupation Convention, is studying ordinances necessary to be promulgated immediately upon the coming into force of the treaty.

The American member of these and similar Peace Conference committees will be placed in a very embarrassing position unless the United States will be prepared to take part, at least informally, on the permanent commissions upon the coming into force of the treaty, and we consider that unless there is a probability that the American selection for these various commissions can be made promptly, it might even be better for the United States to withdraw at the present time from active participation in all matters relating to the execution of the treaty.

Our national prestige and interests will, we consider, be less prejudiced by this course and, from a practical standpoint, the personnel of the Mission is now so depleted, particularly in respect of technical experts, that by attempting to participate in current matters of the character above described me [we] risk committing the United States, at least morally, to cou[r]ses of action, the full significance of which it is impossible for us adequately to appraise.

Dulles, the American member of the temporary reparation commission, the committee on execution of the treaty and the Rhineland Committee, adds that for personal reasons it will be absolutely impossible for him to remain more than a few weeks longer and he would probably feel justified in doing this if it were probable that, by the end of that time, definite selections for the various commissions would be here so that his serving in the interval would afford an easy transition.

In view of this situation we should appreciate your personal advice as to the course which we should follow. Polk. Dulles.

American Mission.

T telegram (SDR, RG 59, 763.72119/5905, DNA).
    [1] J. F. Dulles to RL, No. 3298, July 24, 1919, T telegram (SDR, RG 59, 763.72119/5812, DNA), and JFD to RL, No. 3320, July 26, 1919, T telegram (SDR, RG 59, 763.72119/5829, DNA). Copies of these telegrams were sent to Wilson. They are not in WP, DLC.

To Robert Lansing, with Enclosure

My dear Mr. Secretary,   The White House, 4 August, 1919.

The answer to this is plain. The truth is that, until the Scapa Flow incident,[1] *no* agreement was arrived at. It was *our* decided opinion that the ships ought to be broken up or sunk, and I think that that was also the judgment of Mr. Lloyd George (personally, if not as a representative of the British Admiralty). When the Scapa Flow incident occurred Mr. Lloyd George was so mortified that it should have happened under the eyes of British guards that he did say what Mr. Clemenceau here quotes him as saying, but no general policy with regard to the ships was even discussed, and I drew no tacit inference even from what was said that would affect the policy of the other powers that might receive, or might have received, some of the ships. I think that I can say with confidence that Mr. Lloyd George knew that we still held our original view as to what the British, at least, ought to do with those that fell to them, and that he agreed with that view,—if British opinion would let him act on it. America would get none of the ships anyway,— and I did not understand whether Italy was to get any or not. We were tacitly agreed, I should say, to let France do what she wished.

Faithfully Yours,   W.W.

WWTLI (SDR, RG 59, 763.72119/6065, DNA).
    [1] About which, see n. 8 to the minutes of the Council of Four printed at June 21, 1919, 3:45 p.m., Vol. 61.

E N C L O S U R E

Paris. July 31, 1919.

Urgent. 3436. Confidential. The Council of Heads of Delegations at its meeting yesterday afternoon had again before it the question of the disposal of the German and Austro-Hungarian fleets.

In accordance with the decision taken at the afternoon meeting of July 28th (see point two of Mission's telegram number 3412, of July 31st),[1] extracts from the texts of Sir Maurice Hankey's and Mr. Montoux's minutes were read. Those of Sir Maurice Hankey will be found in the I.C.A. minutes 176E of April 25th; C.F.90 of June 24th, and C.F.91, paragraph two, of June 25th.[2] Mr. Montoux's minutes were virtually in accord with Sir Maurice Hankey's.

Mr. Balfour said that Mr. Clemenceau had accurately remembered the discussion of June 25th. Nevertheless, it seemed that previous to the Scapa Flow incident the Council of Four had been uncertain as to the ultimate action to be taken with German vessels. The French evidently had desired that they should be distributed. The Italian and Japanese did not appear to be of the same opinion. While the Scapa Flow incident may not have been the fault of the Admiralty, it was none the less a fact that the German fleet had been sunk in British waters by its own crews. The minutes showed that Mr. Lloyd George had evidently spoken with great feeling and had renounced in favor of France, the British share in any compensation obtainable. On the extracts now before the Council Mr. Clemenceau based his views; viz, first, that no destruction should take place; and second, that England renounce all claims to vessels which would have fallen to her share but for the Scapa Flow incident. He personally was in entire agreement with the second point. There remained, however, the question of: first, disposal, and, second, proportion of division. He did not think that Mr. Lloyd George's remarks could be regarded as a statement of a considered policy for the reason that when he made it he defined only the French position and made no mention of Italy, Japan or America. Mr. Scialoja,[3] the Italian delegate, pointed out that Italy had not been represented at the Conference on June 24. Italy's position today was the same as that of France. Mr. Clemenceau referred to conversations he had had with Mr. Lloyd George and President Wilson and stated that it was his conclusion from the discussion that a tacit understanding had been reached between them to the effect that the enemy vessels should be divided and not destroyed. Then the Scapa Flow incident occurred. It could never have upset Mr. Lloyd George as much as it did had any form of destruction been previously decided upon. He was surprised to hear the Italian claim now put forth for the first time. He admitted it, however, but insisted that if it were maintained a pool of all enemy vessels should be made.

Mr. Balfour reported that the Admiralty had advised him that no request had been made for a copy of their report on the Scapa Flow incident. When it was received he would furnish it to Mr. Clemenceau. He also asked Mr. White for the American view.

Mr. White stated that he was unacquainted with the discussions which had been referred to but he always believed that the United States advocated the sinking or destruction of the warships.

Mr. Clemenceau said that he would agree to submit to President Wilson any proposal which might be put forth but that he would never agree to the sinking or destruction of the warships.

Mr. Balfour stated that the quotations from the minutes were not sufficient authority for him to act. He proposed to send a telegram to Mr. Lloyd George asking for further instructions.

Mr. White and Mr. Polk stated that they would send a telegram in the same terms to President Wilson.

It was agreed that the discussion should be adjourned until the British and American delegates had received answers to their telegrams. Mr. Balfour has furnished me with a copy of the telegram that he has sent to Mr. Lloyd George, reading as follows:

"Paris, July 30, 1919.

The question of the disposal of German vessels has come up and the Conference has been endeavoring to extract from the records of the proceedings of the 'Four' what was their policy; in my opinion, with imperfect success.

It is quite clear that you laid it down that all the loss consequent on the Scapa Flow disaster should fall on Great Britain in the event of a distribution. But it is not so clear what opinion the Four held as to whether there ought to be a distribution or whether the ships should be sunk; and if there was a distribution on what principle it should be conducted and whether the ships distributed should be broken up or on the other hand used at the discretion of the power to whom they were alloted.

Phrases were certainly employed at the meeting on the twenty-fifth June, which, if taken strictly, meant that France should have all the ships she wanted irrespective of the claims of the other Allies. But this can hardly have been intended, and the whole conversation was clearly of a loose and informal character, which leaves much doubt as to what was the settled policy of yourself or of the President. Nothing on the subject appears to have been said to the naval authorities, either in America or England.

Clemenceau will, I think, fight to the last for the right to use, for whatever purpose he likes, the share of enemy ships, Austrian and German surface and submarine, which is assigned to France. On the principles of distribution he may perhaps be more malleable.

If you wish the Conference to discuss the question further please let me know your views."

We should be very grateful if you will be good enough to let us have instructions in the matter as soon as you can conveniently do so. Signed Polk, White.

T telegram (SDR, RG 59, 763.72119/5922, DNA).
    [1] Ammission to RL, No. 3412, July 31, 1919, T telegram (SDR, RG 256, 180.03501/17, DNA), Section II of which reads as follows:
    "The Council had before it the question of the disposal of the German and Austro-Hungarian fleets.
    "The Admirals who had discussed the question on several occasions had not been able to agree except on one point, namely, that before they could deal with the matter, they must know the decision with regard to the general policy.
    "Mr. Clemenceau stated that he did not see how the question could again be raised. It had already been discussed by the Council of Four and finally, in reply to the French request, it had been decided that the vessels should be distributed and that each recipient country might do what it liked with the vessels allotted to it. There could be no doubt on the question, because when the Scapa Flow incident occurred, Mr. Lloyd George had expressed his regret for what had happened, in view of the fact that France was to receive a certain number of the vessels sunk.
    "Mr. Lloyd George had again renewed his promise and had given Mr. Clemenceau a list of vessels that might finally be given to France by way of compensation.
    "The Council, he pointed out, had never received the promised report from the British Government regarding the Scapa Flow incident, in order that responsibility for the affair might be determined. It seemed clear that the German Government was responsible for the action of the German Admiral. After some further discussion it was agreed that the Secretariat should examine the minutes of proceedings in order to report on all that had been said by the Council of Four. It was further decided that Mr. Balfour should ask the British Government for the report on the Scapa Flow incident."
    [2] See the minutes of the Council of Four printed at April 25, 1919, 5:30 p.m., Vol. 58; June 24, 1919, 11:15 a.m., Vol. 61; and June 25, 1919, 11 a.m., *ibid.*
    [3] That is, Vittorio Scialoja.

To Robert Lansing, with Enclosure

My dear Mr. Secretary,   The White House, 4 August, 1919.

When you [do] you think we ought to let Reinsch come back?[1] He cannot be of much further use in his present frame of mind, and yet it will hardly do to let affairs over there get into temporary hands.   Faithfully,   W.W.

WWTLI (B. Long Papers, DLC).
    [1] For Reinsch's letter of resignation, see Enclosure I printed with WW to RL, July 25, 1919 (second letter of that date), Vol. 61.

E N C L O S U R E

Peking. Aug. 1, 1919.

Confidential. Please communicate to the President I should be greatly obliged if you could give me an indication as to the approximate date when I can be released and hope it may not be later than September first.   Reinsch.

T telegram (B. Long Papers, DLC).

To Robert Lansing, with Enclosure

My dear Mr. Secretary,   The White House, 4 August, 1919.

I do not know to what this refers. I made no statement to Lodge on this subject.[1] Baruch's statement must be referred to, and that was to the effect that no distribution had yet been agreed upon.[2]

I have no objection to letting the Committee on Foreign Relations see the agreement here quoted, if they ask us about the matter.   Faithfully,   W.W.

WWTLI (WP, DLC).
[1] However, see WW to HCL, July 25, 1919, Vol. 61.
[2] For Baruch's statement in his testimony before the Senate Foreign Relations Committee on July 31, 1919, see *Treaty of Peace With Germany: Hearings Before the Committee on Foreign Relations, United States Senate*, 66th Cong., 1st sess., Senate Document No. 106, pp. 5-7.
    Wilson had obviously read the report of Baruch's testimony in the newspapers, e.g., the *New York Times*, Aug. 1, 1919. Baruch had said only that, while the question of whether the United States would receive a share of reparation payments was still an open one, he believed that it would not receive any share if the decision was left to Wilson.

E N C L O S U R E

Paris July 31, 1919.

3413. Very Confidential.

For the Secretary. Department's 2662 July 29, 2 P.M.[1] With reference to statement of the President to Lodge that he has not yet learned of any agreement having been arrived at with reference to distribution of indemnity pursuant to article 237 of the Peace Treaty, you may perhaps wish to recall to the President's attention a memorandum signed by him, Mr. Clemenceau, and Mr. Lloyd George dated May 1st 1919 reading as follows:

"The proportions in which receipts from Germany are to be divided between the Allied and Associated Governments in accordance with article 7 of the reparation chapter of the draft treaty with Germany, shall be those which the aggregates of the claims of each accredits Germany which are established to the satisfaction of the Reparation Commission in accordance with annexes one and two of the reparation chapter, bear to the aggregate of the claims of all against Germany which are established to the satisfaction of the Commission."[2]

Article 7 referred to in the quotation corresponds to article 237 of the Peace Treaty. It is my understanding that the British and French regard this agreement as governing the distribution of indemnity. The French have within the last day or two expressed themselves to me to this effect. Dulles.

                                    American Mission.

T telegram (WP, DLC).
    [1] RL to Ammission, No. 2662, July 29, 1919, T telegram (SDR, RG 256, 811.9111/
146, DNA). This telegram included a paraphrase of WW to HCL, July 25, 1919, Vol.
61.
    [2] See Appendix III to the minutes of the Council of Four printed at May 1, 1919, 11
a.m., Vol. 58.

To Robert Lansing

My dear Mr. Secretary,   The White House, 4 August, 1919.

I should very much like you to tell me just what you think ought to be done in this matter.[1]

I fear that it would be most unwise to put before Congress just at this stage of its discussion of the Covenant either a proposal to promise to assume the Mandate for Armenia or a proposal to send American troops there to replace the British and assume the temporary protection of the population; and yet will our own public opinion tolerate our doing, at least our attempting, nothing?

Faithfully Yours,   W.W.

WWTLI (SDR, RG 59, 860J.01/26½, DNA).
    [1] Wilson enclosed J. S. Williams to WW, Aug. 1, 1919, with its Enclosure, about
which see WW to J. S. WIlliams, Aug. 2, 1919, n. 1.

From Robert Lansing

My dear Mr. President: Washington August 4, 1919.

I return your note of today with a copy of your letter to Senator Lodge[1] under date of July 25th which was published in the NEW YORK TIMES. I think this must have escaped your memory. Undoubtedly it is to that letter that Dulles refers in his telegram of the 31st July. I am telegraphing Dulles to ask if that is the complete memorandum signed by you, Mr. Clemenceau and Mr. Lloyd-George and if it is not to telegraph the entire memorandum.[2] Until I hear from him I do not think it would be well to furnish the Committee with anything on the subject.

Faithfully yours,   Robert Lansing

TLS (WP, DLC).
    [1] It is a TCL copied from the New York Times, July 27, 1919. Lansing's letter was
prompted by D. H. Miller, "Memorandum for the Secretary," Aug. 4, 1919, TI MS (SDR,
RG 59, 763.72119/5904, DNA).
    [2] RL to JFD, No. 2715, Aug. 4, 1919, T telegram (SDR, RG 59, 763.72119/5904,
DNA).

From Joseph Patrick Tumulty, with Enclosure

Dear Governor: [The White House] 4 August, 1919.

I have just read your reply to the Senate resolution asking for information with reference to the Shantung settlement,[1] and have read the letter of General Bliss to you of April 29th.[2] To put it mildly, his reply is astounding. I am wondering how Japan will feel about his statement "If we support Japan's claim, we abandon the democracy of China to the domination of the Prussianized militarism of Japan." "It can't be right to do wrong even to make peace. Peace is desirable, but there are things dearer than peace,—justice and freedom."

This reply of General Bliss's is bound to make a profound impression on the Senate and on the country itself. I am wondering whether your reply touches the point at issue. Is it not possible to withhold the dispatch of this answer for a week, with the hope that Japan will be heard from in the meantime? Or if this does not seem advisable to you, do you not think that your own letter of transmission should explain more clearly the circumstances of General Bliss's letter and your subsequent action with regard to it? As it stands now, the people will be right in believing that the Shantung settlement was made in the face of the burning, detailed protest joined in by General Bliss, Mr. Lansing, and Mr. White. If publication is given in its present form, I feel strongly that the thought of the country will support the closing paragraph of General Bliss's letter, in which the flat statement is made that the price is too great to pay even for peace.

Is it not the case that the Bliss letter was acted upon by you and that the Shantung settlement, as it now stands, met many of the objections set down by General Bliss? Will not the minutes of the Council show that Japan agreed to the return of Shantung and also met many of the other objections set down by General Bliss?

Let me further emphasize the international aspect of this letter. Aside from the insult to Japan that I have noted, there is the reopening of the whole Italian matter, for, as General Bliss says, "if it be right for Japan to annex the territory of an Ally, then it cannot be wrong for Italy to retain Fiume taken from the enemy."

                              Sincerely yours,   J. P. Tumulty

TL (WP, DLC).
  [1] See G. A. Sanderson to JPT, July 16 and 17, 1919, Vol. 61.
  [2] THB to WW, April 29, 1919, Vol. 58.

ENCLOSURE

To the Senate: The White House 4 August, 1919.

I have received the Resolutions of the Senate, dated July 15th and July 17th, asking:

First, for a copy of any treaty purporting to have been projected between Germany and Japan, as was referred to in the press dispatch enclosed, together with any information in regard to it which may be in possession of the State Department, or any information concerning any negotiations between Japan and Germany during the progress of the war. In reply to this resolution, I have the honor to report that I know of no such negotiations. I had heard the rumors that are referred to, but was never able to satisfy myself that there was any substantial foundation for them.

Second, requesting a copy of any letter or written protest by the members of the American Peace Commission or any officials attached thereto, against the disposition or adjustment which was made with reference to Shantung, and particularly a copy of a letter written by General Tasker H. Bliss, Member of the Peace Commission, on behalf of himself, Hon. Robert Lansing, Secretary of State, and Hon. Henry White, Members of the Peace Commission, protesting against the provisions of the Treaty with reference to Shantung.[1] I take pleasure in transmitting a copy of the letter from General Bliss referred to. I beg leave to say that this letter was not a protest against the Shantung decision, but an expression of the views of my fellow-commissioners, written at my request before the Shantung decision was agreed to and before all the elements in the final decision were determined. I have received no written protests from any officials connected with or attached to the American Peace Commission.[2] I am also asked to send you any memorandum or other information with reference to an attempt of Japan or her Peace Delegates to intimidate the Chinese Peace Delegates. I am happy to say that I have no such memorandum of information.

T MS (WP, DLC).

[1] Obviously, someone had shown Senator Borah, the author of this resolution, a copy of Bliss' letter to Wilson of April 29, 1919, or had at least told him of its contents.

[2] However, see S. K. Hornbeck to WW and RL, May 27, 1919, printed as an Enclosure with RL to WW, June 3, 1919 (second letter of that date), Vol. 60.

Gilbert Fairchild Close to Robert Lansing

Dear Mr. Secretary: The White House 4 August, 1919.

The President asks me to send you the enclosed letter[1] and documents which he expects to send to the Chairman of the Senate

Committee on Foreign Affairs, in answer to requests for data from that Committee. Will you not look over the letter and let me know of [if] you have any suggestions to make?

Sincerely yours,   Gilbert F. Close

TLS (WP, DLC).
¹ This was a draft of WW to HCL, Aug. 8, 1919, in reply to HCL to WW, July 15, 1919, Vol. 61. We have not found the draft of Wilson's letter to Lodge. For the letter sent, see WW to HCL, Aug. 8, 1919.

From Robert Lansing

My dear Mr. President: Washington August 4, 1919.

I have read your letter to Senator Lodge as Chairman of the Committee on Foreign Relations, enclosing copies of the various drafts of the Covenant.

My only criticism is that you indicate that there were memoranda relating to the debates in the Commission on the League of Nations which you cannot deliver to them on account of their being in the hands of your colleagues in Paris. I think that this may result in their saying to you that they wish to have copies of these memoranda and would like you to telegraph for them.

My own view is, in regard to the proceedings which took place before the Commissions, that they are all of a confidential nature and would require the assent of all the other nations before you could present them to a Senate Committee. This, as you will recall, is the position we took when Mr. Clemenceau asked whether we would be willing to consent to the submission of the minutes on the League of Nations to the French Senate. I fear that putting it solely on the ground of the memoranda not being in your hands will compel you later to refuse on the ground which I have stated.

My suggestion is that you state that ground in your letter and in that way prevent a further request.

Faithfully yours,   Robert Lansing.

TLS (WP, DLC).

A Memorandum by Alexander Comstock Kirk

[Washington, Aug. 4, 1919]

Telephone message from President. President desires Mr. Long to procure from Japanese Chargé the text of the statement published in the morning papers, and any explanation he may have regarding possible discrepancies between statement handed to Mr.

Long by Debuchi and published statement. The President desires
a memo on this matter. K.

Hw MS (SDR, RG 59, 793.94/94b, DNA).

From Robert Lansing, with Enclosure

My dear Mr. President: Washington August 4, 1919.

I enclose the public statement of the Japanese Government in
regard to Shantung which was given out in Tokio and which will
probably be published here by the Associated Press tomorrow
morning.

It does not seem to me satisfactory in that no time of surrendering sovereignty to China is indicated and the proposed negotiation
for the surrender is to be based apparently on the iniquitous treaty
of May, 1915, and the supplementary agreement of September,
1918. There are other features of the statement which I do not like.

The issuance of this statement, however, puts us in a decidedly
advantageous position. To remain silent in the face of the statement would be an admission on your part that it set forth the
agreement reached at Paris. If it does not state the agreement fully
or accurately, you are, in justice to yourself, bound to make public
the terms on which you assented to the Shantung articles in the
treaty. While there might have been ground for complaint if you
had made public a statement as to Japan's promises before the Japanese Government had made one, there can certainly be none now,
because to do so would be to admit that their statement was either
inaccurate or incomplete.

We hold the strategic position and, I feel, we should use it. I
would suggest, therefore, that you prepare a statement of your understanding of their agreement which can be published on the
heels of their statement when it appears in our newspapers with
the assertion that you find it necessary to do this in order to avoid
the charge of having given your assent to the treaty provisions on
the basis of the statements of the Japanese Government issued at
Tokio.

For your information I am enclosing a copy of a draft of a declaration to be made by the Japanese regarding the Shantung question which I submitted to Baron Makino, Mr. Balfour and finally to
Mr. Clemenceau before my departure from Paris.[1]

Faithfully yours, Robert Lansing.

TLS (WP, DLC).
[1] It is printed in n. 5 to the memorandum by RL printed at June 28, 1919, Vol. 61.

ENCLOSURE

PRIVATE & CONFIDENTIAL.   (8/3/19.—Handed
me by Mr. Debuchi.—
Not for publication.—
B.L.)[1]

IMPERIAL JAPANESE EMBASSY
WASHINGTON

(Text of the statement made to the press in Tokio,
August 2, by Viscount Uchida.)

It appears that, in spite of the official statement which the Japanese Delegation at Paris issued on May 5[2] last and which I fully endorsed in an interview with the representatives of the press on May 17, Japan's policy respecting the Shantung question is little understood or appreciated abroad.

It will be remembered that in the ultimatum which the Japanese Government addressed to the German Government on August 15, 1914, they demanded of Germany "to deliver on a date not later than September 15, 1914, to the Imperial authorities without condition or compensation the entire leased territory of Kiaochow with a view to eventual restoration of the same to China." The terms of that demand have never elicited any protest on the part of China or any other Allied or Associated Powers.

Following the same line of policy, Japan now claims as one of the essential conditions of peace that the leased territory of Kiaochow should be surrendered to her without condition or compensation. At the same time, abiding faithfully by the pledge which she gave to China in 1915, she is quite willing to restore to China the whole territory in question and to enter upon negotiations with the Government at Peking as to the arrangement necessary to give effect to that pledge as soon as possible after the Treaty of Versailles shall have been ratified by Japan.

Nor has she any intention to retain or to claim any rights which affect the territorial sovereignty of China in the Province of Shantung. The significance of the clause appearing in Baron Makino's statement of May 5 that "the policy of Japan is to hand back the Shantung Peninsula in full sovereignty to China retaining only the economic privileges granted to Germany" must be clear to all.

Upon arrangement being arrived at between Japan and China for the restitution of Kiaochow, the Japanese troop[s] at present guarding the territory and the Kiaochow-Tsinanfu railway will be completely withdrawn.

The Kiaochow-Tsinanfu railway is intended to be operated as a joint Sino-Japanese enterprise without any discrimination in treatment against the people of any nation.

The Japanese Government have moreover under contemplation proposals for the establishment in Tsingtao of a general foreign settlement in stead of the exclusive Japanese settlement which by the agreement of 1915 with China they are entitled to claim.

T MS (WP, DLC).
 [1] That is, Breckinridge Long.
 [2] See Hankey's minutes of the Council of Four printed at April 30, 1919, 12:30 p.m., Vol. 58.

Sir William Wiseman to Arthur James Balfour

[New York, Aug. 4, 1919]

Following for Mr. Balfour from Sir W. Wiseman.

Personal and Secret.

An important movement is being started to force the Administration to withdraw recognition from Carranza.[1]

American ambassador to Mexico has advised this course.[2]

The President will not accept this proposal at present but he has lost all faith in Carranza and is perplexed as to right solution.

In spite of statements to the contrary the Administration is much concerned about Mexican situation and rising public indignation in this country.

Hw telegram (W. Wiseman Papers, CtY).
 [1] Wiseman here probably refers to the movement led by Senator Albert B. Fall of New Mexico; Edward Laurence Doheny, petroleum producer of California and Mexico; and William Frank Buckley, lawyer and petroleum producer in Mexico. It was largely financed by the Association of Oil Producers in Mexico and the National Association for the Protection of American Rights in Mexico. Its ultimate objective was to bring about military and/or political intervention by the United States in Mexico. See Clifford W. Trow, "Woodrow Wilson and the Mexican Interventionist Movement of 1919," *Journal of American History*, LVIII (June 1971), pp. 46-72.
 [2] See H. P. Fletcher to WW, March 1, 1919, printed as an Enclosure with FLP to WW, March 1, 1919, Vol. 55. As WW to RL, Aug. 4, 1919 (second letter of that date), reveals, Wilson read Fletcher's letter on August 3.

Edith Bolling Galt Wilson to Henry White

My dear Mr. White: The White House August 4, 1919

Only this morning Miss Benham and I were talking of you and wishing you might run in and refresh us by one of your welcome visits—and here, as though in answer, comes your gracious letter[1] bringing with it that subtle thing spoken of as *atmosphere* which brings your own personality distinctly and reassuringly near.

What vivid memories crowd one upon the other as I read your word pictures—of Paris, of its gossip, its jealousies, its vari[e]d life and its inevitable charm.

I am afraid you will find Washington dull when you come back, for it seems like a village in comparison, but even so, you are too loyal a friend not to find compensation in the warmth of the welcome which awaits you in our hearts.

No, we did not know of the inside history of Marshal Joffre's riding with Foch,[2] but it does not surprise me, and it is an interesting straw in the wind as to the demand of the people. We went, that night (July 14th) to the French Embassy and the Jusserand's seemed very pleased.[3]

It was our only *social* venture since we got back and was really a very happy one.

Before I say any more of ourselves I want you to know that I share the disappointment of your daughter and grandchildren[4] in your delayed visit to them, and hope with all my heart you *have* been able to go before this, and that you found all as you would have had it?

Also I must tell you that the illness of my husband was not serious, though I think it was due to the long strain rather than as a result of a week-end cruise on the "Mayflower."

He was only in bed one day, but even then he worked—for things here are even more hectic than Paris, and the days of 24 hours each seem far too short for the disposal of the demands made upon him.

He postponed his trip to the Coast wishing to be here in touch with the Senate and do everything he could to assist the ratification of the Treaty. I need not go into the state of things in this matter for I know you are kept informed, but I often long for your deft touch which helped so often to untangle the threads in Paris. Of course I believe it will all come right in the end, but the partisan spirit seems armed to the teeth, and it may take a long time to conquer.

Since we got home, (which is nearly a month now) we have both been tremendously busy and the days have passed swiftly—despite the tremendous heat which held for over two weeks. Now however it is cool and we welcome the relief. Most of *smart* Washington is out of town, and only the slaves of the people remain to work.

I have seen the Lansings twice and, of course, asked for news of you, and got a splendid account.

They both look so well and seem happy to be at home.

My husband is down stairs having a hearing of the Rail Road men,[5] so I cannot give you a direct message from him, but can say that he has told me how splendidly you have handled the new Italian min[i]ster,[6] and how clear and able your cablegrams have been. He said the other night he had just sent you a message to thank you[7] for they were so splendidly done.

Dr. Grayson dined a few nights ago with Senator Gerry in your house, and came back enthusiastic over the beauty of the house and your garden. When you come home I will ask you to let me come and see Mrs. White's portrait[8] some time and the other lovely things I know you have. It will recall our happy day in Paris when we visited, under your guidance, other beautiful spots filled with history and charm.

It was sweet of you to use a holiday to write to me, and I have sent you such a long reply you will probably have to ask the *five* to adjourn for a day in order to read it, but there was much to say, and my thoughts will go on and carry you other messages.

I cannot say goodby, without again thanking you for all your help and generous interest manifested in so many delicate ways, while we were in Paris, and add that our friendship begun here, and ripened there, is a very sacred one.

Please remember me to your brothers[9] if they are with you, and know that I am, with warmest assurances

Faithfully yours,   Edith Bolling Wilson.

ALS (H. White Papers, DLC).

[1] H. White to EBW, July 23, 1919, ALS (WP, DLC).

[2] White wrote of this incident, in the letter cited above, as follows:

"Did you see that dear old Joffre rode in the procession beside Foch at the great Peace celebration on the 14th. It had not been intended that he should do so or appear in any particular place on that occasion. (I think you know that an invitation to the treaty signing at Versailles was only sent to him at 10 that same morning when they knew that he was safely in London!) But this time there were signs of public disapproval and the worthy Poincaré thought he would solve the situation by inviting Joffre to sit near him in the Presidential tribune. That proposal, contained in a letter which was published, only made matters worse and they began to look serious; a debate being threatened in the Chamber and other things not less terrifying to the Government. So it was resolved that Joffre should ride behind Foch, at the head of a number of generals. The Public would not stand that either and insisted that they should both ride side by side which they did."

[3] For Jusserand's report to the Foreign Ministry about this affair, see n. 2 to the extract from the Diary of H. F. Ashurst printed at July 15, 1919, Vol. 61.

[4] That is Muriel White, Countess Seherr-Thoss, wife of Hermann Roger Christow, Count Seherr-Thoss and their children, Hans Christoph, Margaret, and Hermann Seherr-Thoss.

[5] About which, see the second news report printed at August 5, 1919.

[6] That is, Tommaso Tittoni.

[7] WW to H. White, July 25, 1919, Vol. 61.

[8] John Singer Sargent's portrait of Margaret Stuyvesant Rutherfurd White, painted in 1883. It now hangs in the Corcoran Gallery of Art.

[9] Julian Leroy White, who was living in France at this time, and White's half-brother, William Hepburn Buckler, former special assistant in the American embassy in London, who had been assigned to the American Commission to Negotiate Peace in June 1919.

Three News Reports

[Aug. 5, 1919]

WILSON TAKES PERSONAL CONTROL OF THE FOOD SITUATION

The ponderous executive machinery of the government, with President Wilson in direct control, moved speedily yesterday toward definite action to bring down the price of the people's food. Aroused by the insistent and growing rumble of unrest throughout the country the President took command of the situation and accelerated the slow-moving government forces.

Like an avalanche the demand for more wages or lower prices continued to grow throughout the day as additional labor organizations communicated to the President their need for higher pay to meet the growing cost of living.

Hundreds of thousands of organized workers were heard from yesterday, and their demands added weight and impetus to the ominous outpouring of cries for relief which resounded in the ears of the whole government establishment.

Late in the day when the general nature of the demand for relief had become plainly apparent the President, without warning, stepped into the center of things and took charge. He left the White House and hurried to the Federal Trade Commission, where he was closeted for some time with Chairman W. B. Colver, who is a member of the subcommittee framing relief measures for the cabinet conference on living costs, and with Trade Commissioner Victor Murdock.

The President believes it will be a long time, probably several years before the price of foodstuffs and other necessaries of life go back to the level they were on before the United States entered the war. He believes that there can be no sudden lowering of prices, but that whatever is accomplished must be done gradually.

The President made his views in this direction plain to representatives of railroad workers who presented their demands to him at the White House, just before he visited the Trade Commission.

The President made no announcement as to the matters discussed with the trade commissioners, and they declined to talk about the matter beyond saying that prices were under consideration.

It is known, however, that the Trade Commission has in hand very complete reports on production costs in industries which run the whole gamut of national needs, compiled during the war. These figures would be invaluable in a general program for forcing a readjustment of prices generally.

Chairman Colver's subcommittee, which includes Director General of Railroads Hines and Assistant Secretary of the Treasury Leffingwell, is expected to submit definite recommendations to the Cabinet conference today following Colver's talk with the President yesterday. These recommendations will undoubtedly form the basis of a report to the President and the cabinet as a whole later in the day.

With the cabinet conference today, will meet Julius Barnes, chairman of the United States Grain Corporation, C. B. Ames,[1] Assistant to the Attorney General in charge of all anti-trust prosecutions, and W. P. G. Harding of the Federal Reserve Board. The conference will meet at the office of Attorney General Palm[e]r.

While no definite statement of contemplated action was forthcoming yesterday, all discussion of the courses to be pursued was directed along three general lines:

First, drastic and speedy prosecution in the courts of everything resembling profiteering in the necessaries of life.

Second, immediate steps to reduce the tremendous volume of currency which has grown with leaps and bounds since the United States entered the war.

T[h]ird, government action to relieve food prices by throwing open the market for wheat and eliminating the government guarantee of $2.20 per bushel to the farmer, even if the government is forced to absorb the difference between the market price and the guaranteed price.

All three of these projected remedies will be under discussion today. Chairman Barnes is the government official charged with administering the wheat price guarantee. He will be questioned by the cabinet conference. Gov. Harding of the reserve board, is the representative of the whole financial fabric of the country, and has his hand on the pulse of currency and credit inflation. He will be present.

Attorney General Palmer and his chief aid, Judge Ames, with the members of the Federal Trade Commission, are of all officials the closest to possible profiteering. Their views will be presented.

The demand for action against profiteers has been included in every new demand for wages, and every new complaint against living cost which has found its way from the people to the capital.

Profiteering, conscienceless capital—exploiters of labor—all these were the complaint of the railroad unions which first voiced the general demand for relief. Profiteering was the basis of complaints reaching the President yesterday just before he hurried to the trade commission which has made profiteering the basis of a large part of its recent activities.

Significance was seen last night in the announcement that Attorney General Palmer had called to Washington for a conference, District Attorney Clyne,[2] of Chicago. The Federal trade commission has been working with the Department of Justice for some time in connection with the manipulation of meat prices, and the prosecution of the Chicago packers has more than once been seriously discussed.

The summoning of Clyne again revived talk of action along this line. It was suggested, however, that the attorney general will probably call to Washington all Federal district attorneys who have in their jurisdictions large concerns dealing with the necessaries of life, to discuss the strict enforcement of the anti-trust laws and other laws designed to prevent price manipulation and exploitation.

Agrarian representatives in Congress were loud in their defense of the farmer yesterday, and they declared that the government guaranteed price on wheat to the farmer was not a primary cause of high living costs.

In both House and Senate the price problem loomed large and the Senate devoted the whole day to discussion of the situation. The net practical result was an announcement from Chairman Gronna[3] that he had called the Senate committee investigating the high cost of living to meet today.

A new angle of the cost situation developed in the Senate when a resolution was unanimously adopted calling upon the railroad administration to acquaint the Senate with what is being done to relieve a threatened shortage of coal cars.

Senator Pomerene, who presented the situation, indicated that coal production was being curtailed by lack of cars, and he asserted that there was grave danger of a coal shortage during the coming winter.

The House was not in session, but committees and individuals devoted their attention to the problem from various angles.

The House interstate commerce committee recommended the enactment of a resolution by Representative Tinkham[4] providing for a nationwide investigation of the cost of living, particularly sugar, by a commission of twelve, five representatives of executive departments of the government and at least five experts in prices and costs.

The commission would be appointed by the President. The committee also recommended action on a resolution for an inquiry into sugar supply and prices by the Federal trade commission.

There was every indication that both House and Senate are eager to get a definite, concrete plan of action from the President. The clamor for relief from high prices is reaching both Representatives and Senators from "back home" and they are anxious to fix responsibility for conditions, and to relieve them.

Condemnation of extravagance as a general characteristic of the American people was heard in various quarters today.

One official in close touch with the finances of the nation, declared that no relief from high prices could be expected while

"100,000,000 people continue to demand the highest quality of everything, and are willing to pay any price to get it."

A general government campaign for economy among the people has been suggested.

[1] Charles Bismark Ames.
[2] Charles Francis Clyne, United States Attorney for the Northern District of Illinois.
[3] That is, Asle Jorgenson Gronna, Republican of North Dakota, chairman of the Senate Committee on Agriculture and Forestry.
[4] George Holden Tinkham, Republican of Massachusetts.

[Aug. 5, 1919]

BIG BROTHERHOODS MAKE FORMAL DEMAND FOR U. S. TO
RETAIN THE RAILROADS
CALL AT WHITE HOUSE

The threat of a general tie-up of the entire railway system of the country loomed ominously last night before administration officials struggling to deal with the demands of the railroad unions for better wages to meet the increased cost of living.

As the clamor for more wages or lower prices grew tremendously in volume yesterday the railroad unions placed themselves squarely on record as demanding the total elimination of "capital" as such from the management of the roads. In a statement or proclamation to the American people the big railway brotherhoods and the railway unions of the American Federation of Labor demanded that the government take over the railroads and operate them in partnership with the workers for the benefit of the general public.

The railroad unions declared that their demands were embodied in the so-called Plumb plan for the solution of the railroad problem, which they declared would be carried before Congress tomorrow.

"It marks," said the proclamation, "the step by which organized labor passes from demands for wage increases to demands that the system of profits in industry be overhauled."

Promises of government action to alleviate the high cost of living, promises of congressional commissions to determine on possible wage increases, promises of further investigation, all failed to placate the union leaders who are in Washington with practically the whole strength of two and a half million men behind them.

They made it plain that congressional action and investigation mean only delay to them, and that they were not prepared to brook any further trifling with the tremendous demands which they have placed before President Wilson and the country.

Without waiving their demands for immediate wage increases, the big brotherhoods stated unequivocally that the ultimate solution of the transportation problem, the big factor in the cost of living, depended upon the inauguration of a "tripartite" control of the railroads, in which only the government, the workers and the consuming public should share.

The present owners would be eliminated by buying their interest at a "fair valuation" to be paid for in government bonds.

With officials of the union of railroad shop workers in Chicago claiming that 250,000 of their men throughout the country had already walked out, B. M. Jewell, acting president of the railway employes' department of the American Federation of Labor, delivered what amounted to an ultimatum to President Wilson.

It was a letter from the heads of the federated shopmen's unions,[1] declaring that they could not wait for congressional investigation of their demands, but that they would be forced to proceed to a strike vote unless the wage increases for which they have been negotiating with Director General Hines for months are granted promptly.

Printed in the *Washington Post*, Aug. 5, 1919.
  [1] W. H. Johnston *et al.* to WW, Aug. 2, 1919.

[*Aug. 5, 1919*]

WILSON SEES OBSTACLE IN STRIKES.

Washington, Aug. 5. (Associated Press.)—Administration officials feel that one way to decrease the cost of living is to increase production, and President Wilson is understood to feel that strikes now or threats of strikes will interfere materially with any solution of the problem sought by Government agencies.

Conferences with Republican and Democratic Senators on the League of Nations have been definitely abandoned by the President until the problems of the high cost of living are solved, Secretary Tumulty announced. The President, Mr. Tumulty said, is going "to give his whole time to the question of the high cost of living."

Printed in the *New York Times*, Aug. 6, 1919.

To William Bauchop Wilson

My dear Wilson: The White House 5 August, 1919.

I congratulate you on your success in getting through the joint legislation with regard to making arrangements for the convening of the International Labor Conference.[1] I wish I could learn your skill in such matters.

Cordially and faithfully yours,   Woodrow Wilson

TLS (received from Mary A. Strohecker).
  [1] See WBW to WW, Aug. 4, 1919 (first letter of that date).

To John Jacob Esch

My dear Mr. Esch: [The White House] 5 August, 1919.

I thank you sincerely for your kind letter of August 2nd and shall look forward with great pleasure to cooperating with you in the important matters we must now address ourselves to.

I noted with the greatest satisfaction the action of the House in rescinding its recess in order to push forward matters which cannot wait.   Cordially and sincerely yours,   Woodrow Wilson

TLS (Letterpress Books, WP, DLC).

To Albert Baird Cummins

My dear Senator Cummins: [The White House] 5 August, 1919.

I am sincerely obliged to you for your kind letter of the second of August and shall look forward with real pleasure to cooperating with you in any way possible, in the discussion or settlement of the difficult railroad matters which now perplex us all.

I share your feeling that the plan suggested by Mr. Hines is perhaps not comprehensive enough to meet all the present conditions, and I am sure that Mr. Hines himself would subscribe to that judgment, but it seems one of the immediate things to do, and may help us all in thinking towards a comprehensive solution.

Cordially and sincerely yours,   Woodrow Wilson

TLS (Letterpress Books, WP, DLC).

To William Cox Redfield

My dear Mr. Secretary: [The White House] 5 August, 1919.

Thank you for your thoughtful letter about the cost of living.[1] Perhaps it will be well for me to make such an appeal as you suggest, but I am waiting for the development of our plans before deciding just what to do.

Cordially and faithfully yours,   Woodrow Wilson

TLS (Letterpress Books, WP, DLC).
¹ WCR to WW, Aug. 4, 1919.

To Charles Mills Galloway

STRICTLY PRIVATE

My dear Mr. Galloway: [The White House] 5 August, 1919.

You will remember that before I went to Europe I intimated to you that in my judgment it would be best for you to resign your position on the Civil Service Commission.¹ I have not been able to convince myself that I was wrong in that request. Indeed my judgment is confirmed that it would, from many points of view, be best both for you and for the public service, but I wish for your sake to avoid any public insistence upon it, and suggest that you now, as of your own motion, send in your resignation. I will, of course, say nothing to anyone of this additional request if you should act with reasonable promptness on the suggestion, because I sincerely wish to save you any mortification or embarassment.

                           Very truly yours,   [Woodrow Wilson]

CCL (WP, DLC).
¹ See WW to C. M. Galloway, Feb. 28, 1919, Vol. 55, and March 25, 1919, Vol. 56.

To John Knox Coit

My dear Mr. Coit: [The White House] 5 August, 1919.

Allow me to acknowledge the receipt of your letter of July 29th and to say that it gives me pleasure to renew my subscription of a $50. Scholarship for the Nacoochee Institute.

In unavoidable haste,

                           Sincerely yours,   [Woodrow Wilson]

TL (Letterpress Books, WP, DLC).

From the Desk Diary of Robert Lansing

                           Tuesday Aug 5 [1919]

Called up Prest at his request. Discussed Bliss' Shantung letter and decided it was unwise to lay before Senate. Told him I was to appear before Com. tomorrow, not today. . . .

Cabinet meeting—2:30-4:15. Conferred with Prest on Com. hearing tomorrow.

From Royal Meeker[1]

Dear Mr. President: Washington August 5, 1919.

I suggest the advisability of the immediate appointment of a Committee to study plans for the stabilization of the purchasing power of the dollar. I have repeatedly pointed out that it is changing prices which cause distress and not the particular level of prices. We have suffered much hardship through the rapidly rising prices since 1914. It is utterly inexcusable that we multiply the hardships by going through the still more painful process of readjusting prices to a lower level. Declining prices inevitably bring about more distress than advancing prices. Economic and financial forces are operating to prevent the present high prices from falling very much in the near future. The sensible thing to do would be to accept facts as they are and enact legislation for the purpose of stabilizing prices at or near their present high level. Wages and salaries can quite readily be adjusted up to the present level. It would be disastrous to deflate prices suddenly.

With sincerest regards, I am
                         Faithfully yours,   Royal Meeker

TLS (WP, DLC).
  [1] Commissioner of Labor Statistics in the Department of Labor.

From Grosvenor Blaine Clarkson

My dear Mr. President: Washington 5 August, 1919.

The Secretary of War and I discussed this morning the desirability of making public the report on the high cost of living which I gave the Secretary yesterday and which he, in turn, forwarded to you. The Secretary said that such permission should, in this instance, come from you, and I therefore await your wishes in the matter.

I believe that a copious digest of this report, or, say, its insertion in full in the Congressional Record, would tend to a beneficial clarification of the public mind upon the subject in question. There would, of course, need to be deletions of certain statements designed only for official review.[1]

                         Faithfully yours,   Grosvenor Clarkson

TLS (WP, DLC).
  [1] The report (T MS, WP, DLC) was made public on August 30, 1919. The *New York Times*, Aug. 31, 1919, printed a summary of its contents with numerous quotations. The full report was printed as United States. Council of National Defense. Reconstruction Research Division, *An Analysis of the High Cost of Living Problem* (Washington, 1919).

To William Byron Colver

My dear Colver: [The White House] 5 August, 1919.

I have not had time to look through the enclosed, but the men who are connected with the permanent staff of the Council of National Defence are serious and diligent in their desire to serve, and I beg that you will be kind enough to look this paper through for any information or suggestions that may seem to you serviceable.

Cordially and faithfully yours,   Woodrow Wilson

TLS (Letterpress Books, WP, DLC).

From Herbert Clark Hoover

[Paris] August 5, 1919.

#850 In order to maintain the relief in Armenia after the withdrawal of food administration measures it was agreed by Council of Five that Colonel Haskell[1] COMMA U S ARMY COMMA should be appointed High Commissioner in Russian Armenia COMMA representing all the allies jointly COMMA and this has been done and Colonel Haskell is on the ground PERIOD He is being supported by stocks of food which I have provided and by funds from the Near-East Relief Committee PERIOD Owing to the demobilization of the reserve army he will in a few days be without staff and the entire administration will break down PERIOD The only solution is to allow us to secure volunteers from the regular army and navy officers here and have Pershing and Knapp authorized to transfer them to Haskell in name of War and Navy Departments PERIOD The continuance of this service is absolutely necessary and entirely outside General Harbord's Commission of Examination as he only expects to remain a month in the country PERIOD The question has also arisen of providing the new governments in Eastern Europe with technical advisors on transportation and other questions and who will be paid by these governments PERIOD Many of these positions can be best filled with officers from the regular army who have already been conducting these services under my administration. It appears to me no better experience or service could be gained or no more constructive work done by the American army and navy than to fill these positions PERIOD In order to cover both issues your approval to War and Navy Departments is necessary PERIOD I trust you can see your way to recommend these matters to them for prompt action PERIOD HOOVER.

CC telegram (WP, DLC).
    [1] That is, William Nafew Haskell. About his appointment, see NDB to WW, July 15, 1919, Vol. 61, and the Enclosure thereto.

From Elizabeth Merrill Bass[1]

My dear Mr. President: Washington, D. C. August 5, 1919.

A few months ago I ventured to ask you to call Secretary Wilson's attention to the qualifications of Miss Gertrude Barnum[2] for the position of Associate Investigator in the Labor Department. The appointment was made and she gave complete and entire satisfaction I understand, but the service terminated a short time ago. The newspapers several days ago gave the resignation of Miss Mary Van Kleek, Chief of the Women in Industry Bureau of the Labor Department.[3] I am extremely anxious that only those devoted to yourself and your Administration receive appointments now. I feel this is expecially desirable in the Department of Labor, where many opposed to the war and opposed to some of your policies have slipped in. Fearing now that a friend and associate of Mrs. Raymond Robbins's[4] may receive the appointment to Miss Van Kleek's Bureau, I again venture to ask if you will suggest to the Secretary that Miss Barnum might be a satisfactory appointee.

You may remember that I told you Miss Barnum is the daughter of the late Judge Barnum[5] of Chicago; a splendid, charming woman between thirty-five and forty; a college woman; a trained student of labor problems, who has been in practical touch with every phase of them and who is acceptable to women in industry.

Faithfully yours,   Elizabeth Bass

TLS (WP, DLC).

[1] Mrs. George Bass, "chairman" of the Woman's Bureau of the Democratic National Committee. She was following through on what she had said to Wilson in their conversation on August 4, 1919, about the appointment of a new director of the Woman in Industry Service of the Labor Department.

[2] Assistant Director of the Investigation and Inspection Service of the Department of Labor. She had previously served as a settlement house worker in Chicago, an organizer and publicist for the International Ladies' Garment Workers Union, and a special agent for the United States Commission on Industrial Relations.

[3] Mary Abby van Kleeck, the first director of the Woman in Industry Service; both prior and subsequent to this, she was the director of the department of industrial studies of the Russell Sage Foundation.

[4] That is, Margaret Dreier Robins. Her "friend and associate" was of course Mary Anderson.

[5] William Henry Barnum, a judge of the circuit court of Cook County.

Albert Halstead to Robert Lansing

Vienna. Dated August 5, 1919. Via Paris. 6, Recd. 11:45 A.M.

3516. From Vienna. The presence of the Roumanian army in Budapest[1] threatens the peace of that city. Already almost [more than][2] a score of unarmed Hungarians have been killed. I cannot too strongly urge that they (*) [be] required to leave immediately. Otherwise there can be no peace and no steps towards a permanent government. The small force of Allied troops, Roumanians, Czechs (?) Servians (?) is required together with an Allied supervisory commission and the blockade. The effects of Budapest situation upon German Austria is also to be considered. Halstead.[3]

American Mission.[4]

(*) Apparent omission.

T telegram (SDR, RG 59, 864.00/104, DNA).
[1] The Rumanian army had occupied Budapest on August 3.
[2] Additions from the telegram sent, SDR, RG 256, 184.011102/266, DNA.
[3] Albert Halstead, Foreign Service officer, at this time United States Commissioner in Vienna.
[4] A copy of this telegram was sent to Wilson on August 6.

A News Report

[Aug. 6, 1919]

WILSON IS USING EVERY WAR LAW TO SMASH THE HIGH PRICE OF FOOD

Driven by the insistent clamor throughout the country for relief from the constantly mounting prices of the people's food President Wilson yesterday abandoned all other public business to take steps to allay the nation's unrest. At the close of the day the following results had been reached:

The President decided to go before Congress to demand additional legislation to meet the high cost of living situation just as soon as he can frame his views in a message.

A nation-wide drive on profiteers and food hoarders was ordered by the Department of Justice. The whole range of criminal and civil law, including the Sherman antitrust law and the Lever wartime food control act, will be invoked to bring to justice those who are taking extortionate profits from the necessities of the people.

Julius Barnes, director of the United States Grain Corporation, agreed to take steps at once to market standard export flour in every community in carload lots at $10 a barrel, $1 less than any price ruling during the past four months. It was decided to maintain the government guarantee of $2.26 a bushel on wheat as a guarantee against a possible higher price later.

These decisions came at the end of a day of feverish activity. At the White House, the Department of Justice, the Federal trade commission quarters, the Treasury Department and the Capitol officials worked with unwonted vigor.

From the President down Washington seemed to have sensed the deep stirring among the people pressed down by a constantly growing scale of prices and a constantly falling dollar with which to buy.

The clamor of the people made vocal in the Capital by the leaders of the railroad workers, pressing their demands for more wages or lower prices at the point of a threat of a nation-wide strike that would cripple the country.

It was plainly apparent that the grim foreboding of the situation had awakened officialdom to a sense of the grave danger lying beneath the smoldering discontent throughout the nation.

There was no indication last night of what the President will recommend to Congress in the way of additional remedial legislation. His recommendations, however, will be based upon data submitted to him yesterday by the cabinet conference on the high cost of living, which made a special study of the situation under pressure during the past three or four days.

This conference met yesterday with Assistant to the Attorney General Ames, in charge of antitrust prosecutions; Gov. W. P. G. Harding, of the Federal reserve board, and Julius Barnes, of the grain corporation.

It was in session until late in the afternoon preparing a memorandum suggesting remedial measures. This memorandum was submitted to the President by Attorney General Palmer after the cabinet meeting at the White House.[1]

"We prepared a memorandum for the President," said Attorney General Palmer, "in which we stated what the government is doing and proposes to do under existing laws to meet the situation brought about by the high cost of living. Some suggestions of possible additions to the law to cope with the situation were made.

"The Department of Justice is using all of its machinery for the purpose of seeking out violators of the penal sections of the food control act—the horders and the profiteers. We hope to be able to take action to teach them a salutary lesson and one which will have a good effect in reducing the high cost of living."

The President early in the day canceled all engagements not concerned with the high cost of living situation, including appointments with senators with whom he was to discuss the league of nations and the peace treaty.

Printed in the *Washington Post*, Aug. 6, 1919.
  [1] It is printed below.

From the Desk Diary of Robert Lansing

Wednesday Aug 6 [1919]

Prest phoned me about Japanese statement in re Shantung & read me his additional st'mt. He then sent up his statement which I read over & gave to press.

A Statement

6 August, 1919.

The Government of the United States has noted with the greatest interest the frank statement made by Viscount Uchida with regard to Japan's future policy respecting Shantung. The statement ought to serve to remove many of the misunderstandings which had begun to accumulate about this question. But there are references in the statement to an agreement entered into between Japan and China in 1915 which might be misleading, if not commented upon in the light of what occurred in Paris when the clauses of the Treaty affecting Shantung were under discussion. I therefore take the liberty of supplementing Viscount Uchida's statement with the following:

In the conference of the thirtieth of April last, where this matter was brought to a conclusion among the heads of the Principal Allied and Associated Powers, the Japanese delegates, Baron Makino and Viscount Chinda, in reply to a question put by myself, declared that:

"The policy of Japan is to hand back the Shantung Peninsula in full sovereignty to China, retaining only the economic privileges granted to Germany, and the right to establish a settlement under the usual conditions at Tsingtao.

"The owners of the railway will use special police only to insure security for traffic. They will be used for no other purpose.

"The police forces will be composed of Chinese, and such Japanese instructors as the directors of the Railway may select will be appointed by the Chinese Government."[1]

No reference was made to this policy being in any way dependent upon the execution of the Agreement of 1915 to which Count Uchida appears to have referred. Indeed, I felt it my duty to say that nothing that I agreed to must be construed as an acquiescence on the part of the Government of the United States in the policy of the notes exchanged between China and Japan in 1915 and 1918; and reference was made in the discussion to the enforcement of the Agreements of 1915 and 1918 only in case China failed to cooperate fully in carrying out the policy outlined in the statement of Baron Makino and Viscount Chinda.

I have, of course, no doubt that Viscount Uchida had been apprised of all the particulars of the discussion in Paris, and I am not making this statement with the idea of correcting his, but only to throw a fuller light of clarification upon a situation which ought to be relieved of every shadow of obscurity or misapprehension.

Woodrow Wilson.[2]

T MS (B. Long Papers, DLC).

¹ Wilson was quoting from Hankey's notes of the Council of Four printed at April 30, 1919, 12:30 p.m., Vol. 58.
² There is a T copy of this document, with WWhw emendations (incorporated in the text that we print), in WP, DLC.

To Robert Lansing

My dear Mr. Secretary: The White House 6 August, 1919.

I would be very much obliged if you would see that the enclosed statement with regard to the Shantung matter is given to the press and secures as wide publicity as the statement made by Viscount Uchida which, I understand, appears in the American newspapers of this morning, provided, of course, that this form of statement meets with the approbation of your own judgment.

Cordially and faithfully yours,   Woodrow Wilson

TLS (SDR, RG 59, 793.94/964½, DNA).

To Frederick Huntington Gillett

My dear Mr. Speaker: [The White House] 6 August, 1919.

I have had under very serious consideration the proper action of the Government with reference to the high cost of living and feel it is my duty to address a joint session of Congress at the earliest possible moment, to present certain recommendations now ready for submission to Congress.

I sincerely hope, therefore, that you can arrange for a joint session for Friday afternoon next at four o'clock, if that hour is agreeable to the two Houses.

Cordially and sincerely yours,   Woodrow Wilson¹

TLS (Letterpress Books, WP, DLC).
¹ Wilson sent the same letter, *mutatis mutandis*, as WW to T. R. Marshall, Aug. 6, 1919, TLS (Letterpress Books, WP, DLC).

A Memorandum by Alexander Mitchell Palmer

Mem. *High Cost of Living.*¹

[c. Aug. 6, 1919]

If the Government is to accomplish a reduction in the prices of necessities it must set an example by removing its own artificial supports of high prices. To this end the policy of the United States Grain Corporation with reference to wheat and the policies of the

¹ WWhw.

War Department, Navy Department and other Government agencies with reference to their surplus stocks must be controlled by the desire and purpose to secure a prompt and important reduction in prices rather than to sustain existing prices.

Wheat.

The sales of wheat to Europe should be restricted to the absolute minimum and this should be done for the very purpose of producing a surplus of wheat which will aid in getting down the cost of living. The unnecessary purchase of wheat by Europe should not be facilitated through the making of loans to European Governments. Sales to European countries on credit may be made only when approved by the Treasury Department.

The handling of the wheat problem should not be controlled by the question whether the Wheat Administration will show a profit or loss, nor by the consideration that the policy may prove embarrassing in an administrative way.

Governmental Surplus Stocks.

In consonance with the purpose of the Government to reduce the cost of living a uniform policy should be adopted by the War Department and other Departments relative to the sale of surplus stocks, not only of food but of clothing and of other commodities.

Method of Reaching Hoarders and Profiteers.

Pending comprehensive legislation, the speculators, hoarders, and profiteers might be reached through the Department of Justice and Federal Trade Commission, in cooperation.

Section 6 of the Lever Law (H.R. 4961; August 10, 1917) says: That any person who willfully hoards any necessaries shall upon conviction thereof be fined not exceeding $5,000 or be imprisoned for not more than two years, or both. Necessaries shall be deemed to be hoarded within the meaning of this Act when either (a) held, contracted for, or arranged for by any person in a quantity in excess of his reasonable requirements for use or consumption by himself and dependents for a reasonable time; (b) held, contracted for, or arranged for by any manufacturer, wholesaler, retailer, or other dealer in a quantity in excess of the reasonable requirements of his business for use or sale by him for a reasonable time, or reasonably required to furnish necessaries produced in surplus quantities seasonally throughout the period of scant or no production; or (c) withheld, whether by possession or under any contract or arrangement, from the market by any person for the purpose of unreasonably increasing or diminishing the price: * * *

It would seem that this Section might be used to reach any profiteer with reference either to stocks in possession or under contract.

Not only may the contract be attached, but, under Section 7, necessaries which are found to have been hoarded as in Section 6 may be seized and sold by process of libel. This procedure is laid down in Section 7 as follows:

That whenever any necessaries shall be hoarded as defined in section six they shall be liable to be proceeded against in any district court of the United States within the district where the same are found and seized by a process of libel for condemnation, and if such necessaries shall be adjudged to be hoarded they shall be disposed of by sale in such manner as to provide the most equitable distribution thereof as the court may direct, and the proceeds thereof, less the legal costs and charges, shall be paid to the party entitled thereto. The proceedings of such libel cases shall conform as near as may be to the proceedings in admiralty, except that either party may demand trial by jury of any issue of fact joined in any such case, and all such proceedings shall be at the suit of and in the name of the United States. It shall be the duty of the United States attorney for the proper district to institute and prosecute any such action upon presentation to him of satisfactory evidence to sustain the same.

Prosecutions under Anti-Trust Laws.

Investigations made by the Department of Justice and by the Federal Trade Commission make it clear that numerous restraints of trade are being practiced throughout the country in violation of the Anti-Trust Act and its amendments. The Department of Justice might proceed upon the basis of information already collected in many important cases and in addition might issue instructions to the District Attorneys throughout the country to conduct local investigations through the grand juries and otherwise and to institute proceedings civil and criminal in cases indicating clear restraints of trade in violation of the Anti-Trust Act and its amendments.

Particular attention appears to be deserved by the packers, by the manufacturers of leather, coal operators, and probably lumber producers. For example, it is stated that in the last 90 days there have been four advances in lumber prices in the Northwest and that these advances have begun to slow down business.

Query whether the Department of Justice can formulate some general rules on the basis of which local prosecutions and proceedings might be instituted without reference to Washington. If so much greater speed could be obtained.

To a very large extent during the war prices were fixed with Government sanction on levels sufficiently high to encourage production even by the high cost producers. Should not a working rule be established by the Department of Justice that maintenance by concurrent action of various producers of substantially higher prices than those fixed by the Government during the war constitutes prima-facie evidence of excessive prices and that this in itself amounts to an unreasonable restraint of trade?

The attention which the public is now paying to the excessive price of shoes makes it especially desirable to do everything practicable to secure a reduction in that direction. Therefore it would seem that the combination of leather companies particularly deserves attention. It is believed that there would be decided advantage in the manifestation of a purpose to proceed criminally against this leather combination.

Many of the most excessive burdens put upon the consumer are due to the prices and practices of retail dealers. The Anti-Trust Laws of course all apply in the District of Columbia. If these acts of retail dealers in the District of Columbia can properly be proceeded against under the Anti-Trust Laws the result would not only be beneficial in the District but would set a useful example which would speedily be followed under the various state laws in the other important cities in the country. Of course any other laws applicable in the District which could be invoked for protection ought also to be resorted to and would equally stimulate action or efforts to obtain similar legislation in other parts of the country.

It is believed that the prosecutions under the Anti-Trust Act ought to be conducted with exceptional publicity so as to get the fullest psychological value in deterring dealers from illegal practices, in encouraging consumers to detect and resist illegal practices, and in creating the general conviction that a real effort is being made to meet the problem.

Bringing Price Fixing Associations under
Observation of Federal Trade Commission

Manufacturers and merchandisers' associations which were either formed or very greatly strengthened during the War are now being used as the medium for price agreements and as instrumentalities for the raising of prices.

This, of course, brings them under the Sherman Law, but it is desirable, if possible, to take a shorter cut.

Under Section 6(e) the Federal Trade Commission has the power

Upon the application of the Attorney General to investigate and make recommendations for the readjustment of the business of any corporation alleged to be violating the antitrust Acts in order that the corporation may thereafter maintain its organization, management, and conduct of business in accordance with law.

Although this paragraph carries with it no procedure and no provision is made for a decree or an enforcement, yet this paragraph might be used for its psychological effect on the associations and also as preparatory to further proceedings by the Department of Justice under the antitrust laws. As a matter of fact, the mere observation that it would be possible to bring to bear under this paragraph would be extremely embarrassing to price fixers.

Publicity as to Supplies in Existence, as to Evidences of Hoarding.

The idea has been encouraged that there is a great shortage of many of the necessities of life. To a great extent the apparent shortages are due to artificial and illegitimate causes and to an important extent there is a large surplus instead of a shortage. It is important that these facts be made known to the public promptly through the Federal Trade Commission.

The Commission already has a large mass of information on this subject indicating that the supplies of the country are substantially in excess of normal. It can under Section 6(b) of the Act require "Corporations engaged in commerce to file with the Commission, in such form as the Commission may prescribe, answers in writing to specific questions." This power can be exercised by sending out broadcast a questionnaire which will reveal contracts of sale for future delivery and also reveal the prices which the producers of food stuffs and other necessaries receive, which prices can be compared with the prices paid by consumers. In the case of canned vegetables and fish, practically the entire pack is sold on contract on the 1st of May.

In 1917 the Federal Trade Commission was able to trace practically all of the pack of vegetables and fish through a questionnaire.

Publicity as to Prices.

One of the greatest methods of restraining excessive selfishness is publicity. The Federal Trade Commission should begin the publication of facts as to manufacturers and wholesale prices of important necessaries of life together with the cost of transportation to principal destinations. This information should be placed at the disposal of states and municipalities throughout the country and it is hoped that the latter will speedily follow up the matter by showing the retail prices charged to consumers and the profits resulting from the charging of those prices. The Departments of Commerce, Agriculture and Labor will contribute the valuable data currently collected so that it may all be brought together for the purposes of this publicity campaign. State and municipal authorities should be urged to lend their aid so as to bring home to the purchasing public, and also to the consciences of dealers throughout the country, the facts as to existing prices and profits and the reasons therefor, whether sufficient or insufficient.

The increase in the retail price of shoes is especially disquieting and indefensible. It seems particularly important for the Trade Commission to put out at once a clear and concise statement as to the facts of cost to the manufacturer and of price of the manufacturer. It is probable that if this should be followed up vigorously by local publicity agencies it would clearly appear that the most indefensible profits, and the most indefensible increases in profits, are being made by the jobbers, wholesalers and retailers.

The Federal Trade Commission should obtain and publish periodical reports of profits from the Big Trusts.

The effort should be made to have the District of Columbia follow up the matter of publicity in such a way as to set an example to other municipalities throughout the country and so as to give a practical evidence of the good faith of the Administration in urging other municipalities to do the same. It is assumed that through some existing agency of the general Government (if not through any local agency in the District) the necessary inquiries can be made to bring out the facts as to retail prices and other local activities which have a bearing on the cost of living.

Rents.

The profiteering in rents is a serious condition in many parts of the country. Where it exists to a serious extent it probably causes greater unrest than any other sort of profiteering. Any effort to prevent substantial increases in rents involves the risk of discouraging additional building although in nearly all parts of the country there has been a serious shortage in building due to the restrictions placed upon it during the war. It is a question as to what can be done to prevent the unjust increase in rents of existing structures without at the same time discouraging the desired construction of new buildings.

It does not appear that there is any existing Federal law to deal satisfactorily with this subject even in the District of Columbia. It is worthy of consideration whether it would not be in the public interest to adopt legislation putting a restriction on increases in rents for existing structures for a limited period for the purpose of preserving the existing status during the difficult period of readjustment. If such a measure were confined to rents for existing structures it would not directly interfere with rents for new structures. The matter is mentioned for consideration without definite recommendation.

In considering this question the possibility of constitutional lack of power must not be overlooked.

Co-operative Stores.

An important method of avoidance of unnecessary and duplicated expense and unreasonable profit is the establishment of co-operative stores where conditions are favorable for that work. The Department of Labor should (with such aid and information as it can obtain from other departments and agencies of the Government) put before the public the facts, the extent to which cooperative stores are being successfully conducted in this country and the principles which experience has shown it is necessary for it to observe in order to make such ventures successful. It is hoped that this information will prove useful as an example and encouragement for the further development of this important agency of economy.

Appeal to the Business Man.

A general appeal should be issued to the American business men bringing clearly to their attention the menace involved in the present situation, the interference with the rights and the comfort and the peace of mind of the great body of American citizens through the continued drift toward higher and higher prices, the resulting social unrest, the tendency of all such conditions to pile up still higher costs through further increases in wages made for the hopeless purpose of trying to keep ahead of an unjustifiable increased cost of living and the resulting interference with public tranquillity and prosperity, and everyone should be urged, in view of the crisis which actually confronts the country, to exercise self-restraint and moderation and to join in getting prices down rather than in putting them higher. In other words, a "Stop Gouging" campaign should be started.

Speculation and Fraudulent Promotions.

Since the Armistice and the constant decrease of Government expenditures the contraction of credit which would otherwise have taken place has in large measure been prevented by speculation in stocks and securities, in land and produce, which has reached a point justifying grave concern. People are being exploited by those who find a profit in trading on their hopes and expectations and in selling them interests in worthless or extremely hazardous enterprises. This particular class of profiteers have not only used their ingenuity to sell worthless securities, but to induce the holders of Liberty Bonds to part with them at less than their real value. This very great evil which underlies the whole problem of the cost of living should be struck at first, by vigorous publicity, second, by the enforcement by the Postmaster General of the laws now existing against the use of the mails to defraud and, third, by the immediate enactment of a measure such as was proposed by the Capital Issues Committee for the control of security issues.

Conservation.

The public should be emphatically warned that while military hostilities have ceased, the necessity for economy continues to be a matter of great public moment and that as to a very large portion of the public the individual can not only help himself and the country as a whole but defeat the designs of the profiteer by resuming the practice of economy and by adopting careful and businesslike methods of making purchases of all kinds. By economy is meant not alone the expenditure of money but the consumption of goods, in the exact ratio as the demand for goods of all sorts is controlled by the individual the demand will decrease and the pressure for rising prices will be relieved.

The housekeeper will find the adoption of the family budget system, the resumption of the old habit of going to market, the elimination as far as may be of the added prices charged for delivery, and the thoughtful selection of inexpensive cuts and of substitutes for things carrying excessive prices, helpful in getting control of the domestic cost of living.

Coordination.

It is highly desirable to secure continual coordination among the various Government departments and agencies in carrying out any program which may be adopted concerning these matters. Various departments have functions to perform which have an important bearing upon the success of any movements of this character. Without careful coordination it will not always be the case that the work of these various departments and agencies will harmonize. Each Dept naturally has a tendency to emphasize its own particular phase of the subject and it may easily be the case that the sum of the disconnected activities will make a distorted picture of the whole and create erroneous impressions. For example the separate observations of a single department may tend strongly to create an impression that prices are bound to rise and in this way there may be a definite stimulus in aid of increasing prices, whereas a careful survey of the entire subject by all the branches of the Government interested in it would indicate that the situation does not suggest the prospect of higher prices.

Indeed there is much in justification of the view that prices cannot continue to increase over a long additional period, especially sinse [since] there are grave doubts as to how long the large export trade will continue to be developed. Under such circumstances caution in the use of observations encouraging the view of an unlimited prospect of increase in prices ought to be observed and the result of such caution would operate strongly in favor of a campaign to get prices down rather than to send them still higher.

At this time the subject is of such vital importance, and various Government activities interlace in so many ways, that there is a great deal in favor of constituting for the time being a sort of Industrial Conference of the heads of Government departments and agencies which would meet with the President weekly and exchange views as to the policies to be adopted and as to the methods of carrying out the policies adopted.

An important feature of coordination is the coordination of publicity because without this the public announcements of the various departments may be so handled as to get much less attention than they deserve and also as to involve numerous apparent contradictions which would easily be removed through the suggested process of coordination.

SUGGESTED LEGISLATION.[2]

(1) The Food Control Act should be extended both as to the time in which it shall be in operation and as to the commodities to which it shall apply. The provisions against ho[a]rding in that law should be made to cover not only food, but feed, fuel, clothing and other necessaries.

(2) A law similar to the New Jersey Cold Storage regulation law, which controls the time during which goods may be kept in storage, describes a method of disposing of them if kept too long and requires that goods released from storage bear the date of their receipt in storage. There might well be added the requirement that such goods when released from storage should be plainly marked with the selling price when they went into cold storage.

(3) All goods whose form or package or container makes it possible should be marked plainly with the price at which they left the hands of the producer, following the analogy of the Pure Food Act, by which it is required that certain information be given on the labels of packages of foods and drugs.

(4) The appropriation asked for the Department of Agriculture (not granted by Congress) for securing and publishing information relative to stocks of foods and prevailing prices should be made. And appropriation for a similar purpose to the Federal Trade Commission as applying to other commodities.

[2] Wilson put check marks next to each numbered paragraph as he incorporated them in his address to Congress printed at August 8.

(5) Federal licensing law for all corporations engaged in Interstate Commerce under which licensing system regulations designed to secure competitive conditions and prevent gouging profits should be promulgated and enforced and possibly a profit sharing plan or some plan of participation by labor in the profits of such corporations should be made a part of this legislation.

(6) Measure proposed by the Capital Issues Committee for the control of security issues, which bill is now pending in Congress, which would do much to stop speculation and fraudulent promotions.

T MS (WP, DLC).

From Joseph Patrick Tumulty

Dear Governor: The White House 6 August 1919.

In your message dealing with the high cost of living, I hope you will emphasize these points:

I—There can be no approach to normal conditions in this country until the treaty of peace is out of the way and the work of liquidating the war has become the chief concern of the Government as well as of the victims of the existing situation. Business of all kinds is largely speculative because of indefiniteness and uncertainty, and gambling has to be paid for by somebody. In this case it is paid for by the consumer who must take care of both gains and losses. It is futile to expect that peace prices can be approximated under a Government and under a financial and economic system that are still legally on a war basis. (N. Y. World[1])

II—The high cost of living is but a phase of the whole question of social and industrial unrest. It is but a reflex and reaction of what is happening throughout the world. All problems of reconstruction are blocked until definite action is taken on this matter.

III—None of the problems of peace, from the cost of living to the control of the railroads, can be dealt with by the Government of the United States until this treaty is disposed of. The country cannot get back to a peace basis until this treaty is ratified. All this mass of war legislation must remain on the statute books until the Senate has acted and the ratifications are exchanged.

IV—We must have world peace and tranquillity at the earliest possible moment. Here at home we should be made ready for peace by wise legislation dealing with the multitudinous phases of reconstruction and readjustment. Congress alone can quicken this process.

V—Europe will not really get busy again until she knows exactly where she stands on this peace proposition. While there is any possibility that the peace terms may be changed or may be held in abeyance or may not be enforced owing to division of opinion among the Allies, the conditions under which European industry and commerce can resume are so uncertain that only the necessary activities will be revived.   Sincerely yours,   Tumulty

TLS (WP, DLC).
¹ He referred to three recent editorials in the New York *World*: "HOLDING BACK PEACE," July 31, 1919; "WHAT THE SENATE COSTS THE COUNTRY," Aug. 2, 1919; and "WHERE THE BLAME LIES," Aug. 5, 1919.

From Joseph Patrick Tumulty, with Enclosure

Dear Governor: The White House, 6 August 1919.

Mr. Hines asked me to lay before you the attached, which is a proposed measure for the adjustment of the wage dispute. It is necessary to act on this by tomorrow.

Sincerely,   Tumulty

TLS (WP, DLC).

E N C L O S U R E

The labor representatives urge that the constitution of a permanent Wage Board will be a slow process and that its proceedings will be exceedingly tedious and that the work already done by the Director General's Wage Board will be lost.

It may become desirable to suggest that Congress by a special act or joint resolution provide that the President during Federal control may constitute a Wage Board containing adequate representation of the public as well as of labor which may fix wages or which may recommend them to the President to be fixed (this meaning in effect that they will be fixed by the Director General if the President does not care to give the matter personal attention) and that when wages are so fixed the Interstate Commerce Commission shall sanction increased rates where necessary to pay the increased wages.

Such a procedure would accomplish the object of securing adequate Congressional warrant for the grave action which is urged by the labor representatives, and would insure the fixing of rates sufficient to take care of the expense; at the same time it would obviate much of the criticism of the employes that any Congressional action involves serious delay.

Under the plan here proposed the Railroad Wage Board (which now consists of three representatives of labor and three representatives of railroad management) could be enlarged by adding three other representatives of labor and three representatives of the public and the enlarged Board could at once utilize the information already accumulated by the Board and could make much more rapid progress than an entirely new institution.

I believe the Board should be "bi-partisan" i.e. should have an equal number of representatives of labor and of the public.

If the Commission is required to make increases in rates where necessary to pay the increased wages, the interest of the owners of the railroads should be regarded as identical with that of the public and therefore the public one half of the Board should be made up partly of railroad representatives and partly of representatives of the general public.

It is important to have a railroad representation both because of its intimate knowledge of the technical aspects of wages from the standpoint of the railroad managements and from the railroad knowledge as to the extent to which the traffic of the country will be able to stand rates sufficiently high to pay any proposed scale of wages.

There are so many distinct classes of railroad employes that it will probably be necessary to have at least six representatives of labor so as to represent adequately the distinct classes; and the other six members should be divided equally between representatives of the railroad managements and representatives of the public.

If the Commission is unable to act by majority vote an umpire should be selected by the committee or if it can not select then by the President.

The representatives of labor are greatly concerned for fear that the proposal to have wages determined by a Board will have the result of compelling employes to work for these wages. My idea is that this element of compulsion or prohibition of a strike is an entirely distinct question and should be dealt with on its own merits and should not be dealt with as a part of the proposal which has been referred to Congress. The object of the present proposal is to get a tribunal which will be regarded as affording the public, as well as labor, an adequate hearing and which will determine the wage which the public is justified in paying through the payment of railroad rates. It is merely to provide a more perfect plan in place of the existing system of divided and uncertain authority to determine the amount of tax which can properly be put upon the public through an increase in wages.

The question whether employes should strike or not, or be compelled to work or not, at the wages proposed is wholly different and my idea is to have the act specifically provide that nothing contained in the act shall have any such effect.

It is assumed that this plan will be a permanent wage plan which will fit in with any permanent solution which may be made of the railroad problem.

T MS (WP, DLC).

From Albert Baird Cummins

My dear Mr. President: [Washington] 6 August 1919

In accordance with my promise, I called together the Interstate Commerce Committee of the Senate for the purpose of considering the suggestions and recommendations contained in your letter to me of the first instant.

The Committee has carefully gone over the whole subject and has, unanimously, authorized me to make the following further response to your communication.

The Committee recognizes the gravity of the situation and earnestly desires to cooperate with you in bringing about the proper solution of the difficult problems which confront the country. It feels, however, that Congress has already given you complete and plenary authority to deal with the existing situation and that additional legislation at this time can add nothing whatever to your power in the premises. The Director General can fix the wages of all men employed in the transportation service, and it seems to be clear that it is for him to say whether the compensation of these men should or should not be increased. He has all the available information which can possibly be secured, and it is the view of the Committee that he should act in accordance with the public interest and his own judgment. He can be advised upon the subject by any board or tribunal which you may select for that purpose.

The Director General has also the absolute right to initiate rates for transportation and can advance or lower them, as he may think necessary or wise, to meet the requirements of the transportation systems in his charge, and, moreover, he can put the new rates into effect whenever, in his judgment, they should become effective. At the present time, the Interstate Commerce Commission has not the authority to suspend for examination or approval the rates initiated by the Director General; but, even if the act which lately passed the Senate, and which has not yet passed the House, shall become a law and the authority of the Interstate Commerce Commission to suspend rates restored, it will still be true that the

Director General must initiate the rates, and it is entirely impossible to believe that the Interstate Commerce Commission would suspend rates that are necessary in order to pay any increased wages of railway operatives.

The Committee is now diligently engaged in the preparation of a bill for the general reorganization of our system of regulation and control. One common phase of the many plans which have been submitted for our consideration relates to the further direction which ought to be given to the Interstate Commerce Commission for its guidance in determining the reasonableness of rates. Upon that phase of the subject, diverse opinions have been developed, and it is thought to be unwise to bring forward for action by Congress any further legislation in that respect until it can be associated with the general plan of reorganization.

If the Committee felt that there was any lack of power on your part or on the part of the Director General, it would be quick to act; but, inasmuch as it can perceive no want of authority, it has reached the conclusion that no additional legislation is required to meet the particular emergency which you have pointed out.

With high respect, I am,

Yours sincerely,   Albert B. Cummins

TLS (WP, DLC).

From William Gibbs McAdoo

Dear Governor: New York August 6, 1919.

Thank you very much for your recent letters. I notice that you got the message to Congress through your letters to the Speaker and Mr. Esch, so that you accomplished effectively the purpose I had in mind. Your action has been very favorably commented on by all those with whom I have talked here. Many Republicans tell me that they are disgusted with the leadership of their party in Congress. I think the Republican leaders are helping you right along.

I note what you say about the Stone interview.[1] I do not want to urge it, but I think you could well make an exception in this instance. An interview is always more readable than a statement and the fact that you are discussing a subject of such vital concern to the whole world justifies your using the vehicle which will be most effective for your purpose. You know one of your strongest points is that you have never hesitated to disregard precedents.

The railroad difficulties are taking very much the form I expected. I am sorry the properties could not have been returned promptly after the last Congress refused to grant the five year extension. However, that is behind us and the point now is to find the right solution. I think there is some merit in the Brotherhood plan.[2] On the other hand, it needs considerable changing and modification. I have refrained from offering any suggestions as to the solution of the railroad problem. If you think I could be of assistance to you in any way, at any time, I am sure you will not hesitate to call on me.

When I was at Washington I told you of my conviction that it would be helpful to publish to the country the corporation income tax returns, showing the abnormal profits being earned by large numbers of industries engaged in producing the necessaries of life. I believe that the publication of such returns would be immensely illuminating and would have a decided effect upon the prices of such things as food-stuffs, clothing, shoes, coal, steel and other essentials, the manufacturers of which have been earning profits, which, in a large number of instances, if not in all, are simply staggering.

If these facts should be disclosed through the publications of the tax returns, attention would be riveted upon those who are exacting inordinate and unjustifiable profits and would, of itself, prove a corrective. Of course, I realize that the causes of the present high prices are deep-seated and that the restoration of normal conditions of production is vital to the world, and that this cannot be brought about until Peace is thoroughly restored.

I am confident that the League to Enforce Peace News Bureau, which is going to begin work at once in Washington, will emphasize this point in connection with the fight for ratification of the Treaty. At the same time, I also realize that legislation cannot accomplish a great deal but a stiff fight all along the line, and the publication of the profits of the extortionists' will do good.

I would suggest that you ask Secretary Glass to submit to you, for your consideration, a list of the leading corporations engaged in the production of the necessaries of life, including wholesalers and retailers who are making excessive profits. I think that you will find the figures startling.

Nell and I hope to have a chance to run down to Washington in the near future, and have a glimpse of you and Edith. We are hoping to have Margaret with us for a few days.

With best love for all,   Affectionately,   W G McAdoo

TLS (WP, DLC).
   [1] McAdoo had urged Wilson to grant an interview to Melville Elijah Stone of the Associated Press for the purpose of "getting some interpretative statement to the country about the Treaty." "I know you dont care for Stone," McAdoo had added in a pencil note, "but he is doing fine work & ought to be encouraged." WGM to WW, Aug. 4, 1919, TLS (WP, DLC). "I would be perfectly willing," Wilson had replied, "to give Mr. Melville Stone an interview, if I thought it wise or permissible to give an interview to anybody,

but I have never yet, since I became President, given an interview to any news agency on a public question, and I think it would offend various susceptibilities if I were to do so at this critical time. Some form of public statement will no doubt presently be desirable, if not necessary, and I am looking for the right method and occasion. I am pretty sure that an interview would not be the right one." WW to WGM, Aug. 5, 1919, TLS (Letterpress Books, WP, DLC).
    [2] That is, the Plumb plan.

From Robert Lansing, with Enclosure

My dear Mr. President: Washington August 6, 1919.

I am transmitting to you herewith for your consideration a copy of a message regarding the disposal of the German and Austro-Hungarian fleets which it is proposed to send to the American Commission at Paris and which contains the substance of your memorandum on the subject based on the message from the Commission, dated July 31, 1919.[1]

This draft telegram has been prepared after consultation with Admiral Benson, Mr. David Hunter Miller of the Department of State,[2] and Mr. Bradley Palmer, the American member of the so-called Scapa Flow Committee, which met at Paris.

                    Faithfully yours,   Robert Lansing

Approved   W.W.

TLS (SDR, RG 59, 763.72119/6066, DNA).
    [1] See WW to RL, Aug. 4, 1919 (fourth letter of that date), and its Enclosure.
    [2] Miller's memorandum on this proposed dispatch is a TI MS, dated Aug. 5, 1919 (SDR, RG 59, 763.72119/5922, DNA).

E N C L O S U R E

                    Washington, August 5th (8th),[1] 1919.
Your 3436, July 31st, midnight.

The President understands that until the Scapa Flow incident no agreement was arrived at regarding the German and Austro-Hungarian warships. It was and still is the President's opinion that the ships should be broken up or sunk. When the Scapa Flow incident occurred the President understood that Mr. Lloyd George on the part of Great Britain renounced in favor of France the British share in any compensation which might result from the sinking of the German ships, but he did not understand that any general policy with regard to the disposition was even discussed and he drew no inference from what was said that would affect the policy of Powers other than Great Britain that might receive or might have received some of the ships. The President thinks he can say with confidence that Lloyd George knew that we still held our original

view as to what the British at least ought to do with those that fell
to them and that Lloyd George agreed with that view if British
opinion would let him act on it. The President understood that
America would get none of the ships anyway but was not sure
whether Italy would get any or not. The President thinks that he
and Lloyd George were tacitly agreed to let France do as she
wished. STOP. The Department understands that the discussion
now relates solely to surface warships and that it was definitely
understood on April 25th that all of the German and all of the Austro-Hungarian submarines are to be sunk or destroyed, and that
this agreement remains in full force. This point should be clearly
brought out in any subsequent discussion. STOP. The Department
further understands that any definite agreement regarding the distribution or disposition of the surface warships requires the assent
of the five powers. STOP. While the President remains of the opinion that all of the surface warships as well as the submarines
should be sunk or destroyed it would facilitate further discussion
of any French proposal if you could send a complete list or description of the vessels which would be covered by such an agreement.
STOP. A note from the Italian Embassy indicates that Italy would
support the destruction of the enemy fleet as representing the first
step towards limitation of armaments in conformity with the principles which are the basis of the League of Nations.

Lansing

TS telegram (SDR, RG 59, 763.72119/5922, DNA).
  [1] Date changed when the telegram was sent.

Edward Mandell House to Woodrow Wilson and Robert Lansing

London. August 6, 1919.

Urgent. 2717. For the President and Secretary of State, from
Colonel House.

The Commission on Mandates met on the morning and afternoon of August 5th.[1]

The Commission first considered a resolution of the Heads of
Delegations of the Five Principal Powers dated July 21st which
reads:

"It was decided that the supervision of the execution of the colonial clauses of the treaty with Germany should be entrusted to the
Commission on Mandates. The Commission was asked to report to
the Council at an early date."

Because of the vagueness of this resolution it was agreed that
Lord Milner should ask the Supreme Council for a more precise

indication of the nature of the action which they intended the Commission on Mandates to take in this matter.

The Commission then took up the question of draft mandates. You will remember that mandates B and C have already been passed.[2] Mahla [Syria] was on the agenda for discussion and I had circulated a draft. The French Delegate however under instructions from his Government refused by telegram to come and discuss this form of mandate on the ground that it was not yet decided whether there should be mandates for the former Turkish empire or not. Lord Robert Cecil insisted, and I agreed with him, article 22 of the Covenant[3] established the mandatory principle for these territories and that it was our duty as a commission to submit a draft as well. Nevertheless the Commission saw the impossibility of going ahead with a formal discussion until the Supreme Council in Paris should remove the misapprehensions of the French. The issue was therefore referred back to Supreme Council for instruction.

It would be helpful if you would send to Polk instructions to the effect that our commission should draft a mandate otherwise the Ottoman Empire will be divided and distributed without any previous agreement as to the general principles under which it shall be administered and the whole mandatory conception will receive a severe blow which public opinion will hardly forgive.

With regard to B and C, I informed the commission of your approval and Milner said that Lloyd George likewise approved. The Italian delegate was asked to secure the formal approval of his government and I believe this is merely a matter of form. The French Government as you know made a reservation regarding B mandate in order that they might secure the right to use armed forces raised in the mandated territories for the defense of France. The Commission was unanimously against the French delegation but their reservation is still maintained and Balfour has been asked to talk with Clemenceau and have it waived. The Japanese delegation likewise reserved in mandate C the right of free immigration and settlement in all mandated territories. This of course has raised serious objections from the British on behalf of Australia, New Zealand, and South Africa and the Commission has supported these objections. Whether the Japanese will insist upon reservation is still uncertain but if they should the issue will have to be determined by the Supreme Council now sitting in Paris.

The Commission by its terms of recurs was likewise asked to hear and report on Belgian and Portuguese claims in Africa. You will remember that the Conference allocated German East Africa to Great Britain under mandate and Belgium claimed a part of this territory. It was decided that our Commission should resolve the dispute. The British and Belgian Governments came to an agreement by which Belgium was to receive roughly one twentieth of the territory but practically one half of the population under mandate. Because the two principal interested powers had reached this agreement and because the Belgians were in possession and had materially contributed to the campaign against the Germans in East Africa the Commission felt under obligation to accept this division. Though I am personally disturbed at the thought of three million five hundred thousand natives going under the Belgian control I did not feel justified in objecting to the arrangement reached by the powers chiefly concerned.

The Portuguese claim was a double one; first, to the revolution spreading the Kianga territory a small triangle containing from three to five thousand inhabitants which had formerly been Portuguese by (but?) which had been taken over by Germany through diplomatic pressure. The Commission decided that this should be restored to Portugal without a mandate first, because it was actually a restitution of former Portuguese territory; second, because it would be a travesty of the mandatory system to require a mandate for so small a territory. The Portuguese claimed in the second place the right to a mandate over some other portion of ex-German territory in South Africa. The Commission decided to deny this claim first because they had not made out a case and second, because there was not territory to assign to them.   Davis.

T telegram (SDR, RG 59, 763.72119/6024, DNA).
  ¹ The minutes of this meeting are in WP, DLC.
  ² See EMH to WW, July 11, 1919, Vol. 61.
  ³ "Certain communities formerly belonging to the Turkish Empire have reached a stage of development where their existence as independent nations can be provisionally recognised subject to the rendering of administrative advice and assistance by a Mandatory until such time as they are able to stand alone. The wishes of these communities must be a principal consideration in the selection of the Mandatory." PPC, XIII, 93.

A News Report

[*Aug. 7, 1919*]

WILSON ASKS HINES TO ACT
SAYS RAILROAD DIRECTOR HAS POWER
TO PASS ON SHOPMEN'S WAGES.

Washington, Aug. 7.—The situation in regard to the striking railroad employes became so serious today that President Wilson took personal charge of the negotiations and, after a long conference with Director General of Railroads Hines, wrote a communication to the latter, in which he authorized Mr. Hines to proceed with the question of wage adjustments, through the authorized national representatives of the employes, but only in the event that the employes now on strike return to their work.

The President's communication was sent at once to B. M. Jewell, Acting President of the Railway Employes Department of the American Federation of Labor, along with a letter in which Mr. Hines urged upon Mr. Jewell the necessity for immediate action on the lines suggested by President Wilson. Upon the receipt of these statements Mr. Jewell called together a number of the officers of the railway employes' organizations.

At midnight Mr. Jewell sent a message to the officers and members of all shopcraft [unions] affiliated with the Railway Employes' Department of the A. F. of L. in which he asks them to return to their work as requested by President Wilson. He included in the message copies of the letter sent by President Wilson to Director General Hines and of the letter which he, Jewell, had received from Mr. Hines. In his message Mr. Jewell said:

"The action of our membership in striking in violation of the laws of our organizations has been detrimental and embarrassing to your officers in the handling of these negotiations. It is therefore plainly our duty to instruct every member now out to return to work at once in order that we may proceed with negotiations with the hope of securing a satisfactory adjustment. Failure of the membership to comply with these instructions will, in our judgment, impair the usefulness of our organizations as well as having a detrimental effect upon the entire labor movement. We have no hesitancy in saying that we have abiding faith in the loyalty of the great majority of our membership and that they will immediately comply with the instructions contained herein. This information should be conveyed to the membership of all points."

Action on the part of the President came when Mr. Hines called at the White House early in the day and informed the President that 80,000 railway employes had gone on strike against the advice of their national leaders to support their demands for higher wages without the delay which would result from waiting on Congressional action. Mr. Hines said that the number was twice the total on strike yesterday, and that if matters were permitted to follow such a course without strong intervention a situation would be created where the best efforts in other directions to bring down living costs would be absolutely defeated.

To this viewpoint the President subscribed, and he told the shopmen in no uncertain terms that they must be prepared to accept a heavy responsibility for the situation which would be developed if they persisted in crippling the railroad systems.

The President referred to the relations between transportation and the high living costs, and said in his letter to Mr. Hines:

"I need hardly point out how intimately and directly this matter affects every individual in the nation, and if transportation is interrupted it will be impossible to solve it."

In his communication to Mr. Hines the President accepts as final a letter from Senator Cummins, Chairman of the Interstate Commerce Committee, in which Mr. Cummins set forth that the joint request of President Wilson and Mr. Hines for the establishment of a Federal wage adjustment board with rate-making power would not be acceptable to Congress. Under these circumstances, President Wilson told Mr. Hines that he had full authority to proceed with negotiations with the railway employes if they would go back to work.

How the money to meet the wage increase, which Mr. Hines says he has not got, is to be raised in the event that the demands of the employes are met, President Wilson does not say in his communication. The general opinion here was that two courses were open. One would be an increase in freight rates; the other a request upon Congress for an appropriation, thus putting squarely up to Congress the question whether it was willing to supply the money necessary to carry out the decisions made by Mr. Hines in the event that Mr. Hines considered that to be the only manner in which a strike could be averted.

It was noted that there was no mention in President Wilson's communication to Mr. Hines of the agitation which has been started by some branches of the railway employes for the adoption of the Plumb plan for the nationalization of the railway systems as the cure for wage troubles. Mr. Jewell has stated that there was no thought on the part of the men to strike in an effort to force the Plumb plan on the Government, and that the only question which would bring on a general strike would be refusal of the Government to grant wage demands which were considered legitimate to meet present economic standards. . . .

The railroad situation was the subject of prolonged and grave conferences at the White House today. Director General Hines took the matter up with the President, first, placing before him, it is said, the communication received from the four brotherhoods and the railway shopmen, setting forth that they must have cash relief at once, and that in their opinion the adoption of the Plumb plan was the only ultimate solution.

To add to this came the news that the association of railway clerks and affiliated employes was taking a strike vote and that it probably would result in 450,000 of their number going on strike within a month in the event wage increases were not granted.

After talking with the President for a considerable time, Mr. Hines summoned a number of his experts to the White House, where they held a separate conference at which a complete analysis of the situation was drawn up and the opinion of the Railroad Administration as the best course to be pursued prepared. These data were submitted to the President prior to the preparation of his letter to Mr. Hines.

Printed in the *New York Times*, Aug. 8, 1919.

To Walker Downer Hines

[The White House]
My dear Mr. Director General: 7 August, 1919.

I am just in receipt of a letter from Senator Albert B. Cummins, Chairman of the Senate Committee on Interstate Commerce, which sets me free to deal as I think best with the difficult question of the wages of certain classes of railway employees, and I take advantage of the occasion to write you this letter, in order that I may, both in the public interest and in the interest of the railway employees themselves, make the present situation as clear and definite as possible. I thought it my duty to lay the question in its present pressing form before the Committee of the Senate, because I thought that I should not act upon this matter within the brief interval of government control remaining, without their acquiescence and approval. Senator Cummins' letter, which speaks the unanimous judgment of the Committee, leaves me free, and indeed imposes upon me the duty to act.

The question of the wages of railroad shopmen was submitted, you will remember, to the Board of Railroad Wages and Working Conditions of the Railroad Administration last February, but was not reported upon by the Board until the 16th of July. The delay was unavoidable because the Board was continuously engaged in dealing with several wage matters affecting classes of employees who had not previously received consideration. The Board now having apprised us of its inability, at any rate for the time being, to agree upon recommendations, it is clearly our duty to proceed with the matter in the hope of disposing of it.

You are therefore authorized to say to the railroad shop employees that the question of wages they have raised will be taken up and considered on its merits by the Director General in conference with their duly accredited representatives. I hope that you will make it clear to the men concerned that the Railroad Administration cannot deal with problems of this sort, or with any problems affecting the men, except through the duly chosen international officers of the regularly constituted organizations and their authorized committee. Matters of so various a nature and affecting so many men cannot be dealt with except in this way. Any action which brings the authority of the authorized representatives of the organizations into question or discredits it must interfere with, if not prevent action altogether. The chief obstacle to a decision has been created by the men themselves. They have gone out on strike and repudiated the authority of their officers at the very moment when they were urging action in regard to their interests.

You will remember that a conference between yourself and the authorized representatives of the men was arranged, at the instance of those representatives, for July 28th to discuss the wage question and the question of a national agreement, but before this conference took place or could take place, local bodies of railway shopmen took action looking toward a strike on the first of August. As a result of this action, various strikes actually took place before there was an opportunity to act in a satisfactory or conclusive way with respect to the wages. In the presence of these strikes and the repudiation of the authority of the representatives of the organization concerned, there can be no consideration of the matter in controversy. Until the employees return to work and again recognize the authority of their own organizations, the whole matter must be at a stand still.

When Federal control of the railroads began, the Railroad Administration accepted existing agreements between the shopmen's organizations and the several railroad companies, and by agreement machinery was created for handling the grievances of the shopmen's organizations of all the railways, whether they had theretofore had the benefit of definite agreements or not. There can be no question, therefore, of the readiness of the Government to deal in a spirit of fairness and by regular methods with any matters the men may bring to their attention.

Concerted and very careful consideration is being given by the entire Government to the question of reducing the high cost of living. I need hardly point out how intimately and directly this matter affects every individual in the nation, and if transportation is interrupted, it will be impossible to solve it. This is a time when every employee of the railways should help to make the processes of transportation more easy and economical rather than less, and employees who are on strike are deliberately delaying a settlement of their wage problem and of their standard of living. They should promptly return to work, and I hope that you will urge upon their representatives the immediate necessity for their doing so.

Cordially and sincerely yours,   Woodrow Wilson

TLS (Letterpress Books, WP, DLC).

To Bert Mark Jewell

Dear Mr. Jewell: The White House August 7, 1919

I am sending you this letter to aid in giving railroad shop employes a clear understanding of the present situation in the light of action just taken by the Senate Committee on Interstate Commerce.

While the wage matters for the railroad shop men were submitted to the Board of Railroad Wages & Working Conditions of the Railroad Administration last February they were not reported upon by the members of that Board until July 16th, this delay being unavoidable and due to the fact that the Board was continuously engaged in dealing with wage matters for classes of employes who had not previously received increases. The magnitude of the problems involved made me feel that I must give Congress an opportunity to consider them. Yesterday the Senate Committee on Interstate Commerce unanimously decided that no steps were necessary by Congress at the present time. This action gives unmistakable notice that Congress will not take action upon these wage problems and will assent to their being handled by the Railroad Administration and under the war powers conferred upon the President by the Federal Control Act. I feel that this removes the embarrassment which confronted me in dealing with the matter prior to giving Congress an opportunity to consider it, and therefore, I am prepared to proceed through the Railroad Administration to dispose of the subject.

You are, therefore, authorized to say to the railroad shop employes throughout the country that the wage matters will be taken up and considered on their merits with you and your associates by the Director General. In that connection I would like to make it clear to you, and through you to all the railroad shop employes throughout the country, that the Railroad Administration in dealing with the wage problems affecting the railroad shop employes can recognize only the international officers of the shop men's organizations and their authorized committee. Matters so widely extended cannot be dealt with except through representatives selected in due course by the labor organizations and any action which brings in question the authority of the duly selected and accredited representatives is bound to interfere with reaching a prompt conclusion. There is now no obstacle whatever to the immediate entering upon of this matter, except the very serious obstacle which has been created by many of the employes themselves, by going out on strikes at a time when their international officers were endeavoring to represent them.

On July 8th at the instance of you and your associates the Railroad Administration arranged for a conference on July 28th to discuss the wage question and the question of a national agreement. Even before this conference took place numerous local bodies of shop men took action toward a strike on August 1st and as a result of this action various strikes took place before there was any opportunity to act in an authoritative and satisfactory way with respect to the wage matter. This condition at once, of itself, forces a suspension of the consideration of the matter until the employes return to work and thereby recognize the authority of their own regularly accredited officers to represent them.

When Federal control of the railroads began the Railroad Administration accepted existing agreements between the shop men's organizations and the various railroad companies, and by agreement created machinery for the handling of grievances of the shop men's organizations of all railroads, whether they had theretofore had agreements or not. Necessarily problems involving questions of so many employes cannot be handled otherwise than through appropriate organizations. At all times the Railroad Administration has dealt in these matters with you and other duly accredited representatives of the shop men's organizations. In the nature of things we can only deal with the regularly constituted international officers and their authorized committees.

Concerted and most careful consideration is being given by the entire Government to the question of reducing the high cost of living. The efforts in this direction which are of such great importance to every individual can only be hampered and rendered less availing by the present interruptions of transportation. This is a time when every employee should help to make the processes of transportation as smooth and economical as possible. When in addition it is clear that employes on strike are merely delaying a disposition of their own wage problem it is evident that there is urgent need from every standpoint of the employes promptly returning to work, and I wish through you to urge an immediate return to work by every railroad shop employee who has gone on strike.

Sincerely yours,   [Woodrow Wilson][1]

TCL (WP, DLC).

[1] It seems a safe assumption that Wilson's letter to Hines was at least based upon a draft by Hines. The spelling ("employes," e.g.) in Wilson's letter to Jewell indicates that Hines drafted this letter also. There is no signed copy of this letter in WP, DLC.

From Joseph Patrick Tumulty

Dear Governor: The White House 7 August 1919.

I hope you are going to describe in a general way just what the whole economic situation is throughout the world and how necessary the League is to bind up the wounds of war.

Your message not only should contain a warning to those capitalistic interests who profiteer, but there should be in it, also, a warning that labor must not profiteer. Labor can't expect any campaign to reduce the cost of living to win if strikes are to predominate. One way that labor can help is to increase production.

Now, in my opinion, is the time to speak frankly to labor as well as capital.   Sincerely yours,   Tumulty

TLS (WP, DLC).

A Memorandum by Joseph Patrick Tumulty

                                             The White House
MEMORANDUM by Mr. Tumulty: 7 August 1919.

The President's message will fail to steady the country unless there is in it certain ingredients of optimism and of gentle admonition to those who wish hastily and over night to revolutionize the processes of our whole economic life.

These excerpts from newspaper editorials may help a little:

The world has got to pay for the appalling destruction of the great war and we in America have got to pay our share. For five years no country in Europe has raised its normal crops, nor produced its normal quantity of manufactured products. The destruction of property of incalculable value has been accomplished by a decreasing production and by a destruction of the facilities for production. Not until Europe is producing its normal supply of foodstuffs and minerals and manufactured goods will there be a return to approximately normal conditions. America must help to get Europe back to normal. Otherwise there will be chaos there which will inevitably be communicated to this country. There is only one possible answer to this question. We must produce more, both for Europe's use and for our use; both for Europe's sake and our own sake. Increased production is the only answer. That means, as the Springfield Republican put it the other day, that everybody everywhere must go to work and work his head off. It means that every effort and every action tending to curtail production, on the part of the workingmen as well as everyone else, must be so severely frowned upon by the community that it will be promptly abandoned. (Baltimore Sun)

The country is sound. There is plenty in the land. People are enjoying prosperity; health is good. No pestilence rages or impends; crops are bountiful and peace has been restored.

Capital is entitled to a fair return upon its investments and managements. Labor is entitled to a fair return upon its industry and skill. Neither the capitalist who wants to "hog all" nor the wage earner of like disposition, should have his way. There should be, and as matters now stand there must be, an equitable division. The present division is not satisfactory. A revision is demanded. But the question is so large it cannot be decided while you wait. Haste makes waste, and often increases difficulties. (Washington Star)

We are all in the same boat. America must give an example to the world of a self-contained people; of a people who having played a great part in the war, are able with calmness to handle the great problems of peace; and these problems can and must be met. Those who propose radical changes must not expect the Government to act upon threats. The Government is the great depositary of the rights of all, and it must safeguard those rights at all costs. Passion and the disregard of the rights of others have no place in the councils of free people. We need light, not heat, in these solemn matters.   J P Tumulty

TS MS (WP, DLC).

A Memorandum by Alexander Mitchell Palmer

Washington, D. C. August 7, 1919.

MEMORANDUM TO THE PRESIDENT.

I attach

(1) a letter from Secretary Houston,[1] with whose views as therein expressed I am in entire accord.

(2) A copy of a telegram which has been sent to every District Attorney in the United States.[2] Some arrests have already been made and others are imminent. I think the general effect of a rigid enforcement of the penal provisions of the Food Control Act will be good. It is extremely important, however, that it should be extended both as to time and as to commodities so far as this can be done within the powers of Congress.

(3) Draft of telegram to State Food Administrators[3] concerning the fair price committee plan. Unless you disapprove, I will send this out to-day.

Telegrams that I am getting from all over the country indicate that the country will not be satisfied unless you say something that will give indication of a hope, at least, that breadstuffs will not be increased in price. The action of the grain market during the past week in showing a decrease of 32¢ in price of corn since the talk about the wheat problem began indicates the close relation of the price of all foodstuffs to wheat. This is verified by the rise of 9¢ yesterday on the report that the Government would do nothing that could have the effect of reducing the price of wheat. I think we might at least go so far as to give indication that nothing except the barest necessities of Europe will be considered by the Grain Corporation in dealing with exports, and that no artificial stimulation of exports on the extension of credits beyond that necessary to accommodate the barest necessities of our Allies will be permitted.

I do not know whether you plan to touch the railroad wage problem in your message to Congress or not. So far as I can get in touch with the sentiment in the country, I believe there is a general feeling that the railroad workers are overstepping the mark and are getting on such dangerous ground that they cannot and will not receive the support of the sober-minded, thinking people of the country who are not talking much. Their proposals look to the man on the street like the first application of "direct methods," which are not going to be tolerated by the real Americans who are earnestly seeking ways to solve these problems through orderly means.   AMP

TI MS (WP, DLC).
    [1] DFH to AMP, Aug. 6, 1919, TLS (WP, DLC). Houston urged that, in all discussions and public statements on the high cost of living, the cost of farm and food products should not be stressed to the exclusion of manufactured products. To do so was perhaps natural but unwise and unfortunate, as well as unfair, because it aroused justified resentment on the part of farmers and allowed manufacturers to evade their share of responsibility for the high cost of living.
    [2] AMP to All United States Attorneys, n.d., T telegram (WP, DLC). Palmer directed the attorneys to investigate and proceed against hoarders of food products and other "necessaries" in violation of the Food Control Act of 1917.
    [3] AMP to state food administrators, n.d., CC telegram (WP, DLC). Palmer requested the administrators to gather information about instances of alleged profiteering and/or hoarding by dealers in food products, dry goods, and clothing for the use of the United States attorneys in their area.

From Thomas Riley Marshall

My dear Mr. President: Washington. August Seven 1919

    I had left my office when your letter came to hand.[1] There was no session of the Senate and I could not take the matter up. It will be presented promptly at twelve o'clock today and arrangements made for the joint session. I hope, with due justice to all grades of American citizens, you will lend your supreme influence towards stamping out the soviet idea.[2]

    I am grateful to you for your statement that I need not stay here during your absence[3] but in view of the present situation, while I can do nothing, I think that unless sickness compels my leaving no opportunity for criticism should be offered by my going away.

With cordial regards, I am,

Very sincerely yours,   Thos. R. Marshall

TLS (WP, DLC).
[1] See WW to F. H. Gillett, Aug. 6, 1919, n. 1.
[2] A reference to the Plumb plan. Thetus W. Sims, Democrat of Tennessee, had introduced, by request, in the House of Representatives on August 2, a bill which provided for the enactment of the Plumb plan. *Cong. Record*, 66th Cong., 1st sess., p. 3586. On the same date, the leaders of the four railroad brotherhoods (Locomotive Engineers, Railway Trainmen, Locomotive Firemen and Enginemen, and Railway Conductors) had issued a joint statement endorsing the plan and demanding governmental ownership of the railroads on a profit-sharing basis with railroad employees. They also announced the formation of a Plumb Plan League to publicize the project. *New York Times*, Aug. 3, 1919. On the following day, Warren Sanford Stone, the head of the Brotherhood of Locomotive Engineers, announced a nationwide campaign to force Congress to enact the Plumb plan. *Ibid.*, Aug. 4, 1919. See also the news report printed at Aug. 4, 1919.
The demands of the brotherhoods met immediate opposition from business groups and newspaper editorialists. The *New York Times*, for example, denounced the proposal and called for "the firmest resistance to the demand for running the railroads in the interest of a class at the cost of the whole people" and urged American workers to "eschew the dangerous nostrums of socialism." *Ibid.*
On August 4, Bert Mark Jewell commented to newspapermen that the railway shopmen were in a mood to demand the democratization, not only of the railways, but also of basic industries, such as steel, coal, and meat packing, along the lines of the Plumb plan. On the same day, another statement by the Plumb Plan League declared that the demand for the adoption of the plan marked "the step by which organized labor passes from demands for wage increases to demands that the system of profits in industry be overhauled." *Ibid.*, Aug. 5, 1919.
On August 5, Jewell and Glenn Edward Plumb were quoted as saying that the railroad workers intended to raise $2,500,000 by the first of September to "educate" the American public on the Plumb plan. If the present Congress refused to enact the legislation, the unions would work to elect a "Plumb-Plan Congress" in 1920. On August 5 also, the Chamber of Commerce of the United States came out against the plan. *Ibid.*, Aug. 6, 1919.
The editorial writers of the *New York Times* were by this time denouncing the plan in sensational terms. "It is," they wrote on August 6, 1919, "plainly a venture into radical socialism that the Brotherhood Chiefs propose; more than that, it is a long step toward the principles of LENIN and TROTSKY and of Soviet Government." Two days later, they flatly asserted: "The plan in what it immediately proposes and in what it hints at is Marxian socialism; the statement of the Brotherhood Chiefs embodies the Marxian doctrines, almost phrases of KARL MARX's 'Communist Manifesto' and other writings." *Ibid.*, Aug. 8, 1919.
K. Austin Kerr, *American Railroad Politics, 1914-1920: Rates, Wages, and Efficiency* (Pittsburgh, 1968), pp. 160-74, describes the development of the Plumb plan and of the public campaign in its favor in the summer and autumn of 1919, but he gives no hint of the passion which it aroused.
[3] See T. R. Marshall to JPT, July 26, 1919, n. 2.

From Frederick Huntington Gillett

Sir: Washington, D. C. August 7, 1919.

Your letter of the sixth received, and I am sure the House will be glad to have a Joint Session for tomorrow at 4 o'clock to receive your recommendations.   Yours respectfully,   F H Gillett

TLS (WP, DLC).

From Julius Howland Barnes

New York, Aug. 7, 1919.

In your forthcoming statement to Congress and in any reference to wheat and flour may I not rely on your making clear that I am in accord with your views when I state that the protection of a world supply and demand price is all the preference that American consumers ask together with such policies as will protect their home supplies against menacing depletion by undue shipments abroad.

I am led to especially request this for it was clear to me that in conference with the news representatives Tuesday evening after my conference with you that they had been informed by someone on your special committee that a policy of wheat price reduction had been decided upon and at the conference Tuesday which I attended at your request and that of Attorney General Palmer the subcommittee report expressed wheat conclusions already formulated without waiting for the conference requested with me and which conclusions were not defended when the real facts were laid down before that gathering[1] but it is evident that the same embarrassing expressions continue on the part of some members of that committee and in justice to the work this would [should] be stopped.

For instance this morning's New York HERALD states:

"It developed that there is serious doubt whether President Wilson is in full agreement with Julius H. Barnes, United States Wheat Director, in his stand that the price of wheat should not be reduced below the guaranteed price of two-dollars twenty-six. The impression prevailed when Mr. Barnes issued his statement last night after his talk with the President, that he represented Mr. Wilson's views. But this is not the case. Mr. Barnes judgement that the price of wheat should be maintained is being opposed by a large group of officials including Mr. Palmer. However, it is entirely up to the President to decide what will be done about wheat."

I am confident I did not misunderstand you and such attitude and expressions on the part of other officials should not continue to jeopardize and embarrass this difficult administration. If Congress wants to deliberately subsidize bread they should say so and pressure should not be put on the wheat director to use authority which could only inaugurate artificial subsidy by a strained interpretation of the act entirely outside of its moral and economic phases.

                                        Julius H. Barnes

T telegram (WP, DLC).

[1] See the first new report printed at Aug. 5, 1919, and the one printed at Aug. 6, 1919.

From William Byron Colver

My dear Mr. President: Washington 7 August 1919

Your letter of August 5th enclosing a most interesting memorandum by the Reconstruction Research Division of the Council of National Defense:

The memorandum directs attention to the problem of the high cost of living; gives a clear statement of the problem; marshals statistical facts; points out common illusions; discusses the causes of high cost of living, and finally suggests certain remedial measures.

The arrangement and statement of the memorandum compels me to accept it except that I am persuaded that the factor of currency inflation has been quite considerably over-emphasized.

I have heard Governor Harding of the Federal Reserve Board state the case with respect to inflation and I understand that his remarkable statement is to be made public within a day or two. I hope it will receive the widest publicity and that public men will give it the consideration which it surely commands.

To return to the memorandum: The conclusion and the aim and end of the memorandum is a suggestion that provision be made for a constant compilation of basic statistics with respect to production, stocks on hand, costs, prices and other data in a permanent and comprehensive way. It is pointed out that much of this material is already being gathered by the Bureaus of the Census, Crop Estimates and Markets, Labor Statistics, Federal Trade Commission, etc., but that information so gathered and issued, without being brought to focus, results in duplication of labor, in narrowness of view point, and in a distressing multiplication of demands by Government agencies upon busy manufacturing and merchandising concerns.

This same point was strongly emphasized by the subcommittee of which Director General Hines was chairman and which reported to the Attorney General, which report I believe has been placed in your hands.

For a long while it has been generally felt, I believe, that much could be done by concentrating a great many of the information services to a focus. The outstanding objection seems to be fear lest certain information, the value of which depends in a very large part upon the promptness with which it is collected, compiled and distributed, would be slowed down. It is held that it is this particular sort of information that is of the greatest practical value.

We fully agree with the memorandum that this is a subject which is worthy of careful and immediate consideration.

The Research Division of the Council of National Defense did a most notable piece of work during the war and would furnish a fine foundation upon which to build.

Partial statistics are often worse than none and for that reason it would be my opinion that the authority and finality of the contemplated data could be assured by nothing less than operation under the power, now vested only in the Federal Trade Commission but which Congress doubtless would grant, at your request, to some other agency, to require, under penalty, immediate answers to reasonable and continuing requests for trade information.

Faithfully yours,   William B Colver

TLS (WP, DLC).

From Walter Irving Clarke[1]

Dear Sir: New York City August 7, 1919.

The Presbyterian New Era Movement[2] will have an important conference for the middle western states beginning Labor Day, at which the church will attempt to apply Christian principles toward the solution of the world problems of the day.

Will you please send me a message for that conference giving your view of how the Church may best help meet the labor problems and other social crises?

I would appreciate having this before August 25 if possible.

Yours for The Presbyterian Church in the U. S. A.,

Walter I. Clarke

TLS (WP, DLC).
  [1] Publicity Director of the Presbyterian Church in the U. S. A.
  [2] For a description of the New Era Movement, see W. I. Clarke to WW, Aug. 13, 1919.

From the Desk Diary of Robert Lansing

Thursday Aug 7 [1919]

Grasty on Prest's relations to Comrs. Loss of prestige by House. . . .

Tumulty on Col. House and Prest's loss of faith in him. Also Prest's dislike of Auchincloss & Mrs. House. Says House & Mrs. planned to accompany Pres't to London & stay at palace but Prest stopped it. . . .

Wrote letter to Pres't urging him to attack Bolshevist movement. Sent him Poole's memo.

From Robert Lansing, with Enclosure

My dear Mr. President: Washington August 7, 1919.

After a talk which I had this morning with Mr. Tumulty I feel it my duty to write you in the hope that there may be opportunity for you to make a frank declaration against the Bolshevist doctrines which are certainly extending far beyond the confines of Russia. I think it is time for this Government to take a very definite stand since there is growing up a propaganda in favor of classism in contradistinction to nationalism which seems to me to menace our present social order. Your well-recognized position as the principal leader of progressive thought makes you the most effective agent to check this dangerous movement and I sincerely hope that you may seize an occasion to make public your views upon this great world-menace and assume the leadership against it to which your position and record entitle you.

In this connection I am enclosing a memorandum which I asked Mr. D. C. Poole, our former Chargé at Archangel (who had so wide an experience throughout European Russia) to prepare. He apologizes for its incompleteness in that the work was done in about three hours.   Faithfully yours,   Robert Lansing.

TLS (WP, DLC).

E N C L O S U R E

STATEMENT by DeWitt C. Poole, jr., Counselor, American Embassy, Russia.

MEMORANDUM CONCERNING THE PURPOSES OF THE
BOLSHEVIKI ESPECIALLY WITH RESPECT TO A WORLD REVOLUTION

The present startling spread of social and industrial unrest in the United States and throughout the world makes it important to examine anew the purposes and activities of the Bolsheviki. The many healthy democratic currents which have been set up are in danger of being poisoned by a propaganda of violence and unreason which aims to subvert the Government of the United States and other non-Bolshevik governments. The vital problem of the moment is to lead the Government and the people between the Scylla of reaction on the one hand and the Charybdis of Bolshevism on the other.

The theoretical purposes of the Bolsheviki are best set forth in the following statement of aims which was embodied in the call for the Third International as having been "worked out in accordance with the programs of the Spartacus Association of Germany and the Communistic (Bolshevik) party in Russia." As wirelessed from Petrograd January 23, 1919, this statement contained the following:

"The present is the period of destruction and crushing of the capitalist system of the whole world. * * *

"The aim of the proletariat must now be immediately to conquer the power. To conquer the power means to destroy the governmental apparatus of the Bourgeoisie and to organize a new proletarian governmental apparatus. This new apparatus must express the dictatorship of the proletariat.

"The dictatorship of the proletariat must be the occasion for the immediate expropriation of capital and the elimination of the private right of owning the means of production through making them common property.

"In order to protect the socialist revolution against external and internal enemies and to assist the fighting proletarians of other countries, it becomes necessary to disarm entirely the Bourgeoisie and its agents and to arm the Proletariat."

It is of the essence of the Bolshevik movement that it is *international and not national in character*. The Revolution in Russia is but the first incident in the Bolshevik program. This thought occurs repeatedly in the writings of Lenin and his associates. Writing in the Moscow OFFICIAL GAZETTE of March 8, 1918, Lenin says:

"There is no doubt that the Socialist Revolution in Europe must come and will come. All our hopes for the definitive triumph of Socialism are based on this prediction and on this scientific prevision. Our propagandist activities in general, and the organization of fraternization in particular, must be strengthened and developed."

The Bolshevik propagandist, Bukharin,[1] writes in chapter 19 of his pamphlet, "The Program of the Communists," (Moscow, July 19, 1918):

"The program of the Communist party is not alone a program of liberating the proletariat of one country; it is the program of liberating the proletariat of the world."

That the Bolsheviki are playing an international game, and aim directly at the subversion of all governments, is disclosed by the avowed tactics of their foreign policy. In his "Peace Program" published at Petrograd, February, 1918, Trotsky says:

"If, in awaiting the imminent proletarian flood in Europe, Russia should be forced to conclude peace with the present-day Governments of the Central Powers, it would be a provisional, temporary and transitory peace, with the revision of which the European Revolution will have to concern itself in the first instance. Our whole policy is built upon the expectation of this revolution."

A similar attitude with respect to the Allies is disclosed even more strikingly in a speech made by Zionoviev,[2] President of the Petrograd Soviet, speaking February 4th last on the subject of the Princes' Island proposal:

"We are willing to sign an unfavorable peace with the Allies. * * * It would only mean that we should put no trust whatever in the bit of paper we should sign. * * * We should use the breathing space so obtained in order to gather our strength in order that the mere continued existence of our Government would keep up the world-wide propaganda which Soviet Russia has been carrying on for more than a year."

This opportunist policy of the Bolsheviki has been successful. It has been possible for them to establish themselves in power partly by means of collusion with the late Imperial Government of Germany and they have been enabled to continue themselves in power partly by reason of the continued interference of the German Government in Russian internal affairs.

It is not clear what relations exist at the present moment between the Bolshevik movement and the reactionary, imperialistic elements of Germany. Their common aim is subversion.

Taken at their best the Bolsheviki are in essence a small coterie of men who are seeking to profit by the existing unrest to impose upon the world, by any means whatsoever, a preconceived order of existence.

Judged by the fruits of their control of central Russia for more than twenty months, they are pure destructivists. They have destroyed not alone the slowly accumulated savings of the people but the lives of many of those who might some day have aided in reconstruction. They have loosed the most savage and venal instincts of the people to the people's undoing.

That they can still carry on their work of destruction at home and their subversive propaganda abroad is due in part to the fact that final condemnation has not yet been passed upon them by those leaders of progressive thought in whom the great mass of forward-looking people have confidence. It is felt that at the present moment, when the results of the world's upheaval hang in the balance between progress and construction on the one hand and destruction and barbaric reversion on the other, a clear warning is needed.

T MS (WP, DLC).
[1] Nikolai Ivanovich Bukharin, a leading Bolshevik theoretician, member of the Bolshevik Central Committee, and editor of *Pravda*.

[2] Grigorii Evseevich Zinov'ev, also a member of the Bolshevik Central Committee. Like Bukharin, he was at this time a close associate of Lenin.

From Robert Lansing, with Enclosure

My dear Mr. President: Washington August 7, 1919.

I submit for your consideration Despatch No. 3277, of which a copy is attached.

I remain of your opinion, previously expressed, that no territory should be taken by the Conference from Russia until she has a responsible government to deal with, and I think that the reply should reiterate this view.

Regarding the Dobrudja, or rather so much of it as is clearly Bulgarian, I think that it will make for peace in the Balkans if the territory is restored to Bulgaria from whom it was taken through the harsh and unjust circumstances of 1913. This is not only fair but particularly reasonable in view of the large accessions of territory which Roumania is to receive.

                    Faithfully yours,   Robert Lansing

TLS (SDR, RG 59, 763.72119/5793, DNA).

                    E N C L O S U R E

                                   Paris, July 23, 1919

3277. Personal. Please submit following situation to the President and cable his decision as soon as possible:

Roumanian Territorial Commission, after considering the general aspirations of the population, geographic and ethnic character of the regions, as well as the historical and economic arguments, unanimously recommends giving Bessarabia to Roumania. American experts Day, Seymour, Coolidge, Lord, Johnson, all favor assigning Bessarabia to Roumania, although we are not at war with Russia, because of danger to European peace if this question remains unsettled. Our colleagues in Supreme Council appear to be of the same view.

The note of the Principal Allied and Associated Powers to Admiral Koltchak of May 26th 1919[1] contained among other conditions for their continued assistance to Koltchak the demand "that the right of the Peace Conference to determine the future of the Roumanian part of Bessarabia be (*)."

If we assent to giving Bessarabia to Roumania our position regarding the Dobrudja will be strengthened. At present British and

Italians accept American point of view that Bulgarian part of Bessarabia should be restored by Roumania, but claim they can not take territory from a power with which the Allies are not at war. In the case of Bessarabia they have taken a contrary view. By agreeing with them in the Bessarabian case, on condition that they accept our point of view in the case of Dobrudja, we may be able to overcome their technical objection in Dobrudja case and secure the wisest solution for both questions. The President's instructions regarding these two points are awaited before the American position is presented in the Supreme Council. Discussion is set for Thursday July twenty fourth.

I agree with and until now, have sustained your point of view that no territory should be taken by the conference from Russia until she has a responsible Government to deal with and I expressed that view only two days ago to the Roumanian Minister who came to solicit our assent to assignment of Bessarabia to his country; but I admit there is much to be said for the view of our own and all the other experts in which General Bliss concurs. Signed White. American Mission.

T telegram (SDR, RG 59, 763.72119/5793, DNA).
[1] Printed as Appendix I to Hankey's notes of the Council of Four, May 27, 1919, 4 p.m., Vol. 59.

Frank Lyon Polk to Robert Lansing

Paris August 7, 1919

3547 Strictly confidential.
For the Secretary of State from Polk. President's instructions in regard to Thrace[1] give us little latitude. I saw Tardieu last night and will see Balfour this morning. The suggestions are to give the section of southwest Thrace to Greece and either internationalizing west Thrace or give Bulgaria a corridor. It is a difficult situation. Tittoni's experts have come through with a suggestion in regard to Dalmatia, but it is practically the same old story and I have told him we won't discuss it. Tardieu is very anxious, for political reasons, that we shall do all we can to help Tittoni as he says that their government is in a desperate condition. Ammission

T telegram (SDR, RG 256, 868.00/169A, DNA).
[1] See WW to RL, Aug. 4, 1919 (first letter of that date).

A Message to the Senate

To the Senate: The White House, 8 August, 1919.

I have received the resolutions of the Senate, dated July 15 and July 17, asking—

First, for a copy of any treaty purporting to have been projected between Germany and Japan, such as was referred to in the press dispatch inclosed, together with any information in regard to it which may be in possession of the State Department, or any information concerning any negotiations between Japan and Germany during the progress of the war. In reply to this resolution, I have the honor to report that I know of no such negotiations. I had heard the rumors that are referred to, but was never able to satisfy myself that there was any substantial foundation for them.

Second, requesting a copy of any letter or written protest by the members of the American Peace Commission or any officials attached thereto against the disposition or adjustment which was made in reference to Shantung, and particularly a copy of a letter written by Gen. Tasker H. Bliss, member of the Peace Commission, on behalf of himself, Hon. Robert Lansing, Secretary of State, and Hon. Henry White, members of the Peace Commission, protesting against the provisions of the treaty with reference to Shantung. In reply to this request, let me say that Gen. Bliss did write me a letter in which he took very strong ground against the proposed Shantung settlement, and that his objections were concurred in by the Secretary of State and Mr. Henry White. But the letter can not properly be described as a protest against the final Shantung decision, because it was written before that decision had been arrived at and in response to my request that my colleagues on the commission apprise me of their judgment in that matter. The final decision was very materially qualified by the policy which Japan undertook to pursue with regard to the return of the Shantung Peninsula in full sovereignty to China.

I would have no hesitation in sending the Senate a copy of Gen. Bliss's letter were it not for the fact that it contains references to other Governments which it was perfectly proper for Gen. Bliss to make in a confidential communication to me, but which I am sure Gen. Bliss would not wish to have repeated outside our personal and intimate exchange of views.

I have received no written protests from any officials connected with or attached to the American Peace Commission with regard to this matter.

I am also asked to send you any memorandum or other information with reference to an attempt of Japan or her peace delegates to intimidate the Chinese peace delegates. I am happy to say that I have no such memorandum or information.

Woodrow Wilson.

Printed in *Papers Concerning the German Peace Treaty*, 66th Cong., 1st sess., Sen. Doc. No. 72 (Washington, 1919).

An Address to a Joint Session of Congress[1]

Reading copy, 8 Aug. 1919.[2]

Gentlemen of the Congress: I have sought this opportunity to address you because it is clearly my duty to call your attention to the present cost of living and to urge upon you with all the persuasive force of which I am capable the legislative measures which would be most effective in controlling it and bringing it down. The prices the people of this country are paying for everything that is necessary for them to use in order to live are not justified by a shortage of supply, either present or prospective, and are in many cases artificially and deliberately created by vicious practices which ought immediately to be checked by law. They constitute a burden upon us which is the more unbearable because we know that it is wilfully imposed by those who have the power and that it can by vigorous public action be greatly lightened and made to square with the actual conditions of supply and demand. Some of

[1] There was originally in WP, DLC, a folder which included the following documents: JPT to WW, Aug. 6; a memorandum by JPT, Aug. 7; RL to WW, Aug. 7 (first letter of that date), probably with enclosure; and a memorandum by A. M. Palmer, Aug. 6, 1919. All these documents are printed at their dates. These, in addition to the memorandum by Palmer printed at Aug. 7, 1919, seem to have been the basic documents that Wilson used in writing this address.

There is a brief WWsh outline, a WWT outline, and a WWT draft of this address in WP, DLC.

Wilson obviously sent the copy of this address to the Public Printer at the last minute. The copy that he sent consists of unnumbered cards (the Public Printer numbered them), the text of which contained many emendations and additions between the lines and in the margins. In his speech, as delivered, the last sentences read as follows: "In the meantime,—now and in the days of readjustment and recuperation that are ahead of us,—let us resort more and more to frank and intimate counsel and make ourselves a great and triumphant Nation by making ourselves a united force in the life of the world. It will not then have looked to us for leadership in vain." *Cong. Record*, 66th Cong., 1st sess., p. 3721.

We are struck, as we are sure most of our readers are, by several obvious facts about the address. First, as the WWT copy shows, Wilson had great difficulty in writing it. Indeed, he did something he had never done before: he sent an unedited copy to the Public Printer which contained several grammatical errors and at least one garbled sentence. Second, the language is characteristic of some of Wilson's essays of the 1880s and early 1890s: it is rambling, loquacious, repetitive, and chatty. Third, Wilson was obviously unable to focus his thoughts and failed to concentrate his message upon the problem at hand. One has only to contrast the language of this address with, say, that of his speeches in Belgium (printed at June 19, 1919, in Vol. 61) to see the degree to which the dementia resulting from his stroke of July 19 had affected him.

[2] WWhw.

the methods by which these prices are produced are already illegal, some of them criminal, and those who employ them will be energetically proceeded against; but others have not yet been brought under the law and should be dealt with at once by legislation.

I need not recite the particulars of this critical matter: the prices demanded and paid at the sources of supply, at the factory, in the food markets, at the shops, in the restaurants and hotels, alike in the city and in the village. They are familiar to you. They are the talk of every domestic circle and of every group of casual acquaintances even. It is matter of familiar knowledge, also, that a process has set in which is likely, unless something is done, to push prices and rents and the whole cost of living higher and yet higher, in a vicious cycle to which there is no logical or natural end. With the increase in the prices of the necessaries of life come demands for increases in wages,—demands which are justified if there be no other means of enabling men to live. Upon the increase of wages there follows close an increase in the price of the products whose producers have been accorded the increase,—not a proportionate increase, for the manufacturer does not content himself with that, but an increase considerably greater than the added wage cost and for which the added wage cost is oftentimes hardly more than an excuse. The labourers who do not get an increase in pay when they demand it are likely to strike, and the strike only makes matters worse. It checks production, if it affects the railways it prevents distribution and strips the markets, so that there is presently nothing to buy, and there is another excessive addition to prices resulting from the scarcity.

These are facts and forces with which we have become only too familiar; but we are not justified because of our familiarity with them or because of any hasty and shallow conclusion that they are "natural" and inevitable in sitting inactively by and letting them work their fatal results if there is anything that we can do to check, correct, or reverse them. I have sought this opportunity to inform the Congress what the Executive is doing by way of remedy and control, and to suggest where effective legal remedies are lacking and may be supplied.

We must, I think, frankly admit that there is no complete immediate remedy to be had from legislation and executive action. The free processes of supply and demand will not operate of themselves and no legislative or executive action can force them into full and natural operation until there is peace. There is now neither peace nor war. All the world is waiting,—with what unnerving fears and haunting doubts who can adequately say?—waiting to know when it shall have peace and what kind of peace it will be when it comes,—a peace in which each nation shall make shift for itself as it can, or a peace buttressed and supported by the will and concert of the nations that have the purpose and the power to do and to enforce what is right. Politically, economically, socially the World is on the operating table, and it has not been possible to administer any anesthetic. It is conscious. It even watches the capital operation upon which it knows that its hope of healthful life depends. It cannot think its business out or make plans or give intelligent and provident direction to its affairs while in such a case. Where there is no peace of mind there can be no energy in endeavour. There can be no confidence in industry, no calculable basis for credits, no confident buying or systematic selling, no certain prospect of employment, no normal restoration of business, no hopeful attempt at reconstruction or the proper reassembling of the dislocated elements of enterprise until peace has been established and, so far as may be, guaranteed.

Our national life has no doubt been less radically disturbed and dismembered than the national life of other peoples whom the war more directly affected, with all its terrible ravaging and destructive force, but it has been, nevertheless, profoundly affected and disarranged, and our industries, our credits, our productive capacity, our economic processes are inextricably interwoven with those of other nations and peoples,—most intimately of all with the nations and peoples upon whom the chief burden and confusion of the war fell and who are now most dependent upon the cooperative action of the world.

We are just now shipping more goods out of our ports to foreign markets than we ever shipped before,—not food stuffs merely, but stuffs and materials of every sort; but this is no index of what our foreign sales will continue to be or of the effect the volume of our exports will have on supplies and prices. It is impossible yet to predict how far or how long foreign purchasers will be able to find the money or the credit to pay for or sustain such purchases on such a scale; how soon or to what extent foreign manufacturers can resume their former production, foreign farmers get their accustomed crops from their own fields, foreign mines resume their former output, foreign merchants set up again their old machinery of trade with the ends of the earth. All these things must remain uncertain until peace is established and the nations of the world have concerted the methods by which normal life and industry are to be restored. All that we shall do, in the meantime, to restrain profiteering and put the life of our people upon a tolerable footing will be makeshift and provisional. There can be no settled conditions here or elsewhere until the treaty of peace is out of the way and the work of liquidating the war has become the chief concern of our government and of the other governments of the world. Until then business will inevitably remain speculative and sway now this way and again that, with heavy losses or heavy gains as it may chance, and the consumer must take care of both the gains and the losses. There can be no peace prices so long as our whole financial and economic system is on a war basis.

Europe will not, cannot recoup her capital or put her restless, distracted peoples to work until she knows exactly where she stands in respect of peace; and what we will do is for her the chief question upon which her quietude of mind and confidence of purpose depends. While there is any possibility that the peace terms may be changed or may be held long in abeyance or may not be enforced because of divisions of opinion among the Powers associated against Germany, it is idle to look for permanent relief.

But what we can do we should do, and should do at once. And there is a great deal that we can do, provisional though it be. Wheat shipments and credits to facilitate the purchase of our wheat can and will be limited and controlled in such a way as not to raise but rather to lower the price of flour here. The Government has the power, within certain limits, to regulate that. We cannot deny wheat to foreign peoples who are in dire need of it, and we do not wish to do so; but, fortunately, though the wheat crop is not what we hoped it would be, it is abundant if handled with provident care. The price of wheat is lower in the United States than in Europe, and can with proper management be kept so.

By way of immediate relief, surplus stocks of both food and clothing in the hands of the Government will be sold, and of course sold at prices at which there is no profit. And by way of a more permanent correction of prices surplus stocks in private hands will be drawn out of storage and put upon the market. Fortunately, under the terms of the Food Control Act the hoarding of food stuffs can be checked and prevented; and they will be, with the greatest energy. Food stuffs can be drawn out of storage and sold by legal action which the Department of Justice will institute wherever necessary; but so soon as the situation is systematically dealt with it is not likely that the courts will often have to be resorted to. Much of the accumulating of stocks has no doubt been due to the sort of speculation which always results from uncertainty. Great surpluses were accumulated because it was impossible to foresee what the market would disclose and dealers were determined to be ready for whatever might happen, as well as eager to reap the full advantage of rising prices. They will now see the disadvantage, as well as the danger, of holding off from the new process of distribution.

Some very interesting and significant facts with regard to stocks on hand and the rise of prices in the face of abundance have been disclosed by the inquiries of the Department of Agriculture, the Department of Labor, and the Federal Trade Commission. They seem to justify the statement that in the case of many necessary commodities effective means have been found to prevent the normal operation of the law of supply and demand. Disregarding the surplus stocks in the hands of the Government, there was a greater supply of food stuffs in this country on June first of this year than at the same date last year. In the combined total of a number of the most important foods in dry and cold storage the excess is quite nineteen per cent. And yet prices have risen. The supply of fresh eggs on hand in June of this year, for example, was greater by nearly ten per cent. than the supply on hand at the same time last year and yet the wholesale price was forty cents a dozen as against thirty cents a year ago. The stock of frozen fowls had increased more than two hundred and ninety-eight per cent, and yet the price had risen also, from thirty-four and a half cents per pound to thirty-seven and a half cents. The supply of creamery butter had increased a hundred and twenty-nine per cent. and the price from forty-one to fifty-three cents per pound. The supply of salt beef had been augmented three per cent. and the price had gone up from thirty-four dollars a barrel to thirty-six dollars a barrel. Canned corn had increased in stock nearly ninety-two per cent. and had remained substantially the same in price. In a few food stuffs the prices had declined, but in nothing like the proportion in which the supply had increased. For example, the stock of canned tomatoes had increased one hundred and two per cent. and yet the price had declined only twenty-five cents per dozen cans. In some cases there had been the usual result of an increase of price following a decrease of supply, but in almost every instance the increase of price had been disproportionate to the decrease in stock.

The Attorney General has been making a careful study of the situation as a whole and of the laws that can be applied to better it and is convinced that, under the stimulation and temptation of exceptional circumstances, combinations of producers and combinations of traders have been formed for the control of supplies and of prices which are clearly in restraint of trade, and against these prosecutions will be promptly instituted and actively pushed which will in all likelihood have a prompt corrective effect. There is reason to believe that the prices of leather, of coal, of lumber, and of textiles have been materially affected by forms of concert and cooperation among the producers and marketers of these and other universally necessary commodities which it will be possible to redress. No watchful or energetic effort will be spared to accomplish this necessary result. I trust that there will not be many cases in which prosecution will be necessary. Public action will no doubt cause many who have perhaps unwittingly adopted illegal methods to abandon them promptly and of their own motion.

And publicity can accomplish a great deal. The purchaser can often take care of himself if he knows the facts and influences he is dealing with; and purchasers are not disinclined to do anything, either singly or collectively, that may be necessary for their self-protection. The Department of Commerce, the Department of Agriculture, the Department of Labor, and the Federal Trade Commission can do a great deal towards supplying the public, systematically and at short intervals, with information regarding the actual supply of particular commodities that is in existence and available, with regard to supplies which are in existence but not available because of hoarding, and with regard to the methods of price fixing which are being used by dealers in certain food stuffs and other necessaries. There can be little doubt that retailers are in part,—sometimes in large part,—responsible for exorbitant prices; and it is quite practicable for the Government, through the agencies I have mentioned, to supply the public with full information as to the prices at which retailers buy and as to the costs of transportation they pay, in order that it may be known just what margin of profit they are demanding. Opinion and concerted action on the part of purchasers can probably do the rest.

That is, these agencies may perform this indispensable service provided the Congress will supply them with the necessary funds to prosecute their inquiries and keep their price lists up to date. Hitherto the Appropriation Committees of the Houses have not always, I fear, seen the full value of these inquiries, and the Departments and Commissions have been very much straitened for means to render this service. That adequate funds be provided by appropriation for this purpose, and provided as promptly as possible, is one of the means of greatly ameliorating the present distressing conditions of livelihood that I have come to urge, in this attempt to concert with you the best ways to serve the country in this emergency. It is one of the absolutely necessary means, underlying many others, and can be supplied at once.

There are many other ways. Existing law is inadequate. There are many perfectly legitimate methods by which the Government can exercise restraint and guidance.

Let me urge, in the first place, that the present food control Act should be extended both as to the period of time during which it shall remain in operation and as to the commodities to which it shall apply. Its provisions against hoarding should be made to apply not only to food but also to feed stuffs, to fuel, to clothing, and to many other commodities which are indisputably necessaries of life. As it stands now it is limited in operation to the period of the war and becomes inoperative upon the formal proclamation of peace. But I should judge that it was clearly within the constitutional power of the Congress to make similar permanent provisions and regulations with regard to all goods destined for inter-state commerce and to exclude them from inter-state shipment if the requirements of the law are not complied with. Some such regulation is imperatively necessary. The abuses that have grown up in the manipulation of prices by the withholding of food stuffs and other necessaries of life cannot otherwise to [be] effectively prevented. There can be no doubt of either the necessity or the legitimacy of such measures. May I not call attention to the fact, also, that, although the present Act prohibits profiteering, the prohibition is accompanied by no penalty? It is clearly in the public interest that a penalty should be provided which will be persuasive.

To the same end, I earnestly recommend, in the second place, that the Congress pass a law regulating cold storage as it is regulated, for example, by the laws of the State of New Jersey, which limit the time during which goods may be kept in storage, prescribe the method of disposing of them if kept beyond the permitted period, and require that goods released from storage shall in all cases bear the date of their receipt. It would materially add to the serviceability of the law, for the purpose we now have in view, if it were also prescribed that all goods released from storage for inter-state shipment should have plainly marked upon each package the selling or market price at which they went into storage. By this means the purchaser would always be able to learn what profits stood between him and the producer or the wholesale dealer.

It would serve as a useful example to the other communities of the country, as well as greatly relieve local distress, if the Congress were to regulate all such matters very fully for the District of Columbia, where its legislative authority is without limit.

I would also recommend that it be required that all goods destined for inter-state commerce should in every case where their form or package makes it possible be plainly marked with the price at which they left the hands of the producer. Such a requirement would bear a close analogy to certain provisions of the Pure Food Act, by which it is required that certain detailed information be given on the labels of packages of foods and drugs.

And it does not seem to me that we can confine ourselves to detailed measures of this kind, if it is indeed our purpose to assume national control of the processes of distribution. I take it for granted that that is our purpose and our duty. Nothing less will suffice. We need not hesitate to handle a national question in a national way. We should go beyond the measures I have suggested. We should formulate a law requiring a federal license of all corporations engaged in interstate commerce and embodying in the license, or in the conditions under which it is to be issued, specific regulations designed to secure competitive selling and prevent unconscionable profits in the method of marketing. Such a law would afford a welcome opportunity to effect other much needed reforms in the business of inter-state shipment and in the methods of corporations which are engaged in it; but for the moment I confine my recommendations to the object immediately in hand, which is to lower the cost of living.

May I not add that there is a bill now pending before the Congress which, if passed, would do much to stop speculation and to prevent the fraudulent methods of promotion by which our people are annually fleeced of many millions of hard-earned money? I refer to the measure proposed by the Capital Issues Committee for the control of security issues. It is a measure formulated by men who know the actual conditions of business and its adoption would serve a great and beneficent purpose.

We are dealing, Gentlemen of the Congress, I need hardly say, with very critical and very difficult matters. We should go forward with confidence along the road we see, but we should also seek to comprehend the whole of the scene amidst which we act. There is no ground for some of the fearful forecasts I hear uttered about me, but the condition of the world is unquestionably very grave and we should face it comprehendingly. The situation of our own country is exceptionally fortunate. We of all peoples can afford to keep our heads and to determine upon moderate and sensible courses of action which will ensure us against the passions and distempers which are working such deep unhappiness for some of the distressed nations on the other side of the sea. But we may be involved in their distresses unless we help, and help with energy and intelligence.

The world must pay for the appalling destruction wrought by the great war, and we are part of the world. We must pay our share. For five years now the industry of all Europe has been slack and disordered. The normal crops have not been produced; the normal quantity of manufactured goods has not been turned out. Not until there are the usual crops and the usual production of manufactured goods on the other side of the Atlantic can Europe return to the former conditions; and it was upon the former conditions, not the present, that our economic relations with Europe were built up. We must face the fact that unless we help Europe to get back to her normal life and production a chaos will ensue there which will inevitably be communicated to this country. For the present, it is manifest, we must quicken, not slacken our own production. We, and we almost alone, now hold the world steady. Upon our steadfastness and self-possession depend the affairs of nations everywhere. It is in this supreme crisis,—this crisis for all mankind,—that America must prove her mettle. In the presence of a world confused, distracted, she must show herself self-possessed, self-contained, capable of sober and effective action. She saved Europe by her action in arms; she must now save it by her action in peace. In saving Europe she will save herself, as she did upon the battlefields of the war. The calmness and capacity with which she deals with and masters the problems of peace will be the final test and proof of her place among the peoples of the world.

And, if only in our own interest, we must help the people over seas. Europe is our biggest customer. We must keep her going or thousands of our shops and scores of our mines must close. There is no such thing as letting her go to ruin without ourselves sharing in the disaster.

In such circumstances, face to face with such tests, passion must be discarded. Passion and a disregard for the rights of others have no place in the counsels of a free people. We need light, not heat, in these solemn times of self-examination and saving action. There must be no threats. Let there be only intelligent counsel, and let the best reasons win, not the strongest brute force. The world has just destroyed the arbitrary force of a military junta. It will live under no other. All that is arbitrary and coercive is in the discard. Those who seek to employ it only prepare their own destruction.

We cannot hastily and over night revolutionize all the processes of our economic life. We shall not attempt to do so. These are days of deep excitement and of extravagant speech; but with us these are things of the surface. Everyone who is in real touch with the silent masses of our great people knows that the old strong fibre and steady self-control are still there, firm against violence or any distempered action that would throw their affairs into confusion. I am serenely confident that they will readily find themelves, no matter what the circumstances, and that they will address themselves to the tasks of peace with the same devotion and the same stalwart preference for what is right that they displayed to the admiration of the whole world in the midst of war.

And I entertain another confident hope. I have spoken to-day chiefly of measures of imperative regulation and legal compulsion, of prosecutions and the sharp correction of selfish processes; and these, no doubt, are necessary. But there are other forces that we may count on besides those resident in the Department of Justice. We have just fully awakened to what has been going on and to the influences, many of them very selfish and sinister, that have been producing high prices and imposing an intolerable burden on the mass of our people. To have brought it all into the open will accomplish the greater part of the result we seek. I appeal with entire confidence to our producers, our middlemen, and our merchants to deal fairly with the people. It is their opportunity to show that they comprehend, that they intend to act justly, and that they have the public interest sincerely at heart. And I have no doubt that housekeepers all over the country, and everyone who buys the things he daily stands in need of will presently exercise a greater vigilance, a more thoughtful economy, a more discriminating care as to the market in which he buys or the merchant with whom he trades than he has hitherto exercised.

I believe, too, that the more extreme leaders of organized labour will presently yield to a sober second thought and, like the great mass of their associates, think and act like true Americans. They will see that strikes undertaken at this critical time are certain to make matters worse, not better,—worse for them and for everybody else. The worst thing, the most fatal thing that can be done now is to stop or interrupt production or to interfere with the distribution of goods by the railways and the shipping of the country. We are all involved in the distressing results of the high cost of living and we must unite, not divide, to correct it. There are many things that ought to be corrected in the relations between capital and labour, in respect of wages and conditions of labour and other things even more far-reaching, and I, for one, am ready to go into conference about these matters with any group of my fellow countrymen who know what they are talking about and are willing to remedy existing conditions by frank counsel rather than by violent contest. No remedy is possible while men are in a temper, and there can be no settlement which does not have as its motive and standard the general interest. Threats and undue insistence upon the interest of a single class make settlement impossible. I believe, as I have hitherto had occasion to say to the Congress, that the industry and life of our people and of the world will suffer irreparable damage if employers and workmen are to go on in a perpetual contest, as antagonists. They must, on one plan or another, be effectively associated. Have we not steadiness and self-possession and business sense enough to work out that result? Undoubtedly we have, and we shall work it out. In the meantime,—now and in the days of readjustment and recuperation that are ahead of us,—let us resort more and more to frank and intimate counsel and make ourselves a great and triumphant by making ourselves a united force in the life of the world. It will not then have looked to us for leadership in vain.

Printed reading copy (WP, DLC).

To Henry Cabot Lodge

My dear Mr. Chairman: The White House 8 August, 1919.

I have at last been able to go personally over the great mass of papers which remained in my hands at the close of my stay in Paris, and am disappointed to find that it is in no respect a complete file, the complete files remaining with the American Commission.[1]

You ask for all drafts or forms presented to or considered by the Peace Commissioners relating to the League of Nations, and particularly the draft or form prepared or presented by the Commissioners of the United States. There are no formal drafts in my possession, except that presented by the American Commissioners,[2] and this I take pleasure in enclosing, along with the formal Report of the Commission on the League of Nations.

You also ask for all proceedings, arguments, and debates, including a transcript of the stenographic reports of the Peace Commission relating to or concerning a League of Nations or the League of Nations finally adopted, and all data bearing upon or used in connection with the Treaty of Peace with Germany now pending. No stenographic reports were taken of the debates on the League of Nations, and such memoranda as were taken it was agreed should be confidential.[3] The reason for regarding as confidential intimate exchanges of opinion with regard to many delicate matters will, of course, occur to you, and I beg to say that I am following the example of the representatives of the other Governments in making this explanation.

The various data bearing upon or used in connection with the Treaty of Peace with Germany are so miscellaneous and enormous in mass that it would be impossible for me to supply them without bringing from Paris the whole file of papers of the Commission itself, and would include many memoranda which, it was agreed on grounds of public policy, it would be unwise to make use of outside the Conference.   Very sincerely yours,   Woodrow Wilson

TLS (Foreign Relations Committee Papers, RG 46, DNA).

¹ Wilson was replying to HCL to WW, July 15, 1919, Vol. 61. For Wilson's earlier draft of this letter, see the Enclosure printed with GFC to RL, Aug. 4, 1919; and, for Lansing's comment on this draft, RL to WW, Aug. 4, 1919 (second letter of that date).

² Wilson sent a copy of what we call the Third Paris Draft of the Covenant, which is printed at Feb. 2, 1919, Vol. 54, and a copy of the report of the League of Nations Commission, which included the final text of the Covenant. Lodge presented these documents to the Senate on August 11, 1919, and they are printed in LEAGUE OF NATIONS: *American Draft of Covenant of the League of Nations together with the Report of the Commission of the League of Nations*, 66th Cong., 1st sess., Sen. Doc. No. 70 (Washington, 1919). Wilson was, of course, mistaken in saying that this was the draft presented by the American commissioners; in fact, no draft was ever presented by the American commissioners. The draft actually presented to the League of Nations Commission was the so-called Hurst-Miller draft, printed at February 2, 1919, Vol. 54.

³ However, see the stenographic transcripts of the minutes of the League of Nations Commission printed in Vols. 54 and 55 and the transcript of the debates on the Covenant on February 14 and April 28, 1919, in the third and fifth Plenary Sessions of the peace conference, printed in *PPC*, III, 208-39, 285-332.

To Robert Lansing, with Enclosure

My dear Lansing: The White House 8 August, 1919.

I would be very much obliged if you would tell me what sort of reply you think ought to be made to the enclosed letter from Mr. Louis Marshall.

Cordially and sincerely yours,   Woodrow Wilson

TLS (SDR, RG 59, 860c.4016/142, DNA).

E N C L O S U R E

From Louis Marshall

Dear Mr. President: New York August 6, 1919.

One of the most serious questions which has arisen in Eastern Europe is that which relates to East Galicia. The Poles and Ukrainians are both claiming that territory. Approximately 750,000 Jews live in that area and have suffered severely both from Polish and Ukrainian hostility. The Commission designated by the Peace Conference to report as to the future government of East Galicia, of which General La Rond, Dr. Lord and Mr. Paton¹ are members, several weeks ago requested the Jews of East Galicia who were then in Paris, to express their views on this problem, and at their request I accompanied the delegation as their spokesman. We took the position that the Jews, as a minority, could not safely assume an attitude for or against either of the two contending nationalities, who for months have been engaged in a bitter warfare, and that each of them resented any action that the Jews might take, as was evidenced by the series of pogroms which, ever since last November, have from time to time occurred in East Galicia in which the Poles and the Ukrainians both participated. Without undertaking to interfere with the political situation, we tentatively expressed the belief, that until conditions in East Galicia had become settled, and for a period of probably ten years, it might be desirable for the League of Nations to administer East Galicia through a High Commission, and that at the expiration of that period a plebiscite should determine the nature of the future government. That would afford a guaranty for the peaceful development of the country and give assurance of the avoidance of conflict likely to arise at any moment and to degenerate into bloodshed. The Commission intimated that a mandate over East Galicia would probably be given to Poland for a definite period, to be followed by a plebiscite, and that in the meantime the various nationalities would be enabled, by the operation of catastres or electoral colleges, to secure representation in the national and local legislative bodies. In view of the fact that the Jews of East Galicia were prepared to submit to any plan that might prove acceptable to the Peace Conference so long as they were permitted to retain their neutrality until a plebiscite had finally determined the permanent form of government, we stated that if that could be accomplished the Jews would willingly acquiesce in the plan indicated, provided (1) that they likewise were permitted to have a catastre or electoral college of their own; (2) that on account of their exceptional position they were to be exempted from conscription until after the plebiscite, and (3) that, as in the Ukraine and Lithuania, a Jewish secretariat should be created in the provincial cabinet for the protection of the Jews of East Galicia. In addition to these provisions it was contended that the clauses protective of racial, religious and linguistic minorities, contained in the Polish treaty, should be applicable to East Galicia.

I have just received a cablegram to the effect that the Polish leaders are insisting in the Diet at Warsaw that catastres or electoral colleges should be created for the Poles and Ukrainians only, and that the Jews of East Galicia are to be forced to participate either in the Polish or Ukrainian catastres. It is also stated that Mr. Paderewski has expressed his opposition against any measure that would relieve the Jews of East Galicia from conscription and has made disagreeable comments upon the Jews, who desire to be relieved from the jeopardy in which they would find themselves of being ground between the upper and the nether millstones of Polish and Ukrainian agitation.

I am confident that a word from you would assure to these unfortunate people that protection which is essential to them in the extraordinary circumstances in which they now find themselves and would secure to them the right of remaining neutral in the bitter conflict between the two nationalities now struggling for the ultimate sovereignty over East Galicia, one or both of whom will be

swift to resent as hostile and to wreak vengeance upon the Jews
for any action taken that may not be in accordance with the
wishes, policies or prejudices of the contending factions.

I am, with great respect and gratitude,

Cordially yours,   Louis Marshall

TLS (WP, DLC).
   [1] Gen. Henri Louis Édouard Le Rond; Robert Howard Lord; and Herbert James Pa-
ton, Fellow of Queen's College, Oxford University, member of the Intelligence Division
of the Admiralty, 1914-1918, a member of the British delegation to the peace conference since February 1919.

To William Cox Redfield

My dear Mr. Secretary: [The White House] 8 August, 1919.

A misapprehension seems to have arisen as to what we agreed
upon last Tuesday with regard to cooperating in the matter of foreign trade.[1] The Treasury Department seems to have got the
impression that I intended to set up an Interdepartmental Committee on International Credits. International credits are being
studied and handled by the Treasury Department in a way which
is wholly adequate and beyond criticism. But of course that was
not our purpose. Our purpose was to make certain that the various
departments and agencies of the Government acquainted with
conditions of international trade and with the necessities of Europe
at the present time, should confer and devise any sensible or feasible methods of cooperation that might be agreed upon should be
adopted. I am therefore writing letters today to the Secretary of
State, the Secretary of the Treasury, the Chairman of the Federal
Trade Commission, Mr. Eugene Meyer, Governor Harding, Mr.
Baruch, Mr. Vance McCormick, and Mr. Norman Davis, suggesting a conference along these lines, which conference I shall ask
the Secretary of State, as the ranking member of the Cabinet, to
call.   Cordially and sincerely yours,   Woodrow Wilson

TLS (Letterpress Books, WP, DLC).
   [1] That is, on August 5, 1919, at the cabinet meeting on that date.

To Carter Glass

My dear Mr. Secretary: The White House 8 August, 1919.

In view of the many critical and pressing interests connected
with foreign commerce and the attitude and cooperation of the
Government in regard to it, I am going to ask you to attend a conference (to be called by the Secretary of State) consisting, besides

yourself, of the Secretary of Commerce, the Chairman of the Federal Trade Commission, Governor Harding of the Federal Reserve Board, Mr. Eugene Meyer, Jr., of the War Finance Corporation, Mr. Bernard M. Baruch, Mr. Vance C. McCormick, and Mr. Norman Davis, to consider the best means and lines of cooperation between the several agencies of the Government in lending such aid and guidance as may be possible and wise, to our foreign commerce in these critical days of dislocation and exceptional circumstances. The business men of the country who are engaged in or wish to become engaged in foreign commerce are a bit distressed with anxieties of several sorts, and I am sure would welcome a manifestation of the sympathy of all government agencies and their readiness to help and their knowledge of how intelligent assistance can be rendered, and I hope that the conference I am proposing will be productive of happy results.

Cordially and faithfully yours,   Woodrow Wilson[1]

TLS (C. Glass Papers, ViU).
[1] Wilson sent the same letter, *mutatis mutandis*, on the same date to Lansing, Baruch, McCormick, Davis, Harding, Colver, and Meyer; all TLS (Letterpress Books, WP, DLC).

To Grosvenor Blaine Clarkson

My dear Mr. Clarkson: [The White House] 8 August, 1919.

Referring to your letter of August 5th in which you say that the Secretary of War and you were discussing the desirability of making public the report on the High Cost of Living, a copy of which you had the kindness to send me, let me say that I think the report an excellent one, but there is one feature of it which I hope you will reconsider. May I not suggest that you have a conference with Governor Harding of the Federal Reserve Board before forming or expressing a judgment about the alleged currency inflation? I think that he can convince you that there is a misunderstanding with regard to that matter.

In haste,

Cordially and sincerely yours,   Woodrow Wilson

TLS (Letterpress Books, WP, DLC).

To Albert Baird Cummins

My dear Senator: [The White House] 8 August, 1919.

Allow me to acknowledge with appreciation your candid letter of the sixth instant. I felt it my duty to suggest permanent legislation about the wage question before undertaking any action which must of necessity be temporary because limited by the period of the Government control of the railroads, but your letter makes it clear to me that it is the desire of the committee that I should act without further legislation, and therefore I have advised the Director General of Railroads to proceed as indicated in the letter to him, of which I enclose a copy.[1]

With much appreciation,

Sincerely yours,   Woodrow Wilson

TLS (Letterpress Books, WP, DLC).
[1] Wilson enclosed a copy of WW to W. D. Hines, Aug. 7, 1919.

To William Bauchop Wilson

My dear Wilson: [The White House] 8 August, 1919.

I think I have expressed to you before my interest in Miss Gertrude Barnum. I do not know her even by sight, but I have learned enough about her work to become very much interested, and I am now taking the liberty of suggesting that when you consider filling the position of Associate Investigator in the Labor Department you should not overlook her. She seems to me to have peculiar qualifications.

But this is probably carrying coals to Newcastle. You probably know more about her than I do.

Cordially and faithfully yours,   Woodrow Wilson

TLS (Letterpress Books, WP, DLC).

To Royal Meeker

My dear Meeker: [The White House] 8 August, 1919.

I have your letter of August fifth but I must frankly say that I do not quite understand what you mean by "plans for the stabilization of the purchasing power of the dollar." Won't you give me a little exposition?

In haste,   Faithfully yours,   Woodrow Wilson

TLS (WP, DLC).

To William Gibbs McAdoo

My dear Mac: The White House 8 August, 1919.

Your letters are very welcome and I profit in my thought by their suggestions. I am going to take up with Glass your suggestion about the corporation tax returns.[1] I like the idea and hope I can get the concurrence of the Secretary of the Treasury in your judgment.

We all unite in dearest love to you both.

In tearing haste,

Affectionately yours,   Woodrow Wilson

TLS (W. G. McAdoo Papers, DLC).
[1] WGM to WW, Aug. 6, 1919.

To Justina Leavitt Wilson[1]

My dear Mrs. Wilson: [The White House] 8 August, 1919.

I have your letter of August 6th[2] and will be very glad to have you quote the following as my tribute to Dr. Shaw:[3]

It was not my privilege to know Dr. Shaw until the later years of her life, but I had the advantage then of seeing her in many lights, for at the very end I saw her acting with such vigour and intelligence in the service of the Government, and through the Government, of mankind, as to win my warmest admiration. I had already had occasion to see the extraordinary quality of her clear and effective mind, and to know how powerful and persuasive an advocate she was. When the war came, I saw her in action and she won my sincere admiration and homage.

Cordially and sincerely yours,   Woodrow Wilson

TLS (Letterpress Books, WP, DLC).
[1] Mrs. Halsey William Wilson, corresponding secretary of the National American Woman Suffrage Association.
[2] It is missing in WP, DLC.
[3] That is, Dr. Anna Howard Shaw, who had died on July 2, 1919. See JPT to WW, July 3, 1919 (first telegram of that date), Vol. 61.

To H. H. Maughirmalani[1]

My dear Sir: [The White House] 8 August, 1919.

I have received your courteous letter of the 26th of June,[2] suggesting that you translate my book, "The State," into the Indian vernaculars, and I am very much complimented that you should desire to do so, but before you could translate the book it would in effect be antiquated, because of the radical changes which are taking place in the political conditions of Europe, and I do not think that it would be wise to continue it in its present form. It ought to undergo, as soon as possible, radical revision.

Very sincerely yours,   Woodrow Wilson

TLS (Letterpress Books, WP, DLC).

¹ The Editors have been unable to learn anything about him, other than that he was at this time in Karachi, India (now Pakistan).
² H. H. Maughirmalani to WW, June 26, 1919, TLS (WP, DLC). Actually, he only proposed to translate *The State* into his own vernacular, Sindhi.

From John Barton Payne[1]

My dear Mr. President: Washington August 8, 1919.

On behalf of the Board I beg to submit, for your consideration and approval, draft of an Executive Order.

The proposed order contemplates a direction to the Shipping Board to exercise the power vested in you by the Emergency Shipping Fund provisions of the Sundry Civil Appropriations Act approved July 19, 1919 (Public—No. 21—66th Congress), in connection with the disposition of plants and materials acquired by the Emergency Fleet Corporation.

The Order as drawn is intended to supplement your Order No. 3018 dated December 3, 1918, by making the power and authority of the Shipping Board commensurate with the subsequently enacted statute:

The new Order provides:

1. That the Shipping Board shall exercise the power of disposing of plants and materials as defined in the Emergency Shipping Fund provisions of June 15, 1917, as amended;

2. That the Board may exercise this power directly, or at its election through the Fleet Corporation or other designated agency;

3. Ratification of acts heretofore done by the Board or the Corporation, which might have been lawfully performed pursuant to this Order.   Sincerely yours,   John Barton Payne

TLS (WP, DLC).
¹ Lawyer of Chicago and Washington, the new chairman of the United States Shipping Board.

From Raymond Bartlett Stevens

Dear Mr. President: Washington August 8, 1919.

The Shipping Board has carefully considered your letter of August 1[1] and the accompanying memorandum of the Secretary of War on the ultimate disposal of the seized German passenger vessels now operating as troop ships.[2] The Board believes that the adoption of the recommendation of the Secretary of War that these vessels should be

"permanently assigned to the War Department with authority to operate, lease or charter same in any service of the United States

of America or in any commerce, foreign or coastwise, in the manner provided by law."
would be a serious mistake. We believe that the needs of the Army in peace and war times can be met without placing permanently the control of these vessels in the hands of the War Department.

As far as the movement of troops and supplies in peace times to the Philippine Islands and other possessions of the United States is concerned, it is certain that satisfactory arrangements can be made for such service with the Shipping Board.

In time of war, all public vessels which the War Department might require would undoubtedly be put at the disposal of the War Department voluntarily by the Shipping Board or any other Department which had control of the ships. If this were not voluntarily done, it could be done at any moment by Executive Order of the President. Furthermore, in war times the War Department has the right to requisition the use or commandeer the title of any privately owned ships for war purposes. Consequently we believe that the needs of the Army do not require that the permanent control of the ex-German ships should be placed in their hands.

The problem of handling the Government ships in order to secure the best development of our foreign trade and to develop the organizations to handle the ships efficiently is a very difficult one, and it would be further be further [sic] complicated if we had two sources of authority, the Shipping Board for the vessels under its control and the War Department for the ex-German vessels. Above all things there should be uniformity of policy and a centralized control in shipping, which would be impossible to secure if the control of the Government fleet were distributed through several Government Departments rather than centralized in one.

Respectfully,   Raymond B. Stevens, Vice Chairman.

TLS (WP, DLC).
  [1] WW to R. B. Stevens, Aug. 1, 1919, TLS (Letterpress Books, WP, DLC).
  [2] NDB to WW, July 31, 1919, TLS (WP, DLC).

From Walker Downer Hines, with Enclosure

Dear Mr. President: Washington August 8, 1919.

Referring to our interview yesterday I find my office has already prepared and sent you a three-page summary of the Plumb Bill.[1] This summary seems to me correct and sufficient except it inadvertently states that the proposed corporation is to consist of fifteen members, whereas the Bill provides that the corporation is to consist of its directors (who are the fifteen members referred to) and of the offical employes and the classified employes, these two classes covering all railroad officers and employes; and the summary also omits to mention that the provisions of the Bill seem designed to preserve the full right to strike. I think this is the effect of that portion of Section 2 of Chapter II reading as follows:

"That notwithstanding anything in this act, any society of workers, all or some of whose members are wholly or partly employes on the railway lines or properties of the Federal Government, or in any other manner employed by the Corporation, or otherwise under this act, may be registered or constitute themselves or be a Trade Union, and may do anything individually or in combination which the members of a Trade Union may lawfully do. Provided, further, that notwithstanding any act, order, or regulation to the contrary, it shall be lawful for any person employed under this act to participate in any civil or political action in like manner as if such person were not employed by said Corporation.

"Provided, further, that no person shall suffer dismissal or any deprivation of any kind as a consequence of any political or industrial action not directly forbidden by the terms of his employment."

In accordance with my promise I enclose copy of the summary which I made for my own use at the time I read the Bill. This is a practical duplication of the summary which has been sent you and I do not think it is necessary for you to read it.

Cordially yours,   Walker D Hines

TLS (WP, DLC).
 ¹ It is missing in WP, DLC, and Wilson apparently had not seen it. About the Sims bill, which put the Plumb plan into legislative form, see T. R. Marshall to WW, Aug. 7, 1919, n. 2.
 Stockton Axson, in an undated memorandum (T MS in possession of Arthur S. Link), tells the story of how Wilson learned the details of the Plumb plan:
 "The evening after the President delivered his address on the Cost of Living (August 8, 1919) we discussed the PLUMB PLAN for the nationalization of the railroads under tripartite control. (And, by the way, it amused me just the other day when a hot-headed young friend said that he was delighted to see that the President had rapped Plumb in his address on the Cost of Living; I contented myself with saying to the young man that I was sure the President had not rapped Plumb at all. But it would have been indiscreet to add that when the President made that address he did not know what the Plumb Plan was.) The President learned about the Plumb Plan on this very evening that I am talking about. Margaret, my niece, said that she had read a very clear statement of it in some New York paper, and I said that just the day before I had read a very illuminating thing in the Washington TIMES in the form of a questionnaire—a sort of A. B. C. Primer of Questions and Answers, set in a large box and occupying about one-third of a whole page. The President said he would like to see it. The paper was found in the White House, and he began to read it aloud very carefully and to consider as he read. He stopped the reading at one point and said, thoughtfully, rubbing his face with a characteristic gesture: 'It comes over me now that I have met Mr. Plumb; that he came once with a group of men and was quite modest in his attitude when he was introduced as the deviser of a new plan and said that it was not exclusively his plan but something that had been worked out as a thing worth careful consideration.' Before the President

got the paper I had remarked that the plan for the direction of the railroads did not seem to me at all radical; that it provided for fifteen directors—five to be appointed by the President for the people, five to be appointed for the operators, and five for the classified employees. But when Mr. Wilson read the TIMES he called attention to the fact that it was provided that the directors for the operators and the employees were not to be appointed but elected, which he said was a very important point. He commented at various points in detail, but when he had completed reading, he said: 'There is nothing radical in this. It is a proposition for serious consideration, but it comes back more and more clearly to my mind that I did meet Mr. Plumb once and his collaborators, and that it occurred to me then, as it occurs to me now, that there is one essential weakness in the plan—the provision for the purchase of the railroads by issuing government bonds, not at their face value, but at their value with the water squeezed out of the stock. Now, this will wreck the stock market, and the trouble is that the losses will fall on a great many small stockholders who have purchased railroad stock on a small scale as an investment and who will find that on revaluation their securities have shrunk to very much less than they had paid for it. This would be a hardship. Perhaps the way to get around it would be for the water to be squeezed out of all stock down to a certain limit, say to the holder of ten shares, and a time set for that, as, for instance, the holder of ten shares on January 1, 1919, so that there cannot be an opportunity for the big holders to unload and distribute among small holders.' Said he: 'After all, there is another aspect to the matter, because, of all this watered stock the millions of passengers and shippers are paying rates of transportation on an inflated valuation of the roads instead of on an actual valuation, so that all of the stockholders combined would make up a comparatively small body as compared with all the shippers and passengers.' Of course, in a general conversation of this sort the President arrived at no definite conclusions. He could not have done so. But it interested me to see how very open-minded he was towards the whole thing, and, furthermore, it interested me to see how often a President must have his first occasion for getting acquainted with an important pending problem. He had been so occupied with the Peace Treaty, the League of Nations, Cost of Living questions, Strike questions, and so on that he had not had an opportunity until this leisurely evening with his family really to inform his own mind of the Plumb Plan. He did say, by the way, that an enormous batch of literature had been sent over to him on the subject, which he had sent to Mr. Hines, the Director General of Railroads, with the request that a digest be made for him, which digest either had not up to this evening been returned or he had not had an opportunity to see it."

ENCLOSURE

SUMMARY OF THE PLUMB PLAN.

The Government is to acquire the Railroads through a Purchase Board consisting of the Interstate Commerce Commission and of three members selected by the Board of Directors of the "Corporation" from its three classes of Directors.

The Corporation is created and is to consist of its Directors, official employees and classified employees. The Directors are fifteen,—five elected by the official employees,—five by the classified employees and five appointed by the President.

The Railroads are to be divided into operating districts. District councils are to be formed consisting of one third members elected by official employees, one third by classified employees, and one third by the Board; and are to perform such functions as the Board may determine.

The Corporation shall fix rates under direction of the Interstate

Commerce Commission. Corporation subject to the Interstate Commerce Act.

The Secretary of Treasury is to lease all the Railroads to the Corporation to be operated as a single system. Corporation is to pay operating expenses—fixed charges on capital employed—making provision for sinking fund to retire debt, and pay one half of balance to Treasury to be used in new extensions and for sinking fund. Other one half to go as a dividend to employees in proportion to their compensation, except official employees to receive twice the rate paid to classified employees. Whenever the one half paid to Treasury exceeds 5% of operating revenues, Interstate Commerce Commission is to reduce rates to absorb amount so paid.

Board of Directors to agree with employees on three Boards of Adjustment, one half membership from classified employees and one half from official employees, to dispose of interpretations, grievances, etc.; "appeal" to Board of Directors when there is a deadlock.

Board of Directors to create Central Board of Wages and Working Conditions, membership one half official and one half classified employees, to deal with salaries, wages and conditions of employement. If desired, Board of Directors is to determine.

Apparent intention to preserve full right to strike.

T MS (WP, DLC).

From Norman Hezekiah Davis

My dear Mr. President: Washington August 8, 1919.

With reference to Secretary Glass's letters of July 10th and 11th to you relative to advances to Italy,[1] I have informed the Secretary of my conversation with you several days ago and that you agree with us that it is advisable to establish credits and make advances thereunder (as indicated in the above letters) which were substantially promised last April. It is only intended to make advances which are considered necessary to meet commitments made by Italy with American concerns, but it is not intended to make advances other than those contemplated and tacitly promised in the letters written by the Secretary to the Italian representative last April.

As you will recall, a credit of $25,000,000 was established in favor of Italy last winter to cover neutral purchases. I failed to mention this in our conversation, although it is explained in the Secretary's letter to you. All of this credit has not been used, and the Italians are desirous of having the balance transferred for purchases in this country. As we are practically committed to let Italy have this money for neutral purchases, we think it advisable to grant Italy's request that the balance of this credit be used for purchases here instead of in neutral countries.

I am simply writing this letter in confirmation of my understanding, in order that you may correct me if I am wrong.

I am, my dear Mr. President,

Faithfully and cordially yours,   Norman H. Davis

TLS (WP, DLC).
    ¹ C. Glass to WW, July 10 and 11, 1919, both in Vol. 61.

Two Letters from Franklin Delano Roosevelt

My dear Mr. President: Washington. August 8, 1919.

I read in the newspapers of the conferences which have taken place in regard to the cost of living and rates of wages problems. I know you will understand that I do not want you to feel that I would intrude in any way, but, frankly, I would like very much to bring one phase of the question to your attention.

The Navy Department, in peace time, has employed more civilians than any other branch of the Government except the Post Office Department, and in their case the employes have been serving in clerical or technical capacities. These Navy Department employes are scattered throughout Navy Yards in almost all parts of the country and represent nearly every form of labor.

Since 1913, nearly every question affecting these direct Government employes, totaling before the War about 60,000 and since the War over 100,000, has fallen under my jurisdiction and has been handled by me. I do not wish to take any credit for the results which have been accomplished except that I may point out that in six years and a half I have never had a strike or serious difficulty of any kind, with the exception of one walkout affecting one trade at one yard. This difficulty was settled inside of 48 hours.

At the beginning of the War, the general question of wages of shipbuilding workers was taken up by the Navy Department with the other branches of the Government and a solution was reached which has from that time on prevented disagreements or serious trouble not only in the Navy but in the shipbuilding industry in general.

I think I have expressed to you on several previous occasions my belief that one of our weak points is the lack of coordination and agreement between the various executive branches of the Government, a lack not only in relation to the carrying out of agreements but, more important still, a lack of a definitely accepted policy by all concerned.

It is for this reason especially that I am writing to you because I am fearful that some action might be taken by other executive branches of the Government which would necessarily affect the thousands of workmen employed by the Navy Department. I realize, of course, that Mr. Daniels will be away for nearly two months,[1] but I feel sure that were he here he would ask that the Navy be given at least an opportunity to express its views, especially because of the fact that the Navy happens to have had on the whole more experience and more success in dealing with labor than any other department of the Government.

Believe me,   Faithfully yours,   Franklin D Roosevelt

[1] Josephus Daniels had left Washington on August 1 to tour naval installations on the Pacific Coast and at Pearl Harbor in Honolulu.

My dear Mr. President: Washington. August 8, 1919.

I asked Mr. Daniels several weeks ago to speak to you about the desirability of taking a definite stand in favor of the Saturday half-holiday for all Government employes, but I understand that he did not have an opportunity of taking the matter up.

As you doubtless know, the Federation of Labor adopted resolutions at the recent convention in favor of the 44-hour week. After running a dozen or so of large industrial establishments, called Navy Yards, for over six years, I am very certain of the justice and rightness of the contention.

Except for three months during the Summer, all Government employes work eight hours on Saturday as they do on every other week day. I am very sure that they ought to have the half-holiday on Saturday throughout the year, working on that day four hours instead of eight.

I think it would be a pity, however, to treat the matter as one involving a 44-hour week. It would be better to treat it as a half-holiday once a week. It comes to the same thing in the end, of course, but ought not to be confused with the total hours of labor. The present Government standard of eight hours will, I take it, last until there is either a sufficient public opinion or more conclusive data in favor of a shorter working day. The principle of the "one day rest in seven" has been accepted by the Federal Government and by most of the States, and I believe that the time has come to recognize also the principle of the Saturday half-holiday.

Quite aside from the political expediency of a move of this kind,

I believe it to be in every way right and proper and if you could see your way clear to advocating legislation to this end, I think it would be an excellent thing.

Believe me,   Faithfully yours,   Franklin D Roosevelt

TLS (WP, DLC).

From David Franklin Houston

Dear Mr. President: Washington August 8, 1919.

I think you will be interested in reading, whenever you have a moment to spare, the enclosed copy of a letter to Senator Kenyon regarding the bill (H.R.7) proposing to create a Department of Education.[1] I am sending the letter to you at the request of Dr. W. O. Thompson, President of the Ohio State University, who is also Chairman of the Executive Committee of the Association of American Agricultural Colleges and Experiment Stations.

Faithfully yours,   D. F. Houston.

TLS (WP, DLC).
[1] William Oxley Thompson to W. S. Kenyon, July 30, 1919, TCL (WP, DLC). Thompson pointed out that the bill empowered the President to transfer to the proposed Department of Education any offices, bureaus, divisions, boards, or branches of government as he saw fit. Thompson feared that this transfer process would lead to the separation from the Department of Agriculture of all its educational and scientific organizations and activities, such as the experiment stations, the extension services, and the administration of the agricultural colleges. These organizations and activities had been built up over a long history of cooperation between the farmers and the federal government. Thompson believed that their continued juxtaposition and interaction under the supervision of the Department of Agriculture was vital to continued agricultural progress. He argued that all of the proposed special functions of a Department of Education could be carried out just as well by existing agencies, such as the Bureau of Education, if Congress would supply the necessary funding. He doubted that "the dignity of a Cabinet member" would secure for education "any better consideration or administration than at present." He deplored "the general tendency to expand the functions of the Federal Government and to increase expenditures."

From Robert Russa Moton

Dear Mr. President: Cappahosic, Virginia, August 8, 1919

I know you are besieged from many and various angles and touching many phases of life in this country, and I have some slight appreciation of the burdens that you have been carrying, and the fine courage and wisdom with which you have faced the situation. I am very glad you are again back on American soil. We somehow feel happier and safer with you in the country.

I want especially to call your attention to the intense feeling on the part of the colored people throughout the country towards white people, and the apparent revolutionary attitude of many Negroes which shows itself in a reckless desire to have justice at any cost. The riots in Washington and Chicago[1] and near-riots in many other cities have not surprised me in the least. I predicted in an address at the Fiftieth Anniversary of the Hampton Institute on the 2d of May—ex-President Taft and Mr. Peabody[2] were present at the time—that this would happen if the matter was not taken hold of vigorously by the thoughtful elements of both races.

I think the time is at hand, and I think of nothing that would have a more salutary effect on the whole situation now than if you should in your own wise way, something as you did a year ago, make a statement regarding mob law,[3] laying especial stress on lynching and every form of injustice and unfairness. You would lose nothing by specifically referring to the lynching record in the past six months; many of them have been attended with unusual horrors, and it would be easy to do it now because of the two most recent riots in the North, notably Washington and Chicago. The South was never more ready to listen than at present to that kind of advice, and it would have a tremendously stabalizing effect, as I have said, on the members of my race.

Of course you muxt [must] have seen the account of the lynching in Georgia of an old colored man seventy years of age, who shot one of two white men in his attempt to protect two colored girls who had been demanded to come out of their home in the night to meet these two men. The colored man killed the white man after he had been shot at by one of the white men because he had simply protested.

I have not the lynching record for the past six months, and am asking to have it sent on from Tuskegee to you.

I am enclosing an editorial from the Atlanta Constitution.[4]

With all kind wishes, and assuring you of jo [no] desire to add to your burdens, but simply to call attention to what seems to me vital not only for the interest of the twelve millions of black people but equally as important for the welfare of the millions of whites whom they touch, I am,

Very sincerely and gratefully,   R. R. Moton

I am taking the liberty of sending a copy of this to Mr. George Foster Peabody, and also to Secretary Baker.

TLS (WP, DLC).
[1] On the race riot in Washington of July 19-22, see J. R. Shillady to WW, July 21, 1919, n. 2, Vol. 61. Rioting had begun in Chicago on July 27, as the result of the drowning of a black youth in Lake Michigan after he was hit by a stone thrown by a white man. The violence and bloodshed continued almost unchecked for four days until some 6,000 state militiamen went into action on July 30. It was only on August 8 that the situation calmed down enough to allow the withdrawal of the militia. Twenty-three blacks and fifteen whites were killed in the riot, and at least 537 persons of both races

were injured. See William M. Tuttle, Jr., *Race Riot: Chicago in the Red Summer of 1919* (New York, 1970), especially pp. 3-10, 32-64.

² That is, George Foster Peabody.

³ See the first statement printed at July 26, 1918, Vol. 49.

⁴ "NO WONDER," *Atlanta Constitution*, July 25, 1919. The editorial condemned what it characterized as a particularly gruesome lynching in Telfair County, Georgia. The event, the *Constitution* said, made it manifestly necessary for the state legislature to enact the antilynching bill then pending before it. "This monstrous affair," the editorial concluded, "does not concern Telfair county, nor Georgia alone, but it concerns the American republic as a whole; and we might as well look the future squarely in the face and be prepared to accept federal jurisdiction in crimes of this kind, *if our own state has not the courage to meet the situation and apply the remedy.*"

Two Letters to Robert Lansing

My dear Mr. Secretary,   The White House, 8 August, 1919.

The marked paragraph in the enclosed message from House amazes and deeply disturbs me.[1] You will remember that when the Council of Ten adopted the resolutions with regard to mandates which were subsequently embodied in the Covenant of the League of Nations the portions of the Turkish Empire which were to be disposed of were constantly used as illustrations and I have never until this moment heard the least question raised about mandates there. Indeed mandates were the particular subject of discussion in connection with Syria, Arabia, Armenia and the rest throughout my dealings with Lloyd George and Clemenceau. I will tolerate no such suggestion as this message conveys. I will withdraw the French treaty rather than consent to see the Turkish Empire divided as spoils!

Will you not be kind enough to send a message of information on this matter to Polk,[2] with a very strong statement of our inflexible determination to allow nothing that will alter the understandings hitherto reached in this vital matter. I shall not press the treaty with Germany upon the Senate if this is to be the course pursued about the other treaties. The United States will certainly not enter the League of Nations to guarantee any such settlements, or any such intolerable bargains as the Greeks and Italians seem to be attempting.   Faithfully Yours,   W.W.

WWTLI (SDR, RG 59, 763.72119/6294½, DNA).

¹ The message was EMH to WW and RL, Aug. 6, 1919. The copy which Wilson marked does not seem to have survived.

² For the telegram sent, see RL to FLP, Aug. 9, 1919 (first telegram of that date).

My dear Mr. Secretary,   The White House, 8 August, 1919.

Rumania is acting in a perfectly outrageous manner.[1] Do you not think that it might be well to authorize our representatives at Paris to notify the Rumanians that we shall not only not support but shall oppose every claim of theirs to territory or sovereignty anywhere if they continue their present course of outlawry?[2]

Faithfully Yours,   W.W.

WWTLI (SDR, RG 59, 864.00/111½, DNA).

[1] Ammission to RL, No. 3535, Aug. 6, 1919, repeating A. Halstead to Ammission, No. 715, Aug. 6, 1919, T telegram (SDR, RG 256, 184.011102/275½, DNA). Halstead reported that the Rumanians had occupied Budapest (on August 3) on the advice of the French Consul General in Bucharest, and that the Rumanian action had destroyed all chance of "representative government" in Hungary. Moreover, Halstead added, the new Rumanian armistice terms conflicted with the former Allied terms, and the Rumanians should be ordered to evacuate Budapest.

[2] For the telegram sent, see RL to FLP, Aug. 9, 1919 (second telegram of that date).

From Robert Lansing, with Enclosure

My dear Mr. President: Washington August 8, 1919.

I wish to call your attention to this communication (Ammission 3533, Aug. 6, 9 pm) which I have received from Mr. Dulles relative to the Interim Reparations Commission, and to ask you what reply I shall make to it. He is certainly in a very embarrassing position without definite instructions from the Department and I feel that we should give him some direction.

This morning I had a conversation with Senator Lodge on the subject. I read him, in accordance with your request of August 4th, the telegram from Polk and Dulles, dated July 31 (Ammission 3416).[1] I also read him parts of the dispatch from Dulles of August 6th. In addition to that I explained to him the very serious position that the United States was being placed in by not taking part in the work of the Interim Commission.

My interview with him was most unsatisfactory and without result. He said of course that the whole matter was illegal and subject to repudiation. To that I agreed but at the same time said that I did not feel we ought to sacrifice American interests. He said that what the other nations were doing was also illegal and that I proposed to meet illegality with illegality. I told him that even if this was so I did not feel that we should sacrifice the great commercial interests of the United States through failure to do what we could to protect them. He said that he supposed the Supreme Council was creating the Interim Commission and that he thought it was a matter for them not a matter for Congress to decide as to what should be done, although he said he would have to point out that their acts were not under law and might be repudiated. He added that Congress would never consent to take any responsibility in the matter and that it was up to you to act if you saw fit but that he would not pass on the propriety of such action.

In other words he wants to force you to act independently and then if opportunity arises to criticise you for doing so. At least that is the impression I gathered.

Faithfully yours,   Robert Lansing.

TLS (SDR, RG 59, 763.72119/6777, DNA).
  [1] Printed as an Enclosure with WW to RL, Aug. 4, 1919 (third letter of that date).

E N C L O S U R E

Paris. Aug. 6, 1919.

3533. August 6, 9 p.m.
Very confidential, to the Secretary from Dulles as a personal and not as an official cable.

I have refrained from taking notice of the action of the Senate Foreign Relations Committee with reference to a provisional appointment to the Reparation Commission[1] as long as my only knowledge came through press reports. Department's 2679, June [July] 31, noon,[2] however brings the matter officially to my attention and I shall be glad to be advised as to what action I should take.

I have been reporting rather fully to the Department the action being taken by present Interim Reparation Commission, or, as it is likewise called, the Committee on Organization of the Reparation Commission. From these reports it will have appeared that this temporary commission is among other things negotiating with the Germans in respect of labor, coal, dyestuffs, reconstruction materials, restitution, et cetera; that it is occupying itself with deductions to be made from the initial twenty billion marks payment by Germany on account of the expenses of the armies of occupation and of essential imports of food and raw materials; that it is dealing with shipping matters both directly and through the Allied Maritime Transport Executive. In sum, the committee is to all intents and purposes carrying on all of the activities of the permanent Reparation Commission, the only qualification being that its decisions are subject to confirmation, modification or repudiation by the permanent commission when established and that our decisions take the form of an announcement of an intention to recommend to the permanent Reparation Commission.

In view of the resolution adopted by the Senate Foreign Relations Committee and in view of the proposed amendment to that resolution which was voted down by the committee, I feel that I am entitled to some definite instructions which will guide me.

As I trust I have made clear by preceding cables, I am only taking such part in the proceedings as seems to me to be essential to protect our interests and to perform our moral obligations to the Germans; for instance, in such questions as labor, where without my objection the French would have taken the position that the supply of German labor is a condition precedent to the return of prisoners of war.

It is in my opinion absolutely impossible to prevent the current discussion and treatment of matters of the character being handled by the temporary Reparation Commission in view of the economic necessities of the European nations concerned and in particular the necessity of some practical accomplishment before winter. Dulles.   American Mission

T telegram (SDR, RG 59, 763.72119/6027, DNA).
   [1] See HCL to WW, July 22, 1919 (first letter of that date), and the first news report printed at July 23, 1919, both in Vol. 61.
   [2] RL to Ammission, No. 2679, July 31, 1919, T telegram (SDR, RG 256, 185.182/88, DNA), informing Dulles of the action of the Foreign Relations Committee.

From Frank Lyon Polk

                                          Paris August 8, 1919.

Urgent 3582. Confidential for the President.

Following long conference with Mr. Balfour yesterday morning regarding Thracian question, during which Balfour seemed much impressed by arguments supporting American objections to cutting Bulgaria off from Aegean Sea, Major Johnson and Mr. Nicholson,[1] who were present at conference, prepared jointly a solution of Thracian question which left Bulgaria her outlet to the Aegean Sea and at the same time added to Greece a small area around Porto Lagos and gave her much of eastern Thrace as a detached colony like east Prussia. Without committing either Government, Johnson and Nicholson submitted this proposal to Venizelos yesterday afternoon as a possible basis of agreement. Venizelos refused to accept solution, calling it unjust to Greece but said Greece would make no trouble if it were imposed upon her. Balfour approved solution but is unwilling to press it against wishes of Venizelos. In the course of his remarks Venizelos made statements which confirmed Johnson's belief that a secret agreement existed relative to Thrace. After leaving Venizelos Johnson drew from Nicholson the admission that early in the war Lloyd George promised Venizelos that if he would bring Greece into the war on the side of the Allies he should have both Western and Eastern Thrace up to the Enosmidia line and in Asia Minor all the vilayet of Aidin. Nicholson said he understood the agreement regarding Thrace was verbal and not written and he added that Lloyd George had made it impulsively and "on the sly." As to Aidin he thought there was a written understanding. Johnson asked whether (Italian interests?) [the French],[2] were similarly committed but Nicholson evaded giving a direct reply. General Le Rond, the French territorial expert, in conference with Johnson later confirmed existence of oral agreement. Nicholson said that on account of this agreement Great Britain could [never] impose on Greece a frontier which Mr. Venizelos was unwilling to accept. He said that while agreement was secret and purely informal, and not binding in same sense as treaty of London, Greek leading men knowing this [knew of it] and Venizelos would fall from power if promises were not fulfilled. Johnson then said he did not see how America would [could] ever consent to any solution based on the secret agreement. To this Nicholson replied that in that case the British would hold that they must sign the treaty without America. Today Johnson on my advice asked Nicholson whether he really meant that Mr. Balfour *on* (would?) sign treaty without America. Nicholson replied that Mr. Balfour thought it would be a disaster for America not to sign but that [if] America insisted on a solution which Venizelos could not accept Mr. Balfour was certainly prepared to sign the treaty without America. General Le Rond and other French experts as well as British military and technical experts are personally strongly opposed to giving Thrace to Greece. It seems clear that the British authorities recognized [British recognize] the strength and justice of American position and would welcome a compromise which we could accept but that they are embarrassed by argument [agreement] with Venizelos. Our experts are convinced that French and British agreement [arguments] regarding ethnic conditions and supposed wishes of Mussulman majority are designed to give appearance of conformity with your principles. There was long debate at conference yesterday afternoon and I stood out against Greece getting Western Thrace. Tardieu proposed as compromise that part of Western Thrace be given to Greece and the rest made a separate international corridor (?) [state] while a large part of Eastern Thrace should be given to Greece. Balfour and Tittoni seemed willing to discuss this suggestion. Johnson believes creation of one small international state in Western Thrace and another at Constantinople with Greek territory between them is impracticable, could not be permanent and is merely an intermediate step in giving whole territory to Greece. He recommends insisting upon maintaining Bulgarian corridor to sea or on single international state for both East and West Thrace as proposed in your earlier telegram[3] or declining to sign treaty. Personally I do not think for one moment that Balfour would hold treaty should be signed without United States but on the other hand I think we cannot get agreement unless we accept Tardieu's solution or something similar. Am disposed accept this solution as a last resort. A small isolated international state has many objections but it is a compromise which in my opinion can be defended. Please cable as soon as possible whether I am authorized to accept such a compromise solution as Tardieu's or if we can get it a solution giving Greece some area in West Thrace and on each side [much of East] Thrace but maintaining a Bulgarian corridor to the sea. Polk.   American Mission.

T telegram (SDR, RG 59, 763.72119/6078, DNA).
    [1] That is, Douglas Wilson Johnson and Harold George Nicolson.
    [2] Additions and corrections from the telegram sent, in SDR, RG 256, 868.00/170, DNA.
    [3] WW to H. White, July 25, 1919, Vol. 61.

From Newton Diehl Baker

Dear Mr. President: [Washington] August 9, 1919.

I return herewith the cablegram from Mr. Hoover,[1] which Mr. Close left with me this morning. I am by cablegram authorizing General Pershing to detach and assign to Mr. Hoover's various missions such Regular Army officers as are available and can be spared from immediate military needs. These assignments are, of course, in their capacity as officers of the Army, and they will continue to be paid as such. At this end we can not tell how many and which officers are either adapted or available, but General Pershing will work it out with Mr. Hoover.

With regard to Mr. Hoover's suggestion that Army and Navy officers be loaned to the new governments in Eastern Europe as technical advisers and be paid by such governments, I find that it has been consistently held that we may not do this because of the phrase in the Constitution, Article I, Section 9, Paragraph 8, which reads:

"No title of nobility shall be granted by the United States, *and no person holding any office of profit or trust under them shall without the consent of Congress accept of any present, emolument, or title of any kind whatever from any king, prince, or foreign state.*

This has been held to preclude officers of the Army from receiving compensation from any foreign state unless previously authorized thereto by Congress.

Respectfully yours, Newton D Baker

CCL (N. D. Baker Papers, DLC).
    [1] That is, HCH to WW, Aug. 5, 1919.

From Franklin Delano Roosevelt

My dear Mr. President,   Washington. Saturday [Aug. 9, 1919]

The Marine Brigade will be in Washington next Tuesday prior to their demobilization at Quantico.[1] They—and we—are most anxious that they pass before you before leaving the service. Would you care to review them in front of the White House at either 12 or 2 o'clock? It would take not more than half an hour

Faithfully yours,   Franklin D Roosevelt

ALS (WP, DLC).
[1] Tumulty provided further details: "About 5,000 Marines who participated in the Battle of Chateau Thierry are to pass through Washington on Tuesday next, and I have assured the Navy Department that you would be glad to review them. I am supposing that you will prefer to have a stand erected on the Avenue directly in front of the White House and review them from there. The Department is planning to have these Marines pass the White House at about 12:30 o'clock, Tuesday. Please let me know if this is entirely satisfactory." JPT to WW, Aug. 9, 1919, TL (WP, DLC). I. H. Hoover added a pencil note to this document: "The President says 'alright.' "

From John Sharp Williams

My dear Mr. President: [Washington] August 9, 1919.

Here's a telegram from Mr. Gerard, our former Ambassador to Berlin.[1] I think there must be some mistake about "the British troops refusing to help the Armenians," but whether that be true or not, the situation is very bad; and if there is any way in which we could supply them with arms, and munitions, and equipment, I think you will agree with me that it ought to be done. I don't see just how it could be done, because we never have been at war with Turkey and Congress hasn't declared any war, but still I suppose that we could manage, in a spirit of "benevolent neutrality"—*benevolent to the Armenians*—to help them out in all three respects. It strikes me that it would also be right to ask Great Britain, if possible, not to withdraw her troops from Northern Armenia until things are in a more settled condition. There are some things which must be left upon the "laps of the Gods," of course, but I hope this is not one of them.

I am, with every expression of regard,

Very truly yours,   John Sharp Williams

TLS (WP, DLC).
[1] J. W. Gerard to J. S. Williams, Aug. 8, 1919, T telegram (WP, DLC). Gerard quoted a telegram from the delegation of the Armenian Republic in Paris stating that Turkish and "Tartar" forces were attacking the republic, that the Armenians had insufficient munitions and food to allow their forces to resist the invasion, and that the British commander in the area refused to assist them. Gerard urged that the American government take the steps to aid the Armenians which Williams discusses below.

Two Telegrams from Robert Lansing to Frank Lyon Polk

Washington, August 9, 1919.

2771 For Mr. Polk.[1] (Secret in special cipher) In connection with the statement to the effect that the French delegate under instruction from his government refused to come and discuss question of draft mandates on the ground that it was not decided that there should be mandates for former Turkish Empire it will be remembered that when the Council of Ten adopted the resolutions regarding mandates which were subsequently embodied in the Covenant of the League of Nations those parts of the Turkish Empire which were to be disposed of were constantly used as illustrations. Until the present moment no doubts as to mandates in the Turkish Empire appear to have been raised and as a matter of fact mandates were the particular subject of discussion in connection with Syria, Arabia, Armenia, etc. throughout the President's dealings with Clemenceau and Lloyd George.

The President desires me to communicate to you the above information and to emphasize strongly the inflexible determination of the United States to accept nothing which will alter the understanding already reached in this vital matter. The President states that he will not tolerate any such suggestion as is conveyed in the message from Colonel House semicolon that he will withdraw the French treaty rather than consent to see the Turkish Empire divided as spoils semicolon and that he will not press upon the Senate the Treaty with Germany if such course is to be pursued in connection with other treaties. The United States will certainly not enter the League of Nations to guarantee any settlements of this nature or any such intolerable bargains as the Greeks and Italians appear to be attempting.   Lansing

T telegram (SDR, RG 59, 763.72119/6024, DNA).
    [1] Lansing was replying to EMH to WW and RL, Aug. 6, 1919.

Washington August 9, 1919

2772. Strictly confidential. For Polk.

Mission's 3535, August 6, 9 p.m., and next to last paragraph in your 3508, August 5, 7 p.m. You are authorized to make it perfectly clear to the Roumanians that if they continue the present course of action the United States will not only refuse to support but will also oppose every claim of theirs to any territory or sover[e]ignty wherever it may be.   Lansing.

T telegram (SDR, RG 256, 864.00/402, DNA).

From Edward Mandell House

London August 9, 1919

Urgent. 2751. For the President and Secretary of State from Colonel House.

I am sending you the form of mandate A which I offered as the American proposal and had circulated among the Commissioners. It is a composite arbitrament of war [draft][1] made by Beer[2] and its essentials agreed to by Cecil. Milner and the other Commissioners reserved comment until a formal meeting of the Commission is had. Please make such (*) [additions] and eliminations as seem to you desirable.

"Class A (Type of mandate for such territories as may be governed in accordance with paragraph four of article twenty-two of the Covenant of the League of Nations.) The Ottoman Empire having by article blank of the Peace Treaty signed at blank on the blank renounced all rights over blank the Principal Allied and Associated Powers acting on behalf of all the Allied and Associated Powers constitute blank an autonomous territory under the guarantee of the League of Nations and confer upon blank a mandate to advise and assist blank in the development of its administration. Blank accepts the mandate thus conferred upon it and will execute the same on behalf of the League of Nations and in accordance with following provisions.

Article one, Paragraph One. The mandatory power shall be responsible for the peace and good order of the territory and undertakes to frame an organic law within one year from the date of this mandate. This law shall come into force as soon as it has been approved by the Council of the League of Nations. The organic law shall be prepared by the mandatory power in consultation with the native authorities (to be [named?] where possible in each mandate) and in its preparation, the rights, interests and wishes of all the populations inhabiting the territory shall be taken into consideration. The organic law shall contain provisions designed to facilitate the progressive development of blank as a self-governing state and the ultimate cessation of this mandate.

Article two, Paragraph One. The mandatory power undertakes that so far as its responsibility under the foregoing article extends and to the extent that it is compatible with efficient administration representative institutions and responsible government shall be or-

[1] The correction and addition in this paragraph from EMH to WW and RL, Aug. 9, 1919, T MS (E. M. House Papers, CtY). There is no copy of the balance of this telegram, which House sent as a separate telegram, in the House Papers.

[2] That is, George Louis Beer.

ganized with a view to the government of the country by means of the native elements.

Article three, Paragraph one. The mandatory power until the going into effect of the organic law (*) and thereafter the government of blank may organize a local gendarmerie for the preservation of internal peace and order and for the defense of the territory, but with this exception: no military, naval or air forces shall be raised or maintained by blank nor shall any fortification be erected therein. Such forces of the mandatory power as may be stationed in blank shall be for the preservation of internal order and protection of the frontiers.

Article four, Paragraph one. No territory of blank shall be ceded or leased to or in any way placed under the control of the Government of any foreign power.

Article five, Paragraph one. The immunities and privileges of foreigners including the rights of Consular jurisdiction and protection as formerly established in the Ottoman Empire by the adoption of capitulations and by usage shall remain in force in blank, but shall rest in suspense during the continuance of this mandate. In all cases touching the person, status or property of a subject or citizen of any state member of the League of Nations the judge or a majority of the judges, if more than one, shall be a person or persons with *western* legal training nominated upon the recommendations of the mandatory power and by the government of blank to hear such cases.

In no event, however, shall the treaty limitations upon the right of the territory under mandate to impose import tariffs in excess of a certain percentage be revived.

Two. So long as the rights resulting from the regime of the capitulations remain in suspense the extradition treaties now in force between foreign powers and the mandatory power apply to blank.

Article six, Paragraph one. The control and administration of Moslem Wakf[3] property in blank shall be undertaken by the government of blank who will respect Moslem law and the wishes of the founders.

Article seven, Paragraph one. The mandatory power will be entrusted with the control of the foreign relations of blank and the citizens of blank when outside its territorial limits will be entitled to the protection of the mandatory power.

Article eight, Paragraph one. The mandatory power undertakes to insure to all complete freedom of conscience and the free and outward exercise of all forms of worship which are consonant with

[3] Usually spelled "waqf"—an Islamic endowment of property to be held in trust and used for charitable or religious purposes.

public order and morality. No discrimination of any kind shall be made between any citizens of blank on the ground of race or religion. No hindrance shall be offered in spiritual matters to the relations of the different religious communities with their spiritual Chiefs.

Two. The organization of religious communities as *millets* where they exist already shall be maintained by the Government of blank so long as the government of blank shall think it desirable.

Three. The right of every community to maintain its own schools for the education of its members in its own language shall neither be denied nor impaired and the inhabitants of the territory shall have the right to use their own language in any secular educational institutions which they may establish.

Article nine, Paragraph one. Missionaries of all denominations shall be allowed to prosecute their calling and to maintain schools and other institutions employing therein whatever language they may desire. There shall be no discrimination against such schools and institutions as compared with other establishments providing similar standard of education. Missionary bodies shall be allowed to acquire and hold property of every description and to erect buildings for religious, educational and general missionary purposes on an equality with the citizens of blank. But the government of blank shall have the right to exercise such control as may be necessary for the maintenance of public order and good government and to take all measures required for such control.

Article ten, Paragraph one. The mandatory power undertakes to secure to all citizens and subjects of states, members of the League of Nations, the same rights as are enjoyed in the territory by its own nationals in respect to entry into and residence in the territory; the protection afforded to their person and property; the acquisition of property movable and immovable and the exercise of their profession or trade.

Nothing herein shall prevent the government blank from introducing legislation with the specific object of preventing foreigners from speculating in land and from monopolizing or wastefully consuming the natural resources of the territory.

Two. The mandatory power agrees not to attempt to obtain special privileges for its own citizens and further undertakes to insure to all citizens and subjects of states, members of the League of Nations, on the same footing as its own nationals, freedom of transit and navigation and complete economic, commercial and industrial equality. Nevertheless the government of blank shall be free to organize essential public works and services on such terms and conditions as it thinks just and nothing herein shall be construed to prevent the impression [imposition?] of whatever import and export duties may be deemed necessary provided they are not discriminatory.

Three. Concessions for the devastation [exploitation?] of the natural resources of the territory shall be granted by the government of blank without distinction on grounds of nationality between the subjects or citizens of states, members of the League of Nations, but the right is reserved to the local government to impose such conditions as will maintain intact its authority.

Four. The rights conferred by this article extend equally to companies and associations organized in accordance with the law of any of the States, members of the League of Nations, subject only to the requirement of public order and compliance with the local law.

Article eleventh, Paragraph one. In accordance with these the mandatory power undertakes to adhere on behalf of blank to any general international conventions already existing or that may be concluded hereafter respecting the slave traffic, the traffic in arms and ammunition, and the traffic in drugs, as well as the convention relating to commercial equality, freedom of transit in navigation, laws of aerial navigation and postal telegraphic and wireless communications.

Two. The mandatory power undertakes to secure the cooperation of the government of blank so far as religious or other local conditions may permit in the execution of any common policy adopted by the League of Nations for preventing and combating disease, including diseases of plants and animals.

Article twelve, Paragraph one. The mandatory power shall make to the Council of the League of Nations an annual report to the satisfaction of the Council containing full information concerning the measures taken to apply the provisions of this mandate.

A copy of all laws and regulations made in the course of the year shall be communicated therewith.

Article thirteen, Paragraph one. The mandatory power undertakes to secure within twelve months from the date of this mandate the enactment and thereafter the execution by the government of blank of a law of antiquities based on the considerations contained in the annex to this mandate which shall replace the former Ottoman law of antiquities. No attempt shall be made by the mandatory power to obtain for the archeological research of its own citizens treatment more favorable than that which is accorded to the archeological research of other citizens or subjects of states, members of the League of Nations.

Article fourteen, Paragraph one. The consent of the Council of the League of Nations is required for any modification of the terms of this mandate and for any amendments to the organic law.

Article fifteen, Paragraph one. If any dispute whatever should arise between states, members of the League of Nations, relating to the interpretation or the application of this mandate which cannot be settled by negotiation this dispute shall be admitted to the permanent Court of International Justice to be established by the League of Nations.

Two. States, members of the League of Nations, may likewise bring any claims on behalf of their subjects or citizens for infractions of their rights under this mandate before this said court for decision.

Annex. Paragraph one. 'Antiquity' means any construction or any product of human activity earlier than the year 1700.

Two. Any person who having discovered an antiquity without being furnished with the authority contemplated in article five below reports the same to an officer of the 'Department of Antiquities' of the country shall be recompensed according to the value of the object. The principle to be adopted should be totally by encouragement rather than by stunning.

Three. No antiquity may be sold except to the Department of Antiquities of the country, but if this Department renounces the acquisition of any antiquity that antiquity may then be freely sold. No antiquity may leave the countries without an export license from the said Department.

Four. Any person who maliciously or negligently destroys or damages an ancient object or structure shall become liable to a penalty to be fixed by the committee of the country.

Five. No clearing of ground or digging with the object of finding antiquities shall be permitted under penalty of fine, except to persons authorized by the Department of Antiquities of the country.

Six. Equivalent of terms for expropriation, temporary or permanent, of lands which might be of historical or archeological interest shall be fixed severally by the government of blank.

Seven. Authorization to excavate shall only be granted to persons who show sufficient guarantee of archeological experience. No mandatory power shall appeal in granting these authorizations (?) in such a way as to eliminate students of other nations without good grounds.

Eight. The proceeds of excavations may be divided between the excavator and the Department of Antiquities in each country in a proportion fixed by this Department. If for scientific reasons division seems impossible the excavators shall, in lieu of his share of the proceeds, receive a fair compensation."   Davis

T telegram (WP, DLC).

Frank Lyon Polk to Robert Lansing

Paris August 9, 1919

Not to be distributed

3599 for the Secretary of State from Polk. In view of defiant attitude of Roumanian Government urge that any negotiations now pending with them for financial assistance for public or private parties should be suspended. When the crop is received the Roumanians will have enough for their immediate wants, but they will soon be in the market for assistance if not already there and I have already indicated to them that their attitude will undoubtedly result in their not receiving any assistance from the United States.

Polk,   Ammission.

T telegram (SDR, RG 256, 871.51/53A, DNA).

From Cleveland Hoadley Dodge

Riverdale-on-Hudson New York

My dear President   August 10th 1919

I was just on the point of writing to tell you how much I thought of your great message when I received the enclosed cable message,[1] & while it is absurd to think that any "personal influence" is necessary, I think I ought to send it to you to confirm what you have already heard from Hoover & others. The men who sign the cablegram are Mr George Walter Smith one of our commissioners for Near East Relief, a prominent lawyer from Philadelphia & a leading Catholic layman. Mr Vickrey[2] is the Director of the fund.

I sincerely trust that the English may be induced to hold on longer & prevent the awful catastrophe which would result if their troops are withdrawn

In view of all that is happening how can those litigious Senators go on with their miserable debate? "Confound their knavish tricks—confound their politics."[3] You are showing the patience of a Saint & are going to win out, but how you can stand your awful burden I cannot see

We all think of you constantly & if fervent prayers do any good you ought to be helped

We are having a grand reunion of all the family—children & grandchildren & are enjoying a very hectic time   All join with me in best wishes to you & Mrs Wilson

Ever affectionately   Cleveland H Dodge

ALS (WP, DLC).
    [1] Walter George (not George Walter) Smith and Charles Vernon Vickrey (via HCH) to C. H. Dodge, Aug. 7, 1919, T telegram (WP, DLC). They reported that Lloyd George

insisted upon immediately withdrawing British troops from the Caucasus. They warned that this withdrawal would be fatal to the Armenian Republic, which was already under attack from three sides by Turkish and "Tartar" troops. They requested Dodge to urge Wilson to use his influence to persuade Lloyd George to postpone the withdrawal at least until Gen. James G. Harbord could complete his investigation and report on the situation in Armenia.

² Formerly involved in lay missionary work in the Far East, more recently in Armenian and Syrian relief operations.

³ From the British national anthem. The lines of course are "Confound their politics/ Frustrate their knavish tricks."

To Robert Lansing

My dear Lansing: [The White House] 11 August, 1919.

Will you not be kind enough to have the substance of the Secretary of War's statement enclosed herein conveyed to Mr. Hoover through the Mission in Paris, and particularly an explanation made to him with regard to the second part which Baker embodies?

Cordially and faithfully yours, Woodrow Wilson

TLS (Letterpress Books, WP, DLC).

To John Barton Payne

My dear Judge Payne: The White House 11 August, 1919.

I have been very glad to sign the Executive Order, the draft of which you were kind enough to enclose with your letter of August 8th concerning the disposition of plants and materials acquired by the Emergency Fleet Corporation, because I believe that it embodies the proper disposition of the matter.

But I would very much value a brief memorandum as to the policy the Board expects to follow in that matter. I am so deeply interested in the whole question of the continued development, and the continued *independent* development of American shipping, that I would like my mind to go along with yours and the minds of your colleagues in this important matter.

Cordially and sincerely yours, Woodrow Wilson

TLS (ICHi).

To Walker Downer Hines

My dear Mr. Director: [The White House] 11 August, 1919.

Thank you sincerely for your kindness in remembering my desire for a brief summary of the Plumb Plan.¹ Your accompanying letter throws still further light on it.

Cordially and sincerely yours, Woodrow Wilson

TLS (Letterpress Books, WP, DLC).
    ¹ See W. D. Hines to WW, Aug. 8, 1919, and its Enclosure.

To Alexander Mitchell Palmer, with Enclosure

My dear Palmer: The White House 11 August, 1919.

I must say that the enclosed appeals to me, and I would be very much obliged if you would look into the statements of fact contained in it, as to Debs being confined for fourteen consecutive hours daily in a cell.

Cordially and faithfully yours,   Woodrow Wilson

TLS (A. M. Palmer Papers, DLC).

E N C L O S U R E

Pasadena, Calif., August 10, 1919.

I beg you for immediate action in matter of amnesty for Debs, an old man in weakening health, confined fourteen consecutive hours daily in cell in midsummer of southern climate. This means practically death sentence inflicted upon a man of finest sensibility for indubitably sincere conscientious objections to war. This is causing truly frightful embitterment in entire radical movement. If Debs should be allowed to die in jail I believe that a peaceable solution of social problem would be impossible in America. Please do not misconstrue this statement. I am appealing to you as a statesman to avoid a calamity which I clearly foresee. I am also appealing to your heart for a man older than yourself who has won the affectionate regards of millions of the plain people.

Upton Sinclair.

T telegram (WP, DLC).

To William Howard Taft

My dear Mr. Taft: [The White House] 11 August, 1919.

Secretary Wilson has transmitted to me your letter to him dated August 1, 1919.¹ In this letter you agree with Secretary Wilson that a formal dissolution of the National War Labor Board should be made at this time. I concur with Secretary Wilson, yourself and Mr. Manly that the work of the Board has now been completed and that the Board should cease to function as of August 15, 1919.

Will you not, therefore, kindly turn over to the Secretary of Labor all of the records of the National War Labor Board, together with such odds and ends of the business as may be undisposed of, so that the Department can make a proper disposition of the same.

I take this opportunity of commending very warmly the Joint Chairmen and the individual members who have been representing the business interests on that Board, as well as the representatives of organized labor, for the very able, efficient and impartial manner in which they have conducted the work of the Board.

Cordially and sincerely yours,   Woodrow Wilson

TLS (Letterpress Books, WP, DLC).
[1] W. H. Taft to WBW, Aug. 1, 1919, TCL, enclosed in L. F. Post to JPT, Aug. 8, 1919, TLS, both in WP, DLC.

To Charles Mills Galloway

My dear Mr. Galloway: [The White House] 11 August, 1919.

Acknowledging your letter of August 7th,[1] I hereby accept your resignation as a member of the United States Civil Service Commission, to take effect September 7, 1919.

Very truly yours,   Woodrow Wilson

TLS (Letterpress Books, WP, DLC).
[1] C. M. Galloway to WW, Aug. 7, 1919, TLS (WP, DLC).

To Walter Irving Clarke

My dear Mr. Clark: [The White House] 11 August, 1919.

My absorption on the public business has been such that I am constrained, with a good deal of shamefacedness, to admit that I know nothing more than your letter[1] tells me of the "New Era Movement" of the Presbyterian Church, and your letter tells me hardly enough to enable me to judge whether I could send you any intelligent message about it, which would be of service to you. I would be very much obliged for a little further information.

Cordially and sincerely yours,   Woodrow Wilson

TLS (Letterpress Books, WP, DLC).
[1] W. I. Clarke to WW, Aug. 7, 1919.

To Norman Kemp Smith

My dear Professor Smith: [The White House] 11 August, 1919.

I am heartily glad to know that you have been elected to the Chair of Logic in Edinburgh.[1] I congratulate you most sincerely, though I am unaffectedly sorry to see you leave the United States. Having been happily instrumental in bringing you here, I regret to see you go away. I shall always remember our association at Princeton with the greatest pleasure, and my interest and friendship will follow you always.

Cordially and sincerely yours,   Woodrow Wilson

TLS (Letterpress Books, WP, DLC).
  [1] See N. K. Smith to WW, July 13, 1919, Vol. 61.

From Robert Underwood Johnson

Dear Mr. President: Tannersville, N. Y. August 11. 1919.

Now that you have so fine a man as Whitlock for the Ambassadorship at Rome may I venture to express the hope that something fine and helpful on large lines may be organized for Italy, to meet a little more than half way the generous and statesmanlike overtures of Premier Nitti as reported this morning in the Associated Press dispatch.[1]

For some time, on my own initiative, I have been trying to arouse some of our captains of industry and bankers to the great opportunity of the present situation, which is also a great peril. Germany is moving heaven and earth to regain her ante-bellum commercial control of Italy, and if we do not soon respond to Italy's appeals that effort will succeed, bringing seeds of future ills to the world. While she is calling for coal the West Virginia mines—according to James W. Ellsworth[2] and others who know—have many of them shut down for lack of a market! It ought not to be a question of Italy's credits here or for much longer of our transportation facilities, which Mr. Hurley tells me are soon to be more and more available. Some one hinted to me the other day at some governmental unwillingness to let this problem be solved by private combinations of capital. I know nothing of this, but I am sure that the splendid good sense which you have exercised in the Brotherhood affair would set the wheels going. I only see a brave, self-sacrificing, sensitive, proud, ambitious, liberty-loving and really conservative people longing to be part of the new order. I am sure you could both do and say something naturally and very soon that would bind Italy to us, and—what is little to you compared with considerations of right—restore your personal prestige in the Peninsula. And your prestige in Italy is a national asset, which your friends value very highly.

In conclusion, and now that the matter is, I am told, *fait accompli*, I wish to thank you for the consideration you have given to my name in the matter of the Italian embassy, on the initiative and suggestion of my friends. It is an honor not to be worked for, and I have the satisfaction that my relation to the matter has been one of dignity and self-respect. I consented to the presentation of my name only because I thought that in this special direction I might *be of use*. But Whitlock will give, as well as take, distinction in the post, and through him I am confident you will do great things for America and Italy.

In all sincerity and with deep appreciation believe me, Mr. President, respectfully and faithfully yours,

Robert Underwood Johnson

ALS (WP, DLC).

[1] Datelined Rome, August 8, 1919, the dispatch consisted of a lengthy interview with Nitti in which he discussed Italy's sacrifices in the war, her postwar reconstruction, her aspirations for the future, and his hopes for close economic and political relations with the United States. *New York Times*, Aug. 11, 1919.

[2] James William Ellsworth of New York, owner and operator of coal mines in Pennsylvania, Ohio, and West Virginia; also well known as a philanthropist, bibliophile, and art collector.

From the Desk Diary of Robert Lansing

Monday Aug 11 [1919]

Conference at W. H. 3-3:45. Thrace. Roumanian violations. Arrange for daily meetings. . . .

Drafted in the evening a strong instruction Am mission on Balkans & Roumania, threatening even to draw out of League of Nations if settlements not just.[1]

[1] See RL to FLP, Aug. 12, 1919 (second telegram of that date).

From Robert Lansing

My dear Mr. President: Washington August 11, 1919.

The Italian Ambassador[1] has received a cable from Signor Tittoni directing him to ask for an audience with you in order to explain the coal situation in Italy, and their needs in regard to it. The Ambassador has asked for an interview with you, and if you will let me know your pleasure in regard thereto, and the time at which you will receive him, I will be glad to make the necessary arrangements.   Faithfully yours,   Robert Lansing

TLS (WP, DLC).

[1] That is, Count Macchi di Cellere, who had returned to the United States on July 13.

From Edward Mandell House, with Enclosure

Ashdown Forrest, Withyham, Sussex.

Dear Governor: August 11, 1919.

I am enclosing you a copy of a cable which I sent you on the 9th.[1]

Haldane telephoned this morning and asked me to come to London to lunch at the Prime Minister's with Grey and himself. I had a chill day before yesterday and was not quite equal to the trip but Grey is coming down here this afternoon. Before I close this letter I will let you know the final outcome and will also send you a cable tomorrow.

I am very happy at the turn things have taken. It is not only that Grey's going[2] has brought George and his Ministers to terms regarding the essential questions between our two countries, but since I last wrote you the Government have been hammered mercilessly by the Liberals.

A week or ten days ago a dinner was given me at the Reform Club to meet most of the representative liberal writers in England. I am enclosing you an extract from a letter which I have just received from Sir George Paish[3] giving the result of the conference. I gave these men sufficient information to guide them in their editorial work; and I am already beginning to see the result. The atmosphere has cleared considerably and with Grey in Washington with you I have no doubt but that everything will come right.

It is my intention to sail for home around the middle of September. There is no need of remaining longer than that. If Mandate A is to be finished before the Turkish Treaty is formed as we desire, there will be ample time to accomplish it before then. If the Council of the League of Nations should sit before our Senate ratifies the Treaty, it would not do for me to sit with them although it has been intimated that as a matter of courtesy they would like a representative of the United States to be present.

We are having a difference of opinion in regard to the time of the meeting of the Assembly. I am urging that it sit in Washington just as soon as the Treaty is ratified by the Senate and enough of the other powers to put it into force. Cecil and Drummond take a contrary view. They do not want it to be called until early next year or in the Spring. I consider that this would be a great mistake, and every liberal in England with whom I have talked have expressed an agreement with me. This includes Grey and Haldane and the liberal group of editors whom I met at the Reform Club. To delay the meeting of the Assembly as long as Cecil and Drummond desire would be to disappoint the world and make it feel that the League was to be another Hague Conference fiasco.

Cecil's argument is that there ought not to be a meeting until an agenda of sufficient importance is worked out to make it impressive. My contention is that an agenda can be formulated within an hour and then committees can be appointed at the Washington meeting to report if necessary at the next meeting of the Assembly which could be held in Geneva in the early winter or spring. The world would then have an assurance of the things that were in contemplation and under way. Happily, the matter is in your hands and the meeting can be called when in your judgment it seems best to do so.

My principal activities with the League now are to delay action and thus far I have been successful.

Affectionately yours,   E. M. House

P.S. Grey has decided to go as Special Envoy about September fifteenth. Do you expect to make your speaking tour, and will you be back by then? He is laying down conditions which will be of the greatest advantage in the settlement of controversies.

TLS (WP, DLC).
    ¹ It is printed at Aug. 9, 1919.
    ² Curzon and Lloyd George had decided in late July to ask Grey to serve as Ambassador to the United States and requested Haldane to persuade Grey to accept. Haldane in turn asked House to assist in the persuasion. Haldane and House agreed that Grey, because of his failing eyesight, would never accept a permanent ambassadorial post, but that he might be coaxed into going to America for a few months as a special envoy. House and Haldane met with Grey in London on July 27. Lloyd George and Curzon wanted Grey to hold discussions with American officials on the Irish question, the naval building program, and the League of Nations. House, Haldane, and Grey agreed on the twenty-seventh that talks on the League of Nations posed no great difficulty, but that Grey should request from Curzon and Lloyd George a statement on their Irish policy and that Grey should submit to them a memorandum of his own views on the naval program. Grey outlined a naval policy which asserted that Great Britain should, as she had done in the past, base her building program on the European naval situation and make no attempt to match any American naval buildup.
    By August 4, Grey and Lloyd George had agreed on Grey's outline of naval building policy, but a mutually acceptable statement of Irish policy proved more difficult. Grey drew up a statement on this subject on August 5, and Haldane presented it to the Prime Minister two days later. The two men failed to reach agreement, and, on August 11, Grey prepared a new statement with House's collaboration. By that date, Grey had decided to accept the mission and to take Sir William Tyrrell with him as secretary.
    Curzon presented Grey with his instructions on September 9. These included a statement of the naval policy mentioned above. The instructions further stated: "His Majesty's Government believe that the League of Nations can be made the means of achieving great good. But to secure this it must be made a reality and must be prevented from becoming an instrument to further separate national interests. . . . His Majesty's Government are therefore determined to pursue no separate or selfish national policy themselves inside the League and to be influenced by no motive that does not conform to the ideal with which the League was founded. It should be the constant effort of Your Lordship to convince the United States Government that this is the desire of His Majesty's Government, just as the latter are convinced that the same desire animates the Government of the United States."
    The instructions discussed Irish policy in general terms. "Absolute independence is impossible," the statement began. "But His Majesty's Government recognize," it continued, "that the question of Ireland is not only urgent but must be considered in the light of changed conditions. . . . As far as Great Britain is concerned some concessions that were impossible before are possible now." A more detailed outline of policy would be issued in a short time. The most concrete paragraph of the statement read as follows:

"The Irish Administration will be chosen by the Irish people, and Ireland will be in the hands of the Irish themselves, with the reservation that army, navy and foreign policy must certainly remain in the hands of the Imperial Government, and that the area of Ulster which desires to be excluded must not be forced under another rule against its will. This area forms a unit in which the majority is separate from the rest of Ireland in feeling and in religion." Ernest Llewellyn Woodward and Rohan Butler, eds., *Documents on British Foreign Policy, 1919-1939*, 1st series, V (London, 1954), 997-1000.

For further details of the origins of Grey's mission, see the entries in the Diary of Colonel House for July 28 and August 7, 12, and 16, 1919 (not printed in this series). See also George W. Egerton, "Britain and the 'Great Betrayal': Anglo-American Relations and the Struggle for United States Ratification of the Treaty of Versailles, 1919-1920," *The Historical Journal*, XXI (Dec. 1978), 885-911, and Keith Robbins, *Sir Edward Grey: A Biography of Lord Grey of Fallodon* (London, 1971), pp. 351-52.

³ About whom, see G. Paish to WW, Dec. 26, 1918, n. 1, Vol. 53.

E N C L O S U R E

Sir George Paish to Edward Mandell House

Reform Club, Pall Mall, S.W.

Dear Colonel House: August 8, 1919.

I should like you to know how very much "the writers" appreciated your visit and talk to them. If you had been present at the meeting we held when the terms of the Peace Treaty were first known you would realize how much you have accomplished. Then it was generally held that the Peace Treaty had given away practically all that we stood for; now the Treaty is accepted with a determination to get it amended in the manner Mr. Wilson desires.

You can, I am convinced, rely upon Liberal England. If you are writing to Mr. Wilson I should be grateful if you would tell him that we now realize the greatness of his difficulties and how much he has really accomplished and that we thank him with all our heart for his great efforts on behalf of liberal principles and of humanity. The fight has not yet been won but a good beginning has been made and the result is not in doubt.

Sincerely yours,   George Paish.

TCL (WP, DLC).

To Robert Lansing, with Enclosure

My dear Mr. Secretary,   The White House, 11 August, 1919.

Will you not be kind enough to have the enclosed put into code and sent to House, in the care of our Embassy at London? It is, as you see, about the <u>mandates</u> and the <u>French attitude</u>.

Faithfully Yours,   W.W.

WWTLI (SDR, RG 59, 763.72119/6114, DNA).

ENCLOSURE

CABLEGRAM (to be coded).

The White House.

For Colonel House, Care American Embassy, London.

I am amazed and deeply disturbed by your message concerning the French attitude towards mandates for the Turkish territories and hope that there is some mistake and that they merely deem it premature to formulate those mandates before it is known who will take them and how they will be defined territorially. The position indicated in your message they cannot maintain without going back on the most explicit though sometimes tacit understandings between Lloyd George, Clemenceau and myself. The very classification of mandates in the Covenant was based upon considerations arising out of the stage of development of the several parts of Turkey and throughout every discussion of Syria, Arabia and the rest it was taken for granted that the basis of final settlement would be mandates. It was to inquire the state of opinion about mandates that the commission went to Syria. Of course we must insist. I hope that further inquiry will put the French position in a different light[1]   Wilson

WWTS telegram (SDR, RG 59, 763.72119/6114, DNA).
  [1] This was sent verbatim as WW to EMH, No. 5793, Aug. 11, 1919, T telegram (SDR, RG 59, 763.72119/6114, DNA).

From Frank Lyon Polk

Paris August 11, 1919

3624. For the President and Secretary of State from Polk.

Your 2771, August 9.[1] Saw Clemenceau this afternoon at conference and asked him privately if it were true that French representative had been instructed to refuse to discuss at London draft for mandates A. He said it was and that he was glad to explain his reasons. He then reviewed his fight with Lloyd George as to the part of Syria which is to go to France and said George had broken faith with him. He said the President knew of his difficulties with George as he explained the matter to the President, when the President had suggested that Cilicia should be part of Armenian mandate. As a result of his treatment by George he had declared he would discuss no matter relating to Turkey with the British until the Syrian situation had been arranged. He was very anxious to impress me with the fact that this refusal to discuss mandates meant no unfriendliness to the United States or to the ultimate adoption of draft of mandates but that it was solely directed against the British. I pointed out that a discussion and settlement of this question in no way prejudiced his case whereas it had direct bearing on the League of Nations section of the treaty of peace with Germany; that if it were known that France had refused to settle the question of mandates the position of the League of Nations would be seriously affected. I did not use your threat as to withdrawal of treaties quite as you sent it as I thought I would hold that threat until Clemenceau's attitude became defiant, but I intimated it might become necessary to withdraw German treaty, in which case treaty for the protection of France would also be withdrawn. Clemenceau agreed not to block the consideration of mandates if we wished it to proceed and he said that if I would write him a letter containing just a few lines stating that in our opinion it was important that the draft of mandates should be determined he would immediately withdraw all objection and have the French representative proceed with negotiations. I will send Clemenceau such a letter tomorrow evening unless I hear from you to the contrary. This is very urgent.   Polk   American Mission.

Prest.

Appreciation of Clemenceau's action. No change as it would make matters more difficult RL[2]

T telegram (R. Lansing Papers, DLC).
 [1] That is, RL to FLP, Aug. 9, 1919 (first telegram of that date).
 [2] RLhw.

A Memorandum by Robert Lansing

NO COMPROMISE: NO RATIFICATION.
August 11, 1919.

I have taken occasion to tell the President that in my opinion the Senate would never assent to ratification of the Treaty without reservations and that we could not lose a moment in coming to an agreement with the "mild reservationists," who were in the mood now to compromise on reasonable terms.

The reception of my suggestion was far from reassuring. I think that he was resentful that I advise any compromise. At any rate he would have none of it, and his face took on that stubborn and pugnacious expression which comes whenever anyone tells him a fact which interferes with his plans. His obstinacy is often utterly unreasonable and defeats his purposes. He seems to lack the faculty of concilliation.

The way I see it, the President is "riding to a fall" and a pretty bad one too. His uncompromising attitude and his unwillingness to confer with anyone who disagrees with him in the slightest particular will, I believe, force the Republican "moderates" into the ranks of the radicals who oppose ratification of any sort or ratification without reservations so drastic as to destroy the Covenant. This impolitic policy of the President's will, if it continues, defeat the Treaty in all probability, and will certainly do so if he decides to make his western trip and appeal to the people, because the "moderates" will feel personally insulted by thus going over their heads. I hope the postponement of his trip means abandonment as that would remove one cause of irritation.

We ought to accept the fact, which seems to me so manifest, that there will be no Treaty of Peace without reservations. We can obtain moderate ones now, if we are willing to come half way. Unless the present opportunity is seized, it will be too late. Only the President's obstinate spirit and belief that he can, even with a minority, force his will upon the Senate prevent a satisfactory settlement and speedy ratification. I wish that his nature was more flexible and his temper less defiant.

T MS (R. Lansing Papers, DLC).

To Louise Whitfield Carnegie

The White House, 12 August, 1919.

May I not express my deep sympathy at the loss of your distinguished husband?[1] His death constitutes a very serious loss to the forces of humanity and enlightened public service, and takes out of the world a force which it could ill afford to spare.

Woodrow Wilson

T telegram (WP, DLC).
[1] Andrew Carnegie had died at his summer home near Lenox, Mass., on August 11.

To John Sharp Williams

My dear Senator: The White House 12 August, 1919.

Unfortunately, it is true that the British Government is proposing to withdraw its troops almost immediately from the region in which they can act as protectors of the Armenians, and I am making every effort to bring about a re-consideration of the matter on their part.[1]

In the present situation of things out there, it does look as if the only effectual assistance would be the assistance of an armed force to subdue those who are committing outrages more terrible, I believe, than history ever before witnessed, so heartbreaking indeed that I have found it impossible to hold my spirits steady enough to read the accounts of them. I wish with all my heart that Congress and the country could assent to our assuming the trusteeship for Armenia and going to the help of those suffering people in an effective way.

Cordially and sincerely yours,   Woodrow Wilson

TLS (J. S. Williams Papers, DLC).
  [1] See J. S. Williams to WW, Aug. 9, 1919.

To Robert Russa Moton

My dear Dr. Moton: [The White House] 12 August, 1919.

Thank you sincerely for your letter of August eighth. It conveys information and suggestions, the importance of which I fully realize and for which I am sincerely obliged. I will take the suggestions you make under very serious consideration, because I realize how critical the situation has become and how important it is to steady affairs in every possible way.

Again thanking you for your public-spirited cooperation,

Cordially and sincerely yours,   Woodrow Wilson

TLS (Letterpress Books, WP, DLC).

From Robert Lansing

My dear Mr. President: Washington August 12, 1919.

I feel exactly as you do about Doctor Reinsch, but I do not think that we can let him leave there before the middle of September.[1]

The question of his successor comes immediately to the front because it would not be right to trust those matters to temporary hands. In this connection I wonder if you would consider Mr. Norman Davis? Doctor Reinsch suggests, and I think properly so, that the person who is to succeed him must have a fundamental idea of finance and industry. Mr. Davis has had a very recent diplomatic experience, and is very well qualified in many ways. He knows something of the Consortium,[2] and that in itself when the part which it will play in the future in China is considered, will add considerably to his utility.

Unless I hear from you to the contrary I will cable Doctor Reinsch that he may leave Peking as soon after the 15th of September as convenient for him to do.

Faithfully yours,   Robert Lansing.

TLS (WP, DLC).
[1] Lansing was replying to WW to RL, Aug. 4, 1919 (fifth letter of that date), and its Enclosure.
[2] About which, see n. 3 to the extract from the Diary of E. T. Williams printed at April 22, 1919, Vol. 57, and RL to WW, May 26, 1919 (second letter of that date), Vol. 59.

From Newton Diehl Baker

CONFIDENTIAL.

Dear Mr. President: Washington. August 12, 1919.

The uncertainties caused by the delay in the approval of the peace treaty, so far as the War Department is concerned,[1] are two in number:

(1). There is pending in Congress a Bill for the entire reorganization of the Military Establishment. The purpose of the Bill is to incorporate into our Army those modifications of organization and new forms of activity which this war has shown to be necessary. The size of the Army to be provided, and general form of this organization, cannot be effectively considered until formal peace is restored and a better judgment of the probable international obligations of the United States formed than is possible in the present condition.

(2). The vast surplus supplies of the War Department include not only the relatively small quantities of food and clothing which are being disposed of, more or less, directly to consumers in this country, but great quantities of machine tools, manufacturing establishments, and other supplies for which no ready market can be expected until peace is established and our industry generally feels surefooted, nor can sales be made abroad with confidence until international relations and national credits are in the way of being established.   Respectfully,   Newton D Baker

TLS (WP, DLC).
[1] For Baker's reason for writing this letter, see C. Glass to WW, Aug. 13, 1919.

From Alexander Mitchell Palmer

Dear Mr. President: Washington, D. C. August 12, 1919.

I have your note[1] enclosing a telegram from Upton Sinclair about Eugene V. Debs. I am making inquiry now as to the truth of his statement that Debs is being confined in his cell for fourteen consecutive hours daily. I do not believe it is true. I will advise you later.

As to Debs' physical condition, I recently made careful inquiry and find that he is in splendid shape. Clarence Darrow, who is his close friend and who visited him within the last two or three weeks, reported to me after he came from Atlanta that Debs is in splendid health and there is no possibility of our being criticised on that account for keeping him in the penitentiary.

                    Respectfully yours,   A Mitchell Palmer

TLS (WP, DLC).
 ¹ WW to AMP, Aug. 11, 1919.

From Thomas James Walsh

Mr. President: Washington August 12, 1919

I felt impelled, upon your submitting to the Senate the treaty with France, to communicate with you as herein, but hesitated until the matter has come to seem to me too important not to have your attention.

In your message you assign as a reason for entering into the treaty that no obligation rests upon us under Article X of the Covenant for the League until called upon by the Council. Your language is: "The Covenant of the League of Nations provides for military action for the protection of its members *only* upon advice of the Council of the League." It is argued by the opponents of the League that the second sentence of Article X imposes upon us an imperative obligation to make war whenever the Council so directs. The supporters of the treaty in the Senate have, with practical unanimity, from conviction as well as to meet criticism made against it, maintained that while the obligation rests upon the country and is absolute whenever the conditions exist calling for its action, Congress is required to determine in each instance whether the conditions do, in fact, exist which require us to take action, and that it is equally required to determine just what action we ought to take honorably to fulfill the obligation; that in both of these respects the Council may *advise*, but only *advise*; it has no power to call upon us to do anything.

If no obligation exists *until* the Council *calls* on the members to make war, or "only upon the *advice* of the Council" it is easy to believe that the obligation has been assumed to make war *whenever* the Council so calls on or advises them. From this it is easy to pass to the conclusion that the country will be at war immediately upon the call of the Council without any action upon the part of Congress. Lodge, in his address, yesterday, assailed with much vigor such a straw man and took great credit to himself for his opposition to our soldiers being sent anywhere to fight, except in accordance with the solemn action of the people's representatives in declaring war.

I write about it now because Senator Kellogg, in a speech recently, referred to what you said as inconsistent with the position taken by me in two addresses. This difference of opinion he thought sufficient justification for a "reservation" of clarification. I thought it singularly unfortunate that Senator McKellar should have taken issue with Senator Swanson concerning the proper construction of the withdrawal provision of the Covenant. That difference was also referred to by Senator Kellogg as requiring clarification, by an interpretative reservation. Senator Jones of New Mexico suggests that in practice our country would, in all probability, wait, though acknowledging its liability, until the Council acted and advised, and undoubtedly that is true. I think it vital, however, that no doubt should arise that under the Covenant Congress and Congress alone will determine whether our treaty obligation requires action on our part, and what action should be taken in fulfillment of that obligation from which the conclusion would be irresistible that the status of war would not exist until Congress had passed the necessary resolution declaring war. Moreover we ought not to subscribe to the doctrine that if a powerful nation should be bent on aggressive warfare, it could nullify this great peace-preserving Article by inducing some subservient delegate on the Council to withhold his assent from the course the other members would advise.

In your own time and in your own way it would be advisable to dissipate the apparent contradiction in views concerning this feature of the League.

With assurances of my esteem, I am,

Cordially yours,   T. J. Walsh

TLS (WP, DLC).

From Francis Edward Clark

My dear President Wilson: Boston, August 12, 1919.

Your very cordial letter[1] was read at the great Conference of Christian Endeavorers at Buffalo, and was received with heartiest appreciation and applause. It would have been a memorable time for the young people if you could have addressed them in person, but your letter was gratefully received. A very strong resolution in regard to the League of Nations was passed in the formal list of resolutions, and a spontaneous vote was also taken at the close of Secretary Baker's address, in which he dwelt briefly on that subject. It was a most spontaneous and hearty unanimous approval of the League, and I believe showed how nine out of ten of all the Endeavorers in our country feel in regard to the matter.

A resolution was also passed deprecating intervention in Mexico, which we understand is being urged in some quarters, until every peaceful method of settling the difficulties of the sister republic are exhausted.

With great respect,   Sincerely yours,   Francis E. Clark

TLS (WP, DLC).
[1] WW to F. E. Clark, July 31, 1919.

Two Telegrams from Robert Lansing to Frank Lyon Polk

Washington. August 12, 12 noon

2797. For Polk. Personal and confidential.

In conversation with the President yesterday he asked me if White was taking part with you in your conferences with Tittoni. I said that I presumed so. The President then said that he hoped so because he was very much pleased with White's handling of Tittoni. You might indirectly confirm what I said if I was correct. Confer with the President every day at noon, so that matters will be handled more expeditiously.

Yesterday I was before the Foreign Relations Committee for two and a half hours.[1] I think that the opponents of the treaty were worsted, particularly Borah and Johnson. The reason their questions was manifestly to find grounds to criticize the President's conduct of the negotiations and his indifference to the opinions of the Commissioners other than House. There was practically little attempt made to elucidate provisions of the treaty. I am convinced that it is personal animosity to the President rather than opposition to the treaty which is delaying the report of the committee.

David H. Miller is summoned before the committee today.[2]

Lansing.

T telegram (SDR, RG 256, 185.182/96, DNA).
[1] Lansing's testimony of August 11, 1919, is printed in *Treaty of Peace with Germany. Hearings before the Committee on Foreign Relations, United States Senate*, 66th Cong., 1st sess., Sen. Doc. No. 106 (Washington, 1919), pp. 215-52.
[2] Miller's testimony is printed in *ibid.*, pp. 379-429.

[Washington] August 12, 1919.

2798 STRICTLY CONFIDENTIAL FOR POLK.

Your 3277 July 23, 10 pm;[1] 3547 August 7, 3 am.;[2] 3582 August 8 midnight;[3] 3599 August 9, 6 pm;[4] 3489 August 3, 4 pm;[5] 3516

August 6;[6] 3256 July 22;[7] 3240 July 20 11 pm[8] and my 2772 August 9, 5 pm.[9]

In regard to the determination of the Balkan territorial questions the President holds firmly to the policy that he will not support treaty provisions which do not make for peace. He even goes so far as to say that unjust territorial settlements may possibly compel the United States to withdraw from the League of Nations as he will not permit this country to be a guarantor of unjust settlements. He states that there seems to be lacking among some of the governments the will to do justice to enemies as well as to allies, but it is only by impartial justice to all that the permanency of peace can be insured and it is only settlements based on such justice which can induce the United States to participate in guarantying them. I cannot too strongly urge upon you that the President takes a firm stand in this matter and will not recede from it.

PARAGRAPH. As to Thrace the President considers that Eastern Thrace should be incorporated in the Constantinople state and that Bulgaria should either have a corridor between that state and Greek territory or that the territory of the Constantinople state should extend westward along the Aegean including possibly Kavalla across which Bulgaria would have a right of way and the free use of a port sufficient for her commercial needs. In any event the President is insistent that Bulgaria shall have an outlet to the Aegean but that such outlet should not be over Greek territory and through a Greek port. He is equally convinced that the cession of Eastern Thrace to Greece would not be in the interest of future peace.

PARAGRAPH. The President also is convinced that, unless Roumania recedes to Bulgaria that portion of the Dobrudja which is decidedly Bulgarian in population, a situation will result which will cause continued irritation and hostility. In view of the extensive territorial acquisitions already conceded to Roumania in other directions based primarily on ethnic grounds, it is manifestly inconsistent for her not to apply the same grounds to a region inhabited chiefly by Bulgarians. It should be made clear to the Roumanian delegates that the acquisition of territory in Hungary depends in large measure upon their willingness to transfer the southern portion of the Dobrudja to Bulgaria.

PARAGRAPH. The present conduct of the Roumanian Government in continuing to direct or permit its military forces to advance into Hungary and to occupy Buda-pest contrary to the express wishes of the Allied and Associated Powers has made a most unfavorable impression upon this Government and may seriously affect its attitude toward Roumania. The President authorizes me to say that,

unless the present aggressive policy is abandoned and the Roumanian armies retire as they have been requested to do by the
Council of the Heads of Delegations, Roumania may forfeit the
friendship and friendly aid of this country, for this Government will
not support a nation which seeks to gain by force of arms territory
or political control to which it is not entitled as a matter of right.

PARAGRAPH. The foregoing statements as to Greece, Bulgaria and
Roumania may be considered by you as definite policies which
should be generally followed in your negotiations on these subjects.

PARAGRAPH. I should add that the acquisition of Bessarabia by
Roumania should not be considered because as Russia cannot be
a party to the negotiation it would be wholly improper to transfer
Russian territory to another state. Before leaving Paris I frankly
stated this position to the Council and the President has given it
his full approval.   Lansing

T telegram (SDR, RG 59, 763.72119/6144B, DNA).
    [1] H. White to RL, July 23, 1919, printed as an Enclosure with RL to WW, Aug. 7,
1919 (second letter of that date).
    [2] FLP to RL, Aug. 7, 1919.
    [3] FLP to WW, Aug. 8, 1919.
    [4] FLP to RL, Aug. 9, 1919.
    [5] FLP to RL, Aug. 3, 1919.
    [6] Ammission to RL, Aug. 5, 1919.
    [7] H. White to WW, July 22, 1919, Vol. 61.
    [8] H. White to WW, July 20, 1919, ibid.
    [9] RL to FLP, Aug. 9, 1919 (second telegram of that date).

From the Desk Diary of Robert Lansing

Wednesday Aug 13 [1919]

Noon Conference with Prest—12-12.30. Read me letter he
planned sending to Lodge.[1] Told me of Redfield's plan to resign in
Sept. and his purpose of naming McCormick for place.

    [1] See WW to HCL, Aug. 14, 1919; see also JPT to WW, Aug. 14, 1919 (second letter
of that date).

From Carter Glass, with Enclosure

My dear Mr. President: Washington August 13, 1919.

Responsive to your suggestion at the Cabinet meeting yesterday,
I am submitting briefly the Treasury's view of the way in which,
and generally the extent to which, the failure to ratify the peace
covenant is impeding business in the United States and preventing
things from being done the doing of which promptly is essential to

our immediate welfare, as well as a safeguard against a very real disaster.

These observations, I have no doubt, are in line with your own thought. They are the result of the Treasury's detailed study of the problem of international finance in the light of the rapidly approaching end of direct government loans to Europe. The impressions stated have been derived also from numerous conferences with representatives of the American industrial and banking world, held with a view to devising means to finance Europe's needs and America's exportable surplus.

The wonder is that the Senate apparently does not perceive and appreciate a situation, critical in every aspect, which is so patent to every business man in this country with whom one comes in contact.   Sincerely yours,   Carter Glass.

TLS (WP, DLC).

ENCLOSURE

MEMORANDUM FOR THE PRESIDENT: August 13, 1919.

The war ended in America with the signing of armistice. We had no selfish interest in boundaries and indemnities. For Europe however, the war will not end until the ratification of the peace treaty, determining these questions and carrying with it the assurance of united action upon the part of the great powers of the world, the United States included, to make the peace definitive. In the case of Germany, indeed, the war will not end until the Reparation Commission has delimited the amount of indemnity which Germany will have to pay.

Until ratification, and, in the case of Germany, until definitive action has been taken by the Reparation Commission, a basis for establishment of private credits on a scale at all adequate to meet the needs of the situation will not exist. For the private lender even now the commercial risk has no terrors, but the political risk is prohibitive. There must be the assurance, that ratification will give, that the major political problems have been settled and that a League of Nations, including the United States, has been formed to make the settlement permanent. Uncertainty as to these things deters not only the American producer and exporter and banker from extending credit to Europe, but deters European peoples from resuming their normal lives and going about their business. Only by working and saving can Europe be restored. Men in Europe can have no heart of hope in work or thrift while vital problems of boundaries and indemnities and the very existence of the states under which they live are moot questions. As it took some months from armistice day for the American business man to recover his poise and adjust himself to the new state of peace, so it will be some months after the ratification of the treaty of peace before men in Europe will resume their normal ways.

It is no exaggeration to say that while the Senate discusses the treaty of peace Europe is on the verge of catastrophe, political, economic and social, and that only prompt ratification of the peace treaty, putting an end to immediate political problems and giving assurance of a united effort of the great nations of the world to make peace permanent, can avert the catastrophe.

Should the catastrophe occur, the blight of social disorder will spread to America, directly through evil communications, and indirectly as the consequence of the stagnation of commerce and industry in the United States which must follow the cessation of our war-expanded exports in the event of a European collapse.

C.G.

TI MS (WP, DLC).

From David Franklin Houston

Dear Mr. President: Washington August 13, 1919.

Complying with your request, I send you this hastily prepared statement of matters held up or held in suspense by reason of the failure of this Nation to ratify the peace treaty.

1. The minds of all the peoples of Europe, of this country and of many others, remain in a state of doubt, hesitation, and distress. Some of the nations are waiting for this country to act before they act and all the nations will be uncertain especially as to the future of the League and the execution of the terms of the treaty if this Nation does not enter and enter whole-heartedly. The disturbed condition of things furnishes agitators a very favorable opportunity to conduct their vicious propaganda.

2. The plans of leaders in the industrial world, as well as in the field of agriculture, and all the problems of readjustment can necessarily be dealt with only in a partial and unsatisfactory manner.

3. The systematic planning of financial assistance for European nations who wish to secure raw materials and machinery, and the early promotion of our foreign exports of such things, are obstructed. This is true not only in respect to the Central powers, but also in respect to the Allies and neutrals as well.

4. Obviously the foreign trade of this country with the Central European nations will be greatly handicapped, while at the same time those nations that ratify the treaty, such as England, Belgium,

and France, will be in a position to lay their plans for monopolizing the markets of Central Europe. We have no consular or trade agents in the Central empires. The bearing of this fact is apparent. It need not be emphasized that much more than food exports is involved. There is involved, as I have indicated, machinery of all sorts and raw materials. Among the latter is cotton. The Central empires formerly took from this country nearly 4,000,000 bales of cotton. This market for this commodity is still practically closed.

5. The production plans of particular areas in Europe especially are obstructed. There are areas whose future will not be known until the treaty is ratified and the processes under the Treaty and League are under way. The people in such areas cannot well make their plans until they know with what nations they are to be affiliated.

6. This nation and others cannot rationally consider their plans for army and navy demobilization or their permanent peace military and naval establishments. The important matter of large reduction in armaments cannot be dealt with. If the League of Nations is to be a reality, the adhesion of this Nation is essential. Under the League, with this Nation participating, disarmament in large ways will be feasible. It is imperative that it should take place. The war has shown what preparation means and what sort of armament we shall be compelled to maintain if the regime of competitive military armament persists. Where before the war military establishments entailed a burden of two or three hundred million dollars, they will hereafter, on the competitive military basis, entail expenditures of a billion or more. I do not think the peoples of the world will stand for the continuance of such burdens.

7. It follows from what has just been said that nations cannot plan and readjust their financial budgets, including their schemes of taxation.

8. In this Nation, as well as in other nations, emergency laws were passed for the period of the war. We have several of these on the statute books. Administrative officers and the businesses affected do not know how long these laws will remain in effect. Peace may come and the laws may be inoperative within a few months, or they may continue in effect for a very much longer period. This state of uncertainty is unfortunate from every point of view.

9. This nation will be prevented from participating at the outset in the handling of important business problems contemplated by the terms of the Treaty. It cannot, for instance, officially participate in the Labor Conference, the invitation for which has been authorized to be extended by this Government.

10. The continued intense agitation concerning the Treaty and

the state of suspense prevents the Nation from directing its best energies to the solution of pressing domestic problems.

11. Obviously, existing conditions make for ineffectiveness of national life in every direction and the persistence and perhaps extension of present burdens and sacrifices.

Faithfully yours,   D. F. Houston.

TLS (WP, DLC).

From Walter Irving Clarke

Mr. President: New York City, August 13, 1919.

Replying to your letter of August 11, the New Era Movement of the Presbyterian Church is the official organization set up by the Presbyterian General Assembly to enable the Church to meet its full duty toward the world problems of the day, to foster Christian democracy.

Its slogan is: "The Whole Church Marshalled for Its Whole Task, with a Specific Task for You and Me." It enlists the laity.

Already the New Era Movement has achieved the doubling of the Church's benevolent and educational funds; it aims to Americanize and Christianize America and the world; it has definite goals for community and social service, and would help solve economic complexities.

The New Era Conference opening Labor Day at Lake Geneva, Wis., will take up such matters as the Church's duty to Labor, to immigration and community problems, the League of Nations and worldwide peace. How can the Church best serve America in today's crises?

A message from you would be very, very helpful. If we could have it in advance, we could build part of our programme around it.   Yours Faithfully,   Walter I. Clarke.[1]

TLS (WP, DLC).
  [1] Clarke enclosed Samuel Charles Black, Secretary Metroplitan District, *The New Era Movement of the Presbyterian Church, U.S.A.* (n.p., n.d.), in which Wilson made five marginal marks.

From George Barnett[1]

My dear Mr. President: Washington. August 13, 1919.

May I have the privilege of both personally and officially extending to you, and through you to Mrs. Wilson, the very grateful thanks of the officers and men of the Marine Corps for your great act of courtesy in reviewing the Marine Brigade yesterday. Nearly all of these young men are leaving the service to-day, having enlisted for the period of the war only. They will go to every state in the Union; and from all that I have heard, I can assure you that they will take back to their homes the wonderful memory of their last day in the service, made particularly memorable by the fact that they were reviewed by the President of the United States.

During their service they have, in many cases, been through hard and dangerous times, but all the hardships will fade from their memory and they will remember only what has been good and beneficial; and I am sure that they will take home with them the wonderful memory of the great courtesy extended to them by the President and Mrs. Wilson.

Again expressing to you, Sir, the deep appreciation we all feel, I have the honor to be,

Your obedient servant,   George Barnett.

TLS (WP, DLC).
[1] Major General and Commandant of the United States Marine Corps.

From Louise Whitfield Carnegie

Lenox, Mass., August 13, 1919.

Please accept my sincere thanks for your kind message of sympathy which I deeply appreciate.   Louise Carnegie.

T telegram (WP, DLC).

From Peyton Conway March, with Enclosure

My dear Mr. President: Washington. August 13, 1919.

Secretary Baker has left the city, and in his absence I am forwarding herewith a copy of a cablegram received from General Pershing. The War Department is in accord with the recommendation of General Pershing.   Very sincerely,   P. C. March.

TLS (WP, DLC).

E N C L O S U R E

Paris, August 13, 1919.

To The Adjutant General. Rush Number 2912 August 12th Confidential

For Secretary of War and Chief of Staff. It is understood that the council of 5 have decided that a total force of 13,000 men, composed equally of British, French Italians and Americans, be sent to the plebiscite area in upper Silesia. It has been suggested by the French that this force be taken from the force on the Rhine and the council tentatively adopted this plan. Mr. Polk sent a cablegram this morning to the President asking his decision.[1] As force on Rhine consists of one Infantry regiment plus certain auxiliaries and is an indivisible unit, I recommend that no change whatever be made in the constitution of that force, but that if troops are to be sent to upper Silesia they be taken from elsewhere.

Pershing.

T telegram (WP, DLC).
   [1] FLP to RL, No. 3635, Aug. 12, 1919, T telegram (WP, DLC).

From Joseph Patrick Tumulty, with Enclosure

Dear Governor: The White House, 14 August, 1919.

I am attaching herewith the letter I have drafted. This is the one about which I spoke to you the other day.

Sincerely yours,   Tumulty

TLS (WP, DLC).

E N C L O S U R E

May I urge upon you as Chairman of the Committee on Foreign Relations the following views with reference to the treaty of peace, now awaiting action before your Committee:

It is clear to me that further inaction in this vital matter upon the part of those of us in posts of responsibility can only delay the return of normal conditions throughout this country and the world. Failure to act produces uncertainty and aggravates those conditions which from day to day grow more acute and make definite action absolutely necessary.

The country rightfully expects of us who share the responsibility for legislation and administration in this critical hour to put aside every consideration but that of the public welfare. In a matter so vital as this, which affects the peace and welfare of the world, any thought of personality or partisanship is intolerable. And, unfortunately, the time that is left to us to grapple with the great problems of readjustment which confront us is all too short. Indeed, we cannot afford to lose a single summer's day in doing all that we may to

mitigate the winter suffering which, unless we find means to prevent it, may prove disastrous in a large portion of the world and
which at the worst may bring to Europe conditions even more terrible than the war itself. Until the great masses of the world's populations can and will resume productive efforts, we can only hope
to make conditions more tolerable. If in our own country, where
alone fundamental soundness is untouched, we continue to stand
helpless in the face of our difficulties; if we postpone putting in
action the necessary instrumentalities for the work of restoring
normal conditions; if we find ourselves unable to furnish the guidance and leadership to coordinate effort and harmonize all American interests, those difficulties will be aggravated to a point where
they will be almost insoluble. There are many problems of peace
that must be delayed until the treaty is out of the way and the legislative machinery put in motion for the enactment of measures
that may in some way remedy the conditions which now confront
us.

A problem in point, both difficult and harassing, is the railroad
question, the proper settlement of which is so indissolubly connected with the general welfare of the nation. In a fine spirit of
broad patriotism the heads of the railroads turned them over to the
government. They served a magnificent purpose in the war. Having used them for the public needs in the emergency, we cannot
now treat them ungenerously. In the settlement of the railroad
question, like the settlement of all the other questions affecting the
nation, the general interests of all must be considered, the interests
of capital and of labor, of the shippers and of the users of railroads
alike. Until the treaty is out of the way, it will be impossible to give
to the settlement of this vital question that study and consideration
which its importance demands. The railroad problem should be
taken up promptly and dealt with fearlessly. What is just and fair
and equitable public opinion will ratify; and what is the best enlightenment in the solution may well turn out to be the highest
selfishness for each of the separate interests concerned.

Another question which presses for a solution, and whose settlement will necessarily be delayed unless the track is cleared for its
consideration, is the question of the establishment of an American
merchant marine.

(Give facts.)

(Soldiers and land question)

There are many other questions which press for a settlement but
whose settlement is postponed by reason of the delay in the matter
of the treaty.

Of course the League of Nations is not a perfect thing. None of its advocates claims perfection for it, but it is the only thing at hand that can bring about a settlement of conditions that are pregnant with danger.

In the presence of a world situation that is unparalleled, where the forces of mischief are loosed upon the world, and where the pressure for stabilizing those conditions come from all quarters of the earth, surely, my dear Senator, in this vital matter which involves so much, time is of the essence.

T MS (WP, DLC).

From Joseph Patrick Tumulty

Dear Governor: The White House 14 August, 1919

The Lodge letter is magnificent,[1] but the opportune time to put it out is a matter for serious consideration. In view of Lodge's letter of this afternoon, it might look as if spurred on by the letter you had seen fit to make a public statement; but no doubt you can make a future use of it.

The business part of it is excellent, but I think you could make it stronger by adding the paragraph in my letter on railroads, after the words, "permanent revival of business" on page 3:

["]A problem in point, both difficult and harassing, is the railroad question, the proper settlement of which is so indissolubly connected with the general welfare of the nation. In a fine spirit of broad patriotism the heads of the railroads turned them over to the government. They served a magnificent purpose in the war. Having used them for the public needs in the emergency, we cannot now treat them ungenerously. In the settlement of the railroad question, like the settlement of all the other questions affecting the nation, the general interests of all must be considered, the interests of capital and of labor, of the shippers and of the users of railroads alike. Until the treaty is out of the way, it will be impossible to give to the settlement of this vital question that study and consideration which its importance demands. The railroad problem should be taken up promptly and dealt with fearlessly. What is just and fair and equitable public opinion will ratify; and what is the best enlightenment in the solution may well turn out to be the highest selfishness for each of the separate interests concerned."

On page one you could add the words found in my letter:

"Indeed, we cannot afford to lose a single summer's day in doing all that we may to mitigate the winter suffering which, unless we find means to prevent it, may prove disastrous in a large portion of the world and which at the worst may bring to Europe conditions even more terrible than the war itself."

I do not think you ought to address Lodge as "My dear sir." I know how you feel toward him, but you will remember how the country criticised Justice Hughes when he addressed you in his resignation as "My dear sir." I think you ought to use the words, "My dear Mr. Chairman."

I think you might consider using these words in the conclusion:

"Of course the League of Nations is not a perfect thing. None of its advocates claims perfection for it, but it is the only thing that can bring about a settlement of conditions that are pregnant with danger.

"In the presence of a world situation that is unparalleled, where the forces of mischief are loosed upon the world, and where the pressure[s] for stabilizing those conditions come from all quarters of the earth, surely, my dear Senator, in this vital matter which involves so much, action is of the essence."

Sincerely,   Tumulty

TLS (WP, DLC).
¹ Following the receipt of this letter, Wilson substituted a new first page of the letter that he had read to Lansing and sent to Tumulty, then used old pages 2 and 3, and then added page 3½, which incorporated the extract from Tumulty's letter. Wilson then used the balance of the old pages (4 through 10) to the end of the letter.

Two Letters from Henry Cabot Lodge

My dear Mr. President: [Washington] August 14, 1919

Soon after the Treaty of Versailles had been laid before the Senate, Senator Hitchcock informed the Committee on Foreign Relations that if the Committee desired at any time to see you for the purpose of discussing the treaty you would be glad to receive them if you were given twenty-four hours' notice. Taking advantage of this suggesstion [sic], the Committee this morning instructed me by vote to say to you that they would be glad if they could meet you for the purpose of asking for certain information in regard to the treaty, at such time and place as might be convenient to you. Owing to the necessary absence of one or two Senators I take the liberty of saying that it would be more convenient to the Committee if the appointment could be made for some day subsequent to Monday next.

It was also the general desire of the Committee that I should say to you that it was assumed that nothing said at the meeting would be considered to be confidential. The Senate has ordered the treaty to be considered in open executive session and in consequence

with this order the Committee feel that any information in regard
to the treaty which comes into their possession should not be withheld from the public.

I have the honor to be,

Very respectfully yours,   H. C. Lodge

My dear Mr. President: [Washington] August 14, 1919.

The Committee on Foreign Relations have instructed me to ask
you if you would be kind enough to lay before them any information you may have with regard to what has been done, if anything,
with the German Colonies referred to in Article 119 and 120 of the
treaty of peace.

I have the honor to be,

Very respectfully yours,   H. C. Lodge

TLS (WP, DLC).

A Draft of a Letter to Henry Cabot Lodge

Mr. Chairman,   [Aug. 14, 1919]

I am sincerely glad that the Committee should have responded
in this way to my intimation that I would like to be of service to it.
I welcome the opportunity for a frank and full interchange of
views.

I hope, too, that this conference will serve to expedite your consideration of the treaty of peace. I beg that you will pardon and
indulge me if I again urge that practically the whole task of bringing the country back to normal conditions of life and industry waits
upon the decision of the Senate with regard to the terms of the
peace.

I venture thus again to urge my advice that the action of the
Senate with regard to the treaty be taken at the earliest practicable
moment because the problems with which we are face to face in
the readjustment of our national life are of the most pressing and
critical character, will require for their proper solution the most intimate and disinterested cooperation of all parties and all interests,
and cannot be postponed without manifest peril to our people and
to all the national advantages we hold most dear. May I mention a
few of the matters which cannot be handled with intelligence until
the country knows the character of the peace it is to have. I do so
only by a very few samples.

The copper mines of Montana, Arizona, and Alaska, for example, are being kept open and in operation only at a great cost and loss, in part upon borrowed money; the zinc mines of Missouri, Tennessee and Wisconsin are being operated at about one-half their capacity; the lead of Idaho, Illinois, and Missouri reaches only a portion of its former market; there is an immediate need for cotton belting, and also for lubricating oil which cannot be met,—all because the channels of trade are barred by war when there is no war. The same is true of raw cotton, of which the Central Empires alone formerly purchased nearly four million bales. There is hardly a single raw material, a single important food stuff, a single class of manufactured goods which is not in the same case. Our full, normal, profitable production waits on peace.

Our military plans of course wait upon it. We cannot intelligently or wisely decide how large a naval or military force we shall maintain or what our policy with regard to military training is to be until we have peace not only but also until we know how peace is to be sustained, whether by the arms of single nations or by the concert of all the great peoples. And there is more than that difficulty involved. The vast surplus properties of the army include, not food and clothing merely, whose sale will affect normal production, but great manufacturing establishments also which should be restored to their former uses, great stores of machine tools, and all sorts of merchandize which must lie idle until peace and military policy are definitively determined. By the same token there can be no properly studied national budget until then.

The nations that ratify the treaty, such as Great Britain, Belgium, and France will be in a position to lay their plans for controlling the markets of central Europe without competition from us, if we do not presently act. We have no consular agents, no trade representatives there to look after our interests. There are large areas of Europe whose future will lie uncertain and questionable until their people know the final settlements of peace and the forces which are to administer and sustain it.

Without determinate markets our production cannot proceed with intelligence or confidence. There can be no stabilization of wages because there can be no settled conditions of employment. There can be no easy or normal industrial credits because there can be no confident or permanent rivival [revival] of business.

But I will not weary you with obvious examples. I will only venture to repeat that every element of normal life amongst us depends upon and awaits the ratification of the treaty of peace; and also that we cannot afford to lose a single summer day by not doing all that we can to mitigate the winter's suffering, which, unless we find means to prevent it, may prove disastrous to a large portion of the world, and may, at its worst, bring upon Europe conditions even more terrible than those wrought by the war itself.

Nothing, I am led to believe, stands in the way of the ratification of the treaty except certain doubts with regard to the meaning and implication of certain Articles of the Covenant of the League of Nations; and I must frankly say that I am unable to understand why such doubts should be entertained. You will recall that when I had the pleasure of a conference with your Committee and with the Committee of the House of Representatives on Foreign Affairs at the White House in March last[1] the questions now most frequently asked about the League of Nations were all canvassed, with a view to their immediate clarification. The Covenant of the League was then in its first draft and subject to revision. It was pointed out that no express recognition was given to the Monroe Doctrine, that it was not expressly provided that the League should have no authority to act or to express a judgment on matters of domestic policy, that the right to withdraw from the League was not expressly recognized, and that the constitutional right of the Congress to determine all questions of peace and war was not sufficiently safeguarded. On my return to Paris all these matters were taken up again by the Commission on the League of Nations and every suggestion of the United States was accepted.

The view of the United States with regard to the questions I have mentioned had, in fact, already been accepted by the Commission and there was supposed to be nothing inconsistent with them in the draft of the Covenant first adopted,—the draft which was the subject of our discussion in March,—but no objection was made to saying explicitly in the text what all had supposed to be implicit in it. There was absolutely no doubt as to the meaning of anyone of the resulting provisions of the Covenant in the minds of those who participated in drafting them, and I respectfully submit that there is nothing vague or doubtful in their wording.

The Monroe Doctrine is expressly mentioned as an understanding which is in no way to be impaired or interfered with by anything contained in the Covenant and the expression "regional understandings like the Monroe Doctrine" was used, not because anyone of the conferees thought there was any comparable agreement anywhere else in existence or in prospect, but only because it was thought best to avoid the appearance of dealing in such a document with the policy of a single nation. Absolutely nothing is concealed in the phrase.

With regard to domestic questions Article XVI of the Covenant expressly provides that, if in case of any dispute arising between members of the League the matter involved is claimed by one of the parties "and is found by the Council to arise out of a matter which by international law is solely within the domestic jurisdiction of that party, the Council shall so report, and shall make no recommendation as to its settlement." The United States was by no means the only government interested in the explicit adoption of this provision, and there is no doubt in the mind of any authoritative student of international law that such matters as immigration, tariffs, and naturalization are incontestably domestic questions with which no international body could deal without express authority to do so. No enumeration of domestic questions was undertaken because to undertake it, even by sample, would have involved the danger of seeming to exclude those not mentioned.

The right of any sovereign state to withdraw had been taken for granted, but no objection was made to making it explicit. Indeed, so soon as the views expressed at the White House conference were laid before the Commission it was at once conceded that it was best not to leave the answer to so important a question to inference. No proposal was made to set up any tribunal to pass judgment upon the question whether a withdrawing nation had in fact fulfilled "all its international obligations and all its obligations under the Covenant." It was recognized that that question must be left to be resolved by the conscience of the nation proposing to withdraw; and I must say that it did not seem to me worth while to propose that the Article be made more explicit because I knew that the United State[s] would never itself propose to withdraw from the League if its conscience was not entirely clear as to the fulfilment of all its international obligations. It has never failed to fulfil them and never will.

Article X is in no respect of doubtful meaning when read in the light of the Covenant as a whole. The Council of the League can only "advise upon" the means by which the obligations of that great Article are to be given effect to. Unless the United States is a party to the policy or action in question, her own affirmative vote in the Council is necessary before any advise [advice] can be given, for a unanimous vote of the Council is required. If she is a party the trouble is hers anyhow. And the unanimous vote of the Council is only advice in any case. Each government is free to reject it if it pleases. Nothing could have been made more clear to the Conference than the right of our Congress under our constitution to exercise its independent judgment in all matters of peace and war. No attempt was made to question or limit that right. The United States will, indeed, undertake under Article X to "respect and preserve as against external aggression the territorial integrity and existing political independence of all members of the League," and that engagement constitutes a very grave and solemn moral obligation. But it is a moral, not a legal, obligation, and leaves our Congress absolutely free to put its own interpretation upon it in all cases that call for action. It is binding in conscience only, not in law.

Article X seems to me to constitute the very backbone of the whole Covenant. Without it the League would be hardly more than an influential debating society.

It has several times been suggested, in public debate and in private conference, that interpretations of the sense in which the United States accepts the engagements of the Covenant should be embodied in the instrument of ratification. There can be no reasonable objection to such interpretations accompanying the act of ratification provided they do not form a part of the formal ratification itself. Most of the interpretations which have been suggested to me embody what seems to me the plain meaning of the instrument itself. But if such interpretations should constitute a part of the formal resolution of ratification, long delays would be the inevitable consequence, inasmuch as all the many governments concerned would have to accept, in effect, the language of the Senate as the language of the treaty before ratification would be complete.[2] The assent of the German Assembly at Weimar would have to be obtained, among the rest, and I must frankly say that I could only with the greatest reluctance approach that Assembly for permission to read the treaty as we understand it and as those who framed it quite certainly understood it. If the United States were to qualify the document in any way, moreover, I am confident from what I know of the many conferences and debates which accompanied the formulation of the treaty that our example would immediately be followed in many quarters, in some instances with very serious reservations, and that the meaning and operative force of the treaty would presently be clouded from one end of its clauses to the other.

Pardon me, Mr. Chairman, if I have been entirely unreserved and plain spoken in speaking of the great matters we all have so much at heart. If excuse is needed, I trust that the critical situation of affairs may serve as my justification. The issues that manifestly hang upon the conclusions of the Senate with regard to peace and upon the time of its action are so grave and so clearly insusceptible of being thrust on one side or postponed that I have felt it necessary in the public interest to make this urgent plea, and to make it as simply and as unreservedly as possible.[3]

WWT MS (WP, DLC).
    [1] Actually, the conference had taken place on February 26, 1919. See the extract from the Diary of Dr. Grayson and the news report printed at that date in Vol. 55.

² Either Wilson had forgotten the advice given in J. A. Metzger to RL, July 29, 1919, or else he had decided, at least for the time being, to take this position.
³ There is a WWT outline of this letter in WP, DLC.

To Carter Glass

My dear Glass: The White House 14 August, 1919.

Thank you warmly for your memorandum sent to serve my thought in the matter of presenting to the Senate the exigency of the situation in regard to the Treaty. Apparently Lodge has already agreed to report the Treaty out promptly, but the material you send me will be very useful when the time comes to fire.

Cordially and faithfully yours,   Woodrow Wilson

TLS (C. Glass Papers, ViU).

To Robert Lansing

My dear Mr. Secretary: The White House 14 August, 1919.

Will you not be kind enough to communicate to Reinsch our judgment in this matter?¹ I entirely agree with you in regard to it. Please express our appreciation of his watchful services when you communicate with him.

Cordially and faithfully yours,   Woodrow Wilson

TLS (B. Long Papers, DLC).
¹ See RL to WW, Aug. 12, 1919.

To Robert Lansing, with Enclosure

My dear Mr. Secretary: The White House 14 August, 1919.

I am taking the liberty of returning two documents; first, Mr. Poole's memorandum concerning the purposes of the Bolsheviki,¹ and second, Mr. Long's memorandum of Dr. Reinsch's letter. I have read them both with the greatest interest.

I think that perhaps I shall have an opportunity in a Labor Day Proclamation to warn the country against Bolshevism in some way that may attract attention.

I think that Mr. Long's comments upon Reinsch's letter are very well founded, but Japan certainly has China very much in her grasp, and I am eager to concert methods by which China may be extricated and set free. We must devote our best thought to this matter at the earliest possible moment.

Cordially and faithfully yours,   Woodrow Wilson

TLS (SDR, RG 59, 861.00/5125, DNA).
¹ Printed as an Enclosure with RL to WW, Aug. 7, 1919 (first letter of that date).

E N C L O S U R E

Breckinridge Long to Robert Lansing

Dear Mr. Secretary: [Washington] August 5, 1919.

The letter of resignation of Doctor Reinsch¹ is a very good resume of the situation in China through the first four or five pages.
The latter part of the letter I think indicates some of the antipathy
which Doctor Reinsch feels toward Japan. It is quite natural that
he should feel as he does. He has been in the midst of the intrigues
which Japan has carried on and has been the most active of the
foreigners who have fought it.

His comments on pages seven to nine I think are quite unjustified. Attention has been given to China and has been continuous.
The Consular Service has a few men comparatively who are available for valuable service in China. The student interpreter corps
has not been kept up because it has been impossible for the Department to find men who are desirous of entering that corps. The
last examination was typical. After months of effort we succeeded
in finding three candidates. One was totally unfit by reason of education; another was disqualified because of his birth and long residence in Japan, and his substitution of the Japanese for the American view point and sympathy in every respect; the remaining one
was well qualified, but eventually decided that he did not care to
serve.

Doctor Reinsch says that promises of assistance have been made
him and have been unfulfilled. Personally I do not know to what
he refers. It has been very difficult to find clerks because all of the
good men were in the Army. All of our Missions have suffered from
that cause, but have only suffered proportionately, and as far as I
remember Doctor Reinsch has been given everything he asked for
except the assignment of certain Consular Officers. The trouble is
that he has not delegated responsibility to and accepted the services of men assigned to the Legation as Secretaries. He has gone
to persons on the outside and has taken them into his confidence
and has operated through them rather than through the regular
and organized establishment. He, himself, is very much over-
worked, and has been for several years; has carried on by an enormous nervous energy and is consequently now in a highly nervous
condition; and is tired out and discouraged at the physical impossibility of achieving which was too much for any one man to do.

As regards Doctor Reinsch's other letter, that under date of June 15,[2] I separate it into two categories; first, as to personnel, and second, as to raising the rank of the Mission to an Embassy. My personal feeling is that the latter would be entirely unjustified. The disorganized condition of China from a political point of view, the civil war which it has been through for a year or more, and disorders which prevail throughout China are not such as to warrant the raising of the Mission to an Embassy—important though our relations are with China.

As regards the personnel he has struck the right note in saying that his successor should be a man with sound knowledge of industrial life and commerce. The activities of the Japanese throughout China have been industrial and financial followed by political control, and originating for the purpose of political control. She has made more than four score loans within the last few years, ranging in size from five to fifty million dollars. She has taken as security mining rights, forestry rights, river and waterway rights, railroad privileges, telegraph and telephone monopolies, and exclusive management of industrial concerns, such as iron foundries, and has taken mortgages on the sources of revenue of the provinces and central government. These loans are mostly executory in that contracts have been entered into whereby a large sum is contracted to be loaned and mortgages taken to secure the whole amount, vesting control of the mortgaged property in Japanese hands, and then only a small amount comparatively, usually amounting to five or ten percent of the sum contracted for paid on account. Frequently Japan withholds further advances on the contract and makes additional bargains in consideration of the additional advances. Japan's hold upon China consequently runs through the whole financial, industrial, and economic systems of the country. If China is to be freed from this unfair and unjust influence it must be done through a very careful appreciation of the industrial and commercial conditions of the country which must precede the exercise of a sound judgment. The Minister of the United States must take a leading part in the liberation of China, or at least must do all that can be done to prevent further encroachment and to ameliorate the condition that now exists until such time as the League of Nations has been established and has lived long enough to be a real force and in such position that it can marshal the moral forces of the world and bring them to work for the liberation of China. In glancing through the suggestions as to personnel which Doctor Reinsch makes three of them are outstanding. Mr. Phillips, of course, would make a very able representative. His long diplomatic experience and his large capacity would render him serviceable as Chief of a Mission anywhere. Doctor Barrows of the University of California[3] might be a very able person, but it seems to me that his experience has been rather too theoretical. Mr. MacMurray is needed in an advisory capacity to the Department in Far Eastern matters, and could not at this time well be spared.

Mr. Thomas Lamont seems to me to have the qualification of sound knowledge of industrial life and commerce, to have had a recent diplomatic experience, and to be of such force and character as to serve better than anyone of whom I can think the needs of that particular post. He has a very deep insight into, and knowledge of, the proposed International Consortium, and his presence there might do much to effectuate it as soon as it is established. He might not consider the post, but I feel quite satisfied that he would make a very able and satisfactory representative if he had on his staff persons who were familiar with the Far Eastern situation, and could give him political advice based upon a thorough knowledge of the whole situation.   Breckinridge Long

TLS (SDR, RG 59, 123R271/105, DNA).
    [1] It is printed as Enclosure I with WW to RL, July 25, 1919 (second letter of that date), Vol. 61.
    [2] Printed as Enclosure II, *ibid.*
    [3] David Prescott Barrows, Dean of the Faculties of the University of California at Berkeley, who, among other things, was an authority on the Philippines.

To Louis Marshall

My dear Mr. Marshall: [The White House] 14 August, 1919.

Replying to your letter of August 6th,[1] may I not say that I am going to take pleasure in cabling the substance of it to our Commissioners in Paris, where I am sure it will be handled in the most serviceable way possible in the circumstances.

You will remember that in one of our conversations in Paris I felt obliged to express my judgment as distinctly against the creation of separate Jewish bodies or colleges, and I am sure you will remember the grounds upon which I earnestly argued my judgment in that matter. I am constrained to say that I have had no reason to change that judgment, and believe that it is in the best interest of the people we are trying to serve.

                    Cordially and sincerely yours,   Woodrow Wilson

TLS (Letterpress Books, WP, DLC).
    [1] Printed as an Enclosure with WW to RL, Aug. 8, 1919 (first letter of that date).

To Cleveland Hoadley Dodge

My dear Cleve: The White House 14 August, 1919.

Thank you for your letter of August 10th. The plight of Armenia and the tragical consequences which are likely to ensue upon the withdrawal of the British troops from the Caucasus have been giving me the deepest concern. It is manifestly impossible for us, at any rate in the present temper of the Congress, to send American troops there, much as I should like to do so, and I am making every effort, both at London and at Paris, to induce the British to change their military plans in that quarter,[1] but I must say the outlook is not hopeful, and we are at our wits' ends what to do. I would welcome any advice you might be willing to give me.

Your letters always bring a delightful note of sympathy. You see so clearly just what is happening, and it strengthens me to know that you are thinking about it and pushing with your will.

It is delightful to hear of your family reunion. I wish we might see you in your happiness. Give our love to everybody.

Affectionately yours,   Woodrow Wilson

TLS (WP, NjP).

[1] The American Commission to Negotiate Peace had on August 8 sent the following telegram to Robert Lansing:

"As the embarkation of British troops from Batum begins August 15 and their withdrawal will probably be followed by anarchy and massacres in Armenia, it is suggested that if you appealed through Ambassador Davis to Curzon or Lloyd George for postponement of this withdrawal for at least one month, such request might be granted. Prompt action is necessary since a telegram to Batum revoking order for embarkation, must be August 13 from London. Officials in British Delegation here, who regard withdrawal as a calamity, have confidentially intimated that an American appeal for postponement is the only thing capable of altering the British decision to withdraw on August 15th."

Lansing embodied this message in RL to J. W. Davis, Aug. 9, 1919, printed in *FR 1919*, II, 828, together with the instruction to take the matter up with the Foreign Office "informally and orally and make such representations as seem proper to you under the circumstances without however, pressing the matter in any way." On August 11, Lansing sent a second, briefer dispatch to Davis which read as follows: "In view of gravity of situation and necessity of immediate action you are instructed to urge British Government with all earnestness not to withdraw troops from Batum for time being." *Ibid.*

Lansing almost certainly conferred with Wilson before sending these two telegrams, although we have no written evidence that he did so.

Davis replied on August 12 to Lansing's first telegram as follows: "Conferred with Curzon yesterday, August 11, first opportunity following instructions. I confined myself to inquiring whether order for withdrawal was definite and irrevocable and expressed fears which were entertained as to its consequences. Curzon professed himself fully alive to possibilities, said withdrawal had been definitely decided upon, that men belonging to units [whose] period [of] enlistment had expired, that no forces were at hand for replacement, that Great Britain had given notice of her intention to withdraw and Allies had offered task to Italy, who declined it, that Great Britain would be highly gratified to see America take mandate for Armenia and assume duty of policing. I told him, in response to questions, that [regardless] of future decisions the instant despatch of American forces was in my judgment, a military and political impossibility. [If] matter went to Congress it was unsafe to rely on prompt action." *Ibid.*, pp. 829-30.

On August 15, Davis telegraphed to Lansing again, quoting the following letter of August 13 from Curzon: "My Dear Ambassador: I have received your note of last evening urging the British Government with all earnestness not to withdraw our troops from Batoum for the time being in view of the evident gravity of the situation. As I explained to you in our conversation earlier in the afternoon evacuation has already commenced at the eastern end of the line. In any case, however, its duration must be sufficiently prolonged to relieve us from any immediate anxiety as to the position at Batoum. Should the present programme be carried out unaltered it will not be till the early part or middle of October that the question of leaving Batoum will assume a practical form, and it may be possible at that date, should the conditions in the Caucasus require it, to make arrangements which will not let the place remain without any protection. In the meantime I am making inquiries as to whether, consistent with the broad policy which I have indicated, anything can be done to insure some degree of local security and to prevent the terrible events of which your Government are apprehensive. Any arrangement for this purpose would be much easier were your Government in a position either themselves to put troops into the Caucasus or to assure us that the mandate for Armenia would ultimately be accepted by the United States." *Ibid.*, pp. 830-31.

On August 20, Davis relayed to Lansing another letter from Curzon of August 19 which read as follows:

"My Dear Ambassador: You may remember that in our conversation yesterday afternoon about the Armenian question and the Caucasus I expressed some surprise that if American opinion was as deeply stirred as I was led to believe on the subject, no official representatives [representations] had reached me from the American Government and I was left to gather American sentiment from the reports and appeals and protests of private individuals. I further said that anxious as we were to do everything in our power to satisfy American opinion and to protect the Armenians, it was difficult to modify our announced and already inaugurated policy of evacuation unless we knew for certain for how long a period we were requested or expected to remain and what part the American Government were prepared to play at its close. Later in the evening Mr Bonar Law speaking on the same subject in the House of Commons used the following words:

'I can assure my noble friend that if any sign of help were coming from America as suggested they would only too gladly welcome it. Indeed I think I might say more with the consent of my right honorable friend: it is, if I may be permitted to say so, an American problem rather than a British. They are in a better position to deal with it. They have interests as great as ours. I think greater. I can assure the House that if the President of the United States were officially to say to the British Government, "We wish you to hold the fort for a little until we can make arrangements" we would certainly do our best to meet him.'

"Mr. Bonar Law meant to add what I may here be permitted to add on behalf of His Majesty's Government that in the event of the American Government addressing us in the sense indicated it would seem only reasonable that the financial burden of retaining our forces in the Caucasus beyond the period already fixed by us should not be borne by Great Britain, but should be assumed by the state which expects to be or is likely to become the mandatory for the Armenian people. Our own financial responsibilities in those regions have already been so overwhelming that we should not feel justified in continuing them for a further period. May I suggest to Your Excellency that you should telegraph in this sense to your Government since the matter is one that calls for very early decision." *Ibid.*, pp. 832-33.

For Lansing's (and Wilson's) reply to this last communication, see RL to J. W. Davis, Aug. 23, 1919.

To Atlee Pomerene, with Enclosure

My dear Senator: [The White House] 14 August, 1919.

After our interview the other day, the enclosed came into my hands from Tumulty,[1] and so fell in with some of the thoughts I had expressed that I thought I would take the liberty of sending it to you and ask if you would not glance it through.

Cordially and sincerely yours,   Woodrow Wilson

TLS (Letterpress Books, WP, DLC).

¹ Tumulty had sent a copy of the Enclosure to Hines on August 5. Hines returned it in W. D. Hines to JPT, Aug. 11, 1919, TLS (WP, DLC), with the following comment: "The general view embodied in this interview that labor and the public should participate along with the owners in the management of railroads is in accord with my own view as expressed in a speech I delivered not long ago at Swampscott, Massachusetts. . . . The assumption of success on the part of the English Railway System is not borne out however, by the official estimates for the year ending March, 1920."

ENCLOSURE

In 1916-17 several interviews were cabled by Charles H. Grasty to the New York Times giving the opinions of English railway managers on the American railway problem. One of these was Henry W. Thornton, General Manager of the Great Eastern and formerly of the Pennsylvania. He was afterward put in charge of British railway interests in France and is now Brig. General Sir H. W. Thornton. Mr. Grasty's cable follows:

"London, December 31, 1916. Private control of railroads in England is a thing of the past. Government control was adopted as a war measure in August, 1914. It has worked so well that the principle will be retained when peace returns. So much is certain. When the war broke out, the Government had to get immediate control of the carriers in order fully to command facilities for transporting troops, arms, and supplies. There was not time for elaborating a plan, so the roads were just taken over in the simplest way.

"The net earnings of the previous year (1913) were guaranteed, with certain minor deductions, for the whole period of government control, and the ten general managers of the larger systems were constituted an executive committee with entire managerial charge.

"The whole scheme falls under the department of commerce and transportation, known here as the Board of Trade; but that body names a member of the committee of ten—Sir Herbert Walker—as its representative, holding for itself only reserve powers of control.

"When the new order set up in the hurry and confusion of that fateful August shook down to something like permanency, the managers were surprised to find what a good arrangement it was. Now, after well over two years of trying out, there is practical unanimity in the opinion that the old conditions will never be entirely restored.

"These railroad heads in America who do not need Dr. [Frank A.] Vanderlip's prescription for hardened arteries and who, like the doctor himself, are ever scanning far horizons for signs of the times, have been watching the experience of England for such light as it may throw upon the serious problems which confront the carriers on that side of the Atlantic.

"It happens that there is one man in the railroad service in this country who can speak comparatively and with authority of railroads in America and in England. He is the General Manager of the Great Eastern, Henry W. Thornton, a product of the Pennsylvania Railroad school, and, before coming here two and a half years ago, for some time general superintendent of the Long Island Railroad. As general manager of the Great Eastern his position corresponds to that of a railway president in America, his responsibility being directly to the board of directors.

"Mr. Thornton is one of the Executive Committee operating the roads, each member of which has the military rank of lieutenant-colonel. I may add that Colonel Thornton has won the regard and confidence not only of the Great Eastern interests, but of the British public. He brings with him the American push and go, but fits into his new environment as if to the manner born.

" 'The arrangement between the Government and the railroad companies,' said Mr. Thornton, in reply to my inquiries, 'Has proved a good bargain for everybody. Under it stockholders receive the same return, with minor deductions, that they had in 1913, upon which year the bargain was based. The Government in turn fares well, because the hauling done for it, if it had been paid for at the regular rates, would have amounted to a great deal more than the difference between the present earnings and what it costs to run the railroads and pay the stockholders.'

" 'Will the old conditions ever be restored'

" 'Never,' replied Mr. Thornton, with emphasis.

" 'The position will be different after the war, but exactly what it will be nobody can tell. It will probably be something like semi-nationalization or government partnership. I do not think that either railroad shareholders or the Government need be anxious about the future condition. It will be better than the old relation, because we have had an opportunity to develop the subject under conditions which were peculiarly favorable to this purpose. We ought to work out something that has all the advantages and none of the disadvantages of government ownership.'

"When asked to comment on the situation in America, Mr. Thornton said that, disregarding the position in England, and looking at it only as applicable to the United States, the Interstate Commerce Commission seemed to him to labor under the disadvantage that it was too far away from its subject. It was like a judge on the bench; it did not share in the consequences of its acts; its responsibility was an academic one.

"The railroad interest, according to Mr. Thornton, divides itself into four distinct parts.

"1—The interest of the shippers.

"2—The railway staff, including labor and all employees.

"3—The proprietors, including the shareholders and bondholders, and the general financing.

"4—The Government, which in Europe already has, and in America will come to have, a military interest.

"The various interests are diverse and often in sharp opposition. The shippers always want low rates and care nothing about the other interests; the shareholders look to dividends; the employees want more wages, and do not worry themselves about the other points of view; the Government had [has] a many-sided interest, which may be one thing to-day and quite another thing tomorrow. Its main interest, of course, is to represent the general public, from which all railway revenue must be derived.

" 'The problem is to bring all these factors together,' said Mr. Thornton, 'so that they will appreciate the different points of view instead of always standing each for its own. My study of the American problem has carried me almost to the conviction that instead of the Interstate Commerce Commission there should be a body representing the four interests to which I have referred.'

" 'It might be well to carry the scheme even nearer to government control. Assuming some form of financial participation on the part of the Government, there is at once a stabilizing of railway securities. They are taken out of the field of speculation. The raising of capital becomes easy and its hire cheap. The Government has then a stake in the proposition. Moreover, each of the interests involved watches the other, and sees that no interest gets more than its share.'

" 'What about the general public in this scheme of control and management?' Mr. Thornton was asked.

" 'The public is represented by the Government, and that ought to be adequate in a democracy. What I have outlined in the way of a possible solution of the railway problem in America may not fit when laid down on the ground, but it seems to me that you have got to devise some scheme of automatic justice in a railway management, or else you will have a breakdown somewhere that will be very serious in its effects on the whole country.

" 'Our problem in England is much easier, because it is simpler here than it is in America to concentrate authority. I have no doubt that if the reorganization of the Interstate Commerce Commission were attempted, there would be a general demand to have local bodies with subordinate authority in the various sections. That would have its advantages, but it would interfere with concentration of authority and ease of control.

" 'The big thing, it seems to me, is that the Interstate Commerce Commission should have a real and practical interest in the administration. For example, in the labor fight recently neither the President nor Congress was directly interested in what happened after the settlement was secured; what they wanted was to get from under the difficulty. A continuing body, charged with permanent responsibility, would have an entirely different outlook on the question.

" 'A body composed of the best available men, appointed for life and adequately paid, would be in a position to get the best results. For example, a labor leader (and there are many good ones in America) might go into this body prejudiced, but his association with the others would broaden and mellow him. Precisely the same thing could be said of the representative of capital.

" 'It has worked out that way in England. Never anywhere has there existed such severe competition as there was here among the railroads, and yet the ten general managers, when brought together to operate the railroads of England, have all come to see one another's point of view, and as a matter of practical experience, every decision reached by them has been unanimous.' "

T MS (WP, DLC).

To Franklin Delano Roosevelt

My dear Mr. Secretary: The White House 14 August, 1919.

I have your note[1] about the recommendation of the Governor of American Samoa[2] that certain Samoa Chiefs be awarded gold medals for meritorious services in connection with the exclusion of influenza from American Samoa, and am puzzled, as you are, how to comply with the request. I could not give them Government medals—there are none to give—and personal medals would hardly be very significant, would they? What do you think?

                    Cordially and faithfully yours,   Woodrow Wilson

TLS (F. D. Roosevelt Papers, NHpR).
    [1] FDR to WW, Aug. 8, 1919, TLS (WP, DLC). Roosevelt forwarded the recommendation to Wilson with the comment that he did not know any way that the request could be complied with except by Wilson. However, he did believe that the chiefs should have "some sort of recognition" for their "excellent work."
    [2] Commander Warren Jay Terhune, U.S.N., to WW, June 12, 1919, TLS (WP, DLC). Terhune explained that the three chiefs had prevented the spread of the influenza epidemic to American Samoa by persuading their peoples to observe the quarantine restrictions. "The fact," he wrote, "that American Samoa excaped the INFLUENZA, whereas Western Samoa, the Fijis, and other Polynesian groups, suffered losses of from thirty to forty per cent, has enormously promoted American prestige in the Pacific."

To George Barnett

My dear General Barnett: [The White House] 14 August, 1919.

Thank you for your kind note.[1] You may be sure it was a genuine pleasure to Mrs. Wilson and me to review the splendid body of Marines who have just been mustered out of service. We are intensely proud of their whole record, and are glad to have had the whole world see how irresistible they are in their might when a cause which America holds dear is at stake. The whole nation has reason to be proud of them.

Cordially and sincerely yours,   Woodrow Wilson

TLS (Letterpress Books, WP, DLC).
[1] G. Barnett to WW, Aug, 13, 1919.

To John Barton Payne

My dear Judge Payne: The White House 14 August, 1919.

May I not ask you to read the enclosed memorandum[1] which was brought to me yesterday by the Italian Ambassador? I know from many sources that the situation of Italy in regard to coal supply is truly desperate, and I beg that you will be kind enough to have the shipping question studied with a view to facilitating shipments of American coal to Italy, if it is at all possible to do so.

By the permission of the Italian Ambassador, I am going to suggest that you be kind enough to have a personal interview with him, in order that you may learn with some accuracy the steps which the Italian Government has been taking for the purchase of coal in this country. This will make clearer than it could otherwise be made, the question of the number and kind of ships needed.

With warmest regard,

Cordially and sincerely yours,   Woodrow Wilson

P.S. May I not say how great a satisfaction it affords me to have you in your present post?   W.W.

TLS (ICHi).
[1] It is missing.

To Robert Underwood Johnson

PERSONAL

My dear Mr. Johnson: [The White House] 14 August, 1919.

You may be sure that I have read your letter of August 11th with appreciation of the admirable personal spirit it shows not only, but also in entire sympathy with the interest expressed in Italy.

I am sorry to say that the Italian Representatives have so far insisted upon solutions of the questions which affected them, which were clearly inconsistent with every other territorial or national arrangement we had made in connection with the treaties. I have argued with them in the most earnest spirit of sympathy and with the most sincere wish to be of service to them, because I know the natural links which bind the two countries together and would feel it an honor to be of service to Italy, but so far they have felt it impossible to accept solutions along the new lines of principle and action which the world desires to adopt.

I have not given up my efforts, and you may be sure will continue them until either they are rewarded or I am sure they are of no avail.   Cordially and sincerely yours,   Woodrow Wilson

TLS (Letterpress Books, WP, DLC).

From James Edward McCulloch and Edwin Courtland Dinwiddie

Dear Mr. President: Washington, D. C. August 14, 1919.

On receipt of your highly appreciated letter of August 4th, suggestiong [suggesting] that the Southern Sociological Congress take steps to bring to the attention of the Conference of Governors the matter of race relations and mob violence, we immediately brought your suggestion to the attention of our Governing Board. We are glad to inform you that they have appointed two delegates to represent the Southern Sociological Congress in presenting this matter to the Conference of Governors, namely; Bishop Theodore D. Bratton, President of the Southern Sociological Congress and Dr. Thomas Jesse Jones, who is the secretary of the Phelps-Stokes Fund and Editor of the recent Report on Negro Education, issued by the United States Bureau of Education.[1]

Owing to the acuteness of this question of race relations at this hour, it seems to us desirable that every possible influence be brought to bear to get the public to think calmly and justly on this subject. We are aware that you have doubtless been requested repeatedly to make a statement in regard to the recent outbreaks of mob violence. We fully appreciate the difficulties that might confront you in making any public statement relative to local conditions, where at best, it is all but impossible to know the real facts. We are aware also that it might be undesirable to address a communication on this subject directly to the Conference of Governors. It has occurred to us, however, that there is a channel open through which you might wish to communicate to the public an expression of your attitude, which we are confident would be a most reassuring influence for the entire Nation at this hour. We, therefore, respectfully, express the hope that you may see your way clear to address to Bishop Theodore D. Bratton, President of the Southern Sociological Congress, a letter that he may read in the course of his address to the Governors' Conference at Salt Lake City.

If you think favorably of this suggestion, we shall see to it that a letter addressed to Bishop Bratton, 609 McLachlen Bldg., Washington, D. C., will be placed in his hands before he reaches the Governors' Conference.

Respectfully and gratefully yours,   J. E. McCulloch
Edwin C. Dinwiddie

TLS (WP, DLC).
¹ Jones was a sociologist who had been a social worker in New York and was later director of the Research Department of the Hampton Institute. He had most recently been a specialist in the education of racial groups in the United States Bureau of Education. He was also the educational director of the Phelps Stokes Fund from 1913 to 1946. His report was United States Bureau of Education, *Negro Education: A Study of the Private and Higher Schools for Colored People in the United States* (2 vols., Washington, 1917). It was the first systematic study of Negro education in the United States and presented a stark picture of the total inadequacy of black educational facilities on all levels.

From Alexander Mitchell Palmer, with Enclosures

Dear Mr. President: Washington, D. C. August 14, 1919.

I attach hereto, for your consideration, the following:

1. Suggestions for oil relief legislation considered by representatives of the Departments of Justice, Navy, and the Interior, and oil men. In Section C, I have indicated by the use of brackets the words which may be omitted to meet the suggestion you made at the conference with Daniels, Lane and myself a couple weeks ago.

Sections A, B, C and G I understand to be agreed to by all three of the Departments as well as the representatives of the oil companies affected.

Sections D, E and F, while in their present form not nearly so objectionable as some earlier drafts, I feel are unnecessary. They give relief to persons who, in my judgment, are not sufficiently entitled as a matter of equity to such relief.

2. Memorandum prepared by Secretary Lane, explanatory of the relief measure.

3. Memorandum explaining the objections of the Department of Justice to Sections D, E and F.

Secretary Daniels is apparently opposed to all relief legislation. I would like to give relief only to such of the claimants as seem to have a substantial equity of a kind which justifies a "give and take" settlement of a lawsuit or a prospective lawsuit. My feeling is that Lane's suggestions would give relief to many who have no substantial equity; and yet his proposals do not go so far as the relief measure which reached the conference stage in the last Congress and are probably more conservative than this Congress is likely to pass if left to its own devices. Of course, the Navy Department has no interest in the matter except as to the Naval Reserves and the Department's rights with respect to these are pretty well guarded by this proposed relief legislation.

I would like to act in concert with the Secretary of the Interior in this matter, for if he and I can agree upon a program of recommendation to the Congress with respect to the relief legislation I am hopeful that our views will be accepted. In order to guide us, it is up to you, therefore, to decide

(a) Shall we recommend any relief legislation whatever?

(b) If so, shall we recommend Sections A, B, C and G, as to which we are all in accord, or

(c) Shall we recommend the entire measure, which is earnestly supported by the Secretary of the Interior, but as to which I am very dubious, to say the least, as to Sections D, E and F.

Faithfully yours,   A Mitchell Palmer

TLS (WP, DLC).

E N C L O S U R E   I

Suggestions for oil relief legislation considered by representatives of the Departments of Justice, Navy, Interior, and oil men.

Sec. A. All deposits of coal, phosphate, oil, oil shale, and gas in public lands chiefly valuable therefor shall be subject to disposition only as provided in this Act, except valid claims initiated and maintained in good faith under preexisting law, which claims may be perfected under such law; *Provided*, That the rights of any persons who, at the date of the approval of this Act, is a *bona fide* occupant or claimant of oil or gas bearing lands not embraced in any order of withdrawal, and who, at such date, is in diligent prosecution of work leading to discovery of oil or gas, shall not be affected or impaired by this Act, so long as such occupant or claimant is in diligent prosecution of such work.

Sec. B. Whenever the validity of any placer mining claim to oil or gas land has been or may hereafter be drawn in question in any departmental or judicial proceeding, the President is hereby authorized to settle any such controversy by an exchange or division of lands or by lease or other division of proceeds of operation as may be agreed upon with the claimant.

Sec. C. Upon relinquishment to the United States filed in the General Land Office within ninety days after the promulgation of rules and regulations under this section of any placer mining claim to oil or gas land embraced in any executive order of withdrawal made prior to June 25, 1910, which claim would be valid except for such executive order or for fraud with which the present claimant is not chargeable, and upon payment to the United States of an amount equal to accrued royalties for the oil and gas produced and saved from such land, prior to February 23, 1915, at one-eighth of such production, and thereafter to the date of the lease provided for in this section at the [commercial] rate [prevailing on February 23, 1915, for leases of proven oil or gas lands of similar character and location,] to be finally determined by the Secretary of the Interior, such claimant shall be entitled to a lease of the land embraced in such claim at a royalty to be fixed by the Secretary of the Interior [at the commercial rate prevailing at the date of the lease for leases of proven oil or gas lands of similar character and location:] *Provided*, That the Secretary of the Interior may reduce the amount of royalty on future production at any time when in his judgment successful operations can not be continued on the basis of the royalty fixed in the lease, and may thereafter increase such royalty as conditions may warrant to an amount not exceeding that originally fixed in the lease. No fraudulent claimant shall be entitled to any such lease, but the successor in interest of such a claimant without notice of the fraud at the time such interest was acquired shall not be chargeable therewith. The Secretary of the Interior shall hear and finally determine all conflicting claims for leases hereunder and may grant leases to one or more of such claimants upon such terms and conditions as he may deem just and equitable. All leases hereunder shall inure to the benefit of the claimant and all persons claiming through or under him by lease, contract, or otherwise, as their interests may appear. Upon the granting of leases hereunder all moneys impounded or secured in suits by the United States or under the Act of Congress approved August 25, 1914 (38 Stat., 708), shall be settled, adjusted, and paid over to the parties entitled thereto.

Sec. D. In case of any claim under the placer mining laws for any lands embraced in any Executive order of withdrawal made prior to June 25, 1910, which claim was initiated under the mining laws prior to the withdrawal order of July 2, 1910, and on which, prior to that date, a substantial amount was expended by the claimant or his predecessor in permanent improvements adapted and looking to the production of oil from the land, and upon which a producing oil or gas well was drilled prior to February 23, 1915, the claimant for which is not entitled to a lease under section C hereof, and is not chargeable with fraud, such claimant shall be entitled to lease the smallest legal subdivision (quarter quarter section or lot) containing such producing well, on the same terms and conditions and on compliance with the conditions precedent to the granting of such lease, as are provided for the granting of leases under section C hereof.

Sec. E. That claimants who would be entitled to leases under section C or D of this act, but whose lands are situated in naval petroleum reserves, shall receive leases for only the producing wells, with sufficient surface ground for the operation of such wells, and no additional wells shall be drilled on any quarter quarter section or lot on which one or more such wells is located, except that the drilling of additional wells by the lessee of the producing wells may be permitted by the President, on such terms and conditions as he shall prescribe.

Sec. F. That any person who at the time of any withdrawal order made subsequent to July 3, 1910, was a *bona fide* occupant or claimant of oil or gas lands not withdrawn from entry, and who had previously performed all acts under then existing laws necessary to valid locations thereof, except to make discovery, and upon which discovery had not been made prior to the passage of this act, and who has performed work or expended substantial amounts on or for the benefit of such locations in substantial and permanent improvements looking to the development of the claim, may, if application therefor be made within three months from the date of this Act, be granted prospecting permits for each forty-acre legal subdivision so occupied and improved, upon the same terms and conditions as other permits provided for in this Act: *Provided*, That such lands are not reserved for the use of the Navy; *and provided further*, That no claimant who has been guilty of any fraud or who had knowledge or reasonable grounds to know of any fraud, or who has not acted honestly and in good faith, shall be entitled to any of the benefits of this section.

Sec. G All leases for oil and gas lands under this Act shall be for a term of twenty years, with a preferential right of renewal for successive periods of ten years upon such reasonable terms and conditions as may be prescribed by the Secretary of the Interior, unless otherwise provided by Act of Congress at the expiration of any such period; all such leases shall reserve to the United States the option to take the royalties therein provided in oil or gas; and they shall contain such other appropriate provisions not inconsistent with this Act as may be prescribed by the Secretary of the Interior.

ENCLOSURE II

(2)

MEMORANDUM as to *Oil Relief Bill.*

Aug 2, 19

Appended hereto are Sections A, B, C, D, E, F, and G. A, B, C, E, and G are agreed to by the Department of Justice and the Department of the Interior. Sections D and F are suggested by the Department of the Interior as substitutes of a more conservative character for the provisions which passed both Houses of Congress at the last session.

POLICY OF PROPOSALS.

These sections are all grounded upon this policy:

1. That the President should have power to settle controversies by exchange or division of lands claimed, or otherwise.

2. That the Government should retain title to all the land. (All the early bills gave patents in some cases. The proposed substitutes give no patents whatever.)

3. That the Government should receive royalty on every barrel of oil produced from the beginning to date, and on to the end of production.

4. That no man who is guilty of fraud himself or had knowledge of fraud when he bought his claim should have a lease, or any consideration whatever.

5. That no man who went on the land *after* the Pickett Act[1] withdrawal should have a lease—no matter what his investment, and he must have found oil before the decision in the Midwest case. And all he will receive is a lease, for which he pays all the royalty he would have paid if the Government had leased the lands from the beginning.

6. That no claimant who had not produced an oil well should get a lease.

7. That no claimant should get a lease unless he had initiated a claim and made substantial expenditures for the development of oil on the land prior to the Pickett Act withdrawal.

8. That no claimant should get a patent to any land, no matter when he went on the land or how much money he had invested.

9. That no claimant should get a lease to his entire claim, no matter what his expenditures or how long he had been on the land prior to any withdrawal, unless the only thing against it is the withdrawal of 1909.

10. That no claimant should get anything for any operations after the Supreme Court held the withdrawal of 1909 to be valid.

11. That no claimant in a naval reserve should get anything but a lease for his producing well.

CLASSES GIVEN RELIEF.

The relief extended under the policy proposed would be this:

Men who had claims under the mining laws and had made discovery of oil or were diligently at work attempting to develop oil at the time of the Pickett Act withdrawal will be given a lease for the claims, if not chargeable with fraud, and upon condition that they pay royalties from the beginning of production to the end. (See Section C.)

Men who had initiated claims under the mining laws prior to the Pickett Act withdrawal and had expended substantial amounts in permanent improvements adapted and looking to the production of oil, and who had a producing well prior to the date of the Midwest decision, will be given a lease for 40 acres or a less subdivision containing the well, the rest of the land to revert to the United States. (See Section D.)

Men who had initiated claims in naval reserves prior to the Pickett Act withdrawal, who were not chargeable with fraud and who had performed work as above outlined, will get a lease for the existing producing wells only, all the rest of the land and oil to revert to the Government. (See Section E.)

Men who were at work on unwithdrawn public lands withdrawn long since the Pickett Act, upon which oil has not been discovered, but upon which such parties have expended substantial amounts in improvements looking to the development of oil, will be given a prospecting permit for the smallest legal subdivision they have occupied or improved. This does not apply to any naval reservations, nor to any person chargeable with fraud. (See Section F.)

At the option of the Government the royalties can be taken either in money or in oil. (See Section G.)

CC MSS (WP, DLC).

[1] The Pickett Act, named for its sponsor, Republican Representative Charles Edgar Pickett of Iowa, had been enacted on June 25, 1910. The act allowed the President of the United States temporarily to withdraw from settlement, location, sale, or entry any of the public lands of the United States for any public purpose stated in the orders of withdrawal. However, a key provision of the Act declared: "That the rights of any person who, at the date of any order of withdrawal heretofore or hereafter made, is a bona fide occupant or claimant of oil or gas bearing lands, and who, at such date, is in diligent prosecution of work leading to discovery of oil or gas, shall not be affected or impaired by such order, so long as such occupant or claimant shall continue in diligent prosecution of said work." 36 *Statutes at Large* 847. See also J. Leonard Bates, *The Origins of Teapot Dome: Progressives, Parties, and Petroleum, 1909-1921* (Urbana, Ill., 1963), pp. 28-29.

ENCLOSURE   III

(3)

OIL RELIEF LEGISLATION:

Objections to Sections D. E. and F. proposed by Secretary Lane, August 2, 1919.

Claimants who violated the first withdrawal of September 27, 1909, in the mistaken belief that it was invalid, but who were in diligent prosecution of discovery work on July 2, 1910, the date of the second withdrawal, and who continued such work to a discovery, would get a lease under Section C. Section D would give a lease for one-fourth of the claim on the same terms and conditions to a claimant who violated not only the first withdrawal but also the second. It is not clear just what is meant by the phrase, "a substantial amount expended in permanent improvements adapted and looking to the production of oil from the land." Evidently it means something less than the diligent prosecution of discovery work as required by the law, because the claimant is further described as one "not entitled to a lease under Section C." It seems to be intended to apply to a case where a number of claims were being held at the date of the second withdrawal without discovery work except on one, with the intention to drill on the others if oil should be discovered on the one, but not otherwise—a plain violation of the law. However, there is no justification for a lease of any sort to any claimant who was not in diligent prosecution of work at the date of the second withdrawal leading to discovery on each claim. That was a plain and unmistakable requirement of the law.

Section E would give a lease of the wells on the naval reserves to both classes without distinction. It is therefore subject to the same objection as Section D with respect to the class there provided for. As to the class provided for in Section C, they may be given substantially the same relief on naval reserves under Section B but not in the same way. The policy of conservation in the ground for future needs can be maintained in part by exchange or division of land or extinguishment of certain claims by compensation from the royalty proceeds of others under Section B. But if Section E were enacted this policy would have to be abandoned as to Naval Reserve No. 2, the most valuable one.

Section F would grant a prospecting permit to any claimant with a paper location made prior to an unquestionable withdrawal "who has performed work or expended substantial amounts on *or for the benefit of* such location in substantial and permanent improvements looking to the development of the claim." Those who have prosecuted discovery work with diligence are fully protected under

Section A, and where there is a substantial dispute on that point it may be compromised under Section B. A prospecting permit on proven oil land is the equivalent of a lease at a flat one-eighth royalty, since the permittee has only to make a discovery to secure such a lease under other provisions of the pending leasing bills.

T MS (WP, DLC).

From David Franklin Houston

Dear Mr. President: Washington August 14, 1919.

I am very glad that you have been able to find time to see the Committee representing the Farm Bureaus.[1] I had a two-hour talk with them yesterday. They are intelligent, reasonable, and public-minded. I think they intend to seek only what is right. They came here with the impression, gained from reading the newspapers, that the efforts to reduce the cost of living would react exclusively against the farmer. Most of the discussion in the press has been about foodstuffs. Perhaps also they had a suspicion that this was the intention of the public as well as of the Government. They assert, quite emphatically, that they are willing to do their part in increasing production and in reducing prices, but they wish the other parts of the community to go along at the same time. I pointed out to them that the aim of the Government is primarily to eliminate and prevent hoarding, manipulation, and profiteering in all necessaries of life; that it was not the view of those charged with responsibility that in the circumstances the farmers themselves were receiving unduly high prices; and that the Government did not believe that it was either expedient or just for the public to ask the farmers to produce with the assurance that the prices of their products would fall and that thereafter the rest of the public would consider what could be done with reference to the prices of other products.

I hope you will find it possible to let the members of the Committee state, in summary fashion, what is in their minds. I may say that the Bureaus which they represent are county farm organizations composed of real farmers. They cooperated very effectively with the Department and the agricultural colleges in building up the county agent system. It is the intention of the Farm Bureaus throughout the country to form a national organization.

I attach hereto a copy of a statement which the members of the Committee have prepared.

Faithfully yours,   D. F. Houston.

TLS (WP, DLC).

¹ Wilson met at the White House at 2:15 p.m. on August 14 with Oscar Edwin Brad-
fute, president of the Ohio Farm Bureau Federation; John G. Brown, president of the
Indiana Federation of Farmers' Associations; David O. Thompson, secretary of the Illinois Agricultural Association; James Raley Howard, president of the Iowa Farm Bureau
Federation; and F. C. Crocker, president of the Nebraska Farm Bureau Association.

The first county farm bureau had been organized in Broome County, New York, in
1911 for the purposes of cooperating with the county agricultural agent and of improv-
ing agricultural methods and rural life in general. The idea spread rapidly, especially
after American entrance into the war created the need for greatly expanded food production. In 1915, the first state federation of county farm bureaus was formed in Missouri, and the farmers of other states soon formed state federations also. In February
1919, representatives of twelve state federations met to plan for a national American
Farm Bureau Federation. The national organization was established at a meeting in
Chicago on November 12-14, 1919. See Orville Merton Kile, *The Farm Bureau Through
Three Decades* (Baltimore, 1948), pp. 24-54.

The farm bureau leaders' discussion with Wilson apparently followed closely the
statement mentioned by Houston in the last paragraph of the above letter: O. E. Brad-
fute *et al.*, Aug. 13, 1919, TS MS (WP, DLC). This memorandum sought to prove that
the American farmer was not primarily responsible for the high cost of living in the
United States. It placed the blame instead on the high wages demanded by labor, the
high profits extracted by middlemen in the processing and distribution of food products,
and the extravagance of most consumers. The American farmer was prepared to do his
share to cut prices by increasing the production of food, but other groups in the American economy would have to do their share as well. See also the *New York Times*, Aug.
15, 1919.

From Charles Sumner Hamlin

PERSONAL AND CONFIDENTIAL.

Dear Mr. President: Washington August 14, 1919.

For your confidential information, I would say that the National
Farmers Grange has sent out letters to all the granges in the country, asking that the members of each grange at once write to Senators, and demand immediate ratification of the peace treaty, without reservation and without amendment.

Last Thursday evening, the Grange at Mattapoisett, Mass.,
where I live, had a meeting to pass upon a motion of some of the
members to rescind a resolution passed by it over a month ago, in
favor of the Peace Treaty. I took occasion to be in Mattapoisett at
that time, and, as a member of the Grange, was asked to express
my views. The particular information which the Grange desired
was whether the allegation of some of the members that, under the
League of Nations, the Pope of Rome would be the universal sovereign of the world was true. I had little difficulty, however, in satisfying them upon this point, and on the conclusion of my address,
the member who made the motion to rescind withdrew his motion,
and said he was absolutely satisfied.

Sometimes I wonder if Senator Lodge has any sense of humor.
His frantic wailing at the possibility of the United States becoming
involved in some petty war under the Treaty, and his eagerness to
avoid this contingency by rejecting the Treaty, thus plunging the

United States and the whole world into incessant wars, reminds
me of an ode of the Latin poet Martial, which, as translated by John
Godfrey Saxe, is as follows:
　　"Poor Pannius who greatly feared to die.
　　Embraced the enemy he fain would fly.
　　Strange contradiction, weary of the strife.
　　He ceased to live for very love of life!
　　With his own hand he stops his vital breath;
　　Madness extreme! To die for fear of death."
　　　　　　　　　　　　　　　　Sincerely yours,　C S Hamlin

TLS (WP, DLC).

From J. D. Sanders

　　　　　　　　　　　　　　　Chicago, Ills., Aug. 14, 1919.
　　WHEREAS, Because of the railroad strike a very grave state of affairs exists in these United States and is bound to result in serious
effects to our country if continued, and
　　WHEREAS, you have used your good offices in trying to bring
about a satisfactory settlement, and
　　WHEREAS, We have the fullest confidence that you will exercise
your power and influence to bring about a speedy and satisfactory
settlement of this state of affairs; be it, therefore
　　RESOLVED, That we, the delegates of the shopcrafts on strike to
whom you addressed your appeal to go back to work, in convention
assembled at Chicago this, 14th day of August, 1919, from all parts
of the United States, notify and urge those whom we represent
who are out on strike to respectfully accede to your wishes and
return to work Saturday morning at the usual hour, August 16th,
1919, and with the assurance you have given us¹ you will use your
power and influence to have immediately granted by the Railroad
Administration our original demands as made to them ie. 85 cents
per hour for mechanics, 60 cents per hour for helpers, 10 cents per
hour increase for apprentices and proportionate increases for other
shop employees retroactive to January 1st, 1919.
　　Be it further RESOLVED, That we will not tolerate any discrimination in any way whatsoever against anyone who has participated
in this demonstration and take it for granted to be a part of your
request that it will be mandatory upon the Railroad Administration
to see that no discrimination is practised.
　　Be it further RESOLVED, That we, believing that there is a great
deal that should be told you regarding this question, that you en-

tertain a delegation of three from this convention to confer with you at the earliest possible time hereafter.[2]

J. D. Sanders,   Secretary,
Chicago District Council of Railroad
Shop-Crafts of Chicago and vicinity.

T telegram (WP, DLC).
  [1] During his meeting with the leaders of the shopmen's unions at the White House on August 4, about which, see the news reports printed at Aug. 4 and 5, 1919.
  [2] Insofar as we know, Wilson did not meet with any delegation from the convention at this time.

From Ellen Duane Davis

My dear Friend,   Martha's Vineyard [c. Aug. 14, 1919]

It has seemed wiser, until now, not to trouble you even with notes from those who care for you and Mrs Wilson, but your loving letter to E.P.[1] *makes* me write a line to thank you for it and to tell you how glad we are you like your little book.[2] Cyrus McC.[3] had them printed but E.P. sent your's to you. We are having a sort of a holiday. The pleasantest thing to us is being so near Jessie and E.P. sees little Woodrow[4] every day. We are both well and E.P. looks much more rested than he did when we came up here. In my feeble brain wanders a thought & strong hope that you and *Yours* may be able to get a few days off and come here so that your name sake may be baptized. Of course we are all eager to see you aside from the baptism but it would be wonderful if you could come. This is not to require an answer, but to tell you both God bless you. We are looking forward to seeing Margaret. E.P. goes to Phila. on Aug. 18. to be gone 3 days so do not think of coming then. Please forgive letter paper and with best love to you both from us both I am always gratefully and sincerely   Yours   Ellen Duane Davis

ALS (WP, DLC).
  [1] WW to E. P. Davis, Aug. 1, 1919.
  [2] See n. 2 to the letter just cited.
  [3] That is, Cyrus Hall McCormick.
  [4] That is, Woodrow Wilson Sayre, about whose birth see F. B. Sayre to WW, Feb. 23, 1919, n. 1, Vol. 55.

From Robert Lansing

Dear Mr. President: Washington August 14, 1919.

I beg to acknowledge the receipt of your letter of August 11, transmitting a statement by the Secretary of War regarding the proposed assignment of Regular Army officers to Mr. Hoover's missions, and Mr. Hoover's suggestion that military officers be loaned to new governments in Europe as technical advisers and be paid by such governments, and asking me to communicate the substance of Mr. Baker's statement to Mr. Hoover, through the Mission in Paris, with an explanation with regard to the second part which Mr. Baker embodies.

In reply I beg to say that I have taken pleasure in complying with your request, and to enclose for your information a copy of my telegram to the Mission in Paris, in relation to the matter.[1]

Faithfully yours,   Robert Lansing

TLS (WP, DLC).
[1] RL to HCH, Aug. 13, 1919, CC telegram (WP, DLC).

Robert Lansing to Frank Lyon Polk

[Washington] August 14, 1919.

STRICTLY CONFIDENTIAL.

Your 3624 August 11, 11 p.m.[1] For Polk. Your action in sending Clemenceau a letter stating importance of determining draft of mandates is approved and Mr. Clemenceau's agreement not to block the consideration of this matter is highly appreciated. The President feels that any deviation from attitude adopted at the time when this subject was discussed by President in Paris would be highly inadvisable as it could only result in serious complications.

Robert Lansing

TS telegram (SDR, RG 59, 763.72119/6114, DNA).
[1] FLP to WW and RL, Aug. 11, 1919.

A Veto Message

[Aug. 15, 1919]

I return this Bill, H.R. 3854, "An Act for the repeal of the daylight-saving law," without my signature, but do so with the utmost reluctance. I realize the very considerable and in some respects very serious inconveniences to which the daylight-saving law subjects the farmers of the country, to whom we owe the greatest consideration and who have distinguished themselves during these recent years of war and want by patriotic endeavours worthy of all praise. But I have been obliged to balance one set of disadvantages against another and to venture a judgment as to which were the more serious for the country. The immediate and pressing need of the country is production, increased and increasing production, in all lines of industry. The disorganization and dislocation caused by the war have told nowhere so heavily as at the industrial centres,—in manufacture and in the many industries to which the country and the whole world must look to supply needs which cannot be ignored or postponed. It is to these that the daylight-saving law is of most service. It ministers to economy and to efficiency. And the interest of the farmer is not in all respects separated from these interests. He needs what the factories produce along with the rest of the world. He is profited by the prosperity which their success brings about. His own life and methods are more easily adjusted, I venture to think, than are those of the manufacturer and the merchant.

These are the considerations which have led me to withhold my signature from this repeal. I hope that they are considerations which will appeal to the thoughtful judgment of the House and in the long run to the thoughtful judgment of the farmers of the country, who have always shown an admirable public spirit.[1]

WWT MS (WP, DLC).
[1] Printed in *Cong. Record*, 66th Cong., 1st sess., p. 3980, and the *New York Times*, Aug. 16, 1919. Both houses overrode this veto on August 19-20, 1919.

A News Report

[*Aug. 15, 1919*]

REPORTS WILSON BOUND TO CARRY TREATY UNALTERED
HITCHCOCK SAYS THE PRESIDENT WON'T CONCEDE
EVEN "THE CROSSING OF A 'T.' "
THREAT TO LODGE AND KNOX

Washington, Aug. 15.—President Wilson today made it plain to Senate Democrats that he was not ready to accept reservations to the Peace Treaty, and that he was not even considering the possibility that the acceptance of reservations might in the end be necessary.

At a conference at the White House with Senator Hitchcock, Administration spokesman in the Senate, the President left no doubt that he considered the very thought of reservations by members of his party in the Senate as premature. He emphasized to Senator Hitchcock the fact that the immediate and vital task of the friends of the treaty and the League covenant in the Senate was to accomplish the defeat of every amendment to the text of the treaty or the covenant. Until that had been done, Mr. Wilson clearly indicated, according to Senator Hitchcock, not the slightest consideration could be accorded any suggestion of reservations. They could not even be thought about.

The President's apparent fear that there was still danger of textual amendments of the treaty by the Senate came somewhat as a surprise to most Senators, for it has been rather generally accepted in the Senate for some time that the advocates of amendments cannot muster the necessary votes. President Wilson, however, as Mr. Hitchcock interpreted him, appeared to be concerned over the possibility that the Shantung provision—perhaps the most obnoxious section of the treaty in the eyes of the Senate generally—might actually be amended by the elimination of "Japan" and the substitution of "China" in the clauses transferring German rights in the Shantung Peninsula.

Another possibility of amendment feared by the President was that in respect to British voting strength in the League of Nations assembly, where self-governing British dominions each get a vote, in addition to the one given the British Empire.

Carrying out the President's idea of rallying the treaty's friends to defend it against amendment, Senator Hitchcock announced that he would address the Senate next week, earnestly urging that no consideration be given any proposition for an amendment, no matter how great the need for it may appear to be.

In this speech, Mr. Hitchcock said he intended to point out to the Senate, as President Wilson today pointed out most emphatically to him, the fact that the slightest textual amendment of the treaty meant that it must go back to Germany for reacceptance.

If in the meantime the other great powers have accepted the treaty as it is, and as Germany has accepted it, the United States, the President pointed out to the Senator, will be in the position of going, "hat in hand," to beg Germany's acceptance of a separate peace. And in that event, the President expressed the view, Germany would use to the fullest extent the trading advantage she would have in dealing singly with the United States.

"The President and I concurred fully in the view," said Senator Hitchcock, "that a new treaty would have to be made if the present treaty was amended textually, and that the United States would then lose entirely the benefits accruing under the present treaty. Other nations, having accepted the treaty, would, of course, be enjoying those benefits all the time. In case of rejection of this treaty, or if it is amended so that it must go back to Germany, the United States would be excluded from access to German dyestuffs, which would probably be available to the merchants and manufacturers of other nations.

"The United States would have to go to Germany, hat in hand, and beg her to accept our peace terms."

According to Mr. Hitchcock, the President said that if the Senate forced the making of a new treaty he would send Senators Knox and Lodge to Berlin to negotiate it.

"The President's view of an amendment of the Shantung provision," said Mr. Hitchcock, "is that in that case Germany would have one treaty with Japan and the Allies, transferring the German rights in China to Japan, and then would be asked to sign another treaty with the United States transferring those rights to China.

"In the opinion of the President, no compromise issue is now before the friends of the treaty and the League. This is not even the time to think of a compromise, much less to discuss it or negotiate for it. The time for reservations to the treaty is still far off. There may have to be a compromise in the end, but at the present that bridge is not being crossed.

"Both the President and I agreed that the immediate task is to see to the defeat of the proposed amendments. We've got to remove absolutely any probability of the dotting of an 'i' or the crossing of a 't.'

"As to reservations, the President has not changed the position he has always occupied, that even mild ones would prove tremendously embarrassing. They would, in his opinion, create in Europe the feeling that the United States entered the League of Nations and accepted the Peace Treaty without confidence in either, in a half-hearted and suspicious spirit."

The President also discussed the importance of expediting as much as possible the report of the Foreign Relations Committee which will bring the treaty directly before the Senate. When asked how much longer he though[t] the committee would keep the treaty, Senator Hitchcock said he hoped it would be out in about ten days. He declined to state whether he had discussed with the President measures to force it out of the committee's hands if it has not been reported within that time.

Mr. Hitchcock laid before the President such information as he had concerning the Senate's demand for reservations. Just before going to the White House, Mr. Hitchcock conferred with Mr. McNary, leader of the group of "mild reservationists," who for several weeks have been trying to work out a middle ground program to which it was hoped Democratic Senators might assent in the interest of ratification.

Senator Hitchcock asked Senator McNary how many Republicans now favored the mild reservation program. Mr. McNary said that from twenty to twenty-five had come over to it. He also informed the Democratic leader that Senator Lodge had a new set of reservations, somewhat different from those drawn up by the McNary group, which had not yet been passed upon by Republican Senators generally.

After having gathered this information Senator Hitchcock stated that his estimate of the situation showed that forty-odd Senators were standing for unqualified acceptance of the treaty, twenty-five wanted reservations, and the remainder, about thirty, wanted the treaty killed. He intimated that this was the view he intended to lay before Mr. Wilson.

He also carried with him the warning, given him about the same time, by one of the treaty's stanchest Republican friends, that ratification without reservations was an impossibility.

This Republican Senator declared today that in the event of a "showdown"—a vote on acceptance or rejection of the treaty as it now stands—only three Republican votes could be counted on in favor of ratification. An equal number of Democrats, this Senator said, might vote against the treaty. Therefore, he said, a two-thirds vote for ratification was impossible unless the safeguarding reservations were made.

Senator McNary promptly denied a report that Senator Hitchcock had asked him whether twenty Republican Senators would unite with the Democrats to take the treaty out of the Foreign Relations Committee's hands and put it before the Senate, if the delay in reporting it lasted much longer. Mr. McNary said Senator Hitchcock did not in any way suggest such a course, nor would Republicans support any such move at this time.

From another Senator it was learned that word was carried to Senator Lodge recently that five Republicans were ready to unite with the Democrats to discharge the committee, but on investigation Senator Lodge learned, it was stated, that not only were the Republicans not willing to do that, but many Democrats would oppose it, as an affront to the committee and a wholly unwarranted interference with the orderly and regular machinery of the Senate.

The mild reservationists today were awaiting a copy of the so-called Lodge reservations, which the Massachusetts Senator is understood to have drafted from ideas and suggestions presented from a number of sources.[1] Senator Lodge today notified Mr. McNary that he had the reservations and would furnish him a copy, at the same time expressing the hope that they would prove acceptable to Senators McNary, Kellogg, McCumber, Lenroot, and others of the "mild" group. Senator Lenroot alone of this group has seen the Lodge proposals. When the others of the group have read them they will hold a conference to determine how far they will concur in them. From what they have been told of Senator Lodge's reservations some of the mild reservationists said they were doubtful regarding his treatment of Article X. Senator McNary said that, while he had not seen the reservations, he understood that the one referring to Article X virtually nullified its provisions.

Senators close to Mr. Lodge said that he was not the author of the new reservations. They implied that Elihu Root's program[2] was the groundwork of the so-called Lodge reservations, and that some ideas suggested by others, in and out of the Senate, were embodied in them.

Mr. Lodge himself said today that if it became apparent that a majority of the Senate favored ineffective reservations he would be forced to vote against the whole treaty, although he wished it ratified, and favored strongly the creation of a League of Nations. But he would not assent, he intimated, to present provisions which he regarded as certain to prove extremely dangerous to the perpetuity of American institutions.

Printed in the *New York Times*, Aug. 16, 1919.

[1] Actually, the so-called Lodge reservations were put in final form only shortly before they were made public in the report presented to the Senate on September 10 by Lodge in his capacity as chairman of the Foreign Relations Committee. As is indicated in the following paragraph of this news report, Lodge had adopted the strategy of reservations to the Covenant of the League of Nations to be embodied in the resolution of consent to ratification which Elihu Root had proposed in his letter to Lodge of June 19, 1919 (about which, see JPT to WW, June 21, 1919, n. 3, Vol. 61). This strategy had the advantage of allowing both moderate Republicans and those determined to defeat the treaty to remain united at least until the proposed reservations could be voted upon. It was also alleged that reservations, unlike amendments to the treaty, would not necessitate the reopening of negotiations to secure the assent of the other signatories of the treaty. Lodge was strengthened in his strategy by William Howard Taft's advocacy in July of reservations to secure the consent of the Senate to ratification of the treaty, about which, see JPT to WW, with Enclosure, July 23, 1919, and the memorandum by W. H. Taft, printed following Tumulty's letter and Enclosure, and the notes for these documents, all in Vol. 61. For a discussion of Lodge's evolving strategy, see Lloyd E. Ambrosius, *Woodrow Wilson and the American Diplomatic Tradition: The Treaty Fight in Perspective* (Cambridge, New York, etc., 1987), pp. 148-61 *passim*.

[2] That is, the program set forth in his letter to Lodge of June 19, 1919.

From Joseph Patrick Tumulty

Dear Governor: The White House 15 August 1919.

The more I think of the suggestion I made this morning,[1] the more anxious I am to have you carry it out. An additional reason for urging the matter is this: It may be that in the conference some suggestion of compromise by way of interpretative resolutions may come from the Republicans, and you would be put into the position of having to defer to them. Whereas, if you give out the statement to the country outlining your attitude in the matter of reservations, amendments and interpretative resolutions, the initiative will be with you. This is very important as part of our offensive.

Sincerely yours,   Tumulty

TLS (WP, DLC).

[1] Tumulty had obviously advised Wilson either to issue his proposed letter to Lodge, printed at Aug. 14, 1919, in the form of a statement to the country or else to read it in the form of an opening statement to the Senate Foreign Relations Committee when he would meet with its members on August 19.

To Henry Cabot Lodge

My dear Mr. Chairman: The White House 15 August, 1919.

I have received your letter of yesterday, and in reply hasten to express the hope that the Senate Committee on Foreign Relations will give me the pleasure of seeing them at the White House on Tuesday morning next, the 19th, at ten o'clock.

I also welcome the suggestion of the committee that nothing said at the conference shall be regarded as confidential. In order that the committee may have a full and trustworthy record of what is said, I shall have a stenographer present, and take the liberty of suggesting that if you should wish to bring one of the committee's stenographers with you, that would be entirely agreeable to me. The presence of the two stenographers would lighten the work.

It will be most agreeable to me to have an opportunity to tell the committee anything that may be serviceable to them in their consideration of the treaty.

Very truly yours,   Woodrow Wilson

TLS (Foreign Relations Committee Papers, RG 46, DNA).

From Henry Cabot Lodge

Dear Mr. President: [Washington] August 15, 1919

I am very much indebted for your kind note received this morning. The Committee will do themselves the honor to meet you at the White House at ten o'clock next Tuesday, as you so kindly suggest, and will bring their own stenographer.

I have the honor to be

Very respectfully yours,   H. C. Lodge

TLS (WP, DLC).

From Key Pittman

My dear Mr. President: [Washington] August 15, 1919.

Upon yesterday you permitted me to place in your hands a memorandum setting forth the divisions of the Senate with regard to the ratification of the treaty. As I was about to leave you asked me if there was any change in the sentiment of the Senate towards the ratification of the treaty. I then stated that I had noticed very little change since your prior conference with me. My investigations today have caused me considerable uneasiness, and I feel it my duty to bare my thoughts to you.

The desire upon the part of a number of Democratic Senators to pass the treaty with reservations is steadily, if not rapidly, growing. If upon next Tuesday you make any statement that may be construed into a determination upon your part not to ratify the treaty with any reservations, an immediate and definite alignment in the Senate will follow. Senators will be called upon to take a stand either for or against your position. Those Senators who agree with you will, of course, throw off all restraint and support your position. Other Democratic Senators, who fear the indefiniteness of some of the terms of the covenant and who prefer reservations for such reasons, will nevertheless, by reason of their loyalty to you, come out firmly on your side. There will, in my opinion, however, I regret to say, be a number of Democratic Senators who will come out openly for reservations.

The fact that you, together with more than one-third of the Senate, declare unalterably against any reservations will assure the Borah faction of their safety in voting for the placing of amendments and reservations of every character, either weak or strong, upon the treaty. If through such combined vote the so-called Kellogg reservations[1] are reported out of committee and adopted by a majority of the Senate, what then will be the situation? The treaty will then be upon its passage with reservations supported by a majority of the Senators. What shall we minority Democrats do? We may either debate the question or vote. If we vote the treaty will fail to receive the necessary two-thirds. If, as I fear, a number of Democrats will vote for the reservations then we minority Democrats will be in the attitude of delaying the ratification of the treaty when such ratification may only require a few votes. I then fear that, in such event, the pressure upon some of our Democratic minority will become too strong and they will go over to the majority and thereby constitute the necessary two-thirds.

As I have suggested before, I do not believe that Borah and his faction or any of the Senators who are absolutely opposed to the entire League of Nations will vote for any reservations so long as they fear that such reservations may obtain the necessary two-thirds.

I believe, and I have expressed it in my speeches, that the Senate should adopt a resolution setting forth its present and future construction of any indefinite provisions of the treaty. I am of the opinion, however, that this may be accomplished by a separate resolution. If a majority of the governments who will be represented upon the council adopt a similar resolution then we will know the action that the council will take in the event that any of these indefinite articles come before it for construction.

For instance, many of the absolute opponents of the covenant have pub[l]icly admitted that there would be little danger to the

United States by reason of the indefinite articles if it were definitely understood that the United States could withdraw from the League upon two years' notice without regard to its obligations and without the consent or approval of the council or other governments.

The resolution, of course, would recite that each of the governments held itself liable to fulfill any and all obligations incurred during its membership in the League. If a resolution of this character alone were adopted immediately by the parliaments of France, Great Britian [Britain], Italy and Japan all fear as to the right of the United States to extricate itself from the League within two years would cease to exist.

With the treaty in this position we could go before the country with an assurance, I believe, of winning the overwhelming support of our people. This form of separate resolution, in my opinion, would accomplish the purpose and yet would not, as a reservation in the resolution of ratification would, open the door for Germany and all of the other countries to demand changes in the treaty.

I know, Mr. President, that you understand the motives that prompt me in laying frankly before you the situation as I see it. I do not have to assure you of my loyalty or with regard to my entire fearlessness as to the effect upon me of any action that I may conscientiously take. I hope that you will not consider it presumptuous upon my part when I say that I am urged by my faith in your wisdom and my heartfelt desire to see you sustained not only in the Senate but in the country, as well as by an intense desire for an early peace.

I have an abiding fear of releasing Germany from the present treaty that was forced upon her and again submitting to her the consideration of a treaty under the usages of international law. And yet there are some things in the treaty that are subject to constructions which would not meet the approval of our citizens. In my humble opinion we should attempt to protect our Government against misconstruction, and yet in a way that will not jeopardize the treaty.

I have suggested a plan that appeals to me. I fully recognize, however, your far superior ability and experience in these matters, and I, for one, will bow to your judgment.[2]

Very sincerely yours,   Key Pittman

TLS (WP, DLC).
[1] For which, see the news report printed at Aug. 2, 1919. Kellogg had presented the reservations in a speech to the Senate on August 7. *Cong. Record*, 66th Cong., 1st sess., p. 3690. See also Herbert P. Margulies, *Senator Lenroot of Wisconsin: A Political Biography, 1900-1929* (Columbia, Mo., and London, 1977), pp. 273-74.
[2] For Pittman's further action, see the news report printed at Aug. 21, 1919.

To Charles Sumner Hamlin

My dear Mr. Hamlin: The White House 15 August, 1919.

Your letter of August 14th has given me solid satisfaction. The support which the National Farmers' Grange is giving us will be of the greatest influence, and I for one am most deeply grateful.

I was greatly amused by the ode from Martial. It is certainly most apposite. I shall be tempted to quote it to Mr. Lodge himself.

With warm appreciation,
                              Sincerely yours,   Woodrow Wilson

TLS (C. S. Hamlin Papers, DLC).

To Walter Irving Clarke

My dear Mr. Clarke: The White House 15 August, 1919.

Thank you sincerely for your letter of August 13th. I am deeply interested in what you tell me of the character and purposes of the New Era Movement of the Presbyterian Church in the U. S. A. I shall follow that movement with the greatest interest and, I need not add, with the deepest sympathy. That the church should devote itself to these great purposes of service and enlightenment is an evidence, it seems to me, of its true interpretation of the spirit of the Gospel and of its vitality as an instrument of high public service in the Nation.
                              Cordially and sincerely yours,   Woodrow Wilson

TLS (WC, NjP).

To James Edward McCulloch

My dear Mr. McCulloch: [The White House] 15 August, 1919.

Thank you for your letter of August 14th. I realise the importance of your suggestion about a statement from me. I have been thinking the matter over a great deal lately, but have not yet been able to come to a conclusion which satisfies me with regard to the best occasion or medium.[1]
                              Cordially and sincerely yours,   Woodrow Wilson

TLS (Letterpress Books, WP, DLC).
   [1] Wilson chose to speak out against lynching and mob violence in his address at Helena, Montana, on September 11, 1919.

From Carter Glass

Dear Mr. President: [Washington] August 15, 1919.

Prof. Irving Fisher[1] is the author of a plan for what he calls a "compensated dollar," which he has been agitating for a number of years. Recently, on account of the general interest in the problem of the high cost of living and because the Professor says his plan is a sure specific for that problem, it has obtained considerable support from people who do not understand the practical financial and currency questions involved. One of these is Royal Meeker, Commissioner of Labor Statistics, who has written to me upon this subject. I am sure you will agree with me that this is no time for tampering with our currency system, and that the Commissioner of Labor Statistics is transcending his legitimate functions in advocating a currency plan.

The cause of the present high cost of living lies far deeper than Prof. Fisher sees. Your own recent address to Congress admirably stated the causes and the cure. The Federal Reserve Board in its letter of August 8th to Senator McLean, of which a copy is enclosed herewith,[2] has amply demonstrated that the fault of the present situation does not lie with our banking and currency system. Prof. Fisher would treat a symptom rather than the disease.

Cordially yours,   Carter Glass

TLS (WP, DLC).
  [1] Professor of Political Economy at Yale University.
  [2] W. P. G. Harding to G. P. McLean, Aug. 8, 1919, TCL (WP, DLC). Harding discussed the various kinds of currency then in circulation in the United States and sought to prove that none of them, and especially the Federal Reserve notes, was responsible for the high cost of living. Harding concluded his analysis as follows: "The Federal Reserve Board believes that any currency legislation at this time is unnecessary and undesirable, and would suggest that whether viewed from an economic or financial stand-point, the remedy for the present situation is the same, namely, to work and to save; to work regularly and efficiently in order to produce and distribute the largest possible volume of commodities; and to exercise reasonable economies in order that money, goods, and services may be devoted primarily to the liquidation of debt and to the satisfaction of the demand for necessaries, rather than to indulgence in extravagances or the gratification of a desire for luxuries." The complete letter was published in many newspapers on August 11, 1919. See, for example, the *New York Times* of that date.

From Elizabeth Merrill Bass

My Dear Mr. President: Washington, D. C. August 15, 1919.

Referring to the part of our conversation last week[1] which concerned the appointment of a new head for the Bureau of Women in Industry Service, I am enclosing a letter from Secretary Wilson[2] indicating that he had done just what I feared that he would do,— appoint the friend and protege of Mrs. Raymond Robins.

This careless placing of women in all parts of the public service is, I believe, one of the worst things being done. I could give many examples of enemies of the Administration being given important posts, not only during the war, but now. I think it comes partly from the fact that public officials, as well as other men, are not accustomed to thinking of women in terms of politics. A lot of careless endorsements are made to officials constantly for women on account of their general abilities or personal traits, with no thought given to whether they are our friends or not.

I am wondering whether it would be entirely impractical to have a committee consisting in part of women to whom all nominations of women for important positions should be referred for an investigation and report upon their qualifications. The Department of Labor is not the only offending department in the line referred to. I became much disquieted while I was in California about some appointments made or in prospect of making by the Department of the Interior. There were some phases in connection with that matter to which I would like to call your attention in person. Perhaps you will permit me to explain my own plan for a representative, nation-wide advisory committee to this Bureau, which can come frequently to Washington during the next year. This will be in addition to our Associate National Committeewomen, one from each State, who, you may have been told, came to the joint session in Chicago the latter part of May and sat in and voted with the Committeemen on all questions.

Referring again to the appointment of Miss Mary Anderson in the Department of Labor, she is not only the friend of Mrs. Raymond Robins and a member of her Trade Union League, but is herself absolutely uneducated and has no mental backgrounds. She has a value but quite obviously should not be the head of an important Bureau in one of the principal government departments.

May I call your attention to the value of the services rendered in many ways to the Administration by Eugene Meyer, of New York? I served with him on the National War Savings Committee, of which Frank Vanderlip was Chairman, and he was my partner in the unsuccessful struggle we made to prevent Mr. Vanderlip's adoption of a plan we knew was foredoomed to failure. He has a mind of absolute clarity and the most illuminating touch on all questions within the line of his experience. I have seen him in many companies of distinguished men, both Americans and foreigners, during the past year, and his phrases of defense of the Administration and its policies and the work of the War Commissions have been so discriminating, worded with such limpid purity of expression and at the same time so trenchant, that they literally disarmed all criticism. I saw him before he went to Europe three months ago and gathered from him that he had never had a talk with you and I venture to suggest that you would enjoy speaking with so faithful a friend and servant of your Administration. If I seem enthusiastic, it is because he has opened a new and fascinating world of business and economics to my vision.

Faithfully yours,   Elizabeth Bass

TLS (WP, DLC).
¹ See Elizabeth M. Bass to WW, Aug. 5, 1919, n. 1.
² It is missing.

From the Desk Diary of Robert Lansing

Friday Aug 15 [1919]

Conf. with Prest—12-12.35. Hapgood's record and danger to his confirmation. Approaching conf. of Prest with Senate Com.

Lunch 12.40-1.40.

To Edward Mandell House

My dear House: The White House 15 August, 1919.

I am glad that your letters have begun to come, though the movement of mail between us is sure to be very slow. I have been very well satisfied with the mandates that you have sent me, and am in hopes that the difficulties raised by the French Government will be overcome by patience and argument. I am very glad indeed that you find your other associates on the Mandate Commission so much of our mind in respect to the full protection of the natives and a liberal administration of the various mandate areas.

I wonder if it would be possible to get your colleagues to assent to putting in each mandate an express provision that the mandate is revocable by a majority vote of the Council, or at least such a vote as would not necessarily include the Power exercising the mandate. If a unanimous vote is required in this matter, it would of course always be possible for the Power exercising the mandate to veto any revocation or even alteration of the mandate.

We have been very much interested to learn within the last two or three days, through the newspapers, that we are likely to have Viscount Grey as the Ambassador of Great Britain. I am delighted to believe that his health permits him to accept this appointment and shall look forward with great pleasure to being associated with him.

I hope that you and the family keep well. We are going through a tremendous storm of all sorts of difficulties here, but the ship is steady and the officers not dismayed. We unite in the warmest messages.   Affectionately yours,   Woodrow Wilson

P.S. Thank you for sending me accurate copies of Mandates B and C.[1] I am heartily glad you liked the Address to Congress.

TLS (E. M. House Papers, CtY).
[1] See EMH to WW, July 17, 1919, n. 1, Vol. 61.

To the Most Reverend Aluigi Cossio, with Enclosure

My dear Monsignor Cossio: [The White House] 15 August, 1919.

Under date of July 28th you were kind enough to send me an autographed letter of Pope Benedict XV, received for me from the Papal Secretary of State. The receipt of the letter gave me great pleasure, and I now avail myself of the opportunity to request you to return to His Holiness, the Pope, the enclosed answer.

Sincerely yours,   Woodrow Wilson

TLS (Letterpress Books, WP, DLC).

E N C L O S U R E

To Benedict XV

Your Holiness: [The White House] 15 August, 1919

I have had the pleasure of receiving at the hands of Monsignor Cossio the recent letter you were kind enough to write me, which I now beg to acknowledge with sincere appreciation. Let me assure you that it was with the greatest pleasure that I lent my influence to safeguarding the missionary interests to which you so graciously refer, and I am happy to say that my colleagues in the Conference were all of the same mind in their wish to throw absolute safeguards around such missions and to keep them within the influences under which they had hitherto been conducted.

I have read with the gravest interest your suggestion about the treatment which should be accorded the ex-Kaiser of Germany and the military officers of high rank who were associated with him in the war, and beg to say that I realize the force of the considerations which you urge. I am obliged to you for stating them so clearly, and shall hope to keep them in mind in the difficult months to come.

With much respect and sincere good wishes for your welfare.

Respectfully and sincerely yours,   [Woodrow Wilson]

TCL (WP, DLC).

From Robert Lansing, with Enclosure

My dear Mr. President: Washington August 15, 1919.

I am transmitting to you herewith a copy of a telegram which has been received from the American Commission to Negotiate Peace regarding the carrying out of the terms of the Treaty with Germany regarding Penalties, and I should be glad to have your views on the suggestions contained therein.

You will recall that it was agreed by the Allied and Associated Governments to submit a list of those who must be handed over to justice under the above-mentioned terms of the Treaty, and I have cabled to Paris to ascertain if this list has been prepared and, if so, what names appear thereon.

Faithfully yours,   Robert Lansing

Aug 18—Prest
Only a few of most guilty should be called. RL[1]

TLS (SDR, RG 59, 763.72119/6373, DNA).
  [1] See RL to FLP, Aug. 21, 1919.

E   N   C   L   O   S   U   R   E

Paris. August 14, 1919.

Urgent. 3682. Confidential for Lansing.

Please refer to section one of Mission's telegram number 3472 August 3, section one of Mission's 3594 August 9 and section four of Mission's 3660 of August 13.[1]

In his letter of August 4 addressed to Marshal Foch[2] General Dupont stated that he found Erzberger's argument well founded; namely, that the handing over of the guilty will bring about a crisis; disorders followed by a Haase Government with the most communistic of the independents as members, the revolt of a large majority of the troops on whom the present government now relies, then communism if not anarchy. Dupont recommended we compromise and proposed that we ask for the Emperor, Tirpitz, if we insist upon it, also the commanders of submarines who torpedoed hospital ships, commanders of prison camps distinguished by excessive harshness, commanders of lines of communications personally guilty of assassination and theft and the judges of Miss Cavell and of Captain Fryatt.[3]

Clemenceau stated that he believed that what Erzberger had said was true and was confirmed by both civil and military French agents. For his part he would abandon nothing given under the treaty. What he proposed was to execute the treaty bit by bit. In order to help the Erzberger government to live on for a few months he proposed that we ask for a few prominent culprits and defer the demand for the rest.

Mr. Balfour stated that he could not himself take a decision on the point in view of British public opinion and that he would have to consult Mr. Lloyd George.

There seemed to be three possible plans: first, to carry out the treaty to the letter and ask for the culprits at once; second (Clemenceau's plan), to ask for a few and put off the demand for the remainder; and third, to abandon that part of the treaty entirely and only insist on the surrender of a very few.

From the information in my possession it would seem to be true that the Erzberger Government will fall if it loses the support of the army. Please let me know the President's wishes in the matter as soon as possible.   American Mission.

T telegram (SDR, RG 59, 763.72119/6373, DNA).
  ¹ Ammission to RL, No. 3472, Aug. 3, 1919, T telegram (SDR, RG 256, 180.03501/21, DNA); FLP to RL, No. 3594, Aug. 9, 1919, T telegram (SDR, RG 256, 180.03501/25, DNA); and Ammission to RL, No. 3660, Aug. 12, 1919, T telegram (SDR, RG 256, 180.03501/28, DNA).
  ² Referred to in the last telegram just cited.
  ³ About these cases, see, respectively, R. U. Johnson to WW, Oct. 22, 1915, n. 1, Vol. 35, and n. 9 to the Enclosure printed with RL to WW, Aug. 22, 1916 (second letter of that date), Vol. 38.

Two Telegrams from Frank Lyon Polk to Robert Lansing

Paris August 15, 1919

3705. Strictly confidential for the Secretary of State from Polk.

Your 2797, August 12 noon not received here until 11:20 p.m. 14th.

I have kept in close touch with White in Italian matter and usually have had him see Tittoni outside of conferences. White left yesterday for a week as he was tired out.

Am sending you today a telegram in regard to Thracian situation. Please do all you can to get the President to make a prompt decision. Situation very irritating personally as I have to fight hard with all the other delegates and now find that no compromise is possible although I asked over a week ago what the scope of my authority was. Do not see how it is possible to insist on East and West Thrace being included in the international state. The compromise proposed has objections but has practically been accepted by the other governments and will be accepted at a pinch by Venizelos. I am perfectly willing to accept the plan put up by Venizelos which will be cabled later today, if the President so decides but think it is poor plan from many angles. What we need is a decision and I beg that you will help me all you can.

Polk,   Ammission.

T telegram (SDR, RG 256, 186.3411/750A, DNA).

Paris August 15, 1919.

3702. Strictly Confidential for the Secretary of State from Polk. Your 2798, August twelfth just received. Our delegation has been embarrassed this week as all parties have been pressing for a settlement of the Thracian question and we had no instructions as to the scope of our authority to compromise the proposal that all of Eastern Thrace and West Thrace should be part of the international state of Constantinople was strenuously opposed by all the European Governments. It is probable that the main objection rests on the doubt as to who will have the mandate of Constantinople if the United States does not take it. The European Governments are so jealous of one another that they would not be willing that such a large state should be in the hands of a European power. In other words France does not want Great Britain to have this large state and Great Britain does not want France to have it. For that reason the suggestion that the line be extended to Kavalla could not be forced on the Peace Conference and also because the Greeks already possessed Port and it would make Venizelos position absolutely impossible at home if it were taken away from them. In the absence of an answer to our request for instructions and in view of the fact that the whole Bulgarian treaty was held up on account of this matter we have been trying to work out a compromise. The compromise which is acceptable to the commission and to Coolidge (Johnson is absent)[1] is in the rough, to leave the southern coast of Bulgarian Thrace to Greece as far as Maronia with a territory to the north sufficiently ample to protect the line of the railroad. The eastern portion of Bulgarian Thrace is to form an international state bounded on the west by the new Greek frontier as far as its northeastern corner, then by a line running east and north to the Maritza River. International state to be bounded on the east by the Turkish Bulgarian frontier according to the arrangement of 1915. Cession to Greece in East Thrace of territory east and south of Bulgarian frontier of 1915 to include Adrianople to line running roughly from a little below Midia to Gulf of Saros. The territory east of this line to go to the Constantinople mandatory. More exact details follow immediately.[2]

We quite see that the compromise has many objections but in

view of Venizelos position at home and in view of the Greek population in the southern part of East Thrace we felt that this was the best that could be done. Bulgarian access to the sea is protected and the access from East Thrace to West Thrace is also assured. If this compromise is not accepted we are frankly at a complete loss as to how to move as we are convinced that the powers will not accept an international state for East and West Thrace and we must confess that their objections under the circumstances are reasonable. All agree that the fate of Venizelos is sealed in Greece if it were known that they were to lose both East and West Thrace. This compromise also tentatively reached only after arduous and, at times, acrimonious negotiations by the experts and after repeated discussions in the Supreme Council. It is accepted by the British (*) obligations to Venizelos in regard to this territory. The British are not bound by any formal obligation to support him.

The compromise that appeals to us has been set forth roughly in this telegram and will be more fully set forth in later telegram. Venizelos acutely opposed to this plan will probably accept it if he feels he can do no better. In view, however, of his strong feeling on the subject and in view of the fact that he has repeatedly said that if the President were only here he would have fared better, I have requested him to send me a letter setting forth his arguments in favor of the so called Tardieu-Venizelos plan and have promised to forward it immediately to President for his consideration with such arguments as he chose to make. The details of this plan will be set out fully and will be cabled today or tomorrow.[3] Roughly it gives the major part of West Thrace, including the whole coast, to Greece and it interna[tional]izes Dedeagatch and the railroad, but does not give as much to East Thrace as contemplated in our compromise.

I earnestly hope that some decision can be sent us at the earliest possible moment as the Bulgarian treaty is being held up by this question alone. The compromise plan is far from perfect, but it will, we believe, insure peace in this section of the Balkans, which has been a consideration we have tried to keep in mind.

Polk.[4]

T telegram (SDR, RG 59, 763.72119/6198, DNA).
    [1] That is, Archibald Cary Coolidge and Douglas Wilson Johnson.
    [2] FLP to RL, No. 3703, Aug. 15, 1919, T telegram (SDR, RG 256, 868.00/178A, DNA).
    [3] FLP to RL, Aug. 16, 1919.
    [4] A copy of this telegram was sent to Wilson on August 18, 1919.

From Robert Lansing

My dear Mr. President: Washington August 15, 1919.

In accordance with the directions contained in your letter of August 8th, a conference, at which I presided, was held on August 14th at the Department of State. It was attended by the Secretary of the Treasury, the Chairman of the Federal Trade Commission, Governor Harding of the Federal Reserve Board, Mr. Bernard M. Baruch, Mr. Eugene E. Meyer, Jr., of the War Finance Corporation, Mr. Norman Davis, Doctor Kennedy,[1] in behalf of the Secretary of Commerce and Mr. Lawrence Bennett,[2] in behalf of Mr. Vance C. McCormick.

The problems and difficulties confronting American interests in connection with foreign commerce were thoroughly discussed. It was the opinion of the conference and particularly that of Mr. Baruch, Mr. Davis, the Secretary of the Treasury and Mr. Meyer, that the nature of these problems is such that the different branches of the government can render no really material aid to American firms engaged in foreign trade until the ratification of the Treaty of Peace removes many doubts and settles many questions now pending which tend to disturb the confidence of the banking and business world.

The question of a closer coordination of the efforts of the different government agencies to aid foreign commerce was taken up and the conference believes that the Economic Liaison Committee, which was formed in March last and which meets every Wednesday in the Office of the Foreign Trade Adviser[3] of the Department of State, is competently fulfilling this need. This committee was organized by the Foreign Trade Adviser and is composed of representatives of the following government agencies; Treasury Department, War Department, Navy Department, Department of Commerce, Department of the Interior, Department of Agriculture, Department of Labor, United States Tariff Commission, Federal Trade Commission, Federal Reserve Board, United States Shipping Board, United States Railroad Administration, and the War Finance Corporation. Its members, who were designated by the chiefs of their respective departments, meet to exchange information and discuss questions arising in connection with the foreign trade of the United States.

The question of American representation on the Reparations Commission was also taken up. Its great importance was fully realized by the members of the conference and, at my request, the Secretary of the Treasury, Mr. Baruch and Mr. Davis have been constituted a committee to consider the selection of a representative to replace Mr. Dulles on the Interim Reparations Commission.

It was the opinion of the conference that American interests would be gravely jeopardized by the omission of American representation on the Interim Reparations Commission and that some one should be selected to replace Mr. Dulles who will eventually become the American member of the permanent commission. I shall not fail to acquaint you with the result of the recommendations of the committee on this subject.   Faithfully yours,   Robert Lansing

TLS (WP, DLC).
    [1] Philip Benjamin Kennedy, director of the Bureau of Foreign and Domestic Commerce.
    [2] Lawyer, formerly secretary of the War Trade Board, at this time chief of the War Trade Board Section of the Department of State.
    [3] Julius Gareche Lay, career officer in the consular service and Acting Foreign Trade Advisor in the State Department.

From Peyton Conway March

My dear Mr. President: Washington. August 15, 1919.

In accordance with your letter of August 15th,[1] I have cabled General Pershing directing that he retain five thousand combatant troops, with the necessary auxiliary force, in addition to those in the occupied region on the Rhine.

                              Sincerely yours,   P. C. March

TLS (WP, DLC).
    [1] It is missing in both the Wilson and March Papers, DLC.

Edward Mandell House to Robert Lansing

                              London. August 15, 1919.

Important, 2818. I would appreciate a cable giving your forecast of the situation regarding the Treaty, when will the Committee report it and when will the Senate come to a vote, what will be the probable result, would it be of advantage or otherwise for Great Britain, France and Italy to ratify soon. I hope that the President and you are keeping well. Edward House.   Davis.

Aug 20—Prest No definite opinion Let them ratify RL

T telegram (R. Lansing Papers, DLC).

From Robert Lansing

My dear Mr. President: Washington August 16, 1919.

I enclose a second memorandum from Mr. Poole containing the draft of a statement on Bolsheviks.[1] I asked him to prepare this draft because I thought it was the best way to have his ideas in definite form. The draft begins on page 2 of the memorandum and ends on page 8. It impresses me as a very well tempered document and worth careful consideration.

Faithfully yours,   Robert Lansing

TLS (WP, DLC).
  [1] It is printed as an Enclosure with WW to RL, Aug. 21, 1919.

From Francis Patrick Walsh, with Enclosure

Dear Mr. President: New York August 16, 1919.

Enclosed please find statement issued today by the American Commission on Irish Independence.

The Commission desires to call your attention to the suggestions made in the statement, with the hope that you will use your powerful influence to the end that the intolerable conditions with reference to the free movement of citizens of the world, and especially the representatives of small nations and struggling peoples, may be removed.

With considerations of our great respect and esteem, we are,

Sincerely,   AMERICAN COMMISSION ON
IRISH INDEPENDENCE,
By Frank P. Walsh Chairman.

TLS (WP, DLC).

ENCLOSURE

New York City, August 16, 1919.

STATEMENT OF AMERICAN COMMISSION ON IRISH INDEPENDENCE.

The first thing the liberty-loving people of the United States and the world must do is to demand, as a matter of inherent right, that any human being has a right to go freely into any country upon the face of the globe, being strictly amenable to the laws of the jurisdiction in which he happens to be, whether those laws are good or bad.

At the present time, this world is one vast jail. The jailer is King George V. Passports in and out of Great Britain, as well as all of the countries in which England claims the right to rule, in any form, must run in his name. Any man or woman that does not think and speak in the language of British imperialism, is actually imprisoned within the boundaries of the country in which he or she may be at the time of the discovery of democratic tendencies or thought. No Irish man or woman is allowed to leave the shores of England, Ireland, Scotland, or Wales, except by the consent of the English Government, which consent is always withheld unless the person is known to be bereft of any national spirit. England has now extended her influence in this respect throughout the world.

John A. Murphy, a distinguished American citizen desires to go from Paris to London. He must request the American State Department to issue him his passport. Mr. Murphy, a resident of Buffalo, New York, is a law-abiding citizen, whose whole life stamps him as a man of unblemished reputation and splendid character; but he sympathizes with Ireland in its struggle for freedom and speaks plainly in support of the right of self-determination for all peoples. Mr. Murphy applied to the United States Government, his own country, for a passport to England. The American State Department, to his amazement, submitted his request to the English Government. The passport was refused. This estimable man must realize, so far as he is concerned, that human liberty is not for him. Liberty cannot be defined as merely permitting one to remain outside of a jail or penitentiary, but must be held to be the right of a man to come and go freely, without let or hindrance, anywhere or everywhere, answerable for his conduct to the laws of any country in which he may be.

Take the case of the representatives of small and oppressed nations, who found their way to Paris for the purpose of appealing to the powers for the relief of oppressed people, whom they represent. England lets them step into France, and then raises its barrier against them, so that they cannot return to their homes, nor can they come to America, for a century and a half the refuge of the oppressed of all nations; nor can they go to any of the English possessions which now cover the world, so they become virtual prisoners in a foreign land, away from home and friends. This is the case today of the Egyptian Delegation, composed of the highest elected officials of the Egyptian people, and men distinguished for their work along the line of education and other ameliorative activities in behalf of their own people.

Imagine the situation if the League of Nations in its present form is adopted. The Secretariat is in London under the shadow of the steeple of Westminster. The Secretary General is Sir Eric Drummond. What chance has a small nation, or its representatives, to get before that body? They would not only be excluded from the building, but they would be excluded from the country, in which the Secretariat is located.

Before a League of Nations is adopted, provision should be made for a joint Secretariat. If an English nobleman *must* be one, then America, with one voice should demand that an American democrat be another. Many of our national boards, during the war, had joint chairmen and joint secretaries. It is absolutely essential, in the case of any international body which is given power to act in matters that affect the lives of millions of people, that they ought not to be subjected to the sole domination of a monarchy.

If the League of Nations is ratified, a distinguished American appointed by our Government and devoted to the principles for which 300,000 American men were killed, gassed and wounded, should have joint control of the executive operations of such a body. The demand for this must be nationwide. It will be difficult enough, at best, for the representative of any nation oppressed by England, or any of the powers dominant in the League of Nations, to get before it. Under the unchecked domination of King George and his titled servants, it will be absolutely impossible.

To begin a true reign of democracy in the world, the jail doors erected throughout the world by the passport system must be battered down by democrats who understand the true meaning of the words "liberty" and "freedom."   Frank P Walsh

TS MS (WP, DLC).

From John Barton Payne

Dear Mr. President: Washington August 16, 1919

Answering your very kind letter of the 14th enclosing the statement from the Italian Ambassador as to the coal situation in Italy:

I have conferred fully with our Division of Operations and we are prepared, beginning September 1, to take for Italy from 75,000 to 100,000 tons per month. This is probably more than they will supply, so that I think you may say that we will provide the facilities for the transportation of such coal as Italy may provide.

Seventeen ships, deadweight tonnage of 105,503, are now actually in coal service for Italy or have been fixed for the Italian coal service. This, however, is for commercial coal and not for the Italian Government as such.

In providing for the tonnage beginning September 1, I take it the Italian representatives will give us adequate notice so that there may be no hitch.

Please accept my cordial thanks for your kind personal expression.   Yours very truly,   John Barton Payne

TLS (WP, DLC).

Frank Lyon Polk to Robert Lansing

[Paris] 16 August 1919

3704. PRIORITY STRICTLY CONFIDENTIAL FOR THE SECRETARY OF
STATE FROM POLK

Referring to my 3702 August 15, 8:00 p.m.

The Tardieu proposal very roughly given is for Greece to receive
the whole of western Thrace south of line starting below the northeast corner of present Greek-Bulgarian frontier, this line to run east
to point north of Gumuljina then northeast to Bulgarian frontier
and then following a curve which passes about half way between
Adrianople and Kirk Kilisse and ultimately comes out on the Gulf
of Saros. The part of Thrace east of this curved line to go to the
International State. The city and port of Dedeagach and the railway connecting with Bulgaria to be internationalized. I quote the
following letter just received from Venizelos:

"As I had the honor to explain to you in person this morning I
consider that Mr. Tardieu's proposal of internationalizing the city
and port of Dedeagatch and the railway connecting this port with
Bulgaria is unquestionably the best of the two proposed solutions
and at the same time it fully assures to Bulgaria an economic outlet
to the Aegean Sea.

The other solution, namely, that of the creation of an International State comprising the eastern half of Western Thrace, is an
unnatural solution and severing as it does, the territorial connection of Greek Eastern Thrace from the rest of the Greek state, cre-
ates a condition full of dangers which, I am informed, Mr. Clemenceau has already pointed out.

In case however, the American Delegation would insist on their
opinion to create this International State, may I be allowed to remark that there is no reason whatever why any part of northern
Thrace should be attributed to Bulgaria. This northern territory in
question contains 100,000 of purely Musselman population, after
subtracting the 13,000 Bulgarians in Achi-Tselombi, which district
can be attributed to Bulgaria. Bearing in mind the repeatedly expressed desire of the Musselman deputies of Western Thrace, and
also their last cable to the President of the Peace Conference under
date of August 12, 1919, there can remain no doubt as to the persistence of the desire of this Musselman population to be permanently delivered from the Bulgarian rule. It would therefore be
wholly unjustifiable not to include this Turkish population—according to the principle of self-determination—in the International
State to be created. Moreover, their inclusion in this International
State, would materially lessen the common frontier between

Greece and Bulgaria, especially at the point where the projected new frontiers of Greece, will be weakest.

Permit me once more, my dear Minister, to point out that Bulgaria, even after the loss of Thrace—to which country she has no ethnical right whatever—will have a population of 4,500,000, a figure which corresponds exactly with that of the whole of the Bulgarian nation, whereas Greece, even after the probable realization of her national claims, will have a population of 6,700,000 in Greek territory out of a total existing number of 8,300,000 Greeks.

And what I ask in the name of Greece is not that she should be favored because she waged a just war on the side of the victors, but that she should not be treated with less consideration and with a spirit of lesser justice than that with which Bulgaria is being treated, which latter country has waged an unjust war."

Polk   Ammission

T telegram (SDR, RG 256, 868.00/178B, DNA).

From Robert Lansing, with Enclosures

My dear Mr. President: Washington August 16, 1919.

You asked me to secure Mr. Baruch's comment on the attached telegram. It was submitted to Mr. Baruch and I return it herewith with his memorandum.   Faithfully yours,   Robert Lansing

Aug. 18. Prest Advise Dulles accordingly   RL[1]

TLS (SDR, RG 59, 763.72119/6810, DNA).
   [1] Baruch's comments were conveyed to Dulles in RL to Ammission, No. 2876, Aug. 19, 1919, T telegram (SDR, RG 256, 181.73/13, DNA).

E N C L O S U R E   I

Paris. August 12, 1919.

3627. German Government has submitted to committee on minutes [motion] of reparation commission a list of food and raw material required to be bought abroad, which list is summarized below. German note further asks whether supplies listed can be furnished by Allied and Associated Governments and if so quantity, quality and price. It is further stated that the German Government will subsequently state the extent to which it will request that the food and raw material be paid out of the initial twenty billion marks payment pursuant to Article 235 of the treaty.

Following is a summary of the list a complete copy of which is being forwarded by pouch:

Elihu Root

William Howard Taft

Gilbert Monell Hitchcock

Henry Cabot Lodge

Philander Chase Knox

Key Pittman

Porter James McCumber

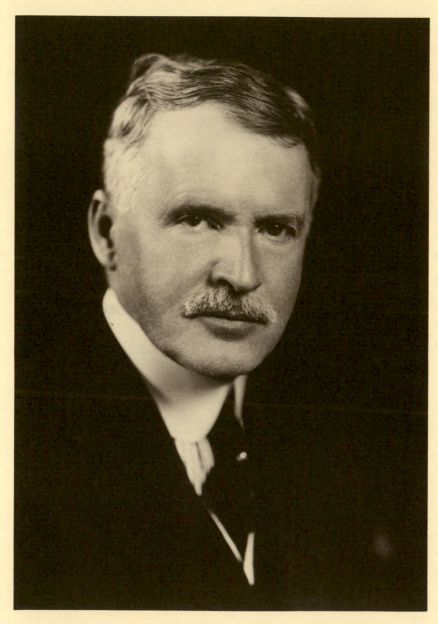

Selden Palmer Spencer

One. Foodstuffs for next four months; meat 160,000 tons, fat 60,000 tons, cereal (including rice and dried vegetables) 800,000 tons, milk the value of six million marks gold, potatoes not yet determined.

Two. Forage and fertilizer for next twelve months; meal cakes 900,000 tons; bran 600,000 tons, maize 1,200,000 tons, barley 850,000 tons, "Thomas" phosphates one million tons, raw phosphates 1,500,000 tons.

Three. Raw material for coming two months: cotton, forty-two thousand tons, East India cotton twenty thousand bales, nako cotton twenty thousand bales, qualities of cotton thread two thousand tons, fine thread one thousand tons, flax six thousand tons, flax thread five thousand tons, lybor sisal fiber *thousand five hundred thousand* soft hemp, five thousand tons, jute fifteen thousand tons, oakum, three hundred tons, cocoa fiber six hundred tons, silk, all kinds, three hundred and fifty tons, bourettee Schaomae three hundred and fifty tons, Schaomaeges piche three hundred fifty tons, washed wool fifteen hundred tons, spun and combed wools two thousand tons; materials for fancy fabrics, seven thousand tons.

Four. Raw materials per month: Heavy leathers, seven thousand nine hundred tons; upper leather (bachettepe) six hundred and thirty-seven thousand pieces; (?) sserfelle, two hundred tons; Horse leather, eight thousand five hundred pieces; sheep and lamb skins (quantity not specified); goat skins five hundred thousand pieces; kid (quantity not specified); vegetable tanning matter (?) hundred thousand, or, pure tanning matter twenty-five thousand tons.

Five. Metals required by Germany in next six months lead forty thousand tons; nickle nine hundred tons; pewter, six thousand tons; tin, fifteen thousand tons; electrolized copper, twenty-four thousand tons; copper ore twenty-four thousand tons; zinc ore, eighteen thousand tons; antimony eighteen hundred tons; aluminum nine thousand tons; mercury three thousand tons; bismuth seven thousand two hundred tons; silver eighteen tons, platinum one hundred and fifty kilograms.

Six. Miscellaneous: Raw rubber two thousand five hundred tons; bone four thousand two hundred carloads; raw glue thirty-four hundred car loads; turpentine three thousand tons; residues sixteen thousand tons; copal seven hundred and fifty tons, lacquer gum three hundred tons; asbestos thirty-six hundred tons.

Polk.

T telegram (SDR, RG 59, 763.72119/6131, DNA).

E N C L O S U R E   I I

A Memorandum by Bernard Mannes Baruch

New York [c. Aug. 15, 1919]

Referring to the list of materials requested by the German Government, a large amount of these could be furnished by American producers if assurances were given that payment would not be interfered with by The Interum [Interim] Reparation Commission. As the United States does not deal in these materials, the Germans should get in touch with American producers and exporters. We should advise the Allies and the German Government to this effect.

This demand shows the extreme necessity and advisability of having an American representative on the Interum Reparation Commission in order that American interests may receive fair treatment in the sale of these large amounts of food and raw materials.

Among the items which we could supply largely, are cotton, lead, nickel, copper, zinc, aluminum, mercury, phosphate and turpentine. We could also furnish to some extent, some of the other articles.

T MS (SDR, RG 59, 763.72119/6811, DNA).

From Robert Lansing, with Enclosure

My dear Mr. President: Washington August 16, 1919.

I enclose herewith a communication from the British Chargé here in relation to the formation of an International Economic Council to act pending the organization of the League of Nations.

Will you be good enough to indicate to me what reply I should make and what action, if any, I should take in the matter?

Faithfully yours,   Robert Lansing

Aug 18—Prest
Has any scheme been proposed & if so what   RL

TLS (SDR, RG 59, 763.72119/6517, DNA).

ENCLOSURE

Ronald Charles Lindsay to Robert Lansing

URGENT.

No. 603.

Dear Mr. Secretary:　　　　　　　　[Washington] August 15, 1919.

I have received a telegram from Earl Curzon of Kedleston informing me that the Supreme Economic Council, acting on instructions from the Council of the Heads of States (Mr. Wilson being present)[1] prepared a scheme for forming an International Economic Council pending the Constitution of the League of Nations. The first meeting of this was intended to take place at Washington on or before September 15th.

Great Britain, Italy, France and Belgium have signified their adherence but it is stated that Mr. Hoover, the American Delegate, is without instructions. I am therefore instructed to enquire unofficially how the United States Government regard the scheme, and to express the hope that they may at an early moment be in a position to announce a decision in this matter.

Believe me, my dear Mr. Secretary,

　　　　　　　　　Very sincerely yours,　　R. C. Lindsay

TLS (SDR, RG 59, 763.72119/6517, DNA).
[1] See Mantoux's and Hankey's notes of a meeting of the Council of Four printed at June 28, 1919, 10:30 a.m. and 11 a.m., Vol. 61.

From Arthur James Balfour

PRIVATE.

Dear President Wilson,　　　　　　　Paris. August 16th, 1919.

I have been asked by the Glasgow University Unionist and Liberal Clubs to forward to you the enclosed request[1] to accept nomination as their joint candidate for the Lord Rectorship of the University of Glasgow.

I have ventured to accede to the request made to me, for I feel that the honour which your tenure of the office of Lord Rector would confer upon the University is one which I, as a past Lord Rector myself, should endeavour to secure. On the other hand, I fully realise that circumstances may make it inconvenient or impossible for you to accept the nomination; and, though I, in common with the Students of the University, shall in that case be deeply disappointed, we must all recognise that your decision must depend upon other circumstances than our personal wishes.

I ought perhaps to add that the Address, which is the only work required of a Lord Rector, may be delivered at any period of his three years' tenure of office which suits.

Yr sy   Arthur James Balfour

TLS (WP, DLC).
¹ It is missing in WP, DLC.

From Robert Lansing, with Enclosure

My dear Mr. President: Washington August 18, 1919.

I have had Mr. Fletcher prepare a direct reply to the questions asked in your memorandum of August fourth on the subject of Mexico, which I beg to enclose. I return also his previous memorandum.¹   Faithfully yours,   Robert Lansing

Aug 26/19

Prest has seen this but does not think it time to act now   RL

¹ See WW to RL, Aug. 4, 1919 (second letter of that date).

E N C L O S U R E

From Henry Prather Fletcher

CONFIDENTIAL MEMORANDUM

My dear Mr. President: [Washington] August 18, 1919.

The Secretary of State has referred to me for direct reply your memorandum of August 4th last, in which you ask, in reference to my memorandum on Mexico, dated March 1st,

(a) Whether I would now make the same analysis and the same suggestions as to courses of action,

and,

(b) If the same course of action were still suggested, what I would propose to do if Mexico did not respond to our "call" upon her to do her duty internally and externally.

In respectful reply, I beg to state that the analysis of the Mexican situation as presented in my memorandum of March 1st (returned herewith) need not be essentially changed. Conditions have rather deteriorated than improved since that time.

POLICY.

I do not believe that the doubt as to whether the Carranza Government would or could respond to our "call" to perform its duty as a government internally and externally, etc., relieves this Government of the responsibility and duty of making every effort to secure relief, through the agencies of government now dominating that country, from the almost intolerable conditions existing in Mexico.

The alternative to our calling upon the recognized Government of Mexico to perform its duties is, I fear, a gradual drifting until, by some sudden emergency, intervention is forced upon us. To avert this I believe the Government of the United States should make every effort to impress upon the Carranza Government, and incidentally the Mexican people, the grave responsibility resting upon them.

The warning served upon the Carranza Government in our note of July 22nd in the Catron case (this note being based upon a telegram which had received your previous approval)[1] seems to have had an awakening and beneficial effect, in spite of Mr. Carranza's characteristically impertinent and evasive reply.[2]

The press of Mexico and such public opinion as exists there is greatly aroused by the agitation in Congress and in the press of this country of the Mexican question. I believe our "call," if Mr. Carranza can be made to believe that it is earnestly made and seriously meant, has at least a chance of success.

I would respectfully suggest, however, that upon the next serious occasion the Department address a carefully prepared note to the Mexican Government, reviewing temperately and in detail the history of our relations since the failure of the Atlantic City Conference,[3] and making therein a last effort to avert intervention.

I would further suggest that a copy of this note be given confidentially to the other Latin American Governments.

Should this last effort prove unavailing, I would propose that this Government then take, alone or in conjunction with other governments, steps to restore orderly conditions in Mexico.

Henry P. Fletcher

TLS (SDR, RG 59, 812.00/23111b, DNA).
  [1] For which, see the Enclosure printed with FLP to WW, July 18, 1919, Vol. 61. The note sent on July 21, not 22, 1919, is printed in *FR 1919*, II, 572.
  [2] Printed in *ibid.*, pp. 573-74.
  [3] That is, the negotiations of the Joint High Commission of the United States and Mexico about an agreement for the withdrawal of the American troops from Mexican territory and the protection of the American-Mexican border. About these negotiations, which took place in New London, Conn., and Atlantic City, N. J., in the autumn of 1916, see the index references under "Mexico and the United States" in Vols. 38 and 40.

Edward Mandell House to Woodrow Wilson and Robert Lansing

London. August 18, 1919.

Important. 2819. For the President and Secretary of State.

The Supreme Economic Council wish to meet in Washington during (September?) provided you approve. They are awaiting word from you before making definite plans. Will you not let me know your wishes? Edward House.   Davis.

Aug. 20—Prest
No decision until treaty ratified   RL

T telegram (R. Lansing Papers, DLC).

John William Davis to Robert Lansing

London. Aug. 18, 1919.

Urgent. 2831. At interview this afternoon for that purpose Curzon states that French sentiment seems hostile to Anglo-Persian agreement[1] and French Minister at Teheran[2] disposed to foment dissatisfaction, in which he hopes for assistance of American Minister.[3] Requests that latter be put on guard and asked to preserve friendly attitude.   Davis.

Aug 20/ Prest. Do not approve at all. Secrecy. Impair friendly peace   RL

T telegram (R. Lansing Papers, DLC).
  [1] In this agreement, negotiated secretly and concluded and published on August 9, 1919, the British government promised again, "in the most categorical manner," to respect the independence and territorial integrity of Persia. It promised, moreover, to lend administrative and military advisers to the Persian government; to furnish it with munitions and military equipment; to provide or arrange a "substantial loan" for Persia; to encourage joint Anglo-Persian enterprises aimed at the improvement of the Persian railroad system, the extension of trade, and the prevention of famine; and to cooperate in the revision of the existing customs tariffs which would take into account the legitimate interests of Persia and promote the prosperity of the country. In addition, in two separate letters, addressing the demands which Persia had intended to present to the peace conference, the British government pledged to work toward the abrogation of the Anglo-Russian agreement of 1907, which had established British and Russian spheres of influence in Persia; to support Persia's claim for reparation of damages suffered at the hands of other belligerents; and to cooperate in the rectification of Persia's frontier at certain points. For this agreement, the reaction to it, and its ultimate fate, see H. W. V. Temperley, ed., *A History of the Peace Conference of Paris* (6 vols., London, 1920-1924), VI, 211-17.
  [2] Charles-Eudes Bonin.
  [3] John Lawrence Caldwell, American Minister at Teheran since 1914.

Robert Lansing to Frank Lyon Polk

Washington, August 18, 1919.

2866 With further reference your 3682 August 14, 12 pm.[1]
President favors Clemenceau plan namely to ask for only a few of most conspicuous culprits.   Lansing

TS telegram (SDR, RG 59, 763.72119/6178, DNA).
  [1] Printed as an Enclosure with RL to WW, Aug. 15, 1919 (first letter of that date).

Two News Reports

[*Aug. 19, 1919*]

PRESIDENT DEFENDS TREATY TO SENATORS
FOR 'INTEPRETATIVE RESERVATIONS' ONLY

Washington, Aug. 19.—In an epoch-making conference at the White House today between President Wilson and members of the Foreign Relations Committee of the Senate the President urged the ratification of the treaty with Germany without change, saying he believed it a formidable vehicle for preventing a future world war.

He made it plain that he would not oppose interpretative reservations, which would embrace the "understanding" of the United States as to certain features, but he was unalterably opposed, he told the Senators, to any reservations or amendments that would have the effect of recommitting the treaty to the signatory powers.

The President agreed, after being pressed by Senator Fall, Republican of New Mexico, that to make changes in the League of Nations covenant would not necessitate obtaining the assent of Germany. The President had hitherto been quoted as maintaining that Germany would have to pass on any reservations the Senate might make. His acknowledgement was hailed by the Republican Senators as a gain in the battle for changes in the covenant.

The President, amplifying his point that Germany's consent would not be necessary in any changes made to the League covenant, said that Germany had already agreed to accept any amendments made in the covenant, up to the time she entered the League. The President insisted that no amendment ought to be embraced in the resolution of ratification, as that would affect the treaty itself, and necessitate sending it back, not only to Germany, but all other signatories. But as to the League covenant, he said, any reservations the United States desired to make could be inserted without obtaining Germany's assent, before the latter is admitted to the League.

During three hours and a half of discussion and questions the President dwelt with the utmost candor on the various phases of the treaty, replying frankly and freely to the interrogations put to him on the entire range of the treaty, from the League of Nations covenant to the Shantung agreement.

The conference was characterized by an entire lack of antagonism on the part of Senators who have bitterly assailed the treaty in the Senate debates. The President was in an amiable mood, smiling often as he answered pertinent queries and dealing at all times with the committee in a genial spirit.

The President at the start assured the Senators that he was eager to reply to all questions. The Republican Senators met him full way and fired innumerable questions, always couched in courteous language. Only once, when Senator Harding, Republican, of Ohio asked the President about the moral obligations which the President said were imposed upon the United States under the League covenant, did the Chief Executive appear to lose patience.

Before the questions began, the President read from a memorandum he had prepared urging that the Senate come to a speedy ratification of the treaty. On opening the conference, he explained that he thought it advisable to make a statement, after which he would answer any questions.

JOVIAL LUNCHEON AFTER CONFERENCE

[*Aug. 19, 1919*]

Washington, Aug. 19.—Members of the Senate Foreign Relations Committee were guests of President Wilson at luncheon at the White House for an hour immediately following the conclusion of the East Room conference over the treaty situation.

Before luncheon there had been a straightaway discussion of the treaty for three hours and twenty-five minutes, the conference having opened promptly at 10 o'clock and closed at 1:25 o'clock. At that hour Senator Lodge, addressing the President, said:

"Mr. President, I do not wish to interfere in any way, but the conference has now lasted about three hours and a half, and it is a half an hour after the luncheon hour."

The President was too genial a host not to be prepared to entertain his guests after such a hard session.

"Will you gentlemen not come in to lunch with me?" he replied to Senator Lodge. "It will be very delightful."

The President and the Senators went into the State dining room, where a table had been spread for the entire committee.

There were just three members of the Senate committee absent from the luncheon, Senator Shields, who was unable to attend the conference; Senator Williams, who had a prior engagement, and Senator Fall, who excused himself from the conference because he had arranged to meet his wife, who is not well.

Mrs. Wilson was not present, but luncheoned in another part of the White House with Private Secretary Tumulty and Director of the Mint Baker.[1]

President Wilson and his guests sat down at the table at 1:30 o'clock, and luncheon was not over until 2:45 o'clock. There was

[1] Raymond Thomas Baker.

some speculation as to whether the subjects of the conference might not have been discussed at the luncheon. Some were even suggesting that the President might find it convenient to tell the Senators at this conference some State secrets that he would not tell them in the wide-open conference that preceded the luncheon. But this was far from the truth. The luncheon was a thoroughly informal and genial social gathering, without any serious discussion of the treaty, and at the conclusion all the Senators were in good humor when they emerged from the White House.

The Senators said afterwards that the President was in a most happy frame of mind and that the luncheon was a delightful function at which the President was a good-natured host and that he and his guests exchanged many stories. The President told of the amazement that was created among many men in Paris over the freedom with which he walked around the streets of the city, saying it was frequently pointed out to him that President Poincaré did not do that. Part of the talk related to the sense of humor of the English. This grew out of a remark made by one of the Senators to the President. The President said that he found that the British had a very fine sense of humor, and went on to mention various of the British periodicals in support of his statement.

The President's spread for his guests included cantaloupe, spring lamb chops, peas, rice, cold Virginia ham, a salad, an ice, and coffee. It was also a "dry" luncheon, no liquors being served. One of the Senators present said tonight it was a meal that could not be duplicated at any leading Washington hotel for $5 a plate at regular menu prices.

Immediately after the conference and just before going into the dining room with his guests, the President, who, of course, was fully cognizant of all the plans that had been made for making the stenographic report of the conference public, descended from the East Room into the basement where the newspaper men were crowded around the tables of the stenographers.

"Is this novel experiment measuring up to your satisfaction," the President asked, addressing the newspaper men, who were soon thronging about in from all parts of the corridors.

"Yes," came the response from several at once.

"You have been getting the report of the proceedings right along?" the President then asked.

"Yes, everything is entirely satisfactory," he was assured.

"I am very much gratified," continued the President.

"Do you care to make a statement," one newspaper man asked.

"I think," replied the President, with a smile, "I have talked quite enough for one day."

The President then joined the Senators to go in to luncheon with them. After that meal, the President asked Senator Lodge: "Shall we resume the morning conference," saying he would be very glad to do so.

Senator Lodge assured the President that they had no further questions to ask.

After an exchange of pleasantries the President and members of the committee parted.

Unprecedented in every respect as was the conference between President Wilson and members of the Senate Foreign Relations Committee, not less so were the scenes and incidents in the basement floor of the historic mansion, where the dignified main corridor and an oval anteroom were temporarily transformed into a veritable beehive of activity in connection with the carrying out of plans for giving fullest publicity to everything that had occurred.

Both the President and the committee had reached an understanding in their exchange of correspondence in advance of the conference for a shorthand record of every word said so that it might be given to the press as soon as the transcript could be prepared. As time was an essential condition of the requests made by representatives of the press it was incumbent upon those in charge of the arrangement for stenographers to have them record the proceedings in relays, one stenographer from the Senate Committee corps making shorthand notes while four others were transcribing their notes for delivery to the press.

The President had his own stenographer present, but no attempt was made by the White House to duplicate the feat of the Senate stenographers in giving out the record of the proceedings as soon as transcribed. The White House made its own record, which was sent to a downtown office to be mimeographed, after having been transcribed at the White House, and this White House transcript was made public after 9 o'clock tonight.

As considerable room was needed for the working operations of the official stenographic corps and to accommodate the many newspaper men, a large portion of the basement floor was given over to their respective uses. The conference proper was held in the historic East Room, where the bodies of three martyred Presidents—Lincoln, Garfield, and McKinley—had reposed in state; where the weddings of daughters of Presidents have taken place, the room in which brilliant state receptions at the White House are held.

No one was present but the President, sixteen of the seventeen members of the Senate committee, and the officially accredited stenographers. Photographers and members of the press were not admitted. The seventeen men, other than the stenographers, sat most of the time in a circle at the southern end of the East Room. The President sat nearest the southeast corner. On his right sat Senator Lodge, next to Senator Williams. On the President's left sat Senator Swanson, at whose left elbow sat Senator Knox, who was the end man on that part of the interlocutory line. On the west side of the circle, facing the President, sat Senator Borah, with Senator Hitchcock on his left and Senator Brandegee on his right, Senator Brandegee being the other end man. Between Senators Knox and Brandegee stood the tables on which the stenographers worked, one table for the President's stenographer, another for the Senate stenographers. The other Senators completed the north side of the circle, sitting between Senators Hitchcock and Williams.

Five stenographers constituted the Senate's corps, while Charles L. Swem, the President's own stenographer, one of the swiftest in the country, took the entire testimony for the three and one-half hours that the committee talked with the President. Mr. Swem, who was thus pitted against the whole corps of five representing the Senate, has accompanied the President on his trips throughout the United States and went abroad with him to serve as his personal stenographer at the Peace Conference.

A copy of the Senate stenographers' transcript was furnished to him late this afternoon and Mr. Swem went over it for the purpose of endeavoring to ascertain whether any vital errors had been made in the rush of its preparation in carbon copies for the use of the press. Mr. Swem also sent the White House transcript to be mimeographed so that copies also might be available at the White House for reference use later in the evening.

Printed in the *New York Times*, Aug. 20, 1919.

A Conversation with Members of the Senate Foreign Relations Committee

CONFERENCE AT THE WHITE HOUSE.

TUESDAY, AUGUST 19, 1919.

The committee met at the White House at 10 o'clock a.m., pursuant to the invitation of the President, and proceeded to the East Room, where the conference was held.

Present: Hon. Woodrow Wilson, President of the United States, and the following members of the committee: Senators Lodge (chairman), McCumber, Borah, Brandegee, Fall, Knox, Harding,

Johnson, of California, New, Moses, Hitchcock, Williams, Swanson, Pomerene, Smith, and Pittman.

STATEMENT OF THE PRESIDENT.

THE PRESIDENT. Mr. Chairman, I have taken the liberty of writing out a little statement in the hope that it might facilitate discussion by speaking directly on some points that I know have been points of controversy and upon which I thought an expression of opinion would not be unwelcome.[1] I am sincerely glad that the committee should have responded in this way to my intimation that I would like to be of service to it. I welcome the opportunity for a frank and full interchange of views.

I hope, too, that this conference will serve to expedite your consideration of the treaty of peace. I beg that you will pardon and indulge me if I again urge that practically the whole task of bringing the country back to normal conditions of life and industry waits upon the decision of the Senate with regard to the terms of the peace.

I venture thus again to urge my advice that the action of the Senate with regard to the treaty be taken at the earliest practicable moment because the problems with which we are face to face in the readjustment of our national life are of the most pressing and critical character, will require for their proper solution the most intimate and disinterested cooperation of all parties and all interests, and can not be postponed without manifest peril to our people and to all the national advantages we hold most dear. May I mention a few of the matters which can not be handled with intelligence until the country knows the character of the peace it is to have? I do so only by a very few samples.

The copper mines of Montana, Arizona, and Alaska, for example, are being kept open and in operation only at a great cost and loss, in part upon borrowed money; the zinc mines of Missouri, Tennessee, and Wisconsin are being operated at about one-half their capacity; the lead of Idaho, Illinois, and Missouri reaches only a portion of its former market; there is an immediate need for cotton belting, and also for lubricating oil, which can not be met—all because the channels of trade are barred by war when there is no war. The same is true of raw cotton, of which the Central Empires alone formerly purchased nearly 4,000,000 bales. And these are only examples. There is hardly a single raw material, a single important foodstuff, a single class of manufactured goods which is not in the same case. Our full, normal profitable production waits on peace.

[1] At this point, Wilson began reading the document printed as the draft of a letter to HCL, Aug. 14, 1919.

Our military plans of course wait upon it. We can not intelligently or wisely decide how large a naval or military force we shall maintain or what our policy with regard to military training is to be until we have peace not only, but also until we know how peace is to be sustained, whether by the arms of single nations or by the concert of all the great peoples. And there is more than that difficulty involved. The vast surplus properties of the Army include not food and clothing merely, whose sale will affect normal production, but great manufacturing establishments also which should be restored to their former uses, great stores of machine tools, and all sorts of merchandise which must lie idle until peace and military policy are definitively determined. By the same token there can be no properly studied national budget until then.

The nations that ratify the treaty, such as Great Britain, Belgium, and France, will be in a position to lay their plans for controlling the markets of central Europe without competition from us if we do not presently act. We have no consular agents, no trade representatives there to look after our interests.

There are large areas of Europe whose future will lie uncertain and questionable until their people know the final settlements of peace and the forces which are to administer and sustain it. Without determinate markets our production can not proceed with intelligence or confidence. There can be no stabilization of wages because there can be no settled conditions of employment. There can be no easy or normal industrial credits because there can be no confident or permanent revival of business.

But I will not weary you with obvious examples. I will only venture to repeat that every element of normal life amongst us depends upon and awaits the ratification of the treaty of peace; and also that we can not afford to lose a single summer's day by not doing all that we can to mitigate the winter's suffering, which, unless we find means to prevent it, may prove disastrous to a large portion of the world, and may, at its worst, bring upon Europe conditions even more terrible than those wrought by the war itself.

Nothing, I am led to believe, stands in the way of the ratification of the treaty except certain doubts with regard to the meaning and implication of certain articles of the covenant of the league of nations; and I must frankly say that I am unable to understand why such doubts should be entertained. You will recall that when I had the pleasure of a conference with your committee and with the Committee of the House of Representatives on Foreign Affairs at the White House in March last[2] the questions now most frequently

[2] Actually, on February 26, 1919. See the news report printed at that date in Vol. 55.

asked about the league of nations were all canvassed with a view to their immediate clarification. The covenant of the league was then in its first draft and subject to revision. It was pointed out that no express recognition was given to the Monroe doctrine; that it was not expressly provided that the league should have no authority to act or to express a judgment on matters of domestic policy; that the right to withdraw from the league was not expressly recognized; and that the constitutional right of the Congress to determine all questions of peace and war was not sufficiently safeguarded. On my return to Paris all these matters were taken up again by the commission on the league of nations and every suggestion of the United States was accepted.

The views of the United States with regard to the questions I have mentioned had, in fact, already been accepted by the commission and there was supposed to be nothing inconsistent with them in the draft of the covenant first adopted—the draft which was the subject of our discussion in March—but no objection was made to saying explicitly in the text what all had supposed to be implicit in it. There was absolutely no doubt as to the meaning of any one of the resulting provisions of the covenant in the minds of those who participated in drafting them, and I respectfully submit that there is nothing vague or doubtful in their wording.

The Monroe doctrine is expressly mentioned as an understanding which is in no way to be impaired or interfered with by anything contained in the covenant and the expression "regional understandings like the Monroe doctrine" was used, not because anyone of the conferees thought there was any comparable agreement anywhere else in existence or in contemplation, but only because it was thought best to avoid the appearance of dealing in such a document with the policy of a single nation. Absolutely nothing is concealed in the phrase.

With regard to domestic questions article 16 of the covenant expressly provides that, if in case of any dispute arising between members of the league the matter involved is claimed by one of the parties "and is found by the council to arise out of a matter which by international law is solely within the domestic jurisdiction of that party, the council shall so report, and shall make no recommendation as to its settlement." The United States was by no means the only Government interested in the explicit adoption of this provision, and there is no doubt in the mind of any authoritative student of international law that such matters as immigration, tariffs, and naturalization are incontestably domestic questions with which no international body could deal without express authority to do so. No enumeration of domestic questions was undertaken because to undertake it, even by sample, would have involved the danger of seeming to exclude those not mentioned.

The right of any sovereign State to withdraw had been taken for granted, but no objection was made to making it explicit. Indeed, so soon as the views expressed at the White House conference were laid before the commission it was at once conceded that it was best not to leave the answer to so important a question to inference. No proposal was made to set up any tribunal to pass judgment upon the question whether a withdrawing nation had in fact fulfilled "all its international obligations and all its obligations under the covenant." It was recognized that that question must be left to be resolved by the conscience of the nation proposing to withdraw; and I must say that it did not seem to me worth while to propose that the article be made more explicit, because I knew that the United States would never itself propose to withdraw from the league if its conscience was not entirely clear as to the fulfillment of all its international obligations. It has never failed to fulfill them and never will.

Article 10 is in no respect of doubtful meaning when read in the light of the covenant as a whole. The council of the league can only "advise upon" the means by which the obligations of that great article are to be given effect to. Unless the United States is a party to the policy or action in question, her own affirmative vote in the council is necessary before any advice can be given, for a unanimous vote of the council is required. If she is a party, the trouble is hers anyhow. And the unanimous vote of the council is only advice in any case. Each Government is free to reject it if it pleases. Nothing could have been made more clear to the conference than the right of our Congress under our Constitution to exercise its independent judgment in all matters of peace and war. No attempt was made to question or limit that right. The United States will, indeed, undertake under article 10 to "respect and preserve as against external aggression the territorial integrity and existing political independence of all members of the league," and that engagement constitutes a very grave and solemn moral obligation. But it is a moral, not a legal, obligation, and leaves our Congress absolutely free to put its own interpretation upon it in all cases that call for action. It is binding in conscience only, not in law.

Article 10 seems to me to constitute the very backbone of the whole covenant. Without it the league would be hardly more than an influential debating society.

It has several times been suggested, in public debate and in private conference, that interpretations of the sense in which the United States accepts the engagements of the covenant should be embodied in the instrument of ratification. There can be no reasonable objection to such interpretations accompanying the act of ratification provided they do not form a part of the formal ratification itself. Most of the interpretations which have been suggested to me embody what seems to me the plain meaning of the instrument itself. But if such interpretations should constitute a part of the formal resolution of ratification, long delays would be the inevitable consequence, inasmuch as all the many governments concerned would have to accept, in effect, the language of the Senate as the language of the treaty before ratification would be complete.[3] The assent of the German Assembly at Weimar would have to be obtained, among the rest,[4] and I must frankly say that I could only with the greatest reluctance approach that assembly for permission to read the treaty as we understand it and as those who framed it quite certainly understood it. If the United States were to qualify the document in any way, moreover, I am confident from what I know of the many conferences and debates which accompanied the formulation of the treaty that our example would immediately be followed in many quarters, in some instances with very serious reservations, and that the meaning and operative force of the treaty would presently be clouded from one end of its clauses to the other.

Pardon me, Mr. Chairman, if I have been entirely unreserved and plain-spoken in speaking of the great matters we all have so much at heart. If excuse is needed, I trust that the critical situation of affairs may serve as my justification. The issues that manifestly hang upon the conclusions of the Senate with regard to peace and upon the time of its action are so grave and so clearly insusceptible of being thrust on one side or postponed that I have felt it necessary in the public interest to make this urgent plea, and to make it as simply and as unreservedly as possible.

I thought that the simplest way, Mr. Chairman, to cover the points that I knew to be points of interest?

THE CHAIRMAN. Mr. President, so far as I am personally concerned—and I think I represent perhaps the majority of the committee in that respect—we have no thought of entering upon argument as to interpretations or points of that character; but the committee is very desirous of getting information on certain points which seem not clear and on which they thought information would be of value to them in the consideration of the treaty which they, I think I may say for myself and others, desire to hasten in every possible way.

[3] This was, to say the least, a dubious and debatable assertion, but it was a point that Wilson had made and would continue to make during the treaty fight, in spite of advice to the contrary.
[4] As Wilson later admitted in this interview, this was an incorrect statement.

Your reference to the necessity of action leads me to ask one question. If we have to restore peace to the world it is necessary, I assume, that there should be treaties with Austria, Hungary, Turkey, and Bulgaria. Those treaties are all more or less connected with the treaty with Germany. The question I should like to ask is, what the prospect is of our receiving those treaties for action?

THE PRESIDENT. I think it is very good, sir, and, so far as I can judge from the contents of the dispatches from my colleagues on the other side of the water, the chief delay is due to the uncertainty as to what is going to happen to this treaty.[5] This treaty is the model for the others. I saw enough of the others before I left Paris to know that they are being framed upon the same set of principles and that the treaty with Germany is the model. I think that is the chief element of delay, sir.

THE CHAIRMAN. They are not regarded as essential to the consideration of this treaty?

THE PRESIDENT. They are not regarded as such; no, sir; they follow this treaty.

THE CHAIRMAN. I do not know about the other treaties, but the treaty with Poland, for example, has been completed?

THE PRESIDENT. Yes, and signed; but it is dependent on this treaty. My thought was to submit it upon the action on this treaty.

THE CHAIRMAN. I should like, if I may, to ask a question in regard to the plans submitted to the commission on the league of nations, if that is the right phrase.

THE PRESIDENT. Yes, sir.

THE CHAIRMAN. You were kind enough to send us the draft of the American plan.[6] When we were here in February, if I understood you rightly—I may be incorrect but I understood you to say that there were other drafts or plans submitted by Great Britain, by France, and by Italy. Would it be possible for us to see those other tentative plans?

THE PRESIDENT. I would have sent them to the committee with pleasure, Senator, if I had found that I had them. I took it for granted that I had them, but the papers that remain in my hands remain there in a haphazard way. I can tell you the character of the other drafts. The British draft was the only one, as I remember, that was in the form of a definite constitution of a league. The French and Italian drafts were in the form of a series of proposi-

---

[5] An incorrect statement. The delay, if there was any, was at this point due to the failure to reach agreement with Italy on Adriatic and other questions, the controversy over western Thrace, and the controversy over mandates in the former Ottoman Empire.

[6] Wilson sent Lodge what is known as the Third Paris Draft of the Covenant, which is printed at February 2, 1919, Vol. 54. For additional information, see WW to HCL, Aug. 8, 1919, n. 2.

tions laying down general rules and assuming that the commission, or whatever body made the final formulation, would build upon those principles if they were adopted. They were principles quite consistent with the final action.

I remember saying to the committee when I was here in March—I have forgotten the expression I used—something to the effect that the British draft had constituted the basis. I thought afterwards that that was misleading, and I am very glad to tell the committee just what I meant.

Some months before the conference assembled, a plan for the league of nations had been drawn up by a British committee, at the head of which was Mr. Phillimore—I believe the Mr. Phillimore who was known as an authority on international law. A copy of that document[7] was sent to me, and I built upon that a redraft.[8] I will not now say whether I thought it was better or not an improvement; but I built on that a draft which was quite different, inasmuch as it put definiteness where there had been what seemed indefiniteness in the Phillimore suggestion. Then, between that time and the time of the formation of the commission on the league of nations, I had the advantage of seeing a paper by Gen. Smuts, of South Africa,[9] who seemed to me to have done some very clear thinking, particularly with regard to what was to be done with the pieces of the dismembered empires. After I got to Paris, therefore, I rewrote the document to which I have alluded, and you may have noticed that it consists of a series of articles and then supplementary agreements.[10] It was in the supplementary agreements that I embodied the additional ideas that had come to me not only from Gen. Smuts's paper but from other discussions. That is the full story of how the plan which I sent to the committee was built up.

THE CHAIRMAN. Of course, it is obvious that the Gen. Smuts plan has been used. That appears on the face of the document.

THE PRESIDENT. Yes.

THE CHAIRMAN. Then there was a previous draft in addition to the one you have sent to us? You spoke of a redraft. The original draft was not submitted to the committee?

THE PRESIDENT. No; that was privately, my own.

THE CHAIRMAN. Was it before our commission?

THE PRESIDENT. No; it was not before our commission.

THE CHAIRMAN. The one that was sent to us was a redraft of that?

[7] About which, see Lord Reading to WW, July 3, 1918 (second letter of that date), n. 1, Vol. 48.

[8] This was Wilson's so-called Washington Draft, printed as an Enclosure with WW to EMH, Sept. 7, 1918, Vol. 49.

[9] Smuts' memorandum is printed at Dec. 26, 1918, Vol. 53.

[10] Again, Wilson refers to the Third Paris Draft.

THE PRESIDENT. Yes. I was reading some of the discussion before the committee, and some one, I think Senator Borah, if I remember correctly, quoted an early version of Article 10.

SENATOR BORAH. That was Senator Johnson.

SENATOR JOHNSON of California. I took it from the Independent.[11]

THE PRESIDENT. I do not know how that was obtained, but that was part of the draft which preceded the draft which I sent to you.

SENATOR JOHNSON of California. It was first published by Mr. Hamilton Holt in the Independent; it was again subsequently published in the New Republic,[12] and from one of those publications I read it when examining, I think, the Secretary of State.

THE PRESIDENT. I read it with the greatest interest, because I had forgotten it, to tell the truth, but I recognized it as soon as I read it.

SENATOR JOHNSON of California. It was the original plan?

THE PRESIDENT. It was the original form of article 10; yes.

THE CHAIRMAN. I was about to ask in regard to article 10, as the essence of it appears in article 2 [3] of the draft which you sent, whether that was in the British plan—the Smuts plan—or the other plans?

Of course if there are no drafts of these other plans, we can not get them.

THE PRESIDENT. I am very sorry, Senator. I thought I had them, but I have not.[13]

THE CHAIRMAN. Mr. Lansing, the Secretary of State, testified before us the other day that he had prepared a set of resolutions covering the points in the league, which was submitted to the American commission. You saw that draft?[14]

THE PRESIDENT. Yes.

THE CHAIRMAN. No specific action was taken upon it?

THE PRESIDENT. Not in a formal way.

THE CHAIRMAN. Mr. President, I have no prepared set of questions, but there are one or two that I wish to ask, and will go to an entirely different subject in my next question. I desire to ask purely for information. Is it intended that the United States shall receive any part of the reparation fund which is in the hands of the reparation commission?

THE PRESIDENT. I left that question open, Senator, because I did not feel that I had any final right to decide it. Upon the basis that was set up in the reparation clauses the portion that the United

[11] Hamilton Holt, "Article X—The Soul of the Covenant," *The Independent*, XCIX (July 5, 1919), 15-16. Holt quoted the text of what was Article III of Wilson's Second Paris Draft, printed at Jan. 18, 1919, Vol. 54.

[12] *The New Republic*, XX (Aug. 6, 1919), 5.

[13] Of course Wilson had all these various drafts in his files.

[14] It is printed as an Enclosure with RL to WW, Jan. 31, 1919, Vol. 54.

States would receive would be very small at best, and my own judgment was frequently expressed, not as a decision but as a judgment, that we should claim nothing under those general clauses. I did that because I coveted the moral advantage that that would give us in the counsels of the world.

SENATOR MC CUMBER. Did that mean we would claim nothing for the sinking of the *Lusitania*?

THE PRESIDENT. Oh, no. That did not cover questions of that sort at all.

THE CHAIRMAN. I understood that prewar claims were not covered by that reparation clause.

THE PRESIDENT. That is correct.

THE CHAIRMAN. I asked that question because I desired to know whether under the reparation commission there was anything expected to come to us.

THE PRESIDENT. As I say, that remains to be decided.

THE CHAIRMAN. By the commission?

THE PRESIDENT. By the commission.

THE CHAIRMAN. Going now onto another question, as I understand the treaty the overseas possessions of Germany are all made over to the five principal allied and associated powers, who apparently, as far as the treaty goes, have power to make disposition of them, I suppose by way of mandate or otherwise. Among those overseas possessions are the Ladrone Islands, except Guam, the Carolines, and, I think, the Marshall Islands. Has there been any recommendation made by our naval authorities in regard to the importance of our having one island there, not for territorial purposes, but for naval purposes?

THE PRESIDENT. There was a paper on that subject,[15] Senator, which has been published. I only partially remember it. It was a paper laying out the general necessities of our naval policy in the Pacific, and the necessity of having some base for communication upon those islands was mentioned, just in what form I do not remember. But let me say this, there is a little island which I must admit I had not heard of before.

SENATOR WILLIAMS. The island of Yap?

THE PRESIDENT. Yap. It is one of the bases and centers of cable and radio communication on the Pacific, and I made the point that the disposition, or rather the control, of that island should be reserved for the general conference which is to be held in regard to the ownership and operation of the cables. That subject is men-

[15] The memorandum summarized in n. 1 to JD to WW, Dec. 3, 1918 (second letter of that date), Vol. 53. Insofar as the Editors know, this memorandum had not been published.

tioned and disposed of in this treaty and that general cable conference is to be held.

THE CHAIRMAN. I had understood, or I had heard the report, that
our General Board of the Navy Department and our Chief of Operations, had recommended that we should have a footing there,
primarily in order to secure cable communications.[16]

THE PRESIDENT. I think you are right, sir.

THE CHAIRMAN. That we were likely to be cut off from cable communication—that is, that the cables were likely to pass entirely into
other hands—unless we had some station there, and it seemed to
me a matter of such importance that I asked the question.

I wish to ask this further question: There was a secret treaty
between England and Japan in regard to Shantung;[17] and in the
correspondence with the British ambassador at Tokyo, when an-
nouncing the acquiescence of Great Britain in Japan's having the
German rights in Shantung, the British ambassador added:

It is, of course, understood that we are to have the islands
south of the Equator and Japan to have the islands north of the
Equator.

If it should seem necessary for the safety of communication for
this country that we should have a cable station there, would that
secret treaty interfere with it?

THE PRESIDENT. I think not, sir, in view of the stipulation that I
made with regard to the question of construction by this cable convention. That note of the British ambassador was a part of the diplomatic correspondence covering that subject.

THE CHAIRMAN. That was what I understood.

SENATOR MOSES. Was the stipulation that that should be reserved
for the consideration of the cable conference a formally signed protocol?

THE PRESIDENT. No; it was not a formally signed protocol, but
we had a prolonged and interesting discussion on the subject, and
nobody has any doubt as to what was agreed upon.[18]

THE CHAIRMAN. I asked the question because it seemed to me a
matter of great importance.

THE PRESIDENT. Yes; it is.

THE CHAIRMAN. As a matter of self-protection, it seemed on the
face of it that the treaty would give the five principal allied and

[16] Lodge was referring to the memorandum just cited.

[17] For which, see the minutes of the Council of Four printed at April 22, 1919, 11:30
a.m., and Appendix II thereto, Vol. 57.

[18] See the minutes of the Council of Ten printed at May 1, 1919, 4 p.m., and of May
2, 1919, 5 p.m.; and the minutes of the Council of Four printed at May 3, 1919, 11:30
a.m., all in Vol. 58. For Wilson's insistence on the internationalization of Yap, see the
minutes of the Council of Four printed at April 15, 1919, 11 a.m., April 18, 1919, 11
a.m., and April 21, 1919, 4 p.m., all in Vol. 57.

associated powers the authority to make such disposition as they saw fit of those islands, but I did not know whether the secret treaty would thwart that purpose. I have no further questions to ask, Mr. President.

SENATOR BORAH. Mr. President, if no one else desires to ask a question, I want, so far as I am individually concerned, to get a little clearer information with reference to the withdrawal clause in the league covenant. Who passes upon the question of the fulfilment of our international obligations, upon the question whether a nation has fulfilled its international obligations?

THE PRESIDENT. Nobody.

SENATOR BORAH. Does the council have anything to say about it?

THE PRESIDENT. Nothing whatever.

SENATOR BORAH. Then if a country should give notice of withdrawal it would be the sole judge of whether or not it had fulfilled its international obligations—its covenants—to the league?

THE PRESIDENT. That is as I understand it. The only restraining influence would be the public opinion of the world.

SENATOR BORAH. Precisely; but if the United States should conceive that it had fulfilled its obligations, that question could not be referred to the council in any way, or the council could not be called into action.

THE PRESIDENT. No.

SENATOR BORAH. Then, as I understand, when the notice is given, the right to withdraw is unconditional?

THE PRESIDENT. Well, when the notice is given it is conditional on the faith of the conscience of the withdrawing nation at the close of the two-year period.

SENATOR BORAH. Precisely; but it is unconditional so far as the legal right or the moral right is concerned.

THE PRESIDENT. That is my interpretation.

SENATOR BORAH. There is no moral obligation on the part of the United States to observe any suggestion made by the council?

THE PRESIDENT. Oh, no.

SENATOR BORAH. With reference to withdrawing?

THE PRESIDENT. There might be a moral obligation if that suggestion had weight, Senator, but there is no other obligation.

SENATOR BORAH. Any moral obligation which the United States would feel, would be one arising from its own sense of obligation?

THE PRESIDENT. Oh, certainly.

SENATOR BORAH. And not by reason of any suggestion by the council?

THE PRESIDENT. Certainly.

SENATOR BORAH. Then the idea which has prevailed in some

quarters that the council would pass upon such obligation is an erroneous one, from your standpoint?

THE PRESIDENT. Yes; entirely.

SENATOR BORAH. And as I understand, of course, you are expressing the view which was entertained by the commission which drew the league?

THE PRESIDENT. I am confident that that was the view. That view was not formulated, you understand, but I am confident that that was the view.

SENATOR MC CUMBER. May I ask a question right here? Would there be any objection, then, to a reservation declaring that to be the understanding of the force of this section?

THE PRESIDENT. Senator, as I indicated at the opening of our conference, this is my judgment about that: Only we can interpret a moral obligation. The legal obligation can be enforced by such machinery as there is to enforce it. We are therefore at liberty to interpret the sense in which we undertake a moral obligation. What I feel very earnestly is that it would be a mistake to embody that interpretation in the resolution of ratification, because then it would be necessary for other governments to act upon it.

SENATOR MC CUMBER. If they all recognized at the time that this was the understanding and the construction that should be given to that portion of the treaty, would it be necessary for them to act on it again?

THE PRESIDENT. I think it would, Senator.

SENATOR MC CUMBER. Could they not accept it merely by acquiescence?

THE PRESIDENT. My experience as a lawyer was not very long; but that experience would teach me that the language of a contract is always part of the debatable matter, and I can testify that in our discussions in the commission on the league of nations we did not discuss ideas half as much as we discussed phraseologies.

SENATOR MC CUMBER. But suppose, Mr. President, we should make a declaration of that kind, which would be in entire accord with your view of the understanding of all of the nations, and without further comment or action the nations should proceed to appoint their commissions, and to act under this treaty, would not that be a clear acquiescence in our construction?

THE PRESIDENT. Oh, it might be, Senator, but we would not know for a good many months whether they were going to act in that sense or not. There would have to be either explicit acquiescence, or the elapsing of a long enough time for us to know whether they were implicitly acquiescing or not.

SENATOR MC CUMBER. I should suppose that when the treaty was signed, under present world conditions, all nations would proceed to act immediately under it.

THE PRESIDENT. In some matters; yes.

SENATOR HARDING. Mr. President, assuming that your construction of the withdrawal clause is the understanding of the formulating commission, why is the language making the proviso for the fulfillment of covenants put into the article?

THE PRESIDENT. Merely as an argument to the conscience of the nations. In other words, it is a notice served on them that their colleagues will expect that at the time they withdraw they will have fulfilled their obligations.

SENATOR HARDING. The language hardly seems to make that implication, because it expressly says, "Provided it has fulfilled its obligations."

THE PRESIDENT. Yes.

SENATOR HARDING. If it were a matter for the nation itself to judge, that is rather a far-fetched provision, is it not?

THE PRESIDENT. Well, you are illustrating my recent remark, Senator, that the phraseology is your difficulty, not the idea. The idea is undoubtedly what I have expressed.

SENATOR PITTMAN. Mr. President, Senator McCumber has drawn out that it is your impression that the allied and associated powers have the same opinion of the construction of these so-called indefinite articles that you have. Is that construction also known and held by Germany?

THE PRESIDENT. I have no means of knowing.

SENATOR PITTMAN. Germany, then, has not expressed herself to the commission with regard to these mooted questions?

THE PRESIDENT. No; we have no expression from Germany about the league, except the expression of her very strong desire to be admitted to it.[19]

SENATOR PITTMAN. And is it your opinion that if the language of the treaty were changed in the resolution of ratification, the consent of Germany to the change would also be essential?

[19] Wilson had obviously forgotten about the German counter proposal on the League of Nations of May 9, 1919, in which the German delegation had put forth an elaborate and altogether different constitution for the league. Similarly, Wilson had failed to remember the detailed comments on the League of Nations contained in the "Observations of the German Delegation on the Conditions of Peace" of May 29, 1919, which had addressed a number of issues in addition to requesting immediate membership in the league. See PPC VI, 765-78, 795-901. See also the draft reply by the Allied and Associated Powers to the German "observations" and their reply to the German scheme for the League of Nations, printed as Appendices II and IV, respectively, to the minutes of the Council of Four printed at June 12, 1919, 11 a.m., Vol. 60.

It is true, however, that the discussion in the Council of Four on this matter revolved mainly around the question of Germany's admission to the League. See, for example, the minutes of the Council of Four printed at June 2, 1919, 4 p.m., June 3, 1919, 4 p.m., June 7, 1919, 4 p.m., and June 12, 1919, 11 a.m., all in Vol. 60.

THE PRESIDENT. Oh, undoubtedly.

THE CHAIRMAN. Mr. President, in that connection—I did not mean to ask another question—I take it there is no question whatever, under international law and practice, that an amendment to the text of a treaty must be submitted to every signatory, and must receive either their assent or their dissent. I had supposed it had been the general diplomatic practice with regard to reservations—which apply only to the reserving power, and not to all the signatories, of course—that with regard to reservations it had been the general practice that silence was regarded as acceptance and acquiescence; that there was that distinction between a textual amendment, which changed the treaty for every signatory, and a reservation, which changed it only for the reserving power. In that I may be mistaken, however.

THE PRESIDENT. There is some difference of opinion among the authorities, I am informed. I have not had time to look them up myself about that; but it is clear to me that in a treaty which involves so many signatories, a series of reservations—which would ensue, undoubtedly—would very much obscure our confident opinion as to how the treaty was going to work.

SENATOR WILLIAMS. Mr. President, suppose for example that we adopted a reservation, as the Senator from Massachusetts calls it, and that Germany did nothing about it at all, and afterwards contended that so far as that was concerned it was new matter, to which she was never a party: Could her position be justifiably disputed?

THE PRESIDENT. No.

SENATOR BORAH. Mr. President, with reference to article 10—you will observe that I am more interested in the league than any other feature of this discussion—in listening to the reading of your statement I got the impression that your view was that the first obligation of article 10, to wit—

The members of the league undertake to respect and preserve as against external aggression the territorial integrity and existing political independence of all members of the league—

was simply a moral obligation.

THE PRESIDENT. Yes, sir; inasmuch as there is no sanction in the treaty.

SENATOR BORAH. But that would be a legal obligation so far as the United States was concerned if it should enter into it; would it not?

THE PRESIDENT. I would not interpret it in that way, Senator, because there is involved the element of judgment as to whether the territorial integrity or existing political independence is invaded or impaired. In other words, it is an attitude of comradeship and protection among the members of the league, which in its very nature is moral and not legal.

SENATOR BORAH. If, however, the actual fact of invasion were beyond dispute, then the legal obligation, it seems to me, would immediately arise. I am simply throwing this out in order to get a full expression of views. The legal obligation would immediately arise if the fact of actual invasion were undisputed?

THE PRESIDENT. The legal obligation to apply the automatic punishments of the covenant, undoubtedly; but not the legal obligation to go to arms and actually to make war. Not the legal obligation. There might be a very strong moral obligation.

SENATOR MC CUMBER. Just so that I may understand definitely what your view is on that subject, Mr. President, do I understand you to mean that while we have two different remedies, and possibly others, we would be the sole judge of the remedy we would apply, but the obligation would still rest upon us to apply some remedy to bring about the result?

THE PRESIDENT. Yes. I can not quite accept the full wording that you used, sir. We would have complete freedom of choice as to the application of force.

SENATOR MC CUMBER. Would we not have the same freedom of choice as to whether we would apply a commercial boycott? Are they not both under the same language, so that we would be bound by them in the same way?

THE PRESIDENT. Only in regard to certain articles. The breach of certain articles of the covenant does bring on what I have designated as an automatic boycott, and in that we would have no choice.

SENATOR KNOX. Mr. President, allow me to ask this question: Suppose that it is perfectly obvious and accepted that there is an external aggression against some power, and suppose it is perfectly obvious and accepted that it can not be repelled except by force of arms, would we be under any legal obligation to participate?

THE PRESIDENT. No, sir; but we would be under an absolutely compelling moral obligation.

SENATOR KNOX. But no legal obligation?

THE PRESIDENT. Not as I contemplate it.

SENATOR WILLIAMS. Mr. President, each nation, if I understand it, is, of course, left to judge the applicability of the principles stated to the facts in the case, whether there is or is not external aggression?

THE PRESIDENT. Yes.

SENATOR WILLIAMS. And if any country should conclude that there was not external aggression, but that France or some other country had started the trouble indirectly, we would have the same right, if I understand it, that Italy had to declare that her alliance with Germany and Austria was purely defensive, and that she did not see anything defensive in it; so when you come to judgment of the facts, outside of the international law involved, each nation must determine, if I understand, whether or not there has been external aggression?

THE PRESIDENT. I think you are right, sir. Senator (addressing Senator Knox), you were about to ask something?

SENATOR KNOX. I only wanted to tell you that I asked that question because I was a little confused by the language of your message transmitting the proposed Franco-American treaty to the Senate,[20] in which you said, in substance, and, I think, practically in these terms, that this is only binding us to do immediately what we otherwise would have been bound to do under the league of nations?

THE PRESIDENT. Yes.

SENATOR KNOX. Perhaps I am mistaken with respect to its having been in that message. I am sure I am mistaken; it was not in that message; it was in the message that Mr. Tumulty gave out—

THE CHAIRMAN. May 10.[21]

SENATOR KNOX. Yes.

THE PRESIDENT. Yes.

SENATOR KNOX. That it was merely binding us to do immediately, without waiting for any other power, that which we would otherwise have been bound to do under the terms of the league of nations.

THE PRESIDENT. I did not use the word "bound," but "morally bound."[22] Let me say that you are repeating what I said to the other representatives. I said, "Of course, it is understood we would have to be convinced that it was an unprovoked movement of aggression," and they at once acquiesced in that.

SENATOR MC CUMBER: Mr. President, there are a number of Senators who sincerely believe that under the construction of article 10, taken in connection with other clauses and other articles in the treaty, the council can suggest what we should do, and of course,

[20] It is printed at July 29, 1919.
[21] Wilson's statement as issued by Tumulty is printed in the *New York Times*, May 10, 1919. See also WW to JPT, May 9, 1919 (second telegram of that date), Vol. 58.
[22] Actually, Wilson did not use these words. He said simply that the French security treaty would be "merely hastening the action to which we should be bound by the Covenant of the League of Nations."

while they admit the council can only advise and suggest, that it is nevertheless our moral duty to immediately obey the council, without exercising our own judgment as to whether we shall go to war or otherwise. Now, the public, the American people, a great proportion of them, have that same conviction, which is contrary to your view. Do you not think, therefore, that it would be well to have a reservation inserted in our resolution that shall so construe that section as to make it clear, not only to the American people but to the world, that Congress may use its own judgment as to what it will do, and that its failure to follow the judgment of the council will not be considered a breach of the agreement?

THE PRESIDENT. We differ, Senator, only as to the form of action. I think it would be a very serious practical mistake to put it in the resolution of ratification; but I do hope that we are at liberty, contemporaneously with our acceptance of the treaty, to interpret our moral obligation under that article.

SENATOR PITTMAN. Mr. President, I understand that, under the former method, in your opinion, it would have to go back to Germany and the other countries; while under the latter method it would not be required to go back for ratification.

THE PRESIDENT. Yes, sir; that is my judgment.

SENATOR KNOX. Mr. President, is it not true that such matters are ordinarily covered by a mere exchange of notes between powers, stating that they understand in this or that sense, or do not so understand?

THE PRESIDENT. Yes, sir; ordinarily.

SENATOR KNOX. That would be a matter that would require very little time to consummate it, if these constructions have already been placed upon it in their conversations with you.

THE PRESIDENT. But an exchange of notes is quite a different matter from having it embodied in the resolution of ratification.

SENATOR KNOX. If we embody in our resolution of ratification a statement that we understand section 10 or section 16 or section something else in a particular sense, and this Government, through its foreign department, transmits the proposed form of ratification to the chancellors of the other nations that are concerned in this treaty, and if those interpretations are the same as you have agreed upon with them in your conversations, I do not see how we would need anything more than a mere reply to that effect.

THE PRESIDENT. It would need confirmation.

SENATOR KNOX. Yes; it would need confirmation in that sense.

THE PRESIDENT. My judgment is that the embodying of that in the terms of the resolution of ratification would be acquiescence not only in the interpretation but in the very phraseology of the interpretation, because it would form a part of the contract.

SENATOR KNOX. It might with us, because we have so much machinery for dealing with treaties, but in other countries where it is much more simple I should think it would not be.

THE PRESIDENT. It is simple legally, Senator; but, for example, this treaty has been submitted to legislatures to which the Government was not, by law, obliged to submit it, and it is everywhere being treated as a legislative matter—I mean, so far as the ratification is concerned.

SENATOR KNOX. You mean in countries where, under their constitutions, there are provisions that treaties ordinarily are not submitted to the legislative branch of the Government, this treaty is being so submitted?

THE PRESIDENT. So I understand.

SENATOR KNOX. Where there are two branches of the legislative department, an upper and a lower branch, do you know whether it is being submitted to both?

THE PRESIDENT. I think not, sir. I am not certain about that; but my memory is it is not.

SENATOR FALL. Mr. President, the idea has struck me and I have entertained the view, since reading the treaty and the league, that Germany having signed the treaty but not being yet a member of the league, any reservations which we might make here would be met by Germany either joining the league or refusing to join the league. It would not be submitted to her at all now, because she is not a member of the league? You catch the point?

THE PRESIDENT. Yes. I differ with you there, Senator. One of the reasons for putting the league in the treaty was that Germany was not going to be admitted to the league immediately, and we felt that it was very necessary that we should get her acknowledgment—acceptance—of the league as an international authority, partly because we were excluding her, so that she would thereafter have no ground for questioning such authority as the league might exercise under its covenant.

SENATOR FALL. Precisely.

THE PRESIDENT. Therefore, I think it would be necessary for her to acquiesce in a league the powers of which were differently construed.

SENATOR FALL. Precisely; but her acquiescence would be by her accepting the invitation, when extended, either to join the league or not to join the league. In other words, upon ratification by three of the powers, a status of peace is established, and as to those three powers and Germany all the rules and regulations contained in the treaty of peace become operative. As to the other nations which have not ratified, the status of peace exists; that is, war has terminated. Now, that being the case, and Germany being out of the league—not having been invited to join the league—if in ratifying the treaty we ratify it with certain explanations or reservations, even in the ratifying resolution, when the time comes and Germany is invited to become a member of the league, or when she applies, under the admission clause of the league, for membership therein, if she enters she of course accepts our reservations. If she makes a qualified application, then it is for the league itself to consider whether she will be admitted?

THE PRESIDENT. I do not follow your reasoning in the matter, Senator, because this is not merely a question of either membership or nonmembership. The covenant is a part of the treaty, it is a part of the treaty which she has signed, and we are not at liberty to change any part of that treaty without the acquiescence of the other contracting party.

SENATOR FALL. Well, Mr. President, of course it is not my purpose to enter into an argument, but we are here for information. There are provisions for the amendment of the articles. Germany is out of the league. Any amendment proposed by the other members of the league prior to her coming into the league would not be submitted to her, would it, she not being a member?

THE PRESIDENT. I will admit that that point had not occurred to me. No, she would not.

SENATOR FALL. Then so far as we are concerned we could make a recommendation in the nature of an amendment.

SENATOR PITTMAN. She has already agreed by this treaty that she has signed that the members may amend it.

THE PRESIDENT. Yes.

SENATOR FALL. Precisely, and we could come in with an amendment.

SENATOR HITCHCOCK. Did I understand your first reply to Senator Fall to be that Germany under this treaty already had a relationship to the league by reason of its international character, and its participation in a number of questions that Germany was interested in?

THE PRESIDENT. Yes.

SENATOR HITCHCOCK. So that it has a relationship to the league of nations even before the time that it may apply for membership.

THE PRESIDENT. Yes.

SENATOR MC CUMBER. Mr. President, you answered one question that I think possibly may need a little elucidation. If I remember rightly, in reference to reparation your statement was that the commission would have to decide whether the United States should claim her proportion of the reparation.

THE PRESIDENT. That the commission would have to do it? No; we decide whether we claim it or not.

SENATOR MC CUMBER. That is what I want to make clear. I think the question was asked if the commission was to decide that, and I thought your answer said yes. That is the reason I asked the question.

THE PRESIDENT. The claim would have to come from us, of course.

SENATOR MC CUMBER. It would have to be through an act of Congress, would it not?

THE PRESIDENT. I would have to be instructed about that, Senator. I do not know.

SENATOR MC CUMBER. Whatever right the United States would receive under the treaty for reparation or indemnity is one that runs to the United States, and therefore to divest ourselves of that right would require an act of Congress.

THE PRESIDENT. To divest ourselves of it? I suppose so.

SENATOR KNOX. In the question of the Japanese indemnity,[23] that was done by a joint resolution.

SENATOR MC CUMBER. I thought the President said it would have to be decided by the constituted authority.

SENATOR KNOX. I did not understand that he said that.

SENATOR SWANSON. I understand that the reparation is to be decided upon a representation made by the associated powers. It would seem that the President under that agreement with France, Great Britain, and other nations would have to submit it to the Senate for ratification, and the agreement would have to be reported.

SENATOR MC CUMBER. In each case it would have the force of law.

SENATOR SWANSON. If the Senate wanted to ratify it, it would take an act of Congress.

[23] Senator Knox here referred to the so-called Shimonoseki indemnity, levied upon Japan by Great Britain, France, the Netherlands, and the United States in October 1864. By the summer of that year, outbreaks against foreigners by opponents of the Shogun's new policy of openness toward western influences had escalated into attacks on French, Dutch, and American ships in Japanese waters. In retaliation, and with the tacit approval of the Shogun's court, British, French, Dutch, and American warships joined in a punitive bombardment of Shimonoseki, the fief of the feudal lord responsible for the assaults. In a subsequent convention, Japan agreed to pay a total indemnity of $3,000,000, of which the United States received $785,000. However, in February 1883, after several unsuccessful earlier attempts, Congress passed a bill which, as a show of goodwill toward Japan, remitted the full share of the United States of the Shimonoseki indemnity. For an elaborate discussion of this affair, see Payson J. Treat, *Diplomatic Relations between the United States and Japan, 1853-1895* (2 vols., Stanford, Calif., 1932), I and II, *passim*.

SENATOR WILLIAMS. This question of reparation does not in any way affect our rights to prewar indemnities?

THE PRESIDENT. That is expressly stated.

SENATOR WILLIAMS. That is expressly stated. Now, then, one other question. Germany has signed this treaty with the covenant of the league in it, and she is subject to be dealt with as a nonmember under the treaty, and has very much fewer privileges than a member?

THE PRESIDENT. Yes.

SENATOR NEW. Mr. President, may I ask a question there? What effort was made by the delegates there to prevent the proceedings of the reparations committee being required to be secret?

THE PRESIDENT. I beg your pardon, Senator.

SENATOR NEW. What effort, if any, was made by the American delegates to prevent the proceedings of the reparation commission from being required to be secret, and did the American delegates protest that America be omitted from this commission on account of that thing?

THE PRESIDENT. Nothing was said about it, that I remember.

SENATOR BORAH. Mr. President, coming back for a moment to the subject from which we were diverted a moment ago, and coupling with article 10 article 11, in order that we may have the construction of the committee which framed the league as to both of those articles, as I understand it from your statement, the committee's view was that the obligations under articles 10 and 11, whatever they are, are moral obligations.

THE PRESIDENT. Remind me of the eleventh. I do not remember that by number.

SENATOR BORAH (reading):

Any war or threat of war, whether immediately affecting any of the members of the league or not, is hereby declared a matter of concern to the whole league, and the league shall take any action that may be deemed wise and effectual to safeguard the peace of nations.

What I am particularly anxious to know is whether or not the construction which was placed upon these two articles by the committee which framed the league was that it was a binding obligation from a legal standpoint, or merely a moral obligation.

THE PRESIDENT. Senator, I tried to answer with regard to article 10.

SENATOR BORAH. Yes; exactly.

THE PRESIDENT. I would apply it equally with regard to article 11, though I ought to hasten to say that we did not formulate these interpretations. I can only speak from my confident impression from the debates that accompanied the formulation of the covenant.

SENATOR BORAH. Yes; I understand; and your construction of article 11 is the same as that of article 10?

THE PRESIDENT. Yes.

SENATOR BORAH. As to the question of legal obligation. That is all I desire to ask at present.

SENATOR HARDING. Right there, Mr. President, if there is nothing more than a moral obligation on the part of any member of the league, what avail articles 10 and 11?

THE PRESIDENT. Why, Senator, it is surprising that that question should be asked. If we undertake an obligation we are bound in the most solemn way to carry it out.

SENATOR HARDING. If you believe there is nothing more to this than a moral obligation, any nation will assume a moral obligation on its own account. Is it a moral obligation? The point I am trying to get at is, Suppose something arises affecting the peace of the world, and the council takes steps as provided here to conserve or preserve, and announces its decision, and every nation in the league takes advantage of the construction that you place upon these articles and says, "Well, this is only a moral obligation, and we assume that the nation involved does not deserve our participation or protection," and the whole thing amounts to nothing but an expression of the league council.

THE PRESIDENT. There is a national good conscience in such a matter. I should think that was one of the most serious things that could possibly happen. When I speak of a legal obligation, I mean one that specifically binds you to do a particular thing under certain sanctions. That is a legal obligation. Now a moral obligation is of course superior to a legal obligation, and, if I may say so, has a greater binding force; only there always remains in the moral obligation the right to exercise one's judgment as to whether it is indeed incumbent upon one in those circumstances to do that thing. In every moral obligation there is an element of judgment. In a legal obligation there is no element of judgment.

SENATOR JOHNSON of California. But, Mr. President, when a moral obligation is undoubted it will impel action more readily than a legal obligation.

THE PRESIDENT. If it is undoubted, yes; but that involves the circumstances of the particular case, Senator.

SENATOR JOHNSON of California. Yes; necessarily.

SENATOR HARDING. In answering Senator Knox a moment ago you spoke of a compelling moral obligation. Would you think that any less binding than a specific legal obligation?

THE PRESIDENT. Not less binding; but operative in a different way because of the element of judgment.

SENATOR HARDING. But not less likely to involve us in armed participation?

THE PRESIDENT. In trifling matters, very much less likely.

SENATOR HARDING. To clear my slow mind, let me take a specific case. Suppose the allotted territory which comes under the control of Italy should in some way be assailed from the Balkan States and the council of the league should immediately look upon that as a threat of war involving other nations and should say that the nations of the league should immediately contribute an armed force to stop that war or to bring the attacking nation to terms, would we be a perfidious people, if I may use that term, or would we violate our obligations, if we failed to participate in the defense of Italy?

THE PRESIDENT. We would be our own judges as to whether we were obliged in those circumstances to act in that way or not.

SENATOR HITCHCOCK. In such a case the council would only act unanimously, and our representative on the council of course would have to concur in any advice given.

THE PRESIDENT. Certainly; we would always in such case advise ourselves.

SENATOR WILLIAMS. But if in such case, Mr. President, we concluded that the case provided for and prescribed had arisen and that the extraneous attack existed and that it fell within the terms of the treaty, then we would be untrue if we did not keep our word?

THE PRESIDENT. Certainly.

SENATOR BORAH. In other words, then, that transfers the power to decide whether we should act from the Congress of the United States to one individual who sits on the council.

SENATOR WILLIAMS. No, it does not; it merely provides that when the council acts in accordance with the prescribed terms and we see that it has acted, then Congress will, as a matter of faith keeping, act itself; and, if Congress does not, Congress will do a dishonorable thing.

SENATOR BORAH. Precisely so; so that the matter gets back to the point where one individual has bound Congress.

SENATOR HITCHCOCK. I hope my question to the President will not be interpreted in that way. My question to the President was whether the matter would even come before this country as the advice of the council until the American representative had concurred with the other eight members of the council. After he had concurred it would then be up to Congress to decide.

THE PRESIDENT. You are quite right, Senator. And let me suggest that I find nothing was more clearly in the consciousness of the men who were discussing these very important matters than that most of the nations concerned had popular governments. They were all the time aware of the fact that it would depend upon the approving or disapproving state of opinion of their countries how their representatives in the council would vote in matters of this sort; and it is inconceivable to me that, unless the opinion of the United States, the moral and practical judgment of the people of the United States, approved, the representative of the United States on the council should vote any such advice as would lead us into war.

SENATOR BORAH. Mr. President, does the special alliance treaty with France which has been submitted to us rest upon any other basis as to legal and moral obligation than that of article 10 and article 11 which you have just described?

THE PRESIDENT. No, sir.[24]

SENATOR BORAH. That is also, as you understand it, simply our moral obligations which we enter into with France?

THE PRESIDENT. Yes.

SENATOR WILLIAMS. All international obligations are moral ones.

SENATOR PITTMAN. There is one thing I do not understand about Senator Borah's question. He has stated that he gathers from what you said that it all rests with our representative on the council. Even if our representative on the council advises as a member of the council, and the council is unanimous, is it not then still up to Congress either to accept or reject that advice?

THE PRESIDENT. Oh, yes; but I understood the Senator to mean that it would be dependent on our representative.

SENATOR JOHNSON of California. May I take the example that was just suggested concerning the Balkan States and a possible attack upon the new territories of Italy. Assuming that that is a case of external aggression by the Balkan States concerning the new territory that Italy has acquired by the peace treaty, upon us rests a compelling moral obligation to do our part in preventing that, does there not?

THE PRESIDENT. Yes.

SENATOR JOHNSON of California. And that compelling moral obligation would require us to use such means as would seem appropriate, either economic or force? Is not that correct?

THE PRESIDENT. Deemed appropriate by whom? That is really the point.

SENATOR JOHNSON of California. Of course, deemed appropriate for the purpose of preventing and frustrating the aggression.

[24] Wilson had obviously forgotten the terms of the treaty, under which the legal obligations of the United States were clearly stated.

THE PRESIDENT. Deemed by us appropriate?

SENATOR JOHNSON of California. I assume of necessity it would have to be deemed by us to bind us as a compelling moral obligation to prevent the aggression in the case named.

THE PRESIDENT. Yes.

SENATOR MC CUMBER. Mr. President, I think, due to my own fault, I do not fully comprehend your distinction between a moral and a legal obligation in a treaty. If we enter into a treaty with France to defend her against aggression from Germany for any length of time, that is a legal obligation, is it not?

THE PRESIDENT. Legal in the sense that a treaty is of binding force; yes.

SENATOR MC CUMBER. Yes; that is what I meant. It is as legal as any treaty could be made legal, and there is also a moral obligation to keep that treaty, is there not?

THE PRESIDENT. Yes, sir. I happened to hear Senator Knox say what I am glad to adopt. It is a legal obligation with a moral sanction.

SENATOR BORAH. That is true generally, is it not?

THE PRESIDENT. Yes, Senator; but I have already defined in what special sense I use the word "legal."

SENATOR MC CUMBER. To my mind those two articles are legal obligations to be carried out by the moral conscience of the American people if the conditions justify it.

THE PRESIDENT. You see we are speaking of two different fields, and therefore the language does not fit. In international law the word "legal" does not mean the same as in national law, and the word hardly applies.[25]

SENATOR BORAH. I wish to ask some questions in regard to the secret treaties. I do not feel as free about those matters as I do about the league, because there are certain things that I recognize may not be entirely open for public consideration; but, nevertheless, in so far as we can, I should like to know when the first knowledge came to this Government with reference to the secret treaties between Japan, Great Britain, Italy, and France concerning the German possessions in Shantung.

THE PRESIDENT. I thought that Secretary Lansing had looked that up and told you. I can only reply from my own knowledge, and my own knowledge came after I reached Paris.[26]

SENATOR BORAH. We did get a reply from Mr. Lansing to the same effect so far as he was concerned. When did the secret treaties between Great Britain, France, and the other nations of Eu-

[25] Sic!
[26] Wilson knew nothing about these treaties until late February 1919. About this matter, see the index references to "Japan" in Vols. 55 and 57.

rope with reference to certain adjustments in Europe first come to your knowledge? Was that after you had reached Paris also?

THE PRESIDENT. Yes; the whole series of understandings were disclosed to me for the first time then.[27]

[27] Wilson's memory may or may not have failed him here.

Arthur Balfour talked with Wilson and Lansing at the White House for three quarters of an hour at 11 a.m. on April 23, 1917. Apparently on his own initiative, Wilson told Balfour that he did not think it would be expedient for him to bind himself to any of the treaty obligations which the Allies had undertaken among themselves. Wilson, Balfour reported, thought that any such engagement would be highly unpopular in the United States. "I did not gather he shared this prejudice himself but he had to count it as political factor which could not be wisely neglected." Wilson, Balfour further reported, was of course "aware of general tenour of mutual engagements by which European Allies have bound themselves and he contemplates possibility that a time might come when though all essential objects of war had been attained one or other of allies relying on strict letter of treaties would show themselves uncompromising and unpractical over some questions of detail. He evidently thought in that event United States being themselves unfettered might exercise powerful and valuable influence." C. A. Spring Rice to D. Lloyd George, April 26, 1917, Vol. 42.

On May 18, 1917, just before he returned to London, Balfour wrote to Wilson as follows:

"I beg now to fulfil, though in somewhat belated fashion, my promise to send you the text of the various Agreements which Great Britain has come to with the Allied Powers. I found that we had not copies with us and it has taken some time to obtain them from England.

"I do not think that they will add much to the knowledge which you already possess of our negotiations since the War began, nor do I think they are likely to modify your general views." AJB to WW, May 18, 1917, ibid.

A complete list of these treaties is printed in n. 1 to the letter just cited. They included all the important secret treaties that Great Britain had concluded with her allies to this point, except the Anglo-Japanese "understanding" of February 16, 1917. In addition, Balfour enclosed a print of a discussion of the Committee of Imperial Defence on March 22, 1917, in which Balfour reviewed British and German war aims and discussed very frankly the embarrassment that could occur on account of the promises made to Italy in the Treaty of London.

Wilson put Balfour's letter and its enclosures in his safe. It is impossible to say whether or not he read the treaties and Balfour's review, but there is no indication by way of marginal or interlinear markings that he did so, and the copies of the treaties and Balfour's review do not give the appearance of ever having been handled. Wilson probably took Balfour at his word: "I do not think that they [the secret treaties] will add much to the knowledge which you already possess of our negotiations since the War began, nor do I think they are likely to modify your general views."

It seems likely that Wilson at this point simply was not interested in the secret treaties. Most important, none of the treaties concerned Germany, except for a treaty, which had long since been published, pledging the Allies not to make a separate peace with the Central Powers; all the other treaties concerned Austria-Hungary and the Ottoman Empire, countries with which the United States was not at war. Wilson had not yet formulated an American peace program; he thought of the United States as strictly and only an associate of the Allies; and he almost certainly envisaged his role at the end of the war as a mediator between them and the Central Powers, a mediator who would not be bound by any treaties, secret or otherwise. And the peace conference lay in the unknown future; at the moment, there were more urgent problems to be faced and overcome.

Wilson did not give copies of the enclosures in Balfour's letter of May 18, 1917, to anyone, and there is not a single mention of them in the entire Wilson corpus or in any correspondence, for example, between Wilson and Lansing and Wilson and House before the date noted below. Wilson's oft-quoted statement in his letter to House of July 21, 1917—"England and France *have not the same views with regard to peace that we have* by any means"—means only what it says.

It is useful to speculate when knowledge of the secret treaties first came to other officials in the United States. Trotsky did of course publish them on November 22, 1917, but publication of them was effectively suppressed in the Allied countries and the United States. Ambassador David R. Francis in Moscow sent copies of them to the State

SENATOR BORAH. Then we had no knowledge of these secret treaties, so far as our Government was concerned, until you reached Paris?

THE PRESIDENT. Not unless there was information at the State Department of which I knew nothing.

SENATOR BORAH. Do you know when the secret treaties between Japan, Great Britain, and other countries were first made known to China?

THE PRESIDENT. No, sir; I do not. I remember a meeting of what was popularly called the council of ten, after our reaching Paris, in which it was first suggested that all these understandings should be laid upon the table of the conference.[28] That was some time after we reached there, and I do not know whether that was China's first knowledge of these matters or not.

Department, and they reached Washington apparently on December 27, 1917. See Arno J. Mayer, *Political Origins of the New Diplomacy, 1917-1918* (New Haven, 1959), p. 278. But they had not come in time for the use of Sidney E. Mezes, David Hunter Miller, and Walter Lippmann of The Inquiry when they prepared the memorandum on war aims (printed at Jan. 4, 1918, Vol. 45) that Wilson used in preparing his Fourteen Points Address, or the additional memorandum by these same authors dated January 2, 1917 [1918], about which see n. 1 to the memorandum printed at Jan. 4, 1918, *ibid*. Moreover, there is no evidence that Lansing sent to Wilson copies of the treaties which he had received from Francis, or of any discussion about them between Lansing and Wilson.

The first mention in the Wilson corpus of the secret treaties was in a memorandum with a series of questions about plans for the peace conference that Lansing sent to Wilson on November 18, 1918, as follows:

"28. How far should treaties and agreements as to territory made since the war began be considered in reaching a final settlement of boundaries? (Particular reference to the London Agreement of 1916 [sic] as to Italy, and the division of German colonial possessions in the Pacific by Great Britain and Japan.)" T MS enclosed with RL to WW, Nov. 18, 1918, ALS (WP, DLC).

Wilson did not answer Lansing's question because a telegram had just come from House (EMH to RL, Nov. 15, 1918, Vol. 53) conveying a memorandum by the French Foreign Office on the organization, scope, etc., of the peace conference, and Wilson answered the queries in this memorandum. The question and answer read as follows:

"B. Release from treaties concluded between them of such groups of states which by the fact of their admission to the Congress shall waive their right thereto. This principle is entirely in accordance with the ideas of President Wilson.

"NOTE: This applies as I read it to all agreements made prior to or during the war— Russia, Italy, Japan and Great Britain in regard to Pacific Islands."

The plain meaning of Wilson's reply is that he *assumed* that there would be general agreement to the French proposal. He did not take up the French proposal with the British and French governments, probably because he thought that there was already firm agreement on it in the terms that House had finally obtained from Great Britain and France as the basis for the Pre-Armistice Agreement, namely that the United States and the Allies would conclude peace with Germany upon a basis of the Fourteen Points, with exceptions relating to the freedom of the seas and reparations. And in fact the question of the validity of secret treaties did not come up during the peace conference until the controversy over a territorial settlement in the Adriatic erupted in April 1919. Wilson then made it clear that he did not consider himself bound in any way by the Treaty of London and also argued that Britain and France were not bound by it. Wilson also said several times in the Council of Four that he did not know the terms of the Treaty of London before the peace conference opened.

[28] Wilson's memory was faulty here. Perhaps he confused this alleged suggestion with the suggestion in the memorandum of the French Foreign Office of November 15, 1918, cited in the preceding note.

SENATOR BORAH. Would it be proper for me to ask if Great Britain and France insisted upon maintaining these secret treaties at the peace conference as they were made?

THE PRESIDENT. I think it is proper for me to answer that question, sir. I will put it in this way: They felt that they could not recede from them, that is to say, that they were bound by them, but when they involved general interests such as they realized were involved, they were quite willing, and indeed I think desirous, that they should be reconsidered with the consent of the other parties. I mean with the consent, so far as they were concerned, of the other parties.

SENATOR MOSES. Were all those treaties then produced, Mr. President?

THE PRESIDENT. Oh, yes.

SENATOR MOSES. Did that include the secret arrangement with reference to Avlona?[29]

THE PRESIDENT. I do not recall that agreement, Senator. You mean with regard to Italy having Avlona?

SENATOR MOSES. Yes.

THE PRESIDENT. If it did, I did not see it. I heard of it, but I can not say confidently that the terms were laid before us.

SENATOR MOSES. I recall in some statements you made in connection with Fiume that you referred to Italy receiving Avlona under some agreement previously arrived at, and in that statement you held that to be part compensation at least for any loss she might sustain in not having Fiume.

THE PRESIDENT. I was referring to what I understood to be the agreement.[30] I am simply now answering your question that I did not see that agreement in written terms.

SENATOR MOSES. Then, they were not produced in textual form?

THE PRESIDENT. I do not know; they may have been and I may not have picked them up in the great mass of papers before me.

SENATOR MOSES. The purpose of my inquiry was to ascertain whether there was laid before the council of ten any textual agreements which transferred parts of the territory of one independent nation to another.

THE PRESIDENT. Only those that have been spoken of.

SENATOR MOSES. That is to say, Shantung and Avlona?

THE PRESIDENT. I say only those that we have had under general discussion. I can not enumerate them, but there are none that

[29] Or Valona, now the chief port of Albania.
[30] That is, Article 6 of the Treaty of London of April 26, 1915, which provided, among other things, that Italy should receive full sovereignty over Valona.

have not been produced so far as I know. That answers the question.

SENATOR MC CUMBER. The secret treaties to which you refer are those treaties which were made from time to time as the exigencies of the war required during the period of the war?

THE PRESIDENT. Yes.

SENATOR MC CUMBER. And not treaties that were made prior to the war?

THE PRESIDENT. Yes.

SENATOR WILLIAMS. Mr. President, I wish to ask you a question in order to see if the facts are clear in my own mind. As I understand the situation—and I should like to have you correct me if I am wrong—France and Great Britain both have stated that they were bound by certain treaties with Japan and they were perfectly willing, with Japan's consent, to reconsider those treaties, but that they were themselves bound if the other party to the treaty did not consent to reconsider. Is that about it?

THE PRESIDENT. Yes.

SENATOR WILLIAMS. That is what I thought. Bound in honor is the only way a nation is bound in international affairs.

SENATOR SWANSON. Can you tell us, or would it be proper to do so, of your understanding with Japan as to the return of Shantung? That is a question which has been very much discussed.

THE PRESIDENT. I have published the wording of the understanding, Senator.[31] I can not be confident that I quote it literally, but I know that I quote it in substance. It was that Japan should return to China in full sovereignty the old province of Shantung so far as Germany had had any claims upon it, preserving to herself the right to establish a residential district at Tsingtao, which is the town of Kiaochow Bay; that with regard to the railways and mines she should retain only the rights of an economic concession there, with the right, however, to maintain a special body of police on the railway, the personnel of which should be Chinese under Japanese instructors nominated by the managers of the company and appointed by the Chinese Government. I think that is the whole of it.

SENATOR POMERENE. That is, that the instructors should be confirmed by the Chinese Government?

THE PRESIDENT. No; not exactly that. The language, as I remember it, was that they should be nominated by the managers of the railway company, and appointed by the Chinese Government.

SENATOR BORAH. Was that understanding oral?

SENATOR WILLIAMS. This rather curious question presents itself

[31] See Wilson's statement printed at Aug. 6, 1919.

to my mind: As I understand, Japan has retained sovereignty for the 99 years of the lease only at Kiaochow, and 5 kilometers, or some such distance, back from the bay.

THE PRESIDENT. She has not retained sovereignty over anything.

SENATOR WILLIAMS. She has not?

THE PRESIDENT. I mean, she has promised not to.

SENATOR WILLIAMS. During the period of the lease?

THE PRESIDENT. No; she has promised not to retain sovereignty at all. Senator Borah asked whether this understanding was oral or otherwise. I do not like to describe the operation exactly if it is not perfectly discreet, but as a matter of fact this was technically oral, but literally written and formulated, and the formulation agreed upon.

SENATOR JOHNSON of California. When, Mr. President, is the return to be made?

THE PRESIDENT. That was left undecided, Senator, but we were assured at the time that it would be as soon as possible.

SENATOR JOHNSON of California. Did not the Japanese decline to fix any date?

THE PRESIDENT. They did at that time, yes; but I think it is fair to them to say not in the spirit of those who wished it be within their choice, but simply that they could not at that time say when it would be.

SENATOR JOHNSON of California. The economic privileges that they would retain would give them a fair mastery over the province, would they not, or at least the Chinese think so? Let me put it in that fashion, please.

THE PRESIDENT. I believe they do, Senator. I do not feel qualified to judge. I should say that that was an exaggerated view.

SENATOR JOHNSON of California. But the Chinese feel that way about it, and have so expressed themselves?

THE PRESIDENT. They have so expressed themselves.

SENATOR KNOX. Mr. President, the economic privileges that they originally acquired in Korea, and subsequently in inner and outer Mongolia, and in northern and southern Manchuria, have almost developed into a complete sovereignty over those countries, have they not?

THE PRESIDENT. Yes, Senator; in the absence of a league of nations they have.

SENATOR KNOX. You think the league of nations would have prevented that, do you?

THE PRESIDENT. I am confident it would.

SENATOR NEW. Mr. President, does not this indefinite promise of Japan's suggest the somewhat analogous case of England's occupation of Malta? She has occupied Malta for something like a century, I believe, under a very similar promise.

THE PRESIDENT. Well, Senator, I hope you will pardon me if I do not answer that question.

SENATOR FALL. Mr. President, speaking of the duty of defense in reference to sovereignty, and of aggression with reference to sovereignty, in construing these different articles of the league, I have been curious to know who will defend the mandate territories or colonies if there should be external aggression.

THE PRESIDENT. Primarily, the mandatory power.

SENATOR FALL. The mandatory power would have that character of sovereignty over the possession which would compel it as a duty to defend the mandate province?

THE PRESIDENT. Yes.

SENATOR FALL. Then a qualified sovereignty would in that instance, at any rate, compel the mandatory of the league first to defend the colony?

THE PRESIDENT. I should put it this way, Senator: We had in mind throughout the whole discussion of the mandate idea the analogy of trustees. The States taking those under mandates would be in the nature of trustees, and of course it is part of the trustee's duty to preserve intact the trust estate.

SENATOR FALL. But out of the funds of the trust estate?

THE PRESIDENT. Oh, yes.

SENATOR FALL. Mr. President, I will not pursue that line at this time. I will say very frankly that I have prepared some questions which I wanted, for my own purposes, to put down in writing, and I had expected to ask them in sequence of you after the other Senators had concluded. It will, however, evidently take quite a long while if we pursue the line which we are now pursuing, and particularly if the Senators themselves argue their own interpretations of the different clauses in the treaty.[32]

SENATOR MC CUMBER. Mr. President, I should like to get as definite an understanding as I can, at least, of how these promises of Japan to return Shantung are evidenced to-day. In what form do they appear?

THE PRESIDENT. They are evidenced in a procès-verbal of the so-called council of four[33]—the name that we ourselves used was very much more pretentious; we called ourselves the council of the principal allied and associated powers—but the four who used to confer, or rather the five, because Japan was there of course at that time.

[32] They are printed as the next document.
[33] See the minutes of the Council of Four printed at April 30, 1919, 12:30 p.m., Vol. 58.

SENATOR MC CUMBER. The principal points were taken down in writing and read over and compared and preserved, were they?

THE PRESIDENT. Not read over and compared, but preserved. The process each day was this, Senator: The matters discussed were summarized, and the conclusions reached were recorded in a procès-verbal, copies of which were distributed within 24 hours; and of course it was open to any one of the conferees to correct anything they might contain. Only in that sense were they corrected.

SENATOR MC CUMBER. Where are those records kept now?

THE PRESIDENT. They are in Paris, sir.[34]

SENATOR MC CUMBER. Is there any objection to their being produced for the committee?

THE PRESIDENT. I think there is a very serious objection, Senator. The reason we constituted that very small conference was so that we could speak with the utmost absence of restraint, and I think it would be a mistake to make use of those discussions outside. I do not remember any blazing indiscretion of my own, but there may be some.

SENATOR MC CUMBER. In those conversations it was fully understood that Japan was to return Shantung as soon as possible?

THE PRESIDENT. Yes, sir.

SENATOR MC CUMBER. Was there anything stated as to what was meant by "as soon as possible"—that is, to place it within any definite period at all?

THE PRESIDENT. No, sir; no. We relied on Japan's good faith in fulfilling that promise.

SENATOR MC CUMBER. Was there anything outside? If I go too far in my questions you can signify it, Mr. President.

THE PRESIDENT. How do you mean outside, Senator?

SENATOR MC CUMBER. Was there anything said by Japan as to anything that she would want to do before she turned the territory over to China?

THE PRESIDENT. No; nothing was mentioned.

SENATOR MC CUMBER. Then "as soon as possible" would naturally mean, would it not, as soon as the treaty has been signed under which she accepts the transfer from Germany?

THE PRESIDENT. Well, I should say that it would mean that the process should begin then. Of course there would be many practical considerations of which I know nothing that might prolong the process.

SENATOR MC CUMBER. And all that Japan reserves is the same that other great nations have reserved—certain concessions?

[34] Actually, Wilson had in his own files a nearly complete set of the official (Hankey) minutes of the Council of Four, as he says below.

THE PRESIDENT. A residential concession and economic concessions: yes, sir.

SENATOR MC CUMBER. The same as Great Britain and France and other countries have retained there?

THE PRESIDENT. Yes; and I ought to say that the representatives of Japan showed every evidence of wishing to put the matter upon just the same basis that the dealings of other nations with China have rested upon for some time.

SENATOR MC CUMBER. The whole purpose of my question, Mr. President, is to satisfy my mind, if I can, that Japan will in good faith carry out her agreement.

THE PRESIDENT. I have every confidence that she will, sir.

SENATOR POMERENE. Mr. President, if I may, I should like to ask a question or two along that same line. If this treaty should fail of ratification, then would not the opportunity be open to Japan to treat the Shantung question just as she has treated the Manchurian situation?

THE PRESIDENT. I think so; yes.

SENATOR POMERENE. So that if the treaty should fail of ratification, China, so far as Shantung is concerned, would be practically at the mercy of Japan; whereas if the treaty is ratified, then at least she will have the benefit of the moral assistance of all the other signatory powers to the treaty to aid in the protection of Chinese rights?

THE PRESIDENT. Senator, I conceive one of the chief benefits of the whole arrangement that centers in the league of nations to be just what you have indicated—that it brings to bear the opinion of the world and the controlling action of the world on all relationships of that hazardous sort, particularly those relationships which involve the rights of the weaker nations. After all, the wars that are likely to come are most likely to come by aggression against the weaker nations. Without the league of nations they have no buttress or protection. With it, they have the united protection of the world; and inasmuch as it is the universal opinion that the great tragedy through which we have just passed never would have occurred if the Central Powers had dreamed that a number of nations would be combined against them, so I have the utmost confidence that this notice beforehand that the strong nations of the world will in every case be united will make war extremely unlikely.

SENATOR MOSES. Mr. President, are these procès verbaux to be deposited anywhere as a matter of public record?

THE PRESIDENT. That had not been decided, Senator. Of course, if they were deposited as a matter of public record, there would be certain very great disadvantages.

SENATOR MOSES. Are they to be deposited with the secretariat of the league of nations?

THE PRESIDENT. No, sir.

SENATOR MOSES. Without some such depository, how otherwise would this engagement of Japan, as embodied in the procès verbal, be brought forward for enforcement?

THE PRESIDENT. There would be as many copies of the procès verbal as there were members of the conference in existence much longer than the time within which we shall learn whether Japan will fulfill her obligations or not.

SENATOR MOSES. You mean in the private papers of the personnel of the council of four?

THE PRESIDENT. I would not call them private papers. I have a copy, Senator. I regard them as a public trust, not private papers, and I can assure you that they will not be destroyed.

SENATOR MOSES. Suppose that each member of the council of four had passed out of office, out of any position of power, at a time when it became evident that Japan was not keeping the engagement as it was embodied in the procès-verbal on the day when this record was made, in what manner would you expect that engagement to be brought forward for enforcement?

THE PRESIDENT. I should deem it my duty—I can not speak for the others—to leave those papers where they could be made accessible.

SENATOR POMERENE. Mr. President, I have another question or two on the Shantung proposition that I should like to ask, if I may.

Assuming for the sake of the argument that there were to be some undue delay on the part of Japan in turning back to China her rights in Shantung, and that China were to make complaint to the council provided for in the league of nations, have you any doubt but that it would be taken up promptly by all the members of that council for their consideration and determination?

THE PRESIDENT. No, sir; I have not any doubt of it.

SENATOR POMERENE. Another question: On yesterday Dr. Millard[35] was before the committee, and he made the statement that there were twenty regional understandings similar to the Monroe doctrine. I desire to say, however, that in answer to a question—

THE PRESIDENT. Did he name any of them?

SENATOR POMERENE. I asked him some questions afterwards, and in explanation he qualified that statement by saying that these were written agreements somewhat akin to the Lansing-Ishii

[35] Thomas Franklin Fairfax Millard, journalist and publisher, unofficial adviser to the Chinese delegation in Paris.

agreement, so-called, and as to these with relation to China a part of them were as between Japan and China, and a part as between Great Britain and China; and he instanced the secret agreement with Japan respecting Shantung. What I desired to ask was this: Did any information come to the commission indicating that there were any regional understandings similar to the Monroe doctrine?

THE PRESIDENT. None, whatever. The only agreements that I can imagine he was referring to are contained in the exchanges of notes which occurred between the Japanese and Chinese Governments in 1915 and 1918 with regard to the method and conditions of the return of Shantung Province to China.

SENATOR HITCHCOCK. Mr. President, I think it should be said also that later on in his testimony, either in answer to a question by Senator Pomerene, or perhaps in response to a question by Senator Swanson, while the witness, Dr. Millard, stated that he deemed them regional understandings—those that he had in mind—he said very emphatically that they were totally unlike the Monroe doctrine, and would not come under that category.

THE PRESIDENT. And in his sense every treaty that concerns territory anywhere affects a region, and is a regional understanding; but that is a very broad and vague meaning to attach to the word.

SENATOR JOHNSON of California. Mr. President, I am quite hesitant about asking certain questions which I wish to ask. I apologize in advance for asking them, and I trust you will stop me at once if they are questions which you deem inappropriate, or that ought not to be asked.

THE PRESIDENT. Thank you.

SENATOR JOHNSON of California. First, we have pending now treaties of peace with Austria, with Hungary, with Bulgaria, and with the Ottoman Empire, all of which involve tremendous new territorial adjustments; and under those new territorial adjustments we will have our obligations, moral or otherwise, under the league of nations, of course. The new territorial adjustments about to be determined upon in these various treaties are really greater in extent, or quite as important, at least, as those that are provided for by the German treaty; are they not?

THE PRESIDENT. I should say so; yes.

SENATOR JOHNSON of California. They will deal not only with the creation of the boundaries of new nations, but possibly with the subject of mandatories, too?

THE PRESIDENT. Well, the treaties will not themselves deal with the mandatories. That is a matter that will be decided by the league.

SENATOR JOHNSON of California. Oh, yes.

THE PRESIDENT. But the treaties will no doubt create certain territories which fall under the trusteeship which will lead to mandatories.

SENATOR JOHNSON of California. So that there is a very important—in fact, the most important—part of the territorial world settlement yet to be made?

THE PRESIDENT. Well, in extent, yes, Senator; so far as the amount of territory covered is concerned, yes.

SENATOR JOHNSON of California. Not only in extent, but in their character, and in the numbers of peoples involved, too, Mr. President. Is not that accurate?

THE PRESIDENT. Well, you may be right, Senator; I do not know.

SENATOR JOHNSON of California. I think you answered to Senator Borah the question I am about to ask, so pardon me if it is repetitive. It is this: Was the United States Government officially informed, at any time between the rupture of diplomatic relations with Germany and the signing of the armistice, of agreements made by the allied Governments in regard to the settlement of the war?

THE PRESIDENT. No; not so far as I know.

SENATOR JOHNSON of California. So far as you are aware, was it unofficially informed during that period?

THE PRESIDENT. I would be more clear in my answer, Senator, if I knew just what you were referring to.

SENATOR JOHNSON of California. I am referring to the so-called secret treaties which disposed of territory among the belligerents.

THE PRESIDENT. You mean like the treaty of London?

SENATOR JOHNSON of California. Yes; like the London pact.

THE PRESIDENT. No; no, sir.

SENATOR JOHNSON of California. Could you state whether or not any official investigation was made by our Government to ascertain whether or not there were any such treaties of territorial disposition?

THE PRESIDENT. There was no such investigation.

SENATOR JOHNSON of California. These specific treaties, then— the treaty of London, on the basis of which Italy entered the war; the agreement with Roumania, in August, 1916; the various agreements in respect to Asia Minor, and the agreements consummated in the winter of 1917 between France and Russia relative to the frontiers of Germany, and particularly in relation to the Saar Valley and the left bank of the Rhine—none of these did we (and when I say "we" I mean you, Mr. President) have any knowledge of prior to the conference at Paris?

THE PRESIDENT. No, sir. I can confidently answer that "No," in regard to myself.

SENATOR MC CUMBER. Senator Johnson, may I ask the President

right here whether or not after we entered into the war any treaties were made between any of our cobelligerents that were not given to us.

THE PRESIDENT. No, sir; I do not know of any.

SENATOR MC CUMBER. Then the secret treaties that you have reference to were made prior to the time we entered into the war?

THE PRESIDENT. Yes, sir.

SENATOR MC CUMBER. After that, our cobelligerents withheld nothing from us; did they?

THE PRESIDENT. They entered into no agreements.

SENATOR BORAH. Well, you asked, Senator, if they withheld anything from us. They withheld all that they had had previously?

THE PRESIDENT. No, no; but he means, Did they withhold any agreement that they made after we entered the war?

SENATOR MC CUMBER. That is just what I meant.

SENATOR JOHNSON of California. We do not know of any engagements which have been made subsequent to our entering into the war?

THE PRESIDENT. No, sir.

SENATOR JOHNSON of California. Those that I have referred to—and I say this, Senator, so that you will have no error in respect to it—I referred wholly, I think, to the treaties that were prior to our entry into the war.

THE PRESIDENT. Yes.

SENATOR JOHNSON of California. Were you familiar, Mr. President, please, with any agreements that were made by the allied Governments with the Czecho-Slovak National Council, the Polish National Council, and the Jugo-Slav National Committee?

THE PRESIDENT. I was aware of arrangements similar to those that we had ourselves made recognizing those national committees as provisional representatives of the people.

SENATOR JOHNSON of California. But merely as recognizing governments, and that these committees represented the peoples of the various countries?

THE PRESIDENT. Yes; and the recognition was purely informal. It was not an international recognition, but an agreement to deal with them as representatives.[36]

SENATOR JOHNSON of California. When our Government through you, Mr. President, in January, 1918, made the 14 points as the basis for peace, were those points made with the knowledge of the existence of the secret agreements?

THE PRESIDENT. No; oh, no.

[36] Wilson was mistaken here.

SENATOR JOHNSON of California. It was not intended, then, by the expression of these 14 points, to supplant the aims contained in the secret treaties?

THE PRESIDENT. Since I knew nothing of them, necessarily not.

SENATOR JOHNSON of California. Yes; quite so. Do you know, Mr. President, or is it permissible for us to be told, whether France has special military agreements with Poland and Czecho-Slovakia?

THE PRESIDENT. I know of none, sir.

SENATOR JOHNSON of California. Did China enter the war upon our advice—the advice of the United States?

THE PRESIDENT. I can not tell, sir. We advised her to enter, and she soon after did. She had sought our advice. Whether that was the persuasive advice or not, I do not know.

SENATOR JOHNSON of California. Do you recall, Mr. President, that preceding that advice we had asked China, as one of the neutral nations, to sever diplomatic relations with Germany?

THE PRESIDENT. Whether we had asked her?

SENATOR JOHNSON of California. Yes, sir.

THE PRESIDENT. I do not recall, Senator. I am sure Mr. Lansing can tell, though, from the records of the department.

SENATOR JOHNSON of California. Do you know, Mr. President, whether or not our Government stated to China that if China would enter the war we would protect her interests at the peace conference?

THE PRESIDENT. We made no promises.

SENATOR JOHNSON of California. No representations of that sort?

THE PRESIDENT. No. She knew that we would as well as we could. She had every reason to know that.

SENATOR JOHNSON of California. Pardon me a further question: You did make the attempt to do it, too; did you not?

THE PRESIDENT. Oh, indeed I did; very seriously.

SENATOR JOHNSON of California. And the decision ultimately reached at the peace conference was a disappointment to you?

THE PRESIDENT. Yes, sir; I may frankly say that it was.

SENATOR JOHNSON of California. You would have preferred, as I think most of us would, that there had been a different conclusion of the Shantung provision, or the Shantung difficulty or controversy, at the Paris peace conference?

THE PRESIDENT. Yes; I frankly intimated that.

SENATOR JOHNSON of California. Did it require the unanimous consent of the members of the peace conference to reach a decision like the Shantung decision?

THE PRESIDENT. Every decision; yes, sir.

SENATOR JOHNSON of California. Do you recall, Mr. President, prior to the decision on the territorial question of Shantung, or of German rights in Shantung, the racial equality question coming before the peace conference?

THE PRESIDENT. I remember that at one of the sessions called plenary sessions a resolution regarding that matter was introduced by the Japanese representatives, but rather as an expression of opinion or hope, and it was not pressed for action.

SENATOR JOHNSON of California. Mr. President, the press at that time stated that it had gone to a vote—and I trust some one will correct me if I am in error—and that the vote was 11 to 6 upon the proposition. The dispatches at that time were to that effect.

THE PRESIDENT. I was misled, Senator. You are referring to the commission on a league of nations?

SENATOR JOHNSON of California. Yes.

THE PRESIDENT. There was a vote there. There never was a vote on any subject in the peace conference.

SENATOR JOHNSON of California. I confounded the two.

THE PRESIDENT. Yes.

SENATOR JOHNSON of California. May I ask, if permissible, how the representatives of the United States voted upon that particular proposition?

THE PRESIDENT. Senator, I think it is very natural you should ask that. I am not sure that I am at liberty to answer, because that touches the intimacy of a great many controversies that occurred in that conference, and I think it is best, in the interest of international good understanding, that I should not answer.

SENATOR JOHNSON of California. Do you know, Mr. President, whether or not the American Commission at Paris urged that a definite sum of reparation be fixed in the treaty?

THE PRESIDENT. It did.

SENATOR JOHNSON of California. Will you state, if appropriate, why that view did not prevail?

THE PRESIDENT. No, Senator, I can not; and yet I dislike to decline, because it may create a misapprehension on your part. Let me see if I can explain it, without indiscretion: I would be very glad, gentlemen, to tell you all about it, if you will leave it out of the notes. May I do that?—because I do not wish to leave any wrong impression on your minds. The explanation is perfectly simple.

SENATOR BRANDEGEE. What is the question, please?

THE PRESIDENT. The question is, Why was the policy urged by the United States, that we fix a definite sum of reparation in the treaty, not adopted?

SENATOR BORAH. I would be content to have it left out of the notes upon your request; but I am afraid it would still get to the public, and that would put us in an embarrassing position.

THE PRESIDENT. It is not an explanation discreditable to anybody, but it is an international secret. I am quite at liberty to say that the United States financial representatives—who, by the way, made an admirable impression upon everybody over there—did advocate the fixing of a definite sum for reparation.

SENATOR FALL. Mr. President, may I ask, to clear up a difficulty in my own mind, whether you regard the answering of these questions as an indiscretion because of the fact that there are other negotiations pending which might be affected?

THE PRESIDENT. Oh, no, sir; simply because they affect the internal political affairs of other countries.

SENATOR FALL. Then, in your judgment, these matters should never be given publicity?

THE PRESIDENT. Matters of this sort.

SENATOR FALL. I say, matters of this sort that have been referred to, should, in your judgment, never be given publicity; and it is not because of pending or other negotiations?

THE PRESIDENT. Oh, no; I think they should not be given publicity.

SENATOR JOHNSON of California. I thank you very much, Mr. President. That is all I desire to ask.

THE PRESIDENT. You have been very considerate in putting your questions.

SENATOR FALL. Mr. President, as I suggested, I have prepared several written questions, for the purpose of concentrating my own ideas, and several of them, I may say, are somewhat in sequence, and I feel that if we are going to hold hearings all day—that is, if we are all going to have the time and do not get into arguments among ourselves—possibly it might be just to you to submit these questions, as I have prepared them, to you first, and allow you to look them over before I pursue the line of inquiry. However, that is, of course, entirely with you. They do not all refer directly to provisions of the treaty nor to the construction of the treaty, but to other matters relating to the treaty.

SENATOR JOHNSON of California. Before you do that, Senator, with the President's permission may I ask one or two more questions concerning Shantung which I omitted or forgot?

THE PRESIDENT. Certainly, Senator.

SENATOR JOHNSON of California. First, did Japan decline to sign the award as made or provided in the peace treaty?

THE PRESIDENT. Her representatives informed us, Senator, that they were instructed not to sign in that event.

SENATOR JOHNSON of California. Was the determination finally reached a balancing of the difficulties or the disadvantages that might arise because of the balancing of those advantages or disadvantages?

THE PRESIDENT. I do not know that I could answer that either "yes" or "no," Senator. It was a matter of many conversations and of many arguments and persuasions.

SENATOR JOHNSON of California. Was the decision reached—if you will pardon the perfectly blunt question—because Japan declined to sign unless that decision was reached in that way?

THE PRESIDENT. No; I do not think it would be true to say "yes" to that question.[37] It was reached because we thought it was the best that could be got, in view of the definite engagements of Great Britain and France, and the necessity of a unanimous decision, which we held to be necessary in every case we have decided.

SENATOR JOHNSON of California. Great Britain and France adhered to their original engagements, did they not?

THE PRESIDENT. They said that they did not feel at liberty to disregard them.

SENATOR JOHNSON of California. And you, Mr. President, were the one who was endeavoring to determine—I gather this from the news dispatches—the question upon its merits and its justice.

THE PRESIDENT. Our Government was the only Government free under the circumstances; yes.

SENATOR JOHNSON of California. Yes, sir. Do you mind stating, or would you prefer not, what it was that caused you ultimately to accede to the decision that was demanded by Japan?

THE PRESIDENT. Only the conclusion that I thought that it was the best that could be got under the circumstances.

SENATOR BRANDEGEE. May I interpolate there without disturbing you, Senator Johnson?

SENATOR JOHNSON of California. Yes, sir.

SENATOR BRANDEGEE. In Part 6 of the hearings before our committee, on page 182, Senator Johnson of California questioned Secretary Lansing. (Reading:)

> SENATOR JOHNSON of California. Was the Shantung decision made in order to have the Japanese signature to the league of nations?
>
> SECRETARY LANSING. That I can not say.

---

[37] Wilson soon contradicts this.

SENATOR JOHNSON of California. In your opinion was it?

SECRETARY LANSING. I would not want to say that, because I really have not the facts on which to form an opinion along that line.

SENATOR JOHNSON of California. Would the Japanese signatures to the league of nations have been obtained if you had not made the Shantung agreement?

SECRETARY LANSING. I think so.

SENATOR JOHNSON of California. You do?

SECRETARY LANSING. I think so.

SENATOR JOHNSON of California. So that even though Shantung had not been delivered to Japan, the league of nations would not have been injured?

SECRETARY LANSING. I do not think so.

SENATOR JOHNSON of California. And you would have had the same signatories that you have now?

SECRETARY LANSING. Yes; one more, China.

SENATOR JOHNSON of California. One more, China. So that the result of the Shantung decision was simply to lose China's signature rather than to gain Japan's?

SECRETARY LANSING. That is my personal view, but I may be wrong about it.

SENATOR JOHNSON of California. Why did you yield on a question on which you thought you ought not to yield and that you thought was a principle?

SECRETARY LANSING. Because naturally we were subject to the direction of the President of the United States.

SENATOR JOHNSON of California. And it was solely because you felt that you were subject to the decision of the President of the United States that you yielded?

SECRETARY LANSING. Yes.

SENATOR JOHNSON of California. The decision is his?

SECRETARY LANSING. Necessarily.

Now, I wondered whether Secretary Lansing was well informed about this question or not?

THE PRESIDENT. Well, my conclusion is different from his, sir.

SENATOR BRANDEGEE. You could not have got the signature of Japan if you had not given Shantung to Japan?

THE PRESIDENT. That is my judgment.

SENATOR BRANDEGEE. You say you were notified to that effect?

THE PRESIDENT. Yes, sir.

SENATOR SWANSON. As I understand, you were notified that they had instructions not to sign unless this was included.

THE PRESIDENT. Yes.

SENATOR BORAH. And was it your judgment that after the treaty had been ratified, China's rights would be protected and Japan would surrender to China what she said she would?

THE PRESIDENT. Yes.

SENATOR SWANSON. As I understand it, you consider this verbal agreement effective as relating to Shantung and you understood that this conveyance would be followed by a conveyance to China.

THE PRESIDENT. Not to supersede it, but the action by Japan is to follow.

SENATOR JOHNSON of California. I beg your pardon, what was your question?

SENATOR SWANSON. The conveyance or retransfer of the German possession in Shantung is to be followed by Japan's conveyance of this back to China, according to this agreement. One is as effective as the other.

SENATOR JOHNSON of California. Yes; but, Mr. President, you would have much preferred to have a different disposition, notwithstanding the promise of Japan in the treaty, would you not?

THE PRESIDENT. Yes, sir.

Senator Fall, would this be a practical suggestion? I have no objection to sitting here all day. Indeed, I have taken the liberty of having lunch prepared, if the gentlemen of the committee would be kind enough to join me. But since your questions are written, perhaps you might leave them with me and let me give such answers as I feel I can.

SENATOR FALL. Precisely, Mr. President. I can say to you, sir, that I prepared the questions with some care for the purpose of informing myself, and I think that it might not be entirely fair to you to answer offhand a series of questions, when I have the theory in mind along which I am propounding the questions—that is, one may lead to another—and I think it would be only fair to you that you might have the questions so you can read them and follow it.

THE PRESIDENT. Will you state the theory at the top (laughter)?

SENATOR FALL. There are two or three theories. The first question that I would like to ask is, "In your judgment have you not the authority by proclamation to declare in words that peace exists, and thus restore the status of peace between the Government and the people of this country and those with whom we declared war?" If you choose, I will read the following question.

THE PRESIDENT. That sets the key to them, I suppose.

SENATOR FALL. To several of them. Then there are others along other lines, one of which leads to another.

THE PRESIDENT. I would be happy to answer them as far as I can.

SENATOR FALL. That can be done later or now, just as you please.

SENATOR WILLIAMS. Suppose we take a recess.

THE CHAIRMAN. I do not know whether there are any more questions.

THE PRESIDENT. I had thought that I would send you in the replies.

SENATOR FALL. That would certainly be satisfactory to me. You would have no objection to the same publicity that is being given now?

THE PRESIDENT. No.

SENATOR FALL. There are two or three different lines of questions.

SENATOR MC CUMBER. You would probably get more clear information if you take that method.

SENATOR FALL. I think so. They are not in any sense, Mr. President, prepared as catch questions, otherwise I would not submit them to you. If you were on the stand, and I were cross-examining you as a witness, I would prefer not to let you see the whole series of questions. But I think that is fair, and so far as I am concerned if it is satisfactory to you it would be more satisfactory to me.

SENATOR BRANDEGEE. In reply to Senator Lodge's inquiry I jotted down a few questions at random with the idea of asking some if they had not been touched upon by other members of the committee. I have some that I would like to ask, but I want to conform to the convenience of the President and the committee as to when it shall be done. I do not mean to delay you on your luncheon hour or anything of that kind.

THE PRESIDENT. The luncheon hour is 1 o'clock, and I was in hopes that you gentlemen would remain for lunch.

SENATOR BRANDEGEE. I do not want to absorb the remaining time if other Senators want to go on now. I am perfectly willing to wait until they are finished.

SENATOR HARDING. I would like to hear your questions.

SENATOR BRANDEGEE. I am not sure what questions I will ask except I made some notes.

SENATOR WILLIAMS. I would rather come back to-morrow morning at half past 10.

SENATOR HITCHCOCK. We have an engagement to-morrow morning for the committee.

THE CHAIRMAN. I think we must have some consideration for the President's time.

SENATOR HARDING. I just want to reserve one question.

SENATOR BRANDEGEE. Do you not want to ask it now?

THE CHAIRMAN. We have until 1 o'clock.

SENATOR BRANDEGEE. I have here the President's statement which he read to us when we met here this morning, and in it he states:

> Nothing, I am led to believe, stands in the way of the ratification of the treaty except certain doubts with regard to the meaning and implication of certain articles of the covenant of the league of nations; and I must frankly say that I am unable to understand why such doubts should be entertained.

Now, I do not believe the President is correctly informed as to the situation if he believes that. There are things in the treaty itself which militate against the ratification, in my opinion, of the treaty without amendment. Did you have in mind, Mr. President, when you read that to us, the Shantung provision of the treaty?

THE PRESIDENT. I certainly had that in mind, Senator, but I did not understand that that stood in the way of ratification. I am, of course, acting only upon such information as I have received.

SENATOR BRANDEGEE. I understand—and that is the reason of taking the liberty of suggesting to you that you may not be well informed in this respect. Of course there is opposition by a great many Senators to the entire covenant of the league of nations, which I have no doubt you know, that is, article 1 of the treaty of Versailles. Then there is opposition to the various parts of the covenants of the league and not to the whole league, by other Senators. Then there is a great opposition, fundamental and sincere, to the Shantung provision, which is in the body of the treaty itself, and which can only be cured by an amendment. As I understand it, no reservation that we could make in the resolution of ratification would be effective to strike out the Shantung provision. It must be cured, if it is cured, by a straight out-and-out amendment, striking that from the treaty. That, of course, would necessitate the resubmission of the treaty to the signatories who have already signed it.

Now, you state later on that every suggestion of the United States was accepted, that is after you went back, after you had your conference with us last March, and having obtained our views as to the necessity for certain changes in the first draft of the covenant, you state (reading):

> The view of the United States with regard to the questions I have mentioned had, in fact, already been accepted by the commission and there was supposed to be nothing inconsistent with them in the draft of the covenant first adopted.

And omitting a few lines which do not apply to that you say (reading):

> There was absolutely no doubt as to the meaning of any one of the resulting provisions of the covenant in the minds of those who participated in drafting them, and I respectfully submit that there is nothing vague or doubtful in their wording.

Of course that is your opinion, if I may say so.

THE PRESIDENT. Yes, sir.

SENATOR BRANDEGEE. But you are familiar with the statements, I have no doubt, that ex-Senator Root, Justice Hughes, Mr. Taft, and other able lawyers of the country have made with respect to the necessity for reservations if we are to ratify the treaty, are you not?

THE PRESIDENT. Yes, sir.

SENATOR BRANDEGEE. That is, you admit that there are grave doubts among the ablest lawyers of the country as to the necessity for reservations or the alternative between reservations and ratifying the whole treaty, as it is expressed in the vernacular, without the dotting of an "i" or the crossing of a "t."

THE PRESIDENT. I admit that there are those difficulties in a great many minds.

SENATOR BRANDEGEE. Now, of course, it is true, is it not, that if difficulties arise as to the construction of any provision of the treaty after we have passed from the scene, what we thought the provisions of the treaty or of the covenant meant, will not be very powerful in the construction that may be placed upon it by those who then have to determine what it means, will it?

THE PRESIDENT. The vote of the United States will be essential.

SENATOR BRANDEGEE. I do not mean that. The fact that you think now that everything in the treaty is plain and that there is no doubt about the meaning of any provisions, and the fact that I think there is grave doubt about many of the provisions, will not seriously affect the opinion of the council or of the arbitrator that finally passes upon the true meaning of the treaty when dispute arises.

THE PRESIDENT. No, Senator; but the plain wording of the treaty will have a great deal to do, and the meaning of the wording is plain.

SENATOR BRANDEGEE. That is simply another way of stating, is it not, that you are clear in your opinion that the provisions of the treaty are plain? But I am suggesting that there will be a dispute between nations as to what the treaty means after we have passed from the scene.

THE PRESIDENT. No, sir; it is a question of being confident of what language means, not confident of an opinion.

SENATOR BRANDEGEE. I mean, we derive our opinions as to the meanings of the treaty from the language of the treaty, do we not?

THE PRESIDENT. Yes.

SENATOR BRANDEGEE. Now they would derive their construction of what the treaty means from the language of it, we not being there?

THE PRESIDENT. Yes.

SENATOR BRANDEGEE. So that what we think about it now will not be determinative in an international court or before an arbitrator 20 years hence in case of a dispute between two nations as to the meaning of the treaty?

THE PRESIDENT. Certainly not, but the language will.

SENATOR BRANDEGEE. Of course they will have the language before them, but the language which determines it is now in dispute between you and certain lawyers of the country and certain Senators as to its meaning. Now what provision is there in the treaty for the determination of a dispute as to the interpretation of a clause of the treaty if such dispute arises?

THE PRESIDENT. The covenant states that there are certain questions which are acknowledged as being especially suitable for submission to arbitration. One of those is the meaning of the treaty.

SENATOR BRANDEGEE. What does the treaty provide about that?

THE PRESIDENT. You have it there, sir.

SENATOR BRANDEGEE. Yes, sir; I wondered if you remembered it.

THE PRESIDENT. I think I do so, but you have the language.

SENATOR BRANDEGEE. Yes. Article 12 of the league provides (reading):

The members of the league agree that if there should arise between them any dispute likely to lead to a rupture, they will submit the matter either to arbitration or to inquiry by the council, and they agree in no case to resort to war until three months after the award by the arbitrators or the report by the council.

That is, if there is a dispute, as I construe this, between members of the league as to the meaning of the covenant or any article thereof, it shall be referred to the arbitrators.

THE PRESIDENT. Only if the parties agree.

SENATOR BRANDEGEE. Or to the council?

THE PRESIDENT. Or to the council; yes.

SENATOR BRANDEGEE. That is, the council is to determine the meaning of the covenant?

THE PRESIDENT. No, Senator; I beg your pardon. There are two processes. If the parties agree to submit to arbitration, of course it is submitted to arbitration, and the decision is final. If they think it is a question that they are not willing to submit to arbitration, then they must submit it to the council for an expression of opinion and a recommendation, but that opinion and recommendation do not bind.

SENATOR BRANDEGEE. Is there any possible way authoritatively of determining without war what the treaty means?

THE PRESIDENT. That is true of every treaty, Senator. If you re-express it in the language of the Senators to whom you refer and there is a dispute about the meaning of that, the same would apply. You can not use any language, I assume, which could not possibly give rise to some sort of dispute.

SENATOR BRANDEGEE. I assume that if it provided that if there should arise between the members of the league any dispute in relation to the construction of any article of the covenant of the league of nations, such dispute should be referred to an arbitrator, and the members would agree to be bound by its decision; that would be an agreement for an authoritative determination of what the treaty meant.

THE PRESIDENT. Yes.

SENATOR BRANDEGEE. Now, as it is they will submit the matter either to arbitration or to inquiry by the council, and so forth. Now, you say that the opinion of the council to which the dispute has been submitted is only advisory?

THE PRESIDENT. Yes, sir.

SENATOR BRANDEGEE. Then suppose one party to the dispute against whom the council decides declines to abide by it?

THE PRESIDENT. Then there is war, but not within three months of the opinion of the council.

SENATOR BRANDEGEE. Under article 10 the members of the league undertake to respect and preserve as against external aggression the territorial integrity and existing political independence of all members of the league. That is a contract between the signatories. We say: "We undertake to preserve the territorial integrity of the members against external aggression," which means that we contract to do it, does it not?

THE PRESIDENT. We engage to do it.

SENATOR BRANDEGEE. It means an international contract, does it not, a compact, an agreement?

THE PRESIDENT. Yes.

SENATOR BRANDEGEE. Whether that is a moral or legal obligation, it is an obligation?

THE PRESIDENT. Yes.

SENATOR BRANDEGEE. Of course, it is a moral duty to keep a

promise, and this is an international promise; so that the distinction between a moral obligation and a legal one seems to me to be not of great importance, because we are obligated in any event.

THE PRESIDENT. Pardon me; I think it is of the greatest importance, because the element of judgment enters into it as it does not in the other.

SENATOR BRANDEGEE. You mean the judgment as to whether or not it is a moral obligation?

THE PRESIDENT. No. For example, a question is submitted to arbitration and it is agreed that the decision shall be final. The judgment of one of the parties to the controversy may be that the decision is a very bad one, but it has to accept it; the element of judgment is excluded altogether; but, with regard to the method of fulfilling the obligations of a covenant like that under consideration there is freedom of judgment on the part of the individual members of the league. It seems to me that makes a very considerable difference.

SENATOR HARDING. Will the Senator permit me to interrupt right there?

SENATOR BRANDEGEE. I will.

SENATOR HARDING. I dislike to interrupt the Senator.

SENATOR BRANDEGEE. I yield to the Senator.

SENATOR HARDING. The President expressed a while ago surprise that I raised a question as to the value of this compact because of the moral obligation feature. Let me premise by the statement that I look upon a moral obligation as that which the conscience of the contracting party impels. The conscience of any nation in Europe, for example, may be warped by its prejudices, racial, geographical, and otherwise. If that be true and any nation may put aside or exercise its judgment as to the moral obligation in accepting any recommendation of the league, really what do we get out of this international compact in the enforcement of any decree?

THE PRESIDENT. We get the centering upon it generally of the definite opinion of the world, expressed through the authoritative organs of the responsible governments.

SENATOR HARDING. Another question: That is surrendering the suggestion of a moral obligation for this Republic to the prejudices or necessities of the nations of the Old World, is it not?

THE PRESIDENT. I do not understand that we make such a surrender.

SENATOR HARDING. Would you not understand a decree by the council to be a suggestion of this moral obligation?

THE PRESIDENT. Certainly I would, but we would have to concur in that before it had any force of any kind.

SENATOR HARDING. Would it not be quite as moral for this Republic itself to determine its moral obligations?

THE PRESIDENT. Undoubtedly, Senator; but in the meantime the world would not have the knowledge before it that there will be concerted action by all the responsible governments of the world in the protection of the peace of the world. The minute you do away with that assurance to the world you have reached the situation which produced the German war.

SENATOR HARDING. What becomes of our standing among nations if the council fixes a moral obligation upon us and we reject the judgment of the council as to the moral obligation?

THE PRESIDENT. Pardon me if I remind you that we always have to concur in that.

SENATOR HARDING. Precisely; but the council state what constitutes the moral obligation, if we agree; but if we do not agree, then, in the eyes of the world we have rejected its judgment as to a moral obligation.

THE PRESIDENT. Certainly; and I hold that we are at liberty to do that, if our moral judgment honestly differs from the moral judgment of the world.

SENATOR HARDING. Then, let us go back to the original inquiry. What permanent value is there, then, to this compact?

THE PRESIDENT. The greatest permanent value, Senator, is the point that I have raised. We are assuming that the United States will not concur in the general moral judgment of the world. In my opinion, she generally will. If it had been known that this war was coming on, her moral judgment would have concurred with that of the other Governments of the world, with that of the other peoples of the world; and if Germany had known that there was a possibility of that sort of concurrence, she never would have dared to do what she did. Without such notice served on the powers that may wish to repeat the folly that Germany commenced, there is no assurance to the world that there will be peace even for a generation, whereas if they know beforehand that there will be that concert of judgment, there is the most tremendous guaranty.

SENATOR HARDING. But, Mr. President, nobody expressed for us our moral obligation to enter into this war. That was our own expression, was it not?

THE PRESIDENT. Certainly; it was our concurrence in the judgment of the world.

SENATOR HARDING. One of the points I am getting at, if I can make it clear, is the necessity of a written compact for this Republic to fulfill its moral obligations to civilization.

THE PRESIDENT. Senator, this Republic, if I interpret it rightly, does not need a suggestion from any quarter to fulfill its moral obligations.

SENATOR HARDING. I quite agree with that.

THE PRESIDENT. But it steadies the whole world by its promise beforehand that it will stand with other nations of similar judgment to maintain right in the world.

SENATOR FALL. Mr. President, then if the commissioner of the United States on the council were to join with the other members of the council in fixing a moral obligation upon the United States, and the Congress and the President, acting as part of the legislative branch of the Government, were to reject that judgment, would it not have a very disastrous effect upon the league, throw the world into chaos, and undo all that has been done?

THE PRESIDENT. It might; but you are assuming a case—

SENATOR FALL. Certainly; we have to assume cases.

THE PRESIDENT. Where we would have to assume that responsibility, because, being part of the Government, we would in every case really express the judgment of the American people, and if the unhappy time should ever come when that judgment is against the judgment of the rest of the world we would have to express it.

SENATOR FALL. Certainly. Mr. President, I am possibly looking, as Bacon said, at a distance.

SENATOR MC CUMBER. Would our moral conviction of the unrighteousness of the German war have brought us into this war if Germany had not committed any acts against us, without the league of nations, as, of course, we had no league of nations at that time?

THE PRESIDENT. I hope it would eventually, Senator, as things developed.

SENATOR MC CUMBER. Do you think if Germany had committed no act of war or no act of injustice against our citizens that we would have gotten into this war?

THE PRESIDENT. I do think so.

SENATOR MC CUMBER. You think we would have gotten in anyway?

THE PRESIDENT. I do.

SENATOR BRANDEGEE. If I may be allowed to resume, for I kept still all morning—

SENATOR FALL. If the Senator will pardon me a moment, I am going to ask the President to excuse me, as I have an engagement.

THE PRESIDENT. I am sorry, Senator, that you are obliged to leave.

SENATOR FALL. I regret, sir, that I have an engagement with my wife, who is not in very good health.

SENATOR BRANDEGEE. Now, if I may proceed without interruption, which breaks the continuity of my thought and uses a great deal of time, I will be through in a very few minutes. As I understand the President, his construction of article 10 is that if the council considers the question of external aggression upon a member of the league, we, having signed this treaty with article 10 in it, in which we undertake to preserve against external aggression the territorial integrity of all members of the league, can then say, it is a moral question into which the element of judgment enters and we, considering our judgment binding at the time, do not care to agree to the recommendation of the council. If every member of the league is at liberty to take that view of its moral and legal obligations under article 10, and declines to do what the council recommends, and if it is known in advance that that is the construction placed upon article 10 by those who framed it, it does not seem to me—and this is merely my opinion—that the terror to wrongdoers by what is hoped to be the united, concerted action of the members of the league in the concentration of its powers to suppress the wrongdoer will have the effect that the President thinks it will. In other words, I do not think that Germany would have refrained from war if she had known that article 10 was in existence.

Article 10 says:

In case of any such aggression, or in case of any threat or danger of such aggression, the council shall advise upon the means by which this obligation shall be fulfilled.

There is no doubt that that is an obligation in a contract, and I know of but one way to perform an obligation that you have contracted to perform, and that is to perform it. I do not think that it admits of any qualifications after you sign the treaty. I want to call attention also to the fact that the external aggression which we undertake, if we sign this treaty, to repel or guarantee against is not stated in the treaty at all to be an unwarranted aggression. I wish to ask the President, if the league were in existence and Hungary and Roumania were members of it, and Roumania were in the position she now is, having raided the territorial integrity of Hungary and marched through its capital and occupied it, and the council, as its duty would be under the covenant, considered what was best to be done and advised us to send immediately to cooperate with them 100,000 men, whether we would be at liberty to discuss whether we were morally bound by article 10 of the covenant and decline to send the men, and, if we were, could we do it without risking being called an "international slacker" by the other members of the league?

THE PRESIDENT. Senator, since you have made the case a concrete one I am afraid I ought not to answer it, because it involves a judgment as between Roumania and Hungary.

SENATOR BRANDEGEE. I withdraw the names of the two countries, and assume the circumstances.

THE PRESIDENT. Let me say that I take it for granted that in practically every case the United States would respond; but that does not seem to be the question. I quite agree with you that a moral obligation is to be fulfilled, and I am confident that our Nation will fulfill it, but that does not remove from each individual case the element of judgment which we are free to exercise in two stages: We are, first, free to exercise it in the vote of our representative on the council, who will of course act under instructions from the home Government; and, in the second place, we are to exercise it when the President, acting upon the action of the council, makes his recommendation to Congress. Then, Congress is to exercise its judgment as to whether or not the instructions of the Executive to our member of the council were well founded, and whether the case is one of distinct moral obligation.

SENATOR BRANDEGEE. Suppose that each member of the council, as you say, acting under instructions from its home Government, including our representative on the council, should think, for instance, that Roumania was entirely right in some invasion of Hungary, and public sentiment was that way, but that our Government instructed our representative to vote with the foreign members of the council to support Hungary—suppose the public sentiment of the other members and of the people of this country were in favor of Roumania, what sort of a position would we be in to fulfill our guaranty?

THE PRESIDENT. In order to answer that question I must go a little bit afield. In the first place, I understand that article to mean that no nation is at liberty to invade the territorial integrity of another. That does not mean to invade for purposes of warfare, but to impair the territorial integrity of another nation. Its territorial integrity is not destroyed by armed intervention; it is destroyed by the retention of territory, by taking territory away from it; that impairs its territorial integrity.[38] I understand the covenant to mean that that is in no case permissible by the action of a single nation against another; that there is only one permissible method and that is, if territorial arrangements are unsatisfactory, that they should be brought to the attention of the world through the league and

[38] The plain meaning of this statement is that temporary occupations of the territory of one state by another was not forbidden by Article X, e.g., the occupation of Veracruz by United States forces in 1914. Wilson made a similar statement in his talk to the St. Louis Chamber of Commerce, printed at Sept. 5, 1919.

that then the league should exercise such rights as it may be able to exercise for a readjustment of boundaries.

I believe that territorial aggression, in the sense of territorial capture, is, by the wording of the act, made illegitimate.

SENATOR BRANDEGEE. The words are not "territorial aggression," but "external aggression."

THE PRESIDENT. But it says the preservation of its territorial integrity against external aggression.

SENATOR BRANDEGEE. Suppose the external aggressor, having gotten within the territory of the aggressee, stays there?

THE PRESIDENT. Then that impairs the territorial integrity.

SENATOR BRANDEGEE. Certainly; and then on a call by the council for us to perform our international contract under article 10, if Congress does not favor performing it, you think we would not be subject to criticism by the other members of the league?

THE PRESIDENT. Oh, we might be subject to criticism; but I think Congress would be at liberty to form its own judgment as to the circumstances.

SENATOR BRANDEGEE. I agree with you entirely, and under our Constitution Congress would have to do so.

THE PRESIDENT. Yes; that is understood by all.

SENATOR BRANDEGEE. Of course; but I am assuming if the council should advise us to do a certain thing, and Congress refused to do it—and if every nation's representative assembly can do the same thing, it seems to me like a rope of sand and not an effective tribunal which would result in promoting peace.

THE PRESIDENT. The reason I do not agree with you, Senator, is that I do not think such a refusal would likely often occur. I believe it would be only upon the gravest grounds—and in case Congress is right, I am indifferent to foreign criticism.

SENATOR BRANDEGEE. Of course, we would always think we were right, I assume. Now, I wish to call your attention to article 15. I do this simply because you think all these provisions are clear, and I want to say in that connection that we had Mr. Miller, who described himself as the technical expert or adviser to the American Peace Commission, especially, I think, on questions of international law.

THE PRESIDENT. The league of nations.

SENATOR BRANDEGEE. We had him before our committee, and he answered this question, that I am about to ask, in three different ways, and we could not, of course, get much information from him; and he promised to take it under advisement and to give us his considered opinion, but he has not done so. Now, article 15, in the last two paragraphs provides:

The council may in any case under this article refer the dispute to the assembly. The dispute shall be so referred at the request of either party to the dispute, provided that such request be made within 14 days after the submission of the dispute to the council.

In any case referred to the assembly, all the provisions of this article and of article 12 relating to the action and powers of the council shall apply to the action and powers of the assembly, provided that a report made by the assembly, if concurred in by the representatives of those members of the league represented on the council and of a majority of the other members of the league, exclusive in each case of the representatives of the parties to the dispute, shall have the same force as a report by the council concurred in by all the members thereof other than the representatives of one or more of the parties to the dispute.

Now, in the first place, it says "represented on the council and of a majority of the other members of the league." Does that mean that the various members of the league have got to act upon that as separate Governments, or does it mean the representatives of the other members of the league?

THE PRESIDENT. I do not quite understand that question.

SENATOR BRANDEGEE. It says:

A report made by the assembly, if concurred in by the representatives of those members of the league represented on the council and of a majority of the other members of the league.

Does that mean there "and a majority of the other representatives of members of the league in the assembly"?

THE PRESIDENT. Yes; I assume so.

SENATOR BRANDEGEE. But it does not say so. It leaves it as though the members of the league could act independently of their representatives and the assembly.

THE PRESIDENT. Oh, no.

SENATOR BRANDEGEE. I assume it means what you say.

THE PRESIDENT. Yes; I assume that.

SENATOR BRANDEGEE. Very well. Now, the question: Supposing there were a dispute between the United States and that portion of the British Empire known as the United Kingdom—England, Ireland, Scotland, and Wales—as to some right of one of our ships to enter an English port, for instance, and that dispute should come before the council, and, upon the request of Great Britain, it should be removed to the assembly. The article I have just read provides for a report concurred in "exclusive in each case of the representatives of the parties to the dispute."

THE PRESIDENT. Yes.

SENATOR BRANDEGEE. Now, all the self-governing colonies of England, or at least five of them, have a vote in the assembly, and the British Empire also has a vote. I assume in the case of the dispute which I have supposed, of course, the United States would be excluded from voting, as being a party to the dispute; and I assume the British Empire would be excluded, but I am not sure.

THE PRESIDENT. Yes, sir; that is what I assume.

SENATOR BRANDEGEE. Do you assume also that Australia, New Zealand, Canada, and India would be excluded?

THE PRESIDENT. They are parts of the British Empire.

SENATOR BRANDEGEE. They are parts of the British Empire, but are they parties to the dispute which I have supposed to have arisen between us and England?

THE PRESIDENT. I admit, Senator, that that is a complicated question; but my judgment about it is quite clear. I think I can give one instead of three answers.

SENATOR BRANDEGEE. Yes.

THE PRESIDENT. Disputes can arise only through the Governments which have international representation. In other words, diplomatically speaking, there is only one "British Empire." The parts of it are but pieces of the whole. The dispute, therefore, in the case you have supposed, would be between the United States as a diplomatic unit and the British Empire as a diplomatic unit. That is the only ground upon which the two nations could deal with one another, whether by way of dispute or agreement. Therefore, I have assumed, and confidently assumed, that the representatives of all parts of the British Empire would be excluded.

SENATOR BRANDEGEE. I should think that would be only fair, and I would assume that; but Mr. Miller answered that question by saying, first, that he was in doubt; secondly, that the self-governing colonies of Great Britain or of the British Empire would not be excluded, because they were not parties to the dispute; and then, third, that they would be excluded because they were parts of the British Empire; and if the legal adviser of the commission was that much confused, I feel that I need not apologize for being confused myself.

THE PRESIDENT. No; but the commission was not confused.

SENATOR KNOX. May I say this: I was not present at the meeting when Mr. Miller testified. The fact is that while it is technically true, as the President says, that the British self-governing colonies deal diplomatically through the British foreign office, it is only true in a most technical sense. They are absolutely autonomous, even in their diplomatic dealings, as to matters that affect them. For instance, I remember when the Canadian reciprocity agreement was negotiated in 1911 the delegates sent to negotiate the agreement were from Canada. Great Britain did not appear at the hearings or conferences at all, and in every sense Canada was just as autonomous in conducting her international negotiations as she would have been if she had been an absolutely independent Government.

THE PRESIDENT. Yes; but this, you see, Senator, is a combination of definite Governments that have definite international relations with each other.

SENATOR KNOX. But the fact that you give representation to Canada and Australia and New Zealand and other autonomous self-governing British colonies rather contradicts the idea, does it not, that they are one Government?

THE PRESIDENT. I think not, sir; because in making up the constitution of the council it was provided, to speak with technical accuracy, that the five principal allied or associated Governments should each have one representative in the league; and in the opening paragraph of the treaty itself those powers are enumerated, and among others is the British Empire. "The Empire of Great Britain," I think, is the technical term. Therefore their unity is established by their representation in the council.

SENATOR BRANDEGEE. Mr. President, I read from the treaty—

THE CHAIRMAN. I was going to ask, if I may, what function do these five Dominions of the British Empire have in the assembly?

THE PRESIDENT. None, except the general powers of the assembly itself.

THE CHAIRMAN. They have votes in the assembly?

THE PRESIDENT. They have votes, but in a matter involving the British Empire, they would have but one vote among them.[39]

THE CHAIRMAN. But on all other matters, they would each have one vote?

THE PRESIDENT. Yes.

SENATOR BRANDEGEE. I want to call the President's attention to the first page of the treaty with Germany, which says, after the preamble setting forth the desirability of the condition existing being replaced by a just and durable peace, "For this purpose, the high contracting parties represented as follows," and then it names them, and in the list is "His Majesty, the King of the United Kingdom of Great Britain and Ireland, and of the British Dominions beyond the seas, Emperor of India, by his duly accredited officials, and the Dominion of Canada, the Commonwealth of Australia, the Dominion of South Africa, the Dominion of New Zealand," etc. Now, they are "high contracting parties"?

[39] Wilson was of course mistaken here.

THE PRESIDENT. Yes.

SENATOR BRANDEGEE. And if one of those high contracting parties has a dispute with another of the high contracting parties, by what inference are other high contracting parties made parties to the dispute?

THE PRESIDENT. I think by the inference that I thought I established, sir—

SENATOR BRANDEGEE. But, if you will allow me to say so, it does not say that these parties, the self-governing British colonies, shall be excluded from participating in the deliberations because they may have some interest in the controversy.

THE PRESIDENT. No.

SENATOR BRANDEGEE. They must be parties to the dispute. Now, if we have a dispute with England about the right of an American ship to enter an English port, how can it be said that New Zealand or Australia is a party to that dispute?

THE PRESIDENT. Because, Senator, in case of the worst coming to the worst, and war ensuing, we would be at war with all of them.

SENATOR BRANDEGEE. It may be that a blunder has been made in creating such a situation. It would not be determinative, in my opinion.

Now, on page 7 of the print that I have, which is Senate Document No. 49, Sixty-sixth Congress, first session, the last thing in the treaty is this statement:

From the coming into force of the present treaty the state of war will terminate. From that moment and subject to the provisions of this treaty, official relations with Germany, and with any of the German States, will be resumed by the allied and associated powers.

The treaty itself provides that when Germany and three of the allied and associated powers have ratified the treaty it has come into force.

THE PRESIDENT. As between those parties.

SENATOR BRANDEGEE. It does not say so.

THE PRESIDENT. I beg your pardon, I think it does.

SENATOR BRANDEGEE. Here it is, Mr. President. (Handing pamphlet to the President.) I have read it, and there is no such language in it that I can discover.

THE PRESIDENT. No; not the part that you read; I did not mean that; but in the part where the provision is referred to about ratification by Germany and three of the principal allied and associated powers.

SENATOR BRANDEGEE. I have read that with some care, and I have not seen it.

SENATOR KNOX. The language to which the President refers is in the concluding paragraph of the treaty, and it provides that when the process of ratification shall have been completed by Germany and any three powers, the treaty shall come into force.

THE PRESIDENT. As between them.

SENATOR KNOX. No; I beg your pardon, Mr. President. In a subsequent clause dealing with what I think is an entirely different matter—that is, the adjustments as between the nations, not adjustments as between the allied and associated powers and Germany—it comes into force whenever the ratifications are made; but if you will take the body of the treaty you will find that everything that Germany is to do is to be done within a certain number of days after the ratification has been made; and a certain number of months afterwards she is to demobilize, give up her ships, and do all things that will make her practically a noncombatant, within a number of days after ratification by three of the powers; so she is either at peace with the world, or she is only partially at peace with the world; and as the requirements of the treaty are specific that she is to go out of the war business altogether, there is a conclusive inference in my mind that she is at peace with the world when those three ratifications have been made.

THE PRESIDENT. I can not agree with you there. You see, the theory is this: That when three of the principal allied and associated powers ratify this treaty, Germany having ratified it, then the treaty is in force; that is to say, she has then engaged to do the things provided in the treaty, and her engagement is with those three powers, among the rest, and she must then proceed to do what she has promised; but it does not establish peace between her and other countries.

SENATOR KNOX. I think that language shows that it establishes peace and provides for a resumption of diplomatic and all other relations with Germany. I intend, within a short time, to try to make my views upon that clear.

THE PRESIDENT. Yes.

SENATOR BRANDEGEE. I went into that question rather thoroughly—"from the coming into force of the present treaty the state of war will terminate." Then it says, "From that moment, and subject to the provisions of this treaty, official relations with Germany and with any of the German States will be resumed by the allied and associated powers," which I assume means all of them.

Now, to revert to another point, Mr. President, have you any knowledge—and I ask all these questions, of course, subject to your determination as to whether it is proper for you to answer them, or to make any statement about them—

THE PRESIDENT. Yes.

SENATOR BRANDEGEE. Are the Austrian, Bulgarian, and Turkish treaties, which I assume are in the process of being made—

THE PRESIDENT. Yes.

SENATOR BRANDEGEE (continuing). Intertwined with the covenant of the league of nations as is the treaty with Germany?

THE PRESIDENT. The covenant of the league constitutes a part of each of those treaties.

SENATOR BRANDEGEE. Would you feel at liberty to state what percentage of progress they have made up to the present time, or how nearly completed they are?

THE PRESIDENT. I think they are all practically completed, Senator, with the exception of some debatable questions of territorial boundaries.

SENATOR BRANDEGEE. Inasmuch as our Constitution provides that treaties shall be made by the President by and with the advice and consent of two-thirds of the Senators present, do you think that it is constitutional for us to approve the Franco-American treaty which provides that before it goes into operation—or substantially, I would say, before it goes into operation—it must secure the approval of the council of the league of nations?

THE PRESIDENT. Why, yes; we can consent. We have the sovereign right to consent to any process that we choose, surely.

SENATOR BRANDEGEE. We have the right to consent, but of course the Senate has the constitutional right to ratify the treaty, negotiated and presented by the Executive; but my point is, have we a right to provide that in addition to the constitutional requirements for the making of a valid treaty there shall also be required the consent of the council of the league of nations, which the Constitution was not aware of?

THE PRESIDENT. If that is a part of the treaty; yes, I think we have.

SENATOR BRANDEGEE. But you do not think that the treaty can in any way amend the Constitution or the constitutional requirements for executing a treaty.

THE PRESIDENT. No.

SENATOR BRANDEGEE. Then by what process of ratiocination do you assume that the treaty can compel the consent of the council before this covenant is approved?

THE PRESIDENT. Suppose you would determine that when any group of nations adopted a treaty then we could adopt the treaty that contained certain provisions that we wished to put in, and to make the operation of the treaty contingent upon its acceptance by the other nations in the group. It seems to me that that is an entirely analogous case. In other words I am assuming that we adopt the treaty with Germany. In that case we will be members of the league. We are in effect saying that we have become members of the league. If the council of the league accepts this we agree to put it in force. It is a means of being consistent with the thing that we have already done in becoming a member of the league.

SENATOR BRANDEGEE. I get your viewpoint about that. Now, do you think it is wise for us to adopt the Franco-American treaty which in substance provides that we can not denounce it until the council of the league of nations gives us permission to do so or agrees to denounce it.

THE PRESIDENT. I do, Senator. I have a very strong feeling with regard to our historical relations with France, and also a very keen appreciation of her own sense of danger, and I think it would be one of the handsomest acts of history to enter into that.

SENATOR BRANDEGEE. I feel just as cordially toward her heroic conduct as anybody can. But that was not the question. The question was whether it was wise to so tie ourselves to any foreign nation as that we never could repudiate—I will not use the word "repudiate"—can never cancel our treaties without due notice, without the consent of a body not yet created.

THE PRESIDENT. Of course I am assuming that body will be created before we adopt the Franco-American treaty, and in that case that provision that you are alluding to is only a completion of the idea of the treaty, namely, as I have been quoted as saying, this is an agreement on our part to anticipate the advice of the council of the league, as we shall take such and such measures to defend France. Inasmuch as we are anticipating that, we are assuming the action of the league, and therefore it is with the league and its action that the whole matter is bound up, and I think that the provision you allude to, therefore, is consistent and almost logically necessary.

SENATOR BRANDEGEE. Well, now, inasmuch as you have stated in your message—and I have of course agreed to it and have no doubt that it is true—that the Franco-American treaty is only designed for temporary purposes, the defense of France until the league says that it is competent to do it, or words to that effect—

THE PRESIDENT. Yes.

SENATOR BRANDEGEE. Would it not be the part of prudence for us to include in the Franco-American treaty, if it should be ratified, a provision that it shall have some time limit put upon it, that it shall exist for not more than 10 years, say. I assume if the league is ever going to be effective to preserve the territorial integrity and political independence of its various members, it will be in the course of 10 years, and there is no objection to having some time limit on the treaty.

THE PRESIDENT. Only a psychological objection, the sentiment between the two countries.

SENATOR BRANDEGEE. The other alternative is to guarantee it forever or until the council of the league loosens us from it, is it not?

THE PRESIDENT. Yes; when the council of the league will exist, among other uses should be that the whole international influence that could be brought to bear for the management of all these things will be present there to bring about this rearrangement.

SENATOR BRANDEGEE. Yes; I understand that. But the fact that we have a vote to loose ourselves does not help us, as unanimous action is required by nine gentlemen, any one of whom can prevent us.

THE PRESIDENT. No, Senator; but the diplomatic relations of the different countries in that council will be such, if I may judge, that those things may be accomplished.

SENATOR BRANDEGEE. That is an optimistic view to take, if you will pardon my opinion about it.

THE PRESIDENT. Perhaps it is.

SENATOR BRANDEGEE. I want to call your attention to the fact that this era of good feeling which exists between the allied and associated powers after their common experience and suffering in this great war may not always exist, in view of future commercial contests and separate interests of different nationalities which may occur in the future, and what some of us feel is that we ought to be careful in making these definite international engagements, which we are wisely determined to carry out in good faith if we should make them, and we feel that now is the time to understand exactly the obligations we are to be held to before we affix our signature, and I have no doubt that you agree to that.

THE PRESIDENT. Yes.

SENATOR BRANDEGEE. I want to ask you a word or two about this so-called American draft. The American draft of the league which was sent to us in response to Senate resolution was the draft which was submitted by the American commission to the conference abroad?

THE PRESIDENT. No.

SENATOR BRANDEGEE. It was the draft which was submitted by you as the head of the American commission to the American commission. Is that correct?

THE PRESIDENT. Why, Senator, it was done as all other things of this sort were done over there. We circulated the draft among the representatives of the 14 States who were represented in the general league of nations, and they had 10 days or more to examine it. I also submitted it to my colleagues, not for any formal discussion but in order to have their opinion if they chose to express it.[40] Then when the commission got down to its real work they appointed a committee.

SENATOR BRANDEGEE. Of the commission?

THE PRESIDENT. No; of two officers of the commission. Well, they did form a committee, but that committee employed the services of two technical advisers. Mr. Miller was one of them and Mr. Hurst—not the Mr. Hurst that Mr. Miller mentioned.[41]

SENATOR BRANDEGEE. He gave his initials as C. J. B.

THE PRESIDENT. I have forgotten the initials.

SENATOR BRANDEGEE. He said he was an employee of the British State Department.

THE PRESIDENT. Yes; he is a very able man. He was on the general drafting committee of the treaty, and Mr. Miller took the various documents that we have been reading and discussing and made a combined draft and it was that combined draft which was the subject of formal discussion and amendment and addition by the committee.[42]

SENATOR BRANDEGEE. And that was the combined draft, the one that you sent to us the other day?

THE PRESIDENT. No; Secretary Lansing was asked for it.

THE CHAIRMAN. It was a composite draft. It came in yesterday.

SENATOR BRANDEGEE. I beg your pardon, I did not know about it. Was there any draft, no matter how incomplete, any skeleton draft or enumeration or substance for a draft for the so-called American plan for the covenant of the league of nations which you took with you from this country or was prepared over there by you?

THE PRESIDENT. Only the one that I referred to earlier in this conference, Senator, when I had taken the Phillimore report as more or less of a basis of my work.

SENATOR BRANDEGEE. That was the only thing that you had in the nature of a skeleton draft when you left the country?

THE PRESIDENT. Yes.

SENATOR BRANDEGEE. Did the Phillimore draft or report, what-

[40] Wilson was confused here. He did not submit any of his drafts to the League of Nations Commission, which saw only the Hurst-Miller draft, printed at Feb. 2, 1919, *ibid.* Wilson did send copies of his First Paris Draft, printed at Jan. 8, 1919, Vol. 53, to the other American Commissioners.

[41] Miller, in his testimony before the Foreign Relations Committee on August 12, could not remember the first name of Cecil James Barrington Hurst and had become embroiled in a contretemps with Brandegee, who thought that C. J. B Hurst was Francis Wrigley Hirst, the British liberal journalist. In a letter to Lodge on August 15, Miller cleared up the confusion over Hurst's identity.

[42] That is, the Hurst-Miller draft.

ever the proper term may be, contain anything like what is now article 10 of the covenant of the league?

THE PRESIDENT. I do not remember.

SENATOR BRANDEGEE. You do not remember whether there was anything like that in that?

THE PRESIDENT. Let me say this in regard to article 10. I believe this to be a part of the history of it. It is so far as I am concerned. Early in my administration, as I think many of the members know, I tried to get the American States, the States of Central and South America, to join with us in an arrangement[43] in which a phrase like this constituted the kernel, that we guaranteed to each other territorial integrity and political independence. "Under a republican form of government" was added in that case. But that is another matter. As I represented to them at that time, it was a desire on my part at any rate to show the way to them of keeping things steady and preventing the kind of aggression they have had.

THE CHAIRMAN. That was the subject of the Niagara conference?[44]

SENATOR BRANDEGEE. The A.B.C. powers.

THE PRESIDENT. I do not think it was discussed there, Senator. We discussed it diplomatically.

THE CHAIRMAN. It was taken up at that time?

THE PRESIDENT. It was taken up at that time.

SENATOR BRANDEGEE. Who was the author of article 10?

THE PRESIDENT. I suppose I was as much as anybody.

SENATOR BRANDEGEE. And you recommended it to your fellow American commissioners?

THE PRESIDENT. Yes.

SENATOR BRANDEGEE. How many Americans were on the commission which framed the covenant for the league of nations?

THE PRESIDENT. Two—Col. House and myself.

SENATOR BRANDEGEE. The total membership was what? Fifteen, was it not?

THE PRESIDENT. Fourteen nations, and five principal nations had two members, which would make 19, would it not? Yes, 19 members.

SENATOR BRANDEGEE. Did they have the unit rule, so to speak, casting one vote for each member?

THE PRESIDENT. In only one or two instances did we vote at all. I presided and the final form was this, "If there are no objections we will regard that as accepted."

[43] The so-called Pan-American Pact, about which see the index references to it in Vols. 39 and 52.

[44] About which see the index references, "Mexico and the United States—ABC Mediation," Vol. 39.

SENATOR BRANDEGEE. As we say in the Senate, "without objection it is agreed to."

THE PRESIDENT. Yes; and that is the way the whole thing was agreed to.

SENATOR BRANDEGEE. Did these commissions to which the plenary conference delegated certain subjects to prepare reports upon have any coordination with each other? Did each commission know what the other commissions were doing?

THE PRESIDENT. No; the subjects were too unlike.

SENATOR BRANDEGEE. Was there any debate on the completed draft of the covenant of the league of nations when it was submitted to the plenary council just before you came over in March?

THE PRESIDENT. Yes; there were speeches.

SENATOR BRANDEGEE. I do not call those debates. I read that there were no debates as to what each particular government demanded.

THE PRESIDENT. No; because there were so many of those represented, and they had all been canvassed in the process of formulation.

SENATOR BRANDEGEE. You replied to a resolution of the Senate requesting a copy of a letter of Gen. Tasker H. Bliss, which was also signed by Secretary Lansing—

THE PRESIDENT. And Mr. White.

SENATOR BRANDEGEE. And Mr. White—you stated, if I recollect, in substance, that you would be glad to furnish us with a copy of it but for the fact that Gen. Bliss had mentioned the names of certain Governments and you thought it was a matter of delicacy not to make it public. Would it not be possible to furnish us with the general drift of the arguments, leaving out the names of the Governments, etc.?

THE PRESIDENT. There was not any argument. He said flatly that it was unjust. It was not a reason.

SENATOR BRANDEGEE. It was an opinion.

THE PRESIDENT. An opinion.

SENATOR BRANDEGEE. A conclusion.

SENATOR JOHNSON of California. With that, you agreed, Mr. President, did you not?

THE PRESIDENT. Senator, I do not think I ought to say any more than I have said.

SENATOR BRANDEGEE. I do not think I care to ask anything more.

SENATOR HITCHCOCK. Will you permit me to read into the record these two paragraphs from the conclusion of the treaty and ask whether they are what you refer to when you express the opinion that the treaty would go into effect when Germany and three of the contracting parties had signed it, and only as to them?

THE CHAIRMAN. That is explicitly stated.

SENATOR HITCHCOCK. I thought it was left in some doubt. I would like to read them into the record (reading):

A first procès-verbal of the deposit of ratifications will be drawn up as soon as the treaty has been ratified by Germany on the one hand, and by three of the principal allied and associated powers on the other hand.

From the date of this first procès-verbal the treaty will come into force between the high contracting parties who have ratified it. For the determination of all periods of time provided for in the present treaty this date will be the date of the coming into force of the treaty.

I just wanted to make it clear that the treaty is not in effect except as to those that have ratified it.

THE PRESIDENT. I could not put my hand on it, but I was sure.

SENATOR MC CUMBER. Mr. President, just one question on this French treaty. If we should adopt this present treaty with the league of nations and with section 10 in it, which brings all of the great nations of the league to the protection of France, if war should be made against her by Germany, what necessity is there for any other special treaty with France?

THE PRESIDENT. To meet the possibility of delay in action on the part of the council of the league.

SENATOR MC CUMBER. But the agreement of section 10 comes into effect, does it not, the moment we adopt the treaty?

THE PRESIDENT. Yes; but the council has to act and formulate its advice, and then the several Governments have to act and form their judgment upon that advice.

SENATOR MC CUMBER. Do you not think under the present situation that that could be done as quickly as Germany could get ready for a second war on France?

THE PRESIDENT. Oh, as quickly as she could get ready, yes; but not as quickly as she could act after she got ready.

SENATOR BRANDEGEE. Mr. President, the situation is this: If Germany has surrendered her navy, demobilized her army, and been shorn of large portions of her territory; if we have no demand for reparation or indemnity against her; if, as you stated in your addresses to the Congress, the war is over; if there is no fighting going on; if Germany has signed the peace treaty, and you have signed the peace treaty; if, in fact, there is a condition of peace, and only the joint resolution of Congress that a state of war existed a year ago—if that is all so, is there no way by which the condition of peace which actually exists can be made legally effective except by the adoption of the proposed treaty?

THE PRESIDENT. Senator, I would say that there is no way which we ought to be willing to adopt which separates us, in dealing with Germany, from those with whom we were associated during the war.

SENATOR BRANDEGEE. Why?

THE PRESIDENT. Because I think that is a moral union which we are not at liberty to break.

SENATOR BRANDEGEE. If we have rescued our fellow belligerents from the German peril voluntarily and without any charge, and if we prefer not to have any entanglements or connections with European powers, but to pursue our course as we did before the war, where is the moral obligation to merge ourselves with Europe forever?

THE PRESIDENT. I do not construe it as merging ourselves, but I do think we are under the plainest moral obligation to join with our associates in imposing certain conditions of peace on Germany.

SENATOR BRANDEGEE. Even if we ratify the German so-called peace treaty, with or without the Shantung provision in it, and strike out article 1 of the peace treaty, the covenant of the league of nations, we still join with those with whom we have cooperated in establishing peace with Germany, do we not, and are at liberty to trade with her?

THE PRESIDENT. An unworkable peace, because the league is necessary to the working of it.

SENATOR BRANDEGEE. Well, suppose they have a league, and we ratify the treaty with the reservation that we are not bound by article 1, which is the covenant of the league—then they have a league of nations covenant.

THE PRESIDENT. Yes, and we are tied into every other part of the treaty by reason of the fact that we are supposed to be members of the league of nations.

SENATOR BRANDEGEE. Suppose we also adopt the 21 amendments that Senator Fall has pending before the Committee on Foreign Relations, striking us out of these commissions to which we are tied, and just cutting the Gordian knot which ties us to the covenant: We establish peace with Germany just the same, I fancy. The other powers could accept our amendments to the treaty or not, as they chose. In either case Germany would be at peace, and they would be in the league, and we would be out of it. We could have peace, and resume all our business in relation to copper mines and zinc mines, etc., and we could export to Germany, and reestablish the consular service; could we not?

THE PRESIDENT. We could, sir; but I hope the people of the United States will never consent to do it.

SENATOR BRANDEGEE. There is no way by which the people can vote on it.

THE CHAIRMAN. Are we not trading with Germany now, as a matter of fact?

THE PRESIDENT. Not so far as I know, sir.

THE CHAIRMAN. Licenses certainly have been issued. It is advertised in all the New York papers.[45]

THE PRESIDENT. We removed the restrictions that were formerly placed upon shipments to neutral countries which we thought were going through to Germany.

THE CHAIRMAN. Yes; I see them advertised broadly in the New York papers.

SENATOR JOHNSON of California. Mr. President, does the moral obligation to which you have alluded compel us to maintain American troops in Europe?

THE PRESIDENT. Which moral obligation, Senator?

SENATOR JOHNSON of California. You referred to the moral obligation resting upon us to carry out the peace terms and the like in conjunction with our associates, and felt that it would be, as I understood you, a breaking, a denial of that moral obligation to make a separate peace or to act by ourselves.

THE PRESIDENT. Yes.

SENATOR JOHNSON of California. Does that obligation go to the extent of compelling us to maintain American troops in Europe?

THE PRESIDENT. Such small bodies as are necessary to the carrying out of the treaty, I think; yes.

SENATOR JOHNSON of California. And will those troops have to be maintained under the various treaties of peace until the ultimate consummation of the terms of those treaties?

THE PRESIDENT. Yes, Senator; but that is not long. In no case, as I remember, does that exceed 18 months.

SENATOR JOHNSON of California. I was rather under the impression that the occupation of Germany was to be for 15 years.

THE PRESIDENT. Oh, I beg your pardon.

THE CHAIRMAN. Along the Rhine.

THE PRESIDENT. Along the Rhine; yes. I was thinking of Upper Silesia, and the other places where plebiscites are created, or to be carried out. It is the understanding with the other Governments that we are to retain only enough troops there to keep our flag there.

SENATOR JOHNSON of California. The idea in my mind was this: Will we be maintaining American troops upon the Rhine for the next 15 years?

[45] Lodge was of course right. In fact, Wilson had worked hard to open up all channels of trade with Germany. For the status of German-American trade at this time, see E. F. Sweet to WW, Aug. 20, 1919, and its Enclosure.

THE PRESIDENT. That is entirely within our choice, Senator; but I suppose we will.

SENATOR JOHNSON of California. Do you know, Mr. President, whether or not we have American troops in Budapest at present?

THE PRESIDENT. We have not. There are some American officers there, Senator, sent with a military commission, but no American troops.

SENATOR JOHNSON of California. Returning, if you do not mind, Mr. President, to one last question about Shantung, do you recall the American experts reporting that the Japanese promise, the verbal promise, which has been referred to, to return Shantung, meant in reality the returning of the shell but retaining the kernel of the nut?[46]

THE PRESIDENT. I remember their saying that; yes, sir.

SENATOR JOHNSON of California. That is all.

THE PRESIDENT. But I do not agree with them.

SENATOR NEW. Mr. President, if no one else has any questions to ask, I have a few.

THE PRESIDENT. Proceed, Senator, if you will.

SENATOR NEW. These questions, Mr. President, are more or less general and haphazard, referring to no particular feature of the treaty, but to all of them.

First, was it the policy of the American delegates to avoid participation by the United States in strictly European questions and their settlement; and, if so, what were the matters in which America refused to participate, or endeavored to avoid participation?

THE PRESIDENT. I could not give you a list in answer to the last part of your question, sir; but it certainly was our endeavor to keep free from European affairs.

SENATOR NEW. What did the American delegates say or do to secure nonparticipation by the United States in the cessions of Danzig, Memel, and in the various boundary commissions, reparations commissions, and other agencies set up in the treaty for the disposition of questions in which America has no national interest?

THE PRESIDENT. I did not get that, Senator, it is so long.

SENATOR NEW. I will divide it. What did the American delegates say or do to secure nonparticipation by the United States in the cessions of Danzig and Memel?

THE PRESIDENT. Why, Senator, the process of the whole peace was this: Each nation had associated with it certain expert advisers, college professors and bankers and men who were familiar

[46] Actually, the saying going around the American delegates was that the Japanese proposals amounted to "offering China the shell and securing for Japan the oyster." See the extract from the memorandum of R. S. Baker printed at April 29, 1919, Vol. 58.

with ethnical and geographical and financial and business questions. Each question was referred to a joint commission consisting of the specialists in that field representing the principal allied and associated powers. They made a report to this smaller council, and in every instance the American representatives were under instructions to keep out of actual participation in these processes so far as it was honorably possible to do so.[47]

SENATOR NEW. The second half of the question is this: What did the American delegates do to secure nonparticipation by the United States in the reparations commission?

THE PRESIDENT. Why, we were disinclined to join in that, but yielded to the urgent request of the other nations that we should, because they wanted our advice and counsel.

SENATOR NEW. What agreement, written or verbal, has been entered into by the American delegates touching the assignment to various States of mandatories under the provisions of article 22?

THE PRESIDENT. None whatever.[48]

SENATOR NEW. If it be understood that Great Britain or her dominions will act as mandatories of the territory in Africa lately held by Germany, what advantage of a practical nature is expected to accrue, and whom will it benefit, from subjecting the British or dominion administration to the mandatories of such nations as Liberia, Italy, or any others?

THE PRESIDENT. Mandatories of Liberia?

SENATOR NEW. Yes.

THE PRESIDENT. I do not understand, Senator. The whole system of mandates is intended for the development and protection of the territories to which they apply—that is to say, to protect their inhabitants, to assist their development under the operation of the opinion of the world, and to lead to their ultimate independent existence.

SENATOR NEW. Mr. President, it seems that there is more than a suspicion; there is a general conviction in the world, I think, that Germany is promoting the dissemination of Bolshevist propaganda in the countries of the Allies, including the United States. That being the case, I am prompted to ask what provision in the treaty obligates Germany to prohibit Bolshevik propaganda from German sources in the United States and allied countries?

THE PRESIDENT. None.

SENATOR NEW. No provision? Was any proposal considered by the peace conference directed toward securing the names of German propaganda agents in the United States and the allied coun-

[47] *Sic!*
[48] Again, *sic!*

tries, or to obtain the records of the disbursements made in support of Bolshevik or other propaganda intended to weaken or disrupt the United States?

THE PRESIDENT. We made every effort to trace everything that we got rumor of, Senator; and traced everything that we could; but no provisions were feasible in the treaty itself touching that.

SENATOR NEW. Did not France yield under pressure at least partly exerted by the American delegates to abandon certain guaranties of the security of her German frontiers which she had been advised by Marshal Foch were indispensable; and is not the present frontier, in French military opinion, less secure than the one which France was induced to abandon?

THE PRESIDENT. Senator, do you think I ought to redebate here the fundamental questions that we debated at Paris? I think that would be a mistake, sir.

SENATOR JOHNSON of California. Mr. President, it is on that very theory that I refrained from asking many of those things, the thoughts of which crowd one's mind, and which one would like to ask.

THE PRESIDENT. Of course. You see, you are going into the method by which the treaty was negotiated. Now, with all respect, sir, I think that is a territory that we ought not to enter.

SENATOR NEW. Of course, if there is any reason why it should not be answered, I will withdraw it. Is there objection to answering this, Mr. President: What was France's solution proposed for administration of the Saar Basin?

THE PRESIDENT. I do not think I ought to answer those questions, Senator, because of course they affect the policy and urgency of other Governments. I am not at liberty to go into that.

SENATOR NEW. Mr. President, would our position in the War of 1812 and the Spanish-American War have been secure under the league covenant?

THE PRESIDENT. Oh, Senator, you can judge of that as well as I could. I have tried to be a historical student, but I could not quite get the league back into those days clearly enough in my mind to form a judgment.

SENATOR NEW. What would have been the procedure under the covenant in those two cases, in your opinion?

THE PRESIDENT. Why, Senator, I could figure that out if you gave me half a day, because I would have to refresh my mind as to the circumstances that brought on the wars; but that has not been regarded as a profitable historical exercise—hypothetically to reconstruct history.

SENATOR NEW. Well, I do not want to press for answers, then.

SENATOR MOSES. Mr. President, under the terms of the treaty, Germany cedes to the principal allied and associated powers all of her overseas possessions?

THE PRESIDENT. Yes.

SENATOR MOSES. We thereby, as I view it, become possessed in fee of an undivided fifth part of those possessions.

THE PRESIDENT. Only as one of five trustees, Senator. There is no thought in any mind of sovereignty.

SENATOR MOSES. Such possession as we acquire by means of that cession would have to be disposed of by congressional action.

THE PRESIDENT. I have not thought about that at all.

SENATOR MOSES. You have no plan to suggest or recommendation to make to Congress?

THE PRESIDENT. Not yet, sir; I am waiting until the treaty is disposed of.

THE CHAIRMAN. Mr. President, I do not wish to interfere in any way, but the conference has now lasted about three hours and a half, and it is half an hour after the lunch hour.

THE PRESIDENT. Will not you gentlemen take luncheon with me? It will be very delightful.

(Thereupon, at 1 o'clock and 35 minutes p.m., the conference adjourned.)

Printed in U. S. Senate, 66th Cong., 1st sess., Doc. No. 76, TREATY OF PEACE WITH GERMANY: *Report of the Conference between Members of the Senate Committee on Foreign Relations and the President of the United States* . . . (Washington, 1919).

A Memorandum by Albert Bacon Fall

[Aug. 19, 1919]

1. In your judgment, have you not the power and authority by a proclamation to declare in appropriate words that peace exists, and thus restore the status of peace between the governments and peoples of this country and those with whom we declared war?

2. Could not in any event, the power which declared war, that is Congress, joined by the President, (as you affixed your approval to the declaration of war,) by a resolution, or act of Congress, declare peace, (as Germany did not declare war upon us)?

3. Is not the pending treaty, aside from the league covenants, merely a set of agreed rules and regulations, to be observed *after* peace is established, and is not the state of war terminated merely by the filing of the first procès verbal?

4. The state of war being thus terminated by the filing of the procès verbal, although we may not yet have ratified the treaty, Germany not having declared war upon us, could you not appoint

or reappoint consular officers and agents in Germany, and by a proclamation of the status of peace, authorize our citizens to do business with and without further delay resume governmental relations with Germany? And would we not then be off of "a war basis" as to business?

5. The agreement of the signatories to the treaty is that:

"From the coming into force of the present treaty, the state of war will terminate."

And under Article 440, it is provided that as soon as the treaty shall have been ratified by Germany on the one hand and by three of the principal allied and associated powers on the other hand, the first procès verbal of the deposit of ratification will be drawn and

"From the date of this first procès verbal, the treaty will come into force between the high contracting parties who have ratified it."

Am I correct in assuming:

(1) That when three of the principal allied powers shall have ratified the treaty with Germany and the procès verbal is filed, the league of nations is then established?

(2) That all the other provisions of the treaty with Germany are in full force as to such ratifying powers?

(3) That as to the two remaining powers, should they not have ratified it, (the one being the associated power—the United States) "the state of war will terminate" although the particular *terms* of the treaty itself will not be in force as to such nonratifying powers?

(4) That such last powers will *not* be members of the league until and unless thereafter they shall have either *ratified* the treaty and the *league* articles, or shall have been *otherwise* accepted into the league under the provisions of the league articles as they now stand, or as they may be in force at the time of admission?

6. However desirable it might be to have the treaty immediately adopted, with the articles of the covenants of the league as written, by what process will this, in view of your statement as to largely increased exports, within the near future or within one or two more years, reduce in this country the rentals, costs of necessaries, etc?

7. Have you heard from Norway, Sweden, Denmark, Holland, and Switzerland or either, as to whether they will join the league, and when?

8. Are you issuing, or allowing to be issued, en bloc or otherwise, licenses to do business with those recently our enemies, and are you allowing ships and cargoes destined to ports of Germany or other recent enemy ports to clear from our ports?

9. Have you requested consular representatives of other countries to act for us in Germany?

10. Among the documents forwarded on the 8th instant to the chairman of the committee by yourself,[1] under Number 6,[2] following the final report of the commission upon the league articles, I find the following recommendation; to wit:

"Resolved, that in the opinion of the commission, the President of the commission should be requested by the conference to invite seven powers, including two neutrals, to name representatives on a committee, (a) to prepare plans for the organization of the league; (b) to prepare plans for the establishment of the seat of the league; (c) to prepare plans and the Agenda for the first meeting of the assembly."

Was this committee appointed and have they reported tentatively to the commission or to yourself; and if so, is a copy of such report available?

11. Under Article 118 of the Peace Treaty, Part IV, there is a general renunciation of all German rights to territory formerly belonging to herself or to her allies and a renunciation of all her rights, titles and privileges outside of her boundary as fixed by the treaty which she held as against the allied and associated powers. There is no cession, apparently, of the territory to any particular power or association of powers, but there is an undertaking on the part of Germany to recognize and conform to the measures which may be taken "now or in the future by the 'Principal Allied and Associated' powers in agreement, where necessary, with third powers in order to carry the above stipulation into effect."

To what nation, nations, or association of nations does the territory renounced under this Article go, aside from such portions as are specifically assigned to certain nations or plebiscite commissions by the particular articles of the German treaty, and by what character of title; and what part, if any, does the United States take, or has she taken, with reference to the disposition of such property?

12. Article 119, Section 1 of Part IV reads:

"Germany renounces in favor of the Principal Allied and Associated Powers all her rights and titles over her oversea possessions."

This appears to be a direct cession of the German overseas possessions to the principal allied and associated powers, of course the United States being the associated power. What character of title does the United States receive to any part of the overseas possessions ceded by Germany through Article 119?

[1] The so-called American Draft of the Covenant and the Report of the League of Nations Commission, cited in n. 2 to WW to HCL, Aug. 8, 1919.
[2] "Number 6" was the "Recommendation of the Commission," which Fall quotes below, except for the last line: "This Committee shall report both to the Council and the Assembly."

13. Has there as yet been any agreement, tentative or otherwise, as to the disposition or the government of such overseas possessions, or any part of same, to which the United States is a party?

14. Will you inform the committee whether, through an agreement between France and Great Britain, any disposition, or agreement for the disposition of all or any part of the German overseas possessions in Africa has been arrived at; and if so, whether the United States has tentatively, or otherwise, consented thereto and whether possession has been taken by either France or Great Britain of any such German territory under any such agreement or tentative agreement?

15. Was it, or is it now contemplated that of the commission composed of five members to be chosen by the council of the league of nations for the government of the Saar Basin, one of said commission to be a citizen of France, one a native of the Saar basin not a native of France, and the three other members belonging to three countries other than France or Germany, there should be one American commissioner among the membership of five; and if so, why is it necessary that America should be represented upon this commission?

16. Why should the United States be represented by one member of the commission for the settling of the new frontier lines of Belgium and Germany under Articles 34 and 35?

17. As Article 48 of the treaty provides for a boundary commission for the Saar Basin to be composed of five members, one appointed directly by France and one directly by Germany, why was it not provided that the other three, to be nationals of other powers, should each be named in the article, to be appointed by some particular country, as is done with reference to the other two, rather than to leave the selection of such three to the council of the league of nations with the restrictive provision that the said three should be selected from nationals of other powers than France or Germany?

18. Why was it necessary to provide in Article 83 that of the commission of seven members to fix the boundaries between Poland and the Czeco-Slovak state, one should be named by Poland, one by such Czeco-Slovak state and the other five named by the principal allied and associated powers, rather than that certain countries specifically named should nominate the five, as well as the two?

19. Has such commission been appointed tentatively or otherwise and has it proceeded to the performance of any of its duties either in a temporary manner or otherwise?

20. Why was it necessary to form a commission of four mem-

bers, one to be designated by each the United States, France, the British Empire and Italy to exercise authority over the plebiscite area of Upper Silesia; that is to say, why was it necessary to name the United States as one of the powers which should appoint one of the four commissioners and then leave the decision of such commission to a majority vote?

T MS (WP, DLC).

From Newton Diehl Baker

My dear Mr. President: [Washington] August 19, 1919.

You will recall that early in 1918 four death sentences were presented to you from France;[1] two for disobedience of orders you remitted to terms of imprisonment, and two young boys, Sebastian and Cook, who were convicted of sleeping on outpost duty, you fully pardoned.

It will interest you to know that upon restoration to duty both made good soldiers. Sebastian died in battle in the Aisne Offensive in July, 1918. Cook was wounded in that battle and restored to health in time to fight in the Meuse-Argonne battle, when he again fought gallantly and was the second time wounded. He has been now restored to health through medical attention and has been honorably discharged from the service.

Respectfully yours,   Newton D. Baker

CCL (N. D. Baker Papers, DLC).
[1] See NDB to WW, May 1, 1918 (first letter of that date), and WW to NDB, May 4, 1918, both in Vol. 47.

From Cleveland Hoadley Dodge

My dear President: New York August 19, 1919.

It is awfully good in you, with all your other cares, to write me such a good letter,[1] and I can thoroughly sympathize with you in the difficulty which you have in knowing what to do in the Near East. Of course, the delay in ratifying the Treaty and the Covenant of the League is one which is aggravating the situation, and it is awfully difficult to know what to advise. You have so much more light on the whole question than I have that I hesitate to suggest anything. I am enclosing, however, copy of a cable which has just come from Mr. Walter George Smith, who is now in London. His suggestion that America assume the burden of expense is of course a very easy one to make, but where is the money coming from. Another suggestion has been made which might possibly be considered, and that is to send some American men-of-war to Batoum, in hopes that the mere fact of their being there, would have a moral effect upon the Turks.

I am leaving this afternoon to be gone for the rest of the month to take the first vacation I have had for a good many years, and I can only hope and pray that your friends in the Senate will "accelerate their speed."

With renewed thanks and best wishes

Yours affectionately,   Cleveland H Dodge

Copy of Cablegram

"London, Aug. 16, 1919.

Cleveland H. Dodge,
    99 John St., New York.
Withdrawal British troops from Caucasus beginning tomorrow. Gravest danger of complete evacuation unless assurance is given by America that she will assume the burden of expense of maintaining troops there. English friends of Armenia doing their utmost.   Walter George Smith."

TLS (WP, DLC).
    ¹ WW to C. H. Dodge, Aug. 14, 1919.

Frank Lyon Polk to Robert Lansing

Paris August 19, 1919

3769. Confidential. The Secretary of State from Polk. Referring to your 2867, August 18, 4 p.m.¹ and my 3703, August 15, 8 p.m. The proposed eastern boundary for the new international state is as follows: from the Aegean Sea to the Salient about twenty kilometers west of Adrianople, the Bulgarian Turkish frontier to 1915; thence southward to the Maritsa a line to be fixed on the ground passing west of Viraanteke, thence to the point where the Maritsa is cut by the Bulgarian Turkish frontier of 1913, the course of the Maritsa.

It will be noticed that Bulgarian Turkish frontier line of 1915 of which the lower half was also that of 1913 starting from the Aegean coast west of Enos keeps in the main just to the east of the Maritsa River as far as the corner of the Saleratus projecting twenty kilometres west of Adrianople. This point near Viraanteke is about two kilometres north of the river. It will be necessary to draw a line from here to the Maritsa and to follow the stream westward about six kilometres until it cuts the Turkish Bulgarian frontier of 1913. From there on the new frontier follows the one of 1913 first; a little further up stream and then when it crosses it to the southward as described in the next section of 3703. The whole of the territory ceded is in 215 except the small bit north of the Maritsa and west and north of the Adrianople salient which would make an undesirable appendage, would thus come within the international state and form the northerly portion of Italy.

Polk.

T telegram (SDR, RG 59, 763.72119/6273, DNA).
    [1] "Proposed eastern boundary of Western Thrace not clear. Further description and explanation desired." RL to FLP, Aug. 18, 1919, T telegram (SDR, RG 59, 763.72119/6199, DNA).

To Albert Bacon Fall

My dear Senator Fall: The White House 20 August, 1919.

You left yesterday in my hands certain written questions which I promised you I would answer. I am hastening to fulfil that promise.

I feel constrained to say in reply to your first question not only that in my judgment I have not the power by proclamation to declare that peace exists, but that I could in no circumstances consent to take such a course prior to the ratification of a formal treaty of peace. I feel it due to perfect frankness to say that it would in my opinion put a stain upon our national honor which we never could efface, if after sending our men to the battle field to fight the common cause, we should abandon our associates in the war in the settlement of the terms of peace and dissociate ourselves from all responsibility with regard to those terms.

I respectfully suggest that, having said this, I have in effect answered also your second, third, and fourth questions, so far as I myself am concerned.

Permit me to answer your fifth question by saying that the provisions of the treaty to which you refer operate merely to establish peace between the powers ratifying, and that it is questionable whether it can be said that the League of Nations is in any true sense created by the association of only three of the Allied and Associated Governments.

In reply to your sixth question, I can only express the confident opinion that the immediate adoption of the treaty, along with the Articles of the Covenant of the League as written, would certainly within the near future reduce the cost of living in this country as elsewhere, by restoring production and commerce to their normal strength and freedom.

For your convenience, I will number the remaining paragraphs of this letter as the questions to which they are intended to reply are numbered.

Seven. I have had no official information as to whether Norway, Sweden, Denmark, Holland, or Switzerland will join the League.

Eight. I answered your eighth question in reply to a question asked me at our conference the other day.

Nine. In February, 1917, Spain was requested to take charge of American interests in Germany through her diplomatic and consular representatives, and no other arrangement has since been made.

Ten. The committee to prepare plans for the organization of the League, for the establishment of the seat of the League, and for the proceedings of the first meeting of the assembly, has been appointed but has not reported.

Eleven. Article 118 of the peace treaty, Part IV, under which Germany renounces all her rights to territory formerly belonging to herself or to her allies was understood, so far as special provision was not made in the treaty itself for its disposition, as constituting the Principal Allied and Associated Powers the authority by which such disposition should ultimately be determined. It conveys no title to those Powers, but merely entrusts the disposition of the territory in question to their decision.

Twelve. Germany's renunciation in favor of the Principal Allied and Associated Powers of her rights and titles to her overseas possessions is meant similarly to operate as vesting in those powers a trusteeship with respect of their final disposition and government.

Thirteen. There has been a provisional agreement as to the disposition of these overseas possessions, whose confirmation and execution is dependent upon the approval of the League of Nations, and the United States is a party to that provisional agreement.

Fourteen. The only agreement between France and Great Britain with regard to African territory, of which I am cognizant, concerns the redisposition of rights already possessed by those countries on that continent. The provisional agreement referred to in the preceding paragraph covers all the German overseas possessions, in Africa as well as elsewhere.

Fifteen. No mention was made in connection with the settlement of the Saar Basin of the service of an American member of the Commission of Five to be set up there.

Sixteen. It was deemed wise that the United States should be represented by one member of the Commission for settling the new frontier lines of Belgium and Germany, because of the universal opinion that America's representative would add to the Commission a useful element of entirely disinterested judgment.

Seventeen. The choice of the Commission for the Saar Basin was left to the Council of the League of Nations, because the Saar Basin is for fifteen years to be directly under the care and direction of the League of Nations.

Eighteen. Article 83 does in effect provide that five of the members of the Commission of Seven to fix the boundaries between Poland and Czecho-Slovakia should be nominated by certain countries, because there are five Principal Allied and Associated Powers, and the nomination of five representatives by those Powers necessarily means the nomination of one representative by each of those Powers.

Nineteen. No such commission has yet been appointed.

Twenty. It was deemed wise that the United States should have a representative on the commission set up to exercise authority over the plebiscite of Upper Silesia, for the same reason that I have given with regard to the commission for settling the frontier line of Belgium and Germany.

Sincerely yours,   Woodrow Wilson

TLS (A. B. Fall Papers, CSmH).

From Joseph Patrick Tumulty, with Enclosure

Memorandum for the President: [c. Aug. 20, 1919]

The Secretary begs to lay before the President the attached memorandum prepared by the Vice-President which shows the condition of affairs on the Hill regarding the status of the treaty.

E N C L O S U R E

A Memorandum by Thomas Riley Marshall

The present condition of the Peace Treaty is lamentable. It accomplishes nothing to endeavor to diagnose the situation and determine whether it is political or patriotic. All patriotism ought to be political and all politics ought to be patriotic.

The President has very definitely stated that the League of Nations does not morally bind the United States to make war in the future unless at the time the Congress of the United States believes such a war necessary and justifiable; that the Monroe Doctrine is preserved in all its vigor; that internal questions, such as immigration and tariff, can never be taken before the League and that if the United States chooses to withdraw from the League upon the two-years notice it is the sole judge as to whether it has kept its obligations.

On the surface of affairs it appears that all proposed amendments to the Treaty itself can be defeated but that it can not be ratified without the above constructions being definitely stated, not by way of reservation but, as the rules of the Senate provide, by amendments to the article of ratification.

The President is loath to accept these amendments to the document of ratification. Certain Senators voice the fear that the President's construction is erroneous. The President voices the fear that, if embraced in the article of ratification, the whole question will be opened up. Today it looks as though two minds were trying to pass each other on a single track.

Believing that the President has fairly expressed the views of the Peace Conference upon the binding force of the League of Nations upon the American Republic, with great hesitation, I suggest for consideration as a solution of the question the following:

Ratify the Treaty without amendment either to the body thereof or to the article of ratification. At the same time pass a statute authorizing the appointment of American representatives in the Assembly and on the Council, with instructions to proceed no farther on behalf of the United States than the organization of the League and the presentation of the President's construction as amendments to the League covenant; if such amendments are not promptly agreed to by the League the service of notice of withdrawal therefrom. Having done nothing more than join in the organization of the League, no controversy could arise as to the right of the government to withdraw in two years therefrom.

T MSS (WP, DLC).

From Newton Diehl Baker

My dear Mr. President: Washington August 20, 1919

Mr. Elmquist, Chairman of the Federal Electric Railways Commission, brought me the attached letter[1] and asked me to present it to you. I do so by memorandum rather than verbally because in this form the subject is available for consideration at your leisure.

The substance of this communication is that the Federal Electric Railways Commission finds the $10,000 which you placed at its disposal inadequate to permit it to make all the inquiries it believes it profitably could make into the subject committed to it, and it therefore desires you to ask the Congress to make an appropriation for the continuance of its work.

The Commission in its letter cites the condition of the street railway industry in the country at this time. It is admittedly very bad.

Many of the properties are in the hands of receivers; few of them are earning dividends, and many of them claim not to be earning operating expenses. In the meantime, rates of fare have been advanced generally and in my judgment, in many instances, the point of largest return has been passed and fares are charged which discourage traffic.

Since the Commission for some reason selected me to present this matter to you, I feel obliged to state my own views about it.

The street railway question is essentially local. The fact that the same question exists in a large number of localities does not make it a national question. The conditions under which street railways are operated throughout the country vary with State laws, local franchise and regulatory ordinances to such an extent that very few generalizations are possible on the subject, but in practically every community the street railway question is one of intense local feeling, and any intervention by the Federal Government would, I think, be misunderstood if not resented unless it were made very clear that the purpose of the intervention was to be helpful to the localities in the solution of their problem, and the justification of such intervention clearly stated. There are two aspects in which the street railway problem has national significance. (1) The very large issues of bonds and stocks of street railway companies must be considered as affecting all questions of national finance. (2) Labor controversies and business disorganizations growing out of street railway difficulties affect the aggregate national strength and well being. Neither of these considerations, in my judgment, justify any assertion of national control, though they obviously create national concern.

If the Federal Electric Railways Commission limits its report to such a statement of existing conditions as will impress upon local communities the fact that their local problem is important and its right solution desirable as a constituent part of a larger problem, and if the Commission's further findings are merely exhibitions of several types of relationship between street railway corporations and their local communities which can be studied helpfully by local authorities facing such problems, the work will be helpful. If the Commission were, however, to undertake a definite finding in favor of or against municipal ownership, in favor of or against the so-called Cleveland or Chicago plan of public control[2] in the sense of recommending any course to other communities, the result, in my judgment, would be unhappy. I therefore venture to suggest, if the continuance of this Commission meets with your approval and you desire to ask the Congress to make an appropriation for its expenses, that a carefully drawn statement be made by you to the

Congress as to the limitations upon the inquiries to be made by the Commission, so that neither the Congress nor the local communities will misunderstand either the activities of the Commission or the scope of its subsequent findings. I will be very glad to prepare for your consideration a suggested statement of this kind if you determine to act affirmatively in the matter.

Respectfully yours,   Newton D Baker

TLS (WP, DLC).
[1] Charles Emil Elmquist *et al.* to WW, Aug. 19, 1919, TLS (WP, DLC).
[2] The so-called Cleveland plan of public control of street railways provided for a pool of all the income from the city's street railway system. From this pool were subtracted the operating costs, maintenance costs, taxes, and 6 per cent interest on the stock of the operating company, the Cleveland Railway Company. The balance went into a fund known, somewhat confusingly, as the interest fund. When this fund reached $700,000, the fare per rider was reduced according to a sliding scale; when the fund fell to $300,000 the fare was increased according to the same scale. In practice, the individual fare had fluctuated between three cents and five cents in recent years. See *Proceedings of the Federal Electric Railways Commission Held in Washington, D. C., during the months of July, August, September, and October 1919, together with the Final Report of the Commission to the President* (3 vols., Washington, 1920), I, 590; II, 995-1003.
The Chicago plan in contrast provided for a fixed five-cent fare per rider. After all expenses were paid, the city and the private operating company shared the profits in the proportion of 55 per cent to the city and 45 per cent to the company. The city by 1919 had accumulated some twenty million dollars, which was held in a fund which would enable it in time to purchase its street railroad system outright. *Ibid.*, I, 280-81.

From Alexander Mitchell Palmer

Dear Mr. President: Washington, D. C. August 20, 1919.

Referring to your note to me of August 11th, enclosing telegram from Upton Sinclair, who made complaint that Eugene V. Debs is being confined fourteen consecutive hours daily in a cell, I submit herewith a letter from the Warden of the Penitentiary which gives the facts.[1] I think this will satisfy Mr. Sinclair that Debs is being properly treated.   Faithfully yours,   A Mitchell Palmer

TLS (WP, DLC).
[1] Frederick G. Zerbst to AMP, Aug. 13, 1919, TLS (WP, DLC). Zerbst confirmed that all prisoners at his facility were locked in their cells from approximately 5 p.m. to 7 a.m. daily because of a shortage of guards. Zerbst commented specifically on Debs as follows:
"Eugene V. Debs is employed in our clothing store-room where his duties are semi-clerical and yet gives him the opportunity for such physical exercise as he feels he should take. I have consulted with him several times and in view of his advanced age, have offered to change him to duty in the hospital which would keep him from being locked in a cell, but he prefers his present assignment, the working conditions there being entirely satisfactory. He is in fully as good health as when he came here, and in a recent conversation he stated that he had met more human kindness in prison, both at Moundsville [West Virginia] and here, than he had ever found outside of prisons."
Wilson requested the White House staff to send a copy of Zerbst's letter to Upton Sinclair. GFC to White House Staff, Aug. 25, 1919, TL (WP, DLC).

From William Gibbs McAdoo

Private

Dear Governor,   New York Aug 20, '19

I understand that Benj. Strong[1] is being considered for the Reparation Commission or some important post in Europe. I sincerely hope it is not true. It would, in my judgment, be a most unfortunate appointment. If you have any such thing in contemplation, please give me an opportunity to "put you wise."

I must be in Washington next Tuesday, August 26th. Nell would like very much to run down with me, so if it would be entirely agreeable to you and Edith we should be glad to spend next Monday night with you. We expect to arrive about 5 pm, Aug. 20. If not entirely convenient, dont fail to let us know as we shall understand.

I have read the account of your conference with the Senators—and with great satisfaction. I dont see how they can fail to take the way out you have so wisely indicated to them. I am sure that your whole exposition of the subject will have a great effect on the country. It was very convincing and illuminating and your poise throughout added greatly to its force.

Nell joins in dearest love to Edith and yourself.

Affectionately Yours   W G McAdoo

ALS (WP, DLC).
[1] Benjamin Strong, Governor of the Federal Reserve Bank of New York.

From Edwin Forrest Sweet,[1] with Enclosure

My dear Mr. President: Washington August 20, 1919.
Attention of Mr. Close

Confirming the telephone conversation between Mr. Close and the Private Secretary of the Secretary of Commerce today in which an inquiry was made regarding the issuing of licenses for the transaction of business with those recently our enemies, and as to whether or not ships and cargoes destined to ports of Germany or other recent enemy ports are allowed to clear from our ports.

In reply to the first inquiry regarding licenses for the conduct of business with the recent enemy powers, there is attached hereto a copy of War Trade Board ruling No. 802 dated July 14, 1919, under the caption of "Resumption of Trade with Germany." This fully outlines the present policy of the issuing of licenses for the conduct of business with the former enemy powers.

In response to the second inquiry dealing with the clearances of ships and cargoes destined to ports of Germany or other recent enemy ports, I am advised by the Commissioner of Navigation as well as the Division of Customs of the Treasury Department that as the prohibition has now been removed on commodities, vessels destined to former enemy ports are now allowed to clear in the usual way. As a matter of substantiating this, I wish to call attention to recent publishing of sailings in New York papers of vessels so destined, as this would point toward a verification of information as given above. Respectfully, E. F. Sweet

TLS (WP, DLC).
[1] Assistant Secretary of Commerce, at this time Acting Secretary of Commerce.

E N C L O S U R E

(For immediate release)
DEPARTMENT OF STATE
WAR TRADE BOARD SECTION
WASHINGTON

(W.T.B.R.802) July 14, 1919.
RESUMPTION OF TRADE WITH GERMANY.

The War Trade Board Section of the Department of State announces that a General Enemy Trade License has been issued authorizing all persons in the United States, on and after July 14, 1919, to trade and communicate with persons residing in Germany and to trade and communicate with all persons with whom trade and communication is prohibited by the Trading with the Enemy Act; *subject, however*, to the following specific limitations and exceptions, to wit:

1. The above mentioned general license does not authorize the importation into the United States from Germany or wlsewhere [elsewhere] of dyes, dyestuffs, potash, drugs or chemicals which have been produced or manufactured in Germany.

2. The above mentioned general license does not modify or affect in any respect present restrictions against trade and communication between the United States and Hungary or that portion of Russia under the control of the Bolshevik authorities.

3. The above mentioned general license does not authorize trade with respect to any property which heretofore, pursuant to the provisions of the Trading with the Enemy Act as amended, has been reported to the Alien Property Custodian or should have been so reported to him, or any property which heretofore, pursuant to the provisions of said Act, the Alien Property Custodian has seized or has required to be conveyed, transferred, assigned, delivered or paid over to him.

Exports to and imports from Germany may take place under Special Export License R.C. No. 77 and General Import License PBF No. 37 as announced in W.T.B.R.803 and W.T.B.R.804, respectively.

T MS (WP, DLC).

From Robert Lansing, with Enclosure

Urgent.

My dear Mr. President: Washington August 20, 1919.

I enclose herewith a copy of a letter which I have received from the British Chargé[1] requesting a message to be placed in the corner-stone of the new Parliamentary Buildings at Ottawa on September 1st.

You will note that if a message is to be sent they desire that it should be communicated not later than the 25th instant.

I also enclose a suggested draft for such a message and would ask if it meets with your approval.

                          Faithfully yours,   Robert Lansing

TLS (WP, DLC).
[1] R. C. Lindsay to RL, Aug. 18, 1919, TCL (WP, DLC).

E N C L O S U R E

May I on this occasion give expression anew to the strong feeling of kinship and friendship we Americans feel for our comrades in the mighty conflict now ended? May the victory achieved by the united peoples of the Old and New World be fruitful of enduring good, so that our sacrifices and those of our brave associates will not have been in vain, but will be glorified in the establishment of a lasting code of international morality and good will.[1]

T MS (WP, DLC).
[1] This was sent as WW to the Governor General of Canada [Victor Christian William Cavendish, 9th Duke of Devonshire], Aug. 22, 1919, TL (Letterpress Books, WP, DLC).

From Edward Mandell House

                                    London Aug. 20, 1919

Urgent. 2850. For the President from Colonel House. The question of permitting conscription in some of the mandate territories has become acute. After a consultation with Lord Grey, Lord Robert Cecil, Ambassador Davis and Raymond Fosdick we have concluded, for reasons which appear in the following statement, that it is best to yield to the wishes of the French only as far as the narrow strip in Togoland is concerned. We have reason to believe that Frank Polk and Mr. Balfour both consider that this slight compromise is necessary. This matter will be handled in Paris and Polk is being sent a duplicate of the following statement:

"The question has arisen over claim by the French Government to be allowed to raise black troops in the portion of Togoland for which they expect a mandate. They do not desire to raise black troops in any portion of the Cameroons which may be assigned to their care. They base their claim as far as Togoland is concerned upon a conversation which took place in the spring in Paris at which it is said that both Mr. Lloyd George and the President agreed that they should be allowed to raise black troops in the mandate D territories assigned to them[1] and there is sufficient ambiguity in the report of what passed to make it difficult to contradict them effectively. Assuming that in this state of things a concession must be made to the French two suggestions have been put forward. In the first place it is suggested that the portion of Togoland assigned to them might be assigned in full sovereignty and not as a mandate. This seems objectionable as infringing the express terms of Article 22 of the Covenant and as making an exception to the principle that in future territories such as these should not be annexed. Moreover, it would be rather difficult for the British to consent to accept the rest of Togoland, subject to mandate, if the French had obtained full sovereignty over their part. The other suggestion is that the French part of Togoland should be subject to a C mandate and that by a special exception, so described in the mandate, the French should be allowed to raise black troops in it. It would be provided that they were not to be used outside of Togoland, except in case of a world war and the defense for allowing it would be that in the adjoining territory belonging to the French black troops were raised without restriction and that the tribal divisions do not correspond with the geographical boundaries and that you might easily have a part of a tribe in the French colony subject to military service and that other part of the tribe in the mandate territory not so subjected, a situation which would be very difficult to administer there. On the whole, therefore, the latter seems the better solution of the two, though it is realized that neither of them are satisfactory."

If you are not in accord with the suggestion made please take it up directly with Polk in Paris.

We are holding a final meeting on mandate A September ninth.

Davis

T telegram (SDR, RG 59, 763.72119/6294, DNA).

¹ See the minutes of the Council of Ten printed at Jan. 30, 1919, 3:30 p.m., Vol. 54, and Minute 1 of the minutes of the Council of Four printed at May 5, 1919, 11 a.m., Vol. 58.

From Norman Hapgood

Dear Mr. President: Copenhagen, August 20th, 1919.

As I have been listening to the interesting but discouraging accounts of Russia given to me by the group that has just arrived from Moscow, and particularly as I have been trying to realize what will happen if Denikin is successful,¹ there have come into my mind in this connection two quotations that I thought might interest you, if you have forgotten them. One is what Lorenzo de' Medici said after foiling the Pitti conspiracy against his house: "He only knows how to conquer, who knows how to forgive." The other, what Caesar said, in letting his enemies of Pompey's party go free after they had fallen into his hands: "I will conquer after a new fashion and fortify myself in the possession of the power I acquire, by generosity and mercy."

A letter received today from Mr. Brandeis says: "The President seems to have grappled effectively with domestic labor outbreaks, and will doubtless secure ratification of the treaty. But Peace can come only with good-will; and it is through moral regeneration that we may hope for the world I had thought nearer of attainment than now appears. Perhaps the Master of Ballantree² was right in his contempt for the human reason."

He speaks very courageously of Palestine. Indeed, he is one of the men whose courage never flags.

With all best wishes,
                    Yours faithfully,   Norman Hapgood

TLS (WP, DLC).
¹ Gen. Denikin, encouraged by earlier military successes, had on July 3, 1919, issued his so-called "Moscow order" which outlined strategy for the advance of his armies to capture that city. During the summer, his forces continued to move forward; they seized Odessa on August 23 and Kiev on August 31. The furthest point of Denikin's advance was to be the town of Orel, two hundred and fifty miles from Moscow, captured on October 13. See William Henry Chamberlin, *The Russian Revolution, 1917-1921* (2 vols., New York, 1935), II, 244-49.
² Robert Louis Stevenson's *The Master of Ballentrae*.

Robert Lansing to John William Davis

[Washington] August 20, 1919

5844 Your urgent 2831, August 18, 7 p.m.

The Anglo-Persian agreement has caused a very unfavorable impression upon both the President and me and we are not disposed to ask our minister at Teheran to assist the British Government or to ask him to preserve a friendly attitude toward this agree-ment. At Paris I asked of Mr. Balfour three times that the Persians have an opportunity to be heard before the Council of Foreign Min-isters because of their claims and boundaries and because their territory had been a battle ground. Mr. Balfour was rather abrupt in refusing to permit them to have a hearing. It now appears that at the time I made these requests Great Britain was engaged in a secret negotiation to gain at least economic control of Persia. The secrecy employed and the silence observed seem contrary to the open and frank methods which ought to have prevailed and may well impair the bases of a peace inspired by friendliness. We can-not and will not do anything to encourage such secret negotiations or to assist in allaying the suspicion and dissatisfaction which we share as to an agreement negotiated in this manner.

Paragraph. You will respond to Lord Curzon's request in this general sense.   Lansing

T telegram (SDR, RG 59, 741.91/23, DNA).

A Memorandum by Robert Lansing

THE PRESIDENT'S FEELINGS AS TO
THE PRESENT EUROPEAN SITUATION

August 20, 1919.

Today at my daily conference with the President we were dis-cussing the rapacity of Roumania, the apparent weakening of Cle-menceau at the Paris Council toward the defiant attitude of the Roumanians in Hungary, and the deep concern of Masaryk that the Arch-duke Joseph[1] was accepted by the Roumanians as the head of the Hungarian Government.

The President said that Roumania's conduct was insufferable, that he had for that Government a feeling of contempt and indig-nation, and that he considered Roumania the most despicable of the Balkan nations. He added that the Roumanians had a German king,[2] that the Arch-duke was German, that his success might in-duce Austria to turn to the Hapsbergs again, and that these com-bining with the Germans might again raise the standard of Pan-Germanism.

He said with considerable heat: "When I see such conduct as this, when I learn of the secret treaty of Great Britain with Persia, when I find Italy and Greece arranging between themselves as to the division of western Asia Minor, and when I think of the greed and utter selfishness of it all, I am almost inclined to refuse to per-mit this country to be a member of the League of Nations when it is composed of such intriguers and robbers. I am disposed to throw up the whole business and get out."

This is the *third* time that the President has said to me that the present conduct of the nations makes him consider withdrawing from the League, though he never before spoke so emphatically. The other occasions were when the Greeks were demanding all of eastern Thrace and when France was insisting on her claim to Syria.

I believe that the idea of guarantying unjust territorial arrangements brought out his earlier statements, but what he said today seemed to go more to the root of the matter, namely, the inordinate cupidity and disregard of right by all nations.

"Foreign affairs certainly cause a man to be profane," he commented.

T MS (R. Lansing Papers, DLC).
  [1] The Rumanians, after entering Budapest on August 3, had arrested most of the Hungarian officer corps and made such extravagant demands upon the Peidl government that it resigned on August 6. On August 7, following a right-wing coup, the Hapsburg Archduke Joseph had accepted the provisional governorship of Hungary and asked Stephen Friedrich, a right-wing leader to form a new government. Friedrich did not succeed in forming a government until August 16. Meanwhile, the Rumanians had been systematically looting Hungary. Deák, *Hungary at the Paris Peace Conference*, pp. 112-18. For a different view, see Arno J. Mayer, *Politics and Diplomacy of Peacemaking: Containment and Counterrevolution at Versailles, 1918-1919* (New York, 1967), pp. 827-52.
  [2] Ferdinand I, grandson of Prince Charles (or Carol) of Hohenzollern-Sigmaringen, the first King of Rumania.

A News Report

OFFER A COMPROMISE
League Adherents Propose Separate Interpretive Measure.
TO PRECEDE RATIFICATION

[Aug. 21, 1919]

The first open move for a compromise in the league of nations fight came from administration quarters yesterday, embraced in a proposal that the Senate adopt interpretive reservations, but that they be kept apart from the actual ratification of the treaty.

The overture met with no immediate success on the Republican side of the chamber, Senators of the Republican reservation group declaring they could not recede from their position that to be effective the reservations must go into the ratification itself.

Senator Pittman, of Nevada, a Democratic member of the foreign relations committee, presented the compromise proposal in the form of a resolution embodying in effect the four reservations agreed on by seven Republican senators and declaring them to constitute the Senate's understanding of disputed points in the covenant.[1]

In the Republican draft, however, it is expressly provided that the reservations "be made a part of the treaty by the instrument of ratification," a proviso which Senator McNary, of Oregon, and others of the group of seven Republicans said they considered absolutely necessary if enough Republican votes are to be gained to secure ratification of the treaty.

To overcome this objection Senator Pittman proposed in a speech in the Senate that the resolution be adopted at once and submitted to the other powers who will be represented on the league council. A general debate developed, during which Senator Borah, Republican, Idaho, and others, took exception to President Wilson's distinction between moral and legal obligations under the covenant as expressed in yesterday's White House conference between the President and the foreign relations committee.

Although Senator Pittman said he had not submitted his resolution for the President's approval, he asserted that it carried into effect Mr. Wilson's views on the subject of reservations as expressed to the committee Tuesday. He indicated his firm belief that the administration would go no further toward a compromise because it feared that inclusion of the reservations in the ratification would reopen the negotiations with Germany.

Leaders of the McNary group, nevertheless, insisted they had information that in the end their plan would have Democratic support.

In his argument that reservations should not be incorporated in the ratification itself, Senator Pittman declared Germany was awaiting an opportunity to attach "hundreds of reservations," and that to reopen the subject would submit the United States to a needless risk. His resolution went over without action.

Questions by Senator Borah turned the debate to a discussion of the moral and legal obligations assumed under Article 10 of the covenant, by which the members agree to preserve one another's territorial integrity against external aggression. The article, Mr. Pittman asserted, had no legal force because it "doesn't carry the essentials of a contract."

"You couldn't take it into a court of law," he said, "and find any means by which it could be enforced except by the conscience of the parties affected."

"But when Germany actually invaded France," replied Senator Borah, "it seems to me that under Article 10 we would have been obligated to go at once to aid France."

"The matter would have been laid before Congress," said Senator Pittman, "and Congress would have decided we should act, and it would have been a godsend."

"I agree with that, but still Congress would have had no real discretion. It would have been compelled to act if it were going to carry out its contract," returned Mr. Borah.

Senator Pittman said that in his resolution he had "conformed as nearly as practicable" to the reservations drawn by the McNary reservation group.

"I believe there are 46 Democratic senators," he said, "who will support a separate resolution such as I have suggested, and I am convinced that if those on the other side, who have been supporting reservations to be contained in the resolution of ratification, and who I know to be sincerely in favor of the league of nations, will join with us, the ratification will soon be accomplished."

Senator Pittman attacked the position taken by Senator Fall, Republican, New Mexico, in Tuesday's White House conference, that amendments to the league covenant need not go back for German acceptance because Germany is not a league member. The impression that President Wilson agreed with that stand was erroneous, Senator Pittman said. Senator Fall took issue with this assertion, saying the President had agreed Germany need not accept covenant changes.

A separate resolution expressing reservation to the treaty also was introduced by Senator Owen, Democrat, Oklahoma, who has been an advocate of unreserved ratification. The reservation as proposed would cover the same general ground as those included in the Pittman resolution. . . .

Senator Pittman's resolution follows:[2]

That when the Senate of the United States shall advise and consent to the ratification of the treaty of peace with Germany signed at Paris on the 28th day of June, 1919, now pending in the Senate, that it be done with and in consideration of the following understanding as in the present and future construction and interpretation to be given to the treaty:

1. That whenever the two years' notice of withdrawal from the league of nations shall have been given by any member of the league, as provided in Article I, the government giving such notice shall be the sole judge whether all its international obligations and all its obligations under the covenant shall have been fulfilled at the time of withdrawal.

2. That the suggestions of the council of the league of nations as to the means of carrying into effect the obligations of Article X, the execution of which may require the use of military or naval forces, or economical measures, can only be carried out through the vol-

untary separate action of each of the respective governments, members of the league, and that the failure of any such government to adopt the suggestions of the council of the league, or to provide such military or naval forces or economical measures, shall not constitute a moral or legal violation of the treaty.

3. That all domestic and political questions relating to the internal affairs of a government which is a member of the league, including immigration, coastwise traffic, the tariff and commerce, are solely within the jurisdiction of such government and are not by the covenant of the league of nations submitted in any way either to arbitration or to the consideration of the council or assembly of the league of nations, or to the decision or recommendation of any other power. If a dispute arises between parties with regard to a question other than those which are herein specifically exempted as domestic questions, and it is claimed by one of the parties that such question is a domestic and political question, relating to its internal affairs, then the council shall not consider or make recommendations thereon, except upon the unanimous vote of the council, other than the representatives of the disputants.

4. There shall not be submitted to arbitration or inquiry by the assembly of the council any question which, in the judgment of the United States, depends upon or involves its long-established policy, commonly known as the Monroe doctrine, and it is preserved unaffected by any provisions of the said treaty.[3]

Printed in the *Washington Post*, Aug. 21, 1919.
[1] About which, see the news reports printed at July 31, 1919, and Aug. 2, 1919.
[2] The text of this resolution, S. Res. 168, printed in *Cong. Record*, 66th Cong., 1st sess., p. 4035, conforms to this version.
[3] Pittman, in a statement issued on August 21, said that Wilson had had no knowledge of his resolution. In addition, Hitchcock "indicated" to reporters that Pittman's move was in no way inspired by the administration. "There was no formal expression from the White House." *Washington Post*, Aug. 22, 1919.
   We can find no explicit evidence that Pittman had any form of communication with Wilson about his resolution. We are, however, struck by the fact that Pittman's four "interpretive" reservations parallel exactly Wilson's own "interpretive" reservations, which he drafted and gave to Hitchcock before he went on his western tour. They are printed at Sept. 3, 1919. It is entirely possible that Pittman did see Wilson on August 19 or 20, and that his visit to the White House was not recorded in the Head Usher's Diary. That diary seems to be incomplete for this period. Or Pittman could have talked to Wilson over the telephone about his resolution, and Wilson could have encouraged Pittman to introduce it. Finally, the letter printed as the following document makes it clear that Wilson strongly approved the Pittman resolution. However that might have been, no action was taken on it because Pittman had requested that it lie on the table.

To Thomas William Lamont

My dear Lamont: The White House 21 August, 1919.

Thank you for your note from North Haven.[1] I do not know whether you have seen the detailed report of my "conference" with the Senate Committee, but I hope when you do see it, you will think that it cleared the air.

I hope now that all forces will be concentrated upon promoting the policy of keeping all reservations or interpretations out of the formal act of ratification, and embodying those that can reasonably be accepted in a separate document.

I am glad to see that you are having a vacation. Please present my warm regards to Mrs. Lamont.[2]

Cordially and sincerely yours,   Woodrow Wilson

TLS (T. W. Lamont Papers, MH-BA).
  [1] It is missing.
  [2] That is, Florence Haskell Corliss Lamont.

To Newton Diehl Baker, with Enclosure

My dear Baker: The White House 21 August, 1919.

I think you personally saw the signers of the enclosed petition. They were very earnest in their representations to me,[1] and I dare say we have no choice but to bring back the men enlisted or drafted for the period of the war, so soon as peace shall have been proclaimed. I shall look forward to consulting you about this matter, because it involves the whole question of the maintenance of American forces in Siberia. I am a good deal perplexed in judgment about it.

The temper of these people varied a little, but for the most part they were sensible and appealing.

Cordially and faithfully yours,   Woodrow Wilson

TLS (N. D. Baker Papers, DLC).
  [1] Wilson had seen the signers of the petition printed as the Enclosure at the White House at 2:15 p.m. on August 20.

ENCLOSURE

Chicago
To the President of the United States: August 20, 1919.

We come, a committee from Chicago, Illinois, delegated by a mass meeting of the 27th and 31st Infantry Siberian Expedition Auxiliary, on a mission of mercy to ask the immediate return of the American troops from Siberia who were drafted or enlisted for the period of the war.

We most respectfully represent to you that there are over 4,000 Illinois troops in Siberia. The organization which delegates us as a committee consists of fathers, mothers, wives, brothers and sisters of these men in service in Siberia. Our people are poor in purse but patriotic and loyal to this government and have voluntarily taxed themselves to send this committee to Washington to present this petition to you in person.

We further represent to you that everyone in our organization is a patriotic American citizen, that their sons and husbands were ready to make any sacrifice during the war even to the extent of losing their lives, without questioning either the wisdom or policy of sending these troops to Siberia. Since the signing of the armistice and the army of the enemy has been demobilized, we have for the past nine months been hoping and praying daily that our boys in Siberia would be returned to the states.

Our boys in Siberia have made piteous appeals to us to do something to hasten their return home to their loved ones and the land they love. In answer to their appeals, we herewith present to you petitions containing over one hundred thousand names attesting to the sincerity of purpose in which this petition was circulated in [sic] for this appeal. We have written and petitioned the War Department. We do not intend in this petition to raise or discuss the question as to the motives for sending our troops to Siberia, nor the reason for keeping them there—we come only as human beings with the natural affection for our boys and husbands, and beg and implore of you as Commander-in-Chief to return our boys to their homes immediately.

We place our complete confidence in you and feel that we will be able to return to Chicago with a message of good cheer from you to the relatives of the boys in Siberia who are broken in spirit, shattered of health, and those who need their loved ones.

We are most loyally yours,   Fred McAver President
Mrs. K. Alexander Vice-Pres.
Margaret Murray, Secretary
Mrs. Mary A. Healy Fin. Secy.
Jas Eagan

A Mincer   A. Greenstone
William G. Bobeng, Treasurer   Mrs A. Mincer

TS MS (N. D. Baker Papers, DLC).

To Newton Diehl Baker

My dear Baker: The White House 21 August, 1919.

Thank you for your thoughtfulness in telling me about the records made by Sebastian and Cook,[1] the two youngsters who were pardoned for sleeping on outpost duty. It is very delightful to know that they redeemed themselves so thoroughly, and it was very thoughtful of you to give me the pleasure of learning about it.

Cordially and faithfully yours,   Woodrow Wilson

TLS (N. D. Baker Papers, DLC).
  [1] See NDB to WW, Aug. 19, 1919.

To Joseph Patrick Tumulty

Dear Tumulty: [The White House] 21 August, 1919.

You can reply to this,[1] please, that I did present the Bible, and the gift was very cordially accepted by the President of the Peace Conference, Mr. Clemenceau; and that every effort was made by the Peace Conference to secure the complete religious freedom throughout the world. Particular attention was paid to the matter in the Treaties formulated with the new countries where religious minorities were particularly protected, and also in the provisions for territories which were to be put under mandate.

The President

TL (WP, DLC).
  [1] Frank Hurt Mann to JPT, Aug. 15, 1919, TLS (WP, DLC). Mann, the general secretary of the American Bible Society, wished to know if a "specially bound and cased" Bible, sent to Wilson by the Society "to be used on the table at the peace conference," had been so used. He also asked whether the conference had discussed the subject of "complete religious freedom throughout the world," about which the society had sent a memorial to Wilson.

To John Work Garrett

My dear Garrett: [The White House] 21 August, 1919.

It is with the greatest regret and reluctance that I yield to your desire to retire from the diplomatic service,[1] and I hope most sincerely that this is only a temporary withdrawal. Your long training and experience ought not to be lost to the service of the Government, and I want you to know how highly your ability and devotion to the interests of the country have been valued by those who have had the privilege of knowing and directing your work.

I can readily realize how you have grown to feel out of touch with American affairs, and I hope that renewed contact will yield you everything you desire.

Cordially and sincerely yours,   Woodrow Wilson

TLS (Letterpress Books, WP, DLC).
  [1] Wilson was replying to J. W. Garrett to WW, Aug. 10, 1919, ALS (WP, DLC). Garrett was resigning from his post as Minister to the Netherlands and Luxembourg after more than eighteen years in the Foreign Service.

To the Librarians of the United States

To the Librarians: [The White House] 21 August, 1919.

I welcome this opportunity to send greetings to the librarians of the United States.[1]

The help you gave the Government during the war in placing before millions of people authentic Government messages warrants the publication of a bulletin, which may serve as a guide to information that the Federal Government is ready to place at your disposal.

As duly appointed messengers to the people you have the power of showing that while our Government may make mistakes, its works are open to the day and a knowledge of its purposes and of its acts is accessible to the humblest citizen.

Sincerely yours,   Woodrow Wilson

TLS (Letterpress Books, WP, DLC).
[1] Wilson's message was inspired by F. K. Lane to WW, Aug. 19, 1919, TLS (WP, DLC). Lane had provided a draft of the message with the suggestion that it be included as a forward to a pamphlet explaining the kinds of information available from various federal agencies to be sent to the libraries of the country. "They did fine work during the war, these Libraries," Lane commented, "and we are now compelled to cut off all connection with them because of no money."

To Francis Edward Clark

My dear Dr. Clark: [The White House] 21 August, 1919.

You know how to cheer me, and the information brought me by your kind letter of August 12th has indeed done so. I thank you with all my heart.

Cordially and sincerely yours,   Woodrow Wilson

TLS (Letterpress Books, WP, DLC).

To William Bauchop Wilson

CONFIDENTIAL

My dear Wilson: [The White House] 21 August, 1919.

Of course I always rely on your judgment in appointments. If you have thought Miss Mary Anderson better fitted than Miss Barnum, I have no criticism to make, but I think that it would be very useful for you to know that Miss Anderson is thought to be very much under the influence of Mrs. Raymond Robins, whose influence is not likely to lead in the direction of which our judgment would approve. I know that you will keep your eye on this.

Cordially and faithfully yours,   Woodrow Wilson

TLS (Letterpress Books, WP, DLC).

To Elizabeth Merrill Bass

My dear Mrs. Bass: [The White House] 21 August, 1919.

I wrote to the Secretary of Labor about Miss Barnum[1] and learned,[2] as you have learned, that he had practically already settled upon Miss Anderson. My suggestion evidently reached him too late, but I think that now it will be sufficient to apprise him of the influences which have to be guarded against.

Cordially and sincerely yours, Woodrow Wilson

TLS (Letterpress Books, WP, DLC).
[1] WW to WBW, Aug. 8, 1919.
[2] There is no correspondence in Miss Barnum's case file in WP, DLC, to explain how Wilson learned of Secretary Wilson's decision.

To Ellen Duane Davis

My dear Friend: [The White House] 21 August, 1919.

Thank you for your note,[1] which has pleased and cheered me. You may be sure that if I followed my heart I would come at once to see the dear ones and the dear friends at Martha's Vineyard, but unhappily everything is problematical with me, including my own personal plans, and I can only hope, and hope without confidence. I am heartily glad to hear that E.P. is getting some real rest, and I hope that you yourself are getting more rambunctious every day.

With affectionate messages from us all,

Faithfully yours, Woodrow Wilson

TLS (Letterpress Books, WP, DLC).
[1] Ellen D. Davis to WW, Aug. 14, 1919.

From Newton Diehl Baker

My dear Mr. President: Washington. August 21, 1919.

You may be interested to glance at the enclosed figures which show the relative length and cubical mass of the "Wilson Dam" which we are now constructing at Muscle Shoals, in comparison with other great structures of the kind in this country and the world.[1] Respectfully yours, Newton D Baker

TLS (WP, DLC).
[1] Harry Taylor to NDB, Aug. 20, 1919, TL (WP, DLC). Col. Taylor, Assistant Chief of Engineers, U.S.A., presented figures for length at top, maximum height, and cubic yards of masonry for the Assuan (usually spelled Aswān) Dam in Egypt and seven dams (including Wilson Dam) in the United States. Wilson Dam ranked second only to Assuan in cubic yards of masonry, third in length, and seventh in height. For an earlier reference to the Muscle Shoals dam project, see WW to W. C. Adamson, March 29, 1918, Vol. 47.

From Alexander Mitchell Palmer, with Enclosures

Washington, D. C. August 21, 1919.

MEMORANDUM FOR THE PRESIDENT.

Here is a memorandum from Mr. Lane which continues the debate on Sections D, E and F of the draft of the oil relief legislation, sent you with my recent memorandum. I am sending it to you as per the request of the Secretary of the Interior, though I think the former memorandum covered the whole situation exactly.

AMP

TI MS (WP, DLC).

E N C L O S U R E   I

Franklin Knight Lane to Alexander Mitchell Palmer

My dear Palmer: Washington August 16, 1919.

Here is a memorandum of answers to objections which were raised to Sections D, E, and F. I trust that you will let this go the way of the memorandum which it deals with.

Cordially yours,   Franklin K Lane

TLS (WP, DLC).

E N C L O S U R E   I I

OIL RELIEF LEGISLATION.
Answer to Objections to Sections D, E, and F,
as Stated by the Department of Justice
in Undated Memorandum Accompanying Attorney General's
Letter of August 14, 1919.

It is unwarrantably assumed that Section D is intended to apply to cases where groups of claims were held at date of second withdrawal without discovery work except on one and with the intention to drill on the others. Section D is intended and does apply only to cases where claims have been located before the second withdrawal, where a substantial amount had been expended in permanent improvements adapted and looking to the production of oil on the claim for which a lease is sought, and no lease is proposed to be given for any claim that has not upon it a producing well brought in prior to February 23, 1915, and furthermore, in that event a lease issues only for the 40 acres containing the producing well. The equities are just as great as the class relieved in Section C, and the difference is simply a degree of diligence or continuity in performing the work. In both cases the location must have been made before the second withdrawal and work performed looking to the development of the location. Subsequently, a producing well must have been brought in on the land. Section C gives a lease to this class of claimants with the only added condition that the locator must have been diligently at work or continuously at work; while Section D would give the smaller relief of a lease upon one-fourth the area to the man who has performed just as much work, and spent just as much money, and has just the same equities as the claimant under Section C, except that he was not as diligently or continuously at work.

Section E does give a lease on all existing wells within naval reserves coming under Sections C and D. That was the plan agreed upon last winter by the House and Senate Committees and was understood to have had the President's approval. It takes care of producing wells which, so far as I know, must and should be operated, and which the Government is not prepared to handle.

Comment on Section F unfairly states the purpose of the section. It has no relation to the original Taft withdrawals or the naval reserves. It is simply designed to recognize the equities and give a small measure of relief to men who in good faith went upon the open public land, made a location under the mining laws, which they had a right to do, and performed work or expended substantial amounts on or for the benefit of their location in substantial and permanent improvements looking to the development of the claim. After they had made such expenditures without warning, the lands are withdrawn, simply to await legislation. If this bill passes, such lands will be subject to prospecting, because Section F relates only to unproven lands which do not have upon them wells. Why should not the man who went there in good faith, in strict compliance with the law, and who spent his money and time prior to the withdrawal, not be given an opportunity to secure a prospecting permit to further explore the land in preference to a stranger?

The whole matter in relief legislation is based upon equities, as evidenced by good faith and expenditures, and equities are undoubtedly present in each one of the classes provided for in Sections C, D, E, and F.

T MS (WP, DLC).

From John Charles Shaffer[1]

My dear Mr. President: [Denver?] August twenty-one 1919.

Permit me to congratulate you on the conference at the White House on Tuesday. The candid and direct way in which you answered the questions put to you by Senator Lodge and others has cleared the atmosphere in regard to the League of Nations and has made the general public much stronger for the adoption of the Peace Treaty, including the League of Nations.

I have just written a letter to Mr. Will H. Hays, chairman of the National Republican Committee, whom I know intimately, and was a factor in having him elected to that office; I felt at liberty to write him on this important matter. I called his attention to the fact that the attitude of Senators Lodge, Johnson, Borah and others was dividing the Republican Party, and if they persisted in their attitude toward the Peace Treaty and the League of Nations they would divide the Republican Party's vote in the next national election. I suggested that the Republicans as a unit in the Senate ratify the Peace Treaty as it now stands, giving it united support and then pass a bill at the same time making such reservations as in their judgment and wisdom were wise for the protection of the Monroe Doctrine and other interests of our government and stating very plainly that unless these reservations were accepted by the other members of the League of Nations that the United States would withdraw at the end of two years from the League of Nations.

This would give us an opportunity, as set forth in your address to the Senators, of at once coming to peace terms with Germany and the other governments in Europe and would permit us to open up commercial relationships with the governments in Central Europe and would give the senators who feel that our interests are not as well defined and protected in the Peace Treaty and the League of Nations as might be desired the opportunity of placing before the other nations the reservations which they feel are essential to our taking part in the councils of the League of Nations.

May I call your attention to the fact that I have from the very beginning of the discussion of the League of Nations supported it in all my papers and expect to do so until the consummation of this great work. I congratulate you, Mr. President, on the large part you have taken in this great work.

Very sincerely,   John C Shaffer

TLS (WP, DLC).
    [1] Of Chicago, president and publisher of the *Rocky Mountain News*, the *Denver Times*, the *Chicago Evening Post*, and other newspapers in Louisville, Indianapolis, Terre Haute, and Muncie.

To Robert Lansing, with Enclosure

My dear Mr. Secretary: The White House 21 August, 1919.

Thank you sincerely for having let me see the enclosed. I am returning it for your files.

Cordially and faithfully yours,   Woodrow Wilson

E N C L O S U R E

DeWitt Clinton Poole, Jr., to Robert Lansing

MEMORANDUM

My dear Mr. Lansing: Washington

Supplementing my memorandum of the 7th instant,[1] and in compliance with your request, I have the honor to submit herewith a draft of a statement such as the President may find it desirable to make with respect to Russia.

I believe that a statement of this kind, if coupled with positive measures of economic assistance, would serve not only to warn people in general against the evil fatuity of Bolshevism, but would also be effective in hastening a solution of the Russian difficulty. Seeming uncertainty in the attitude of the United States has long been a reliance of the Bolsheviki and a source of confusion to their opponents. A statement from the President would have great moral weight.

We are already giving economic aid. It is desirable that this be extended, as a deterrent to Bolshevism and a means of bringing about normal conditions of life which will enable the people to choose a representative government.

It would be desirable to give economic aid also to the people within the Bolshevik lines, if this can be done with the assurance that the goods will not fall into Bolshevik hands and be inequitably distributed for the furtherance of their political ends. Aside from humanitatian [humanitarian] considerations, it is important from the point of view of policy to avoid the charge of starving the people of Central Russia. The responsibility should be placed where it belongs—upon the Bolsheviki. I believe that Mr. Miles[2] is about to recommend an experiment with the cooperatives.

The statement proposed herewith and economic relief are interdependent measures. The promise of something concrete will give force to the statement. The statement is indispensable in connection with relief within the Bolshevik lines, if this is not to react so

[1] The Enclosure printed with RL to WW, Aug. 7, 1919 (first letter of that date).
[2] That is, Basil Miles.

as to strengthen the very evil we wish to abate. It must be clear that assistance is given not in recognition of the Bolshevik government, but rather in mitigation of it, and through agencies that are quite independent of its control.

The numbers in parentheses in the following draft of a statement refer to subsequent notes embodying such authority for the facts related as it has been possible for me to get together in a very limited time. They are intended only for your convenience and not for publication in case a statement is made.

DRAFT OF STATEMENT.

With the termination of the war and the impending resumption of trade relations throughout the world, it becomes necessary once more to define the attitude of the United States toward Russia.

The Government and people of the United States have watched the development of events in Russia during the last two years with the sympathy which they have traditionally shown toward all efforts for political and social betterment. More particularly, the purposes of the so-called Bolshevik group have been the subject of study; their methods before their accession to power and during the 22 months which have since elapsed have been scrutinized and an estimate made of the actual results of their control of the Russian governmental machine. There has been no lack of patience. The experiment has been given full time for fruition.

It has been found that the purposes of this group of men lie not in the direction of reasoned reform but are primarily destructive (1). Their methods are opportunist and unmoral, arbitrary and coercive. The results of their exercise of power have been demoralization, wide-spread slaughter and economic collapse (2).

Following the revolution of March, 1917, the Bolshevik leader, Lenin, returned to Russia in collusion with the late Imperial Government of Germany. Apparently with the continued clandestine assistance of that Government, which sought its own ends in the disruption of Russia (3), he and his associates took forcible control of affairs at the beginning of November, 1917, and shortly thereafter dissolved the Constitutional Assembly which had been elected by the people of Russia to select a representative government. Though nearly two years have since elapsed, no important changes have taken place, except by death, in the personnel of the group which thus established itself in power.

In June, 1918, at the instigation it is believed of the Government of Germany (4), the Bolshevik Government attempted to arrest a body of Czecho-Slovak troops which were seeking to retire from the eastern front through Siberia, with the ultimate purpose of reaching France and continuing there the struggle against the

Central Powers. Under cover of the resistance which these troops set up, the people of Siberia drove out the commissioners of the Bolshevik Government and organized at several points liberal governments of their own choosing. The chief of these, at Omsk, endeavored to establish peaceful relations with the Bolsheviki at Moscow, offering to furnish them grain if the latter would not seek to spread their doctrines by force in Siberia. This offer was rejected (5) and military operations, including the arming of enemy prisoners of war, were set on foot by the Bolsheviki, which necessitated the despatch of American and Allied troops to Siberia to protect the Czecho-Slovak rear.

During July, 1918, attempts were made by liberal and advanced elements in Central Russia to throw off the Bolshevik yoke. The so-called Left Social Revolutionists, who had theretofore collaborated with the Bolsheviki, broke from them, for the more special reason that shipments toward Germany of food and other articles vitally needed in Russia now revealed the extent to which the opportunist policy of the Bolsheviki had betrayed Russia into German hands (6). The Bolsheviki replied by a reign of terror (7). During the late summer and autumn of 1918 and until the popular sentiment against the Bolsheviki was thereby thoroughly cowed, an unknown number of people, which must, however, be counted by many thousands, were killed in cold blood, some for alleged crimes against the Bolshevik government, some because they were considered potentially dangerous to the Bolshevik power, and many as simple hostages (8). The victims of the terror did not belong, for the most part, to the class which had misruled Russia under the Czars, but to those liberal elements which some day, it might be hoped, would play a leading part in the upbuilding of Russia along modern democratic lines (9).

The Bolsheviki began, also, in the fall of 1918, a system of discrimination in the distribution of food which operated, on the one hand, to lessen opposition through starvation and, on the other, to bring into the ranks of their active supporters many unconvinced but despairing recruits. By this system which still subsists (10), the population is divided into categories along occupational and class lines and receives food, so far as food may be available, in accordance with a scale which is adjusted with a view to the maintenance of the Bolsheviki in power and in fulfilment of their program for the extinction of the middle classes. The ration given to members of the Red Army is estimated by the Bolshevik Official Gazette of February 6, 1919, to be three times the average for the several categories of the civil population.

The Bolsheviki have built up the Red Army by means of this

discrimination and by forced conscription, including the taking of hostages among the wives and children of former officers for whose technical knowledge there is need (11). This army has served to maintain the defence of Bolshevik Russia and to put down the peasant revolts which have occurred not infrequently within its lines (12).

Economic ruin has gone on apace. Factories are shut down or are running at a small fraction of their former output. Transportation is seriously crippled. The currency is debauched. Famine and disease are widespread. In the country much of the livestock has been killed. The peasants are indisposed to produce beyond the requirements of their own consumption, as the currency has little or no value in exchange, cloth and manufactured goods are hardly to be had and stocks of grain are taken by the Red Army or by committees of requisition carrying out armed raids from the cities (13).

These conditions are in part the result of Russia's participation in the war and of general revolutionary upheaval. It is beyond question, however, that they have been intensified and maintained by the misgovernment of the Bolsheviki and that the continuance of the Bolsheviki in control of Central Russia is an obstacle to the alleviation of this tragic distress. The Government of the United States, together with the Associated Governments, endeavored within recent months to arrange for a cessation of internal warfare and the feeding of the population, but without success.

The problem is not one for Russia alone. The whole economy of eastern Europe is thrown out of gear by Russia's paralysis and cannot be set properly going until order is reestablished in that country. Moreover, the purposes of the Bolsheviki are not confined to the borders of Russia. Russia is but the first incident in their program. Their aim is world-wide revolution, to be accomplished through a forcible usurpation of power on the part of a single class. They use their possession of the Russian governmental machinery first of all as a means of universal propaganda. Their doctrine aims at the destruction of all governments as now constituted. Poland and the other new states of eastern and central Europe are under the direct menace of their destructive teachings. The successs [sic] everywhere of the healthy democratic movements of the day is endangered by an insidious suggestion of violence and unreason emanating from Moscow.

We are impelled by every consideration of a humanitarian and moral order to endeavor to relieve the economic want of the Russian people. Their unhappy lot is in part a direct result of their contribution to the success of the war from which we have emerged victorious. At the same time it lies within the interest and duty of every orderly government to take measures which, while not interfering with the right and duty of the Russian people to work out their own destiny, will hasten the movement of events along the paths marked out by internal factors toward the restoration of the national economy and the establishment of a government having the popular mandate, a government which will concern itself exclusively with the well-being of the Russian people and abstain from attempts to effect the overthrow of the institutions which the peoples of other countries have chosen for themselves.

Having regard to these considerations, it will be the policy of the United States to seek, on the one hand, to relieve in every practicable way the economic distress of the Russian people and, on the other, to hasten the end of the Bolshevik régime in Central Russia.

Support will continue to be given to such elements in Siberia and elsewhere as are working for the restoration of order throughout Russia and the setting up of government under adequate democratic guarantees. Material relief will be provided in every possible way for the population of regions liberated from Bolshevik domination. Private enterprise desiring to trade with these regions will have the cooperation of the Government.

The relief of the people within the Bolshevik lines is made very difficult by the Bolshevik nationalization of foreign trade and their discriminating system of food distribution, but the Government will continue to study means by which these people may be helped and it is hoped that concrete measures will from time to time be found possible.

NOTES RELATING TO THE FOREGOING DRAFT.

1. This is made clear, I believe, by the extracts quoted in my memorandum of the 7th instant. As showing that the Bolshevik attitude remains as uncompromising as ever, I insert herewith an interview recently given by Lenin via wireless to a newspaper man in Budapest.

2. The Department's files contain much first-hand evidence as to conditions in central Russia. One of the most recent reports received from Mr. Hapgood, summarizes the observations of Gregor Alexinsky, who recently came to Copenhagen from Russia.[3] I have

3 Grigorii Alekseevich Aleksinskii, a Social Revolutionary who had broken with Lenin in 1909 and the author of several books on Russian political and foreign affairs which had been published in English translation between 1913 and 1917. A news report, "Workmen and Peasants Rebel," *New York Times*, Aug. 25, 1919, had the following comment on Aleksinskii and his reports: "Washington, Aug. 24. That strong opposition against the Bolsheviki is developing in European Russia is the report brought out of Russia by G. A. Alexinsky, a member of the second Duma, who recently escaped from the country. Mr. Alexinsky is a socialist revolutionist and was imprisoned for ten

read several of Alexinsky's books on Russia and know him as an objective observer with radical sympathies. A summary of his report, as prepared in the office of Foreign Intelligence, is inserted.[4]

3. There can be no doubt of collusion in the case of Lenin's return. Obviously the German Government did not send Lenin across Germany in a sealed car without the definite expectation of profit. That it was not a mere passive acquiescence on the part of Germany appears from the testimony of Mr. Roger Simmons before the Senate Investigating Committee (Hearings on Bolshevik Propaganda, page 343 et seq.)[5]

The subsequent relations of the Germans with the Bolsheviki are not so clearly established but the evidence in hand is sufficient to prove beyond any reasonable doubt that the Bolsheviki received aid from time to time from Berlin. My own intimate contact with the Bolsheviki during five or six months convinced me of the existence of a special obligation owed by the Bolsheviki in that quarter.

4. Chicherin[6] admitted to me personally that the Germans had brought pressure to bear concerning the Czecho-Slovaks and I had confirmation of this through other channels.

5. The offer of the Siberian Government and its rejection were published in the Moscow Izvestia (the official gazette of the Bolsheviki) for June 11, 1918.

6. This is all brought out in the proceedings of the Fifth All-Russian Soviet Congress (Moscow, July, 1918).

7. This Congress resolved: "Bolshevik Russia must reply to all crimes of the people's enemies with wholesale terror against the bourgeoisie." (Pravda, July 14, 1918.)

8. See my cablegram No. 2, September 3, 1918, from Moscow, embodying personal observations.[7] A circular telegram of the Bolshevik Commissar for home affairs sent to all Soviets September 2, 1918 points out that "nothwithstanding frequent pronouncements urging *mass terror* against the Social Rdvolutionists [Revolutionists], White Guards and bourgeoisie, no real terror exists," and continues:

---

months by the Bolsheviki before he made his escape. A summary of his report has reached Washington by official channels."

[4] It is missing.

[5] 66th Cong., 1st sess., Sen. Doc. No. 62, *Brewing and Liquor Interests and German and Bolshevik Propaganda: Report and Hearings of the Subcommittee on the Judiciary, United States Senate, Submitted Pursuant to S. Res. 307 and 439, Sixty-Fifth Congress. . . .* (3 vols., Washington, 1919), III, 343-44. Roger E. Simmons, a trade commissioner in the Bureau of Foreign and Domestic Commerce of the Department of Commerce, had been in Russia from July 1917 to January 1919 to study Russian economic resources, especially timber. He testified before the Senate Subcommittee on the Judiciary, headed by Lee S. Overman of North Carolina, on February 15 and 17, 1919. His complete testimony is printed in *ibid.*, pp. 293-319, 339-62.

[6] That is, Georgii Vasil'evich Chicherin.

[7] D. C. Poole, Jr., to RL, Sept. 3, 1918, printed in *FR 1918, Russia*, I, 681-82.

"A stop must be put to this situation. There must be an end of wealness [weakness] and mercy. All Right Social Revolutionists known to local Soviets should be arrested immediately. Numerous hostages should be taken from the bourgeoisie and officer classes. At the slightest attempt to resist or the slightest movement among the White Guards, shooting of masses of hostages should be begun without fail. Initiative in the matter rests especially with the local executive committees. Indecisive action on the part of the local Soviet must be immediately reported. Not the sloghtest [slightest] indecision in using mass terror!"

It is difficult, if not impossible, to estimate the number of victims of the terror. I believe that a conservative estimate would put it in the tens of thousands. Replying to a protest by Major Wardwell,[8] commanding the American Red Cross, Chicherin wrote under date of September 11, 1918:

"You speak of execution of 500 persons in Petrograd as of one particularly striking instance. (This set of executions had been announced in the official press.) As for the number, it is only one. Among these five hundred, two hundred were executed on the ground of the decision of the local organization to whom they were very well known as most active and dangerous counter-revolutionaries and three hundred had been selected already some time ago as belonging to the vanguard of the counter-revolutionary movement."

Major Wardwell has of all Americans the widest personal knowledge of the terror. He was associated with Colonel Robins[9] and cannot be accused of prejudice against the Bolsheviki. If you or the President should still have any feeling of doubt as to the extent and horror of Bolshevik repressions during the fall of 1918, I can arrange for Major Wardwell to come to Washington and to give you an account of what he himself saw.

9. This was a matter of widespread comment among foreign observers in Russia. Mr. Roger Simmons, Special Agent of the Department of Commerce, gives first-hand evidence in his testimony before the Senate Committee (Hearings on Bolshevik Propaganda, page 313):

"In Lubanka prison where I had eighty-five fellow prisoners, the personnel surpised me. I expected to find princes and men of all titles. There were a few of these, but the majority I would term middle-class—mechanics, printers, peasants—many peasants—small manufacturers, soldiers, priests, workmen, officers (army and navy), and professional men, students, etc."

[8] That is, Allen Wardwell.
[9] That is, Raymond Robins.

The Bolsheviki find their chief enemies in the middle classes. Before the Central Executive Committee at Moscow, April 29, 1919, Lenin said in substance: "Our great and principal enemy is the small proprietor. The small bourgeoisie is the only force capable of upsetting us."

10. This system is described in the Izvestia for September 11, 1918. See also Food Supplement to the Review of the Foreign Press (U. S. General Staff) April 7, 1919, page 593; May 26, 1919, page 107; May 12, 1919, page 48.

11. Report on visit to Finland by Lieutenant Commander John A. Gade, U.S.N., now demobilized; Reports in possession of Military Intelligence Division, War Department, including No. 2023-76, Military Attaché Record Section.

12. Military Intelligence Division files 2070-1158; 2070-1409. Report of Dr. Davidson[10] from Legation, Stockholm, April 16, 1919, respecting admissions in Bolshevik official press of frequent peasant revolts.

13. See decree concerning "harvesting and requisitioning detachments," original signed by Lenin, August 6, 1918. Translation in Russian Division, State Department.

14. This was emphasized by Mr. Eugene Meyer of the War Finance Corporation, whom I met in London recently. He had been studying the possibility of assisting Poland and the countries in the region of the Baltic. He said that he feared that there was nothing to be done until the Russian problem was settled.

Respectfully,   D C Poole

TLS (SDR, RG 59, 861.00/5126, DNA).
    [10] That is, M. Davidson, about whom see n. 5 to the minutes of the Council of Ten printed at Jan. 21, 1919, 10:30 a.m., Vol. 54.

To John Barton Payne

My dear Judge Payne: [The White House] 21 August, 1919.

Thank you for your letter of August 16th about the shipping to carry coal to Italy. I am heartily glad the arrangements could be made.   Cordially and faithfully yours,   Woodrow Wilson

TLS (Letterpress Books, WP, DLC).

To Count Vincenzo Macchi di Cellere

My dear Mr. Ambassador: [The White House] 21 August, 1919.

I am very happy to learn from the Chairman of the United States Shipping Board that the Board feels that there will be shipping, beginning September 1st, to take from 75,000 to 100,000 tons of coal per month to Italy. If the Italian representatives will give the Board adequate notice, so that there may be no interruption to the arrangement, this tonnage can certainly be made available.

Seventeen ships of the dead-weight tonnage of 105,503 tons are now actually in the coal service for Italy or have been alloted to the Italian coal service. This, however, is for commercial coal, not for the Italian Government as such.

Cordially and sincerely yours,   Woodrow Wilson

TLS (Letterpress Books, WP, DLC).

Robert Lansing to Frank Lyon Polk

[Washington] August 21, 1919.

Confidential. Your 3797 August 20, 10 pm.[1]

Presidents idea is to ask for most notorious culprits and question of making demand for others to be decided later. It was not understood from your 3682 August 14[2] that Clemenceau planned that at the time when the request is made for the few conspicuous culprits the German Government should be informed that a further demand for remainder will actually be made.

T telegram (SDR, RG 59, 763.72119/6373, DNA).
  [1] "Clemenceau's plan is to ask for a few now and the remainder later. You state President believes we should ask for only a few of the most conspicuous culprits, and presumably forego any demand for the remainder. If so, this would be third alternative stated in my 3682 Aug. 14 and not Clemenceau's plan. Please instruct." FLP to RL, No. 3797, Aug. 20, 1919, T telegram (SDR, RG 256, 185.118/141, DNA).
  [2] Printed as an Enclosure with RL to WW, Aug. 15, 1919 (first letter of that date).

From Robert Lansing, with Enclosure

Personal and Confidential.

Dear Mr. President: [Washington] August 21, 1919.

I enclose an important memorandum prepared by Ambassador Fletcher exposing President Carranza's attitude of hostility to the United States and its citizens, and his belief, expressed over his own signature, that you are responsible for what he is pleased to call the tortuosity of American policy with regard to Mexico.

The memorandum encloses translations of two notes,[1] the originals of which are in the possession of the War Department, written by Mr. Carranza to a literary woman whom he has employed to prepare in book form[2] his propaganda against the United States, which is to be circulated in Latin America with the idea of injuring our prestige.

A series of articles from the pen of his chief of cabinet, explaining the Carranza Doctrine, which he has set up to destroy the Monroe Doctrine, and which is thoroughly anti-American and seeks to replace Pan-Americanism by what he calls Indo-Latinism, is also attached.[3]

While you may not have time to read all these articles, I think it worth your while to glance at the editorial dated June 30th, which summarizes the so-called doctrine, important portions of which have been marked.   Faithfully yours,   R.L.

CCLI (SDR, RG 59, 812.00/23111C, DNA).
    [1] V. Carranza to Hermila Galindo, June 29 and July 31, 1919, T MSS (SDR, RG 59, 812.00/23111C, DNA).
    [2] It appeared as Hermila Galindo, *La Doctrina Carranza y el Acercamiento Indolatino* (Mexico City, 1919).
    [3] These are missing in both the Wilson Papers and the State Department files.

E N C L O S U R E

From Henry Prather Fletcher

SECRET.

Dear Mr. President: [Washington] August 20, 1919.

I hand you herewith translations of two notes which were written by President Carranza to a Miss Hermila Galindo, a Mexican literary woman, who is preparing for secret circulation a book called the "Carranza Doctrine and the Indo-Latin Rapprochement."

In these notes reference is made to a Blue book which has been secretly printed by the Mexican Government,[1] and which I am reliably informed contains the correspondence of the Carranza Government with its representatives at the American-Mexican Conference at Atlantic City; the Mexican Government's proposals in regard to the Great War and the Conference of Neutrals; the various high-toned notes which the Mexican Government has addressed to the United States and British Governments, and extracts from President Carranza's public utterances on international affairs.

I also attach hereto transcripts of a series of leading articles which appeared in the official Mexican Government newspaper EL PUEBLO, explanatory of the so-called Carranza Doctrine, and which were written by Aguirre Berlanga, the Minister of Government, who was almost openly pro-German, and Mr. Carranza's principal lieutenant in all his anti-American work.

Fearing that you may not have time to read the whole series, I have marked certain salient paragraphs which I believe too important to be overlooked, if a correct understanding of Mr. Carranza's position is desired.

The Mexican Government is preparing to launch an active, perhaps secret, anti-American campaign throughout Latin America, and will attempt to misrepresent and impugn the good faith of the efforts of this Government to bring about a better understanding with Mexico, and will seek to make capital propaganda of Carranza's steadfast independence and disregard of the advice, assistance, and in many cases the representations of this and other governments.

I believe it should be made plain to the Mexican people and to the people of this continent that Carranza's obstinacy and hatred of the United States is the principal cause of Mexico's troubles, and that instead of the Hero and Great Patriot he wishes to be considered, he is merely a stumbling block in the path of Pan Americanism, and is ruining his country to gratify a blind hostility to and distrust of the United States.   Henry P. Fletcher

CCLS (SDR, RG 59, 812.00/23111C, DNA).
¹ Secretaría de Relaciones Exteriores, *Labor Internacional de la Revolución Constitucionalista de México* (Mexico City, 1919); also published as *Diplomatic Dealings of the Constitutionalist Revolution in Mexico* (Mexico City, 1919).

From Edward Mandell House

London August 21, 1919.

Urgent 2861. For the President from Colonel House. Drummond is anxious to secure answers to the following questions: "1. Assuming that the Senate ratifies the treaty would the President have any objection if an American were appointed as High Commissioner of Danzig. 2. Assuming that the Senate ratifies the treaty would the President have any objection to an American being appointed an agent Sarre Valley Government Commission." It is of course possible that the appointment of Americans to posts above named would not be acceptable to other powers. Drummond feels very keenly that the appointment of a Frenchman as Chairman of the Sarre Valley Government Commission would jeopardize the League in the eyes of neutral powers and that a compromise could perhaps be effected with the French if an American was to be appointed. He will have to be a man of exceptional qualifications if possible with a knowledge of French and German. If you agree with Drummond's point have you anybody in mind for the position.
            Davis

T telegram (R. Lansing Papers, DLC).

Two Telegrams from Robert Lansing to
Edward Mandell House

[Washington] August 21, 1919.
(Not for distribution)

Strictly Confidential. For Colonel House. Your 2818 August 15.

I have shown your message to the President and we feel that at the present moment it is not possible to give a definite opinion when ratification of the treaty will come to a vote but there is some reason to hope that action will be taken in the near future. As to the probable result of the vote no prophecy can be ventured until there is a clear manifestation of the effect of the conference which the President held Tuesday with the Foreign Relations Committee of the Senate. We consider that it would be a distinct advantage if England France and Italy would ratify the Treaty as soon as possible.

The President and I are both well and I hope to take a short vacation in September.   Robert Lansing

[Washington] August 21, 1919.

Confidential for Colonel House.

Your 2819 August 18, 11 am.

The President and I feel that no decision can be reached regarding the meeting of the Supreme Economic Council until the ratification of the Treaty is settled.   [Robert Lansing]

T telegrams (R. Lansing Papers, DLC).

Isaiah Bowman to Robert Lansing

Sir: New York City. August 21, 1919.

In continuation of our conversation of this morning, I beg to submit the following facts regarding the Persian situation. They are from published sources, that is, English blue books and other Government publications, etc. They are summarized in a report presented to the American Commission at Paris in January of this year. The report is from the Persian Relief Commission which went out to Persia under President Judson.[1]

The main points are as follows:

1. The principal oil company in Persia today is the so-called Anglo Persian Oil Company, Ltd. The shares of the company are held chiefly by the British Government, one of the rare instances in

which a government is directly concerned in a foreign investment. The reason for this action of the British Government is that the Persian oil fields are among the richest in the world. They are producing at the present moment sufficient oil to meet the needs of the entire British Navy for fuel as well as for petroleum by-products. English concessions in Persia total 500,000 square miles of oil-bearing land out of a total of over 700,000 square miles of Persian territory. Enormous refineries have been built at Abadan on the Shott-el-Arab.

2. By the terms of the agreement between Persia and the Anglo Persian Oil Company, Persia was to obtain in exchange as compensation for the concessions 16% of the annual net profits. The Persian Government guaranteed police protection and this has been made the basis of charges against the Persian Government equal to or in excess of its share of the net annual profits. The result is that though the company's estimated annual net profits during the past year have been close to a million pounds or five million dollars and smaller amounts in preceding years, the Persian Government has never obtained anything.

3. Naturally, the Persian Government has made many bitter protests against the action of Great Britain and all the more because the British Government is the chief stockholder in the oil company and, therefore, combines with its commercial interest a political interest and influence which amounts practically to ownership of Persian land and sovereign control of Persian people.

4. It should be noted that the British Government purchased the controlling shares of the Anglo Persian Oil Company, Ltd. in 1914 and increased its holdings in 1917 to twenty-five million dollars.

Yours very truly,   Isaiah Bowman

Read by Prest Aug 21/19. RL

TLS (R. Lansing Papers, DLC).
¹ We have not found the report of the Persian Relief Commission. Judson was Harry Pratt Judson, President of the University of Chicago.

From the Desk Diary of Robert Lansing

Thursday Aug 21 [1919]

Dr. Bowman on Thracian and Adriatic Questions. Came at my request from NY. He told me much which confirmed my views as to House's plan to take dip. negotiations out of State Dept. & give it to League of Nations. I shall tell Prest. . . .

Conference with Prest. 12-12:25. Discussed League of Nations bureaus. Prest said if one established here it would be under the

State Dept. Told him I considered delegates to League would be diplomatic officers under Dept. He assented. Show[ed] him British oil concessions in Persia. Told him Armenia should be attached to some paying region if under mandate. No answer. . . .

Tumulty phoned me as to necessity of resisting RR men's demands and asked me to speak to Prest.

A Memorandum by Robert Lansing

BOWMAN'S VIEWS AS TO COLONEL HOUSE.

August 21, 1919.

Dr. Isaiah Bowman, the executive head of the group of experts at the Peace Conference, who was in Washington today to advise as to Thrace, gave me some interesting information which supplemented his statements made to me in Paris the night before his departure for the United States in June.

He told me that he knew from conversations which he had with several of the Experts that Colonel House had been favorable to the Shantung decision in order to persuade the Japanese to recede from their determination to press for an article in the Covenant declaring for equal treatment for the nationals of all the members of the League and that he had strongly urged the President to accede to the Japanese demands not only as to Shantung but also as to the Pacific Islands north of the equator.

He also said that Colonel House favored giving over Fiume to Italy; that the experts were all against it and did not feel that their views reached the President because Dr. Mezes, the head nominally of the Inquiry, [who] did whatever he was told to do by the Colonel or by Auchincloss, had on previous occasions changed expert memoranda to meet the Colonel's views without consulting the authors; that to avoid this improper censorship, which they bitterly resented, the experts prepared and signed a joint memorandum against the cession of Fiume to Italy[1] and sent it directly to the President through Grayson or Close without informing Mezes or House of their action; that a few days later the President issued his public statement as to Fiume[2] which caused such furor in Italy; and that Colonel House, when he found out what had been done, "came as near losing his temper," as he (Bowman) ever knew him to and bitterly complained that the memorandum had not passed through Mezes' hands since the experts had upset his plans when he had reached "a satisfactory settlement" with the Italians for Italian control of Fiume which only required his obtaining the President's assent.

Dr. Bowman, who was very bitter at the way expert opinion had been distorted, added that the Colonel's method of negotiation, as he knew from months of association, was to accept the other party's demand and then to seek a formula for it with which he could go to the President and obtain his assent; and that he (Bowman) considered that such a policy was most dangerous to American interests and made House an impossible representative for the United States in all foreign affairs.

Bowman also told me that at one time he was discussing the Council of the League of Nations with the Colonel, who mentioned a plan to establish League Bureaus of Information and Correspondence in the various capitals, which could deal directly with the departments of Government; and that the Colonel said that he was strong for such bureaus although he was afraid of opposition in Washington because it would of course take away a good deal of control of affairs from the Department of State.

This information confirmed a warning which I had received yesterday in a letter from L. H. Woolsey (now in Paris) who said that the Commission on Organization, on which are Cecil, Drummond, Fosdick and House, was planning to constitute bureaus which were to be independent of all foreign offices reporting to and receiving instructions from the Secretariat of the League.

The matter seemed to be sufficiently serious for me to lay it before the President, which I did at our noon conference at the White House today, though I did not mention the name of my informants.

The President seemed to be much concerned at my statement as to the plan of the Commission on organization in London, and said that bureaus of that sort could not be independent, and that, if one was set up in Washington it would have to be in the Department of State and subject to the complete control of the Secretary. As a departmental bureau the idea might work out all right. The original proposition is, however, preposterous since I trust that this country will not permit the authority to conduct our foreign affairs to be confided in any degree to a bureau reporting to and acting for the Secretariat or Council of the League. It looks to me as if Sir Eric Drummond and Colonel House were endeavoring to increase the powers of the Secretariat beyond reason, so that the Council of the League rather than the Governments would manage all world matters. If this is attempted, I shall declare the truth, point out the danger, and fight to defeat the scheme. I have reached the conclusion that Drummond is a dangerous man and ought not to be Secretary General.

T MS (R. Lansing Papers, DLC).
  [1] I. Bowman et al. to WW, April 17, 1919, Vol. 57.
  [2] Printed at April 23, 1919, Vol. 58.

From the Desk Diary of Robert Lansing

Friday Aug 22 [1919]

Japanese Chargé with memo. on basis of negotiations between China & Japan. Told him it was not satisfactory.

Conf. at W H with Prest, 12-1. Mrs. W. came in for a moment Discussed state of unrest in country. Pres't indicated socialistic tendencies. Discussed Jap. memo. & other matters. . . .

Dr Matthews[1] on Bolshevik danger in this country and from Judaism. Said he had talked to Prest yesterday very frankly about Brandeis, who [he] says is dishonest, and other Zionists.

[1] The Rev. Dr. Mark Allison Matthews, pastor of the First Presbyterian Church of Seattle, Wash., a long-time acquaintance of Wilson. Matthews saw Wilson at the White House at 2:45 p.m. on August 21 and apparently stayed for a long visit.

Frank Lyon Polk to Robert Lansing

Paris August 22, 1919.

3834 Confidential for the Secretary of State from Polk.

As the Italians are pressing for a settlement in view of the fact that their House of Deputies meet on August 28, General Bliss and Polk suggest that we be authorized to submit to Tittoni some proposition as our last word on the Adriatic settlement, our acceptance to be on condition that Tittoni also accepts proposal as final settlement of all Italy's claims in Adriatic.

The following is submitted for your consideration: Italy to receive the territory west of the American line in Istria and Julian Venetia, and in addition the region about Albona lying between the bay of Fianona and the American line, along the Arsa river, on condition that this latter area and its territorial waters are permanently neutralized.

A free state of Fiume under control of League of Nations to be established with area and government corresponding to that already proposed by President Wilson, the area to include islands of Cherso and Veglia. Plebiscite to determine ultimate fate of the state according to terms already suggested by President.

All other territory east of American line, including the Assling Triangle, to go to Jugo-Slavia, except as provided below:

The town of Zara, including only its immediate suburbs, but not the district nor any of its included islands, to be made a free city under the League of Nations with charter which will guarantee full protection to Italians of Zara without establishing Italian sovereignty over city.

The Island of Lissa and the Pelagosa group of islands to be assigned to Italy in full sovereignty.

The Lussin Islands to be assigned to Italy providing a plebiscite (by individual islands or by the group as a whole, as Italy may prefer) under control of League of Nations shows that the people desire Italian sovereignty, and providing further that these islands and their adjacent waters are permanently neutralized. All other islands to go to Jugo-Slavia.

Italy to have the mandate for any Albanian state which may be established by the Conference.

The above proposal involves as new concessions from President's present stand the giving of Albona region to Italy, the possible cession to Italy of Lussin Islands, and giving Italy mandate over Albania. Johnson regards Italian claim to Albona district as very objectionable and supported by no just grounds, with which view I agree. But we both agree that it may be wise to make this concession in interests of a prompt settlement, particularly as Tittoni seems to lay some stress on the political importance of this small section. Johnson would also approve proposed concession regarding Lussin islands if this alone stood in way of settlement. He thinks Italian protectorate over Albania exceedingly dangerous, as Italy desires it for colonization and future expansion in the Balkans. On the other hand he feels French mandate is absolutely impossible, and English acceptance of mandate highly improbable. Albanians greatly desire American mandate and are bitterly opposed to Italian mandate. But if American mandate is out of question, there is left as only practicable solution an Italian mandate under such safeguards as we can erect. We urgently need your advice on this point. Have you also any opinions as to proper frontiers for Albanian state, or will you trust to our opinions on this matter.

This telegram prepared by Johnson and Coolidge.

Marconi[1] told me last week that of course they would have to sign what we handed to them, but he begged us to be as generous as possible. Both he and Tittoni have been most conciliatory—begging rather than urging concessions.

It may be that the President would feel that the question of Albania should be held for decision by the League of Nations and should not be discussed at this time, in which case I feel Tittoni should be told. Clemenceau told me to-day he saw no reason for discussing Albania at this time. I raise question in order to ascertain your views.   Polk.

T telegram (SDR, RG 256, 186.3411/755A, DNA).
[1] That is, Guglielmo Marconi.

An Aide-Mémoire

IMPERIAL JAPANESE EMBASSY
Washington.

[Aug. 22, 1919]

The Honorable the Secretary of State in the course of his conversation with the Japanese Chargé d'Affaires at Washington on July 28[1] called the attention of the Japanese Government to the information received from the American Minister at Peking to the effect that the Japanese Government have opened negotiations with the Chinese Government for the restitution of Kiao-chou on the basis of the Sino-Japanese agreements of 1915 and 1918. Secretary Lansing understood that it had been agreed at the Paris Conference that the question of Shantung was finally to be adjusted independently of and without reference to the arrangements of 1915 and 1918. He therefore asked for explanations respecting the reported action of the Japanese Government which seemed to him to be inconsistent with the understanding reached at Paris.

The Japanese Government desire to point out in reply that it is not true that negotiations had been opened at Peking for the restitution of Kiao-chou. In their statement issued to the press on August 2[2] they have made it clear that such negotiations could only be entered into after the treaty of peace with Germany shall have been ratified by Japan.

At the same time, they confirm that, in response to the desire of President Hsu, informally conveyed to the Japanese Minister at Peking[3] toward the latter part of May, Mr. Obata expressed his readiness to address an official communication to the Chinese Acting Minister of Foreign Affairs[4] in the sense that the Japanese Government were prepared to enter into negotiations with the Chinese Government as soon as practicable after the ratification by Japan, China and Germany of the Treaty of Versailles, in pursuance of Japan's engagement to China.

It will be recalled that the legal obligation undertaken by Japan toward China to return Kiao-chou originates from the arrangement of 1915. Japan is firmly determined to abide by her pledged word consecrated in that arrangement and it was this sincere determination that Mr. Obata's proposed communication was intended to re-affirm. Nor was any exception then taken by the Chinese Government to the substance of the communication thus suggested. These informal conversations were, however, eventually abandoned by the Chinese themselves owing apparently to the change of the situation caused by their failure to sign the Treaty of Versailles.

The question now raised by the Secretary of State seems further to rest on the presumption that it was admitted by the Japanese delegation in Paris that the validity of the Sino-Japanese arrangements of 1915 and 1918 was at least questioned. Careful research of the reports so far received in Tokio on the proceedings of the Paris Conference has failed to disclose anything which indicates such an admission on the part of the Japanese delegation. On the contrary, Viscount Chinda at the close of the discussion on the Shantung clauses on the 30th of April defined the position of Japan in the matter "to remove any moral obligation on behalf of Japan not to invoke the agreements in question."[5]

Contentions are often advanced in this connection that China was compelled to accept the arrangement of 1915 under conditions which deprived her of a free choice of any other alternative. It is, however, evident that if such contentions were adopted to challenge the validity of treaty solemnly entered into by a sovereign power, dangerous precedents would be set with grave consequences upon the stability of the existing international relations.

In offering foregoing explanation, the Japanese Government are happy to believe that the spirit of entire frankness and confidence in which it is submitted will not be misunderstood by the American Government.

T MS (R. Lansing Papers, DLC).
    [1] About this conversation, see the news report printed at July 28, 1919.
    [2] The Enclosure printed with RL to WW, Aug. 4, 1919 (third letter of that date).
    [3] That is, Torikichi Obata.
    [4] That is, Ch'en Lu.
    [5] For this statement, see the minutes of the Council of Four printed at April 30, 1919, 12:30 p.m., Vol. 58.

To Robert Lansing

CONFIDENTIAL

My dear Mr. Secretary: [The White House] 22 August, 1919.

This is all exceedingly serious.[1] Do you not think it would be best for Mr. Fletcher to return at once to his post at Mexico City? I fear that there is not sufficient restraining influence upon Carranza in his absence, and that there is a possibility that he may feel freer than he would feel if Mr. Fletcher were there, to express publicly this outrageous attitude.

Cordially and faithfully yours,   Woodrow Wilson

TLS (Letterpress Books, WP, DLC).
    [1] See RL to WW, Aug. 21, 1919, and its Enclosure.

To Franklin Delano Roosevelt

PERSONAL AND CONFIDENTIAL

My dear Mr. Secretary: The White House 22 August, 1919.

My eye was caught by this advertisement in one of the maga-
zines, and I am writing to ask whether the Department had any
knowledge of this literary plan of Admiral Sims or whether the Department approved of it before he made this engagement with The
World's Work.[1] I am sure that you will agree with me that plans of
this sort should certainly be submitted to the Department before
they are put into execution.

                    Cordially and sincerely yours,   Woodrow Wilson

TLS (F. D. Roosevelt Papers, NHpR).
  [1] William Sowden Sims, *The Victory at Sea* (Garden City, N. Y., 1920), was serialized
in *World's Work*, XXXVIII-XL (Sept. 1919-July 1920).

To Josephus Daniels

TO BE SENT THROUGH THE NAVY DEPARTMENT

                              The White House, 22 August, 1919.
Hon. Josephus Daniels, Secretary of the Navy,
Honolulu, Hawaii.

Please convey following message to Governor McCarthy:[1] "Pray
accept my warm congratulations upon the completion of the great
drydock. The development of Pearl Harbor Naval Base is most opportune and necessary because of the coming of the great fleet to
the Pacific. The whole nation is deeply interested in the constitution of this fleet and is happy to see the Pacific Coast and the
American Islands of the Pacific accorded the advantage of its
presence."[2]   Woodrow Wilson

CC telegram (WP, DLC).
  [1] Charles James McCarthy, Governor of the Territory of Hawaii.
  [2] Daniels, on June 16, had announced the division of the existing Atlantic Fleet into
two new units: an Atlantic Fleet, under the command of Admiral Henry Braid Wilson,
and a Pacific Fleet, commanded by Admiral Hugh Rodman. Each fleet would have an
equal number of battleships and smaller supporting vessels. A group of smaller ships
already operating in the Far East would continue to be designated as the Asiatic Fleet,
under the command of Admiral Albert Gleaves. This arrangement went into effect on
June 30. Later public statements in June revealed that the Pacific Fleet would have
greater speed, range, and firepower than its Atlantic counterpart since it was to have
the navy's newest, oil-burning battle cruisers and battleships. The new Pacific Fleet
sailed from Hampton Roads, Virginia, on July 19 and passed through the Panama Canal
on July 26. By mid-August the fleet was calling at port cities on the West Coast of the
United States. See the *New York Times*, June 17, 18, 23, and 29; July 10, 17, 20, and
28; and Aug. 8 and 11, 1919.
  Daniels presided at the ceremonies opening the new drydock at Pearl Harbor on August 21. The drydock, designed to accommodate the navy's largest ships, had been under construction since 1909. *Ibid.*, August 22, 1919. For the background of the long-

delayed completion of the drydock and the creation of the Pacific Fleet, see Harold and Margaret Sprout, *Toward a New Order of Sea Power: American Naval Policy and the World Scene, 1918-1922* (Princeton, N. J., 1940), pp. 85-90, William Reynolds Braisted, *The United States Navy in the Pacific, 1909-1922* (Austin, Tex., and London, 1971), pp. 40-42, 208-24, 505-10; and Paolo E. Coletta, ed., *United States Navy and Marine Bases, Domestic* (Westport, Conn., 1985).

To Newton Diehl Baker

My dear Baker: The White House 22 August, 1919.

Thank you for your letter of the 20th accompanying the Report of the Federal Electric Railways Commission. I have just received the enclosed letter from Mr. Sweet,[1] and you will notice that he proposes that the Commission should sit in various cities in order to afford public opinion a clearer view of the whole problem. I would very much like to know your judgment as to whether it is wise to continue the activities of this commission or whether it may be said to have accomplished all that it is possible to accomplish.

I hesitate to approach Congress on the subject unless there is a clear case of useful, if not indispensable, service which can be demonstrated to them as a sufficient argument for and [an] appropriation and authorization.

Cordially and faithfully yours,   Woodrow Wilson

TLS (N. D. Baker Papers, DLC).
[1] E. F. Sweet to WW, Aug. 20, 1919, TLS (WP, DLC).

To Albert Sidney Burleson

My dear Burleson: [The White House] 22 August, 1919.

I am sending this letter of Mr. Hooker's to you, because I asked him to write it to me[1] and because, as I now see the case, I fully agree with his judgment that the ruling of the Department is wholly wrong in this matter.

Of course you will understand that I await your own judgment before forming a conclusion, but I hope that you will look into it from the point of view of men who, like myself, have spent a large part of their lives writing books and for whom book reviews are given a very great additional value by enabling them to know whether the purchase price of the book is within their reach or not.

Cordially and faithfully yours,   Woodrow Wilson

TLS (Letterpress Books, WP, DLC).
[1] Wilson saw Richard Hooker, editor of the *Springfield* (Mass.) *Republican*, at the White House on August 14. The Editors have not found Hooker's letter.

To Benjamin Franklin Buchanan[1]

[The White House] 22 August, 1919.

May I not take the liberty of expressing my profound interest in the action which the Legislature of my native State is to take in the matter of the Suffrage Amendment to the Constitution of the United States? It seems to me of profound importance to our country that this amendment should be adopted, and I venture to urge its adoption upon the Legislature with the utmost respect and with the greatest earnestness.   Woodrow Wilson

T telegram (Letterpress Books, WP, DLC).
[1] Lieutenant Governor of Virginia and President Pro Tempore of the Virginia State Senate. Wilson on the same day sent the same telegram, *mutatis mutandis,* to Harry R. Houston, Speaker of the Virginia House of Delegates (Letterpress Books, WP, DLC).

From Alexander Mitchell Palmer, with Enclosure

Dear Mr. President: Washington, D.C. August 22, 1919.

This memorandum of suggestions for your statement is pretty poorly done, but I hope it may be of some little service.
                         Faithfully yours,   A.M.P.

TLI (WP, DLC).

E N C L O S U R E[1]

The railroad shopmen have demanded a large increase in wages. Receiving now 68 cents per hour, they demand an additional 17 cents, which would make their wage 85 cents per hour. This demand has been given careful and serious consideration by the Board of the Railroad Administration constituted to adjust all questions of wages and consisting in equal parts of representatives of the employees and the operating managers of the companies. This Board has been unable to come to an agreement and the Director General of Railroads and the President have therefore been obliged to make careful examination of the merits of the claim.

End[3] At the time of the general readjustment of railroad wages following the report of the Lane Commission,[2] the shopmen insisted that if the same principle of settlement had been applied to them as was applied to the other classes of railroad employees, their wages would have been increased at that time by 4½ cents per hour. This

[1] Words in angle brackets in this document deleted by Wilson; words in italics added by him.
[2] United States Railroad Administration, *Report of the Railroad Wage Commission to the Director General of Railroads, April 30, 1918* (Washington, 1918). Franklin K. Lane was the chairman of the commission.
[3] WWhw.

claim has been insisted upon ever since, but the shopmen now declare that in order to equalize their wages with the increased scale in private employment in other lines of industry and to make up for the decreased purchasing power of their wages by reason of the increased cost of living, they should have at this time a general increase of twenty-five per cent.

The Railroad Administration and the President have given careful and sympathetic consideration to all of these claims and are forced to the conclusion not only that the demand is not justified, but that in all fairness to the Government, the taxpayers and the other wage workers of the country, it ought not to be pressed at this time. If such a general increase were allowed, it would immediately result in demands from other employees, both in public and private employment, to make their wages conform to the new rates thus established, for wage workers generally insist on the differentials between the trades which now obtain. The consequent additional burden upon transportation and industry in the United States would be almost incalculable. Any substantial increase of wages in leading lines of industry at this time would utterly crush the general campaign which the Government is waging, with energy, vigor and substantial hope of success, to reduce the high cost of living. Only by keeping the cost of production on its present level, by increasing the supply for consumption in the country and by rigid economy and saving on the part of the people, thus decreasing the demand, can we hope for large decreases in the burdensome cost of living ⟨heretofore existing⟩ *now weighing us down.*

The earnest efforts which are being made by the Department of Justice and other agencies of the Government, and by State and municipal authorities everywhere, have already had the effect of considerably decreasing prices in many lines and, if conditions of production can remain as at present, the indications are that in a very short time these considerable reductions will reach the point of substantial and satisfying relief. This will be relief afforded through the orderly processes of government, through which alone permanent relief can come. By increasing wages of particular classes of employees, a temporary adjustment to living conditions may be attained, only to be destroyed immediately by the very consequences of that temporary adjustment. It is nothing short of a patriotic duty on the part of Americans in every line of industry and trade to restrain their desire for their immediate selfish gain, so that the general and final result may be enjoyed by all alike.

If wages are increased to meet what is now unquestionably the maximum cost of living, we shall soon find prices forced to a new and larger maximum, and this proceeding will be repeated as wages follow prices in their flight. At the end must come an industrial paralysis, which will destroy our whole commercial structure. Somewhere this process must be stopped. While the Government is exerting every effort to reduce the cost of living, the whole people in whose interest the effort is being made, will ask that labor withhold its demands for permanent wage settlements until normal and settled conditions permit us to take stock of the possibilities of the situation and deal justly and fairly not alone with one class, but with all classes of our people.

Every sign points to an early return of these normal conditions. When the peace treaty shall have been finally ratified and the normal flow of trade shall be no longer impeded by the uncertainties which follow in the wake of war, we can measure with accuracy the share which both labor and money shall receive out of the product of its joint contribution to industry. Then the problem of proper adjustment of the relations of these two necessary ingredients of the capital which is the basis of all production, can be settled in a spirit of just dealing and with exact knowledge of conditions which are likely to be permanent. And it will be the first business of our great political democracy to see that a just industrial democracy shall prevail along with it. This cannot be done piecemeal or in haphazard fashion without making matters worse instead of better. It can and will be done in normal times of peace through the orderly processes established by the people for the very purpose.

To work out the problems which are the aftermath of war, we must have peace. It must be a peace not political alone, but industrial also. Settlements and adjustments are never made while men are at war. There must be a truce, heads must cool and anger spend itself, before men will see clearly what is best for themselves or can give honest consideration to the rights of others.

Whatever methods the wage workers may feel to be justified in private employment, there can be no justification for anything but obedience to the orderly forms of law made by the people themselves when the Government is the employer. The Government is now endeavoring through the processes set up by the law to adjust the cost of living to the wage-earner's capacity to pay. If that adjustment cannot be made in the way now proposed, it will be made in another. These processes may at times seem slow to impatient minds, but they are more certain and more safe than plans which will inevitably result in the disordered operation of the functions of government.

The President cannot now consent to the increases demanded. There is merit, however, in the contention that the same principle of adjustment of wages should be applied to the shopmen as to other railroad employees. He has concluded from an examination of the record that this was not done in the adjustments reached by the Lane Commission. To put the shopmen, therefore, upon the same wage basis as their fellow employees, the Director General of Railroads will increase their wages at the rate of 4½ cents per hour, effective as of the date of the increase heretofore granted to all railroad employees.

T MS (WP, DLC).

From Alexander Mitchell Palmer

Dear Mr. President: Washington, D. C. August 22, 1919.

I have carefully considered the case of Edgar C. Caldwell, who was convicted in the Circuit Court of Calhoun County, Alabama, of the murder of a street car conductor in Anniston, Alabama, and was sentenced to be hanged.[1] This case is now pending in the Supreme Court of Alabama on a petition for rehearing.

I am unable to find any authority warranting interference by the Federal Government with the decision in this case. Should you desire to go more fully into this phase of the subject, I am attaching hereto a memorandum prepared by Assistant Attorney General Stewart, reviewing fully the authorities relating thereto.

Faithfully yours, A Mitchell Palmer

TLS (WP, DLC).
[1] About Wilson's original involvement in this case, see WW to T. E. Kilby, Feb. 28, 1919, Vol. 55. The enclosure with the above letter, Robert P. Stewart, "MEMORANDUM FOR THE ATTORNEY GENERAL. *In the matter of Edgar C. Caldwell*," Aug. 16, 1919, TS MS (WP, DLC), discussed the possible ground for federal intervention in the case. On December 15, 1918, the date of the killing, Caldwell had been a soldier in the United States Army. Stewart concluded that, even though the United States was on that date still legally in a state of war with Germany, Caldwell's military status was not sufficient ground for federal interference in the judicial process of the State of Alabama, especially in view of the fact that the military authorities had freely surrendered Caldwell to the civil authorities of that state.

A Memorandum by John Barton Payne

Washington August 22, 1919

JBP

MEMORANDUM FOR THE PRESIDENT:

(1) The President Director of the Division of Operations is Mr. J. H. Rosseter[1] of San Francisco; absent on the Pacific Coast since June 19; expects to return early in September. While I have no official knowledge, have learned that he expects to remain only a

short time; is connected with Grace & Company, ship operators. I take it you will want a Director of Operations not interested in private shipping. It will be necessary, therefore, to find a new Director, a most important and responsible post.

(2) The financial and accounting work of the Shipping Board and Fleet Corporation is not in a satisfactory condition. The account to be made to the Treasury Department, suggested by you in May 1918 and required by the Congress later, has not been satisfactorily made, and the voyage accounts are in bad shape,—out of a total of some 15,000 voyages, 7,000 are not accounted for. Judge Nevin,[2] Comptroller, has resigned and I have secured Major Thomas L. Clear, head of Panama Canal accounting system both during its construction and during its operation. He is highly recommended by Treasury officials.

Treasurer Reed[3] has also resigned and we are considering Alonzo Tweedale, Auditor of the District of Columbia, as his successor.

(3) I appointed a small committee here and another in Philadelphia on Organization and Efficiency, for the purpose of cutting out duplication and effecting a compact, efficient organization. Already a reduction of some $600,000 has been made in payroll and rentals. You will doubtless be appealed to in this connection, but it seems to me imperative that we should go through the entire organization and secure a compact working force.

(4) I am particularly desirous of having your advice as to the policy to be pursued re the sale and operation of the ships.

We have built 1040 steam vessels, 6,085,000 deadweight tons. Of these 224 are wood, 13 composite, and 280 small Lake type, leaving of desirable ocean-going steamers suitable for Merchant Marine 523 steel vessels of 4,205,000 d.w.t.

There are still under construction 75 wood, 18 composite or concrete, 121 of the Lake type, and 970 suitable ocean-going vessels, 7,933,000 d.w.t. These are being completed from time to time and will probably be all finished by the end of 1920. This will give us 1493 good steel ships with a deadweight tonnage of 12,138,000. Besides the above we have a number of wooden hulls, 8 sailing vessels, with tugs and barges.

Chairman Hurley established a large sales organization in New York for the purpose of pushing the sales of the ships. This we have reduced to about one-third. It is still sufficiently large to deal with all current questions.

The following prices for the various types of ships were fixed during Chairman Hurley's administration and have not been changed:

Steel Vessels

Lake Type 3000/4200 D.W. Tons	$200 per d.w.t.
Submarine Boat Corp. Type 5350 DW Tons	$210 per d.w.t.
American International SB Corp Type 7800 dwt.	$215 per d.w.t.
Skinner & Eddy Type, 8800 D.W. Tons	$220 per d.w.t.
Skinner & Eddy Type, 9600 (10096) D.W. Tons	$225 per d.w.t.

Wooden Vessels

Ferris Type, single screw, 3500 d.w.t.

$90 per d.w.t.—Cash Payment on Delivery.

$100 per d.w.t.—On delivery of vessel, 50% of purchase, price to be paid in cash; balance, 50%, to be paid in quarter-annual installments of 8⅓% extending over period of 18 months.

$115 per d.w.t.—On delivery of vessels, 25% to be paid in cash; balance, 75%, payable in quarter-annual installments of 6¼% extending over period of 36 months.

We have sold 64 wooden ships and 24 steel ships and have made a contract with the Anderson Overseas Corporation for the sale of 100 Lake type vessels. This, however, is not an actual sale,—it is little more than an option giving it the right to sell the ships to foreign purchasers. Unless it can make such sales, nothing will result from the transaction. No money is to be paid until the Overseas Corporation makes sales.

We come then to the question as to a permanent policy.

I concur in Chairman Hurley's views that private ownership and operation is highly desirable, but this is hardly the immediately practical question.

We have the ships and if, as I believe, you desired to create a permanent Merchant Marine, we must operate them, because it is physically impossible to sell this entire fleet within a relatively short time. Indeed, if it is decided to sell, it is probable that prices must be substantially reduced. The indications are that ships can now be built for substantially less than our prices, probably as low as $165 a deadweight ton.

If we can successfully operate the fleet through private companies it will encourage our people to enter the business, and in my view will be the most effective way of ultimately disposing of the ships. The country must grow up to the subject of a Merchant Marine. There is now no system of creating and financing ship paper, such as exists in England. Time is required to get financial people in the habit of thinking and investing along such lines. The question, therefore, for you to determine is, what action we shall take in leading up to and carrying out your permanent policy.

For the most part, the people now considering the purchase of ships are not the substantial going concerns, but are new people who are attracted to the business by present high rates. It is possible that such concerns, if competition arises or rates are reduced, may go out of the business or fail. The utmost care should be taken to deal with substantial people, as well as to encourage deserving new concerns.

(5) *Competition.*

If we continue to operate the ships to what extent shall we refrain from competing with private concerns now operating established trade routes? This question is frequently asked and should be answered.

(6) *The manufacture of ships for foreign account by American shipbuilders.*

To what extent, if any, shall restraint be exercised in this regard?

(7) *Large passenger ships.*

The suggested construction through the Navy Department of two 1,000 foot ships.

This has been discussed in the press and our records indicate has your approval. It seems to me it is involved with the broad question as to a future policy. If our primary purpose is to dispose of the ships, the construction of new ships is of doubtful wisdom.

T MS (WP, DLC).
  [1] That is, John Henry Rosseter.
  [2] John J. Nevin.
  [3] Waldo Reed.

From Count Vincenzo Macchi di Cellere

My dear Mr. President,   Washington August 22nd, 1919

Allow me to express to you my warmest thanks for your goodness in informing me that the United States Shipping Board feels that, beginning from September 1st, there will be shipping to take from 75.000 to 100.000 tons of coal per month to Italy, in addition to the tonnage already allotted for supplying commercial coal.

I hasten to convey to my Government this communication, and, knowing how welcome it will be to them, I desire to interpret to you from this moment their appreciation for the assistance you have been so kind to grant us in this matter which is of such vital importance to my Country.

I have put myself in touch with the proper officials of the Italian Government here, and wish to assure you that everything will be done to the end that the Shipping Board will be given adequate notice so that there may be no interruption whatever to the arrangement and the tonnage made available.

Respectfully and sincerely Yours   V. Macchi di Cellere

TLS (WP, DLC).

From Charles Howard Shinn[1]

Dear old Classmate,   Northfork, Calif. August 22, 19.

You are *all right*. Stick to it: Heaven bless you!

When you come to Calif. I simply must see you a few minutes. Shall not live forever—we two. Let's meet again!

Please ask Mr Tumulty to write me, here—or you write. Have an *appointment* made, with *you in San Francisco*. Notify me in care U. S. Forest Service, 114. Sansome St San Francisco.

I enclose an envelope for that last.

From the high hill-places I write.

As ever yours   Charles H Shinn

ALS (WP, DLC).

[1] Wilson's old friend and fellow graduate student at The Johns Hopkins University, 1883-1885. At this time a forest examiner for the United States Forest Service in California.

A Memorandum by Walker Downer Hines

Mr. President: [Washington, Aug. 23, 1919]

I have been working throughout the day on the matters to which your draft of statement relates. I have not yet been able to complete some specific suggestions which I think it highly important to submit to you both as to the substance of the matter and as to procedure. I feel it is so vital that you have before you the best possible advice which I can formulate that I believe it would be better for me to postpone submitting a suggestion until a little later in the day, when the work upon which I am now engaged can be brought to a conclusion. If, however, you prefer to take the matter up in the meantime, I believe it would be better, if convenient to you, for me to come over and discuss the situation with you.

T MS (WP, DLC).

From Walker Downer Hines, with Enclosure

Dear Mr. President: Washington August 23, 1919.

I return memorandum which you sent over to me today. I have made some suggestions and in order to put them in the form most easily understood I have made them by interlineations and riders on your own draft. The last paragraph on my rider "B" page 3 is important, because there are probably some other rather glaring inequalities which we ought to correct in regular course and it would be unfortunate to give out any statement indicating that the door was closed to such correction.

However, I strongly advise a different procedure which I believe will be far more effective. There are at present in Washington not only the chief executives of the six shopmen's organizations, but a committee of about 100 general chairmen. I recommend that I submit a report to you stating my conclusions and reasons and that you thereupon send for the chief executives and the committee of 100 and orally state the situation to them. This will not only have much more weight with these representatives of the shopmen, but it will also have much more weight with the shopmen themselves. While my relations with railroad labor have been entirely satisfactory and I believe the labor representatives have a reasonable degree of confidence in me, still in the last analysis they probably regard me as a railroad man. They will feel much better satisfied that the disposition of this matter represents an independent personal judgment on your part if you personally talk to them. There is another highly important reason for this course. The strike ballot which is just being concluded merely presented the issue between (a) the proposal that Congress appoint a Commission to pass upon railroad wages and (b) the shopmen's original proposal for the increase of 85¢. If a strike should now be called it would be called on the strength of affirmative votes based upon this issue which has disappeared. I believe you should definitely request the representatives of the shopmen to submit your determination of the subject to their entire membership and take no action in advance of a consideration of your determination by the entire membership. I do not believe they could refuse such a request. If they should refuse it would put them in a most unfavorable light. If they accede to the request there will be afforded an opportunity, which otherwise would be lacking, for sober second thought.

Mr. Carter,[1] Director of our Division of Labor, strongly advises in favor of this course but makes the point that if the course be adopted it be done in such a way as to let the Committee feel that you are not trying to "go behind them" but are really trying to aid them in getting a difficult situation considered in such a way as will be best for the shopmen's organizations and their membership as well as for the general public.

I enclose tentative draft of a report in which I deal with the various contentions presented by the shopmen.[2]

I ought to add that Mr. Carter believes that a proposal to pay temporarily to all railroad employes the estimated increase in the cost of living (amounting since midsummer 1918 to from 6¢ to 7¢ per hour) would go far towards securing the warm support of all other railroad employes, although he does not believe that even that offer would gain acceptance by the shopmen's representatives. I have carefully weighed this suggestion. I believe the public would accept it as merely another method of making a general increase of, say, 7¢ per hour in the wages of all railroad employes. This would probably represent an annual burden of $450,000,000 or more. No matter how well guarded the offer might be the strong probability is that it would constitute a permanent addition to the wages of all railroad employes. The public would feel that the specific action thus taken would constitute a negation of the general principle laid down. I am not therefore able to recommend this course but I feel I ought to call your attention to the fact that Mr. Carter, who is well advised as to the state of mind of the employes, feels that the method proposed in my report[3] will not only be unacceptable to the shopmen but will be coldly received by all railroad employes, whereas the other plan would meet their warm support even though it is not accepted by the shop employes.

I shall be glad to confer with you about this matter either this evening or tomorrow (Sunday) if you wish to consider it further prior to Monday morning. I am satisfied that final action ought to be taken on Monday, but I attach so much importance to your personal statement to the representatives of the employes, that I think matters should wait until Monday for that purpose.

Cordially yours,   Walker D Hines

TLS (WP, DLC).
    [1] That is, William Samuel Carter, the former president of the Brotherhood of Locomotive Firemen and Enginemen.
    [2] [W. D. Hines] to WW, Aug. 23, 1919, T MS (WP, DLC). Hines summarizes this report in W. D. Hines to WW, Aug. 25, 1919.
    [3] See the final paragraph of W. D. Hines to WW, Aug. 25, 1919.

E N C L O S U R E

A situation has arisen in connection with the administration
of the railways which is of such general significance that I think
it my duty to make a public statement concerning it, in order that
the whole country may know what is involved.

The railroad shopmen have demanded a large increase in wages.
58, 63 and
They are now receiving 68 cents per hour. They demand 85 cents per
hour. This demand has been given careful and serious consideration
by the Board which was constituted by the Railroad Administration to
adjust questions of wages, a Board consisting of an equal number of
representatives of employees and of the operating managers of the
railroad companies. This Board has been unable to come to an agreement,
and it has therefore devolved upon the Director General of Railroads
and myself to act upon the merits of the case.

~~The chief argument used by the shopmen for an increase in
wages is, of course, the very serious increase in the cost of living,
and~~ This is a very potent argument indeed. But the fact is that
the cost of living has certainly reached its peak, and will probably
be lowered by the efforts which are now everywhere being concerted
and carried out. It will certainly be lowered so soon as there are settled
conditions of production and of commerce: that is, so soon as the Treaty
of Peace is ratified and in operation, and merchants, manufacturers,
farmers, miners all have a certain basis of calculation as to what
their business will be and what the conditions will be under which it
must be conducted. The demands of the shopmen, therefore, and all
similar demands are in effect this: that we make increases in wages,
are likely to
which ~~will in all probability~~ be permanent, in order to meet a temporary

A

The shopmen urge that they are entitled
to higher wages because of the higher wages
for the present received by men doing similar
work in shipyards, navy yards, and arsenals,
as well as in a number of private industries,
but I concur with the Director General in
thinking that there is no real basis of comparison between the settled employment afforded mechanics by the railroads under living conditions as various as the location
and surroundings of the railway shops themselves and the fluctuating employment afforded in industries exceptionally and temporarily stimulated by the war and located almost
without exception in industrial centres where
the cost of living is highest.

The substantial argument which the shopmen urge is the very serious increase in the
cost of living

2.

situation which will last nobody can certainly tell how long, but in
all probability only for a limited time. Increases in wages will,
moreover, certainly result in still further increasing the costs of
production and, therefore, the cost of living, and we should only have
to go through the same process again. Any substantial increase of wages
in leading lines of industry at this time would utterly crush the general
campaign which the Government is waging, with energy, vigor and substantial hope of success, to reduce the high cost of living. Only by keeping
the cost of production on its present level, by increasing the supply for
consumption in the country and by rigid economy and saving on the part of
the people, thus decreasing the demand, can we hope for large decreases
in the burdensome cost of living now weighing us down.

     The Director General of Railroads and I have felt that a peculiar
responsibility rests upon us, because in determining this question
we are not studying the balance sheets of corporations merely, we are
in effect determining the burden of taxation which must fall upon the
people of the country in general. We are acting, not for private
corporations, but in the name of the Government and the public, and must
assess our responsibility accordingly. For it is neither wise nor
feasible to take care of increases in the wages of railroad employees
at this time by increases in freight rates. It is impossible at this time,
until peace has come and normal conditions are restored, to estimate what
the earning capacity of the railroads of the country will be when ordinary
conditions are not up again. There is no certain basis, therefore,
for calculating what the increases of freight rates should be, and it is

3.

necessary, for the time being at any rate, to take care of all increases

in the wages of railway employees out of the guarantee of the Government

to the railroads while they remain under federal administration, that

is, out of the taxes. Clearly it would not be right to meet what will

certainly be a temporary condition of things by such means.

In such circumstances it seems clear to me, and I believe will

seem clear to every thoughtful American, including the shopmen them-

selves when they have taken second thought, and to all wage earners

of every kind, that we ought to postpone questions of this sort until

normal conditions come again and we have the opportunity for certain

calculations as to the relation between wages and the cost of living.

It is the duty of every citizen of the country to insist upon a truce

in such contests until intelligent settlements can be made, and made

by peaceful and effective common counsel. I appeal to my fellow-citizens

of every employment to cooperate in insisting upon and maintaining

such a truce, and to cooperate also in sustaining the Government in what

I conceive to be the only course which conscientious public servants

can pursue. Demands unwisely made and passionately insisted upon

at this time menace the peace and prosperity of the country as nothing

else could, and thus contribute to bring about the very results which

such demands are intended to remedy.

There is, however, one claim made by the railway shopmen which

ought to be met. At the time of the general readjustment of railroad

wages following the report of the Lane Commission, the shopmen insisted

that if the same principle of settlement had been applied to them that

-4-

There is, however, one claim made by the railway shopmen which ought to be met. They claim that they are not enjoying the same advantages that other railway employees are enjoying because their wages are calculated upon a different basis. The wages of other railway employees are based upon the rule that they are to receive for eight hours' work the same pay they received for the longer workday that was the usual standard of the pre-war period. This claim is, I am told, well founded; and I concur in the conclusion of the Director General that the shopmen ought to be given the additional four cents an hour which the readjustment asked for will justify. There are certain other adjustments, also, pointed out in the report of the Director General, which ought in fairness to be made, and which will be made.

Let me add, also, that the position which the Government must in conscience take against general increases in wage levels while the present exceptional and temporary circumstances exist will of course not preclude the Railroad Administration from giving prompt and careful consideration to any claims that may be made by other classes of employees for readjustments believed to be proper to secure impartial treatment for all who work in the railway service.

T MS, with WWT, WWhw, and WDHhw (WP, DLC).

From Atlee Pomerene

Dear Mr. President: [Washington] August 23, 1919.

Thank you very much for your favor of the 14th inst., enclosing typewritten memoranda of Mr. Charles H. Grasty's cable to the New York Times, on the subject of railway management, which I herewith return.[1] I have read it with very great interest.

I agree with what seems to be his thought, that there must be a closer relationship between government and railroads in their administration, than heretofore.

Our Sub-Committee, which is now framing a bill to be presented to the full Committee, is providing for a transportation board which shall have a larger control of the administration of the railroads than heretofore. We shall aim to provide for a greater consolidation of the railroads under the direction of this board, first by voluntary processes, and later by compulsion, where necessary and advisable.

I do not believe the Congress would ever be willing to go back to the old system as it existed prior to the War. My belief is that the best thought of the day is in favor of greater unification of the roads, and placing them under closer governmental control and regulation.

We hope to be able to report to the full Committee during the coming week, and I shall be glad to have an opportunity for fuller conference with you when our plan is completed.

Very sincerely,   Atlee Pomerene

TLS (WP, DLC).
  [1] It is printed as an Enclosure with WW to A. Pomerene, Aug. 14, 1919.

From Henry Cabot Lodge

My dear Mr. President: [Washington] August 23, 1919

I am instructed by the Committee on Foreign Relations respectfully to request you to send to the Senate the Treaty with Poland, signed at Versailles on the 28th of June;[1] the Agreement between the United States, Belgium, the British Empire and France of the one part and Germany of the other part, with regard to the military occupation of the territories of the Rhine, also signed at Versailles on the 28th of June;[2] and the Declaration of the 16th of June, signed by you, M. Clemenceau and Mr. Lloyd George.[3] They desire that these documents may be before them officially. The treaty with Poland is referred to in the treaty with Germany, and the other two documents appear to be concerned exclusively with matters included in the treaty with Germany. The Committee therefore are desirous of considering them in connection with the treaty of peace with Germany.

I am further instructed to say that as the treaties with Austria, Hungary, Bulgaria and Turkey are all closely connected, if not interlocked, with the treaty with Germany, the Committee would be obliged, if it is not incompatible with the public interest, if you could send them any drafts or any information in regard to the terms and provisions of those four proposed treaties, which the Committee are certain would be of great help to them in hastening action upon the treaty of peace with Germany.

I have the honor to be

Very respectfully yours,   H. C. Lodge

TLS (WP, DLC).
  ¹ Printed in *PPC*, XIII, 791-808.
  ² See Appendix II to the minutes of the Council of Four printed at June 13, 1919, 12 noon, Vol. 60.
  ³ Printed at June 16, 1919, Vol. 60.

From Newton Diehl Baker

My dear Mr. President: [Washington] August 23, 1919

I have your note of the 21st, inclosing to me the petition left with you by the committee from Chicago seeking to bring about the return to the United States of the enlisted personnel of the 27th and 31st Infantry Regiment[s] now constituting parts of the Siberian Expeditionary Force.

The total enlisted strength of the American Army in Siberia is 8,153 men. Of these, 6,500 are estimated to be emergency men. We have forwarded to Vladivostok 2,001 replacements, and we now have available for shipment to Siberia 1,410 men. The total number of men who have voluntarily enlisted in the Regular Army and expressed a preference to be sent to Siberia is the aggregate of these two; that is, 3,411. We are receiving recruits in the Regular Army now at about the rate of 800 men a day. Of these from fifty to sixty enlist explicitly for Siberian service. Assuming these rates of enlistment to remain constant, we would get about 1,500 men a month for Siberia, and as we have already sent or have to send about 3,500, it would take approximately three months to secure the men to replace the temporary men now there. So that if it be determined to maintain the present force, there will be no difficulty in returning the emergency men by the expiration of the emergency as those terms are defined in the Military Act. I do not make any comment in this note on the general question of the Siberian force because I understand that you desire to discuss that question with me at a later date.

I take the liberty of suggesting the inclosed letter to your petitioners for their information.[1]

Respectfully yours,   [Newton D. Baker]

CCL (N. D. Baker Papers, DLC).
[1] Wilson sent it as WW to F. McAver, Aug. 26, 1919.

From James Cardinal Gibbons

My dear Mr. President: Baltimore. August 23, 1919.

I am honored and gratified by your very thoughtful letter of July 25th.,[1] in which you express your sincere appreciation of my interview upon the Peace Treaty and League of Nations.

It was my intention to write to you sooner, but I was away from the city most of the time, and furthermore I held back feeling that you were too heavily burdened during these days for correspondence. It is my earnest hope that we will see quickly the fruit of your tireless labors and that the Senate and yourself will soon arrive at a satisfactory conclusion of the very weighty questions now confronting you.

With sentiments of highest esteem and warm regards, I am,

Very faithfully yours,   J. Card. Gibbons.

TLS (WP, DLC).
[1] WW to J. Card. Gibbons, July 25, 1919, Vol. 61.

From Cyrus Townsend Brady[1]

Dear Mr. President: Yonkers, N. Y. August 23rd, 1919

It is a long time since I have troubled you with a letter. I think I have never had any real business to write, I have only done so from time to time because the spirit moved me.[2] It moves me hotly in this instance. Hence this letter.

A friend of mine who is sometimes mistaken in his course as all people are, wrote me a letter the other day in which it was definitely stated that on one occasion while you were President of Princeton you begged ex-President Cleveland not to attend a Princeton faculty meeting—weather being inclement and Cleveland ill. It is stated that you assured Cleveland that some proposition to which he was opposed and of which you were in favor was not to be considered at that particular evening meeting if Cleveland would remain absent for his health's sake. Notwithstanding your action and your promise it is alleged this proposition was brought up and put through by, taking advantage of Mr. Cleveland's absence which you had procured.

My correspondent wrote me that the information came to him from a man who had it from some one entitled to know and so on back through the usual line. He further added as a corollary to the story that thereafter no important conference between yourself and Cleveland was had unless Cleveland provided himself with a witness. Such is the degrading story.

I heard this story first some years ago, from the same man. I laughed it out of court then. Now, I am mad all through as he states that another man has just retold it to him.

Mr. President, I am not writing this to you to elicit from you a denial of the story. I do not need or require such a denial, nor would I insult you by asking it. Still I think you ought to know it. It may come to you from some other source. And when I inform you of it I think it proper to let you have my frank opinion of the situation which I do in the copy of the letter to my friend which I enclose.[3] Naturally, you will see the propriety of my withholding names.

I do not think you are always right, Mr. President, in everything that you do—nobody is—but I think you are nobly intentioned and so generally right that the wrongs do not count and I assure you of my sincere, hearty and single-hearted support.

I trust I have not troubled you with an over-long letter but the situation has seemed to warrant it.

Yours very sincerely,   Cyrus Townsend Brady

TLS (WP, DLC).
    [1] Episcopal minister and prolific author of popular novels and biographies.
    [2] There are four letters in WP, DLC, from Brady to Wilson prior to the date of the one printed above, the earliest dated Dec. 22, 1915, the most recent, April 2, 1918. All are on trivial subjects.
    [3] C. T. Brady to "My dear Friend," Aug. 23, 1919, TCL (WP, DLC).

From Charles James McCarthy

Honolulu, August 23—Received August 24, 1919.

The people of this crossroads of the Pacific appreciate the sentiments conveyed in your today's congratulatory cable upon the developments of the Pearl Harbor Naval Base. We hope that it is but a herald of the great future business both naval and commercial which will come to these Pacific waters. The Territorial government is endeavoring to do its full share to make this section of the Pacific Ocean great emporium commerce.

Charles J. McCarthy

T telegram (WP, DLC).

To Robert Lansing, with Enclosure

Dear Mr. Secretary,   The White House, 23 August, 1919.

Will you not be kind enough to have the enclosed sent as promptly as possible to House, and oblige,

Yours faithfully,   W.W.

WWTLI (SDR, RG 59, 763.72119/6482½, DNA).

ENCLOSURE

CABLEGRAM (to be coded).[1]

The White House, Aug. 23, 2 p.m.[2]

For Col. House, (Care American Embassy, London)

From the President:

I greatly regret necessity for compromise permitting French to raise troops in mandate portion of Togoland but do not know that we can avoid it in view of the oral assurances given in the Council of Ten. No concession of the kind should be made outside Togoland.

Personally I think it desirable to have American Commissioner at Danzig and at the head of the Saare Basin Commission, but hope that Drummond will not raise the question in any form now because of the present state of emotion in the Senate.

Lansing.[3]

WWT MS (SDR, RG 59, 763.72119/6482½, DNA).
 [1] Wilson was replying to EMH to WW, Aug. 20 and 21, 1919.
 [2] Date added in the State Department.
 [3] Signature added in the State Department.

From Herbert Bruce Brougham[1]

Dear Mr. Wilson: Chevy Chase, Maryland [c. Aug. 24,1919].

The issue which you raised at Princeton, and which it was my singular privilege to bring to public view,[2] is being converted into industrial terms and centers, as you are aware, in the demand of the railway labor organizations for democratic control.

It would afford me a very deep personal satisfaction, if it would be of service, to bring Mr. Glenn E. Plumb to see you. His program for the railroads, to my knowledge, has had more than its share of misrepresentation, in the press and elsewhere. Its root principle, the consent of the governed in industry, attacks so directly the fundamentals of privilege and of unwarranted profits in the industry now concerned, that no effort or expense is being spared to marshal against it the best-trained minds of the country. As Mr. Plumb is giving the intellectual direction to this movement I can see a hope of clarifying the issue in such a meeting with you as I suggest. A quiet half-hour devoted by you in this way would, I am sure, be not ill-spent.

Very sincerely yours,   H. B. Brougham

TLS (WP, DLC).
    [1] Former editorial writer for the *New York Times*; more recently associate editor and Washington correspondent of the Philadelphia *Public Ledger*. At this time a free lance journalist.
    [2] About which, see the index references to "Brougham, Herbert Bruce" in Vol. 26.

Suggestions by Walker Downer Hines for a Talk to Railway Shopmen

(Dictated by Mr. Walker D. Hines, 24 August, 1919)[1]

1. When we were engaged in actual hostilities against the enemy, our country was actuated by a wonderful spirit of self-sacrificing community of purpose. We were all trying to protect the country's interests in a time of great national crisis. The painful processes of bringing the country back to normal after the greatest upheaval known to history will make the coming winter an even more critical time than the war period itself. Never was there greater need for common purpose and self-sacrifice in order to promote, and indeed in order to safeguard, the public interest, the every-day needs of our citizens. The paramount necessities are to increase production in order to make up for the destruction wrought by the war and for the scarcity created by it, and to reduce the cost of production so as to relieve our people of the cruel burden of an ever mounting cost of living. Nothing will do more to defeat these purposes than to start again upon another ascending spiral of increased wages and increased prices. No industry would suffer sooner from such a policy than the railroads and their employees. Anything that slows down production means less business and employment on the railroads, less earnings for railroad employees, and increased costs for what must be purchased.

2. A reasonable time must be afforded within which to work out

the policies of the Government to protect the public against the evils of profiteering and to give the public the benefit of every facility for increasing production. Favorable results are already beginning to appear. It is confidently hoped and believed that substantial relief will be achieved in increasing measure. The movement must not, however, be defeated in its very beginning, and it will be threatened with such defeat if there is now a general increase in levels of wages, for that will necessarily give a new start to the increase in the cost of living, which will in turn slow down production. All such interferences with the resumption of normal conditions will give capital innumerable additional pretexts for increasing its own profits and will continually confuse the efforts to measure and supervise those profits which amount to profiteering. Certainly it is reasonable to ask railroad labor to do its part in this important work which is so largely for its own benefit, and not to insist upon a course which, if adopted, would threaten to defeat this great public movement in its inception. I confidently believe the movement will be eminently successful and will bring great and lasting benefit to the people.

3. It goes without saying, however, that if I should be disappointed in this respect, it will then be necessary to accept as a permanent basis the existing higher levels of cost, and in that event railroad wages should be readjusted so as to reflect that permanent condition. But we must not incur the inconsistency of making general increases in wages on the assumption that the present high cost of living will be permanent at the very time when we are trying with great confidence to reduce the cost of living and are seeing it actually beginning to diminish. I am aware that railroad employees have a sense of insecurity as to the future of the railroads and have misgivings as to whether their interests will be properly safeguarded after the end of the present form of Federal control. It is not unnatural that this feeling of uncertainty may prompt them to be particularly insistent that their wage matters shall be adjusted at the present time rather than to postpone the matter and incur the risk of a termination of the present Federal control. I anticipate that legislation dealing with the future of the railroads will in itself afford adequate protection for the interests of railroad employees, but entirely aside from that, it is important for the railroad employees to bear in mind that the President of the United States, whether in possession and control of the railroads or not, will always have the opportunity to exert a weighty influence in the solution of the wage questions which may arise between the railroads and the railroad employees. The railroad employees may rest assured that during my term of office I will exert

the influence of the office, whether in actual possession of the railroads or not, to see that justice is done to the railroad employees. Therefore, I believe they are justified in having every confidence that hearty cooperation with the Government at the present time in its efforts to reduce the cost of living will not be prejudicial in any sense whatever to their own interests, and indeed will merely prepare the way for a more favorable and satisfactory disposition later on of their wage problems, if, contrary to our confident expectations, it shall develop that the cost of living maintains or goes above its present level.

T MS (WP, DLC).
    [1] Dictated to C. L. Swem during or after a conference with Wilson at the White House which began at 2:15 p.m. and ended about three-thirty.

A News Report

WILSON CALLS A HALT ON RAILWAY WAGE INCREASES; TELLS SHOPMEN TO WAIT

[*Aug. 25, 1919*]

Washington, Aug. 25.—President Wilson told the representatives of the railroad shop crafts, 100 of whom he received today at the White House, that the demands they had made for wage increases of from 15 to 27 cents an hour could not be met without perpetuating the high living costs by a further tax upon all the people of the nation, and that therefore he had decided that the requests must be refused.

The President said that he acquiesced in a suggestion made by Director General of Railroads Hines that the shopmen should be [paid] on the same basis as other railroad employes by receiving for eight hours work the same pay which they received for the longer work day of ten hours, which was the usual standard of the prewar period. This would mean an additional 4 cents an hour, to be made retroactive as of May 1.

To that extent, the President said, he was willing to meet the request for higher wages. He emphasized, however, that the Administration had adopted, as a national policy, applicable to all labor organizations, that large wage increases which would keep up living costs and must ultimately result in disaster to the nation, could not be granted at this time. The President added that he felt the question of adjusting wages to a scale which probably would remain a permanent one could not be fairly approached until it was determined to what extent living costs would be reduced. He expressed the belief that living costs were already on the downward trend and that, if there was co-operation on the part of railway workers to prevent a tie-up of transportation, radically lower levels soon would be reached.

The members of the railway shop crafts, about 500,000 in number, have just completed a strike vote in which 98 per cent. of the membership cast ballots in favor of a strike beginning Sept. 2, in the event the demands they made for increased wages were not granted and adhering to the policy of providing, by Congressional action, a board of review to consider their claims.

President Wilson, however, held that an entirely new situation has been created, to which the recent strike vote was not applicable, inasmuch as the idea of establishing a board of review, which had formed the basis of the strike vote, had been abandoned, and an entirely new proposition, that of awaiting decision on further large wage increases until more normal conditions prevailed in the economic world, had been placed before the men. In view of this situation he expressed the hope that the leaders of the employes in the shop crafts would accept his judgment as to what was right and fair, at least to the extent of placing the matter again before the men, prior to authorizing a strike.

The leaders of the shop crafts, headed by Bert H. Jewell, acting President of the Railway Employes Department of the American Federation of Labor, obviously were somewhat startled by the announcement of the principles which the President laid before them and found it difficult to make an immediate reply. They went from the White House to the National Hotel, where a conference was held and then proceeded to the offices of the Railroad Administration to confer with Director General Hines.

Mr. Jewell asked Mr. Hines if the decision by the President was final and was assured that such was the case. Mr. Hines added that the stand taken by the President marked the adoption of a national policy in regard to the Administration's dealings with labor, and that it would be adhered to, in any event.

Mr. Hines then asked the leaders of the employes—there were six, headed by Mr. Jewell—if they would submit the statement by President Wilson and the memorandum appended by the Railroad Administration to the various unions. This the leaders agreed to do. They did not, however, offer any prediction as to what the future held in store. The leaders left the Director General's office obviously under a severe strain and refused to discuss the situation.

Another conference of the leaders was held tonight at which, it is said, it was decided to telegraph the various statements to the unions throughout the country and withhold any official announcement until it was possible to determine the attitude which the workers of the shop crafts would assume.

The situation was critical tonight. The President said Director

General Hines appeared confident that the majority of the shop men would recognize the position taken by the President as the only sane course to follow in view of the economic crisis now faced by the nation and withhold the decision to go on strike Sept. 2. But it was admitted also that no definite knowledge as to what will happen could be expected much before Sept. 2, when the real test will come.

During the recent crises, when from 20,000 to 80,000 shop men walked out at different times, because an immediate surrender was not made to their demands for heavy increases, Mr. Jewell and other accredited national officials of the shop crafts labored long and hard to get the men back to work pending the completion of the strike vote and further conferences with the Railroad Administration. They succeeded in breaking the backbone of this unauthorized strike, the men finally consenting to return until they were informed as to the attitude which the Railroad Administration would take. There the situation stood when President Wilson's announcement that the full demands of the workers could not be met without bringing disaster to the nation was made known today.

That President Wilson was fully cognizant of the situation which confronts him was evident in the extreme care with which he dealt with his subject and the appeal which he made to the patriotism of the men.

The President did not confine his utterances to the statement which he made to the workers, but in addition issued a open appeal to the people of the nation, in which he set forth the dangers which were attached to recent developments, including the cost of living and the increasing demands on the part of labor. He emphasized the fact that in his mind it would be ruinous at this time to increase transportation rates, a course which must be adopted in the event the demands of the railroad men were granted.

The statements issued by the President and the memorandum analyzing the wage situation by Director General Hines made the issue as to the Government's attitude toward organized labor other than as represented by the shopmen a clean-cut one. There are pending, in addition to the increases demanded by the shopmen, which would total about $165,000,000 annually, demands by the four brotherhoods and other railroad organizations which would bring the grand total increases up to at least $800,000,000.

It was such demands, the President pointed out in his statement, which tended to create an impossible situation, if the Administration was to continue its efforts to reduce living costs and meet the wage increases asked.

It was made doubly plain by the President that the new policy of not considering large wage increases until more normal economic conditions had been brought about extended not only to the shop crafts, but to the four Brotherhoods and other branches of organized labor as well. This, in a sense, was a notice to the Brotherhoods that it would be futile for them to press wage increases at this time.

The President decided to adopt the stand he took today in face of the knowledge that his Director General of Railroads and the representatives of the shop crafts had failed to come to an agreement during the conferences which have been in progress for the last week.

In his plea to the railway workers to co-operate with the Administration the President said: "If we fail, it will mean national disaster," and added that unless a solution was reached, and a strike averted, "the Winter just ahead of us may bring suffering infinitely greater than the war brought upon us."

There was reference made by President Wilson in his statement to the employes' representatives to the situation which confronts the nation in solving the problem of returning the railroads to their former owners on a sound economic basis, and he expressed the belief that the fear of the men that their interests would suffer once the Administration let go its control was not well founded.

The men, he said, might rest assured that during his term of office, whether the Government maintained control of the railroads or not, justice would be done. His present attitude, he said, did not prejudice any further requests which might be made when more normal conditions were brought about, and the demands could be considered without passion.

There was a very distinct impression tonight that President Wilson will in no way alter the stand which he has taken in regard to the wage question as applicable to all workers, and to the best means of the solution of the problem of bringing down high living costs, no matter what developments may follow. His open address to the people, issued in addition to his statement to the workingmen, has placed him on record, it was pointed out, as unalterably wedded to the course which he has joined.

Director General of Railroads Hines has taken just as firm a stand in his memorandum.

At least the developments today have served to bring the situation to an issue where the occurrences of the next week must determine whether labor will accept the President's edict or defy him in face of the declaration that such action on the part of a group will bring about a dangerous economic crisis for the nation.

The President indicated in his statements that the situation in industries other than the railroads were engaging his attention in seeking for a general solution of the living cost situation and that he did not regard all the levels which have been reached as permanent, especially if there was brought about a considerable reduction in living costs.

The belief was expressed in some quarters that the President felt the time had come when the conditions brought about by the many factors contributing to the disturbed economic situation must be faced without faltering, and that to delay further in taking a definite stand against continuous wage increases which could mean only advanced living costs, which in turn would pave the way for more wage demands—the "vicious circle"—could lead only to nation-wide disaster.

It possibly will be two or three days before the national leaders here are able to determine whether the members of the shop crafts throughout the country will consent to remain at work pending the taking of another vote to determine whether a majority of the men are willing to agree to the new program put forward by President Wilson. If the workmen agree to such a course it will at least assure an adjournment of a strike until October.

The Administration hopes, in the event that the men agree to take another vote, that economic conditions will be such before October that an agreement on wage schedules which will be acceptable to the workmen can be arrived at.

Printed in the *New York Times*, Aug. 26, 1919.

From Walker Downer Hines

Dear Mr. President: Washington August 25, 1919.

Before you see the shopmen's representatives this afternoon, I think it important for you to have in mind the following.

The increases in pay which will come about by reason of my report, which is herewith inclosed,[1] are after all very substantial in many respects. There is a basic increase of 4 cents, but as to important classes of employes in the shop crafts the increase is 9 cents. This comes about because experience has convinced us that the differentials which our orders have made among the different classes of freight car repairmen and as between them and car inspectors are unfair, are the source of pronounced discontent and bring about costly methods of doing our work.

The last three or four pages of my report state the details of these increases, but I do not believe it will be necessary for you to examine them.

Assuming you may not have an opportunity to read the tentative draft I sent you of my report[2] (and the final draft herewith inclosed is not different in substance excepting in the more specific statement of the increases) I summarize the matter for you as follows:

I first decide that the rates of pay in shipyards, navy yards and arsenals cannot be accepted as a standard for railroad shops because of radically different conditions, the outstanding differences being that railroad shop work is done in practically every city and railroad town of importance in the United States and that the work offers a permanent career; and that a standardized uniform wage for the railroads cannot be controlled by wages so largely the product of special and different conditions.

I next decide that there is no convincing proof that the average rates of pay in private industries throughout the country is in excess of the rates proposed and indicate that information now available in the Department of Labor shows that the rates offered are probably slightly higher than the average of union scales throughout the country, although there are of course numerous instances of higher rates.

I next take the position that at this time it is not proper to make an increase in the railroad wages to bring them up to the level of what is apparently the top notch in the high cost of living, especially in view of the present movement which promises so soon to make substantial reductions in the cost of living. I also point out, however, that it appears that the railroad shop employes as a whole have already had increases which on the average bring their wages up to the present high level of the cost of living, although I concede that as to some of the classes this is not the case.

I then point out the specific increases which I think should be made, the basic increase being 4 cents, but the increase to an important proportion of the freight car repairmen and car inspectors being 9 cents.   Cordially yours,   Walker D. Hines

TLS (WP, DLC).
  [1] W. D. Hines to WW, Aug. 23, 1919, TLS (WP, DLC). This is the revised version of the letter cited in n. 2 below.
  [2] See W. D. Hines to WW, Aug. 23, 1919, n.2.

Remarks to Railway Shopmen

August 25, 1919.

If I were the president of the railways of the country and were considering the question of railway administration by itself, that would be one thing. I hold the present administration and decision of the railroads through the Director General by a statute which has something beyond that in it. It does not go into the balance sheets simply of the corporations. It does not consider their earning capacity. It takes certain prewar periods and says to the railroads, "the government guarantees the net result of their business in dollars as it stood during these prewar years." So that whether the railroads can earn what it is costing to run them or not, is, so far as the law is concerned, neither here nor there. The Government of the United States, that is to say, the people of the United States have to pay the bill. And if there are increases in that cost, you have got to put them on the railroads in increased rates, or you have got to put them on the general body of the taxpayers of the country, out of the federal treasury. There are no other ways of meeting these charges. If you put them directly on the freight rates, then you immediately increase the cost of living, because you increase the cost of transportation of all sorts of goods, and I need not tell you how prompt shippers are to add that and a little more to what the goods will cost when they reach the consumer.

So that you are at the very outset caught in a quandary. The men whom you represent say to us, "The cost of living has gone up, and we think that our wages ought to be increased to meet this increased cost." They thereupon propose a remedy which will increase the cost of living—which will certainly increase the cost, and then we will have to face this question all over again, and that at the very time, gentlemen, when the government is making efforts which are beginning to be successful, to bring down the cost of living.

The picture I have in my mind is this. We have been climbing a peak in respect to the cost of living, and I am convinced we have reached the top of it and are beginning to go down on the other side. We won't go down very fast, I am afraid, until all the conditions of our life are settled. They cannot be settled until we know the basis of peace, for one thing, not only for ourselves but for others, because commerce depends upon having a calculable element in its business, eliminating uncertainties, knowing what is to happen tomorrow. And I am convinced that as soon as those conditions of uncertainty are eliminated, the cost of living will go steadily down, because production will increase, the channels of commerce will be opened and broadened, and the whole process will set in which was uninterruptedly in operation before we plunged into the war.

But even now and under the existing uncertainties, the cost of living is beginning to go down. I can assure you that there is tremendous pressure being brought to bear. You see how promptly Congress has responded to some of the suggestions I made to them as to the means of bringing it down.[1] I do not think there ought to be any interruption in the process at the very time, therefore, that we have passed the peak itself. It is proposed that we destroy that very process by beginning to raise the cost of living again. We must not allow ourselves as intelligent men to be caught in that quandary. That is an impossible situation.

Now there is another element in it that I wanted to talk to you men about. Our common enemy is the profiteer. Whenever we can find him, we will deal with him. But every time you change the conditions in the cost of production, you make it harder to find him. He has then a new hiding place and a new excuse and, having changed the conditions, you confuse your own mind and your own methods in catching up with him and bringing him to book. And, therefore, if you want to check profiteering, which is what all of us want to check—we do not want to check the honest earning of reasonable profits, because that is what keeps business going. But we do want to check the dishonest earning of unreasonable profits—because unreasonable profits are necessarily dishonest, and not playing fair with the country.

There is another element that I want to speak to you about. I conjecture what is in your minds is partly this. I am not telling you things that you do not know, for in dealing with men like you I have found that you were just as acute as any men I have dealt with in knowing what is going on. I am trying to set the picture for

[1] See the address printed at Aug. 8, 1919. Initially, it had appeared that Congress would take quick action on Wilson's recommendations. Leaders of both houses had promised to do so in public statements on August 9. Senator Kellogg, on August 11, had introduced a bill for the licensing of corporations engaged in interstate commerce. Bills to prevent profiteering in food, fuel, and wearing apparel in the District of Columbia had been introduced in the Senate on August 15 and in the House of Representatives on August 18. Representative Elijah Cubberly Hutchinson, Republican of New Jersey, on August 21, had introduced a bill to regulate foods in cold storage. However, none of these bills ever emerged from the committees to which they were referred. A second bill to regulate cold-storage foods, introduced by Hutchinson on September 25, was several times debated and amended in both houses but never achieved final passage during the life of the Sixty-sixth Congress.

The only measure recommended by Wilson in his address of August 8 which had made substantial progress in Congress by this time was the bill to extend the scope of the Lever Food and Fuel Control Act of 1917 (about which see the index references under "Lever bill" in Vol. 52). Gilbert Nelson Haugen, Republican congressman of Iowa, on August 21, had reported from the House Committee on Agriculture H.R. 8624, a bill which amended the Lever Act to extend its scope to clothing and food containers and provided for a prison term of up to two years and a fine of up to $5,000 for profiteering and/or hoarding of products covered by the amended Lever Act. The bill did not, however, prolong the life of the Lever Act beyond the formal declaration of peace, as Wilson had also suggested in his message. The House debated the bill at length in the committee of the whole on August 22 and, with some minor amendments, passed it on that same date. The Senate approved the bill on September 12. After it passed through two separate conference committees, both houses approved the final version of the bill on October 11, and Wilson signed it on October 22. See the *New York Times*, Aug. 10, 11, 12, 15, 19, and 23, Sept. 13, and Oct. 12, 1919; *Cong. Record*, 66th Cong., 1st sess., pp. 3748, 3885, 3976, 4140, 4228, 5304, 6727, and 6760; and 41 *Statutes at Large* 297.

you. There is another thing that I conjecture to be in your minds. You expect the federal control of railroads to end presently, and you think that you are more likely—I do not know whether I am correct in interpreting your minds or not, but I suspect that this is in your minds—you think you are more likely to get advantageous adjustments from the public authority than from a private authority like the managers of the railroads; that the general public interest will be more in its mind than it will be in the minds of the owners of the railways; and you are expecting that if you do not get the increases of wages which the men whom you represent have demanded, you will have more difficult conditions to deal with after the railroads cease to be under federal control. I want to say that I think you are mistaken about that. No legislation can change the character of the railroads, and the character of the railroads is that they are a public instrumentality in which every community in the United States is interested. That being the case, it is not likely, to judge by my past experience, that the President of the United States will lack influence. Perhaps I am justified in saying that it is not likely that he will lack authority in assisting at the settlement of questions like wages in the future as in the present, and I am free to promise you that so long as my term of office lasts, at any rate, all the influence of the Executive will be on the side of assisting to see that justice is done the railway employees.

My argument against present action is that it will upset the very processes by which we are trying to serve the whole country as well as ourselves. I remember telling a friend of mine who was opposing certain legislation that I thought essential (he was opposing it on inconsistent grounds) that he reminded me of the hero of a well-known novel, in which the hero, who, when he had been rejected by the heroine, rushed from the house and "rode off in every direction." You can't do that. You cannot go in several directions, and in particular you can't go in opposite directions. This is something like going in opposite directions and would defeat the process which the government is now pressing, and pressing with increasing success.

Now, that does not mean, gentlemen, that there ought not to be certain minor adjustments. I understand that you have claimed, and that it is true that you are quite correct in it, that, whereas the wages of other railway employees are now being calculated upon the basis of paying the same wage for an eight-hour day that was paid before the war for a longer day, the wages of the railway shopmen have not been exactly adjusted to that basis. That being the case, they ought of course to be adjusted to that basis, and the Director General of Railroads informs me that the result will be a basic increase of four cents an hour, in some cases amounting to nine cents an hour. That is an adjustment that ought to have been made originally and ought, of course, to be made now. And I want to say that the Director General has made a report to me on all the elements in this case, which will be placed in your hands immediately after the meeting and which you can of course make any use of you please. But what I have asked you to come here for, gentlemen, is this: I have told you the elements of the case as they seem to me. I am a public servant, and I cannot exercise my preferences. I have got to do my duty as I see it, my duty as a servant of all the people as well as a friend of the shopmen, and therefore I am going to ask you gentlemen who are in authoritative positions in relation to the shopmen, to ask them to reconsider this question in this new light. The question, as I understand it, to which their answers were returnable yesterday, was the question whether they would insist upon the increases of wages which they had suggested or would consent to submit them to a new tribunal to be created by legislation. Now, that is a dead question, because, as you know, when we suggested to a committee of one of the houses that they consider the creation of such a tribunal, they said they did not care to consider it, and therefore no such legislation is now in contemplation or can for the present be in contemplation.[2] Now for that reason, in order that what I say may be available to you in something other than the haphazard way in which I have extemporaneously expressed it, I want to read you this little paper[3] and request that you lay the matter before the men as it is stated in this paper, as a service to all of us. You will see that the paper sums up the greater part of what I have been saying, and, I hope, in a clearer and more consecutive way.

T MS (WP, DLC).

[2] See WW to J. J. Esch, Aug. 1, 1919; J. J. Esch to WW, Aug. 2, 1919; A. B. Cummins to WW, Aug. 2, 1919; and A. B. Cummins to WW, Aug. 6, 1919.
[3] A copy of the message printed as the next document.

A Message to Railway Shopmen[1]

[Aug. 25, 1919]

Gentlemen: I request that you lay this critical matter before the men in a new light. The vote they have taken was upon the question whether they should insist upon the wage increase they were asking or consent to the submission of their claims to a new tribunal, to be constituted by new legislation. That question no longer has any life in it. Such legislation is not now in contemplation. I request that you ask the men to reconsider the whole matter in view of the following considerations, to which I ask their thoughtful attention as Americans, and which I hope that you will lay before them as I here state them.

We are face to face with a situation which is more likely to affect the happiness and prosperity, and even the life, of our people than the war itself. We have now got to do nothing less than bring our industries and our labor of every kind back to a normal basis after the greatest upheaval known to history, and the winter just ahead of us may bring suffering infinitely greater than the war brought upon us if we blunder or fail in the process. An admirable spirit of self-sacrifice, of patriotic devotion, and of community action guided and inspired us while the fighting was on. We shall need all these now, and need them in a heightened degree, if we are to accomplish the first tasks of peace. They are more difficult than the tasks of war,—more complex, less easily understood,—and require more intelligence, patience, and sobriety. We mobilized our man power for the fighting, let us now mobilize our brain power and our consciences for the reconstruction. If we fail, it will mean national disaster. The primary first step is to increase production and facilitate transportation, so as to make up for the destruction wrought by the war, the terrible scarcities it created, and so as soon as possible relieve our people of the cruel burden of high prices. The railways are at the center of this whole process.

The Government has taken up with all its energy the task of bringing the profiteer to book, making the stocks of necessaries in the country available at lowered prices, stimulating production, and facilitating distribution, and very favourable results are already beginning to appear. There is reason to entertain the confident hope that substantial relief will result, and result in increasing measure. A general increase in the levels of wages would check and might defeat all this at its very beginning. Such increases would inevitably raise, not lower, the cost of living. Manufacturers and producers of every sort would have innumerable additional pretexts for increasing profits and all efforts to discover and defeat profiteering would be hopelessly confused. I believe that the present efforts to reduce the costs of living will be successful, if no new elements of difficulty are thrown in the way; and I confidently count upon the men engaged in the service of the railways to assist, not obstruct. It is much more in their interest to do this than to insist upon wage increases which will undo everything the Government attempts. They are good Americans, along with the rest of us, and may, I am sure, be counted on to see the point.

It goes without saying that if our efforts to bring the cost of living down should fail, after we have had time enough to establish either success or failure, it will of course be necessary to accept the higher costs of living as a permanent basis of adjustment, and railway wages should be readjusted along with the rest. All that I am now urging is, that we should not be guilty of the inexcusable inconsistency of making general increases in wages on the assumption that the present cost of living will be permanent at the very time that we are trying with great confidence to reduce the cost of living and are able to say that it is actually beginning to fall.

I am aware that railway employees have a sense of insecurity as to the future of the railroads and have many misgivings as to whether their interests will be properly safeguarded when the present form of federal control has come to an end. No doubt it is in part this sense of uncertainty that prompts them to insist that their wage interests be adjusted now rather than under conditions which they cannot certainly foresee. But I do not think that their uneasiness is well grounded. I anticipate that legislation dealing with the future of the railroads will in explicit terms afford adequate protection for the interests of the employees of the roads; but, quite apart from that, it is clear that no legislation can make the railways other than what they are, a great public interest, and it is not likely that the President of the United States, whether in possession and control of the railroads or not, will lack opportunity or persuasive force to influence the decision of questions arising between the managers of the railroads and the railway employees. The employees may rest assured that, during my term of office, whether I am in actual possession of the railroads or not, I shall not fail to exert the full influence of the Executive to see that justice is done them.

I believe, therefore, that they may be justified in the confidence that hearty cooperation with the Government now in its efforts to reduce the cost of living will by no means be prejudicial to their own interests, but will, on the contrary, prepare the way for more favourable and satisfactory relations in the future.

I confidently count on their cooperation in this time of national test and crisis.   Woodrow Wilson

TS MS (WP, DPC).
    [1] There is a WWT draft, with numerous WWhw emendations, of this message in WP, DLC. It is printed, along with Hines' revised letter of August 23, in STATEMENT BY PRESIDENT WILSON TO REPRESENTATIVES OF THE RAILWAY EMPLOYEES' DEPARTMENT, AMERICAN FEDERATION OF LABOR, AND REPORT OF WALKER D. HINES, DIRECTOR GENERAL OF RAILROADS, TO THE PRESIDENT, AUGUST 25, 1919 (Washington, 1919).

A Statement on the Railroad Crisis

The White House, Aug. 25, 1919.

My Fellow Citizens: A situation has arisen in connection with the administration of the railways which is of such general significance that I think it my duty to make a public statement concerning it, in order that the whole country may know what is involved.

The railroad shopmen have demanded a large increase in wages. They are now receiving 58, 63, and 68 cents per hour. They demand 85 cents per hour. This demand has been given careful and serious consideration by the board which was constituted by the Railroad Administration to adjust questions of wages, a board consisting of an equal number of representatives of employees and of the operating managers of the railroad companies. This board has been unable to come to an agreement, and it has therefore devolved upon the Director General of Railroads and myself to act upon the merits of the case.

The shopmen urge that they are entitled to higher wages because of the higher wages for the present received by men doing a similar work in shipyards, navy yards, and arsenals, as well as in a number of private industries, but I concur with the Director General in thinking that there is no real basis of comparison between the settled employment afforded mechanics by the railroads under living conditions as various as the location and surroundings of the railway shops themselves and the fluctuating employment afforded in industries exceptionally and temporarily stimulated by the war and located almost without exception in industrial centres where the cost of living is highest.

The substantial argument which the shopmen urge is the very serious increase in the cost of living. This is a very potent argument indeed. But the fact is that the cost of living has certainly reached its peak, and will probably be lowered by the efforts which are now everywhere being concerted and carried out. It will certainly be lowered so soon as there are settled conditions of production and of commerce; that is, so soon as the Treaty of Peace is ratified and in operation, and merchants, manufacturers, farmers, miners, all have a certain basis of calculation as to what their business will be and what the conditions will be under which it must be conducted.

The demands of the shopmen, therefore, and all similar demands, are in effect this: That we make increases in wages, which are likely to be permanent, in order to meet a temporary situation which will last nobody can certainly tell how long, but in all probability only for a limited time. Increases in wages will, moreover, certainly result in still further increasing the costs of production and, therefore, the cost of living, and we should only have to go through the same process again. Any substantial increase of wages in leading lines of industry at this time would utterly crush the general campaign which the Government is waging, with energy, vigor, and substantial hope of success, to reduce the high cost of living. And the increases in the cost of transportation which would necessarily result from increases in the wages of railway employees would more certainly and more immediately have that effect than any other enhanced wage costs. Only by keeping the cost of production on its present level, by increasing production and by rigid economy and saving on the part of the people can we hope for large decreases in the burdensome cost of living which now weighs us down.

The Director General of Railroads and I have felt that a peculiar responsibility rests upon us, because in determining this question we are not studying the balance sheets of corporations merely, we are in effect determining the burden of taxation which must fall upon the people of the country in general. We are acting, not for private corporations, but in the name of the Government and the public and must assess our responsibility accordingly. For it is neither wise nor feasible to take care of increases in the wages of railroad employees at this time by increases in freight rates. It is impossible at this time, until peace has come and normal conditions are restored, to estimate what the earning capacity of the railroads will be when ordinary conditions return. There is no certain basis, therefore, for calculating what the increases of freight rates should be, and it is necessary, for the time being at any rate, to take care of all increases in the wages of railroad employees through appropriations from the public treasury.

In such circumstances, it seems clear to me, and I believe will seem clear to every thoughtful American, including the shopmen themselves when they have taken second thought, and to all wage earners of every kind, that we ought to postpone questions of this sort till normal conditions come again and we have the opportunity for certain calculation as to the relation between wages and the cost of living. It is the duty of every citizen of the country to insist upon a truce in such contests until intelligent settlements can be made, and made by peaceful and effective common counsel. I appeal to my fellow-citizens of every employment to cooperate in insisting upon and maintaining such a truce, and to cooperate also in sustaining the Government in what I conceive to be the only course which conscientious public servants can pursue. Demands unwisely made and passionately insisted upon at this time menace the peace and prosperity of the country as nothing else could, and thus contribute to bring about the very results which such demands are intended to remedy.

There is, however, one claim made by the railway shopmen which ought to be met. They claim that they are not enjoying the same advantages that other railway employees are enjoying because their wages are calculated upon a different basis. The wages of other railroad employees are based upon the rule that they are to receive for eight hours work the same pay they received from the longer workday that was the usual standard of the pre-war period. This claim is, I am told, well founded; and I concur in the conclusion of the Director General that the shopmen ought to be given the additional four cents an hour which the readjustment asked for will justify. There are certain other adjustments, also pointed out in the report of the Director General, which ought in fairness to be made, and which will be made.

Let me add also that the position which the Government must in conscience take against general increases in wage levels while the present exceptional and temporary circumstances exist will of course not preclude the Railroad Administration from giving prompt and careful consideration to any claims that may be made by other classes of employees for readjustments believed to be proper to secure impartial treatment for all who work in the railway service.   Woodrow Wilson.

Printed in the *New York Times*, Aug. 26, 1919.

Two Letters from Carter Glass

My dear Mr. President: Washington August 25, 1919.

In compliance with your note of July 19,[1] transmitting a letter from Senator Owen, I am enclosing herewith a letter to you, setting forth the general position of the Treasury Department in respect to foreign finance, which I think, in effect, answers most of the questions raised by Senator Owen.

I am inclined to think that the policy of the Treasury concerning this vital matter should be made public and I should like to have your permission to give the accompanying letter to the press, if you approve.

In this letter to you Senator Owen, referring to the Bill (S.3928, now S.2582), introduced by him, to establish a Federal Reserve Foreign Bank, says that the Comptroller of the Currency made a favorable report on this Bill to you. I have not seen that report. Secretary McAdoo emphatically disapproved this Bill in his letter to you, dated September 26, 1918.[2] The Comptroller of the Currency at no time had to do with the formulation or execution of the Treasury's policies with respect to foreign exchange or foreign loans.

Senator Owen's suggestion that you cancel the original executive orders relating to foreign exchange transactions and the shipment of coin, currency and bullion seems to have been anticipated and met by your proclamation issued on June 26, 1919, by which were revoked and cancelled the proclamation dated August 27, 1917, as amended by a subsequent proclamation dated September 7, 1917, issued under an Act approved June 15, 1917, known as the Espionage Act, and the executive orders of September 7, 1917, October 12, 1917, and January 26, 1918, except in so far as they may be necessary to enable the Secretary of the Treasury and the Federal Reserve Board to control any and all transactions in Russian rubles, transactions with that part of Russia now under the control of the so-called Bolshevik Government, and any and all transactions with territories in respect of which such transactions were at the time of the proclamation permitted only through the American Relief Administration. By virtue of the proclamation of June 26, 1919, and subsequent orders issued by the Federal Reserve Board in pursuance thereof, the only transactions now restricted in any way by the proclamation and executive orders above referred to are foreign exchange transactions or dealings in Russian rubles and any transfers of credit or exchange transactions with, or exportations of coin, bullion and currency to, that part of Russia now under the control of the so-called Bolshevik Government.

I am, my dear Mr. President,
                    Cordially and faithfully yours,   Carter Glass.

P.S. Senator Owen's letter is returned herewith.

[1] WW to C. Glass, July 19, 1919, Vol. 61.
[2] About which, see R. L. Owen to WW, July 16, 1919, n. 2, *ibid.*

Dear Mr. President: Washington August 25, 1919.

I received your letter of July 19th, with the enclosed letter dated July 16th from Senator Owen, concerning the needs of Europe and the financing of our exports.

Since the armistice the United States has advanced to the Governments of the Allies, as of the close of business August 15, 1919, the sum of $2,141,996,211.55, and there remained on August 15 an unexpended balance of $780,889,038.45 from the total loans of

$10,000,000,000 authorized under the Liberty Loan Acts. The Treasury sees no need of an additional appropriation for government loans, though, it may later have occasion to ask the Congress to make some further modification of the terms under which the existing appropriation is available.

The Treasury asked and obtained power for the War Finance Corporation to make advances up to the amount of $1,000,000,000 for non-war purposes and the War Finance Corporation is prepared to make such advances.

The Secretary of War is authorized to sell his surplus stores on credit.

The United States Wheat Director is authorized to sell wheat to Europe on credit.

The power which at present exists in the Government or Governmental agencies to make loans and extend credit to Europe is, therefore, considerable. This power must, of course, be exercised with extreme caution and with the most careful regard for the urgent needs of our own people for an ample supply of foodstuffs and other necessities of life at reasonable prices.

The Treasury is prepared, at the convenience of the Governments of the Allies, to take up with their representatives the funding of the demand obligations which the United States holds, into long-time obligations, and at the same time the funding during the reconstruction period, or say for a period of two or three years, of the interest on the obligations of foreign Governments acquired by the United States under the Liberty Loan Acts.

The Treasury's present understanding of the situation does not lead it to believe that action on the part of this Government additional to that above described will be either necessary or desirable.

The Treasury believes that the need of Europe for financial assistance, very great and very real though it is, has been much exaggerated both here and abroad. Our hearts have been so touched by the suffering which the war left in its train, and our experience is so recent of the financial conditions which existed during the war (when men were devoting themselves to the business of destruction) that we are prone to overlook the vast recuperative power inherent in any country which, though devastated, has not been depopulated, and the people of which are not starved afterwards. We must all feel deep sympathy for the suffering in Europe today, but we must not allow our sympathy to warp our judgment and, by exaggerating Europe's financial needs, make it more difficult to fill them.

Men must go back to work in Europe, must contribute to increase production. The industries of Europe, of course, cannot be set to work without raw materials, machinery, etc., and, to the extent that these are to be secured from the United States, the problem of financing the restoration of Europe belongs primarily to our exporters. Governmental financial assistance in the past and talk of plans for future government or banking aid to finance exports has apparently led our industrial concerns to the erroneous expectation that their war profits, based so largely on exports, will continue indefinitely without effort or risk on their part. To them will fall the profits of the exports and upon them will fall the consequences of failure to make the exports. So soon as domestic stocks, which were very low at the time of the armistice, have been replenished, those industries which have been developed to meet a demand for great exports, paid for out of government war loans, will be forced to close plants and forego dividends unless they maintain and develop an outlet abroad. The industries of the country must be brought to a realization of the gravity of this problem, must go out and seek markets abroad, must reduce prices at home and abroad to a reasonable level, and create or cooperate in creating the means of financing export business.

Since armistice day, the consistent policy of the Treasury has been, so far as possible, to restore private initiative and remove governmental controls and interferences. It has been the view of the Treasury that only thus can the prompt restoration of healthy economic life be gained. The embargoes on gold and silver and control of foreign exchange have been removed, as well as the voluntary and informal control of call money and the stock exchange loan account. The control exercised by the Capital Issue Committee over capital issues has been discontinued. Thus the financial markets of the United States have been opened to the whole world and all restrictions removed that might have hindered America's capital and credit resources, as well as its great gold reserve, from being available in aid of the world's commerce and Europe's need.

Senator Owen believes that the dollar should be kept at par, no more no less, in foreign exchange. His proposed Federal Reserve Foreign Exchange Bank (Senate Bill 2582), if it took effective action to this end, could do so only by drawing gold out of the United States when the dollar would otherwise be at a discount and by inflating credit when the dollar would otherwise be at a premium.

The support of any foreign exchange in the United States is primarily the business of the foreign government concerned. The support of sterling exchange in this country was discontinued by the British Government on its own initiative, and the abandonment of the support of franc exchange by the French Government and of lire exchange by the Italian Government followed as a matter of course. The view of these Governments, I take it, is that should they, now that war control of their imports has been relaxed, attempt to continue to "peg" their exchanges here at an artificial level by Government borrowing, the effect would be to stimulate their imports and discourage their exports, thus aggravating their already unfavorable international balances.

The dollar is now at a premium almost everywhere in the world. Its artificial reduction and maintenance at the gold par of exchange in all currencies is quite unthinkable unless we propose to level all differences in the relative credit of nations and to substitute for our gold reserve, a reserve consisting of the promise to pay of any nation that chooses to become our debtor. Inequalities of exchange reflect not only the trade and financial balance between two countries, but, particularly after a great war such as that we have been through, the inequalities of domestic finance. The United States has met a greater proportion of the cost of the war from taxes and bond issues than any other country. Largely as a consequence of this policy, the buying power of the dollar at home has been better sustained than has the buying power at home of the currency of any European belligerent. For the United States to determine by governmental action to depress the dollar as measured in terms of foreign exchange and to improve the position of other currencies as measured in terms of dollars would be to shift to the American people the tax and loan burdens of foreign countries. This shifted burden would be measured by the taxes to be imposed and the further loans to be absorbed by our people as a consequence, and by increased domestic prices.

United States Government action at this time to prevent in respect to foreign exchange the ordinary operation of the law of supply and demand, which automatically sets in action corrective causes, and to prevent the dollar from going to a premium when its natural tendency is to do so, would artificially stimulate our exports, and, through the competition of export demand with domestic demand, maintain or increase domestic prices.

These are some of the reasons why the Treasury disapproves of the Federal Reserve foreign exchange bank bill.

The Treasury approves the Bill of Senator Edge (S.2472)[1] to authorize the organization under Federal law of corporations to engage in the business of foreign banking and financing exports, of which corporations the Government would be a stockholder, and the Bill (S.2395) to permit national banks, to a limited extent, to be stockholders in such corporations. There is no need, however, of the creation of a new governmental agency of this sort, now that the war is over, and I am opposed to Senator Owen's plan (S.2590)[2] to create a Foreign Finance Corporation and for the War Finance Corporation to become a stockholder in such a corporation.

The Treasury approves the Senate Joint Resolution No. 31, introduced by Senator Owen, to amend the War Finance Corporation Act, among other things, to remove the fixed minimum on the interest rate charged by it. The Treasury is opposed, however, to Senate Joint Resolution No. 88, subsequently introduced by Senator Owen, which differs from No. 31 by authorizing the War Finance Corporation to buy bonds of the governments of the allies for the purpose of stabilizing the exchanges. If the Congress wishes the Government to invest in further amounts of obligations of foreign governments that should be done directly by the Treasury as heretofore and not through the War Finance Corporation.

It is essential to discriminate between plans, on the one hand, to support exchange by direct action of the United States Government and plans, on the other hand, to facilitate the extension of private credit and the investment of private capital in Europe. To the former the Treasury is utterly opposed. Of the latter the Treasury heartily approves. I believe it will be found that this general principle accords with and helps to explain the opinions above expressed with respect to specific measures to which Senator Owen has directed your attention.

It is not, of course, to be expected that the breach left by the withdrawal of Governmental support of exchange can be filled by private initiative until the ratification of the Treaty of Peace has given reasonable assurance against the political risk which, rather than any commercial or credit risk, now deters private lenders. Some progress has already been made in placing here through private channels the loans of Allied and neutral European countries and municipalities. The Treasury favors the making, in our markets, of such loans, which contribute to relieve the exchanges. I am sure that when Peace is consummated, and the political risk measurably removed, American exporters and European importers will lay the basis of credit in sound business transactions, and I know that American bankers will not fail then to devise means of financing the needs of the situation, nor American investors to respond to Europe's demand for capital, on a sound investment basis.

Meanwhile, it is well to remember the silent factors, which are always at work towards a solution of the problem. Immigrants' remittances to Europe are, and will continue to be a very large item in rectifying the exchanges. As soon as Peace is concluded, foreign travel will be a further item. Another very important factor is the purchase of European securities and repurchase of foreign held American securities by American investors. But the principal factor in Europe's favor is the inevitable curtailment of her imports and expansion of her exports. These processes, of course, are stimulated by the very position of the exchanges which they tend to correct.   Faithfully yours,   Carter Glass

TLS (WP, DLC).
    [1] About which, see R. L. Owen to WW, July 16, 1919, and n. 4 thereto, Vol. 61.
    [2] About which, see n. 3 to the letter just cited.

From Thomas William Lamont

Dear Mr. President: North Haven Maine Aug. 25, 1919.

I attach herewith a statement that I am considering making public, as to the Treaty situation.[1] A number of my friends have, ever since my return from abroad, urged me as a Republican, to make some statement that might serve to appeal to the Republican Senators in Washington; and what is more, to appeal to fair-minded sentiment throughout the country. Hitherto I have refrained from making any such statement. People, for instance, like Senator Root, with whom of course, I have been in disagreement, as he has been still hanging out for firm reservations, told me that if I made a statement, praising your course at Paris, I might get Borah, et al, so angry it would get their backs up still worse against the Treaty. Then Berney Baruch said that if I were to make a public statement, probably Reed of Missouri would make a public attack against my motives.

To tell the truth, I am getting a little tired of being shut up all the time, just because I may get somebody 'mad.' When I left Paris I fully intended, as you know, to go right over to Washington and sit down with the Republican Senators, in order to give them in an informal way, certain information and help the thing along. But when I arrived in New York I was told it would never do for me to be seen in Washington, etc., etc.

Of course I want to be guided by your own judgment in this matter. What I want to do is to help, not hinder. I have a little feeling that if I were to say a few things that are the truth about your course at Paris and about what happened, it might have a favorable rather than an unfavorable effect, even if it made Borah and Reed 'mad.' May I in any event ask your brief perusal of the attached statement and your judgment as to the wisdom of issuing anything of this kind now? I wrote this out before your meeting with the Foreign Relations Committee, revising it only a trifle after that. Of course in this statement I have covered a good deal of the ground that you covered with the Committee, and I can cut a lot of that out. I hate to bother you at this time when you are under such pressure, but my thought was that if you were inclined to think it wise for me to take any step of this kind, I would do so, and issue the statement from up here,—from the coolness of a detached Maine atmosphere.

With great respect and regard, I am,

Very sincerely yours,   Thomas W. Lamont

P S As I wired you, I thought you covered the whole ground admirably in your Conference.[2]

TLS (WP, DLC).
  [1] About this statement as published, see T. W. Lamont to WW, Sept. 10, 1919.
  [2] Lamont's telegram is missing.

From James Edward McCulloch, with Enclosure

My dear Mr. President: August 25, 1919.

I have the honor to present herewith a copy of the program for the improvement of race relations that Bishop Bratton and I submitted to the Governors Conference at Salt Lake City, Utah, August 20th. We were gratified that the Conference received this program with enthusiastic appreciation and ordered that it be incorporated in their annual report. We are confident that the Governors can be relied upon to aid as far as possible in making it effective.

Respectfully and gratefully yours,   J. E. McCulloch.

TLS (WP, DLC).

E N C L O S U R E

A PROGRAM FOR THE IMPROVEMENT OF RACE RELATIONS PRESENTED TO THE GOVERNORS CONFERENCE, SALT LAKE CITY, UTAH, AUGUST 20, 1919.

Recognizing that the Negro is a permanent and increasingly important factor in the development of our National life, the Southern Sociological Congress considers the solution of the problem of race relations as the most delicate and difficult single task for American Democracy. We believe that no enduring basis of good-will between the white and colored people in this country can be developed except on the fundamental principles of justice, co-operation and race integrity. The obligations of this generation to posterity demand that we exert our utmost endeavor to preserve the purity of our Democratic ideals expressed in the American Constitution as well as the purity of the blood of both races. With this belief the Southern Sociological Congress has worked out a program for the improvement of race relations which we respectfully submit to this conference of Governors in the earnest hope that this body of distinguished leaders may lend its powerful influence toward making this program effective throughout the Union.

THE PROGRAM IS:

First, that the Negro should be liberated from the blighting fear of injustice and mob violence. To this end it is imperatively urgent that lynching be prevented.

1—By the enlistment of Negroes themselves in preventing crimes that provoke mob violence.

2—By prompt trial and speedy execution of persons guilty of heinous crimes.

3—By legislation that will make it unnecessary for a woman who has been assaulted to appear in court to testify publicly.

4—By legislation that will give the Governor authority to dismiss a sheriff for failure to protect a prisoner in his charge.

Second: That the citizenship rights of the Negro should be safeguarded, particularly,

1—By securing proper traveling accommodations.

2—By providing better housing conditions and preventing extortionate rents.

3—By providing adequate educational and recreational facilities.

Third: That closer co-operation between white and colored citizens should be promoted, (without encouraging any violation of race integrity).

1—By orgaizing local committees both white and colored in as many communities as possible for the consideration of inter-racial problems.

2—By the employment of Negro physicians, nurses and policemen as far as practicable in work for sanitation, public health and law enforcement among their own people.

3—By enlisting all agencies possible in fostering justice, goodwill and kindliness in all individual dealings of members of one race with members of the other.

4—By the appointment of a standing Commission by the Governor of each state for the purpose of making a careful study of the causes underlying race friction with the view of recommending proper means for their removal.

Southern Sociological Congress.
Theodore D. Bratton, President.
J. E. McCulloch, Secretary.

T MS (WP, DLC).

From the Desk Diary of Robert Lansing

Monday Aug 25 [1919]

Conference with Prest. 12-1. Reply to Jap. memo. Siberian matters. Hapgood &c. Prest very angry at Senators for proposed amendment as to Shantung.[1] Told me most confidentially that he planned to go to the people at once, and that if they wanted war he'd "give them a belly full."[2]

[1] The Senate Foreign Relations Committee, on August 23, had adopted by a vote of nine to eight an amendment proposed by Senator Lodge to the Treaty of Peace with Germany which provided that in Articles 156, 157, and 158 of the treaty, whenever reference was made to "Japan" coming into the economic or other privileges formerly held by Germany in Shantung Province, the word "China" should be substituted. This alteration came to be commonly referred to as the "Shantung amendment." *New York Times*, Aug. 24 and 25, 1919.

[2] This was apparently the moment, or near to it, when Wilson decided to make a cross-country tour on behalf of the League of Nations. Although there had been some correspondence about such a tour between Tumulty and Wilson earlier, while Wilson was in Paris, the subject seems to have dropped out of sight upon Wilson's return to Washington and after his stroke on July 19. In response to Wilson's decision on about August 25, Tumulty and the White House staff must have worked frantically for the next three days to make at least initial arrangements. On August 28, Tumulty told reporters that Wilson would set out on a twenty-five day trip on September 3. Tumulty also said that Wilson would deliver his opening address in Columbus, Ohio, on September 4, "probably in the evening." *New York Times*, Aug. 29, 1919.

Wilson's decision to go to the country was obviously made without much thought, in anger, and on the spur of the moment. The decision was, we have to say, irrational. To begin with, there was absolutely no evidence that a "swing around the circle," however eloquent Wilson's speeches might be and however much he might persuade large crowds, would have any influence upon the nineteen or twenty so-called Republican mild reservationists, whose votes were absolutely essential to the Senate's consent to the ratification of the Treaty of Versailles. In their public statements and letters to Wilson, these senators had made it absolutely clear that they would not vote for ratification of the treaty without appending reservations to the articles of ratification. Democratic leaders in the Senate had also pointed out the realities of the situation to Wilson several times. If further evidence was needed that the treaty would not be ratified without the inclusion of reservations, then the negative reaction of the spokesmen of the mild reservationists to the Pittman resolution (about which see the news report printed at Aug. 21, 1919) should have been conclusive evidence. To repeat, it was by this time perfectly obvious that Wilson could obtain ratification of the treaty only by accepting the procedure demanded by the so-called mild reservationists and, in doing so, forge a senatorial coalition that could put the treaty across in spite of the opposition of the minority of senators who had vowed to vote against it on any terms. Of course, it is possible that Wilson understood these necessities, had decided to go to the country and build as much popular support for the treaty as possible, and intended to sit down with the Republican moderates upon his return and make the best deal possible.

Such a strategy was not without merit and was certainly the sort of tactic that Wilson had used once before, during and after his preparedness tour in late 1915 and early 1916. The success of this strategy of course depended upon the maintenance by Wilson of sufficient mental and physical resources to execute such a plan. As we have seen, Wilson's stroke of July 19 had already caused him considerable dementia; however, he was not aware of this fact. Dr. Grayson tried very hard to make him aware of the dangers of a major breakdown if he undertook a strenuous speaking tour. Obviously, Grayson feared a major stroke. Grayson had been alarmed by the stroke of July 19 and had persuaded Wilson to cancel plans for a western tour in early August. Cary T. Grayson, *Woodrow Wilson: An Intimate Memoir* (New York, 1960), pp. 94-95. The following incident, which Grayson relates in his memoir of Wilson, must have taken place on August 25 or 26:

"Later on, the conviction grew upon him that he must go. Opposition to the Treaty was increasing in the Senate, and he must rally the moral opinion of the country and do it immediately, so he felt. I played my last card and lost. Going into the study one morning I found the President seated at his desk writing. He looked up and said: 'I know what you have come for. I do not want to do anything foolhardy but the League of Nations is now in its crisis, and if it fails I hate to think what will happen to the world. You must remember that I, as Commander in Chief, was responsible for sending our soldiers to Europe. In the crucial test in the trenches they did not turn back—and I cannot turn back now. I cannot put my personal safety, my health in the balance against my duty—I must go.' . . . I paused a moment, and then turning, left the room. There was lead where my heart ought to be, but I knew the debate was closed, that there was nothing I could do except to go with him and take such care of him as I could." *Ibid.*, p. 95.

Wilson paid no more attention to Grayson's warning than he did to the consequences of his absence from Washington for a month. At this very moment, he was facing at least three crises in his foreign relations: the crisis with Japan over Shantung and the crises in Paris over Adriatic and Thracian questions. Perhaps he thought that he would be able to continue to negotiate on these questions while on a strenuous speaking tour. If so, such hopes were to prove to be illusory. In addition, Wilson still faced at home the prospect of a nationwide railroad strike, to say nothing of the accumulated crush of other domestic problems.

A Draft of An Aide-Mémoire[1]

DRAFT OF REPLY TO JAPANESE MEMORANDUM
OF AUGUST 22, 1919

[c. Aug. 25, 1919]

The Secretary of State presents his compliments to the Japanese Chargé d'Affaires and desires to express to his Government the appreciation of the Government of the United States of the frankness with which the attitude of the Japanese Government in regard to negotiations with China as to the restitution of Kiao-Chow and German rights in Shantung are stated in the memorandum handed to the Secretary of State on August 22, 1919.

With the same frankness the Secretary of State has the honor to make the following comments upon the memorandum and to state the views of the Government of the United States as to the situation which has been created by the delivery of the memorandum.

The Government of the United States would be lacking in candor if it failed to disclose the grave concern with which it views the attitude of the Japanese Government as set forth in the memorandum. It was a condition precedent to the assent given by the President to Articles 156, 157 and 158 of the Treaty of Versailles that the Japanese Government should agree that the Sino-Japanese Agreements of 1915 and 1918 should not be referred to in the negotiations for the return to China of Kiao-Chow and the German rights referred to in the statement made to the Council of the Allied and Associated Governments at Paris.[2]

refer to
Makino
& Chinda[3]
The President, after careful consideration of the Japanese memorandum, instructs the Secretary of State to state that he made it clear to the Japanese delegates who participated in the conferences at Paris that his assent to the articles was given solely upon the condition precedent above set forth and that, if that condition is

now repudiated by the Japanese Government after he has given his assent to the articles in full reliance upon the acceptance ⟨of⟩ *by* the Japanese Government of the condition precedent, he may be compelled to consider the advisability of ⟨withdrawing his adherence to⟩ *discontinuing his support of* the articles in question and of demanding their amendment by the signatories to the Treaty before its going into effect.

⟨However great the embarrassment such a course might entail and however loath the President may be to reopening the question at this time, the failure of the Japanese Government to accept without qualification the condition precedent makes such withdrawal and demand almost unavoidable.⟩

It seems needless in this connection to discuss the validity of the Agreements of 1915 and 1918 or whether the assent of the Government of China to those Agreements was obtained voluntarily or by duress, the essential fact is that *it was understood that* they were not to be considered in the negotiations for the return *to China* of Kiao-Chow and ⟨the⟩ *certain* German rights ⟨to China⟩. In the event that the Japanese Government persist in their purpose as set forth in their memorandum, the Government of the United States may then deem it necessary to discuss the validity of such agreements.

It is hoped that the Japanese Government upon further ⟨investigation of the facts⟩ *consultation with their peace delegates* and upon consideration of the views above set forth will frankly assure the Government of the United States that they will not base the negotiations with the Chinese Government for the return of Kiao-Chow and German rights upon the Agreements of 1915 and 1918, and that they will not introduce any terms of such Agreements into the negotiations.

The gravity of the ⟨consequences of⟩ *embarrassments which might follow* the failure of the Japanese Government to give an immediate assurance as outlined above cannot but impress the Japanese Government as it has the Government of the United States, which sincerely hopes that the situation created by the memorandum of the Japanese Government may be ⟨changed⟩ *cleared* and that the understanding, which was reached at Paris, may no longer be a subject of doubt or discussion between the Governments of the United States and Japan, since it is the earnest desire of the President and the Government of the United States to avoid ⟨a situation⟩ *everything* which ⟨would⟩ *could* affect unfavorably the amicable spirit and mutual confidence which have in the past characterized the relations between the two Governments.

T MS (R. Lansing Papers, DLC).

[1] Words in angle brackets in this document deleted by Wilson; words in italics added by him.
[2] For which, see the minutes of the Council of Four printed at April 22, 1919, 11:30 a.m., Vol. 57.
[3] RLhw.

Frank Lyon Polk to Robert Lansing

Paris. August 25, 5 p.m.

3890. Strictly Confidential and personal for the Secretary of State only from Polk.

Situation becoming difficult for us owing to delay in receiving instructions. When I arrived, the Thracian question was being discussed and it was said that it was the only question holding back the Bulgarian Treaty. The President's suggestion of an international state was proposed while White was still signing but the Allies would not listen to it. I sent then a personal cable 3441, August 1, 5 p.m. asking for instructions as to the scope of my authority. This cable was never answered. Negotiations were begun on all sides and great pressure was brought to bear on us. I do not really care how the matter is settled although I think that a free state for West Thrace as suggested in my 3702, August 15, 8 p.m. is the best solution so far, but I hope for some decision so that the matter can be closed one way or another. The longer the Bulgarian Treaty is kept open the more danger there is for trouble in the Balkans.

The Council is being deliberately flouted now by the Roumanians and I see no reason why the other small states should not take the same attitude unless we make our decisions more rapidly. The general feeling is here that if the five powers have so little influence with Roumania, the League of Nations will have even less.

Please believe me, this is not a complaint but a personal message to you for advice. I fear that you are leaving shortly on your vacation and it will then be most difficult to get any decisions. Dulles is leaving Saturday. He had no answer to his message,[1] but I did not feel I could hold him any longer.

In regard to the proposed settlement of Thracian matter, White, Bliss, Coolidge and I were amazed when Johnson told us last week that he had not agreed to the proposed straightening out. He had worked out all details and it was our understanding that he, as we, thought the compromise unsatisfactory but the best that could be done.   Polk.

T telegram (SDR, RG 59, 763.72119/6376, DNA).
[1] That is, FLP and JFD to RL, July 31, 1919, printed as an Enclosure with WW to RL, Aug. 4, 1919 (third letter of that date).

From Frank Lyon Polk

Paris August 25, 1919

3897. Urgent. For the President and The Secretary of State.

Reference your 2771, August 9, 4 p.m. my 3624, August 11, 11 p.m. together with your 2820 August 14, 10 a.m.[1]

To my surprise I received on Saturday a communication from Clemenceau, of which the following is a translation.

"By your letter of the 13 August you have been kind enough to indicate the interest which the American delegation takes in the early determination of the form of mandate: A: (The form of mandates, B and C having already been determined), on the ground that mandates constitute an important part of the work of the League of Nations.

I have, therefore, examined the matter again with the keen desire of giving you every satisfaction and I now ask for the privilege of acquainting (*) with the following result my study.

A preliminary consideration occurred to me when I came to examine the text of article 22 of the covenant of the League of Nations, which lays down the broad rules applicable to different types of mandate.

Here is the text: 'To those colonies and territories which, as a consequence of the late war, have ceased to be under the sovereignty of the states which formerly governed them and which are inhabited by the peoples not yet able to stand by themselves under the strenuous condition of the modern world etc.'

It is clear that these words do not permit us to anticipate a mandate for the Turkish Empire, under the circumstances in which the Turkish Empire exists at present.

My second observation springs from examination of the draft mandate A prepared by Colonel House.[2] His preamble reads as follows 'The Turkish Empire having by article blank of the Treaty of (*) signed at blank the blank renounced all rights over blank the principal Allied and Associated Powers acting in the name of all the Allied and Associated Powers constituted blank arrive autonomous territory under the guarantee of the League of Nations and *upon* and a mandate to advise and assist blank in the development of its administration.'

These words imply that Colonel House's project would not be practicable for any mandate which eventually might be given authority over territories which remain Turkish (inasmuch as it refers

---

[1] RL to FLP, Aug. 9, 1919; FLP to WW and RL, Aug. 11, 1919; and RL to FLP, Aug. 14, 1919.

[2] For which, see EMH to WW, Aug. 9, 1919. The following quotation is obviously badly garbled. For a clear text, see the telegram just cited.

only to territories over which the Turkish Empire has surrendered all rights under the Treaty of Peace).

Therefore we cannot advance the discussion of mandate A until a decision has been reached in America with regard to Turkey and even not then until after the question has been drafted by the conference itself. The substance as well as the form of the Turkish question must remain in suspense as no agreement has yet been reached concerning the entirety or any single part of the Turkish Empire.

Support is lent to my contention by the fact that the preparation of mandates B and C did not prove possible until (one), a decision of the Supreme Council was rendered settling the allocation of the German colonies in Africa and in the Pacific, (two) Germany renounced all her colonies according to the terms of the Treaty signed the 28th of June. Consequently an examination of mandate A will not be possible until we have advanced to the same stage in the Turkish settlement. Indeed how can one lay down the conditions of these mandates now when we do not yet know whether a settlement will be arrived at and what will be its scope?

This conclusion appears to me all the more valid inasmuch as the maintenance of a Turkish state under the sovereignty of a Sultan appears to be in conformity, not only with the wishes of the Turkish people, but also with modern principles of the unity of a compact and self conscious nation.

The Supreme Council has listened to the claims of the Mussulmen of India. They thought it would be very dangerous to infringe upon the integrity of the Ottoman Empire and to destroy the authority of the Caliph.

I must confess that personally, therefore, discussions make me pause particularly when I consider the mad competition between powers which are already disputing, arms in their hands, concerning the territory which they claim but which have not yet been given over to them.

When I see the almost insurmountable difficulties which jeopardize the establishment of a durable peace in the Balkans I am forced to believe that we will not easily arrive at a unanimous decision concerning Turkey unless that decision is based upon the principle of the maintenance [of] the sovereignty of the Sultan. Within the Ottoman Empire itself the disturbance has only begun and from this point of view the inquiry which is now being independently conducted by the American Commission does not appear to have contributed to calm (?) of the people nor to have facilitated a solution.

You can understand that in these circumstances I see neither the point nor the possibility of discussing today a theoretical form of mandate which can only be seriously studied and approved when the Allied Powers have begun to talk (?) terminating of decision and of reality.

Nor can I see how this delay, which is necessitated by the facts as well as by a complete lack of decision with regard to the present situation in the east, can influence American operations or diminish the prestige of the League of Nations. The mandate principle has been accepted and the form of those which are to be applied in Africa and in the Pacific Islands has already been agreed upon. No doubt, therefore, can exist concerning the good faith of the allied powers in following the same course in Asia just as soon as an agreement has been reached upon indispensable preliminary points."

In answer to this letter I have today replied as follows "I have just received your letter of August 22 in which you discuss the practicability of agreeing upon any draft of an A mandate at the present moment. Inasmuch as the conclusion which you reach differs from our understanding of the other day which I communicated to the President and Colonel House I am led to examine the arguments which you adduced in support of advisability present point of view.

In the first place it is my understanding that the draft mandate which Colonel House proposes assumes merely to lay down the broad principles of the administration which shall guide any state which shall act as mandatory power with relation to such portions of the Turkish Empire as the Supreme Council shall decide should be administered under mandate. If the Turkish Empire is completely dissolved this type of mandate is to apply to its several portions—when these powers may be given mandate over them. If the Empire is preserved in part these principles will control almost all of the balance. If the Empire is kept intact the draft mandate will of course prove to be a (?) labor. Lord Milner's commission, with the exception of the Australians, believes that they are in compliance with and instructed by their terms of reference to draft an A mandate. Both the President and I are also likewise strongly of the opinion that the Allied and Associated powers should accept certain basic principles of decent administration in advance of the distribution of territory.

As to your objection to the preamble of Colonel House's draft I feel confident that it can be stricken out or amended in Commission at the instance of your representative should the Commission believe that it is technically inappropriate in the existing situation.

The fact that the United States has not decided whether it will accept a mandate over some portion of the Turkish Empire may indeed be delaying the decision as to the future of the territory. On the other hand I cannot see how it delays the discussion and his acceptance of a general type mandate. Indeed this seems to me to be one substantial *stop* (step?) which the Supreme Council can take in the matter at the present juncture.

Though in point of time the Commission on Mandates did not draft their types B and C until after the several German colonies in Africa and the Pacific had been allocated and until after Germany had renounced title to them, there was no intrinsic reason why they should not have done so. I am sometimes inclined to think that it would have been better if they had. Certainly it would have created a satisfactory impression concerning the good faith of the Allied and Associated Powers than has been created by the procedure which was actually followed.

I am clear in my own mind that the commission should be instructed to draft an A mandate. Of course I do not wish to force them to an idle task. Structure will not be idle, however, unless the Council should agree to your suggestion that the Turkish Empire should be in its entirety, including Eastern Thrace. If that is your considered view it completely alters the aspect of the situation and I should wish to communicate immediately with the President so that he might be saved the embarrassment of even raising the question of an American mandate."

(special cipher) You will see that I have not made use of the President's statement in your 2771, August 9, 4 p.m. for two reasons: first, because I had every reason to expect a favorable written report from Clemenceau, secured without introducing the President's name; second, because I believe Colonel House's 2717, August 6, 10 p.m.[3] was slightly misinterpreted by the Department. Clemenceau does not deny that the mandatory principle may apply to the dismembered Turkish empire but he refuses to discuss the general terms of any such mandate, preferring to delay their discussion until France has been definitely allotted her share. The *evil* seems to me to be exactly of the same character. It is a move to gain the strategic position.

Should Clemenceau remain obstinate and the President is, in light of the above explanation, still of the opinion expressed in your 2771, August 9, 4 p.m., I shall at once make the President's attitude clear to him.

This matter is most urgent.   Polk.

(*) Apparent Omission.

T telegram (SDR, RG 59, 763.72119/6371, DNA).
    [3] EMH to WW and RL, Aug. 6, 1919.

To Fred McAver

My dear Mr. McAver: The White House August 26, 1919.

After you and your associates called upon me and presented the petition for the return of the drafted or emergency enlisted personnel of our troops in Siberia, I asked the Secretary of War to let me know just what the status of our troops in Siberia is.[1] He has just informed me[2] that the total enlisted strength in Siberia is slightly over 8,000 men, of whom emergency men are estimated to be not in excess of 6,500. As soon as the Congress authorized the resumption of enlistments in the Regular Army, the War Department offered to men about to enlist an opportunity to elect Siberian service. 3,411 men have so chosen, and of these men more than 2,000 have already been sent to Vladivostok to relieve emergency men in those forces. Recruits are being received by the War Department at between fifty and sixty per day, and as rapidly as they can be prepared are being formed into companies and transported to Siberia further to relieve the emergency enlisted men there.

At the rate of progress above indicated it is clear that substantial relief will have been afforded to our emergency soldiers before the winter sets in, even though it should not turn out in the public interest to bring about the entire return of our forces at that time. Upon the latter aspect of the question, however, I can give no further assurance at this time than to say that I have the petition and the reasons which were presented by your committee very much in my mind, as indeed I have this whole delicate and difficult matter, and your committee can count upon its having my most earnest and sympathetic consideration.

Cordially yours,   Woodrow Wilson.

TCL (Letterpress Books, WP, DLC).
    [1] See WW to NDB, Aug. 21, 1919 (first letter of that date) and its Enclosure.
    [2] In NDB to WW, Aug. 23, 1919.

To Newton Diehl Baker

My dear Baker: [The White House] 26 August, 1919.

Thank you for the figures about the various dams.[1] I am glad to find that I am not the biggest dam in the world.

Cordially and faithfully yours,   Woodrow Wilson.

TLS (Letterpress Books, WP, DLC).
    [1] See NDB to WW, Aug. 21, 1919, and n. 1 thereto.

To Jessie Woodrow Wilson Sayre

My darling Jessie,   The White House, 26 August, 1919.

I am writing this in the hope that it will reach you on your birthday,[1] though, since I am taking time by the forelock, it may get to you a day too soon. In any case it carries love unmeasured, not only to you, my darling daughter, but also to all the dear ones, of whom I think so often and with such a yearning. It has been delightful to get from Margaret first-hand news of you all! I am so glad that the little lad[2] is gaining now and that your anxiety about him is relieved. May many, many happy birthdays come to you, dear: may they grow happier and richer in love and rewarding experience as they multiply! Our hearts go out to you.

It looks now as if I would have to start across the continent for my long delayed "tour" almost at once and that there is slim chance for me to get to you to take part in the christening. It distresses me beyond measure that it should be so; but the trip will in all probability fill September, and in October both the King and Queen of the Belgians and the Prince of Wales come and must be entertained at the White House (not at the same time, fortunately), so that freedom there is none in sight. Please do not hold essential plans in abeyance for your incalculable father. He goes where he must, not where he would, though he prays some day to be free again.

We are all well. Mac. and Nell came down last night and are with us until four this afternoon (Mac. to argue a case), so that the whole family joins in love messages and loving wishes. And of the family Edith and I claim the privilege of taking precedence!

Your devoted Father

WWTLS (RSB Coll., DLC).
  [1] On August 28.
  [2] That is, Woodrow Wilson Sayre.

From Newton Diehl Baker

Confidential.

My dear Mr. President: Washington. August 26, 1919.

I have your note with regard to the communication from the Federal Electric Railways Commission.[1] I return herewith the letter from Mr. Sweet. I do not think you would be justified in asking the Congress to make an appropriation and authorization for this purpose at this time for the reason that this inquiry is admittedly upon a subject of domestic rather than national concern, and there are so many matters pressing for consideration from the national point of view that I think they ought not to be pushed aside even a little by the introduction of this less important matter.

In addition to that, I believe that the Commission has already heard most of the people who have valuable views on the question and that it can formulate now as comprehensive a report as it could later. This, of course, does not meet Mr. Sweet's suggestion which has merit, but I think not enough merit in the present juncture of affairs to justify its being done.

I venture to suggest the enclosed letters for the Commission and Mr. Sweet.[2]   Respectfully yours,   Newton D. Baker

TLS (WP, DLC).
    [1] WW to NDB, Aug. 22, 1919.
    [2] T MSS dated Aug. 25, 1919 (WP, DLC). Wilson had them copied verbatim and sent as WW to Members of the Federal Electric Railways Commission, Aug. 28, 1919, and WW to E. F. Sweet, Aug. 28, 1919, both printed at that date.

From John Skelton Williams

Dear Mr. President: Washington August 26, 1919.

Please accept my warm congratulations upon your clear, sound and altogether admirable proclamation relative to the high cost of living, and your courageous stand on the question of the wage increase.

Your proclamation and your statement to the railroad shopmen, printed in the morning papers, impress me as being among the most important of your great public utterances which have been so potential in shaping the political and economic policies, not only of our own country but of the world; and I do not see how any citizen of this country who desires to save our civilization from the chaos which now possesses so much of the rest of the world, can withhold from you unlimited support.

I know the enormous pressure upon every moment of your time; but I trust you will pardon me for offering a few thoughts in this connection which may be worthy of your consideration. If asked to name the three special causes which in our own country have contributed more than any other to the present indefensible scales of prices and living costs I should name

1st, the Steel and Iron producers;

2nd, the Coal operators; and

3rd, the operations of the shipping trust—by fixing a wage scale unprecedented in this country, which led in all wage increases without creating a new supply of labor or permanent employment.

The Shipping Board, however, had new and unprecedented

problems to solve in the most difficult times; started without a nucleus upon which to build and inevitably was the prey of profiteers of all classes—of capital and of labor,—and it is, of course, hardly profitable now to discuss what "might have been."

The other two principal causes of our economic unrest are yet with us, and, fortunately, can be handled and remedied,—and I believe by the President.

I took the liberty of sending you, while you were abroad, certain statements relative to the profits in the year 1918 of the great Steel and Iron combinations.[1] My analysis of the report of the U. S. Steel Corporation showed that it made last year a profit of approximately 100 per cent on its common stock and that this stock, furthermore, had represented, at the organization of the Steel Corporation nothing but "water." It was also shown that the U. S. Steel Corporation profits were so enormous that it could have afforded last year to reduce by $30 per ton the price of every ton of steel fabricated and would still have had a sufficient profit remaining to pay about 7 per cent on its common stock.

In answer to the suggestion that the U. S. Steel Corporation could not make a further reduction in the price of the finished products without reducing wages, I have shown by its own figures that the Corporation could have paid every one of its two hundred and sixty thousand employees in the year 1918 100% more wages than they did pay, and would have sufficient profits remaining to yield about 7 per cent on the entire capital.

Mr. President, in my humble judgment, our present grave economic conditions are due principally to the enormous and abnormal profits which have been made and are being made and retained by the so-called trusts and "near" trusts and their allied interests. When the wage earner demands of the great industries which are making these enormous profits a larger proportion of its earnings than has been accorded him in wages these corporations have no defense for a refusal.

Let us take, for example, the Steel Trust. When the laborer calls upon the Corporation for an increase in wages, the reply that the increase would deny capital a fair participation in earnings is impossible because, as I have shown you, that Corporation for last year could have paid 50 per cent, or even 100 per cent, additional wages and would have had enough profit left to pay about 7 per

[1] J. S. Williams to WW, May 29, 1919, TLS (WP, DLC). The enclosures with this letter were a copy of the letter cited in n. 2 below; "Analysis of Earnings for 1918 of the Lackawanna Steel Company"; and "Memorandum Regarding Charges Made for 'Maintenance' and for 'Capital Expenditures' by the United States Steel Corporation for Years 1916, 1917 and 1918 as Compared with Preceeding Fourteen Years," all T MSS (WP, DLC).

cent on the entire capital stock. Therefore, many corporations, such as the U. S. Steel Corporation have been forced to grant swift and extraordinary increases in wages. When these increases are granted, they become known; and then the workmen in other industries which are not trusts and which are making *moderate* profits call for similar increases. But these other industrial establishments, lacking the enormous profits earned by the trusts and certain other industries, must choose between refusing the demands and suffering the disaster of a *strike* or granting them and *facing bankruptcy*. The same figures prove that if the managers had been wisely compliant with the trend of the thought of this time for fair division of the results of good fortune and management they could have reduced the price of fabricated steel to the consumer $15 per ton, increased the wages of their producing workmen 50 per cent and still have paid their stockholders 7 per cent. Or, as already indicated, they could have divided between stockholders and consumers and by the decreased price given powerful impetus to the building and other industries, provided employment for armies of men and helped reduce rents and other costs of living.

You have before you a concrete example of this in the railroads. If they were making 100 per cent on their capital as the steel trust was making last year, they would have no defense for refusing to share these profits with their men by raising wages and raising them heavily. But we all know that the railroads not only are not making 100% but are actually running at a *deficit*. They have no margin of profit from which to pay the further increase in wages which is asked for. The workman in the railroad shop getting, say, 50 cents per hour, does not understand the economic conditions which prevent him from getting, say, $1. per hour, which a workman employed by the Steel Trust receives for work no more skillful nor exacting than that which he is performing. He is not satisfied with the answer that the Steel Trust is getting prices for its products which enable it to make 100 per cent on its stock, and hence can pay its men 50 to 100 per cent more than the railroad employee is paid. *The trust injures the railway first by overcharging it for steel products, thereby improperly increasing its expenses, and again by inflating, from its excessive profit, the wages of its own workmen, thereby causing dissatisfaction and demoralization among the railway's workmen.*

Mr. President, the conclusion is irresistible—that if we intend to make a radical cure of these defects and inequalities, it will be necessary for us by legislation or otherwise *to curb or limit the profits exacted by monopolies or by corporations and associations whose profits are not regulated or governed by the natural laws of competition.*

The Steel Trust cannot claim that its profits are made in fair competition. They are not. It is inconceivable that the railroad operator can ever make profits of 100 per cent. The Interstate Commerce Commission has power to control the rates which any road may receive and the railroad never will be able to compete in the labor market with a monopoly which is exacting for its products prices sufficient to enable it to make 100 per cent on an extravagantly watered capital.

The holders of railroad securities have no opportunity to change their investment by selling their securities and going into the steel business to compete with the steel trust. Steel corporations under other names, perhaps held,—but not independently controlled,—by other owners, operate almost as a unit with the Steel Trust, because the steel combinations already control our country's vast deposits of raw materials so largely as to make them a practical monopoly.

I am impressed with the feeling that it is of the highest importance for the welfare of our country that the U. S. Steel Corporation should be sufficiently disintegrated to bring about real and active competition in the production of steel and iron.

I can find no support for the theory that economic conditions justify this colossal combination on the ground that this two billion dollar corporation can produce steel and iron more cheaply because of its great size. In any case nothing is gained for the country or the public by cheap production if the consumer gets no advantages from it and must pay as much for the product as if the cost were high, or suffer for lack of it. Cheap production is a curse instead of the blessing it should be, if its results are to enrich a few investors and to create an artificially high standard of wages for some thousands of men while disorganizing millions and hampering all industrial enterprise.

In the last analysis every corporation is created and protected by the laws and government on the theory that it will be an instrument for the general welfare. When it is made by short-sighted greed and by skillful use of circumstances, a means for doing and causing evil, law and government should force it to performance of the duties and functions for which it was created. When by extraordinary conditions it is enabled to prevent the operations of great natural laws of commerce, it should be restrained from such interference. When it becomes an actual and active obstacle to enterprise, prosperity and development its power for harm should be limited, if not ended.

I think it can be demonstrated, Mr. President, that ten corporations with 200 million dollars each could produce steel and iron just as cheaply as this one corporation with two billion dollars. In fact, I am inclined to think that if we had ten steel corporations with 200 million dollars each, the healthy competition which would thereby be developed would enable them to produce at less cost than the present monopoly; and I am certain that if we had ten or more such corporations acting independently instead of the big U. S. Steel Corporation the prices of all steel and iron products throughout this country would be from $20 to $40 per ton less than those now being exacted under existing monopolistic or semi-monopolistic conditions.

With lower prices I believe building operations and other enterprises throughout the country would be enormously stimulated, and there would be more homes for the people and more factories in which to work.

The Steel Trust, the coal operators, and other monopolies are causing enormous economic waste by keeping vast bodies of men on their pay-rolls idle for one, two, three or four days per week, while they are curtailing production twenty, thirty, forty or fifty per cent for the express purpose of creating scarcity and thereby enabling them to obtain unjustified pre-armistice prices. In many of these great industries, men who could be producing the materials so urgently needed for the purpose of bring[ing] down the cost of living, are idling, consuming only, and are producing nothing.

I invite your attention to the official figures which show the great curtailment in the production of steel and iron, while old prices are being maintained or in some cases advanced; and I also ask your attention to the records which show the large extent to which the coal operators have closed mines or curtailed their output for the purposes I have stated.

The U. S. Steel Corporation in 1918 converted through the application of human labor the raw materials in their mines valued, *unmined*, at 50 to 100 million dollars into finished products which then sold for approximately $1,500,000,000. If that corporation last year had worked its men only fifty per cent of their time it would have failed to produce $700,000,000 of products which it did produce. The idleness of those men would therefore have entailed an economic loss of $700,000,000. Would this not have been just as much a loss as if that much property had been wiped out by a conflagration?

It would be hard to calculate the economic loss which our people are suffering, and have been suffering, because certain industries have kept and are keeping their works shut down or working at part capacity or for only a few days a week, for the definite purpose of limiting production and keeping up prices.

I trust you will pardon me for imposing upon you this lengthy letter; but the problem which we have before us is, as you so fittingly describe it, "one which is more likely to affect the happiness and prosperity and even the life of our people than the war itself," and I hope that my deep appreciation of the solemnity of the situation may be my excuse for intruding as I am doing upon your valuable time.

Respectfully and faithfully yours,   Jno. Skelton Williams

P.S. For your convenient reference I also inclose with this a copy of my letter of May 5 to Director General Hines[2] in which I analyzed the operations of the U. S. Steel Corporation for the year 1918.

TLS (WP, DLC).
  [2] J. S. Williams to W. D. Hines, May 5, 1919, TCL (WP, DLC).

Robert Lansing to Frank Lyon Polk

Washington August 26, 1919.

For Polk.

2949. President agrees to the final settlement of Italian claims in the Adriatic as set forth in your 3834 August 22nd 2:00 p.m., except that disposition Albania's future should be left to the League of Nations.   Lansing

T telegram (SDR, RG 256, 186.3411/759, DNA).

A Revised Draft of an Aide-Mémoire[1]

August 26, 1919

MEMORANDUM.

The Secretary of State presents his compliments to the Japanese Chargé d'Affaires and desires to express on behalf of his Government its appreciation of the frankness with which the Japanese Government stated its attitude in regard to negotiating with China concerning the restitution of Kiao-chou and German rights in Shantung in the memorandum handed to the Secretary of State on August 22, 1919.

With the same frankness and same desire to avoid misunderstandings the Secretary of State has the honor to present his observations upon the memorandum of the Japanese Government and to state the views of the Government of the United States as to the situation which has been created by the delivery of the memorandum.

The Government of the United States would be wanting in candor if it did not admit that it views with grave concern the present attitude of the Japanese Government since it discloses that there is a radical difference of understanding as to the proposed negotiations with China. The Government of the United States had no doubt that the *representatives of the* Japanese Government *at Paris* clearly understood that a condition precedent to the assent of the President to Articles 156, 157 and 158 of the Treaty of Versailles was that the Japanese Government should agree that the Sino-Japanese Agreements of 1915 and 1918 should not be relied upon or referred to in the negotiations for the return to China of Kiao-chou and the German rights ⟨mentioned⟩ *as dealt with* in the Japanese statement to the Council of the Allied and Associated Governments at Paris.

The President, after careful consideration of the Japanese memorandum, directs the Secretary of State to say that he is deeply concerned that the Japanese Government have without doubt unintentionally declared a policy contrary to the understanding reached with the Japanese delegates at Paris; that during the conferences of the Council of the *Principal* Allied and Associated Governments Baron Makino and Viscount Chinda showed their willingness to accept the condition precedent by stating that their Government would not appeal to the Agreements of 1915 and 1918 in negotiating with China unless the latter refused to negotiate under Articles 156, 157 and 158 of the Treaty; and that the assent of the President to those Articles was given because he believed that the Japanese Government acting through their accredited delegates understood and agreed to ⟨eliminate⟩ *disregard* the Agreements of 1915 and 1918 ⟨from⟩ *in* their ⟨future⟩ negotiations with the Chinese Government relative to Kiao-chou⟨.⟩ *in carrying out the agreement reached at Paris.*

The President further directs the Secretary of State to say that, since his assent to the Articles of the Treaty depended upon the acceptance of ⟨the⟩ *this* condition precedent, the non-compliance with that condition by the Japanese Government may ⟨compel⟩ *oblige* him to consider the ⟨advisability⟩ *necessity* of discontinuing his support of the Articles in question, though he sincerely hopes that the Japanese Government will find it possible to remove the necessity of such action on his part.

The Government of the United States considers it needless in this connection to discuss the validity of the Agreements of 1915 and 1918 or whether the assent of the Chinese Government to those Agreements was given voluntarily or obtained by duress. The fact essential at the present time is that it was understood *at Paris* that they were not to be considered in the negotiations for the return to China of Kiao-chou and certain German rights in Shantung. In the event, however, that the Japanese Government find themselves unable to ⟨recede from⟩ *reconsider* the position set forth in their memorandum, which it is sincerely hoped will not be the case, the Government of the United States may feel it needful to ⟨discuss⟩ *raise the question of* the validity of such agreements though it would do so with reluctance and regret.

It is confidently anticipated that the Japanese Government upon further consultation with their peace delegates and upon consideration of the facts above set forth will find it possible to give a frank assurance to the Government of the United States that in accordance with the understanding reached at Paris they will not base their negotiations with the Chinese Government for the return of Kiao-chou and German rights upon the Agreements of 1915 and 1918 and that they will not introduce any terms of such Agreements into the negotiations.

The grave embarrassments which may result from the failure of the Japanese Government to give an immediate assurance as outlined above cannot but impress that Government with the desirability of preventing the possibility of such embarrassments arising by changing the situation created by the memorandum under consideration and by removing all doubt and uncertainty as to the Japanese Government's intention to abide by the condition precedent as stated in this communication, and which the Government of the United States is firmly convinced is only now a subject of discussion through misapprehension of the facts on the part of the Japanese Government.

The Government of the United States in presenting this statement of the case has done so with all candor because it is not the part of friendship and of good understanding to withhold the truth or attempt to hide existing divergence of views. It is the earnest desire of the President and the Government of the United States to avoid everything which could affect unfavorably the ⟨amicable⟩ *friendly* spirit and mutual confidence which have in the past characterized the relations between the United States and Japan; and it is, because of that desire, which is doubtless shared by the Japanese Government, that they are urged to give the assurance which will bring to an end the difference which has arisen as evidenced by their memorandum.

CC MS (R. Lansing Papers, DLC).
    [1] Words in angle brackets deleted by Wilson; words in italics added by him.

From Edward Mandell House

Dear Governor: London, August 26, 1919.

Grey and I are coming out together. We plan to sail on the Lapland, September 16th.

As I wrote you before, there seems to be no purpose in my remaining after Mandate A has been formed. We should finish this by the tenth. I feel the need of getting out of the European atmosphere as I have been in it too long already.

                    Affectionately yours,   E. M. House

P. S. Our annual falling out seems to have occurred.[1] The Foreign Office received a cable the other day saying that we were no longer on good terms and asking that the Prime Minister and Balfour be informed. The press representatives also told me that they had the same news. I am wondering where this particular story originated and why they wanted the Prime Minister and Balfour to be informed. Tyrrell said it came from one of their men in New York and not from Washington.

TLS (WP, DLC).
[1] House first mentioned the reports of this alleged "falling out" between himself and Wilson in his diary entry of August 22, 1919. The Diary of Edward M. House, T MS (E. M. House Papers, CtY). He noted that on August 19, Henry Wickham Steed, editor of the London *Times*, had told him of a dispatch from one of his correspondents in New York saying that it was "current" that Wilson and House had had "a falling out." House also mentioned that Sir William Tyrrell had told him "later" that the Foreign Office had received a similar dispatch. This dispatch, according to House, "stated that the difference between the President and me had arisen because I had been so pro-British that he considered I had delayed the Peace Conference three months." For more on these rumors, see EMH to WW, Aug. 29, 1919.

To John Charles Shaffer

PERSONAL

My dear Mr. Shaffer: [The White House] 27 August, 1919.

Your letter of August 21st is most welcome, and I am going to carefully digest the suggestions it makes. It is difficult to see how any qualification can be placed upon the adoption of the treaty which would not have to be taken to the Assembly at Weimar and submitted to the judgment of the present German Government. In my own judgment, as you will see, there is no real doubt as to the meaning of the clauses of the Covenant of the League of Nations which have been brought most under discussion, and the plain meaning constitutes, I believe, a sufficient safeguard of the interests of the United States. But the difficulty of finding a way does not render the judgment of men like yourself, whose judgment I greatly respect, any the less necessary or valuable to me.

Cordially and sincerely yours,   Woodrow Wilson

TLS (Letterpress Books, WP, DLC).

To John Skelton Williams

My dear Mr. Comptroller: [The White House] 27 August, 1919.

Your letter of August 26th interests me very much and gives me a great deal to ponder upon. We have a great problem to work out, and I greatly value your thoughtful suggestions based upon genuine inquiry.

Cordially and sincerely yours,   Woodrow Wilson

TLS (Letterpress Books, WP, DLC).

To Cyrus Townsend Brady

My dear Brady: [The White House] 27 August, 1919.

Thank you for your generous letter of August 23rd. I can almost catch the radiation of the generous ardor of friendship that glows all through it, and am greatly cheered and helped by it.

Perhaps if I knew the author of the extraordinary slander which you quote, I might be able to throw some light on it, because even here in Washington I have never known more venomous intrigue than sprang out of the Princeton fight.

That fight, by the way, is not over. I hope there will be enough of me left after the Presidential term is over to make a vigorous presentation to the country of what it is necessary to do to our universities, in order to render them truly American. I can then, if it seems necessary, pay my compliments to the benighted and malicious gentlemen who were ignominiously prominent in that struggle.

With warm regard,

Cordially and faithfully yours,   Woodrow Wilson

TLS (Letterpress Books, WP, DLC).

To Herbert Bruce Brougham

My dear Mr. Brougham: [The White House] 27 August, 1919.

I value your suggestion about my seeing Mr. Plumb, but am sorry to say that I cannot act upon it, at any rate at present, because the consideration of the railway matter has not come to such a point as to crystalize judgment.

In great and unavoidable haste,

Cordially and sincerely yours,   Woodrow Wilson

TLS (Letterpress Books, WP, DLC).

Gilbert Fairchild Close to the White House Staff, with Enclosure

Memorandum.   27 August, 1919

The President would like to have a memorandum of the facts referred to in this letter.   G.F.C.

T MS (WP, DLC).

E N C L O S U R E

From Lillian D. Wald

New York   August Twenty-Fourth

Dear President Wilson: Nineteen Nineteen

No doubt the attack on John Shillady in Texas[1] has been brought to your attention, and I beg the privilege of asking you to state in effective manner the chagrin that all true Americans must feel because of this outrage. We had in mind to send the protest to the Governor of Texas, trusting that he would respond to an appeal from right thinking Americans to take action upon the hideous performance within his state, an offence aggravated because perpetrated by a Judge of the Courts. As reported in this morning's paper, the Governor's answer to the officials of the National Association for Advancement of Colored People, highminded citizens of our Nation, gives no hope of redress from him.

I have known Mr. Shillady in his public service for many years. He is firm and gentle, a wise counselor and profoundly interested in helping the Negroes to maintain their self-respect that they may live within their land unmolested, contributing the best that is in them because of our faith and belief in them.

We have a branch of work among the colored people in New York, and I feel that they, like the law-abiding colored people throughout the country, would be heartened if some ringing message came from you of abhorrence because of an attack upon their friend.

The times are so serious, as you well know, that I am sure you will understand the anxiety within our hearts. I believe that you can carry comforting balm to the colored people in this time, and the attack upon Mr. Shillady gives you a just and imperative opportunity.   Faithfully yours,   Lillian D. Wald

TLS (WP, DLC).
    [1] See the memorandum from the White House Staff printed at Aug. 28, 1919.

From John Barton Payne

Subject: POWER to OPERATE, CHARTER, and SELL SHIPS under
EXISTING LEGISLATION.

Dear Mr. President: Washington August 27, 1919

The Shipping Act, approved September 17, 1916, does not contemplate the construction and operation of commercial ships by the Shipping Board. The act provides for regulation rather than operation. Operation may, however, be accomplished as follows:

(1) Section 11 of the Act authorizes the creation of a corporation (the Emergency Fleet Corporation) for the purchase, construction, equipment, lease, charter, maintenance, and operation of merchant vessels in the commerce of the United States; capital stock not to exceed $50,000,000; but provides that no such corporation shall engage in the operation of any vessel constructed, purchased, leased, chartered, or transferred under the authority of this act unless the Board shall be unable after a bona fide effort to contract with a citizen of the United States for the purchase, lease, or charter of such vessel under terms and conditions prescribed by the Board.

The Board is required to give public notice of the terms and conditions upon which a contract will be made, and to invite competitive offerings. If, after full compliance with this provision, it is unable to enter into a contract with private parties for the purchase, lease, or charter of the vessels, it shall make a full report to the President, who shall examine such report, and if he approves the same, shall make an order declaring that the conditions have been found to exist which justify the operation of such vessels. However, at the expiration of five years after proclamation of peace by the President, the vessels shall revert to the Board, and the Board may sell, lease, or charter the same as provided in Section 7 of said Act.

The effect of this is that if the President shall find, after the prescribed effort has been made, that the vessels of the Fleet Corporation cannot be sold or leased on the terms prescribed by the

Board, they may be operated for five years after the peace proclamation.

(2) The emergency shipping acts authorized the President to
requisition, construct, or otherwise acquire merchant ships. These
powers you delegated to the United States Shipping Board Emergency Fleet Corporation, which by virtue thereof is now in possession of the ships mentioned in my previous memorandum.[1]

Section 4 of the Emergency Shipping Act, after authorizing the
President to delegate power to such agency or agencies as he shall
determine, provides, that all money turned over to the Fleet Corporation may be expended as other moneys of said corporation are
now expended. All ships constructed, purchased, or requisitioned
under this authority are to be managed, operated, and disposed of
as the President may direct; this power (Section 10) will cease six
months after the proclamation of peace.

CONCLUSION

(a) The President may make such order as he deems wise as to
the operation or disposal of the ships constructed or acquired under this emergency legislation.

(b) The Shipping Board may fix the terms for the purchase,
lease, or charter of vessels otherwise acquired, and give public notice that the vessels are offered upon such terms and conditions. If
the ships are not sold to a citizen of the United States on the prescribed terms, and such report is made to, and approved by, the
President, then the ships may be operated by the Emergency Fleet
Corporation for a period of five years. As to existing ships there is,
therefore, no difficulty re their operation for five years.

(c) In view of this legislation, it is doubtful whether new construction should be undertaken in the absence of a specific appropriation. The operation of ships by the Government is, as you will
observe, treated as temporary.

Section 11 providing for the organization of the Fleet Corporation provides that at the end of five years after peace is declared
the operation of vessels on the part of any such corporation shall
cease and said corporation stand dissolved and the vessels and
other property shall revert to the Board, which, under Section 7 of
the Act, is authorized, with the approval of the President, to
charter, lease, or sell to any citizen of the United States; but no
provision is made for further operation.

I trust this will cover what you have in mind.

Respectfully submitted,   John Barton Payne

TLS (WP, DLC).
[1] See Payne's memorandum printed at Aug. 22, 1919.

From Alexander Mitchell Palmer

Dear Mr. President: Washington, D. C. August 27, 1919.

In further reference to the case of Edgar C. Caldwell, a negro soldier who was convicted in the State courts of Alabama on a charge of murder and was sentenced to be hanged, I wrote you on the 22nd that I could find no authority warranting interference by the Federal Government.

If you think it wise, however, I could do this: The case is now pending in the Supreme Court of Alabama on a petition for re-hearing. I could ask leave of the Court to file a brief amicus curiae and, if leave should be granted, I would insist that the record shows the defendant to be guilty only of manslaughter. The only excuse, of course, for going this far is the fact that the defendant, at the time of the commission of the crime, was a soldier and the War Department might have tried him for the offense, but did not.

If we do nothing but file a brief, we will probably be charged with trying to interfere with State courts; if we do nothing, I presume negroes generally will feel that the Government is not much interested in its negro soldiers. Thus a question of rather broad policy is raised. Will you indicate what you think ought to be done?[1]   Faithfully yours,   A Mitchell Palmer

TLS (WP, DLC).
    [1] "Will you please let Mr. Scott know what the Attorney General proposes to do in the case of Caldwell, as per his letter of August 27th attached." WW to JPT, Aug. 28, 1919, TL (WP, DLC). A handwritten notation on Palmer's letter printed above indicates that Tumulty wrote on August 28 to Emmett Jay Scott, formerly special assistant to the Secretary of War to advise on matters affecting Negro soldiers and now secretary-treasurer of Howard University. Tumulty's letter is missing in WP, DLC.

James Grover McDonald[1] to Joseph Patrick Tumulty

My dear Mr. Tumulty: New York City August 27, 1919.

We have today sent the following telegram to President Wilson:

"This Association is being urged to co-operate in a movement to present a petition this week before the Senate Foreign Relations Committee in reference to economic conditions in Russia. Before taking any action in support of this movement we would prefer to discuss situation with you. Would it be possible for you to see at your convenience a small committee of three or, preferably, five persons, including Miss Lillian Wald, Paul Kellogg. Will take no action until we hear from you."[2]

We appreciate fully the many demands which are being made on Mr. Wilson's time, but because of the crisis in the Russian situation, and because of our anxiety to do nothing which might embarrass the working out of the proper solution of that problem, we are very anxious to see the President before we participate in any movement to bring the Russian matter before Congress. We are confident that you will understand the spirit in which we make this request for an interview.[3]

Very sincerely yours,   James G McDonald.

TLS (WP, DLC).
[1] Chairman of the Board of Directors of the League of Free Nations Association.
[2] J. G. McDonald to WW, Aug. 27, 1919, T telegram (WP, DLC).
[3] "Will you not be kind enough to say in reply to this that 'the President greatly appreciates your considerate suggestion about an interview, but is so absolutely overwhelmed with necessary tasks that he hopes you will feel at liberty to take your own course in the important matter referred to in your message.'" WW to JPT, Aug. 28, 1919, TL (WP, DLC).

Peter Michelson[1] to Joseph Patrick Tumulty

My dear Mr. Tumulty: Washington, D. C. August 27, 1919.

The American Jewish Relief Committee, as I mentioned to you at your office the other day, is launching a drive for the relief of Jews in Poland. They feel that an expression from the President, endorsing their work and bringing out in his own forceful way the true conditions as he knows them to exist in the desolated regions, can bring the need for this relief to the American people as nothing else can.

Will you kindly take this matter up with the President and see if he is willing to give us a statement?[2] I am enclosing several news releases showing what the committee has done. Kindly return them when you have finished with them.

Very truly yours,   Peter Michelson.

TLS (WP, DLC).
[1] Washington representative of various charitable organizations such as the National Tuberculosis Association and the American Red Cross.
[2] "I feel that it would be most unwise for me to do what is here suggested, not because I lack the warmest interest in what is proposed, but because there are so many efforts of this sort, and just now the condition in Poland is one so full of dynamite that I think the less publicly said and the more quietly done the better. Won't you please explain this to Mr. Michelson?" WW to JPT, Aug. 29, 1919, TL (WP, DLC).

From the Desk Diary of Robert Lansing

Wednesday Aug 27 [1919]

Conference with President—12-12:55. Approves attempt as to consortium. Last telegram of 8th from House. Other matters. Greek Bulgarian frontiers.

A Memorandum by David Hunter Miller

[Washington] August 27, 1919.

MEMORANDUM FOR THE SECRETARY.

The question of conscription in Togoland involves the so-called "B" and "C" mandates.

"A" mandates (for Turkey) are not involved or discussed.

Colonel House, after consultation with Lord Gray [Grey], Lord Robert Cecil, Ambassador Davis and Raymond Fosdick, recommends a concession to the French.[1]

He says there are two modes of concessions.

1. Annexation of Togoland by France.

The despatch says "This seems objectionable as infringing the express terms of Article 22."

I agree that such a solution is wholly inadmissible.

2. The French part of Togoland to be subject to a "C" mandate and by a special exception, so described, the French allowed to raise black troops—these troops not to be used outside of Togoland except in a world war.

I think Togoland should be under a "B" mandate (Central Africa, 5th Par. Article 22 of Covenant) not under a "C" mandate (6th Par. Article 22).

Aside from this, it seems to me that the whole idea of training black troops in mandate territory to fight in Europe, is contrary to the principle of mandates, which is analogous to that of wardships.

I submit a draft despatch embodying these views.[2]

D.H.M.

TI MS (SDR, RG 59, 763.72119/6886, DNA).
[1] See EMH to WW, Aug. 20, 1919.
[2] D. H. Miller, T MS of draft telegram dated Aug. 27, 1919 (WP, DLC). The revised version, with Wilson's addition, is printed as RL to FLP, Aug. 30, 1919.

To the Members of the Federal Electric Railways Commission

Gentlemen: [The White House] 28, August 1919.

The Secretary of War has transmitted to me the report[1] in which you outline the inquiries you have been able to make and suggesting the advisability of further appropriations in order that your work may be carried to a more comprehensive conclusion by further hearings, both in Washington and throughout the country.

The spirit in which you have approached your work, and the importance of the questions which you are considering, would plainly justify a request from me to the Congress that it provide the means for a continuance of the inquiries until a definite survey could be made, were it not for the fact that so many matters of immediate national concern were pressing for solution. The street railroad question is, after all, largely local in its control, and perhaps the best your Commission could expect to do, under any circumstances, would be to set out helpfully a description of the most sympathetic and successful experiments which have been made throughout the country in placing the relations between communities and such public utilities upon a sound basis. This I hope the Commission will be able to do from the hearings it has already had with such illustrations of the national importance of the problem as can be made in order that communities which are facing the conditions you describe will have the spur of knowing that their action, incidentally but clearly, does affect the general financial and industrial condition of the country.

I am grateful to the members of the Commission for the earnest and intelligent work they have done and trust that it will be possible for them to summarize out of the hearings and deliberations already had a helpful report.

Cordially and sincerely yours,   Woodrow Wilson

TLS (Letterpress Books, WP, DLC).
[1] A summary of which appears in NDB to WW, Aug. 20, 1919.

To Edwin Forrest Sweet

My dear Mr. Sweet: [The White House] 28, August 1919.

I have your note of the twentieth of August with regard to the possible usefulness of hearings by the Federal Electric Railways Commission throughout the country.

After considering the report and recommendations which the Commission handed me a day or two ago, through the Secretary of War, I feel obliged to come to the conclusion that I would not be justified in approaching the Congress to secure an appropriation for further work by the Commission. I have no doubt the hearings would be useful in the way you suggest, and I regret that there are so many pressing demands upon both the Congress and the executive just now that this helpful work seems necessarily pushed aside.   Cordially and sincerely yours,   Woodrow Wilson

TLS (Letterpress Books, WP, DLC).

From Robert Lansing

My dear Mr. President: Washington August 28, 1919.

In accordance with your request I am transmitting to you herewith the certified copy of the Treaty between the United States, the British Empire, France, Italy and Japan on the one hand and Poland on the other hand, as well as a certified copy of the Agreement between the United States, Belgium, the British Empire and France of the one part and Germany of the other part, with regard to the military occupation of the territories of the Rhine.

The Legal Adviser of the Department raises the question of the necessity of submitting to the Senate the Rhine Convention. The argument is that this Convention is an agreement to execute the terms of the Treaty, and that once the Treaty is ratified these arrangements will be justified under the implied authority given to carry out the express provisions of the Treaty. There seems to be no reason, however, why this Agreement should not be submitted to the Senate, and in any case, as a matter of policy, I feel that it would be a grave mistake to withhold it from the Senate.

Faithfully yours,   Robert Lansing.

TLS (WP, DLC).

Gilbert Fairchild Close to Rudolph Forster

Mr. Forster: [The White House] 28 August, 1919

The President asks if you will be kind enough to draw up the proper form of message for transmitting to the Senate the treaty with Poland, signed at Versailles on the 28th of June; and the agreement between the United States, Belgium, the British Empire and France of the one part, and Germany of the other part, with regard to the military occupation of the territories of the Rhine, also signed at Versailles on the 28th of June.

Please say that "this treaty and this convention are ancillary to the Treaty of Peace with Germany, and I am glad to lay them before the Senate now, in order that they may be considered, if possible, in connection with that treaty, and also in order that they may serve to throw further light upon the treaty itself."

G.F.C.

TL (WP, DLC).

To Henry Cabot Lodge

My dear Mr. Chairman: [The White House] 28 August, 1919.

Allow me to acknowledge the receipt of your letter of August 23rd and to say that I shall take pleasure in laying before the Senate the treaty with Poland, signed at Versailles on the 28th of June; and the agreement between the United States, Belgium, the British Empire and France of the one part, and Germany of the other part, with regard to the military occupation of the territories of the Rhine, also signed at Versailles on the 28th of June.[1]

The declaration of the 16th of June to which you refer was a mere declaration of policy and does not become in any way pertinent until the treaty is ratified. My impression is that a certain degree of embarrassment would be caused, not to the United States but to the countries with which we must necessarily cooperate in many particulars in the execution of the treaty, if it were submitted now. It will of course be made public in due time.

With regard to the treaties with Austria, Hungary, Bulgaria, and Turkey, it would be out of the question for me to submit them in their present form, even to the Committee on Foreign Relations. They are in process of negotiation, are subject to change and reconsideration until finally submitted and signed, and therefore are not suitable for submission. I am sure that the Committee on Foreign Relations will appreciate the undesirability of creating the precedent which would be created by submitting treaties in their draft form. It would tend to take the function of negotiating treaties out of the hands of the Executive, where it is expressly vested by the Constitution.   Very sincerely yours,   [Woodrow Wilson]

CCL (WP, DLC).
  [1] Wilson submitted copies of the Rhine convention and of the Polish treaty to the Senate for its advice and consent to ratification on August 29. Sixty-sixth Cong., 1st sess., Sen. Docs. 81 and 82 (Washington, 1919).

From the White House Staff

Memorandum: [c. Aug. 28, 1919]

It appears from the Press dispatches that John R. Shillady, of New York, Secretary of the National Association for the advancement of the colored people went to Austin Texas last week in the interests of securing a State Charter for the Organization; that on August 22, 1919, after holding a meeting with colored people, which was not molested, he was met in front of his hotel by several white men who administered a severe beating with their fists, and ordered to catch the first train out of texas; and not to stop in Texas.

It also appears from the Press that Governor Hobby,[1] in reply to an inquiry as to whether efforts were being made to punish the offenders, stated that Shillady was the only offender and that he had been punished prior to the receipt of the inquiry; he also stated that the organization could do more toward the advancement of the colored people by keeping their representatives out of that State than in any other way.

T MS (WP, DLC).
    [1] That is, William Pettus Hobby.

To Joseph Patrick Tumulty

Dear Tumulty: [The White House] 28 August, 1919.
    Would you be kind enough to acknowledge this letter from Miss Wald[1] for me in some gentle and kindly way, and express our desire to do everything that is possible to moderate and prevent such outbursts of feeling as she alludes to.   The President

TL (WP, DLC).
    [1] The Enclosure printed with GFC to the White House Staff, Aug. 27, 1919.

To Alexander Mitchell Palmer

My dear Palmer: The White House 28 August, 1919
    I sincerely hope that you will do what you suggest in your letter of August 27th about the case of Edgar C. Caldwell, a negro soldier convicted in Alabama on the charge of murder. I think this is the right course to take and am glad you have suggested it.
                    Cordially and sincerely yours,   Woodrow Wilson

TLS (A. M. Palmer Papers, DLC).

From Joseph Patrick Tumulty, with Enclosure

Dear Governor: [The White House] 28 August, 1919.
    These are the Hughes reservations.   The Secretary

TL (WP, DLC).

E N C L O S U R E

RESERVATIONS IN ENTERING LEAGUE OF NATIONS.

Mr. HALE. Mr. President, I have before me a copy of a letter sent by me on July 18 to Mr. Justice Hughes, of New York, asking his opinion about certain reservations to be proposed to the covenant for the league of nations in the peace treaty and also his reply. I ask leave that they be printed in the RECORD.

There being no objection, the letters were ordered to be printed in the RECORD, as follows: UNITED STATES SENATE,
COMMITTEE ON CANADIAN RELATIONS,

July 18, 1919.

Hon. CHARLES EVANS HUGHES,
     96 Broadway, New York City.

MY DEAR JUDGE HUGHES: Many of us in the Senate are in favor of having the United States enter a league of nations, provided that in doing so we do not sacrifice the sovereignty or traditional policies of our country. We believe that the proposed covenant for a league of nations in the peace treaty now before the Senate does make such a sacrifice. Rather than take the covenant as it now stands, I am very certain that considerably more than one-third of the Senate would refuse to ratify the treaty altogether. As far as I am personally concerned, I do not want to see this happen, and I do want to see some plan devised whereby the United States may safely enter the league of nations. It has seemed to some of us that this result could best be accomplished by attaching certain reservations to the proposed covenant which would limit the participation by the United States in the league. I shall be very glad if you will give me your opinion as to the validity of such reservations, and also as to what reservations, in your judgment, should be made to safeguard the interests of our country.

Sincerely, yours,   FREDERICK HALE.

NEW YORK, *July 24, 1919.*

Hon. FREDERICK HALE,
     United States Senate, Washington, D. C.

MY DEAR SENATOR HALE: I am in receipt of your letter of July 18, and it gives me pleasure to comply with your request for my opinion with respect to the validity and advisability of reservations on the part of the United States in entering the proposed league of nations.

Permit me to state at the outset the point of view from which I think the questions should be approached. There is plain need for a league of nations, in order to provide for the adequate development of international law, for creating and maintaining organs of international justice and the machinery of conciliation and conference, and for giving effect to measures of international cooperation which from time to time may be agreed upon. There is also the immediate exigency to be considered. It is manifest that every reasonable effort should be made to establish peace as promptly as possible and to bring about a condition in which Europe can resume its normal industrial activity.

I perceive no reason why these objects can not be attained without sacrificing the essential interests of the United States. There is a middle ground between aloofness and injurious commitments.

I share the regret that suitable steps have not been taken for the formulation of international legal principles and to secure judicial determinations of international disputes by impartial tribunals, and that the hope of the world in the determination of disputes has been made to rest so largely upon the decision of bodies likely to be controlled by considerations of expediency. There is merit enough in the proposed plan to make it desirable to secure it, if proper safeguards can be obtained, but it is just as futile to exaggerate its value as it is to see nothing but its defects. One must take a light-hearted view of conditions in the world to assume that the proposed plan will guarantee peace or bring about a cessation of intrigue and of the rivalries of interests or prevent nations which can not protect themselves from being compelled to yield to unjust demands where for any reason great powers deem resistance inexpedient. Rather, the proposed covenant should be viewed as a mere beginning, and while it is important that we should have a beginning, it is equally important that we should not make a false start.

I think that the prudent course is to enter the proposed league with reservations of a reasonable character, adequate to our security, which should meet ready assent, and thus to establish a condition of amity at the earliest possible moment.

As to the validity of reservations, this question has two aspects—first, with respect to the action on our part which is essential to the making of reservations and, second, as to the effect of reservations upon other parties to the treaty.

As to the first question it is manifest that attempted reservations will be ineffectual unless they qualify the act of ratification. The adoption of resolutions by the Senate setting forth its views will not affect the obligations of the covenant if it is in fact ratified without reservations which constitute part of the instrument of ratification.

If the Senate should adopt reservations by a majority vote, I assume that these will be made part of the proposed resolution of assent to the treaty, and the question will then be whether the Senate will give its assent with these reservations by the requisite two-thirds vote. If the proposed reservations are reasonable, the responsibility for the defeat of the treaty, if it is defeated, will lie with those who refuse the vote essential to the assent. If the Senate gives its assent to the treaty with reservations, the concurrence of the President will still be necessary, as ratification will not be complete without his action, and the responsibility for a refusal to give the ratification with the reservations as adopted by the Senate as a part of the instrument of ratification would thus lie with the President.

Assuming that the reservations are made as a part of the instrument of ratification, the other parties to the treaty will be notified accordingly. As a contract the treaty, of course, will bind only those who consent to it. The nation making reservations as a part of the instrument of ratification is not bound further than it agrees to be bound. And if a reservation as a part of the ratification makes a material addition to or a substantial change in the proposed treaty other parties will not be bound unless they assent. It should be added that where a treaty is made on the part of a number of nations they may acquiesce in a partial ratification on the part of one or more.

But where there is simply a statement of the interpretation placed by the ratifying State upon ambiguous clauses in the treaty, whether or not the statement is called a reservation, the case is really not one of amendment, and acquiescence of the other parties to the treaty may readily be inferred unless express objection is made after notice has been received of the ratification with the interpretative statement forming a part of it.

Statements to safeguard our interest which clarify ambiguous clauses in the covenant by setting forth our interpretation of them, and especially when the interpretation is one which is urged by the advocates of the covenant to induce support, can meet with no reasonable objection. It is not to be supposed that such interpretations will be opposed by other parties to the treaty, and they will tend to avoid disputes in the future. Nor should we assume that a reservation would lead to the failure of the treaty or compel a resumption of the peace conference when the reservation leaves unimpaired the main provisions of the covenant looking to the peaceful settlement of disputes and the organization of conferences, and simply seeks to avoid any apparent assumption of an obligation on our part to join in a war at some indefinite time in the future for a cause the merits of which can not now be foreseen, as it is evident that in such case we must inevitably await the future action of Congress in accordance with what may then be the demand of the conscience of the Nation. In contemplating this experimental, albeit hopeful, enterprise, our security and good faith are primary considerations. Those, either here or abroad, who would oppose such reasonable interpretations or reservations on our part would take a heavy responsibility.

The question is then what specifically should the reservations be:

First. With respect to the right of withdrawal (Article I). It is reasonable to provide that a member withdrawing from the league should not be released from a debt or liability previously incurred. But it should not be possible that through a claim of the nonperformance of an obligation a member desiring to withdraw should be kept in the league, perhaps indefinitely. I understand that different interpretations have been put upon the clause in question, and I think that there should be a clarifying statement as a part of the ratification.

Second. The clause relating to domestic matters, such as immigration or tariff laws is ambiguous (Article XV), as it provides for a finding by the council whether the question is one solely within the domestic jurisdiction. There should be a clear statement of our understanding that such matters, where no international engagement has been made with respect thereto, are not submitted for the consideration of action of the league or any of its agencies.

Third. It is urged by the advocates of the covenant that article 21 recognizes and preserves the Monroe doctrine. But the descriptive phrase employed in the article is inaccurate, and the meaning of the article is far from clear. There should be an interpretative statement which will remove all doubt that the traditional policy of the United States as to purely American questions is still maintained. I fully indorse Mr. Root's proposed statement of reservation and understanding upon this point, but in the view that an alternative form of statement may be helpful, I submit one below.

Fourth. I agree with Mr. Root that it would be desirable to eliminate article 10, with its guaranty to "preserve against external aggression the territorial integrity" of all members of the league. My views as to this article were stated in the inclosed address before the Union League Club (Mar. 26, 1919), and I need not repeat them at length. I still think that article 10 is a trouble breeder and not a peacemaker.

If we are entering upon a new world order of democracies, the inevitable consequences should be recognized. Democracies can not promise war after the manner of monarchs. It is idle to attempt to commit free peoples to the making of war in an unknown contingency when such a war may be found to be clearly opposed to the dictates of justice. The limitation with respect to "external aggression" is important, but does not meet the difficulty. As the most earnest supporters of the article admit, it may be invoked against a power which has performed all its obligations under the other provisions of the covenant and be the victor "in a war 'legal' under articles 12, 13, and 15."

While the importance of article 10 is strongly emphasized by its supporters, it is said at the same time that the fulfillment of the engagement would be only according to the plan advised by the council of the league, and as this must be a plan upon which the members of the council unanimously agree we could veto any proposal calling for an intervention in what we deemed to be an unsuitable case. Again, it is freely recognized that war can only be declared by Congress.

Article 10 is objectionable because it is an illusory engagement. Whether we shall go to war to preserve the territorial integrity of another State in a situation not now disclosed or described so that the merits of the case may be judged will depend upon the action of Congress, and that action will be taken according to the conviction of our people as to our duty in the light of the demands of justice as they appear when the exigency arises. The general guaranty of article 10 can not be relied upon to produce action contrary to its judgment. We should not enter into a guaranty which would expose us to the charge of bad faith or of having defaulted in our obligation, notwithstanding that Congress in refusing to make war had acted in accordance with its conception of duty in the circumstances disclosed.

Of course a limitation of the operation of article 10 to a period of years would be preferable to the indefinite obligation proposed. But in my judgment it would be better that if article 10 is not eliminated a reservation and interpretative statement should be adopted which would adequately recognize the limitations I have mentioned. Further, it is possible that such a reservation and interpretative statement, while sufficient for our protection, would make acquiescence easier than if the elimination of the article were required. I append the form of such a statement for your consideration.

The resolution embodying the reservations and interpretations thus suggested might be in some such form as the following:

"The Senate of the United States of America advises and consents to the ratification of said treaty with the following reservations and understandings as to its interpretation and effect to be made a part of the instrument of ratification:

"First. That whenever two years' notice of withdrawal from the league of nations shall have been given, as provided in article 1 of the covenant, the power giving the notice shall cease to be a member of the league, or subject to the obligations of the covenant of the league, at the time specified in the notice, notwithstanding any claim, charge, or finding of the nonfulfillment of any international obligation or of any obligation under said covenant: *Provided, however,* That such withdrawal shall not release the power from any debt or liability theretofore incurred.

"Second. That questions relating to immigration, or the imposition of duties on imports, where such questions do not arise out of any international engagement, are questions of domestic policy, and these and any other questions which, according to international law, are solely within the domestic jurisdiction are not to be submitted for the consideration or action of the league of nations or of any of its agencies.

"Third. That the meaning of article 21 of the covenant of the league of nations is that the United States of America does not relinquish its traditional attitude toward purely American questions, and is not required by said covenant to submit its policies regarding questions which it deems to be purely American questions to the league of nations or any of its agencies, and that the United States of America may oppose and prevent any acquisition by any non-American power by conquest, purchase, or in any other manner of any territory, possession, or control in the Western Hemisphere.

"Fourth. That the meaning of article 10 of the covenant of the league of nations is that the members of the league are not under any obligation to act in pursuance of said article except as they may decide to act upon the advice of the council of the league. The United States of America assumes no obligation under said article to undertake any military expedition or to employ its armed forces on land or sea unless such action is authorized by the Congress of the United States of America, which has exclusive authority to declare war or to determine for the United States of America whether there is any obligation on its part under said article and the means of action by which any such obligation shall be fulfilled."

With high regard, I am,

Very sincerely, yours,   CHARLES E. HUGHES.

Tearsheet from *Cong. Record*, 66th Cong., 1st sess., pp. 3511-12.

From Joseph Patrick Tumulty, with Enclosures

Dear Governor: The White House 28 August 1919.

I hope you can act upon this suggestion of Mr. Hines. If you decide that a proclamation is wise, I think you ought to warn the country against Bolshevist propaganda.

I am calling your attention to Mr. Poole's statement[1] which contains facts that would be of great value to the country.

I think a point that might be emphasized is very clearly expressed in the following editorial from the New York World:

"The question before them (railroad shopmen) is whether they will help to cure a most serious situation or whether they will employ the brute power of organization to make it immeasurably worse. They can strike if they are so determined. They can tie up the vast transportation systems of the country, cause great suffering, enormous financial losses and even destroy human life. But they are bound to share in all the misery they create. Neither they nor their families can escape.

"The railroad employees have recently petitioned Congress to allow them to take over the management of the railroads. Before there can be any serious discussion of the Plumb plan, or any plan to give the railroad employees a voice in the management of the properties, they must prove that they are fit for management and can be intrusted with power. The test of their responsibility has come in the issue that the President has decided. If they deliberately elect to take the country by the throat and try to choke it into submission, they may be able to inflict immense damage but they will have completely destroyed themselves as organizations that merit either the confidence or the friendly consideration of the American people."[2]

Sincerely yours,   Tumulty

[1] See the Enclosure printed with WW to RL, Aug. 21, 1919.
[2] "A TEST OF LABOR," New York *World*, Aug. 27, 1919.

E N C L O S U R E   I

Joseph Patrick Tumulty to Walker Downer Hines

My dear Mr. Hines: The White House 27 August, 1919

I think that now that the question of an increase for shopmen is again up for submission, we ought to follow up our statement of Monday by another, particularly addressed to the shopmen themselves, along these lines:

(As a preface, appreciation might well be expressed of the action of their officers and executive committee in resubmitting the matter of a strike to a vote of the people, following the President's statements the other day)

"When the Government is taking unusual and vigorous measures to reduce the cost of living, it is not the time for organized labor or any portion of organized labor to stay the Government's hand and to insist upon increased wages, which inevitably will go into the costs and be multiplied time and again in the prices to be paid by the consumer. This is a critical time not only in the affairs of the world but in the affairs of our own country. Your Government asks for time to make its campaign against the cost of living effective. I am confident that the fighting spirit and united effort which made it possible for the American people to rise as a unit to make successful war upon German tyranny are not dead but only sleeping. Only by cooperation between all phases of our life,—labor, management and capital,—can we work out the difficult problems which press for solution. We shall not make progress by arraying conflicting interests in battle against each other at home. The line of progress is the line of cooperation.

"The Government represents the whole people, and the duty of those in authority of protecting the people in every emergency is obvious. The railroads must be kept running, so that the needs of the people in our great cities and towns, which affect their very lives, may be taken care of. All interests alike would be affected by a strike of this character, and the victims of it would not be the rich, but the poor and the weak, the people who have to earn their daily bread in the sweat of their faces.

"Any attempt to enforce these demands by 'direct action' would be considered an unfriendly act against the United States of America, and in these circumstances it would be the business of the Government of the United States at all costs to protect the rights of all the people against the unfriendly aggression of any class."

Sincerely yours,   Tumulty

E N C L O S U R E   I I

Maurice Brice Clagett[1] to Joseph Patrick Tumulty

PERSONAL & CONFIDENTIAL

My dear Joe: Washington August 27, 1919.

Returning herewith your letter to Mr. Hines of today.

After consideration, he is doubtful of the advisability of getting this out in the form suggested. Probably it would be construed as a sign of weakness on his part. As far as the shopmen's immediate matter is concerned, he has said about all he could say in his address to the shopmen the other day.

The Director General thinks it advisable, however, and that it would prove very helpful, if the President could get out a Labor

Day message or proclamation which would apply equally to everyone. Following out the practice in connection with the Thanks Giving Day Proclamation, such a statement or proclamation could be gotten out in advance of Labor Day, say tomorrow, and this would be very helpful in connection with the vote now being taken by the shopmen.

Mr. Hines' suggestions for such a proclamation are that, first the President review the splendid services performed by labor generally during the war, their patriotic attitude, and the reliance placed upon them during the war by the Government.

The President could then refer to the present situation growing out of readjustments after the war, could stress the difficulties of the problem, and point out how important it is that America pass successfully through the present period.

He could then make a general appeal for sanity, for true Americanism, and for the most careful consideration of the present day problems facing America.

If the President were to issue such a statement or proclamation, Mr. Hines thinks it would be most helpful. If the President decides not to do so, the Director General himself will consider making a Labor Day statement and getting it out soon.

Sincerely yours,   Brice Clagett

TLS (WP, DLC).
[1] Assistant to the Director General of Railroads.

From Newton Diehl Baker

Information

My dear Mr. President: Washington. August 28, 1919.

I have taken the liberty of placing the memorandum[1] which Mr. Sayre left with you the other day about conditions at the Leavenworth Disciplinary Barracks in the hands of General Crowder,[2] whom I have just sent to Leavenworth to make a thoroughgoing inspection for me. General Crowder is personally responsible for the changed character of our military prisons. Some eight years ago, on his recommendation, they were transformed from old-fashioned, hard-and-fast military jails to disciplinary institutions, with a modern attitude toward the inmates, and honorable restoration to the Service as the object of their discipline. I have explained very fully to General Crowder that I do not want the recent disorders at Leavenworth[3] to be the occasion for a reversion to the old type of prison, but as rapidly as possible desire the restoration of the modern, human point of view. On General Crowder's return, I shall make the necessary orders to restore what we have lost by the congestion and consequent disorders which the war brought about.

Mr. Sayre's correspondent, I think, quite frankly fails to grasp the limitations even upon a modern penal institution. Portions of the letter, which I assume Mr. Sayre did not read to you, criticize the management for not supplying to the table of the prisoners "spring broilers, dairy products and more frequent allowance of fresh eggs, since all of these are products of the farm." It would not, I think, be proper to use the products of the farm in this way. The prison fare should be adequate, appetizing, but simple, and the fancy market products produced on the farm should be sold to relieve the Government in some part of the custodial expense which the misconduct of the inmates has imposed on the Government. The other portions of the letter, however, are very serious, and it is to those that I have particularly addressed General Crowder's attention.   Respectfully yours,   Newton D. Baker

TLS (WP, DLC).
  [1] Not found.
  [2] Maj. Gen. Enoch Herbert Crowder, the Judge Advocate General.
  [3] There had been two serious incidents at the disciplinary barracks at Fort Leavenworth, Kan., within the last seven months. Following minor scuffles between inmates, January 25-28, most of the more than 2,000 prisoners there refused to go to work on January 30 and 31. A committee of inmates informed the prison authorities that, in view of the recent release of 113 conscientious objectors formerly detained there, the remaining prisoners wished to know what was to become of them now that the war was over. Many of them had received sentences ranging from fifteen to thirty years' imprisonment for various infractions of military law, and they wished to know whether they would have to spend the rest of their lives in prison for these wartime offenses. The strike soon ended, and the War Department formed a committee of officers to review all court-martial cases. This committee set free some of the prisoners and reduced the sentences of many others. Winthrop D. Lane, "The Strike at Fort Leavenworth," *The Survey*, XLI (Feb. 15, 1919), 687-96; *New York Times*, July 23, 1919.
  A second "strike," that is, refusal to do work of any kind, involving most of the 2,272 prisoners then in the disciplinary barracks began on July 22. This time the strikers demanded to be set free by a general amnesty. The strike was over by July 27, and prison authorities announced that the inmates would go back to work shortly. Baker, on July 25, had signed an order appointing a general court martial to be held at Fort Leavenworth to try "such persons as may be brought before it." *New York Times*, July 23, 26, and 28, 1919.

From Franklin Delano Roosevelt

CONFIDENTIAL

My dear Mr. President: Washington. August 28, 1919.

I have been looking into the matter of Admiral Sims' articles which are about to appear in The World's Work[1] and I have finally had a conference with the Admiral himself. I find that Admiral Sims made an official application to the Secretary for permission to write this book. Mr. Daniels wrote a personal letter to the Admiral giving his cordial endorsement and followed this up by an official approval of the plan.

The first article has been actually printed[2] and sent out for distribution on the news-stands within a day or two.

After my talk with the Admiral, I feel certain that his articles will not contain anything except a popular description of the Navy's part in the war in European Waters—and Mr. Daniels was apparently entirely satisfied

Faithfully yours,   Franklin D Roosevelt

TLS (WP, DLC).
 [1] See WW to FDR, Aug. 22, 1919, n. 1.
 [2] William Sowden Sims, "THE VICTORY AT SEA. I. WHEN GERMANY WAS WINNING THE WAR," *The World's Work*, XXXVIII (Sept. 1919), 488-511.

From Sir Maurice Hankey

Dear Mr. President,   [London] 28 August 1919

I write to thank you most warmly for your photograph and for the very kind inscription which you wrote beneath it. This will remain for me a valued memento of the most interesting episode in my life.

May I take this opportunity of thanking you for your unvarying kindness, encouragement, and confidence towards me in Paris.

We here are watching your campaign for the Peace Treaty with the greatest interest and sympathy.

Yours very sincerely   M. P. A. Hankey

ALS (WP, DLC).

Maurice Brice Clagett to Rudolph Forster, with Enclosures

My dear Mr. Forster: Washington August 28, 1919.

In accordance with our promise, I enclose herewith a copy of the statement issued tonight by the Director General, which was approved tonight by the President. I also enclose a copy of the letter to the President signed by Mr. Hines which the President marked "Approved—Woodrow Wilson."

Very sincerely yours,   Brice Clagett

TLS (WP, DLC).

E N C L O S U R E   I

From Walker Downer Hines

Dear Mr. President: Washington August 28, 1919.

The strike in California, Arizona and Nevada has stopped almost all trains on the Southern Pacific, the Santa Fe and the Salt Lake Railroads. The State of California especially is virtually cut off from the rest of the country. Train loads of passengers have been marooned for two or three days at places in the desert and are still there.

I attach a statement which, after consulting with my associates and with my representatives on the Pacific Coast, I am satisfied ought to be issued immediately. The Brotherhood Chiefs agree that the step is proper and propose to support the Government. They have made and are making strenuous efforts to control their men but the strike, which was unauthorized, spread like wildfire, and so far they have not been able to control the situation. I believe that by sending this message immediately the situation can be speedily controlled.

I have consulted with the Department of Justice and it is in full accord with the position indicated and has already given the necessary instructions to the District Attorneys and United States Marshals.

The pressure from the people on the Pacific Coast is naturally tremendous as the suspension of service is proving almost intolerable.

There has been a question in my mind as to whether it would be more appropriate for you, instead of me, to issue a statement. The Attorney General thinks I ought to issue it and so does Mr. Tumulty. My own view is, in the light of the developments of today, that it will be sufficient for me to do so. Before taking the step, I felt I ought to give you the opportunity to consider it. However, I have not the slightest doubt that the public interest requires that the step be taken immediately.

Cordially and sincerely yours,   (Signed) Walker D. Hines

TCL (WP, DLC).

ENCLOSURE II

UNITED STATES RAILROAD ADMINISTRATION

Washington, D. C., August 28, 1919.

To Public Officers, Railroad Officers and Employes, and Citizens generally in California, Arizona and Nevada:

A strike is in progress on the part of the train and enginemen and yardmen on the steam railroads being operated by the United States Government in parts of California, Arizona and Nevada. This strike began at Los Angeles purely as a sympathetic strike on account of a controversy between the Pacific Electric Railway Company and certain employes of that company. The property of that company is not in the possession or control of the Government of the United States. The strike of the employes on the steam railroads was entered upon without any grievance being presented or alleged. The strike was and is a violation and repudiation of the agreements between the striking employes and the steam railroads upon which they worked and also of the National Agreement between the United States Railroad Administration and the Chief Executives of the organizations to which the strikers belong, such National Agreement providing for the adjustment of all causes of complaint in an orderly manner without suspension of work. The strike is also an illegal strike under the laws of the organizations to which the strikers belong and has been so characterized by the Chief Executives of those organizations.

The Chief Executives of these organizations stated that they believed they could induce their men to go back to work and urged that they be given time to enable them to do this. The Railroad Administration has given the time for this purpose. The Director General has also by publication in the newspapers of San Francisco and Los Angeles urged upon the strikers the absence of justification for their action and the importance of returning to work. Nevertheless many of the strikers have not yet returned to work and to a large extent the public service which the Government must render to the public is at a standstill. It follows that the only course which the Government can adopt is to exercise its entire power for the purpose of rendering the public service and the President has so instructed.

All striking employes who do not report for duty on and after seven o'clock on Saturday morning, August 30th, when and as called for duty, will be regarded as having terminated their employment and their places will be filled.

Anyone who interferes with or impedes the possession, use, operation or control of any railroad property, or railroad under Federal control, commits an offense against the United States, punishable by fine and imprisonment, and will be arrested and prosecuted accordingly. Anyone who obstructs or attacks persons assisting or endeavoring to assist in the possession, use, operation or control of any railroad under Federal control, will be guilty of the offense described and will be dealt with accordingly. Anyone who obstructs or retards the passage of the mail or any vehicle or person carrying the same likewise commits an offense against the United States punishable by fine, and imprisonment and will be arrested and prosecuted accordingly. Instructions have been issued to the United States District Attorneys and to the United States Marshals, to take the necessary steps to enforce these provisions of the Statutes of the United States.

The Governors of the States involved, the Mayors of the cities involved, and all other State and local peace officers are relied upon to lend assistance in the performance of the public service as above outlined in every possible manner, including giving aid in the enforcement of the statutory provisions above referred to, and also in enforcing all State statutes, municipal ordinances and other local public regulations which will aid in protecting the railroad property and its operation and in protecting those assisting or endeavoring to assist in the operation of the railroads.

Walker D. Hines,   Director General of Railroads.

Mimeographed copy (WP, DLC).

Robert Lansing to Frank Lyon Polk and John Foster Dulles

Washington, August 28, 1919.

2980 *Personal for Mr. Polk and Mr. Dulles.*[1]

Your 3416, July 31, 3 p.m.[2] and other messages relating directly or indirectly to the same subject. The policy of the Department is as follows: One. United States should not participate in the work of setting up Commissions, etc. until the Treaty is ratified by the United States. Two. There seems to be no reason why United States representatives cannot discuss with representatives of the other Powers what may be done if and when the Treaty comes into force. Three. Questions regarding the execution of the Treaty and the personnel of the various Commissions, etc., will be studied in the Department, as well as in the American Commission, in order that upon ratification of the Treaty by the United States no unnecessary delay may occur in carrying out the terms thereof. Four.

The President is planning to nominate a successor to Mr. Dulles in a few days and Mr. Dulles will be able to confer with him upon his arrival in the United States.   Lansing

TS telegram (SDR, RG 59, 763.72119/5905, DNA).
    [1] Accompanying this telegram in the State Department files is a T MS, dated August 27, 1919, and entitled "MEMORANDUM FOR THE PRESIDENT." It was a paraphrase of Lansing's telegram. In addition, Lansing suggested a number of persons to succeed Dulles in Paris. Obviously, Lansing had shown the memorandum to Wilson and obtained his approval of the telegram.
    [2] Printed as an Enclosure with WW to RL, Aug. 4, 1919 (third letter of that date).

Robert Lansing to Frank Lyon Polk

Washington August 28, 1919.

2981. Confidential. For Polk.

Your 3702,[1] 3703[2] 3769[3] and 3890.[4] I have with the President been over your telegrams in regard to Thrace and have examined the proposed boundaries on a map marked by Doctor Bowman, and while we appreciate the embarrassment you are in because of the Greek claims in eastern Thrace we are unable to justify in our own minds the acceptance of the compromise suggested.

It should be stated that the rejection of the proposal is not because of sympathy for Bulgaria, or because of lack warm friendship for Greece. We are by no means unmindful of the loyal and worthy service rendered by the Greeks and have considered sympathetically their natural desire to include within the boundary Greece all territories inhabited by those of Greek blood, but we cannot permit sentiments of friendship and regard to affect our judgement as to a settlement on which depends the stability of future peace. If the United States is to be a signatory of the treaties with Bulgaria and Turkey, and one of the guarantors of the territorial settlements declared in them, those settlements must not be based solely on the principle of reward or of the national aspirations of a brave people. They must be based primarily upon the purpose of removing causes for future wars and upon the permanent character of the settlements, because equitable and reasonable. The compromise suggested does not in our opinion meet these conditions. The separation of the territories of the international state and the separation of the Greek territories would not make for stability, or for continued peace. Of such an unnatural arrangement inviting as it would present dissatisfaction and future discord this government could not without doing violence to its sense of justice become a guarantor.

The President moved by a strong desire to meet the wishes of the Greek nation as far as is compatible with his conception of a settlement which is to be permanent in nature would agree that the west portion of western Thrace should be ceded to Greece, while the east portion of western Thrace and all of eastern Thrace should be included in the international state. The division of the territory by this arrangement would be as follows: the eastern boundary of Greece in Western Thrace would be a line running due north from the Aegean Sea through Maronia to a point just south of Chelepi. The line would from that point run westward until it touched the Greek-Bulgar boundary of 1913. The territory of the international state in west Thrace would lie east of the Greek territory and be bounded on the north by line beginning at the north east corner of the Greek territory and running eastward through Karakalissa to the Maritza River and thence northward and following the Turkish-Bulgar boundary to the Black Sea. Bulgaria should be granted a land right of way to the Aegean Sea across the territory of Western Thrace included within the international state and also the free use of the port of Dedeagatch.

The boundaries described only indicate the general plan of territorial settlement and may have to be somewhat modified.

In the opinion of the President the foregoing settlement is one which seems to possess elements of permanency that others lack. It of course denies the Greek aspiration to obtain sovereignty over the greater part of Eastern Thrace, but in view of the mixture of races in that region the grant of the sovereignty to one of the races would be to excite bitterness and hostility. Incorporated in the international state the populations would be free from national intrigues and quarrels.

It may be urged that by the proposed arrangement the territory of the international state would be greatly increased and that such increase is undesirable and contrary to the original plan for the neutralization of the city of Constantinople, the Bosphorus and the Dardanelles. In that connection it may be pointed out that unless a considerable territory is attached to the government of Constantinople its maintenance will be a constant and very considerable expense to the power or group of powers which is charged with the government. The cost of administering the government cannot but be a subject of serious consideration to the power or group which is designated to assume that responsibility. If it can be shown that the resources of the international state are sufficient to meet expenses of administration there will be less objection to assuming it than if it is a continuing liability. If the international state is not self-supporting the difficulties of obtaining consent to becoming a mandatory will be greatly increased.

You may discreetly use this latter argument in favor of the settlement suggested by the President.   Lansing.

T telegram (SDR, RG 256, 868.00/194, DNA).
  [1] FLP to RL, Aug. 15, 1919 (second telegram of that date).
  [2] See n. 2 to the telegram just cited.
  [3] FLP to RL, Aug. 19, 1919.
  [4] FLP to RL, Aug. 25, 1919.

Frank Lyon Polk to Robert Lansing

Paris August 28, 1919

3931. Very urgent. Confidential for the Secretary of State from Polk.

Tardieu told me this morning that Venizelos had told him that he was ready to accept Thracian compromise which provides for International State in West Thrace along the lines indicated in my 3702, August 15, 8 p.m. Tardieu wanted to know whether I was authorized to close the matter so we could proceed immediately with the Bulgarian treaty. I told him that in view of the fact that Venizelos had appealed to the President the matter was before the President for decision and I had no authority to act. Tardieu said and I agree with him that Venizelos fears that the President's decision may be more unfavorable than the proposed compromise.

Polk,   Ammission.

T telegram (SDR, RG 256, 868.00/194A, DNA).

To Edward Mandell House

[Washington, Aug. 28, 1919]

URGENT MESSAGE FOR COLONEL HOUSE'S INFORMATION:

Your telegram concerning Grey[1] did not reach us until your letter enclosing a copy of it was handed to me.[2] If Grey arrives with satisfactory powers on the questions you refer to, the greatest service would be rendered to the two countries. In any case, Grey will be heartily welcomed although the fact that Great Britain continues to send us special envoys instead of a permanent Ambassador is causing a great deal of unfavorable comment on this side. We should all be glad if Grey were able to remain.

I beg you to reconsider your plans. You will make a grave mistake by coming back before the Senate ratifies the Treaty. It would undoubtedly be construed as a breaking up of the American Mission and it would supply great capital. I hoped that you could return to Paris and participate in the work carried on there. You should, in any case, be in reach to cooperate with the Mission in every possible way. The situation here makes this vitally important. I expect that by the early part of October the Treaty will be ratified.

Please acknowledge receipt of note from the President.

Lansing.

TC telegram (E. M. House Papers, CtY).
   [1] EMH to WW, Aug. 8, 1919. The only copy of this telegram now in WP, DLC, is in code and was received on Aug. 10, 1919.
   [2] EMH to WW, Aug. 11, 1919.

To Bernard Mannes Baruch

My dear Baruch: The White House 29 August, 1919.

I hate to see you resign from anything that would bring us into constant contact and consultation, but of course I dare say it is inevitable that the Advisory Commission of the Council of National Defence should now be disbanded.[1]

I subscribe to all that you say about the Council, and I hope some day I shall have an adequate opportunity to express the admiration I have had for the work of the Advisory Commission.

In haste,

Cordially and faithfully yours,   Woodrow Wilson

TLS (B. M. Baruch Papers, NjP).
   [1] Wilson was replying to B. M. Baruch to WW, Aug. 28, 1919, TLS (WP, DLC). Baruch submitted his resignation as a member of the Advisory Commission of the Council of National Defense.

To Charles Howard Shinn

My dear Shinn: [The White House] 29 August, 1919.

Thank you for your letter of August 22nd. Of course I shall try to see you when I am in San Francisco. It is impossible for me to foresee how I shall be handled there, but I am going to beg that you will not hesitate to invade my hotel and demand to see me. We shall be there on the 17th and 18th of September, and I shall look forward with genuine pleasure to seeing my old classmate.

Cordially and faithfully yours,   Woodrow Wilson

TLS (Letterpress Books, WP, DLC).

To Alexander Mitchell Palmer, with Enclosures

My dear Palmer: The White House 29 August, 1919.

I wish you would read this letter and memorandum. Quite aside from any exaggerated feelings in the matter, I believe that Spargo is right and that our action ought to be promptly formulated and taken. Won't you advise me in the matter?

Cordially and sincerely yours,   Woodrow Wilson

TLS (A. M. Palmer Papers, DLC).

E N C L O S U R E   I

From John Spargo

Old Bennington   Vermont

Dear Mr. President: August 25th., 1919

I need not, I hope, assure you that I have no desire to add to your very great burden, nor any other desire than to be of whatever service a humble private citizen may. Certainly, I would not be a nagging, censorious critic.

In begging you to give a few minutes to the reading of the accompanying Memorandum, you will permit me to say, with the utmost possible kindness, that it is becoming increasingly difficult for me, and for a great many of my friends, to refrain from joining in some movement of protest against certain lamentable things which you have the power to end. We are being driven by the irresistible compulsion of conscience into a position of opposition to you at the very time we would gladly be upholding and helping you.

I believe, fully and unreservedly, that you are as truly opposed to anything that savors of injustice and oppression as I or any man living. I believe, fully and unreservedly, that you want to be truly democratic, generous as well as just, and that many of the excessively severe sentences imposed upon men and women who could not make the mental and moral adjustments which the war made necessary have given you genuine pain. Had I never had the privilege of meeting you face to face and feeling the sincerity of your devotion to the ideals of freedom you have so well and so nobly expressed, doubt might have been possible.

It remains to be said that, owing perhaps to the multitude of grave and perplexing problems which have been imposed upon you, you have disappointed every Liberal that I know, just as you have disappointed me. The more they have championed you and tried to sustain and uphold you, the more disappointed are they. Personally, I have eagerly scanned the New York paper every morning since your return, expecting to read that you have proclaimed a general amnesty covering the cases of those who have been sentenced to long terms of imprisonment because of the expression of anti-war views.

I do not want to rush into print with any expression of my feeling. Nor do I want to add one iota to the already too great volume of dissent. But I do beg you to give serious consideration to this very important matter and to permit me in friendship to urge you to act and to act quickly.

If you could find the time for it and cared for me to do it, I should be very glad indeed of the privilege of a personal interview to set before you facts which seem to me to make this a matter of grave national urgency. In any case, I trust you will read the accompanying Memorandum and consider it as the friendly suggestion of a fellow citizen who wishes you only well and who, in availing himself of the high privilege of addressing you thus frankly, desires to aid in bringing about the triumph of your ideals over those who are assailing you.

With assurances of my profound respect,

Very sincerely yours,   John Spargo.

TLS (JDR, RG 60, Straight Numerical Files, File No. 197009-1-3, DNA).

E N C L O S U R E   I I

Memorandum for the President's Consideration

SUBJECT: Relation of continued punishment of war offenders to Bolshevism and other forms of Social Unrest

THEME: The well-being of the nation, political expediency, the imperative need of checking the rising tide of discontent which manifests itself in Bolshevism and other dangerous forms of social unrest, here and throughout the world, all point to the need of immediate action by the President and the proclamation, without a day's delay, of a general amnesty covering all those cases of conviction and sentence for seditious utterances and other offenses against the laws relating to sedition and espionage which are not included in the following paragraph.

EXCEPTIONS: Persons actually guilty of crimes involving destruction of life and property; persons guilty of actual communication of military information to the enemy, or attempts to do so; persons actually in the employ of enemy governments. These several groups should be sharply distinguished from the very large class of persons convicted for uttering opinions and statements in opposition to the war, to conscription, to military service, to our government or to our Allies.

The individuals in each of the several groups thus exempted may or may not be deserving of Executive clemency. Each case should be dealt with upon its own merits, due regard being had to the human factor, the immense moral strain imposed upon the individual of German or Austro-Hungarian extraction.

There is no reason for considering individuals in the large class of cases covered by the first paragraph. Justice, Democracy, Humanity and Political Expediency alike require immediate amnesty for the entire class.

ARGUMENT: In support of this contention two sets of reasons are respectfully submitted. These reasons are roughly designated "General" and "Particular," for the sake of convenience.

REASONS: *I General.* (a) Many of the sentences imposed during the war for the utterance of opinions and sentiments which were regarded as disloyal were indefensibly savage and could only have been the result of mass hysteria. The sentences imposed upon Mr. Debs, Mrs. O'Hare, Mrs. Rose Pastor Stokes and the Chicago Socialists, Germer, St. John Tucker, Engdahl,[1] et al, are cases in point. So far as the writer is able to discover, even Germany did not impose such brutal sentences for similar offenses.

A comparison of the sentence imposed upon Mr. Debs with that imposed by Germany upon Karl Liebknecht[2] for an offense of vastly greater gravity shows that there was greater liberality and justice in the German treatment than in our own.

(b) If we take the view that the severity of the sentences in many cases was justified by the exceptional circumstances, it seems clear that with the war ended the only attitude worthy a great democracy is a generous tolerance. There is no reason for continuing any one of these sentences. In this connection it should be pointed out that even under the Czars it was a time honored practice to

[1] Eugene Victor Debs, sentenced to ten years of imprisonment; Kate Richards (Mrs. Francis Patrick) O'Hare, five years; Rose Harriet Pastor (Mrs. James Graham Phelps) Stokes, ten years; Adolph Germer, twenty years; the Rev. Irwin St. John Tucker, twenty years; and John Louis Engdahl, twenty years.

[2] Karl Liebknecht had been sentenced by a military court (he was at that time a soldier on furlough) on June 28, 1916, to two and a half years imprisonment for inflammatory remarks made at an antiwar rally in Potsdam Square in Berlin on May 1 of that year. He had been formally charged with inciting the masses against the government, inciting the army to revolt, resisting arrest, and aiding and abetting the enemy. His defiance of another military court at an appeal hearing caused that body, on August 23, 1916, to lengthen his sentence to four years and to deprive him of his German citizenship for six years. Karl W. Meyer, *Karl Liebknecht: Man Without A Country* (Washington, 1957), pp. 97-104.

celebrate the ending of wars—whether by victory or defeat—by general amnesty to political prisoners. Surely, this great democracy can do no less.

(c) Obviously the war subjected a great many men and women of high purpose and character to a great moral strain. They were called upon to abandon ideas and ideals deeply rooted. Many were able to do this. Others were not. A wise democratic policy would take this great moral overstrain into account.

2 PARTICULAR: (a) Many thousands of Liberals and Radicals who have stoutly and proudly supported the government throughout the war, and who kept silent and refrained from protesting against excessive and brutal treatment of offenses of the kind here considered, lest they injure the national cause, fully expected the President to declare a general amnesty almost immediately after the armistice was signed. They have been grievously disappointed, with very unfortunate consequences. Their support is still needed—perhaps more than ever. It is needed to help the fight for ratification of the Peace Treaty, especially the League of Nations. It is needed as a bulwark against the mounting Bolshevist agitation.

There is no fact more obvious in our American life today than the revolt of this very important group against what they have come to regard as a reactionary and oppressive government. The overwhelming majority of Liberals and Radicals who supported the war with whom the writer is acquainted are in revolt.

(b) In every agitation against the League of Nations (outside of certain reactionary circles—the U.S. Senate, etc) the agitation derives its greatest impetus and force from the appeal against what is regarded as the government's adoption of oppressive and despotic methods. No radical is today able to argue for the League of Nations in the name of democratic idealism without being at once placed on the defensive.

(c) Great radical groups are busy preparing for an immense agitation for amnesty. They will probably have the sympathy of eighty per cent (at least) of those who were in sympathy with the President's ideals throughout the war.

(d) New radical groups and parties are forming everywhere and their strongest appeal in nearly every case is against a continuance of repressive measures now that the war has passed. Every day that Mr. Debs or Mrs. O'Hare remains in prison adds to the discontent.

(e) The demand for amnesty cannot be long resisted without very serious consequences. It would be a very great mistake to wait and later appear to have granted amnesty under pressure from Socialists, I.W.W.'S and certain familiar radical protestors. It would be far better, from every point of view, for the President to take this step freely, of his own initiative, so forestalling a serious agitation.

If the President believes that it would be easier for him to act and make a public pronouncement in response to the request of a group of well-known, influential men, distinguished for their patriotism, rather than without such a request, or rather than in response to a request from men not so wholly identified with patriotic service to the nation, the writer will very gladly arrange to have such an appeal signed and at once presented.

(f) It is the writer's earnest belief that the immediate issuance of a generous statement by the President, setting forth our duty as a nation to return to pre-war ways of freedom; recognizing the great spiritual and mental difficulties under which the minority labored, and urging tolerance and forgiveness now that the peril is past, would be a great blow to Bolshevists and near Bolshevists and would rally to his support a great and very valuable force.

In conclusion the writer begs to ask the President to consider how much evil was wrought by a lack of generous comprehension of the South at the termination of the Civil War, and how Lincoln would probably have acted, with the probable avoidance of infinite difficulties, not yet outgrown. *To breed a single hateful, vengeful thought unnecessarily in these times is dangerous.*

Respectfully submitted,   John Spargo.

T MS (JDR, RG 60, Straight Numerical Files, File No. 197009-1-3, DNA).

To John Spargo

PERSONAL

My dear Mr. Spargo: The White House 29 August, 1919.

I have nothing but thanks for your candid letter of August 25th. It concerns a matter that I have more nearly at heart, I think, than I have been able to make evident. I assure you that I am going to deal with the matter as early and in as liberal a spirit as possible.

Cordially and sincerely yours,   Woodrow Wilson

TLS (J. Spargo Coll., VtU).

To Royal Meeker

My dear Meeker: The White House 29 August, 1919.

Just a line to say that of course I am interested in what you broach to me about the stabilization of the purchasing power of the dollar,[1] but I must say that I do not think that this is the time to take up fundamental changes in the currency. I fear that the adoption of such suggestions as Professor Fisher's will at this time only excite hopes that cannot be fulfilled in time to meet the present emergency, if they can be met at all.

Cordially and sincerely yours,   Woodrow Wilson

TLS (WP, DLC).
  [1] Wilson was replying to R. Meeker to WW, Aug. 12, 1919, TLS (WP, DLC). Meeker's letter was written in reply to WW to R. Meeker, Aug. 8, 1919, which in turn was inspired by R. Meeker to WW, Aug. 5, 1919. Meeker explained in his letter of August 12 that what he meant by "the stabilization of the purchasing power of the dollar" was "a commodity price index number as our standard of values and prices in place of the present single commodity standard, gold." "I know you are familiar," he continued, "with Prof. Irving Fisher's plan for increasing the gold content of the dollar to conform with increases in the price of commodities, thereby holding the exchange ratio between the new gold standard and commodities in general [balance, equilibrium?]. . . . I think it would now be not only safe but very desirable to put into operation a scheme for stabilizing prices by adopting the multiple commodity index number as our standard of value. I think Prof. Fisher's plan of making use of our present gold standard with which our people are thoroughly familiar is the best plan thus far presented for accomplishing this desirable result. However, much careful study needs to be made of his plan, especially of the particular index to be made use of."
  Meeker added the following in conclusion: "Prof. Fisher is to be in town tomorrow and has arranged to talk over with me a plan of campaign for stabilizing the dollar. I trust that you will be able to see him and go over his plan with him in some detail." As the letter printed above implies, Wilson did not see Fisher on August 13 or on the days immediately following.

To Thomas William Lamont

My dear Lamont: [The White House] 29 August, 1919.

I think you are entirely justified in making the statement which I return with this letter,[1] and I cannot help thinking that it will be of real service. On the third page you speak of France, England, and Belgium as having ratified. France has not yet formally ratified, and England has in effect done so, but not in form. Belgium, I believe has just done so. The French vote is expected to come very soon.

May I not say that it is very generously written, particularly with regard to myself, and I hope sincerely that it will serve to clear the clouded air that has now been thrown about every great matter by misapprehensions and misrepresentations of those who have been fighting the treaty.

With sincere regards to you both,
Cordially and sincerely yours,   Woodrow Wilson

TLS (Letterpress Books, WP, DLC).
  [1] Lamont's statement is missing in WP, DLC. About the statement that he issued, see T. W. Lamont to WW, Sept. 10, 1919, n. 1.

To Thomas Nelson Page

My dear Page: The White House 29 August, 1919.

I know that I have expressed to you orally, but I am afraid I have never adequately expressed in writing, the deep regret I feel in accepting your resignation as Ambassador at Rome.[1] I have had reason to know and deeply appreciate the spirit in which you served your own country and sought to serve Italy in that post, and it has excited my genuine admiration. I have felt so thoroughly acquainted with the principles by which you were actuated that I always felt sure of the attitude you would take and of the spirit in which you would serve.

I am sure that in expressing regret at your retirement from the public service, I am expressing the general sentiment of all who have had the benefit of knowing you and the work you have done, and I wish in this simple way to render you this tribute as a friend and as the official head of the Government.

Cordially and sincerely yours,   Woodrow Wilson

TLS (T. N. Page Papers, NcD).
[1] Wilson was replying to TNP to WW, July 19, 1919, Vol. 61.

To the Secretary of Local 78[1]

My dear Sir: [The White House] 29 August, 1919.

May I not express to you, and through you to your fellow-members of Local 78, my admiration of the public-spirited action they have taken, an action which I am sure is in the interest of the whole country as setting an example of patriotic cooperation in relieving, not complicating, a situation which must be dealt with with as much wisdom as energy.

Cordially and sincerely yours,   Woodrow Wilson

TLS (Letterpress Books, WP, DLC).
[1] Of the Brotherhood of Painters, Decorators, and Paper Hangers of Hoboken, N. J. At a meeting held on August 26, Amiel Ratelier, the president of the local, had urged the members to stand behind Wilson's request that unions not ask for higher wages by voting against a proposed demand that their daily wage be increased from $6.50 to $8. One hundred twenty-five of the 155 members present voted against the contemplated wage demand. "UNION WITH WILSON; ENDS WAGE DEMAND," *New York Times*, Aug. 27, 1919, clipping (WP, DLC).

To the Right Reverend Alfred Harding[1]

My dear Bishop Harding: [The White House] 29 August, 1919.

I owe you a humble apology for not having replied sooner to your letter of July 16th about the Thanksgiving celebration in the autumn.[2] The truth of the matter is that your letter got misplaced under a pile of papers and has only just now come to the surface again. I hope that you will forgive a busy man for allowing his papers to get mixed up.

I need not tell you that the idea you suggest seems to me an admirable one; neither need I explain to you, I am sure, why I fear to make any promises with regard to a personal participation in the exercises you are looking forward to and planning. I have found so often that it was imprudent to promise anything outside the beaten path of my official duties that I would be indeed indiscreet if I did not act upon that experience.

I shall hope, nevertheless, my dear Bishop, at least to be present and to share in the enjoyment of the benefits which I am sure will come from the occasion.

Cordially and sincerely yours,   Woodrow Wilson

TLS (Letterpress Books, WP, DLC).
  [1] Protestant Episcopal Bishop of Washington.
  [2] Harding's letter is missing in WP, DLC.

From Newton Diehl Baker

Confidential.

My dear Mr. President: [Washington] August 29, 1919.

I return herewith the papers in the case of Colonel _____.[1] You have the power to direct that he be reprimanded, but you have no power to direct any demotion of numbers or loss of rank. If you determine to direct a reprimand, I suggest that it be administered by the Secretary of War personally.

Upon the wisdom of such a course, I am not certain of the state of my own feelings, since I know Colonel _____ personally and have admired his soldierly bearing and his high professional attainments. I may, therefore, be leaning over backward, but when the matter was presented to me I came to the conclusion that it would not be right for me to interrupt the trial for the following reasons:

The Facts:

Colonel _____ is thirty-two years of age. He was trained at West Point, and is thoroughly familiar with the standards set by the Regular Army for the conduct of officers and gentlemen. He knows that drunkenness is under the severest condemnation, both because of its effect upon officers and its effect upon men. He knows that there is probably no subject upon which the Regular Army is as sensitive as the relations of officers with women. This grows out of the fact that officers are frequently called upon to leave their families for long periods of time, and that nothing but chivalry on the part of their brother officers in their attitude toward women can protect their families in their absence.

In spite of this, on the night in question, Colonel _____, who had been drinking but was not drunk and apparently not at all unaware of what he was doing, while seated in the smoking compartment of a Pullman car talking in French with some of his officer associates, was told by the porter that there was a French lady on board. When asked how he knew that, the porter replied that he had heard her talking in French to her husband. Colonel _____ then asked where her berth was, and found that she was occupying an upper berth opposite his own in the train, and that her husband was occupying an upper berth one or two sections removed.

After everybody in the car had retired, and the woman in question had gone to sleep, Colonel _____ crawled from his berth across the aisle into the woman's berth, without getting down into the car, aroused her and attempted in French to make an improper proposal to her. She was alarmed and became hysterical, repeatedly requesting him to leave her and finally calling her husband; whereupon Colonel _____ got back into his own berth.

The husband, the porter, the conductor, and perhaps others, came to the women's berth, and her husband was obliged to stay in her berth with her during the rest of the night, during which time she was hysterical. Neither the woman nor her husband went to sleep again, but arose early in the morning and identified Colonel _____ on the platform as he was leaving the car as the man who had been in the woman's berth.

The husband of the woman is a florist in New York who had been a soldier in France. The wife is apparently an entirely chaste woman.

The woman and her husband joined in a complaint against Colonel _____, alleging the circumstances above recited. The Inspector General was directed to investigate the matter. Thereafter, one of Colonel _____'s officer associates visited the husband and wife and induced them to write a joint postal card withdrawing the charges.

In addition to these offenses being obviously inconsistent with the conduct which military regulations require of officers and gentlemen, the facts are known to a good many officers. They are, of course, known to the employees and to some of the passengers upon the particular train upon which the incident occurred.

During the present war I have had no subject more on my mind than the character of the Army. Every resource has been appealed to to make the Army sober and decent. A very large number of officers have been dismissed for drunkenness, and a substantial number for irregular sexual relations and improper conduct with or toward women. Of these officers so dismissed, many have been young men brought into the Army by the emergency without the advantage of the training or the traditions which ought to have protected Colonel _____. There is a feeling throughout the country that the Regular Army protects itself, and has been harsh in its treatment of volunteer and emergency officers and men. I did not feel that I could justify myself if I adopted a course with regard to Colonel _____ which would relieve him of the necessity of a trial for conduct so gravely improper. Moreover, I frankly think the conduct of which he has been guilty is inconsistent with the conduct of an officer and gentleman, and I believe that the good name of the Army can only be preserved by insisting upon conduct from officers which is sober with respect to drinking and chivalrous with respect to women. If conduct of this kind were frequently condoned, self-restraint would be hard for other officers to learn and almost impossible to enforce upon enlisted men.

My own thought about the matter is that if Colonel _____ comes to trial he will probably plead guilty in order to avoid the details of his misconduct becoming a matter of record, and that I could then present the matter to you with a recommendation that you approve the sentence but commute it in view of the fine attainments and distinguished conduct of Colonel _____ in France; thus interposing your action at the place where clemency is a recognized function of the executive rather than by having you interfere with the trial itself.

I may be all wrong about this, and it may well be that your intervention having the same justification will be timely to prevent further scandalous discussion of the subject.

Respectfully yours,   [Newton D. Baker]

CCL (N. D. Baker Papers, DLC).
  [1] About which, see WW to J. E. Ransdell, Sept. 1, 1919.

Harper & Brothers to Joseph Patrick Tumulty

Dear Mr. Tumulty: New York, N. Y. August 29, 1919.

We are taking the liberty of enclosing herewith a letter from a firm of Leipzig publishers, Akademische Verlagsgesellschaft.[1] In view of the fact that this is a German translation we hesitated about acting without consulting the President.

As you probably know, we have disposed of the French translation rights to Payot,[2] and would do so under any circumstances regarding translations into other languages as the present contract with us empowers us to act in these matters.

We should, however, like definite instructions regarding this proposed German edition.[3]

Sincerely yours,   Harper & Brothers

TLS (WP, DLC).
[1] The letter is missing. The Leipzig firm wanted to publish a German translation of Wilson's *George Washington.*
[2] *George Washington, Fondateur des États-Unis (1732-1799),* trans. Georges Roth (Paris, 1927). See WW to G. Roth, April 25, 1918, Vol. 47, and G. Roth to WW, Nov. 30, 1918, Vol. 53.
[3] In response to a note from Tumulty on August 30, Wilson replied as follows: "I would be very much obliged if you would say that it would be very much against my taste to have any dealings just now with regard to my books with German publishers." WW to JPT, Sept. 1, 1919, TL (WP, DLC).

From Porter James McCumber

My dear Mr. President: [Washington] August 29, 1919.

I observe by the press that you are soon to start on a speaking tour in favor of the League of Nations. As the treaty is now before the Senate, it is most natural that all criticisms from over the country will be directed to members of the Senate and especially to those who are supporting the League. Therefore, we have exceptional opportunities to guage [gauge] the sentiment of the people and ascertain the principal objections to the treaty and I further believe that you will welcome any suggestions that might come from a supporter of this League of Nations.

The most bitter opposition comes from the Sinn Fein followers in the United States, who have been misled by false assertions and constructions which have been persistently circulated throughout the United States; (a) that Great Britain has six votes to our one in the settlement of international disputes; (b) that Great Britain has acquired millions of square miles of territory as the result of the war; (c) that we bind ourselves to come to the aid of Great Britain if Ireland, Egypt or India should rebel. You of course know the complete answers to these false assertions. The first is untrue because a dispute with a part of an Empire is a dispute with the whole and a dispute with a head of an Empire is necessarily a dispute with each part. Therefore, as you stated in our interview with you, the British Empire must be treated as a single entity under all the provisions of Article 15.

The second is equally untrue because, while Great Britain and British dependencies alone conquered the southern islands and the German possessions south of the equator, Great Britain has asked for nothing and undoubtedly would be very well pleased if the United States, or any other great nation, would accept the mandatory relation to those German colonies.

The third is equally false, as is clearly indicated by the terms of Article 10.

The next serious opposition comes from that class of people to whom the mention of Japan is as a red rag to a bull. The exchanged notes between China and Japan on May 25, 1915, is a pledge on the part of Japan that she will return the German concessions to China. Every official declaration since that date by the Japanese government has verified that purpose. If Japan enters the League of Nations she agrees that she will with scrupulous regard make good her treaty obligations and understandings, and this is a clear understanding with China. If she fails to do so after becoming a mamber [member] of the League, then she has broken her faith with the League and the League, on the complaint of China, is bound to compel her to make good her promise. If we drive Japan out of the League, and by that action make China breach her agreement with Japan, then the latter country is at liberty to hold all she has secured from Germany by right of conquest and will be unrestrained in further encroachments upon Chinese independence. The other great nations cannot assist China because they are tied by their treaties with Japan, made in the stress of combat, and we will not go to war against Japan and upon any Far Eastern question.

I make these brief arguments, Mr. President, not because you are not more thoroughly acquainted with them than I, but simply to indicate to you my own conclusions and to point out that from all the information I have received these are the main objections urged and need the greater attention.

I am enclosing you a slip which reached me in the mail this morning,[1] which will indicate to you not only the character of the weapons they are using, but the source from which they come.

                    Very sincerely yours,   P. J. McCumber

TLS (WP, DLC).
    [1] A one-page, printed leaflet headed "Women of America!" (WP, DLC). It was issued by a group with a New York address called "American Women Opposed to the League of Nations." The opening sentences give the flavor of the whole: "Do you wish your Sons and Brothers, Husbands and Sweethearts, sent to War, not to fight for Liberty, but to uphold Tyranny?—sent to suffer and die in the waterless deserts of Africa, in the feverish jungles of Asia, in the icy fields of Russia, not for America's sake, but for England and Japan and the International Money Power? Women of America! This will happen if America enters the League of Nations." It then quoted Article X of the Covenant as proof of this assertion. The leaflet concluded: "Crush this monstrous thing! ACT—ACT NOW—ORGANIZE—let the Senators in Washington know that you demand the defeat of this un-American League for War." Below this was a tear-off section to send, with one's name and address, to the organization mentioned above.

From Bert Mark Jewell, with Enclosures

Dear Mr. President: Washington, D. C. August 29, 1919.

The attached represent the position taken by the Executive Council of our Department, and committee of approximately one hundred men whom you met.

We have taken this position at the present time not because we feel we have been properly treated in the matter of wage increases, and not because we are sure that you can reduce the high cost of living, the burden of which we have been bearing all during the war, but because we do not desire to be responsible for the upheaval which we can see.

We are at a loss to understand how you can hope to maintain peace in this country when you have put into the mouth of every employer the words which will have caused him to refuse to grant any increases in pay for the time being. This will surely, in our opinion, force the workers to strike in self defense. While it may be true that these workers could be whipped into line for the time being, we fear the result and say frankly that we do not think the present policy can be pursued.

American labor must not forget its responsibility as a citizen, which it surely will do if all other classes are to be arrayed against them.

In all of your proclamations and statements, there is an absence of any specific time within which you desire to try to reduce the high cost of living. There is also an absence of any specific procedure which you expect to follow.

We are daily receiving wires from our Locals wherein they are declining almost unanimously to accept your proposition of an adjustment in wages. While we may be counted upon to do all we possibly can to avert the condition we see ahead of us, yet we cannot be expected to do the impossible.

Our members returned to work the early part of August, after being on an unauthorized strike for several days after we had exerted every persuasive power and used all the force which we could muster, and in practically every instance they wired us saying that they would agree to return to work to a date not later than September 2nd.

We are now very much in doubt as to whether or not they will remain on the job after September 2nd with the present situation.

Yours very truly,   B. M. Jewell
Act'g Pres., Ry. Employes Dept., A. F. of L.

TLS (WP, DLC).

E N C L O S U R E S

Two Letters from Bert Mark Jewell and Others to the
Officers and Members of Railroad Union Locals

Greetings: Washington, D. C., August 26, 1919.

The attached letter of the President of the United States,[1] accompanied by the proposition of the Director General[2] were delivered to your Executive Officers and National Committee in conference at the White House at 3 P.M., August 25th, and are submitted
to the membership at the urgent request of President Wilson, and
it is requested that the contents of these documents be given your
most careful consideration at a summoned or called meeting of
each craft.

Shortly after the conclusion of the conference with the President
and the Director General, another conference was held with the
Director General. In answer to a direct question, the Director General stated that the attached proposition was final and that there
would be no wage increases granted to any other class of railroad
employes, as a class, but in the event of unjust inequalities, as between individuals, adjustments involving increases to equalize
rates of pay would be made where justified, except under the conditions that are clearly stated in the fourth paragraph of the President's letter herewith attached.

Knowing the sentiment of the membership, your committee, after duly considering the proposition, advised the Director General
that they could not accept as a basis of settlement the rates established in his proposition, as submitted by the President.

Practically every class of railroad employes have now submitted
requests for very substantial increases over existing rates of pay. It
is well that our members give very serious consideration to this fact
if there is to be any additional general increase in the wages of
railroad employes, the Federated Shop Trades will receive the
same consideration. Don't fail to give this statement careful
thought and don't forget that if the Federated Shop Trades become
involved in a strike now, you are striking alone to force an increase
for the two million railroad employes.

In view of the foregoing facts, the statements contained in the
President's letter and the responsibility that must be assumed if a
suspension of work is to take place, your Executive Council has
decided that it would fail in its duty were it to authorize a strike

---

[1] A message to railway shopmen, Aug. 25, 1919.
[2] W. D. Hines to WW, Aug. 23, 1919 (revised letter), about which see W. D. Hines to
WW, Aug. 25, 1919.

until the membership has had an opportunity to decide their course of action on this proposition. It is not our intention to shirk any of our responsibilities as Executive Officers, and the wishes of a constitutional majority of the membership, expressed by their vote as hereinafter directed, will be carried out.

Until the wage question has been disposed of, there will be no action taken in connection with reaching a conclusion on the National Agreement.

Immediately on receipt of this letter each craft will hold a summoned or called meeting, appoint a committee of tellers, who will prepare and distribute blank pieces of paper upon which each member shall sign his name and number of lodge in which he holds membership. If the member votes "yes," it will indicate the acceptance of the President's proposition. If the member votes "no," it will indicate the rejection of the President's proposition and that he desires to strike.

Efforts should be made to secure the vote of members located at outside points. Only members employed by railroads are entitled to vote.

This vote shall be taken as a secret ballot, the tellers together with Secretary will tabulate the vote and wire the results by stating the number of members voting "yes" and the number voting "no," name of craft and number of local lodge. This vote to be confirmed by letter under seal of Lodge.

Pending the issuance of the official strike order (provided the members vote to strike), it is earnestly requested that every member shall remain at work.

Owing to the large number of members involved, it must be understood and agreed that the respective International organizations will not be obligated to pay regular strike benefits beyond the limits of the funds available for that purpose.

Wire vote and send letter of confirmation to John Scott, Room 507 A. F. of L. Building, Washington, D. C. *at once.*

> J. F. Anderson,
> International Association of Machinists,
> F. C. Bolam,
> International Brotherhood of Blacksmiths
> and Helpers,
> Wm. Atkinson,
> International Brotherhood of B. I. S. B. &
> H. of A.
> J. M. Burns,
> Amalgamated Sheet Metal Workers' Int.
> Association,

James P. Noonan,
International Brotherhood of Electrical
Workers,
Martin F. Ryan
Brotherhood Railway Carmen of America,
B. M. Jewell,
Act. President Railway Employes' Department,
A. F. of L.

Greetings: Washington, D. C., August 27, 1919.

The following important communication has been sent to the Chief Executive Officers of all organizations representing railroad employes by the Board of Railroad Wages and Working Conditions.

"UNITED STATES RAILROAD ADMINISTRATION
"Walker D. Hines, Director General of Railroads

"Washington, D. C. August 26, 1919.

"Mr. A. O. Wharton, Chairman, Board of Railroad Wages and Working Conditions, Washington, D. C.,

"Dear Mr. Wharton: It is desirable respecting claims now pending or to be filed before your Board, to define the functions which it is appropriate for your Board to perform, in view of the decision announced by the President yesterday with reference to the policy which the Government must pursue in regard to railroad wages as a part of the general campaign which the Government is waging to reduce the high cost of living in the interest of all wage earners as well as all other Americans.

"The position of the Government is that in view of its campaign to reduce the cost of living and of the strong prospects that substantial relief will be achieved, it is not proper now to make general increases in wages on the assumption that the present cost of living will be permanent, and that pending the efforts of the Government to bring down the cost of living the higher costs of living ought not to be accepted as a permanent basis of wage adjustment, although it is recognized that if the efforts of the Government to bring down the cost of living should fail, railroad wages should be readjusted in the light of any permanent higher living cost, which would thereby have to be recognized.

"The President has also made it clear, however, that the Railroad Administration is not precluded from giving prompt and careful consideration to any claims that may be made by the various classes of employes for readjustments believed to be proper to secure impartial treatment for all railroad employes.

"I therefore request that you take up promptly the claims which have already been presented, and those which are to be presented by any classes of railroad employes to the effect that either for their classes as a whole or for any subdivisions of these classes readjustments ought to be made in order to make sure that equal treatment is done on the basis of the general principles of wage adjustment which the Railroad Administration has already established.

"It has been our constant endeavor since the first wage adjustments were made by the Railroad Administration to deal fairly and impartially with all classes of railroad employes. The situation is so complex that absolute perfection in this regard is unattainable. Nevertheless our experience up to the present time may in all probability develop that certain relative injustices may have been unintentionally done, and it should be our purpose to promptly correct these injustices.

"The Railroad Administration has been firmly committed to the policy since last September that it cannot make wage adjustments retroactive back of a date approximating the date upon which your Board makes its reports, because otherwise there would be unending confusion and all effort to get a measure as to the cost of conducting the railroads at any given time in the past would be rendered hopeless. I therefore hope that your Board will be able to report promptly upon any inequalities which may be found to exist to the end that any correction which the Director General may find appropriate can be made effective at the earliest justifiable date in accordance with the policy of the Railroad Administration.

"In all such matters the Board will be expected to report not only a statement of facts and its conclusions upon the facts, but also its recommendations.   Sincerely, yours,   WALKER D. HINES."

In our opinion the importance of this communication warrants the placing of it in the hands of the entire membership.

It must be understood that practically every class of railroad employe has presented demands for substantial increases in wages or have notified the Administration of their intention to do so at an early date. In effect, it is our understanding that this letter is a notice to all railroad employes that there shall be no further general increases in railroad wages unless the efforts of the United States authorities prove unavailing in reducing the present high living cost.

The Federated Shop Trades represent approximately 22 per cent of the total number of railroad employes. It must be obvious that in the event living costs are not reduced, wage increases must and will be made, and if that is done it must also be obvious that the

Railroad Administration must give equal consideration to all classes of employes.

As you are well aware, President Stone of the Brotherhood of Locomotive Engineers and President Lee of the Brotherhood of Railroad Trainmen, are on record to the effect that wages must go up or living costs go down. Coupled with this fact practically 78 per cent of the railroad employes have made requests for wage increases that equal or are greater than the requests submitted by the Federated Shop Trades.

Their requests have been denied except where it can be shown that they have not been given relatively the same consideration. This means that only adjustments of inequalities will be made where it can be demonstrated that such inequalities exist.

If the Federated Shop Trades strike now, they carry the full burden of securing the same general increase for the 78 per cent of the railroad employes who have not yet decided what action they propose to take. We do not believe that we should allow ourselves to be placed in that position. In our opinion, the next 90 days will bring the entire situation to a head, and if a strike is to take place every class of railroad employes should be willing to join in the movement, share their full measure of responsibility and not leave the issue to be decided by the 22 per cent of the railroad employes represented by the Federated Trades.

The adjustment in wages that has been offered to the Federated Shop Trades, if accepted, will establish increases that are practically equivalent to the increases granted any other class of railroad employes. This must not be lost sight of in considering the situation we now face. It is conceivable that men may decide to do a thing in a manner that will lessen their chances of ultimate success, but common sense dictates that 22 per cent of the railroad employes should not undertake to fight the battle for the 78 per cent who have asked for general wage increases, and who have been denied, as we have, any further general increases, unless the effort to increase the purchasing value of the dollar by reducing living costs proves unsuccessful.

With a reasonable degree of certainty, we recognize that this letter, coupled with the recommendation we propose to make will draw criticisms from the individuals in our organizations who have not as yet indicated a desire to listen to reason or abide by any criticism not of their own making. There is not now, nor has there ever been objection to honest criticism. Such criticism is not objectionable; on the contrary, is welcome, and this comment is made for the express purpose of directing the attention of the membership to members who have by various means introduced methods of procedure which must appeal to every right-thinking union man as being detrimental to the organization that we have perfected as the result of 30 years' untiring effort and generally against every obstacle that could be invented to defeat us.

In view of the facts as above stated, your Executive Officers and National Agreement Committee recommend that the question of suspending work be left in our hands with the understanding that no strike order will be issued unless such action becomes absolutely necessary to meet the conditions arising from the present situation, or in joint action with other railroad organizations for a general wage increase.

The above recommendation is made after mature deliberation and consideration of all the elements entering into this controversy. It is our honest judgment that a fatal mistake would be made by our members to assume the responsibility of tying up the railroads at this time, when the President is evidently doing all possible to reduce the high cost of living. It is but fair to assume that the President will have the loyal support of a majority of the American public in his effort to procure this much-needed relief. We would, no doubt, be charged with obstructing his efforts.

It should be understood, however, that if the Government fails to effect a substantial reduction in the cost of living within a reasonable time we reserve the right to put the strike vote into effect.

We sincerely trust that the contents of this letter will be given the consideration that this important subject merits.

Yours, fraternally,

J. F. Anderson,	J. M. Burns,
International Association of Machinists,	Amalgamated Sheet Metal Workers' Int. Association,
F. C. Bolam,	James P. Noonan,
International Brotherhood of Blacksmiths and Helpers,	International Brotherhood of Electrical Workers,
Wm. Atkinson,	Martin F. Ryan,
International Brotherhood of B. I. S. B. & H. of A.	Brotherhood Railway Carmen of America,

B. M. Jewell,

Act. President Railway Employes' Department, A. F. of L.

Printed copies (WP, DLC).

From Edward Mandell House

London August 29, 1919

Urgent. 2914. For the President from Edward House.

The New York SUN story concerning a breach between us[1] is being generally published over here. The representatives of the

American papers have asked me for a statement and among them the New York AMERICAN. I merely want to say that I have refused to comment upon the story and anything appearing to the contrary is without foundation.   Davis.

T telegram (SDR, RG 59, 811.911/101, DNA).
[1] "WILSON-HOUSE BREAK IS NEAR," New York *Sun*, Aug. 27, 1919. The report by Laurence Hills, dated Paris, August 26, began as follows: "No open break has occurred in the relations between Col. E. M. House and President Wilson, but the two men for the first time in their long acquaintance no longer are en rapport. The Colonel virtually has ceased to function as the President's unofficial diplomatic agent in Europe." This fact, Hills contended, was becoming more obvious every day. The latest evidence of House's "complete and sudden effacement from the stage of diplomatic Europe" was the Colonel's refusal to come to Paris from London to sign the Austrian peace treaty, although he was still an official member of the American peace commission. Hills attributed House's loss of influence with the President to his alleged compromise agreement with Clemenceau and Lloyd George to postpone consideration of the League of Nations, to his role in the Italian crisis and, above all, to his advice to Wilson on the Shantung settlement.

From the Desk Diary of Robert Lansing

Friday Aug 29 [1919]

Conference with Prest. 12-12:30. Prest much incensed at press report he had broken with House. Gave me Matthews' papers on Brandeis to examine.[1]

[1] See the extract from the Lansing Desk Diary printed at Aug. 22, 1919.

From Frank Lyon Polk

Paris August 29, 1919

3946 Strictly, Confidential. No distribution
For the President and Secretary of State.
Following résumé of negotiations regarding Adriatic situation shows present situation according to our information:
Italian and Jugoslav commercial representatives have been for some time negotiating in London through Mr. Steed,[1] seeking basis of agreement in order that both might unite in appeal to Powers for favorable action on their claims to Adriatic shipping. No final agreement was reached, but notable progress toward an understanding appears to have been made. The Jugoslav representatives report that Italians agreed to renounce their claims to Assling Triangle and accept simply a guarantee of unhampered railway transit across that area. Also that both Italians and Jugoslavs favorably considered, although not definitely accepting, idea of abandoning large international state of Fiume in favor of giving to city and district of Fiume alone a status like that of Danzig but possibly with greater local power to Italians of the town, although no Italian

sovereignty. Italian claim to Idria mining region reported as having been renounced, and claims to Cherso and Zara not pressed. On other hand, Italians insistent on obtaining Lussin Islands and Lissa. Jugoslavs agreed to make commercial concessions to Italy as regards wood, Dalmatian coal, cement and other raw materials.

On returning from London to Paris the conferees talked with Smodlaka[2] of Jugoslav delegation. The progress toward agreement was considered by both sides to warrant conversations with Tittoni, and the Italian conferees agreed to arrange an informal meeting with Tittoni. The Jugoslavs report that Tittoni replied he could not consider these negotiations at the present time, and they explain his attitude by saying that Tittoni is engaged with the French and British in developing an agreement for the Adriatic solution, and does not want to consider a compromise agreement which might give Italy less than he can secure through some other arrangement.

The French are very anxious for a speedy solution of the Adriatic problem, even if necessary to concede much to Italy. Two weeks ago Tardieu urged the importance of a speedy settlement and arranged a meeting at which Scialoja[3] presented a proposition which was almost identical with that presented by Tittoni and rejected by Mr. White some weeks ago.[4] Tardieu's anxiety to get a solution by compromising with the Italians was made very manifest at this meeting. Shortly after Clemenceau urged the necessity of a settlement and told me that he would even be willing to give Fiume to the Italians if necessary. The anxiety of the French is variously attributed to a natural desire to reduce the anti-French sentiment now strong throughout Italy, and to the fear that Italy may not ratify the German treaty until she gets some of her claims in the Adriatic satisfied. Tittoni and Clemenceau are now preparing a telegram to be sent to the President proposing some solution of Italy's claims. On the other hand, Marconi told me that Italy would have to accept any line which America insisted upon and would sign the treaty; but he urged me to keep in mind Italy's needs when reaching our final conclusions. The Jugoslavs are apprehensive over the French-Italian negotiations, and urge that America stand firm, saying that we alone can protect them from a compromise which would inflict great wrong upon them and prove a source of irritation and danger in the future.[5]   Polk.

T telegram (SDR, RG 256, 186.3411/765A, DNA).

[1] Steed had for several months been working with the Italians and Yugoslavs to reconcile their differences. See Ivo J. Lederer, *Yugoslavia at the Paris Peace Conference: A Study in Frontiermaking* (New Haven, 1963), *passim.*

[2] Josip Smodlaka, a member of the Yugoslav delegation.

[3] Vittorio Scialoja, a member of the Italian delegation.

[4] About which, see H. White to WW, July 19, 1919, Vol. 61.

⁵ A draft of this telegram by Douglas Wilson Johnson is filed with the one just printed: T MS (SDR, RG 256, 186.3411/765, DNA).

To Edward Mandell House

The White House, [Aug. 29, 1919]

For Col. House, Care American Embassy, London.

Am deeply distressed by malicious story about break between us and thank you for your message about it. The best way to treat it is with silent contempt.   Wilson.¹

WWT MS (SDR, RG 59, 811.911/101½, DNA).
¹ Wilson's message was conveyed to House in RL to Amembassy London, No. 5896, Aug. 29, 1919, T telegram (SDR, RG 59, 811.911/101a, DNA). The copy received by House, dated August 30, 1919, is in the E. M. House Papers, CtY.

Charles Warren Fowle¹ to Joseph Patrick Tumulty, with Enclosure

My dear Mr. Tumulty: New York August 29, 1919.

As you know, President Wilson has asked Mr. Cleveland H. Dodge of our Committee to keep him advised regarding information which may reach him or us bearing on the extremely serious situation in Armenia and the Southern Caucasus, and to make any suggestions which might prove helpful in dealing with this extremely difficult and complicated question. Mr. Dodge is absent from New York on a brief vacation, but we feel that he would like to have us transmit through you to the President attached copy of a cablegram which reached his office today through the Department of State. The President will doubtless remember that Dr. Barton and Dr. Peet,² who send this message to Mr. Dodge, are members of our Commission which went out last January to investigate conditions in the Near East and lay the foundations for our relief work, Dr. Barton being Chairman of the Commission as well as Chairman of our Commitee. Both these gentlemen have resided in Turkey for a great many years, and are thoroughly familiar with many phases of the problems of the Near East, and can therefore speak with considerable authority.

It is apparent to various members of our Committee that a systematic effort is being made to place the United States in a position of responsibility for any untoward events which may occur in the Armenia region, and we feel that it is only right to suggest that in case the British troops are withdrawn, it should be clearly understood throughout our country, as well as abroad, that the United

States has not as yet assumed responsibility for the safety and welfare of any portion of that region, and in case massacres or destruction of life and property should occur, the responsibility therefore
must be laid upon the shoulders of the Council in Paris whose duty
it is, before the whole World, to provide for the safety of defenseless
peoples whose fate has not yet been determined by the Peace Conference. Any attempt, on the part of Great Britain or other powers,
to lay at America's door the burden of guilt, in case terrible events
do occur, can be far better refuted if this responsibility of the Council in Paris is made clear both to our people and to the leading Governments abroad. Our purpose is not to shirk or shift responsibility,
but to have people understand where it properly and unquestionably lies.

We appreciate the extreme difficulties, if not absolute impossibility, of the United States undertaking the military occupation of
any portion of that region before its ultimate status is determined
by the Peace Conference, and we should be called upon only to
take our share rather than the whole of any such responsibility.

We would deeply appreciate any information which the President wishes to convey to us in this connection or any suggestions
which you care to make, which may help us to a more intelligent
and effective handling of our part of this problem. Naturally our
Committee and our thousands of supporters throughout the country are much concerned at the threatening disaster to our work in
that region, and to several hundred thousand helpless people
whom we are endeavoring to save from starvation, and bring back
to some hope of normal living.

Very respectfully,   Charles W. Fowle

TLS (WP, DLC).
    [1] Foreign Secretary of the American Committee for Armenian and Syrian Relief.
    [2] Rev. Dr. James Levi Barton, Foreign Secretary of the American Board of Commis-
sioners for Foreign Missions and chairman of the American Committee for Armenian
and Syrian Relief; and William Wheelock Peet, treasurer and business manager of the
American Board of Commissioners for Foreign Missions in Turkey.

E N C L O S U R E

Paraphrase of confidential message sent Mr. Dodge by Barton and
Peet, telegraphed from Constantinople on the 23rd inst.

"The following communication to Cleveland Dodge is sent by
Barton and Peet.

Our Caucasus tour has just been finished and to our horror and
surprise we have found that the forces of Great Britain which have
up to the present time been doing police duty in the Caucasus re-

gion are actually in process of evacuation. Some posts important in character have already been evacuated and soon they will evacuate all of them.

The Turks and Tartars are combining their efforts to destroy the remnant of the Armenians in the Caucasus who are thus in a state of being surrounded by their enemies who are determined to destroy them. Even while the British troops were occupying the country, atrocities have recently been committed, and this shows what will take place after the foreign forces which have restrained the Tartars and Turks, shall withdraw. The Turks are on the Western and the Tartars on the Eastern front, and the Armenian Army which is small and badly equipped is totally unable to resist them. The Turks and Tartars are combining with the evident purpose of totally destroying all the Christian population in the southern Caucasus region. Unless the powers shall take steps which are radical in character and take them at once, when the foreign troops withdraw from the Caucasus a massacre of Christians will take place surpassing the atrocities previously committed by the Turks in horror and extent. Intervention has been refused by Italy and France, and so far no response has been received by Colonel Haskell[1] to an appeal made by him to the Paris Conference. Colonel Haskell and many other Americans who are acquainted with Caucasus affairs, and we, ourselves, entertain the opinion that the only hope of saving these Christians is based upon action by the United States. We think that only the President is able to prevent hostilities from breaking out which will certainly become widespread and thus save the world from being startled by a new horror.

Unless a military force is sent to back them, nothing can be accomplished, either by General Harbord or by Colonel Haskell. Adequate equipment should be furnished the small Armenian Army and the United States should immediately send troops.

It is the opinion of Colonel Haskell, with which we agree, that the Armenian Army should receive five million rounds of ammunition for the United States rifles, ten thousand rifles, one hundred machine guns and ammunition, also ammunition for their Russian rifles to the extent of five million rounds, which latter should be delivered by the British authorities at Ericic (Erivan) before they leave the country.

Thirty thousand units of clothing and equipment, followed by blankets, overcoats etc. should be at once sent to the Armenians.

Within a month the forces of the United States should be on the ground and an announcement should be made with[in] a week that they are coming. Their number should be as follows: One batallion field artillery with shrapnel and gas shells, one machine gun battalion, one reinforced brigade consisting of two regiments of infantry, one company of signal field troops, one squadron of reconnaissance planes, and the whole complete with transports, supplies, etc.

It is the opinion of Colonel Haskell that these men should be immediately sent from France. Volunteers, if necessary, can replace them at a later date. Order would be assured if these men were now here or even if their coming and progress were officially announced. Persuasion should be used with the British Government to induce them to cease moving their troops out from the areas which are threatened until the above suggestions are carried out.

If the outbreak takes place it will be dangerous to seventy American[s] engaged in relief work, more than twenty thousand orphan Armenians, not omitting to mention three hundred thousand refugees. If the outbreak takes place it will result in the destruction of the result of three years' work carried on by American philanthropy with the expenditure of over ten million dollars. We urge you most solemnly to make an immediate call on the President, who is the only man in the opinion of all of us who can make the situation in the Caucasus safe, where a world menace is threatening, by maintaining order in that region."

T MS (WP, DLC).
  ¹ That is, Col. William Nafew Haskell, U.S.A.

Woodrow Wilson and Robert Lansing to Edward Mandell House

[Washington] August 29 [1919]

No. 5897 From the President and Secretary of State for Colonel House:

In consideration of the nature of Mandate (A) (set forth in your 2751 of August 9, 8 p.m.) would it not be feasible to insert some provision for possible amendment, revision or recall of Mandate by Council after a term of years has elapsed?

T telegram (E. M. House Papers, CtY).

Robert Lansing to Frank Lyon Polk

Washington, August 29, 1919.

2796 Your 3897, August 25, 6 p.m.
The views of the President and the Secretary of State are as fol-

lows: Clemenceau's present attitude for delay regarding consideration of the form of mandate "A" on its face is based upon the theory that no decision has been reached as to the abandonment of Turkish sovereignty over any part of Turkey. This is erroneous as the first and fourth paragraphs of Article 22 of the Covenant show conclusively that at least a portion of the Turkish Empire is to be placed under mandatory Powers. Accordingly, the consideration of the form of mandate "A" should proceed at this time and you will support this view STOP In view of the fact that the attitude of Clemenceau appears to be one, strictly speaking, for delay rather than of entire opposition, the use of the President's statement contained in 2771 August 9, 4 p.m. will be left to Mr. Polk's discretion.

Lansing

T telegram (SDR, RG 59, 763.72119/6371, DNA).

From Edward Mandell House

London. Aug. 30, 1919.

Urgent. 2934. For the President. Today's papers carry news that you will definitely tour the States. My best wishes go with you. I believe that the people throughout the country are tired of the technical controversies into which discussion has lately been drawn in Washington and will welcome a reassertion of the ideals America fought for and the broad principles upon which the league is based. There is a noticeable sag in popular interest in Europe as well as in America and your voice is eagerly awaited.

The world needs to be reminded of the way in which the League will serve to avoid war through discussion, delay and publicity; it needs to be assured that some program of world disarmament is really contemplated which will contribute to remedy the cost of living; it needs to be shown the closely interwoven economic relations between countries which make international cooperation not only a moral choice but a shelter and even a selfish necessity.

From this distance it seems to me that hostility to the League in America is almost wholly based upon article ten. You will best know after your tour regarding whether or not the American people show response to the argument that we are for the first time making order out of anarchy in international relations and are laying down the principle that territory is no longer to be acquired by force of arms. It would seem that our people have not yet grasped the limitations and significance of the external aggression clause. I cannot help feeling that you will find response to the argument that we are now taking in international relations the first primitive step which the state took in requiring its citizens to go to law for the vindication of their claims. Edward House. Davis.

T telegram (R. Lansing Papers, DLC).

From Robert Lansing

My dear Mr. President: Washington August 30, 1919.

In connection with my letter dated August 28, 1919, transmitting certified copies of the Rhineland Agreement and the Polish Treaty, I am sending you herewith, as of possible interest, a copy of a memorandum regarding the Rhine Agreement which may be found in the Minutes of the Council of Four of the day on which the Agreement was passed upon.[1]

Faithfully yours, Robert Lansing.

TLS (WP, DLC).
[1] "MEMORANDUM DEFINING THE RELATIONS BETWEEN THE ALLIED MILITARY AUTHORI-TIES AND THE INTER-ALLIED RHINELAND HIGH COMMISSION," June 13, 1919, T MS (WP, DLC). This memorandum is printed as Appendix III to the minutes of the Council of Four printed at June 13, 1919, 12:00 noon, Vol. 60.

From Joseph Patrick Tumulty

Dear Governor: [The White House] 30 August, 1919

Our friend Mr. Baruch saw Mr. Gary yesterday, and Mr. Gary said he appreciated your attitude in the matter,[1] but said that his reluctance to meet these men was based on the fact that they represented only 15 percent of the men employed in the steel plants; that the Steel Corporation had never had any difficulty with any of their workmen; that within the plants various organizations had been established for the setting forth of grievances, and that all grievances had been acted upon when set forth; that there are no differences now between their men except that which is the result of an attempt on the part of the American Federation of Labor to unionize these shops, an effort they have been making for years and in which they have been unsuccessful. He said they had made a canvass of the situation and that over 85 percent of the men were against any strike and will not support the American Federation of Labor in case one is decided upon. Mr. Gary is writing the President a personal letter, setting forth the situation, so that the President may be in possession of all the facts. I think the President ought not to make up his mind until he has heard from Mr. Gary, and Mr. Baruch agrees with me in this.

Sincerely yours,   [J. P. Tumulty]

CCL (J. P. Tumulty Papers, DLC).
¹ Wilson was much concerned about the possibility of a strike against the United States Steel Corporation and had sent Baruch to confer with Elbert Henry Gary, chairman of the corporation's board of directors, presumably to try to persuade Gary to do everything possible to avoid a strike. For the background, see S. Gompers *et al.* to WW, Sept. 4, 1919.

From William Bauchop Wilson, with Enclosure

My dear Mr. President: Washington August 30, 1919.

I am inclosing you herewith proposed letters to Mr. Homer L. Ferguson, President of the Chamber of Commerce of the United States of America, Mr. Magnus W. Alexander, Managing Director of the National Industrial Conference Board, and Mr. Samuel Gompers, President of the American Federation of Labor, calling a conference to deal with the relationship between capital and labor.

It is proposed that the National Industrial Conference Board name five members, the United States Chamber of Commerce five members, the American Federation of Labor ten members, and the President ten members, making a body of thirty persons. The suggestion is made that the conference meet in Washington on the 24th of September. It would not be advisable to call it earlier than that date because the Presidents of these respective organizations would undoubtedly desire to canvass the available men and consult with their associates before naming their representatives.

I have taken your message to Congress of May 20th as the basis of the communication, and have either paraphrased or quoted the language, adding only the last two paragraphs.

I am inclosing you a number of names¹ of persons who suggest themselves to me as being suitable for selection by you as members of the conference.   Faithfully yours,   W B Wilson

TLS (WP, DLC).
¹ Not printed.

ENCLOSURE

Mr. Magnus W. Alexander, Managing Director,
National Industrial Conference Board,
15 Beacon Street,
Boston, Massachusetts.

Dear Sir:

In my message to Congress under date of May 20, 1919, I laid particular stress upon the fact that there is a real community of interest between capital and labor but that it has never been made evident in action, and that it can be made operative and manifest only in a new organization of industry. The genius of our business men and the sound practical sense of our workers can certainly work out such a partnership when once they realize exactly what it is that they seek and sincerely adopt a common purpose with regard to it.

The new spirit and method of organization which must be effected are not to be brought about by legislation so much as by the common counsel and voluntary cooperation of capitalist, manager and workman. Legislation can go only a very little way in commanding what shall be done. The organization of industry is a matter of corporate and individual initiative and of practical business arrangement. Those who really desire a new relationship between capital and labor can readily find a way to bring it about, and perhaps Federal legislation can help. The object of all reform in this essential matter must be a genuine democratization of industry based upon the full recognition of the rights of those who work in whatever rank to participate in some organic way in every decision which directly affects their welfare or the part they play in industry.

The Congress has already shown the way to one reform, which should be nation-wide, by establishing the eight-hour day as the standard day in every field of labor over which it can exercise control. It has served the whole country by leading the way in developing a means of preserving and safeguarding life and health in dangerous industries. It can now help in the difficult task of giving a new form and spirit to industrial organization by coordinating the several agencies of conciliation and adjustment which have been brought into existence by the difficulties arising between employers and employees and by setting up and developing new Federal agencies of advice and information which may serve as a clearing-house for the best experiments and best thought on this most important matter, upon which every thinking man must be aware that the future of society so greatly depends.

I desire to get the combined judgment of representative employers and representative employees and representatives of the general public conversant with these matters, and for the accomplishment of that purpose I have decided to call a conference of five persons to be selected by the Chamber of Commerce of the United States of America, five persons to be selected by the National Industrial Conference Board, and ten persons to be selected by the American Federation of Labor, to confer with ten representatives of the general public whom I shall select, these representatives to meet in the City of Washington on September 24, 1919, for the purpose of counselling together on the great and vital questions affecting our industrial life and their consequent effect upon all our people, to the end that we may work out if possible a genuine spirit of cooperation and partnership based upon a real community of interest which will redound to the welfare of all our people.

The wastages of war have seriously interfered with the natural course of our industrial and economic development. The nervous tension of our people has not yet returned to its normal condition. The necessity of devising at once methods by which we can speedily recover from this condition and obviate the wastefulness caused by the continued interruption of many of our important industrial enterprizes by strikes and lockouts emphasizes the need for a meeting of minds in a conference such as I have suggested. I am sure that your organization will gladly bear the expenses of its own representatives to a conference called for such an important purpose, and I would therefore request that you select five persons to act as the representatives of the employers connected with your organization in the conference, and advise the Secretary of Labor of the names and addresses of the persons selected so that he may make the necessary arrangements for the meeting.

T MS (WP, DLC).

From William Bauchop Wilson

My dear Mr. President: Washington August 30, 1919.

I have found it very difficult to add anything to what you have already said, except by way of elaboration, concerning the effect of the failure to promptly ratify the Peace Treaty, and feel guilty of taking up your time without adding to your thought in sending this statement.

The World War aroused our people to a high nervous tension

which has greatly accentuated the spirit of unrest. It cannot be allayed until the terms of peace are definitely known and accepted. We are no longer isolated. Inventive genius has eliminated space. Men and material can be transported across the Atlantic in one-tenth of the time that was required in the days of Washington or Monroe, and thought can be transmitted instantly by the pressing of a button.

Our people is cosmopolitan. They or their forebears have come from all nations of the earth. Their sympathies go out to other nations accordingly. Matters of minor importance in the League of Nations are magnified into major principles because they affect these countries. The unsettled political and economic conditions of Europe have a direct effect upon the minds of our people. Hence, we have the Irish situation, the Italian claims, the anti-British feeling, the opposition to the Shantung arrangement distracting their attention from the problems at home, and these things can only be allayed when the Peace Treaty has been definitely disposed of.

The establishment of new States and new boundary lines in central Europe and the Balkan States may or may not be permanent. If there is no League of Nations to hold these lines with a firm hand until they have been stabilized, if it is to be a case of each nation for itself as it has been heretofore, Europe will soon be in turmoil again, and experience has demonstrated that Europe at war is a menace not only to our commerce but to our institutions. Our business men realize this fact, and until the question of the League of Nations has been determined they cannot seek European business for future delivery. All these affect production at home and have a direct connection with the cost of living.

With Europe in a condition of upheaval, it is not only the production of her foodstuffs that is interfered with, but also the production of other materials that are recognized as necessaries of life. She cannot proceed to make good the wastes of war or to supply current needs, and that situation means a continuation of high prices if the law of supply and demand follows its natural course. Furthermore, with Europe in a condition where she cannot produce the material necessary to supply her own needs, and having no surplus or but a small surplus to put into the markets of the world, there need be no fear of foreign competition with our business men. That makes a condition that is conducive to the formation of combinations at home that result in profiteering. There has been an artificial stimulation of demand and an artificial restriction of supply incident to the war, which we can only begin to remove when the terms of peace are proclaimed.

One of the things that has to be avoided is the reaction that would follow giving the impression that the signing of the Peace Treaty would immediately restore prices to their pre-war condition. That can only be secured when peace has been restored, the wastage of the war made good, and the industries of the world restored to a basis where they can meet the current demands.

Faithfully yours,   W B Wilson

TLS (WP, DLC).

From Walker Downer Hines

Dear Mr. President: Washington August 30, 1919

Mr. Jewell and his associates are fearful that their constituents will still vote largely in favor of a strike and are exceedingly anxious that you make some further statement which will aid in arresting this tendency.

I understand you have reached the conclusion that is [it] is not expedient for you to make a Labor Day Statement. It occurs to me, however, that what Mr. Jewell and his associates have in mind could be substantially accomplished through a statement issued by you now, commenting further upon the progress of the campaign for a reduction in the cost of living. Such a statement would be read by most of the shop employes as well as by workers generally, and I believe would have a wholesome effect on the deliberations concerning the shop wage matter and also on the Labor Day celebrations.

In order to make my suggestion more concrete, I take the liberty of submitting a tentative draft of a statement along the lines I have in mind.[1]   Cordially yours,   Walker D Hines

TLS (WP, DLC).
    [1] It is missing.

From William Cox Redfield

Dear Mr. President   Washington August 30. 1919

I did not intend to recall quite so soon the substance of my note to you of first August asking my release from official duties about the middle of October nor shall I forget your generous and cordial reply.

In view, however, of your approaching absence throughout September on a mission in which my hopes and prayers go with you, a further word may be ventured.

I shall be glad to defer my withdrawal until the latter part of

October in order that opportunity may be had after your return for any conference or action you may desire.

Meanwhile there is no reason on my part why the fact of my resignation should not be made known

Cordially Yours   William C. Redfield

ALS (WP, DLC).

From Homer Stillé Cummings

Stamford, Connecticut,

My dear Mr. President: 30 August 1919.

I had hoped to see you again before you began your Western trip, but perhaps the matters I have in mind will keep and be more completely matured when you return. I am just now planning a meeting of the Executive Committee[1] which I expect to call to meet at Atlantic City, on the 26th of September, at which time I am hoping that we shall be able to develop our budgets and lay out the details of temporary sub-headquarters and attend to other pressing matters. Our chief difficulties just now, from the standpoint of the Committee, have to do with matters of finance. Our income is just about sufficient to maintain our present running expenses. It is highly important, however, to develop and extend some of our branches, especially those dealing with publicity and the work amongst the women. I shall hope to lay before you, upon your return, a rather complete outline of our plans.

Of course, it is unnecessary to say so, but I was delighted and encouraged by the manner in which the interview with the Foreign Relations Committee was handled. It has had a wonderfully beneficial effect, while the swift and decisive manner in which you met the high cost of living issue and the critical railroad condition, was beyond all praise.

The real purpose of this note, however, is to wish you God speed upon your Western journey. The stage is set and I am confident, from what I know of Western conditions, that your tour, burdensome and taxing as it is certain to be, will be replete with dramatic instances and wonderfully effective in advancing the cause which is so close to all our hearts.

Very sincerely yours,   Homer S. Cummings

TLS (WP, DLC).
[1] Of the Democratic National Committee, of which he was the chairman.

From Lyon Gardiner Tyler

Dear Mr. President,   Charles City Co., Va., August 30, 1919

I am authorized by the Board of Visitors of William and Mary College to inform you that at the meeting of the Board held in June last the degree of Doctor of Laws was conferred upon you by that body, on the nomination of the Faculty. As soon as I am notified of the acceptance of the honor, the Diploma attesting the fact will be transmitted to you.

It gives me great pleasure to add that this action of the constituted authorities of the College marks the last of my active connection with the Institution. At the same meeting I tendered my resignation, after a service of thirty one years.

With high regard, I am
          Yours Sincerely   Lyon G. Tyler, President Emeritus.

ALS (WP, DLC).

From Robert Lansing, with Enclosure

Dear Mr. President: Washington August 30th, 1919.

I am enclosing a copy of the telegram dispatched today to Tokio. It is the one which on Thursday, you approved in principle. The text remains unchanged except for one suggestion you made and for one additional paragraph and a few changes in phraseology.

I have consulted with the Secretary of War and his objections as to the time of making any public statement have been met by a slight modification of language which, while eliminating the necessity for any public statement leaves us free to make one if and when it should be deemed advisable.

The matter I now desire to bring to your immediate attention is important, particularly in view of your prospective absence from Washington.

I take it that withdrawal from Siberia has been decided upon. There remains only to determine the time at which it shall be done. We have not asked for a reply from the Japanese Government and we probably will not receive one at all satisfactory, even if they make any answer. There will certainly not remain time for them to minifest [manifest], by their actions in Siberia a change of heart before Vladivostok shall be frozen in.

Consequently, it seems to me, you may want to give definite instructions to the Secretary of War. Transports must be provided and must reach Vladivostok before the ice sets in and a period of thirty days may elapse before the transports can even reach that port. Otherwise our troops will be dependant [dependent] on the use of railroads in Manchuria along which Japanese troops are stationed, and on the line owned by the Japanese which connects Harbin with open ports to the south in Korea and China. Reliance on this means of exit seems inadvisable.

The inference is that the withdrawal should be directed immediately, to take place as soon in the future as practicable.

I am sending a copy of this cable to the Secretary of War for his confidential information.

Faithfully yours,   Robert Lansing

TLS (WP, DLC).

E N C L O S U R E

[Washington] August 28, 1919. 4 P.M.

AMEMBASSY TOKYO.

Following is the text of a note which you will please leave with the Minister of Foreign Affairs at once:

QUOTE: Excellency: Under special instructions from my Government, I am directed to call Your Excellency's attention to the developments which have attended the joint efforts of Japan and the United States to render assistance to Russia first, through the sending of their military forces and second, through the adoption of the Siberian railway plan in conjunction with the other Allied Governments.

You will recall the circumstances which attended the joint decision of our two Governments in regard to the sending of military forces. The purpose of the expedition was fully expressed, on the part of the United States, in an Aide Memoire handed to the Japanese Ambassador at Washington July 17, 1918[1] and, subsequently, in an official statement given to the press by the Acting Secretary of State.[2] In both of these statements of policy it was made clear first, that military action in Siberia was admissable, as the Government of the United States saw the circumstances at the time, only to help the Czecho-Slovaks consolidate their forces and get into successful cooperation with their Slavic kinsmen and to steady any efforts at self-government or self-defense in which the Russians themselves might be willing to accept assistance.

At the same time, the Japanese Ambassador at Washington, on behalf of his Government, submitted to the Secretary of State a

---

[1] See the Enclosure printed with WW to FLP, July 17, 1918, Vol. 48.
[2] See the press release printed at Aug. 3, 1918, Vol. 49.

declaration of purpose on the part of Japan[3] which was fully consonant with the purpose of this Government and which was based upon a sentiment of sincere friendship towards the Russian people.

As time passed it became more and more evident that the restoration of railway traffic in Siberia was not only a vital element in such military assistance to the Russians and Czechs as had already been afforded, but equally so in connection with any economic assistance in Siberia, such as was contemplated by this Government and expressed in an Aide Memoire to the Japanese Ambassador at Washington August 10, 1918.[4]

My Government has instructed me to reiterate to Your Excellency the gratification with which, consequently, it received the plan for supervising the Siberian railways, which was proposed by the Government of Japan[5] and which so fully accorded with the purpose of the United States as outlined at some length in a copy of a circular telegram which was handed to the Japanese Ambassador at Washington September 14, 1918.[6] As Your Excellency will recall, the plan proposed by Japan was supplemented by a memorandum submitted by Ambassador Morris and fully concurred in by the Japanese Foreign Office.[7]

The plan provides that the general supervision of the railways shall be exercised by a special Inter-Allied Committee—the Committee which is now actually established at Vladivostock. It further stipulates that a Technical Board and an Allied Military Transportation Board shall be placed under the control of the Committee. The duties of these two boards and also of the Committee are outlined quite simply and clearly. Under the plan, the protection of the railways is placed under the Allied military forces.

The memorandum supplementing the plan, in addition to fixing an understanding as to the membership of the Inter-Allied Committee and the two boards under its control, and also giving assurance for effective use of the services of Mr. John F. Stevens, provides that the plan itself shall be interpreted as a sincere effort to operate the Chinese Eastern and Trans-Siberian Railways in the interest of the Russian people with a view to their ultimate return to those in interest without impairing any existing rights. It fur-

---

[3] See the Enclosure printed with FLP to WW, July 24, 1918 (first letter of that date), Vol. 49.

[4] Apparently a garbled reference to FLP to Diplomatic Representatives of Great Britain, France, Italy, Japan, Russia, and China, October (not August) 10, 1918, printed in FR 1918, Russia, III, 147-50.

[5] About which, see FLP to RL, Dec. 30, 1918, n. 4, Vol. 53.

[6] RL to K. Ishii, Sept. 14, 1918, printed in FR 1918, Russia, III, 253-54, enclosing RL to WHP, Sept. 13, 1918, printed in ibid., 249-52.

[7] About which, see the note cited in n. 5 above.

thermore stipulates, without any possibility of misinterpretation, that in entrusting to Mr. Stevens as President of the Technical Board, the technical operation of these railways, it is to be understood that the Governments of Japan and the United States are prepared to give him the authority and support which will be necessary to make his efforts effective.

The Government of the United States views the operation of the Chinese Eastern and Trans-Siberian Railways as the one element most necessary to economic and political prosperity in Siberia today; as the fundamental condition precedent to the restoration of normal economic life and the reestablishment of political stability. Without it it does not seem possible that there can be the slightest improvement in the present distressing conditions. Clothes, medical supplies and goods cannot be shipped into Siberia nor can the produce of the country itself be shipped out. The railways are the only avenues of communications. Consequently, my Government considers as of the utmost importance any developments which may tend to block them.

The developments to which I am directed to call Your Excellency's attention have to do with the radical difference of interpretation, with its consequent difficulties of friendly cooperation, which have been placed upon the duties required of the Allied military forces in protecting the railways and also in giving to Mr. Stevens the authority and support necessary to make his efforts effective. As you are aware, the United States understands the Allied military forces are not only obligated to protect the railways, free from interruption, but also wherever they may be in control to forward the operation of the general plan. This is especially true as regards the duties of the United States and Japan in their mutual obligations to give to Mr. Stevens the degree of authority and support necessary to make fully effective the efforts of himself and, consequently, of the Allied Engineers under his direction. The Engineers are to be protected as a vital element in the protection of the railways.

On the other hand the Imperial Government seems to understand that the protection of the railways, so far as it may concern Japanese troops, is limited strictly to safeguarding railway property and keeping the line open and entails no obligation whatever for cooperation on the part of Japanese forces in furthering the general operation of the plan itself. To illustrate one of the phases of this question, allow me to recall to Your Excellency the instructions which the Japanese military representative at Omsk has now received to the effect that any disagreement between a Russian under the authority of the Omsk Government and a National of any country engaged in the operation or protection of the railways, must be a matter for discussion between the Omsk Government and the Government of the other persons involved. In practice this understanding has resulted in a definite refusal on the part of Japanese military commanders to protect the lives and property of the Allied inspectors in the territory controlled by General Semenoff.[8]

Such an understanding seems to the United States to be wholly inadmissable. As Your Excellency is aware, the Omsk Government is not recognized by the United States nor is my Government advised that recognition has been accorded it by Japan. Furthermore, the Omsk Government is not referred to in the plan proposed by Japan and it is only by a later development of circumstances that the Russian Chairman[9] has any connection with Admiral Kolchak. But quite aside from any suggestion to abandon the definite character of the plan by injecting into it new elements of authority it is as well known to the Government of Japan as to that of the United States that the Government of Admiral Kolchak is wholly favorable to the Allied operation of the railways and has only recently testified to this attitude conclusively by ordering Russian railway authorities to waive all existing Russian legal restrictions or regulations which might otherwise interfere with our present efforts. Hostile actions of Russian authorities acting in the name of the Omsk authorities can, therefore, only be in disobedience to express instructions. Nevertheless, Japanese military commanders have allowed conditions to arise in sections of the railways guarded by Japan which have threatened the withdrawal of Allied Engineers, because of the refusal of these commanders to protect the lives and property of the Engineers in the performance of the duties imposed upon them by the plan proposed by Japan.

Consequently, the continued disposition, now apparent as a definite policy, on the part of Japan through its military commanders in Siberia, to refuse the support of its military forces in making effective in practice the declared purposes of the agreement, has been viewed by my Government with the grave[st] concern, especially so as the United States has hitherto been confident in the hope that a consistent policy of frankness might lead to a clear and thorough accord on all questions in which the United States and Japan are both obligated to assume responsibilities.

The United States Government feels it cannot be held responsible for that for which it is not in fact responsible. The entire plan was predicated on the cooperation of the two governments. With

[8] That is, Grigorii Mikhailovich Semenov.
[9] That is, Leonid Aleksandrovich Ustrugov, chairman of the inter-Allied committee to supervise the operation of the Trans-Siberian Railway and Minister of Communications in the Omsk (Kolchak) government.

the failure of the Japanese officials to lend its cooperation in such an elemental manner a situation is created which the Government of the United States must immediately consider from the point of view of fixing the responsibility for the failure of the enterprise which has been the cause of so much labor and from which so much of benefits was to be expected for the Russian people.

It is, nevertheless, in a spirit of sincere friendship that the Government of the United States desire me to bring to Your Excellency's attention the fact that it is now confronted with the necessity of deciding, after repeated and frank efforts to arrive at a mutual understanding of purpose as regards an international undertaking which was accepted only after searching discussion and consideration, whether it may not be the only course practicable for the United States to pursue is an entire withdrawal from all further efforts to cooperate in Siberia to be followed if need be, by a public statement of the reasons for such action since it might be misunderstood if no explanation is made.

I am directed to add that the Government of the United States has a clear appreciation of the consequences of such action, especially as it is burdened with a deep sense of obligation towards Russia, whose people contributed such a vital share in the triumph of the Allied and Associated Governments over the Central Powers. Moreover, my Government is firmly convinced that the future welfare of all Governments is to be based upon a community of interest which is about to replace permanently the former balances of power and other bargains of self-interest and aggrandizement on the part of one nation or group of nations at the expense of others. With the deepest regret my Government finds that the attitude of Japan in this matter raises the question as to whether this view of international relations is shared by the Imperial Government. At the same time, I am to assure you that this perfectly clear and frank statement of the circumstances of the case, as the Government of the United States sees them, and of the only course of action which seems logically to follow, are presented in the firm belief that the traditional friendship of our two countries will assure a thorough understanding on the part of Japan.

In conclusion allow me to add for Your Excellency's information that copies of this note are being communicated to the Governments of Great Britain, France, Italy and China and to the Russian Ambassador at Washington. Unquote   (signed)[10]

T MS (WP, DLC).

[10] Sent as RL to Amembassy, Tokyo, Aug. 30, 1919, T telegram (SDR, RG 59, 861.77/1056a, DNA); it is printed in FR 1919, Russia, pp. 573-78.

From Robert Lansing, with Enclosure

My dear Mr. President: Washington August 30, 1919.

You requested comment on the attached telegram of August 25th from Archangel[1] and I attach hereto the comment of our Russian Division,[2] as well as a draft of a telegram to our representative at Archangel, for your consideration.

Faithfully yours,   Robert Lansing

Sept 2/19 *Prest* Make this a little warmer   RL.

TLS (SDR, RG 59, 861.00/5282, DNA).
   [1] P. P. Skomorokhov, president of the Conference of Zemstvos and Municipalities of the Northern Region, *et al.* to WW, Aug. 25, 1919, T telegram (SDR, RG 59, 861.00/5282, DNA), printed in *FR 1919, Russia*, pp. 655-57. This telegram related in grim detail the history of the advance of the Red Army in the northern regions and predicted the annihilation of the anti-Bolshevik people of that area unless the Allied military forces presently there were allowed by their governments to remain.
   [2] It is missing.

E N C L O S U R E

Washington, September 3, 1919.

751 The President has received a telegram from representatives of the conference of Zemstvos and Municipalities making a fervid appeal for retention of Allied troops. Please consult your British Colleague and if you then deem it advisable inform President of Zemstvos Conference that American troops were sent to Archangel to assist Russians in safeguarding supplies and in such efforts as might be made to restore normal conditions. American troops were withdrawn after cooperating with Allied forces in North Russia for nine months, only because of conditions over which this Government had no control. You may assure the President of the Conference that our action was dictated by stern necessity and only because we had reached the limit of time when our military activities had perforce to cease. This Government understands that every possible effort is being made to offer a refuge for those Russians who are in danger. While this Government regrets most keenly that it cannot render the assistance asked for and which it thoroughly appreciates is very greatly needed, you may say that the Government and people of the United States continue to regard with deep and sympathetic interest the efforts now being made by the Provisional Government of Northern Russia and those other elements associated with Admiral Kolchak, and is hopeful that means will develop by which Russia may be assisted towards a happy outcome of the efforts of her people to regain control of their own affairs.   Lansing[1]

T telegram (SDR, RG 59, 861.00/5282, DNA).
¹ This was sent as RL to Felix Cole, Sept. 4, 1919, and is printed in *FR 1919, Russia*, p. 660. Lansing made only a few minor changes in the draft of the telegram sent; they did not change the tone of the message at all.

Robert Lansing to Frank Lyon Polk

Washington, August 30, 1919.

3001 Referring to the statement sent to you by Colonel House and quoted in our Despatch from London 2850, August 20, 9 p.m.,¹ the President thinks that the first suggestion that the portion of Togoland assigned to France might be assigned in full sovereignty is directly contrary to the terms of the Covenant and is inadmissible. As to the second suggestion, the President understands that this portion of Togoland should be under a B Mandate and not under a C Mandate. Aside from this, however, the President believes that the whole idea of training black troops in Mandate territory to fight in Europe is contrary to the principle of mandates and to the spirit of the Covenant which regards the welfare of the people in the territory covered by the Mandate as paramount to other considerations. It does not seem to the President that the question of the boundary raises any more difficulties than existed when Togoland was German. While the President feels that he cannot consistently with his remark in the Council of Ten refuse France's request in regard to this particular territory, he is by conviction entirely opposed to the idea or the practice.²

Lansing

T telegram (SDR, RG 59, 763.72119/6294, DNA).
¹ That is, EMH to WW, Aug. 20, 1919.
² Last sentence added by Wilson to the draft referred to in n. 2 to the memorandum by D. H. Miller printed at Aug. 27, 1919. The addition is a WWhw MS (SDR, RG 59, 763.72119/6886, DNA).

A Labor Day Message

[*Aug. 31, 1919*]

I am encouraged and gratified by the progress which is being made in controlling the cost of living. The support of the movement is widespread and I confidently look for substantial results, although I must counsel patience as well as vigilance because such results will not come instantly or without teamwork.

Let me again emphasize my appeal to every citizen of the country to continue to give his personal support in this matter, and to make it as active as possible. Let him not only refrain from doing anything which at the moment will tend to increase the cost of living, but let him do all in his power to increase his production; and further than that, let him at the same time himself carefully economize in the matter of consumption. By common action in this direction we shall overcome a danger greater than the danger of war. We will hold steady a situation which is fraught with possibilities of hardship and suffering to a large part of our population; we will enable the processes of production to overtake the processes of consumption, and we will speed the restoration of an adequate purchasing power for wages.

I am particularly gratified at the support which the government's policy has received from the representatives of organized labor and I earnestly hope that the workers generally will emphatically indorse the position of their leaders and thereby move with the government instead of against it in the solution of this greatest domestic problem.

I am calling for as early a date as practicable a conference in which authoritative representatives of labor and of those who direct labor will discuss fundamental means of bettering the whole relationship of capital and labor and putting the whole question of wages upon another footing.   Woodrow Wilson.[1]

Printed in the *Washington Post*, Sept. 1, 1919.
[1] There are no drafts or copies of this statement in WP, DLC, which fact raises the question of the authorship of the statement.

From Elbert Henry Gary

PERSONAL AND PRIVATE.

My dear Mr. President: New York, August 31st, 1919.

It has been suggested to me that you would be pleased to receive in confidence a statement of the present labor situation as we see it from the viewpoint of our Corporation and its subsidiaries, and I hasten to comply.

We have now about 250,000 employes, perhaps more, and are operating our works at about 80% of full estimated capacity. The number mentioned is the average for the last six or eight years or more. During the war, at the peak, we had say 285,000.

Since 1901 we have had very little labor trouble; nothing of great importance, and the few slight disturbances, which were invariably disposed of promptly by the voluntary action of the men themselves, were brought about by the efforts of labor leaders to induce our men to join the labor unions. In a letter I cannot be specific or exact, but the above is substantially accurate.

When the Corporation was organized in April, 1901, many of the works were dealing with labor unions as such, and we adopted the policy of leaving the situation precisely as we found it and never departed from this course except as hereinafter mentioned. The labor unions immediately attempted to extend the recognition of unions (that is, contracting through leaders) to all our works and this resulted in "calling out" men from several places where union labor was employed. A strike resulted during the summer of 1901 which was entirely sympathetic, based on no claim of injustice, or request for benefits or relief of any sort. It lasted in some degree for perhaps four to six weeks, at the end of which time the remainder of the men who had been on strike voluntarily resumed work without making any demands for or receiving any changes in wage rates or otherwise. From this time on the men who belonged to unions in considerable numbers continued to withdraw from the unions until about twelve or fourteen years ago there was only one mill (and that not large, located in or near a small place in Ohio) that was operated as a union mill. At this time, because of the violation of the regular annual contract between the operating company and the union leaders and at the request of the majority of the workmen, it was announced by the employers that at the end of the term of the contract the mill would be operated as an "open shop," and this was carried into effect. On the date fixed for the change the men were called out by the labor leaders. Soon after a majority of the men asked to have the mills opened, whereupon work was resumed. Then a number of men, selected from the few who still desired a continuance of union labor, probably some or all holding positions in the unions which afforded salaries, began to attack and club the workmen on their way to and from work, and many were seriously injured. Protection was asked of and refused by the city officials; and the mill was then shut down and the large majority of men given and retained in employment at our mills in other locations. The mill in question has never been operated since, though succeeding city officials and the Chamber of Commerce have frequently requested it. The reason is that it is not a good point for assembly, production and delivery to markets. Since then we have never operated any of our manufactories with labor dominated by the unions. We have been opposed to the "closed shop" system and have steadfastly adhered to the "open shop," which employs and retains one in the mill whether one does or does not belong to a labor union. The employes are not, in any respect, discriminated against or favored in consequence of being union or non-union. The contrary is sometimes stated by union leaders, but there is no justification in fact for the assertion. Our orders to this effect are positive and clear.

For many years last past, antedating the war and continuing without much interruption throughout the war, the labor leaders have been carrying on a drive at or in the vicinity of our works to induce our workmen to join the unions, but without much success. This has been advertised by the leaders in public speeches on the platform, at street meetings, in periodicals and otherwise. It has been especially directed against our Corporation and subsidiaries. During the last six months the campaign has been more vigorous than ever before. Threats, boasts and promises have been made to the men. Misrepresentations as to the facts have been common. During all this time no agitation has been started or carried on by the body of workmen. They have not sought the labor leaders, but the latter have importuned the former wherever and whenever opportunity offered.

The leaders, through the public press and public speeches, have made claims, demands and threats calculated to influence the employers. These leaders have in no true sense represented the workmen. According to my information, which I believe to be reliable, not over 20%, and probably not exceeding 10%, are members of labor unions.

Now in all these years why have not the men risen in the strength of their numbers and insisted upon changes? The answer is obvious. The large majority of the men do not desire to become members of labor unions. They do not wish to pay the dues imposed. They object to being dominated by the labor leaders. They demand freedom from tyranny. And, above everything else, our workmen generally are satisfied with their conditions and terms of employment. They know, what is the fact, that any man, or number of men, whom they select as a committee, can see the foreman, superintendent or head officer of the employing company and present any suggestion or claim with the full assurance, obtained by long and practical experience, that they are welcome and will receive patient attention, full consideration and fair results. Within a few weeks the men at one of our works appointed their own committee to see a superintendent, who called in consultation the President.[1] They asked for the reinstatement of a man who had clearly and inexcusably violated an important order. The President came to me for advice. On the statement of the man that he personally regretted the occurrence and had been influenced by an "outsider"

[1] James Augustine Farrell, president of the United States Steel Corporation since 1911.

and would hereafter carefully observe all directions in regard to his work, I recommended he be taken back, and this was adopted. He still occupies the same position.

There is only one way the labor unions can induce the majority, or a large number by comparison, to join the labor unions and to bring about the "closed shop," viz: If they could secure recognition of the unions by the employers, which means making contracts with the leaders concerning conditions and terms of employment of their workmen and operation of the works, then, of course, no one could obtain employment except through the unions and therefore all would be forced to join the unions. With such support in numbers the leaders might fix dues, salaries for themselves, etc., etc., and that is really, though not admittedly, the principal purpose of their present efforts. This recognition is what is now attempted. Any step in that direction would be misrepresented and misused. A few months since I received a letter from a labor leader asking for a conference. I replied briefly and politely that I could not confer with him as representing our workmen; that we stood for the "open shop"; but I did not immediately publish the correspondence. This gentleman promptly advertised in the papers that, for his union, he had received recognition by me. Thereupon the press concluded and published that we had changed our policy and would hereafter deal with unions as such. Consequently I was compelled to publish the exact correspondence. However, in the meantime, a number of our men, as they stated, had signed with the unions, though comparatively few had paid their dues.

I have no personal feeling against any of the labor leaders, but the system is bad. However much it may be denied, it is labor unions that largely have brought about existing conditions in regard to prices. Labor receives 85 to 90% of the total cost of production from the raw to the finished material. The prices of labor have advanced by leaps and bounds. Carpenters and painters are demanding $1. and more per hour. Most of the other lines and departments correspond. If a union man employed to paint a surface should depart from his particular work for a moment to drive a nail which would prevent large damage or even disaster, he would be reprimanded or fined by the labor leader and would never again repeat the offense. Every housekeeper, every foreman or superintendent or employer, has had experiences like this. Cases could be multiplied; they are familiar. If we should now recognize labor unions as such, the whole steel industry, of which our Corporation is perhaps 40 or 45 per cent, would become unionized, and this would spread to all other lines. The influence has been more and more extended during the war, for its necessities have frequently subordinated principle. If this country should become generally unionized it would mean the commencement of industrial decay. I think it would mean in the international contest for a fair position of influence, much more than it would be wise for me to publicly state at this time. The high moral ground, and the sound economic position to occupy cannot be successfully attacked if the general public will continue to approve the "open shop" policy.

The reason our men generally do not join the labor unions is that they are satisfied with their present conditions. We have done many things for their benefit and advantage, and so far as the substantials are concerned, voluntarily and without previous request. In wage rates, living and working conditions, conservation of life and health, care and comfort in times of sickness or old age, providing facilities for the general welfare and happiness of the employes and their families, our companies have taken advanced positions. The labor leaders have, with emphasis, opposed all our welfare work on the announced ground that we were bribing our workmen, absurd as this appears.

During the war our manufactories were devoted to supporting your efforts to win the war. Our mills were in continuous and full operation turning out steel products to supply the military necessities of our Government and its associates. Our men, nearly 300,000 strong, performed loyal and efficient service and contributed largely to the purchase of bonds, and many to charity, unyielding to the persistent efforts of labor leaders to join labor unions and to strike. This is denied in some quarters, but my statement is exact and true. The wages paid seemed large and at times were criticised by other employers, but we believed them necessary on account of the high cost of living. Of course, high wages helped to increase living expenses, as it always does, but there were so many men in other departments like shipbuilding, etc., which were under labor unions, taking advantage of war conditions, and there were so many other conditions which could not be controlled, that prices got beyond the control of the natural laws of trade.

Speaking for myself, I am willing to have Governmental supervision and regulation of industry, provided it can be under a well organized, non-partisan body of men selected because of their peculiar fitness, and subject to review by the Federal Courts as to certain fundamentals. Moreover, if at any time complaint is made to you that we are not treating our men right or are not managing our affairs in accordance with the rules of justice, equity or good morals, and you will inform me of the same and permit a full investigation of the facts, we will show you, or a fair-minded, competent representative to be selected by you, that the complaint is unwarranted, or we will make the necessary change.

I am familiar with the facts and have intended and attempted to correctly represent the situation. I am, of course, anxious that nothing should be done by you to injure our interests, or those of our employes, and still more especially, the general industrial situation, which you, by action or non-action, have done so much to encourage.

With high esteem, I am,

Sincerely yours,   Elbert H. Gary
By JHO

P.S. I shall not have the opportunity to read and sign this letter, as I am in the country and desirous of having it sent today.

TL (WP, DLC).

From Benjamin Bright Chambers[1]

Philadelphia, Pa.

My dear President Wilson,   August 31, 1919.

I sincerely hope that you will pardon this delay in my writing to thank you for seeing me.[2] Due to the heat and overwork, I have been for a month really ill, and I have had to make a special trip to New York to see a physician.

It was very unfortunate that upon the only occasion I have talked to you in nearly eight years, I happened to be so run down. But far from the conversation not meaning anything, it ment more to me than anything else in that period.

I hope that you understood why I told you all I did. It was not to make parade of pain, or to seek your sympathy at all, but since a person like you offered me your friendship and trusted me, it of course presupposed that I am at every turn a gentlemen, and if I met the sort of trouble that I did, it seemed to me that I was bound in honor to tell you all of it. But having told it, I shall never, if or when you allow me again to see you, mention anything unpleasant, and my mind shall be directed, as only I wished I had the time then, to the delightful sides of life, and to carrying out what I have wished.

May I, however, now add to that conversation the fact that the lawyer from the east who was sent west secretly by my sister,[3] deceived me when he saw me, as to the amount of money which I had in the east, to the amount of several thousand dollars. He later died and it was found that he had embezzled a number of thousands of dollars, as I had predicted would be the case. This was an added circumstance that embarrassed me (when in Oregon last): indeed it was a combination at one time of a number of very unfortunate circumstances which threw me into such a position.

As to the man in the west who threatened me I am sure you understand that my only object, which led me into the trouble, and indeed kept me in it, was a clearly charitable desire to help him and a few of his family. It was five years ago. I of course do not communicate with him, and only one other person in the west knew of it, whom I saw in Philadelphia last autumn, and who told me that not one word concerning it had ever gotten out or been mentioned. Nothing now will ever come of it. In the East only three or four people know of it, and I want to assure you that I shall never mention one word of my last conversation with you to any one.

I shall probably accept your advice, of teaching for one more year. As to your keeping a memoranda, I do not know what I can add, now at least. As you know my whole life has been profoundly influenced by your ideas.[4] I have no other purpose than to accomplish as much good as I can. I have a good deal of ability and now a number of friends. But partly on the theory that a man should be careful in choosing his life work, and partly because of the opposition of my sister and her husband, I held off after graduation in making a start for five years, at which very time I met with all of this trouble. Yet I cannot see that to loose ten years in a sense is an overwhelming handicap, and that there is not such a thing as starting at 32 or even 33, and succeeding nobly, in a life well spent for other people, and the world's good. The whole difficulty just now is to get well and get into a position where I would be on my feet.

If you will see me at some much later period, I shall in all probability accept any advice you would give and do anything which you would suggest. But may I repeat that I shall not again say anything of an unpleasant nature; and you know I do not want to bother you. I know now, as I knew full well when at college, that you are one of the few really great men in the world's history.

Will you please accept my best wishes for yourself and Mrs. Wilson, and allow me to thank you once more for the interview which ment so very much to me.

Cordially and respectfully yours,   Benj. B. Chambers

ALS (WP, DLC).

[1] Princeton 1909, formerly in the lumber business in Oregon, at this time engaged in secondary school teaching in the Philadelphia area.

[2] Wilson had met with Chambers at the White House from noon to 12:30 p.m. on August 11.

[3] Eleanor Chambers (Mrs. John Findlay) Van Lear.

[4] Chambers had earlier consulted Wilson for guidance on various problems. He later (1932) wrote a memoir of his relationship with Wilson: "The Character of Woodrow Wilson," T MS (NjP-Ar and WC, NjP). It is a warm portrayal of Wilson as the person who, Chambers says, had the greatest influence in shaping his life.

Frank Lyon Polk to Robert Lansing

Paris, Aug. 31, 1919

Confidential. #3975. For the Secretary of State from Polk. "Your 2981 Aug. 28, 4 p[m] received. Does the President intend to send any personal message for me to transmit to Venizelos in reply to Venizelos plan submitted in my 3704, Aug. 15, 8 p.?.[1] I think it would help if he would.   Polk.

T telegram (SDR, RG 59, 763.72119/6453, DNA).
  [1] Actually, FLP to RL, Aug. 16, 1919.

From Frank Lyon Polk

Paris August 31 1919.

3774, Confidential for the President and Secretary of State.

Following memorandum handed me yesterday by Clemenceau, who told me that he, Tittoni, and Balfour had had a conference on the Italian situation, and that this was Tittoni's proposal.[1] I put the paper in my pocket without reading it, so made no comment to him. Tittoni is to see Lloyd George today, and apparently Tittoni, Lloyd George, and Clemenceau are immediately to join in a telegram to the President on the subject of the proposed settlement. Tardieu has asked to see me tomorrow to discuss it. I shall take the position that the Wilson line and Zara demarcations in detail in our telegram 3834, August 22nd 2 P.M. is as far as we will go, but that of course if they wish to appeal to the President it is entirely their right to do so. The memorandum in translation follows:

"Proposed note to Mr. Polk August 29th.

One. President Wilson's line.

Italy accepts as her eastern boundary President Wilson's line. She asks only that to the north of Albona this line shall reach the sea at a point to the south of the Chersono-Fianona road, thus leaving to Italy the town of Albona which is Italian and from which there were many Italian volunteers. *If the coast strip is neutralized.*[2]

Two. Fiume.

So far as Fiume is concerned two solutions are possible.

(A). An independent state with the boundaries as fixed by President Wilson (except for the slight rectification of Albona), the island of Cherso to be part of the independent state in accordance with the line of President Wilson; a special status for the city of Fiume. *Agreed to without a special status for Fiume*

(B). The city of Fiume itself to be given outright to Italy, the administrative district of Susac to be left to Jugo-Slavia. Under this arrangement no independent state, all the territory east of President Wilson's line and the Island of Cherso to go to Jugo-Slavia. As a military guarantee, Italy asks under this plan that all that part of the Jugo-Slav territory which, under the other plan, would have constituted the independent state, shall be neutralized. *No.*

(C). In either case very precise guarantees for the ethnic minorities. *Yes*

Three. Dalmatia.

All of Dalmatia to go to the Jugo-Slavs, except the town of Zara and the island of Uglian, immediately in the vicinity of Zara, which shall be under the sovereignty of Italy. The existing economic interests of Italy in Dalmatia and the rights of Italian minorities shall be guaranteed. *No, but willing that Zara should be accorded independent status.*

Four. Islands.

The only Italian islands would therefore be (Luteo) *Lussin & Unie, & Lissa Yes,* Lagosta *No.* and Uglian. *No.*

Five. Albania.

Italian mandate over the territory as defined by boundaries of 1913. *This would be most dangerous to the peace of the Balkans*

Six. Valona.

Italian sovereignty over the town together with such part of the hinterland as is strictly necessary to its economic life and security. *Yes.*

Seven. Railroads.

As far as the Assling railroad is concerned, Italy withdraws any territorial demand, and asks only for precise gua[ra]ntees as to the use of the railroad. Conversely, no cession of territory in dispute to the Jugo-Slavs in the valley of the Drin will be agreed to, but they shall receive with respect to the use of the proposed railroad the same guarantees which are given to Italy in the case of the Assling railroad. *Yes, if Jugo-Slavs agree*

Eight. Neutralization.

Italy proposes the general neutralization of all the coast and the islands from the southern extremity of Istria to Cattaro. *Yes as far S. as the Austrian island fortifications extended.*

Nine. Summary.

Italy makes the following concessions: (A) She withdraws her territorial claims to the Assling triangle. (B) She accepts the line of President Wilson from Idria to a point north of Albona. (C) She consents to the Island of Cherso forming part either of the independent state or of Jugo-Slavia. (D) She gives up all of Dalmatia except Zara and the Island of Uglian.

On the other hand, she asks for the sovereignty over Zara (with the island of (*), the mandate over Albania (with boundaries as fixed in 1913) and Valona with its hinterland.

As to the Albanian frontier on the side of Greece, Italy consents to the adoption, in the place of the 1913 frontier, of the frontier as proposed by the American Delegation which leaves Koritza to Albania and gives Argolic Cassandra to Greece." Polk.[3]

(*) APPARENT OMISSION.

T telegram (SDR, RG 59, 763.72119/6458, DNA).
  [1] All underlinings by WW.
  [2] This and subsequent italicized answers WWhw.
  [3] Henry White probably wrote this telegram. There is a copy of it edited by him in the H. White Papers, DLC.

From Francesco Saverio Nitti

Rome. August 31, 1919.

4021. Strictly private for President Wilson.

Sunday night. Prime Minister Nitti requested me this evening to send for him following confidential personal message to President. Text was in Italian but acting Minister of Foreign Affairs and I have gone over translation together and shown it to Nitti who reads English though he does not speak it.

He does not wish this step of his generally known and prefers to send message through me rather than in the usual way through Foreign Office and Italian Embassy Washington. Very confidential. He seems to hold very decided views about Italian (*) here.

Following is message:

"May I express to you at this time my personal opinion, my intimate *preoccupation*, my hopes. I address myself to you, my dear Mr. President, with sincere faith. You know my ideas and you know my sentiments toward you and toward America. What I am doing is not exactly according to diplomatic customs but I desire to (*) myself personally to you with sincerity of sentiment. I am profoundly convinced that your most cordial intention has never been lacking for a moment towards the Italian people. You know better than anyone else the greatness of our country and future civilization. You are too just a man not to feel the effort which Italy has made during the war. I consider you as a friend of our people and of Italy. I believe also that some Italian agents in high and low positions may have given by certain of their acts the impression of a tendency and a policy which are not Italian. I confess to you that I always deemed it dangerous to request territories in Dalmatia since others could have seen in this a pretention of ours toward an advance on the other coast but in your spirit of justice you must think what other powers would have done if they had had like us sacred traditions on an opposite shore created by *same* profound sincerity. I tell you however that justice has not been received in persuading you that our Istria, which Dante declared all Italian, should be broken up. People live above all in sentiment and in tradition and Italy wishes to maintain her old and great civilization which shall still give so much light to the world. I must also take away a doubt from your mind. They are not few in America who believe in good faith that Italy may still desire new war adventures, several organs of little authority of the Italian press (what country does not have its yellow press) have by their language authorized this absurd conception. The near future will show *who* (you?) where in Europe is a more profound will for progress, for concord and for peace. We must be great democracy of work and the road of Italy is sure. I hold above all for a sincere union with the United States of America which you so worthily represent. And it also is for this reason that I would wish for *who* (you?) to render justice to Italy by your own initiative and that you should give us the proof of your benevolent interest when the passions, excusable in part, of certain minorities shall be cooled off all will be happy to render justice to your work as I render it to you now. Believe me *may* (my?) dear Mr. President, he who has painted for you an imperialistic Italy, which wishes to oppress other peoples, has lied to you. This is not the noble and democratic Italy which I represent at this hour in the world but also the real Italy, in the name of which I speak to you as to a friend, feels that there is a minimum to which she has a right. This Italy serene and hard working. This Italy of thinkers and of workers you will see within a few years the cordial friend of the Slavs but she must feel that it was not wished to wrong her. I know Lloyd George and Clemenceau have understood the spirit of some of our requests but I trust that you will feel the personal appeal which I address to you. You can accept the moderate requests of Minister Tittoni with full serenity. In any case you must understand that the personal appeal which I am addressing to you is inspired by the same ideals as yours and by the same sentiments as direct your conduct and I hope that I have not appealed to you in vain. Nitti."   Jay.

(*) apparent omission.

T telegram (SDR, RG 59, 763.72119/6473, DNA).

From Edward Mandell House

London. Aug. 31, 1919.

Urgent 2938. For the President from Colonel House.

In reply to your telegram 5882.[1] I shall be glad to remain as desired when we finish the mandates on September 9th and 10th. I shall return to Paris. If you approve I shall not plan to sail until after October 1st. In view of the statements I have made about date of return, would it not be well for White House or State Department to say that: "The statement that Colonel House is about to return to the United States is incorrect. It will be necessary after he has finished his work on the Mandate Commission in London for him to return to his duties in Paris."

T telegram (R. Lansing Papers, DLC).
  [1] WW to EMH, Aug. 28, 1919.

From Charles Richard Crane

Paris August 31, 1919.

3976. Please transmit to the President the following from Charles Crane:

"Situation in Turkey so serious your commission decided to return to report as soon as it had covered essentials. Report well founded on vital human facts not in harmony with many things the Allies are doing or planning to do. I believe it would help your campaign to have it published. Doctor King sailing in few days with report[1] and inspiring message. He might make part of campaign with you. Outside of Armenia and Constantinople the former Turkish state must be kept for the Moslem world or there will be no peace there nor in any other part of the world. The flouting of the doctrine of no annexations will horrify millions of people, whose only trust now is in America and in you. It is not fair to the Turks to add to the strain already caused by the Greek landing and killing at Smyrna,[2] where one hundred ten thousand troops have demoralized a country kept well in hand by twelve British officers. A general American mandate would be received with such joy (by all?) *but all* kinds of people that little trouble and few troops would be required to administer it.

We are recommending for Syria:

First. That (?) administration go in accordance with desires to be a true mandatory under League of Nations.

Second. That Syria, including Palestine and Lebanon, be kept a unity according to desires of great majority.

Third. That Syria be under a single mandate.

Fourth. That Emir Feisal be King of the new Syrian State.

Fifth. That extreme Zionist program be seriously modified.

Sixth. Democratic America be asked to take the single mandate for Syria.

Seventh. That if for any reason America does not take mandate then it be given Great Britain.

We are recommending parallel policy for Mesopotamia, Great Britain as mandatory, in strict fulfillment spirit of Anglo-French declaration November 9th 1918.[3]

We are recommending for Turkey:

First. Separate Armenian state under mandate limited in area for their own sakes.

Second. Separate international Constantinopolitan state under League of Nations administered through mandatory.

Third. Mandatory for continued Turkish state according to their own desire.

Fourth. That no independent territory be set off for Greeks for the present.

Fifth. Appointment of commission on precise boundary.

Sixth. A general, but composite mandate for non-Arabic speaking portions of Turkish Empire, to include subordinate mandates as indicated with Governors and Governor General.

Seventh. That America be asked to take the whole if reasonable conditions can be fulfilled; not to take any part if not the whole. Charles Crane."   Polk.

T telegram (WP, DLC).
[1] It is printed in *PPC*, XII, 751-863. The appearance of this volume in 1947 marked the first official publication of the complete, *verbatim* text of the report of the King-Crane Commission.

A copy of the report was presented to the American peace commission in Paris on August 28, 1919. Henry Churchill King sailed from Brest for New York on September 5, carrying with him the original copy of the report. King wrote to Wilson while at sea on September 10 as follows: "Mr. Crane and I have supposed ourselves to be making our report primarily to yourself and to the American Delegation at the Peace Conference, and that you and the Delegation must decide how our report might be further used. But as the American Section of the projected Inter-Allied Commission on Mandates in Turkey, we have aimed so to prepare our report, that (with the exception of the Confidential Appendix to the Report on Syria) it could be put in its entirety in the hands of British, French or Italian representatives, if you so desire. Mr. Crane and I have also regarded ourselves as not free to give to the press any statement of our recommendations without your express permission; but have supposed there would be no objection, but might rather be some advantage, in giving some suggestion of the actual conditions found in Syria and Turkey." Quoted in Harry N. Howard, *The King-Crane Commission: An American Inquiry in the Middle East* (Beirut, 1963), p. 258. This letter is not in WP, DLC. The report was delivered to the White House on September 27, 1919, by Capt. Donald Melrose Brodie, U.S.A., a member of the staff of the King-Crane Commission. Because of Wilson's illness, it is doubtful if he ever read the document. *Ibid.*

At some subsequent date, the copy of the report delivered to the White House was transmitted to the State Department, and there it remained. Ray Stannard Baker wrote to King on May 4, 1922, to ask what had become of the report, whether any part of it had ever been published, and if he might have a copy for his study of Wilson at the Paris Peace Conference. King responded on May 6 with the following comment: "The State Department have never published any part of [the report], and seem to have adopted the policy of not giving anyone access to it. Under those circumstances Mr Crane and I have felt that about all we could do was to say to those who inquired of us about it, that so far as we were concerned we were perfectly ready to have the report seen by any inquirer, but that we did not feel at liberty to publish our findings until the State Department had released the report, although a few individuals had seen the report." Quoted in *ibid.*, p. 311. King and Crane decided to refer Baker's request for a copy of the report to Wilson. Wilson responded to Crane on July 6 saying that he had "no objection to Baker's making public the report on Syria"; indeed, he thought it "a very timely moment for its publication." WW to C. R. Crane, July 6, 1922, CCL (WP, DLC). Baker evidently got his copy of the report from King or Crane. He published extracts and summaries from it in *Woodrow Wilson and World Settlement* (3 vols., Garden City, N. Y., 1922), II, 205-219, and in the serial publication of that work in the *New York Times*, Aug. 20, 1922, Sect. 7, p. 4.

Baker's extracts in the *New York Times* in turn inspired James Wright Brown, the proprietor of *Editor & Publisher*, a trade journal of the newspaper publishing industry, to write to Wilson to request a copy of the report and permission to publish it in full. Wilson immediately agreed. J. W. Brown to WW, Sept. 27, 1922, TLS, and J. R. Bolling to J. W. Brown, Sept. 28, 1922, CCL, both in WP, DLC. Brown printed substantially the entire prose text of the report as a supplement to *Editor & Publisher*, LV (Dec. 2, 1922), omitting the extensive statistical material presented in tabular form in the original report, and paraphrasing a few sentences and paragraphs to avoid specific references to the statistical material. Brown's version was reprinted in the *New York Times*, Dec. 3 and 4, 1922.

[2] About which, see the index references to "Smyrna, Greek landing at," in Vol. 59 of this series.

[3] For the text of which, see the memorandum printed at March 25, 1919, Vol. 56.

To Joseph Patrick Tumulty

Dear Tumulty: [The White House] 1 September 1919

I wish you would handle this[1] for me in some considerate way. Reading the dispatches, as I do, every day, I know what a delicate and dangerous situation exists throughout the world with regard to the Jews and the activities of the promoters of the Zionist movement, and I think it would be most imprudent for me to make any public expression of opinion.

These gentlemen know the helpful position which the Government of the United States has assumed in this matter and are a little too insistent upon a constant asseveration of our interest and sympathy.   The President

TL (WP, DLC).

[1] Samuel Max Melamed to WW, Aug. 25, 1919, TLS (WP, DLC). Melamed, the editor in chief of the Chicago *Daily Jewish Courier*, a newspaper printed in Yiddish, informed Wilson that the twenty-second annual convention of the Zionist Organization of America was to take place in Chicago on September 14 and would, in his opinion, "in all probability . . . lay the foundations for a Jewish home-land in Palestine." He requested Wilson to send a message "of encouragement or assurance" to American Jews to be included in a special convention issue of the *Jewish Daily Courier*.

To William Cox Redfield

PERSONAL

My dear Mr. Secretary: The White House 1 September, 1919.

Thank you for your letter of August 30th. It is generous of you to consent to postpone your retirement, and I want to assure you how much I appreciate the generous suggestion. I shall hope to have a little conversation with you about this very important matter before I leave.

Cordially and faithfully yours,   Woodrow Wilson

TLS (W. C. Redfield Papers, DLC).

To Bert Mark Jewell

My dear Mr. Jewell: [The White House] 1 September, 1919.

Thank you for your frank letter of August 29th. I realize the serious elements in the situation, but must believe that the shopmen will act as other responsible American citizens would act in the existing critical situation.

Cordially and sincerely yours,   Woodrow Wilson

TLS (Letterpress Books, WP, DLC.)

To Joseph Eugene Ransdell

My dear Senator: [The White House] 1 September, 1919.

I was very much impressed by what you and your senatorial colleagues said to me the other day about Colonel _____, and immediately after your visit I took the matter up with the Secretary of War in the sincere hope that after I learned all the circumstances of the case, I would feel free to take the course that you and your colleagues suggested. But I am sorry to say, my dear Senator, that a full recital of the facts of the case[1] makes it seem to me most unwise to do what you urged, notwithstanding my great admiration for the unusual and admirable record of Colonel _____ and my full appreciation of the fact that one error, however serious, does not establish a presumption as to a man's character or usefulness.

The fact seems to be that, while Colonel _____ had been drinking, he was by no means under the influence of liquor in the sense that his actions were irresponsible or that he was unaware of what he was doing. There were many elements of plan and deliberation in the circumstances as disclosed, and I feel that a very vital matter of morale is involved in every case of discipline of this sort.

I believe that it would be seriously demoralizing to the service, were I to intervene and prevent a court martial, and I want to suggest that if Colonel _____, as is probable, pleads guilty before the court, many unpleasant circumstances of publicity will be avoided, and it will then be possible to consider any modifications of punishment which may be thought desirable in view of his admirable record.

With unaffected regret that I cannot take the course you urge,
Cordially and sincerely yours,   Woodrow Wilson

TLS (Letterpress Books, WP, DLC).
¹ NDB to WW, Aug. 29, 1919.

To Porter James McCumber

[The White House]
My dear Senator McCumber: 1 September, 1919.

I deeply and warmly appreciate your letter of August 29th. It is very stimulating to get such suggestions and such guidance, and they are most cordially welcome. I know the disinterested and patriotic spirit in which you are approaching this whole matter of the Treaty, and am particularly gratified that you should put your thoughts at my service in the important mission I am about to undertake. Your suggestions are very much to the point indeed and constitute an admirable analysis, it seems to me, of the points at issue upon which the country will be most desirous of being fully informed.

Cordially and sincerely yours,   Woodrow Wilson

TLS (Letterpress Books, WP, DLC).

From Henry Cabot Lodge

[Washington]
My dear Mr. President: September 1, 1919

I am indebted to you for your letter of August 28, which reached me last evening. I also have to thank you for sending to the Senate the treaty with Poland, signed at Versailles on the 28th of June, and the agreement between the United States, Belgium, and the British Empire, of one part, and Germany, of the other part, with regard to the military occupation of the territory of the Rhine, also signed at Versailles on the 28th of June. The declaration of the

16th of June was printed some time ago in the Record from the English "White Book," the declaration having been submitted to the House of Commons on the 4th of July I believe. The Committee asked for it merely because they thought it better that it should be officially before them.

As to the request of the Committee for drafts or information regarding the treaties with Austria, Hungary, Bulgaria and Turkey: the Committee of course were aware that negotiations are wholly in the hands of the Executive and there was no thought of trespassing upon your jurisdiction. You noticed, of course, that the request asked merely for such information as you could give them if it was not incompatible with the public interest. The four treaties still to be made are so closely connected with the German treaty that many Senators have thought that all the peace treaties should be considered together, and the request was made merely for such information as you felt could be properly given in regard to those treaties not yet submitted in the hope that it might hasten action upon the treaty of peace with Germany. If it is not compatible with the public interest to give any information in regard to them, that is a matter upon which, of course, your decision is final.

I have the honor to be
Very respectfully Yours   H. C. Lodge Chairman

TLS (WP, DLC).

From a Memorandum by Robert Lansing

TENDENCY TOWARD COMMUNISTIC IDEAS.

September 1, 1919.

I wonder how long we can tolerate the radical propaganda which is being carried on in this country and is teaching the laboring class to revolt against the present economic order. How long can we go on this way without a disaster? The peril seems to me very great. On the other hand the President has as much as said that he is not afraid of this growing tendency but on the contrary he feels that it springs from the awakening consciousness of a right which is essentially just. He speaks of "industrial democracy" as necessary to perfect "political democracy," and he indicates that he is prepared to go a long way in securing to the working man control over and profit in the production of his labor. Secretary Baker, whose social and political principles are even more radical than those of the President, announced today that he had been experimenting with one of the factories of the War Department in wage-fixing, product-controlling and general participation in the management by the employes, and that the venture had been entirely successful. He too used this newly coined shibboleth of "industrial democracy."

If this sort of thing keeps on and leaders of political thought encourage such ideas we are about to enter upon one of the most critical periods in our history. We will be faced with the greatest labor strikes that this country has ever seen. I do not doubt that there will be serious disorders, violence and blood-shed, because the demands of Labor will be beyond reason. Then the reformers, who started this movement, will too late attempt to check it, because they will find that the laborers have turned to new leaders with communistic if not Bolshevik doctrines. I do not believe that the President will be listened to as he has been in the past. He will issue appeals but they will not be as effective as they were in the past. Then what will happen?

The consequence of this approaching state of industrial unrest and bitter antagonism is, as I see it, a political party with communistic principles which intends to break down the present economic order and supercede it with a new order which will be founded on the theory that the laboring class should be not only masters of their own toil but also of the accumulated wealth of others without which they would lack opportunity to labor. The right to possess capital is ignored, and the possessors of capital become the servants of those who desire to use it for their own benefit and claim the right to such benefit because they work with their hands. . . .

T MS (R. Lansing Papers, DLC).

A News Report

[*Sept. 2, 1919*]

WILSON STILL DEAF TO TREATY CHANGES
Voices Particular Disapproval of Amendments Affecting Votes in League Council.
WARNED OF RESERVATIONS

Washington, Sept. 2.—After a talk of an hour with President Wilson at the White House late today, Senator Swanson of Virginia, one of the leaders in the fight for ratification of the Versailles treaty as written, declared that the President was as unalterably opposed as ever to any changes that would involve recommitting the treaty to the Paris Conference.

Mr. Swanson went to the White House to take up the Senate situation with the President prior to the latter's departure tomorrow on his month's trip through the West. The President, he said, once more expressed the hope that the majority of the Senate would accept the treaty as it stood. If interpretative reservations were deemed imperative, the President said he would not oppose them, but he frowned upon the threatened program of direct amendments and drastic reservations that would send the treaty back to Paris.

The Shantung amendment,[1] Senator Swanson told the President, had no chance of being accepted by the Senate. Its supporters, he said, could not command anywhere near a majority of votes for it.

The President voiced disapproval of the amendment offered in the Foreign Relations Committee by Senator Johnson of California to provide that the United States have equal representation with Great Britain in the League of Nations Council.[2] This amendment, if adopted, the President said, would throw the entire treaty back to Paris and reopen it to long controversy.

Although Great Britain with her colonies has six votes in the Council and Assembly, the President said, the fact was that the delegates, in effect, would vote as one, and that the United States would be at no actual disadvantage.

Senator Swanson predicted, in his talk with the President, that none of the other amendments advocated by the majority Senators would obtain a favorable vote in the Senate. As to reservations, he frankly told the President that there was an appreciable drift toward others than interpretative ones, but the Administration Senators had concentrated their forces in an effort to defeat them.

At the Capitol during the day Administration Senators had a series of conferences with several of the Republican reservationists. Talk of compromise on the part of Democrats was in the air, but none of the Democratic leaders would admit that they were making any overtures.

The majority leaders complacently predicted that their policy of drastic reservations would win. As to amendments, none of them would prophesy on any but that sponsored by Mr. Johnson, to give the United States six delegates in the League Council. There was a general tendency manifested to regard the Johnson amendment as likely to be adopted by the Senate.

The Foreign Relations Committee expects to complete its executive sessions over the treaty by Thursday. After that reservations will be considered. With speed the treaty may be reported to the Senate by Saturday. . . .

Printed in the *New York Times*, Sept. 3, 1919.
    [1] See n. 1 to the extract from R. Lansing's desk diary printed at Aug. 25, 1919.
    [2] The Senate Foreign Relations Committee on August 29 had adopted, by a vote of nine to eight, an amendment to Article III of the Covenant of the League of Nations offered by Johnson which read as follows: "Provided that when any member of the League has or possesses self-governing dominions or colonies or parts of empire which are also members of the League, the United States shall have votes in the assembly or council of the League numerically equal to the aggregate vote of such member of the League and its self-governing dominions and colonies and parts of empire in the council or assembly of the League." *New York Times*, Aug. 30, 1919.

Gilbert Fairchild Close to the White House Staff

2 September, 1919

Memorandum.

The President would like to see Senator Hitchcock tomorrow, Wednesday, at the afternoon hour which will least interfere with his work in the Senate, though as long before seven o'clock, his leaving time, as possible. The President's own preference would be 2.15.[1]   G.F.C.

T MS (WP, DLC).
    [1] The Head Usher's Diary does not record Hitchcock's visit on September 3, about which see n. 1 to Wilson's memorandum printed at that date.

To James Campbell Cantrill[1]

The White House, 2 September, 1919

Both as the leader of the party and as a student of existing conditions throughout the world, I venture to urge with the utmost earnestness that the State Convention include in its platform a plank in favor of the Suffrage Amendment. It would serve mankind and the party by doing so.[2]   Woodrow Wilson

T telegram (WP, DLC).
    [1] Democratic congressman from Kentucky.
    [2] The Kentucky State Democratic Convention, which met in Louisville on September 4, did include a plank which called upon the legislature to ratify the woman-suffrage amendment. Louisville *Courier-Journal*, Sept. 5, 1919.

To Henry van Dyke

My dear Dr. van Dyke: [The White House] 2 September, 1919.

I know that you will be generous and pardon my delay in replying to your letter of the thirteenth of July,[1] because you will be able to realize how full my days have been and how necessary it has been for me to devote my whole time to other things than my private correspondence.

But I must not altogether neglect to acknowledge a letter which I very warmly appreciated. I know what earnest work you have been doing on behalf of the League of Nations, and therefore know how to value your kind letter of the thirteenth of July and its thoughtful suggestions.

Cordially and sincerely yours,   Woodrow Wilson

TLS (Letterpress Books, WP, DLC.)
    [1] It is printed at that date in Vol. 61.

To Benjamin Bright Chambers

My dear Chambers: [The White House] 2 September, 1919

Just a line to acknowledge your letter of August 31st and to say that I am heartily glad that you are going to teach for another year.

With the best wishes,

Cordially yours,   Woodrow Wilson

TLS (Letterpress Books, WP, DLC).

To Samuel Isett Woodbridge[1]

                                    The White House
My dear Woodbridge: 2 September, 1919

I need hardly tell you that I have read your letter[2] very carefully and thoughtfully, and with a very full appreciation of the spirit which prompted it.

But what you say leads me to believe that you have not thought the matter through. France and Great Britain absolutely bound themselves by treaty to Japan with regard to the Shantung settlement as it stands in the Treaty with Germany. What would you propose that we should do? To refuse to concur in the Treaty with Germany would not alter the situation in China's favor, unless it is your idea that we should force Great Britain and France to break their special treaty with Japan, and how would you suggest that we should do that? By the exercise of what sort of force?

Japan, as you know, has promised to retain much less than the terms of the treaty give her. She has consented to bind herself by all the engagements of the Covenant of the League of Nations, and if the United States is to be a party to this treaty and a member of the League, she will have an opportunity for serving China in all matters of international justice such as she has never had before, and such as she could not obtain by the course you suggest.

I beg that you will think these things over.

All the news you give us of the family is most welcome, and I hope you will give my most affectionate messages to them all.

With best wishes,   Faithfully yours,   Woodrow Wilson

TLS (WC, NjP).
  [1] Presbyterian missionary in Shanghai, at this time on furlough in the United States. His deceased wife, Jeanie Wilson Woodrow Woodbridge, was a first cousin of Woodrow Wilson.
  [2] S. I. Woodbridge to WW, Aug. 26, 1919, ALS (WP, DLC). An excerpt from this letter follows:
  "In my newspaper work I have observed very carefully the trend of events for the past thirty years. Wilson, Japan will *never* relax her hold on China. Ask any body who has ever lived a dozen years in the Far East, and you will discover that rational people in any profession or trade will agree with this statement. The people who love their country the most are the ones who have been trained by missionaries. The best commercial assets America has in China are American Hospitals, Colleges, Schools and printing presses. These have been the main factor in creating and cementing China's love for our American people. It seems to me that putting our *imprimatur* on the Shantung Agreement will forever crush our commercial hopes and aspirations. It puts *you* in a terrible light in the eyes of four hundred millions of people. But more important in God's sight is this—Agreement to this unjust agreement will put back the work the Church has been doing, for many years."

From Franklin Knight Lane

My dear Mr. President: Washington September 2, 1919.

I have had a group of men who are familiar with the world situation as to petroleum at work on the problem you gave me as to supplying our ships with fuel oil.[1] The Shipping Board has not yet given any exact data as to its needs. But I have taken their rough estimate at the amount of fuel oil needed and had the problem worked out on that basis. The survey made by these experts accompanies this letter.[2]

Permit me to supplement what they have said with a few suggestions of my own:

1. That the first duty is to secure a more profitable use of of [sic] the oil available.

To burn oil under a boiler and convert it into steam secures but ten per cent of the heat units in the oil. Whereas if a Diesel Engine were used 30 to 35 per cent would be secured.

Therefore, our first duty is to develop the Diesel Engine and educate men who can handle it. This I am satisfied will be the policy of other countries and we should be forehanded.

A campaign should be made under your leadership and direction to secure Diesel Engines and engineers, both for our shipping program and for stationery plants.

2. That we should save oil.

Millions of barrels now are wasted yearly which could be saved by demonstrating that it can be done. Most of the operators would be agreeable to such a program because it would mean money to them. We have been carrying on such a campaign on the Indian lands of Oklahoma very successfully. It should be extended over all fields. Money to hire experts is all that is needed to make such an effort. And if permission and demonstration will not do the work, then we should try the potency of the law.

3. That we should buy fuel oil by the millions of barrels *now* while it is cheap—cheaper than it probably will be two years hence and at any time after the Shipping Board's program is fully developed.

It can be stored in covered earth reservoirs for comparatively little money, from which, if carefully made, the loss will be almost negligible.

4. That we should contract for foreign fuel oil for as long a term of years as possible. This can be done as to Mexican oil. Either the price can be fixed in advance or the market price at the time be the price. The former I would believe to be the wiser policy.

5. Induce the building of hydro-electric plants along the lines of those railroads which are now great consumers of fuel oil. Passage of a proper power bill would greatly help.

6. Assure American capital that if it goes into a foreign country and secures the right to drill for oil on a legal and fair basis (all of which must be shown to the State Department) that it will be protected against confiscation or discrimination. This should be a known published policy.

7. Deny by law the right of any nationals of any foreign country to have any stock or other interest in an American producing, selling or refining company, when such foreign country does not permit Americans to have a stock or other interest in a foreign oil property.

8. Require every American corporation producing oil in a foreign country to take out a Federal charter for such enterprise under which whatever oil it produces should be subject to a preferential right on the part of this government to take all of its supply or a percentage thereof at any time on payment of the market price.

9. Sell no oil to a vessel carrying a charter from any foreign government either at an American port or at any American bunker when that government does not sell oil at a non-discriminatory price to our vessels at its bunkers or ports.

10. Discover oil if possible in the Philippines. This could be done through private capital, I believe, if properly approached. If not, the government should make the effort.

With the Gulf and Caribbean supply I believe the Atlantic needs can be taken care of under this program. The Mediterranean needs may be cared for in the new strike in Palestine if this field keeps its promise and we can tie it to us. (It is a Standard oil enterprise.) The Indian Ocean could be supplied from the Persian field if we compelled it by some such legislation as that suggested above, or secured guarantees of supply by diplomacy, a thing quite possible, I believe, if we evidenced a determination not to supply English ships at our ports or bunkers unless they supplied ours at theirs. The Pacific can be cared for immediately from the California field and the possible Philippine field. In the interior of China there is said to be oil which could be brought out by pipe line and water if we would guarantee the funds by making a long term contract. But this would be very costly.

On the whole I do not think the situation is a desperate one provided we take advantage of our present relations with Great Britain to compel fair play, and make our own people feel certain that they will be protected in foreign investments when they comply with the re[a]sonable regulations we should make as to their duty toward other countries and nationals.

As to the machinery for carrying out these and other suggestions as to policy and planning, I would think it could be done if you were to call in the Secretary of State, Secretary of Navy, Secretary of Interior, and Chairman of Shipping Board. You could then determine on a policy and select some man as an executive officer who would carry out your decisions and work with and through the different departments to secure their fullest help.

Cordially and faithfully yours,   Franklin K. Lane

TLS (WP, DLC).
    [1] See WW to FKL, Aug. 2, 1919, and FKL to WW, Aug. 4, 1919.
    [2] David White et al., "Preliminary Draft of Report to the Secretary of the Interior on the FUEL OIL SUPPLY FOR THE MERCHANT MARINE," Aug. 20, 1919, T MS (WP, DLC). This thirty-three-page report concluded that the domestic sources of oil known at that time could not come even close to providing the estimated 100,000,000 barrels of fuel oil per year needed by 1922 to operate the American navy and merchant marine. Therefore, the United States would have to compete with the other nations of the world for the necessary crude oil, with all the political problems and uncertainties that that would entail. The report put forth various proposals to deal with the situation, some of which are mentioned by Lane in the above letter. The most notable suggestion not mentioned was that it might be necessary for the United States Government to establish an oil board and a corporation, somewhat similar to the United States Shipping Board and its Emergency Fleet Corporation, to deal in foreign oil markets.
    David White was the Chief Geologist with the United States Geological Survey.

Woodrow Wilson and Robert Lansing to Frank Lyon Polk

Washington, September 2, 1919.

3074 CONFIDENTIAL FOR POLK FROM THE PRESIDENT AND SECRETARY OF STATE.

Your 3774. August 31, 10 p.m.

Point one: Acceptable if the coast strip is neutralized.

Point two: Fiume. Paragraph a agreed to but without a special status for Fiume.

Point two: Paragraph b not acceptable.

Point two: Paragraph c agreed to.

Point three: Dalmatia. Cannot be accepted but would be willing that Zara should be accorded an independent status.

Point four: Islands. Acceptable that Lussin, Unie and Lissa should be Italian; but not Lagosta and Uglian.

Point five: Albania. An Italian mandate over this territory would be most dangerous to the peace of the Balkans and should not be accepted.

Point six: Valona. This is acceptable.

Point seven: Railways. This arrangement is acceptable if the Jugo-Slavs agree to it.

Point eight: Neutralization. This may be accepted as far south as the Austrian island fortifications extended.   Lansing.

T telegram (SDR, RG 59, 763.72119/6458, DNA).

Robert Lansing to Frank Lyon Polk

Washington. Sept. 2, 1919.

3012. CONFIDENTIAL. For Polk from Lansing.

Your 3927, August 28, 11 a.m.[1]

After talking over the matter of an international government of large Constantinople State with the President, his opinion is adverse to Johnson's suggestion because he considers that international administrative control cannot successfully operate. While I am in general accord with his views, which are supported by previous experiments, and realize the danger of intrigues and jealousies, I am not at all certain that some plan like the one proposed might not temporarily bridge over the present situation until matters become more normal and a better and more stable arrangement can be reached.

I wish you would consider the question further and possibly make a new suggestion as originating with you which I can lay before the President.   Lansing.

T telegram (SDR, RG 59, 763.72119/6438, DNA).
[1] FLP to RL, Aug. 28, 1919, T telegram (SDR, RG 59, 763.72119/6438, DNA). In this telegram, Douglas Wilson Johnson suggested that the legitimate objections of France and England to a large State of Constantinople would be satisfied by a form of international government of the state in which both France and England were represented. A copy of this telegram was sent to Wilson on August 29.

A Memorandum[1]

[Sept. 3, 1919]

Suggestion

The Senate of the United States of America advises and consents to the ratification of said treaty, with the following understanding of the Articles of said treaty mentioned below; and requests the President of the United States to communicate these interpretations to the several States signatory to said treaty at the same time that he deposits the formal instrument of ratification with the Government of the French Republic at Paris:

Inasmuch as Article One of the Covenant of the League of Nations provides no tribunal to pass judgment upon the right of a Member State to withdraw from the League, the Government of the United States understands the provision of Article One with regard to withdrawal as putting no limitation upon the right of a Member State to withdraw except such as may lie in the conscience of the Power proposing to withdraw with regard to its having fulfilled "all its international obligations and all its obligations under the Covenant" in the sense intended by the instrument.

It understands that the advice of the Council of the League with regard to the employment of armed force contemplated in Article Ten of the Covenant of the League is to be regarded only as advice and leaves each Member State free to exercise its own judgment as to whether it is wise or practicable to act upon that advice or not.

It understands that under Article Fifteen of the Covenant of the League no question can be raised either in the Assembly or in the Council of the League which will give that body the right to report or to make any recommendation upon the policy of any Member State with regard to such matters as immigration, naturalization, or tariffs.

It understands, also, that the reference to the Monroe Doctrine in Article Twenty-one of the Covenant of the League means that nothing contained in the Covenant shall be interpreted as in any way impairing or interfering with the application of the Monroe Doctrine in the American Hemisphere.

WWT MS (WP, DLC).
  [1] There is a first draft of this memorandum in WP, DLC. Wilson gave this memorandum to Hitchcock on September 3. Hitchcock returned it in G. M. Hitchcock to EBW, Jan. 5, 1920, and it is filed in WP, DLC, as an enclosure with his letter.

To Newton Diehl Baker

My dear Mr. Secretary,

The White House.
3 Septem[be]r, 1919.

Will you not be kind enough, when you welcome General Pershing at New York,[1] to convey to him the following message from me.

My dear General Pershing, I am distressed that I cannot greet you in person. It would give me the greatest pleasure to grasp your hand and say to you what is in my heart and in the hearts of all true Americans as we hail your return to the home land you have served so gallantly. Notwithstanding my physical absence, may I not, as your commander-in-chief and as spokesmen of our fellow countrymen, bid you an affectionate and enthusiastic welcome,—a welcome warmed with the ardour of genuine affection and deep admiration? You have served the country with fine devotion and admirable efficiency, in a war forever memorable as the world's triumphant protest against injustice and [as its][2] vindication of liberty, the liberty of peoples and of nations. We are proud of you and of the men you commanded. No finer armies ever set their indomitable strength and unconquerable spirit against the forces of wrong. Their glory is the glory of the nation, and it is with a thrill of profound pride that we greet you as their leader and commander. You have just come from the sea and from the care of the men of the Navy, who made the achievements of our arms on land possible, and who so gallantly assisted to clear the seas of their lurking peril. Our hearts go out to them, too. It is delightful to see you home again, well and fit for the fatigues you must endure before we are done with our welcome! I will not speak now of our associates on the other side of the sea. It will be delightful on many occasions to speak their praise. I speak now only of our personal joy that you are at home again and that we have the opportunity to make you feel the warmth of our affectionate welcome.

I envy, my dear Mr. Secretary, the privilege you are to have.

Faithfully Yours,   Woodrow Wilson

WWTLS (N. D. Baker Papers, DLC).
    [1] Pershing landed in New York on September 8. For a detailed account of his triumphal arrival, see the *New York Times*, Sept. 9, 1919.
    [2] NDBhw.

To Samuel Gompers

My dear Sir: The White House 3 September 1919.

For the purpose of reaching, if possible, some common ground of agreement and action with regard to the future conduct of industry, I desire to obtain the combined judgment of representative employers, representative employees, and representatives of the general public conversant with these matters, and for the accomplishment of that purpose I have decided to call a conference of five persons to be selected by the Chamber of Commerce of the United States of America, five persons to be selected by the National Industrial Conference Board, fifteen persons to be selected by the American Federation of Labor, three persons to be selected by the farming organizations, and two persons to be selected by the investment bankers, to confer with fifteen representatives of the general public whom I shall select, these representatives to meet in the City of Washington on October 6, 1919, for the purpose of consulting together on the great and vital questions affecting our industrial life and their consequent effect upon all our people, to discuss such methods as have already been tried out of bringing capital and labour into close cooperation, and to canvas every relevant feature of the present industrial situation, for the purpose of enabling us to work out, if possible, in a genuine spirit of cooperation a practicable method of association based upon a real community of interest which will redound to the welfare of all our people.

The wastages of war have seriously interfered with the natural course of our industrial and economic development. The nervous tension of our people has not yet relaxed to normal. The necessity of devising at once methods by which we can speedily recover from this condition and obviate the wastefulness caused by the continued interruption of many of our important industrial enterprizes by strikes and lockouts emphasizes the need for a meeting of minds in a conference such as I have suggested. I am sure that your organization will gladly bear the expenses of its own representatives to a conference called for such an important purpose, and I would therefore request that you select fifteen persons to act as the representatives of the employees connected with your organization in the conference, and advise the Secretary of Labor of the names and addresses of the persons selected so that he may make the necessary arrangements for the meeting.

Sincerely yours, Woodrow Wilson[1]

TLS (S. Gompers Corr., AFL-CIO Archives).
[1] On the same date, Wilson sent copies of this letter, *mutatis mutandis*, to Homer

Lenoir Ferguson, president of the Chamber of Commerce of the United States of America; Magnus Washington Alexander, managing director of the National Industrial Conference Board; William Gideon Baker, Jr., president of the Investment Bankers Association; James Nelson Tittemore, president of the American Society of Equity; Charles Simon Barrett, president of the National Farmers' Union; and Oliver Wilson, president of the National Grange. All are TLS, Letterpress Books, WP, DLC.

In drafting these letters, Wilson heavily revised the draft of the letter to Homer L. Ferguson that William B. Wilson had sent him on August 30. This draft is printed as an Enclosure with WBW to WW, August 30, 1919. Woodrow Wilson then made a new start and used only the last paragraph of W. B. Wilson's draft.

To Henry Cabot Lodge

My dear Mr. Chairman: [The White House] 3 September, 1919.

After sending to the Senate the other day a copy of the Rhine land agreement, it occurred to me that it might be serviceable to your committee to have the enclosed memorandum,[1] which was agreed to on the same day that the Rhine land agreement itself was finally formulated.   Sincerely yours,   Woodrow Wilson

TLS (Letterpress Books, WP, DLC).
  [1] See Appendix III to the minutes of the Council of Four printed at June 13, 1919, 12:00 noon, Vol. 60.

To Albert Rathbone

My dear Mr. Rathbone: [The White House] 3 September, 1919.

I write to ask a great service of you. We very much need a financial advisor to be associated with the Peace Commission in Paris, who will have an adequate knowledge of what has gone before and be also in intimate touch with the financial policy of our own country, and I am writing to express the hope that you will add to the services you have already rendered the country by consenting to go to Paris and act in that capacity. So many of the most substantial interests of the country are involved that it is my desire to have men like yourself of the first capacity in charge of the great matters which are sure to arise on every hand.
               Cordially and sincerely yours,   Woodrow Wilson

TLS (Letterpress Books, WP, DLC).

To Joseph Tyrone Derry[1]

My dear Mr. Derry: [The White House] 3 September, 1919.

I am sincerely distressed that I was not able to see you when you were in Washington. It would have been a real pleasure to grasp your hand once more, but I hasten to send this word of cordial greeting after you.

Cordially and sincerely yours, Woodrow Wilson

TLS (Letterpress Books, WP, DLC).
[1] Formerly proprietor of the Select Classical School in Augusta, Ga., which Wilson had attended from 1867 to 1870.

To Francesco Saverio Nitti

My dear Mr. Secretary, The White House, 3 September, 1919.

Will you not be kind enough to have the following message conveyed to Signor Nitti?

I have received with the greatest gratification your generous message and beg to assure you that I do understand the motives by which the great Italian people are moved. There can never be in America anything but the warmest friendship for Italy, the warmest sympathy for her just ambitions, and the most earnest desire to render the service of friends. The position of the Government of the United States with regard to some of the Italian claims has not been due to any misconception of the spirit of the Italian people or their representatives, but only to the conviction that it would be as harmful to Italy herself as it would be dangerous to the peace and the good understanding upon which peace must rest to make settlements in the Adriatic which could not be squared with the principles elsewhere applied throughout the complicated settlements of the present negotiations. Pray accept assurances of my personal confidence and respect and my sincere thanks for what you so generously say of the motives which have controlled the action of the American Government.[1]

W.W.

WWTLI (SDR, RG 59, 763.72119/6473, DNA).
[1] This was sent as RL to Amembassy, Rome, No. 282, Sept. 3, 1919, T telegram (SDR, RG 59, 763.72119/6473, DNA).

From Edward Mandell House

Dear Governor: London, September 3, 1919.

After receiving your cable I notified Lord Grey that I would not be able to return with him to the United States on September 20th. as I had promised. He seems a little timid about the whole adventure and I hope you will give him the warmest possible welcome. He is one of the finest characters I have ever met, and you will find him the most satisfactory man representing a foreign government with whom you have had to deal. He would like to meet you in a personal way first before discussing business, and if you could have him around some evening alone I think it would be a joy to you both.

I had a talk with Chamberlain,[1] Chancellor of the Exchequer, yesterday. He believes that England can pull through and finally pay all her obligations provided she gets a little helpful consideration from the United States. It is not merely money that they want but at the moment they would like the interest payments deferred, and they would like the use of the American dollars which will come to them in one way or another during the next few months.

I am counting upon going over to Paris on the 13th. It is my intention to be there in an advisory capacity and not to sit in negotiations that are now pending. I shall try to get things so organized as to shorten their labors and bring them to an early conclusion. There is an enormous amount of criticism here and I suppose everywhere because of the delay.

The Hungarian, Bulgarian and Austrian Treaties should be out of the way by the first of the month, and it seems by common consent the Turkish Treaty is to be deferred.

I shall count upon sailing for the United States about the 10th of October. This would bring me there after the Treaty is out of the way.   Affectionately yours,   E. M. House

TLS (WP, DLC).
  [1] That is, (Joseph) Austen Chamberlain.

From the Diary of Dr. Grayson[1]

Wednesday, September 3, 1919.

The President spent the entire day cleaning up all of the loose ends of work about the Executive Offices and left Washington at 7:00 o'clock in the evening in the Private Car MAYFLOWER. The President was accompanied by Mrs. Wilson, myself and Secretary Tumulty, while the Executive office staff usually assigned to a trip of this sort also accompanied the party. The interest in the trip was so great that it was necessary to run the expedition in a special train to accommodate the newspaper men and photographers who had been assigned to cover the trip. There were twenty-one newspaper correspondents representing all of the press associations and the big newspapers. They[2] were as follows:

Byron Price,	Michael Hennessy,
Pierce Miller,	Boston Globe.
Associated Press.	J. Jerome Williams,

Hugh Baillie,
  United Press.
John Nevin,
  International News Service.
A. E. Geldhof,
  Newspaper Enterprise
  Association.
J. J. O'Neill,
  Mt. Clemens News Bureau.
E. C. Hill,
  New York Sun.
Philip Kinsley,
  Chicago Tribune.
Robert T. Small,
  Philadelphia Public
  Ledger.
Robert S. Norton,
  Boston Post.

Universal News Service.
Louis Seibold,
  New York World.
Charles H. Grasty,
Rodney Bean,
  New York Times.
Charles White,
  New York Tribune.
David Lawrence,
  New York Evening Post.
Ben Allen,
  Cleveland Plain Dealer.
Stanley M. Reynolds,
  Baltimore Sun.
Morton M. Milford,
  Louisville Courier-Journal.
Frank R. Lamb,
  Washington Times.

There were also five photographers, who represented the moving picture weeklies and the still picture organizations of the country.

When the President's special halted at Baltimore in order to have the Private Car placed in its regular position on the train, a large crowd of railroad men were in evidence, and they cheered the President for a few moments.

The night trip was uneventful.

T MS (received from James Gordon Grayson and Cary T. Grayson, Jr.).
  [1] About this diary, see n. 1 to the extract from it printed at Dec. 3, 1918, Vol. 53.
  [2] Those whose names can be expanded or corrected are: John Edwin Nevin, John Joseph O'Neill, Jay Jerome Williams, Charles Henry Grasty, Charles Thomas White, Edwin Conger Hill, Philip House Kinsley, Robert L. Norton, Michael Edmund Hennessy, Benjamin Farwell Allen, Stanley Meade Reynolds, and Morton Marshall Milford. O'Neill was better known for his long association with the *Brooklyn Daily Eagle* in various reportorial and editorial capacities.

APPENDIX

Wilson's Neurologic Illness during the Summer of 1919
By
Bert E. Park, M.D.

Three books and appendices to *The Papers of Woodrow Wilson*[1] have established to a reasonable degree of medical certainty that Wilson suffered from long-standing hypertension and cerebrovascular disease, which led to signs of premature brain aging by the time he participated in the Paris Peace Conference. Today's physician would term this an incipient "organic brain syndrome," or "dementia." The latter term is used here in the strictly medical, and not pejorative, sense. Yet as the appendices to Volume 58 of *The Papers* have demonstrated, Wilson was not so compromised during the conference as to prevent him, for the most part, from functioning well. Even so, a rather severe viral infection and accompanying transient delirium in early April 1919 and what was almost certainly a small stroke later in that month contributed to a marked decline in Wilson's physical vigor and mental acuity in May and June.[2] Between his departure from Paris on June 28 and mid-July, Wilson was no longer operating at his normal capacity. Not only did he have great difficulty in composing his forthcoming address of July 10, in which he was to present the Treaty of Versailles to the Senate; he was forever confused about such technical matters as the legal status of reservations and amendments and the degree to which they would affect American ratification. As a result, in part, of his inability to adapt to new circumstances, Wilson failed to develop any realistic strategy to form a bipartisan pro-League coalition in order to assure that the Senate would consent to ratification of the treaty.

On Saturday morning, July 19, the fatigued President suffered yet another physical setback. For reasons which he did not reveal, his physician, Dr. Grayson, hustled Wilson aboard the *Mayflower* for a cruise on the Potomac River and Chesapeake Bay in spite of warnings of an impending storm. The presidential party returned to Washington on Monday, and Wilson canceled all appointments and confined himself to his bedroom. Despite the absence of bona

[1] Edwin A. Weinstein, *Woodrow Wilson: A Medical and Psychological Biography* (Princeton, N. J., 1981); Bert E. Park, *The Impact of Illness on World Leaders* (Philadelphia, 1986), pp. 3-76, 331-42; Kenneth R. Crispell and Charles F. Gomez, *Hidden Illness in the White House* (Durham, N. C., 1988), pp. 13-74; and B. E. Park, "The Impact of Wilson's Neurologic Disease during the Paris Peace Conference"; E. A. Weinstein, "Woodrow Wilson's Neuropsychologic Impairment and the Paris Peace Conference"; and James F. Toole, "Some Observations on Wilson's Neurologic Illness," all in *The Papers of Woodrow Wilson* (hereinafter cited as *PWW*), Vol. 58, pp. 611-38.
[2] Park, "Impact of Wilson's Neurologic Disease during the Paris Peace Conference," *ibid.*, pp. 621-22.

fide medical records and Dr. Grayson's disclaimer that the President was suffering from nothing else than "dysentery,"[3] it seems reasonably certain in retrospect that Wilson may have suffered yet another small stroke. Why else would Grayson whisk him out of the capital on such short notice? Certainly being placed aboard ship in rough waters would not have been beneficial for a patient suffering from an upset stomach and diarrhea.

In view of Wilson's previous medical history, his subsequent behavior during July and August 1919, and the occurrence of large-vessel strokes in late September and early October, few other diagnoses than a small stroke seem plausible. Regardless of the precise nature of his transient incapacity, *and viewing this isolated episode as a continuum of an ongoing disease*, Wilson's biological clock was clearly winding down. Above all, his untreated hypertension and cerebrovascular disease (whether or not an overt stroke actually occurred in July) were taking their toll on the President's intellect and behavior.

Wilson's deterioration—dramatic, as will be seen—on that account is now a matter of record. Specific criteria for an underlying diagnosis of dementia include, in increasing order of compromise, the following: first, loss of ability to recall past events and of recent memory; second, increasingly petulant, irritable, suspicious, and withdrawn behavior; third, the proclivity to become so set in one's ways as to become a caricature of oneself; and finally, a restricted ability at abstract reasoning and subsequent inability to work out new strategies to solve problems as changing circumstances require.[4]

Perhaps the most striking and outwardly visible sign of Wilson's dementia during July and August was his memory loss. The first aberrations for which we have hard evidence occurred on July 25. Senator Lodge had written Wilson on July 22 to inquire whether the arrangements for the distribution of certain reparation payments by Germany had been agreed upon at Paris. Wilson replied that, so far as he knew, no such arrangements had been made. As

[3] Grayson may or may not have understood the cause of Wilson's illness, but he did recognize that he was a very sick man. It must have been at this time that Grayson persuaded Wilson to abandon plans for a speaking tour on behalf of the League of Nations. "I dreaded the extensive journey necessary for this more than I dreaded the plague," Grayson later wrote. "I had already seen that the wear and tear on him of continual controversy over the treaty was undoing the good that had been done by his ocean voyage, and that his vitality was being slowly sapped." Later, when Wilson decided to undertake the tour, Grayson writes, he had to accept the decision, but he did so knowing that doom lay ahead. Cary T. Grayson, *Woodrow Wilson: An Intimate Memoir* (New York, 1960), pp. 94-95.
[4] Any textbook dealing with dementia makes reference to these qualities. See, for example, Charles E. Wells, "Organic Syndromes: Dementia," in *Comprehensive Textbook of Psychiatry*, H. Kaplan and B. Sadock, eds. (Baltimore, 1985).

it turned out, Wilson had not only forgotten the reparation arrangement that had been agreed to, but also that he had written any letter to Lodge on the subject.[5] Similarly, on August 4, in a draft of a letter to the Senate, he denied having received any protests from members of the American commission against the Shantung settlement, which again contradicted the record. Indeed, on that very same day, Wilson was about to send a copy to Lodge of General Tasker H. Bliss' letter of April 29, 1919, protesting against the Shantung provisions of the German peace treaty and characterizing the Japanese government in words so scorching that publication of the letter would have caused a Japanese-American crisis.[6]

It also would seem significant that on August 6 Wilson felt obliged to put check marks by each of the six proposals that Attorney General A. Mitchell Palmer had made for measures to deal with the high cost of living, which Wilson accepted without question and recited virtually verbatim two days later in his address to Congress on the matter. That address in itself is one of his poorest on record, and, as the Editors of *The Papers* have pointed out, contained several grammatical errors and at least one garbled sentence. Indeed, the numerous emendations and notations in the margins and below the lines in the text of this address suggest that Wilson had a great deal of difficulty in systemically marshaling his thoughts, which resulted in a speech that was often rambling and without substance.[7] On the same day, in yet another letter to Lodge, Wilson erred both in denying having any formal drafts of the League Covenant except "that presented by the American Commissioners" (who had never presented one), and in insisting that no stenographic reports had been taken of the proceedings of the League of Nations Commission.[8]

During this same period, Wilson became increasingly irascible, petulant, and suspicious. Again on August 8, he characterized one of Colonel House's disclosures as "amazing" and "deeply disturbing"; lambasted Rumania for acting in a "perfectly outrageous manner"; and threatened to withdraw the French Security Treaty on account of what he perceived to be the sorry sight of other nations fighting over the spoils of war.[9] Three days later, Lansing risked his chief's confidence by alerting him to the need to come

[5] See HCL to WW, July 22, 1919, and WW to HCL, July 25, 1919, both in *PWW*, Vol. 61; and WW to RL, Aug. 4, 1919, and RL to WW, Aug. 4, 1919, both in *ibid.*, Vol. 62.
[6] See JPT to WW, with Enclosure, Aug. 4, 1919, *ibid.*
[7] AMP to WW, "Suggested Legislation," Aug. 6, 1919; Address to a Joint Session of Congress, Aug. 8, 1919, *ibid.*
[8] WW to HCL, Aug. 8, 1919, *ibid.*
[9] Two letters to RL, Aug. 8, 1919, *ibid.*

to some type of agreement with the mild reservationists. Wilson's resentment compelled Lansing to observe that the President's obstinacy was by now "utterly unreasonable" and defeated his purposes, and to lament that Wilson's nature was not more "flexible" and his temper "less defiant."[10] A day later, Wilson threatened to withdraw from the League altogether in the face of "unjust territorial settlements" that were hardly new issues. On August 15, he publicly vowed to send Senators Lodge and Knox to Berlin to negotiate a treaty with Germany if they succeeded in defeating the Versailles Treaty.[11]

No single event was at once more important and yet so revealing of Wilson's increasing deficiencies than his interview with members of the Foreign Relations Committee on August 19. Wilson made at least sixteen overt errors, misrepresentations, and self-contradictions during the three-hour session, which the notes appended to that document in this volume point out in painstaking detail. Whether in recalling dates of what transpired at Paris, what documents he did and did not have in his possession, the role that his advisers allegedly played in the proceedings, or simply forgetting some terms of the treaty itself, Wilson's memory was clearly faulty—almost consistently so. Such mistakes did not pass unnoticed by Lodge, who at one point reminded Wilson of some facts seemingly unknown to the President that were openly advertised in the newspapers of the day. Wilson was unable to perceive either that he had failed to change any senatorial minds or that his performance had been less than exemplary; indeed, he thought that it had been a great success.

By mid-August, Wilson was so set in his beliefs and his ways that he had become a veritable caricature of his former self. Failing to shift reflectively in his thinking as circumstances changed, his frustration boiled over. Just one day after his self-perceived triumph over the Senate Foreign Relations Committee, he declared: "I am almost inclined to refuse to permit this country to be a member of the League of Nations when it is composed of such intriguers and robbers. I am disposed to throw up the whole business and get out."[12] Yet, as is so typical of individuals with evolving organic brain syndromes, what he was not disposed to do was to change—even in the face of advice from senators of both parties who told him that he simply did not have the votes for ratification unless he accepted reservations to the treaty.

[10] Lansing memorandum, Aug. 11, 1919, *ibid.*
[11] RL to FLP, "Strictly Confidential," Aug. 12, 1919, *ibid.*; news report printed in *ibid.*, Aug. 15, 1919.
[12] Lansing memorandum, Aug. 20, 1919, *ibid.*

Not that the "mild reservationists" were themselves refusing to compromise; virtually everyone who had access to Wilson was attempting to meet him halfway. The farthest that he would go was to allow Hitchcock, his Senate minority leader, to offer four interpretive reservations for use as he saw fit.[13] What Hitchcock was *not* allowed to do, however, was the one thing required to break the impasse—to incorporate the reservations into the process of ratification by the United States.

Ironically enough, Wilson had argued years before that it was the Chief Executive's "plain duty" to reach understanding with the Senate on matters that divided them, rather than to go over its head with an appeal to the people.[14] History had earlier told Wilson

[13] Wilson memorandum to G. M. Hitchcock, Sept. 3, 1919, *ibid.*
[14] Woodrow Wilson, *Constitutional Government in the United States* (New York, 1908), pp. 139-41. Wilson's statement in *Constitutional Government* is striking in light of his actions in 1919. The statement follows:

"The Senate has shown itself particularly stiff and jealous in insisting upon exercising an independent judgment upon foreign affairs, and has done so so often that a sort of customary *modus vivendi* has grown up between the President and the Senate, as of rival powers. The Senate is expected in most instances to accept the President's appointments to office, and the President is expected to be very tolerant of the Senate's rejection of treaties, proposing but by no means disposing even in this chief field of his power. Advisers who are entirely independent of the official advised are in a position to be, not his advisers, but his masters; and when, as sometimes happens, the Senate is of one political party and the President of the other, its dictation may be based, not upon the merits of the question involved, but upon party antagonisms and calculations of advantage.

"The President has not the same recourse when blocked by the Senate that he has when opposed by the House. When the House declines his counsel he may appeal to the nation, and if public opinion respond to his appeal the House may grow thoughtful of the next congressional elections and yield; but the Senate is not so immediately sensitive to opinion and is apt to grow, if anything, more stiff if pressure of that kind is brought to bear upon it.

"But there is another course which the President may follow, and which one or two Presidents of unusual political sagacity have followed, with the satisfactory results that were to have been expected. He may himself be less stiff and offish, may himself act in the true spirit of the Constitution and establish intimate relations of confidence with the Senate on his own initiative, not carrying his plans to completion and then laying them in final form before the Senate to be accepted or rejected, but keeping himself in confidential communication with the leaders of the Senate while his plans are in course, when their advice will be of service to him and his information of the greatest service to them, in order that there may be veritable counsel and a real accommodation of views instead of a final challenge and contest. The policy which has made rivals of the President and Senate has shown itself in the President as often as in the Senate, and if the Constitution did indeed intend that the Senate should in such matters be an executive council it is not only the privilege of the President to treat it as such, it is also his best policy and his plain duty. As it is now, the President and Senate are apt to deal with each other with the formality and punctilio of powers united by no common tie except the vague common tie of public interest, but it is within their choice to change the whole temper of affairs in such matters and to exhibit the true spirit of the Constitution by coming into intimate relations of mutual confidence, by a change of attitude which can perhaps be effected more easily upon the initiative of the President than upon the initiative of the Senate.

"It is manifestly the duty of statesmen, with whatever branch of the government they may be associated, to study in a very serious spirit of public service the right accommodation of parts in this complex system of ours, the accommodation which will give the government its best force and synthesis in the face of the difficult counsels and perplexing tasks of regulation with which it is face to face, and no one can play the leading part in such a matter with more influence or propriety than the President. If he

that senators deeply resent such action, a warning he had now forgotten. Wilson was simply no longer responding to political realities and necessities. He was cut off from his own experience and unable to embark on new strategies. In a word, Wilson could not shift reflectively in his thinking to alternatives that circumstances demanded.

Instead, what once was gray became in Wilson's eyes black and white. If the senators really wanted a fight, which only a few diehard opponents of the treaty did, he vowed to "give them a belly full." As the Editors point out, Wilson's decision to go on a speaking tour in the West was "made in anger," "without much thought," and bordered on the "irrational."[15] He was now perversely self-consumed, as impervious to the advice of his physician not to make the trip for reasons of health as he was seemingly unaware of the consequences of his absence from Washington for a month.

Whether in rebukes to the Japanese government or in his intransigence in the face of a threatened railway strike, Wilson's rigidity and anger, bordering on the paranoid, were pervasive influences on his conduct during the summer of 1919. By now, virtually every affront incensed him, including a news release that he had broken with House—despite the fact that the break had been obvious to Wilson and everyone else for some time. Moreover, the President's penchant for underlining important points in memoranda, rather than allowing the heretofore forceful Wilsonian style to speak for itself, reflected his increasingly petulant and inflexible mind-set. The depths to which his impact on others had fallen was highlighted by Lansing's rueful admission that Wilson was no longer likely to be listened to as he had been in the past.[16]

Perhaps the most objective analysis that can be applied to Wilson's underlying medical condition as it impacted on his conduct and duties would be to rate him from the standpoint of what is known today as "a percentage of impairment of the whole person,"

---

have character, modesty, devotion, and insight as well as force, he can bring the contending elements of the system together into a great and efficient body of common counsel."

Moreover, in his address of 1890, "Leaders of Men" (*PWW*, Vol. 6, p. 663), Wilson had written that compromise was "the true gospel of politics." "Do we not in all dealings adjust views, compound differences, placate antagonisms?" he continued. "Uncompromising thought is the luxury of the closeted recluse. Untrammeled reasoning is the indulgence of the philosopher, of the dreamer of sweet dreams."

It might be added that, as a political leader, both as Governor of New Jersey and President of the United States, Wilson had been adept, through compromise, at forging bipartisan coalitions in order to assure passage of all important legislation; also that he had said over and over that expediency is the rule of political life.

[15] See the note to the extract from Lansing's Desk Diary printed at Aug. 25, 1919, *PWW*, Vol. 62.

[16] Lansing memorandum, Sept. 1, 1919, *ibid.*

as it is described in the American Medical Association's standardized *Guides to the Evaluation of Permanent Impairment*.[17] The
Guides go to great lengths to differentiate between *impairment*,
which is "directly related to the health status of the individual,"
and *disability*, which "can be determined only within the context
of the occupational demands . . . or requirements that the individual is unable to meet as a result of the impairment."[18]

In evaluating impairment of brain function, the *Guides* apply
several criteria, including alterations in language, in complex and
integrated cerebral functions, and in emotion, with or without the
presence of episodic neurologic disturbances. If we apply a few of
these criteria to Wilson, his medically-defined impairment can now
not only be substantiated, but quantified. With reference to the
criterion of disturbances in complex integrated cerebral functions,
even before his major strokes in September-October 1919, Wilson
would be conservatively rated as 5 to 15 per cent impaired on the
basis of the following description from the *Guides* equating with
that percentage of impairment: "There is a degree of impairment
of complex integrated cerebral functions, although the individual
still has the ability to carry out most activities of daily living as well
as before onset." Taking the next criteria of emotional disturbances
(likewise obvious in Wilson's case), the first level of that impairment is characterized by "mild to moderate emotional disturbance
under stress," again equating with 5 to 15 per cent impairment of
the whole man. Nor would Wilson's hypertension and early
congestive heart failure,[19] each with its own defined percentage of
impairment, be ignored by today's physician. Moreover, Wilson's
episodic small strokes through the years involving his right hand
are all a matter of record. These would warrant an additional 5 to
15 per cent rating.[20] More important still, percentages from separate categories are cumulative in computing impairment. This
leads to the conclusion that Wilson would have been conservatively certified as being from 15 to 45 per cent impaired as a percentage of the whole man by September 1919.

That Wilson was impaired in the strictest medical sense of the
word during the summer of 1919 is self-evident. Whether or not
his underlying condition led to overt *disability* as the nation's
Chief Executive, however, was raised by Dr. James F. Toole in his
essay in Volume 58. The trail may indeed be "cold," as he termed

[17] American Medical Association, *Guides to the Evaluation of Permanent Impairment*, 2nd edn. (Chicago, 1984); also Bert E. Park, "Presidential Disability: Past Experiences and Future Implications," *Politics and the Life Sciences*, VII (1988), 50-66.
[18] A.M.A., *Guides*, p. x.
[19] Progression of the latter during the western speaking tour will be well documented
in Volume 63. Wilson often had to sleep sitting up to promote blood return to his failing
heart. This symptom first became apparent in April while Wilson was in Paris.
[20] A.M.A., *Guides*, p. 63.

it, but the record is now ample enough to add support to the retrospective diagnostician along the way. The evidence in Volume 62, when combined with clinical observations of demented individuals in general, appears to answer Toole's question in the affirmative.

After all, quite specific *qualitative* criteria can be applied in Wilson's case further to substantiate, not only the degree of his impairment, but its implications for his conduct (i.e., disability) during the period in question. One well-recognized authority on the behavioral correlates of patients with dementia or brain injury from whatever cause has noted that such individuals tend to fail if they are required to:

1. shift reflectively from one aspect of a situation to another;
2. give an accounting of themselves for acts and thoughts;
3. keep in mind various aspects of a task;
4. grasp the essentials of a given whole;
5. voluntarily evoke previous experiences and learn from them;
6. assume an attitude toward accepting the "merely possible," and;
7. detach the ego from the outer world or from inner experiences.[21]

This list is not all-inclusive, but it will at least serve to illustrate the problem at hand. Wilson's inability to shift reflectively was epitomized by his single-minded obsession with the Senate's acceptance of the treaty "as is." He failed to acknowledge what others told him of the necessity to shift gears toward accommodation as the reservationists gained momentum.

Virtually all of Wilson's associates were as one in underscoring Wilson's increasing inability during the summer to give an accounting for his acts and thoughts. As Ray Stannard Baker acknowledged: "He has the artist's temperament," always preferring to work alone. Lansing later added that Wilson's unfounded resentment prevented him from assuming the obligatory role of conciliator.[22] Nor, on occasion, could he give a readily reproducible account of himself to others in a more literal sense. In his meeting with the Senate Foreign Relations Committee, Wilson gave equivocal, contradictory, and incorrect answers when asked to give a full accounting of conference discussions, the existence of secret treaties, the specifics of the United States' role in the reparation agreements, successive drafts of the Covenant, and European territorial settlements.

[21] Kurt Goldstein, "Functional Disorders in Brain Damage," in *American Handbook of Psychiatry*, 2nd edn., Silvano Arieti, ed., 7 vols. (New York, 1974-81), IV, 43-66.
[22] Baker Diary, July 4, 1919, *PWW*, Vol. 61; Lansing memorandum, Aug. 11, 1919, *ibid.*, Vol. 62.

Wilson's faulty memory betrayed him on so many occasions that he was forever asking his associates to send him memoranda of their prior discussions so he could keep in mind details of the task before him. Increasingly so, he found it difficult to compose his speeches. As has been said, earlier that summer he had struggled aboard ship with his message to the Senate, just as he later also had trouble marshaling his thoughts while writing and rewriting his speech of August 8 concerning the high cost of living. More significant still was Wilson's failure to come to effectual agreement with the key leaders of the moderate reservationists. Instead, he obstinately opposed or put off this group of potential supporters.

Grasping the essentials of the given whole was also increasingly difficult for Wilson. On a practical level, making check marks on a memorandum or underlining key points helped him to keep the various aspects of an argument together. Philosophically, his increasing paranoia fostered the delusion that "the given whole" was none other than a monolithic Republican party, embodied metaphorically in the person of Senator Lodge. Had Wilson exercised his previous remarkable powers of political leadership by singling out potential supporters among the Republicans (including former President Taft as well as the mild reservationists) and realistically addressing their concerns, he probably would have achieved speedy ratification of the treaty. Nor was it at all certain that the "whole" of the problem was the renegotiation of the entire treaty should the distasteful reservations be accepted, a position from which Wilson never wavered despite its incorrect assumption.

Evoking prior experiences with an eye to learning from them was also now difficult for Wilson. He had obviously forgotten the lessons of his off-year election appeal of 1918, not to mention his appeal to the Italian people of April 1919. The decision to go to the American public in September 1919 over the heads of the Senate was not only irrational, but in the circumstances, was bound to be futile.

Certainly the beleaguered President refused from beginning to end to assume an attitude of accepting the "merely possible." He had set his course and would accept nothing short of total success on his terms. Neither members of the opposition nor those in his own camp could convince him otherwise. Instead, he chose to listen to the obsequious encouragement of William G. McAdoo, or to Josephus Daniels' overly optimistic assessment that the Republicans were "floundering."[23]

Finally, one is struck in reading Volume 62 by how few letters Wilson wrote during the summer of 1919, and his increasing will-

[23] W. G. McAdoo to WW, July 31, 1919, and J. Daniels to WW, July 30, 1919, both in *ibid.*

ingness to let others draft important documents and statements for him.

With respect to both his functional impairment and disability, Wilson's medical history may be divided descriptively into two periods. The first was roughly a twenty-year interval up to the western tour of 1919, which was characterized by untreated hypertension and a few episodes strongly suggestive of microvascular strokes. Following his large-vessel strokes in late September and early October 1919, Wilson entered the second phase of his illness, after which few observers denied that his mental faculties were compromised. Then, too, the behavior of such demented individuals can be divided qualitatively into four phases. Phases I and II roughly parallel the final year of the first period described above, in which a reduction of what is termed "adaptive versatility" occurs. The afflicted person's capacity to endure frustration declines. He makes unrestrained comments or criticisms and complains of tiring easily after sustained effort in a given task. Accordingly, he concentrates on one issue at a time and becomes increasingly self-absorbed. He pays less attention to detail. His recall is impaired, and he becomes insensitive to the advice and reactions of others.[24] The record suggests that these qualities characterized Wilson's behavior to the letter during the spring and summer months antedating the western tour.

Only with phases III and IV do associates come to realize that there is something definitely abnormal about the person's behavior, which in Wilson's case would apply to his conduct after his strokes in September-October 1919. These latter phases will be the subject of a forthcoming essay in the next volume of *The Papers*. Yet it is of paramount importance concerning all phases of the illness that virtually every investigator of dementia agrees that a major determinant of impairment is the adequacy of adaptive patterns as defined by the underlying personality. Above all, those with rigid adaptive patterns before illness strikes demonstrate greater impairment as a rule.[25] This last observation, of course, has singular implications, given Wilson's personality profile before the onset of his hypertension and cerebrovascular disease.

Woodrow Wilson was both a statesman and a moralist. Long ago, Edmund Burke made a memorable distinction between the two that has peculiar relevance to the President's predicament in 1919:

> The latter has only a general view of society; the former, the statesman, has a number of circumstances to combine with those general ideas, and to take into his consideration. Circum-

---

[24] Loring Chapman and Harold Wolff, "Diseases of the Neopallium," *Medical Clinics of North America*, XLII (1958), 677-89.
[25] *Ibid.*

stances are infinite, are infinitely combined, are variable and transient. . . . A statesman, not losing sight of principles, is to be guided by circumstances.[26]

What the modern-day neuropsychologist would hasten to add is that Burke was pointing to the need of the statesman to use abstractions instrumentally. On the basis of a hypertensive and cerebrovascular-induced dementia, Wilson could no longer do this by the summer of 1919. He remained a moralist to the end; indeed, this one quality that so aptly described him was only magnified by his underlying medical condition. That Wilson would lose his ability to shift reflectively with changing circumstances was an event of considerable significance for the United States and the world.

[26] Quoted in Arthur M. Schlesinger, Jr., *The Cycles of American History* (Boston, 1986), p. 82.

INDEX

NOTE ON THE INDEX

THE alphabetically arranged analytical table of contents at the front of the volume eliminates duplication, in both contents and index, of references to certain documents, such as letters. Letters are listed in the contents alphabetically by name, and chronologically within each name by page. The subject matter of all letters is, of course, indexed. The Editorial Notes and Wilson's writings are listed in the contents chronologically by page. In addition, the subject matter of both categories is indexed. The index covers all references to books and articles mentioned in text or notes. Footnotes are indexed. Page references to footnotes which place a comma between the page number and "n" cite both text and footnote, thus: "418,n1." On the other hand, absence of the comma indicates reference to the footnote only, thus: "59n1"—the page number denoting where the footnote appears.

The index supplies the fullest known form of names and, for the Wilson and Axson families, relationships as far down as cousins. Persons referred to by nicknames or shortened forms of names can be identified by reference to entries for these forms of the names.

All entries consisting of page numbers only and which refer to concepts, issues, and opinions (such as democracy, the tariff, money trust, leadership, and labor problems), are references to Wilson's speeches and writings.

Four cumulative contents-index volumes are now in print: Volume 13, which covers Volumes 1-12, Volume 26, which covers Volumes 14-25, Volume 39, which covers Volumes 27-38, and Volume 52, which covers Volumes 40-49 and 51.

INDEX

Adams-Onís Treaty (1819), 35-36, 37
Adriatic question, 345n1; Balfour on, 22-26; Polk's proposal, 456-57; WW on settlement, 522, 603-605, 625; Polk on, 574-75; Tittoni's proposal, 603-605; Nitti on, 605-606
Aegean Sea, 265
agriculture: see farmers and farming
Agriculture, Committee on (House of Representatives), 491n1
Agriculture, Department of, 213, 214, 233n1
Aidin (Aydin), Turkey, 239-40
Akademische Verlagsgesellschaft, 564-65,n1
Alabama: and Caldwell case, 465,n1, 530, 536
Albania: and Adriatic question, 457, 522, 620
Albert I, King of the Belgians, 516; WW's invitation to visit U.S., 6; accepts WW's invitation, 29
Albona (now Labin, Yugoslavia), 456, 457, 603
Aleksinskii, Grigorii Alekseevich, 445-46,n3
Alexander, James Strange, 34
Alexander, Mrs. K., 434
Alexander, Magnus Washington, 582, 583, 623,n1
Alexander, Will Winton, 106-107,n2
Algeciras, Act of (1906), 39-40, 41
Allen, Benjamin Farwell, 627
Amalgamated Sheet Metal Workers' International Association, 569, 573
Ambrosius, Lloyd E., 308n1
American Bible Society, 435n1
American Commissioners to Negotiate Peace, 219,n2
American Commission on Irish Independence: statement on Irish situation, 324-26
American Committee for Armenian and Syrian Relief, 166, 576-77, n1,2
American Farm Bureau Association, 300n1
American Federation of Labor: and railroad strike crisis, 122, 134-35, 138, 140, 161, 162, 190, 485, 567; F.D. Roosevelt on Saturday as half day of work, 232; and steel industry, 581; and conference on relationship between labor and capital, 582, 584, 623
American Handbook of Psychiatry (Arieti, ed.), 635n21
American Jewish Relief Committee, 531
American Railroad Politics, 1914-1920: Rates, Wages, and Efficiency (Kerr), 198n2
American Red Cross, 34n1
American Relief Administration, 123, 499
American Samoa: escapes influenza epidemic, 290,n2
American Society of Equity, 300n1, 623,n1
American Women Opposed to the League of Nations, 566n1
Ames, Charles Bismark, 169
Amherst College, 82n2

Analysis of the High Cost of Living Problem (report), 165,n1
Anderson, J., F., 568-69, 570-73
Anderson, Mary, 97,n9, 314-15, 436, 437
Anderson Overseas Corporation, 467
Anglo-Persian agreement, 334,n1, 427-28
Anglo-Persian Oil Company, Ltd., 78, 452-53
antilynching bill (Georgia), 234n4
antitrust laws: Palmer on prosecutions under, 173-74
Arabia, 235, 242, 257
Argentina: and wheat situation, 52, 53
Arieti, Silvano, 635n21
Arizona: and railroad strike, 548, 549-50
Armenia: and mandates, 27n1, 149, 235, 242, 257, 285n1, 416, 454, 607; and Turkish invasion of, 116n1, 248,n1; Hoover on relief efforts in, 166; WW's concern over situation in, 259-60, 285; reports and advice on situation in, 576-79; and King-Crane recommendations, 608
arms limitation: House on, 62; and disposal of German and Austro-Hungarian ships, 187; Houston on, 269
Arrogant Diplomacy: U.S. Policy toward Colombia, 1903-1922 (Lael), 5n6
Asia Minor, 25, 141-42, 238
Assling railroad, 604
Assling Triangle, 456, 574, 604
Associated Press, 184n1, 252n1, 626
Association of Oil Producers in Mexico, 155n1
Association of Railway Conductors, 140
Aswan (Assuan) Dam, 437,n1
Atkinson, William, 122, 568-69, 570-73
Atlanta Constitution, 234n4
Auchincloss, Gordon, 202; House's influence over, 454
Australia, 188; and wheat situation, 52, 53
Axson, Stockton (Isaac Stockton Keith Axson II), brother of EAW, 226n1

Baillie, Hugh, 627
Baker, Newton Diehl, 116, 234, 271; on Panama Canal Railroad's steamship operation, 8-10, 97; and "official" name of the war, 69; on Russian situation and Czech troops, 82; and conscientious objectors, 97; issue of making public report on cost of living, 165,n1; army officers to aid Hoover's missions, 240, 249, 303-304; effect of treaty delays on War Department, 261; on record of two soldiers WW pardoned, 415, 434-35; on electric railways, 420-22, 461, 516-17; request for return of U.S. soldiers in Siberia, 433, 478-79; on Wilson Dam, 437; WW answers on dams, 515; on incidents at Fort Leavenworth, 545-46,n3; on scandal involving U.S. Army colonel, 562-64, 610-11; Lansing on "industrial democracy" of, 612-13; and WW's welcome to Pershing, 622
Baker, Ray Stannard, 607n1; on WW, 635

WOODROW WILSON